Forgotten Friends

Forgotten Friends

*Monks, Marriages, and Memories of
Northeast India*

INDRANI CHATTERJEE

OXFORD

UNIVERSITY PRESS

OXFORD
UNIVERSITY PRESS

Oxford University Press is a department of the University of Oxford.
It furthers the University's objective of excellence in research, scholarship,
and education by publishing worldwide. Oxford is a registered trademark of
Oxford University Press in the UK and in certain other countries

Published in India by
Oxford University Press
YMCA Library Building, 1 Jai Singh Road, New Delhi 110 001, India

The international boundaries, coastlines, denominations, and other information
shown on any map in this work do not imply judgement on the part of
Oxford University Press concerning the legal status of any territory or the
endorsement or acceptance of such information. For present boundaries and
other details, please refer to maps authenticated by the Survey of India.

ISBN 13: 978-0-19-808922-3
ISBN 10: 0-19-808922-8

Typeset in Adobe Garamond Pro 11/13.2
by The Graphics Solution, New Delhi 110 092
Printed in India at Rakmo Press, New Delhi 110 020

Contents

List of Figures   vii
List of Abbreviations   ix
Acknowledgements   xi

Introduction   1
1. Monastic Governance, 'Geographicity', and Gender   36
2. Eighteenth-century Shifts of Monastic Governments   81
3. Political Ecology and Reconstituted 'Hindu' Marriage   127
4. Translations of Adherence: From 'Feudalism' and   173
   'Slavery' to 'Savagery'
5. A Fraternity of Tea and the Politics of Monastic   232
   Friendship
6. Undoing Gender? Restoring of Motherhood and Merit   287
   Conclusion: Rule by Ethnology—Forgetting Histories   339
   and Households

Bibliography   372
Glossary   420
Index   425
About the Author   453

Figures

1.1 Physical Contours of Eastern India   37
1.2 Sharecropper's Buddhist Temple, Pilak, Tripura   40
3.1 Navadvip Khunti   130
3.2 Follower of Khunti, Potrait and Image, Navadvip   131
5.1 Mary Winchester in 1871   265
7.1 Modern Political Boundaries of Eastern India   362

Abbreviations

ABHS	American Baptist Historical Society
AGG	Agent of the Governor General
AGG, NEF	Agent of the Governor General in the North-East Frontier
AHR	*American Historical Review*
Asst.	Assistant
BC	Board's Collection
BDRC	*Bengal District Records, Chittagong*
BFP	Bengal Foreign Proceedings
BJC	Bengal Judicial Consultations
BJP	Bengal Judicial Proceedings
BOR	Board of Revenue
BPC	Bengal Political Consultations
BPP	Bengal Political Proceedings
BRC	Bengal Revenue Consultations
BSOAS	*Bulletin of the School of Oriental and African Studies*
CDR	*Kachar District Records* (comp. Debabrata Datta, ed. Sunanda Datta, Kolkata, 2007)
CMA	Church Missionary Archives, Wales.
CNISSAS	Centre for Northeast India, South and Southeast Asia Studies
Collr.	Collector
Commr.	Commissioner
Comp.	Compiled
CSSEAS	Centre for the Study of South-East Asian Societies
CSSH	*Comparative Studies in Society and History*
DHAS	Department of Historical and Antiquarian Studies
Dy.	Deputy
Ed.	Editor
EI	*Epigraphia Indica*

EPW	*Economic and Political Weekly*
FPP	Foreign and Political Proceedings
GG	Governor General
GOB	Government of Bengal
GOI	Government of India
ICSBA	International Centre for the Study of Bengal Art
IESHR	*Indian Economic and Social History Review*
IHRC	*Indian Historical Records Commission*
IOR	India Office Records
Islam *BDR*	Sirajul Islam (ed.), *Bangladesh District Records: Chittagong vol. 1, 1760–1787*
JAAR	*Journal of the American Academy of Religion*
JAS	*Journal of Asian Studies*
JASB	*Journal of the Asiatic Society of Bengal*
JAOS	*Journal of the American Oriental Society*
JARS	*Journal of the Assam Research Society*
LP	T. H. Lewin Papers, Senate House, London
MAS	*Modern Asian Studies*
NAI	National Archives of India, Delhi
NEF	North-East Frontier
NLW	National Library of Wales, Aberstywyth
OIOC	Oriental and India Office Collections, British Library
PP	*Parliamentary Papers*
RDR	*Rangpur District Records*, Walter K. Firminger (ed.)
SDR	*Sylhet District Records,* Walter K. Firminger (ed.)
SRCB	*Select Records of Cooch Behar, vol. 2.* Calcutta, 1869.

Acknowledgements

A FERRY-RIDE ON THE BRAHMAPUTRA sparked off this book. I was visiting Gauhati for its archives, but had decided to take a detour to study the architectural design of a temple on an island off the river. I was unaware that my unpreparedness for such a visit struck other passengers on the ferry as odd until a matron, leading a festive group of young male and female weavers, took me under her protective wing. When we got off the ferry, her group of pilgrims offered their fruit and sweets to the priest within the temple. I had nothing to contribute. But the matron quickly gave me work to do—'click photographs!'—a place to stand in when the offerings were given to the priest, and entered my name alongside those of the other members of the group asking for the deity's blessings. The names, I noticed only then, all ended with 'Bodo'. Even though I had brought nothing to the ritual, they gave me large shares of the fruit and sweets that had been returned by the deity as 'blessings'. Their kindness, unremarkable to those who are not attuned to the social and political hierarchies of the subcontinent, shamed me out of my intellectual and political smugness and torpor. Even if she never reads this book that resulted from her generosity, I thank Rupa Bodo for that instructive gesture of inclusion.

A chain of old and new friends have guided me at every step. Monisha Behal, better known as Ben, assured me a place to stay in Gauhati, and put me in touch with her network of friends and family in many parts of northeastern India. Along with Oli and SP, marvelous and caring hosts in Gauhati, I am especially grateful for the help and sustenance organized by Dingi Sailo, her entire family, Ramdini and Dinkima and everybody who travelled with me between Aizawl and Siaha. I thank Pu T.K., Nonai, and Ma Puia for accompanying me on a hair-raising journey up the hillside to Serkawr. However, I remain especially grateful to the Lha Pi family for their hospitality at the end of that journey—and for permission to photograph their historic home in the hills, their library, and records. I also thank Kalyani Das and Debashish Das for sheltering us in Kalyani and for accompanying me on one of the more daring of my intellectual journeys through the archives and institutions of Navadvip. Their generosity led me to the doors of the Manipuri dham there and to the custodian of the deity (sebait) Tikendrajit, who gave me permission to photograph the metal 'licence' that has been reproduced in this book. I also thank the lineage of Bhattacharyya purohits who spent long hours narrating the histories of each of the sites across Manipur and Tripura for me, for explanations and commentary on the signs and symbols of Buddhist awakening at a formally Vaisnava site. I especially thank them and the sebait, Rajkumar Tikendrajit Simha, for permissions to photograph all the images within.

My undergraduate and graduate students at Rutgers University have borne up with my ideas, tests, and arguments patiently through the years. They are the reason that I have tried to write simply. They are the reason that I wish to write at all. My colleagues in the department, especially Temma Kaplan, Julie Livingston, and Bonnie Smith read through and commented on various segments of drafts. Mia Bay, Paul Clemens, Barbara Cooper, Samantha Kelly, Jennifer Jones, Cami Townsend, and Seth Koven provided dollops of emotional support in the department. I have learnt a great deal from them, as I have from the tireless efforts on my behalf by colleagues in the Interlibrary Loan department of the Alexander Library and members of the Art Library at Rutgers University. This hard-working group of librarians has been heroic in securing copies of books and rare articles for me. I could not have studied what I did without them.

My warm thanks also to a vast network of generous colleagues outside my own university. I have received gifts of books and articles from people across such a wide range of places that I am deeply humbled by them. I wish to acknowledge in particular Robert Linrothe, who gave me his marvelous and illustrated books on Bengal art and archaeology in addition to reading and commenting on early drafts of the first two chapters. Paul Nietupski found and sent me all the articles that I could ever hope to read and digest on Himalayan geographies and monastic regimes. Jacques Leider found manuscripts that would be of special interest and sent them online to me. Elliot Sperling encouraged me by sending along his own unpublished work, as did William Pinch, Dick Eaton, and David Curley.

I also received a great deal of support from South Asian feminist scholars who convened the annual Feminist Pre-Conference at Madison and constituted themselves as my 'sisters under the sari'. I owe a special vote of thanks to Anjali Arondekar, Geeta Patel, and Ramya Sreenivasan for many hours of scintillating conversation; to Minnie Sinha, Barbara Ramusack, and Geraldine Forbes for wise counsel on many aspects of institutional life. Anjali and Ramya bravely committed to reading drafts and gave me the critical comments that only 'sisters' can. I thank them for keeping me honest at all times. I particularly thank Anannya Dasgupta who turns everything she touches into a thing of beauty; she turned a jumble of words into a chapter once and showed me that it could be done. Ramya too committed to reading drafts even as she moved jobs, homes, and cities—and remained a stalwart friend of the project despite all that.

A fellowship at the Institute of Advanced Studies at Princeton and another at the Agrarian Studies Program at Yale University allowed me freedom from teaching commitments and a lively and engaged environment in which to first conceive and then execute different segments of the manuscript. Julia Thomas and Bruce Grant were especially generous in their engagement at Princeton. Sincere thanks go to Kay Mansfield, administrator extraordinaire and friend of scholars at the Agrarian Studies Program, K. Sivaramakrishnan and Jim Scott for cordially nourishing open-ended debate. The most sincerely felt thanks also to Kasturi Gupta, South Asian Studies Council at Yale, for being the centre of home, hospitality, warmth and care for all visitors from South Asia as well as from other American universities to New Haven. Her warm hospitality and care ensured that there was enough laughter with which to recover from bad days.

My heartfelt thanks go to my parents who taught me to resist fear and welcome the unknown and invisible. I am grateful that they let me be curious and that they remained curious about the strange world I inhabited in my work. I am also grateful that they shared at least one trip to a Buddhist site with me. Watching them as they responded to archaeological finds of stones and metal objects in a humble caretaker's trunk in an on-site hut, as well as to Buddhist populations described as 'tribal' in anthropological scholarship, were clarifying moments. I thank them for that memory of Pilak and Unakoti, as much as I remain grateful to Rong-phru-sa and his community for their tenderness and conversation.

I have received so much from Sumit Guha that it is hard to know how to describe it all. Over the years, he has lifted a great deal of responsibility from my shoulders, and encouraged me to explore parts of a world that had been hitherto shut off to us. I thank him for accompanying me also on one of my trips; his presence made the visit to the Buddhist stupa at Baxanagar and its environs especially memorable. In addition to that, he has endured additional hours of intellectual work debating the admissibility of this or that body of evidence, the need for additional language-training, running his razor-sharp eye over my draft chapters. His commitment to the world of learning has been an inspiration. I hope this book compensates in some way for all that he has endured in its making.

However, all things in my life have begun with one good woman and been completed by other expert women. This monograph too would not be complete without the expert cartographic skills of Lois Kain. Nor would it have been clarified without the compassionate expertise of Margaret Case. I thank both women profusely. I remain responsible for all the failures and shortcomings, and would like to ask for my readers' pardon for such in advance.

Introduction

THE BACKBONE OF THIS BOOK is a political and economic order centring on monastic teachers in a variety of disciplines—Buddhist, Vaisnava, Saiva, Tantric, and Sufi. These teachers and their disciples, students, and adherents constituted a basic unit of political society in precolonial India, which lasted in ever-attenuated forms into the twentieth century. Among other things, these monastic teachers and students performed the social labour of evaluating, corroborating, transmitting and storing information; both hermit-like and collective monasticism implied a broad-based organization of life common to many groups in the subcontinent.

Among these, the Sufi, Vaisnava, and Saiva lineages of the fifteenth to nineteenth centuries have received serious historical attention.[1] Such attention has been withheld, however, from the Bon Tantric and Mahayana Buddhist lineages that occupied the same terrain.[2] Moreover, the particular relationships that existed between Buddhists and non-Buddhist others—such as the Sufi or Vaisnava lineages around them—have also been ignored. This deficit is only partially due to post-nationalist distance from the material archaeological and numismatic remains, records, and lived practices in large swaths of the area.[3] The oversight of collocated Buddhist and Bon figures is more likely based on a linear and largely Christian logic of time and history. In its Protestant and post-Reformation aspects, such logic implied the absolute uniformity of the faith of subjects and their sovereigns. Moreover, British colonial scholars in the early nineteenth century constructed a chronology in which a 'Hindu epoch' was followed by a 'Muslim one' and so on. When some texts in the same century were found to describe Buddhist thought and practice, colonial scholars retrofitted Buddhism into this chronology.[4] Accordingly, Buddhism was believed to have 'died' in India and lived outside it after the thirteenth century.[5] This view has been spectacularly influential in shaping postcolonial Indian historical scholarship, especially of eastern India.[6]

Elsewhere, scholars of Tibetan-language records have, however, found that Tantric Buddhist and Bon teachers–disciples and adherent households continued to thrive on the plains of eastern India long after the arrival of Central Asian Sufis.[7] This was especially true of places along the foothills of the Himalayas (Kamarupa, western Assam), but it was also true of places further south, such as Kumilla (centre of colonial Tippera, historically Tipura, transcribed as Tripura in modern India), Chittagong, and the region that modern maps identify as Arakan. Sometime between the seventh and tenth centuries, this entire area had constituted the southern part of a Tibetan empire, whose southern border ran along the river Ganges on the Indian plains.[8] In the sixteenth century, the itinerary of a Tantric Buddhist monk, included long stays at monastic centres in the highlands of 'Bhangala or Tipura', 'Ra'kan (Arakan) and Assam'.[9] This teacher's disciple also wrote a history of the extent of Vajrayana (Tantric) Buddhist settlements in the same region, whose populations he referred to as 'Ku-ki'.[10] In classical and standard Tibetan, 'sKu' (pronounced 'Ku') is shorthand for the Buddha's body, and 'sKyed' (pron. 'Kye') a reference to birth.[11] Together, the term stands for the birth of incarnate Buddhas. By such use, the monk-historian linked the presence of Muslim Central Asian armies (Turuskas) on the plains with the re-invigoration of Buddhist teaching. Monks from Magadha, he wrote, 'returned' to their original homes; the distinction between the different Buddhist teaching traditions was erased and these places were sanctified as homes of reincarnated Buddhas ('Ku-ki')

Such accounts were taken seriously by literate Bengali-speaking men in the late nineteenth century. It was reflected in their sense of social geography. Sarat Chandra Das, who visited some Tibetan Buddhist sites during these years, thus provided three different meanings for a literary term such as 'Kamboja'. The first identified it with a region called 'Upper and Eastern Lushai Hill Tracts lying between Burma and Bengal called Koki land'; a second identified it with 'southeast of Burma and Siam, where the Buddhists of Magadha had taken shelter during the conquest of their country by the Mahomedans in 1202 A.D.'[12] The third identified the term with people from Inner Asia. This expansive sensibility survived till the 1930s, when the historian Benoychandra Sen situated Bengal and Kamarupa (part of modern Assam) within a 'Tibeto-Chinese' Kamboja as well.[13]

This study also presumes upon the expansive temporal and geographical sensibility of the monk-historian as well as that of the late nineteenth-century Bengali-speaking and Tibetan-reading male. The territorial spread inferred by terms such as 'Tipura' and 'Rakhan' is enormous. 'Tipura' referred to Bhatgaon (eastern Nepal); it was the site of the palace of the Saiva lord Anandadeva (1147–67).[14] It was a name also associated with a goddess, Tripurasundari, whose temple in the Tibukche Tol was the centre of the town. Descendants of Anandadeva were identified as 'Tripuri' and alternated in the control of the valley with another family, the Bhonta, with its centre at Banepa (in the east of the valley). Their power-sharing arrangements were disrupted at the end of thirteenth century and the beginning of the fourteenth, when Tipura (Bhatgaon) was repeatedly attacked, with the connivance of its rivals, by Tirhutiya (from plains of Bihar) forces established in the Terai (foothills).[15] Whether as fugitives or as new members of the Tirhut forces, the Tipuria followed Saiva ascetic warriors who travelled between the temples dedicated to the wealthy Visvanath on the plains and Pasupatinath on the mountains.[16] After the Sultan of Bengal raided Bhatgaon in 1349, a female regent in Kathmandu shored up the lineage by arranging a marriage between her seven-year-old granddaughter and an initiated Saiva, Jayasthiti Malla, from the Gangetic plains.[17] The erstwhile dual rule of Tipura-Bhonta was transformed into a form of triple rule, identified as Malla rule within the valley.

Himalayan Malla were important for the history of eastern India for many reasons. At least one of the branches of the Malla dominated a region called 'Khasa or Ya-tshe' in western Tibet between the end of the thirteenth and through the fourteenth century. This region is now divided up between the modern Indian states of Himachal Pradesh, Uttaranchal, Western Nepal, Tibet and the Republic of China. However, in the thirteenth-fifteenth century, these Malla were both lay patrons of, and often ordained monks in, a lineage of Buddhists whose main monastery was at a place called Sa-skya [pronounced Sakya].[18] The Sakya Buddhist hierarchs in turn had been significant mediators in the thirteenth century vis-à-vis Inner Asian armies led by Mongol commanders. Sakya Buddhist proximity to Mongol commanders enabled them to flourish, sometimes in rivalry with other Buddhist ordination lineages in the Kailasa-Mansarovar region, such as the Kagyupa located at monasteries such as Digung-pa (in Tibetan, bKa'-rGyud-pa at 'Bri-gung-pa) or another lineage of Buddhist called the Kadampa.[19] The co-dependence of monastic lineages and laymen's militias shaped the histories of war on both sides of the Himalayas. The ancient Tibetan tantric lineages (called the Nyingma) had developed a reputation for battlefield sorcery. As a scholar puts it, no Himalayan Buddhist lineage was entirely devoid of its own arsenal of harmful magic and functionaries.[20] This must also be kept in mind when speaking of eastern Bengal in the same centuries. For Malla forces were said to have entered Magadha and then reached Gangasagar in Bengal in the fifteenth century. In the early seventeenth century, Mughal armies seeking to oust Afghan sultans from eastern India confronted Tibetan-speaking Bon and Buddhist Tantrics in the same area.[21] Together, this evidence suggests that scholars who argue for the 'Tibetanisation' of regions in the Brahmaputra valley only in the seventeenth century may have under-estimated the historical depth of the process.[22] This monograph attempts to understand why, and to trace its consequences for a postcolonial historiography and politics of the region.

It proceeds by resurrecting an outline of relationships that once linked the coastal plains with the Himalayan societies. It then lays out the conditions that induced postcolonial historians to ignore or forget these relationships. It ends with both explanations for, and implications of, such forgetting in the postcolonial historiography of gender, geography and memory in and across eastern India.

MONASTIC TEACHERS AS FORGOTTEN FRIENDS AND 'GOVERNORS'

Foremost among the forgotten relationships were those that had coalesced around a variety of monastic teachers, some of who were spoken of as 'spiritual friends' (Sanskrit *kalyanamitra*, Bengali-Hindustani *dost*). Each group of disciples, students, and adherents of a teacher was formed by a mode of ritualized initiation, mandatory in all forms of Mahayana (and Vajrayana) Buddhist orders, Vaisnava Bhakti, Saiva and Bon Tantra, and among Sufi *silsilahs*. Empowerment and initiation rituals may or may not have been followed by a second and third, equally formalized, ordination or renunciation ritual, but a basic ritual of initiation was adequate to constitute a relation of power and affection, and had material and political effects.[23] To accept initiation was equivalent to submission to a legal–moral and disciplinary practice that was identified with particular teachers. Thus the 'irony' noted for Mahayana lineages— that 'progress' in training was equated with greater and greater 'dependence' and the merging of the disciple's personhood into that of the teacher's and of the teaching lineage—could be thought of as representative of more than Buddhist traditions.[24] Similar initiation committed disciples of other traditions also to mandated, physical and mental–emotional observances, that dissolved the 'individual self' into a larger and more potent entity, whether that of a guru, or that of the guru's own ritual-intellectual teachers, and through them to an even wider group of followers and disciples. These relationships might have been renewed at various points in the course of the performances enjoined by the initiation itself; these may or may not have varied by season, generation, and gender under the direction of a teacher–guru.[25]

Rituals of initiation, common to most teaching–learning societies in the subcontinent, had a threefold implication for a South Asian history of politics. They shaped subjectivities of entire lineages of students and teachers by means of shared discipline of appetites and desires, bodies and minds. They secured the availability of administrative and military personnel; and they established and elaborated an economic system and network.

The disciplinary and spiritual lineage that each teacher claimed as his own shaped the training of the student and the cultivation of a discipline, often referred to as asceticism.[26] Scholars of Sanskrit texts use the term *yoga* (and *prayoga*) to refer to such regimes of practice or discipline.[27] The doctrines to be cultivated varied from teacher to teacher, from that of generative potency and power over the elements to renunciation of all such power. In some, especially the Vajrayana Buddhist orders, one ultimate goal of such discipline was to make the hierarchical division of male and female itself irrelevant to the goal of achieving liberation from the cycles of birth and rebirth.[28]

An equally important aspect of this form of politics was the availability of trained and disciplined clerical, artisanal, and military personnel that initiation and ordination established. Since the second century CE, monastic ordination lineages of Mahayana Buddhists had developed clerical administrations made up of grades of contemplative, teaching, and service-oriented monks.[29] From the seventh century, this monastic form of government spread through Tibet and Central and Inner Asia. An ubiquitous system of monastic administrations and economies existed in many Asian societies ranging from Mongolia to the islands of Southeast Asia during the late medieval and early modern periods.[30] Copperplate and stone inscriptions, dating between the seventh and thirteenth centuries, and paper and cloth deeds thereafter, found in many parts of eastern India, spelled out identical 'constitutions' of monastic governance.

The third and most important aspect of these ritualized relationships was economic. All initiates paid for their learning and assimilation in some form. Sanskrit legalists used terms such as *dakshina* to refer the exchange of services between a skilled teacher and a lay disciple or 'patron'. The quality, size and nature of these payments separated the humbler initiates from their wealthier counterparts. Biographies of Tibetan and Chinese scholars reveal that some initiates made over cloth, wine, barley, and meat—moveable and useable goods—along with labour services.[31] Wealthier initiates offered 'as remuneration for the initiation rite an image made of gilded bronze, and a golden throne as a thanks-offering (*gtan-rag*), a silver spoon with the image of a stag, a sword with an ornamented hilt, and an armour with the image of a scorpion on it'.[32] Labour-services at one end and precious bullion at another connected the same order of disciples through their common subjection to the adept teacher-master. Commoner labour-providers, wealthy merchants, and fierce warriors could all be counted among the lay (or un-ordained) disciples or 'subjects' (Sanskrit *praja*) and simultaneously patrons and protectors, of a monastic or teaching lineage and all its residential sites, fields, herds, and goods.

The wealthiest however appeared to have given produce of cultivable or uncultivated lands to individual members of a monastic or teaching lineage, declaring the recipients and the lands exempt from taxes and labour-levies. Such deeds and documents were thus economic and political charters. The most effective were those granted by Buddhist monks, either as a collective or as individuals. Such for instance was the case of the first Tibetan abbot of the monastery at bSam.yas (pronounced 'Samye'), who allotted a 'hundred subject households' to the monastic collective.[33] Sometimes these payments were 'fees' for the conduct of an important ritual.[34] These payments and grants enabled heads of monasteries, or their most ardent lay disciples, to assemble a heterogenous and differentially skilled set of people on those lands.[35]

In particular, this pattern of economic activity by monastic men in the early centuries amassed men skilled in arts of physical combat (wrestling, stickwork, archery) and ritual warfare on monastic estates. This was especially true of Vajrayana body-based *tantra*, *kaula*, *siddha* disciplines practiced by some branches of Buddhist and Saiva-sakta lineages at the time.[36] Monastic militias grew out of such estates of Tantric Buddhist and Saiva orders. 'Pala' Buddhist donors, for example, settled 'Vedic' Brahman lineages, skilled in these ritual arts, in the Brahmaputra valley.[37] A lineage of ordained Buddhist tantrics such as the Kargyupa constituted an entire police and military force of the Tshalpa monasteries.[38] Since Vedic Brahmans and Buddhist monks alike originated from lay families and clans that also supported their gurus, both laymen and ordained monks appear to have provided military service to monastic estates and teachers. Each such community was multi-layered: asceticized lay householders followed monks, some of who were preachers while others exercised temporal and 'royal' authority.

Monastic grants which inscribed the 'payments' that all residents of such lands were obliged to make to the 'Brahman' recipient of the gift were most politically potent when accompanied by other provisions that established limits on external authorities. Sometimes these authorities acted on behalf of laymen. Sometimes these were the donors' own bureaucracy, especially those of law-enforcement personnel (*chat-bhat*). Exemption from their ingress into the gifted estate, and exemption from their search warrants, meant that the 'sovereignty' of the recipient was localized, shaped by the terms of the grant, and limited to the territorial boundaries spelled out in the grant.[39] Within these limits, wealthy or powerful monastic donors exchanged their own powers of tax collection or authority over a group of people for the skills and support of a non-Buddhist adept, his teaching–disciple lineage, and the lineage's support and participation in the donor's government. Thus, monks sometimes received the moral authority to punish crimes committed by villagers within their domain, and the economic authority to collect sale taxes and charge fines and arrears.[40] In sum, such grants decentralized the powerful monastic donor's own authority by making his favoured monastic lineage, or another lineage or teacher responsible for many aspects of pastoral care.

This pattern of localized sovereignties also intensified non-sectarianism, characteristic of eastern Indian monastic governments of the 'Pala' as well as of the Saiva Tantric teachers and disciples whose names ended with -sena (Devasena, Buddhasena, and his son or disciple Jayasena).[41] Lay disciples of one teaching lineage patronized skilled adepts of other lineages. A grant of the Buddhist (*paramasaugata*) Mahendrapala, for example, confirmed all the gifts of grain and land that a Saiva subject had earlier made to various working populations.[42] Identical non-sectarianism was noted of the Sena lineage in the thirteenth century. A Tibetan Buddhist monk (Dharmasvamin) who went on pilgrimage to Bodhgaya (Bihar) in 1234–5, *after* the Turko-Afghan Muslim 'conquest' of the region, found one of the Sena disciples as a 'lord of Magadha'.[43] Buddhasena issued orders to the cultivators and others attached to the tax-exempt property owned by the Mahabodhi complex that the income from the property be assigned permanently to yet another Buddhist monastic scholar (*bhikshu pandita*), Dharmarakshita, who had once been the Rajaguru (royal preceptor) of the Kama country. Dharmarakshita, in turn, was advised to care for the elderly monks from Sinhala (modern Sri Lanka), presumably also present on the plains at the same time. Presumably such pattern of non-sectarian gift continued in the Himalayan worlds as well between the thirteenth and seventeenth centuries: for long-haired Saiva Natha ascetics (yogis, bairagis) were painted in Buddhist processions till at least 1712.[44] Such non-sectarian patronage also enabled the establishment of Central Asian Sufis in eastern India.[45] Thus the same actions were spoken of as gift (*dana*) and mandatory charity (*zakat*).

When the term was *dana*, they referred to an invisible but socially valued good called *punya* or merit, a commodity that mitigated the effects of karma, overcame debt—especially to one's ancestors—and overcame bad rebirths for the donor. Like other kinds of capital, merit was produced by the Buddhist monk and acquired by both laity and the ordained in exchange for lands, grain, herds, manufactured goods, labourers, and labour-time given in *dana*. The process of exchange consolidated the political and economic relationships between donor and recipient, as well as tying the present 'long life' and afterlife of both to the future.

Michael Walsh has recently argued that 'merit' was a commodity which was the object of many transactions and exchanges between lay and ordained monastic actors alike.[46] Rather than the division of labour associated with an industrializing economy, Walsh's treatment of merit as a quantum good suggests that labour in a monastic economy was divided between the lay and the ordained, and the returns of labour between the worldly (*laukika*) and the cosmological (*paralaukika*). Work in both domains constituted the merit-making goals of laymen and laywomen. Laymen were expected to conquer greed, desire, and ignorance as they moved towards renunciation of worldly ambitions on their journey towards monastic merit-making. Laywomen, too, were expected to conquer greed, desire, selfhood in their ability to give up the fruits of their work—cattle-wealth, trade goods, cash, and sons that had been generated by their work in the world. Such gifts in turn amassed moral capital, or 'merit', for the lineages in which they were simultaneously daughter and wife, sister and mother.

For lay followers, anonymous gift-giving had little value since such gift-giving had to earn 'merit', which in turn could be accumulated and transferred to the credit of particular persons, lineages, clans. As a 'good', such merit was moral capital that was transferred and transmitted to ancestors, future generations of descendants, disciples as well as teachers and superiors. These dual conceptions of material and future returns shaped the economic actions of both laymen and laywomen and are attested by metal images commemorating such monastic teachers in many parts of Bengal, Assam, and Bihar in the medieval and early modern periods. These images were of the monks themselves.[47] Some of these images bore inscriptions transferring the merit accrued from gifting an image (including a Siva-linga) to a teacher (*acarya*).[48] Susan Huntington's study of medieval sculpture from eastern India found many such inscribed images.[49] Similarly, Gouriswar Bhattacharya's work on an eleventh-century inscription on a slate relief identified a Bouddha *bhikshu* male with shaven head and long ears as that of a tantric acarya, the preceptor of the donor and a worshipper of Tara.[50] These images constituted investments in spiritual futures, and represent an identity of values and wealth-holding by lay males and females in the same period. Both used mobile wealth to invest in meritorious futures, a fact that is also borne out by the names of lay females (*upāsikā*) who sponsored the writing, illustration, and donation of key ritual manuscripts of Mahayana Buddhist orders across eastern India and Nepal in the thirteenth and fourteenth centuries.[51]

Transmissions of 'merit', and generosity as forms of moral capital, distinguished some men and women from others. A reputation for generosity, wisdom, knowledge, or skill was as much part of capital as lands and herds and goods created and earned by such traits. The rules of transmission of each kind of 'good', however, varied from group to group in time. Methods of accounting for transmission of moral capital in spiritual and social lineages fuelled the construction of tradition in the shape of genealogies in the hands of descendants and successors. Such methods of transmission enhanced the generational authority of men and women who alone could 'remember' and transmit genealogies. As in seventeenth-century Vietnamese and Thai societies, post-menopausal women, though female in anatomy and work experience, became 'male' as they aged; their prestige and potency within the household grew as they accumulated hitherto 'male' oral-ritual skills such as those of communal lore, genealogies, and ritual invocations.[52]

Mughal documents and inscriptions from the sixteenth and seventeenth centuries suggest a continuity of this pattern of monastic government and the extension of power through the actions of such teaching-learning lineages. In the eyes of their disciples, all such figures—whether Bonpo or Buddhist, Vaisnava or Saiva, Sufi or *alim*, 'teacher' or 'priest', diviner or prophet—were potent figures with the power to control or avert disease, death, and defeat. They were appreciated and nurtured by all with the means to do so. Some of these men were closer to alchemists, like the Muslim diviner (*qalandar*), an 'expert in the science of necromancy and magic spells', who was the teacher of a highly-ranked Mughal officer, a governor of Bengal. He received a substantial annual stipend (30,000 rupees) from his disciple, and served as both arbitrator of disputes and as a naval commander, as occasion arose and as his Mughal patron-cum-disciple needed.[53] An earlier generation of scholars of Muslim and Hindu lineages had studied mostly male members of such political societies. Following Mills, however, this monograph turns its attention to the women-centred households that constituted the 'base' of support and provisioning for both monastic militias and teaching lineages of males.[54]

FORGOTTEN LAYWOMEN AND MONASTIC CODES OF GENDER

Three concerns in particular drive this monograph. One is that of female donors and the monastic economy. Despite the economic salience of *dana* and *zakat*, the historiography of eastern India has lagged behind that of southern India in its study of gendered economic agency within the terms laid out by monastic constitutions.[55] Recent scholarship on the gendered nature of donative activity in eastern India suggests some parallels with the southern Indian evidence.[56] It appears that though women's public authority over land may have been widely known, women did not liquidate their holdings for their own donative activities. Instead, it is likely that the instance of the landowning female consort of a Buddhist male (Devakhadga) was representative: this female allowed her husband to make gifts of her immobile wealth (land) while she used gold, a mobile and malleable form of wealth in her own donative activity, which comprised the covering of an image of a Brahmanical goddess with precious bullion. This would appear to fit with the record between the seventh and the eighteenth centuries, which indicated that many laywomen acted as donors of valued mobile goods such as manuscripts, lamps, and herds; fewer of them gave lands. From the seventeenth century, however, some female donors also gifted lands to monastic recipients. As with previous regimes of monastic actors, Mughal donors also rendered gifted lands exempt from taxes; imperial and local officials were instructed not to impede the recipient's organization of cultivation and collection of harvests from these lands for their own subsistence (*madad-i-ma'ash*).[57] Women also appeared to have made gifts of their claims in the labour-services of others to their teachers and gurus in the eighteenth century.[58] What happened to such actors in the monastic economy in the nineteenth century?

A second question arises from the recorded involvement of monastic governments in marriages of disciples, members of ordination lineages, and of related laity. Three different kinds of disciples and members of monastic communities have to be distinguished in any group. One was the initiated layman who had sexual partners; the second, the ordained monk who also had sexual partners; and finally, the ordained celibate male or female who did not. Theoretically parallel to each other, ordained monastic and lay householder lineages in fact overlapped in the communities around individual Tantric Saiva, Sakta, Vaisnava, and Tantric Buddhist teachers. One such overlap appeared in the records of an initiated Buddhist tantric lord, the 'king' Dharmapala, whose banner had the goddess Tara represented on it.[59] The same Dharmapala, however, after having visited the pilgrimage sites of Kedara and Gokarna, 'entered the life of a householder' by marrying Rannadevi, daughter of a Rastrakuta. From this marriage was born Devapaladeva, who combined both monastic and temporal authority in himself and was described in the inscriptions as world-conquering ruler.[60] The father's ritual-meditative focus on Tara was shared by the son, whose inscription on an icon of the deity found in Patna district bore Tantric formulae (*Om Tare Tuttare Ture Svaha*).[61] The affinal relationship with the Rastrakuta was inherited and renewed by men in the Pala lineage. These affinal relations were equally marked by an absence of sectarianism. The Pala Buddhist initiates' wives were not themselves initiated Buddhists but 'Hindu', likely Vaisnava.[62]

Cross-lineage affinities suggest that marriages between disciples strengthened the political and economic bases of a teacher and his teaching lineage, perhaps by expanding the sources from which 'gifts' could originate. Sanskrit texts on *dana* authored by learned Saiva tantric 'Sena' men, for instance, recommended endogamous sexual unions for those considered spiritually and ritually distinguished (*kulina*). However, these men of superior moral achievements were also required to accept 'in gift' the hands of maidens from households of lesser moral capital. When Saiva monastic governance thus authorized polygyny and hypergamous relationships for the distinguished and spiritually accomplished men (that is, *kulina* brahmans), they implicitly positioned the supremely disciplined householder male (*kulina* brahman) as the tantric analogue of the supremely disciplined celibate monk. Both received 'gifts' from disciples and acted as a 'field of merit', returning blessings. Since 'gifts' were permanent, the same codes therefore accommodated a variety of arrangements such as single-generation or bi-generational polyandry (*niyoga*). Epic narratives laid claim to arrangements in which supremely disciplined elder males ('sages') were nominated (by elder women) to impregnate childless widows of the elder women's households.[63] Such textual Brahmanic and precolonial provisions are illuminated further by recently found documents which establish explicit contracts of fraternal polyandry in the period between the fourth and eighth centuries CE in and around northwestern Afghanistan.[64] Neither fraternal polyandry nor levirate nor polygyny was unknown to monastic governments. If such was the case, when and why did these marriages acquire 'subaltern' status?[65] Or to put it in another way, when did political and economic institutions become merely 'domestic'? Were eighteenth-century or nineteenth-century British colonial policies responsible for both the degraded status of such marriages as well as the inability of historians to appreciate them in the histories of the seventeenth-nineteenth century?

From the eighteenth century, it is true, individual colonial officials disdained plural partnerships that were 'repugnant to European ideas'.[66] Yet such attitudes were neither uniform nor given effect as policy immediately. A Scottish private trader and official of the East India Company who spent four months at the fifteenth-century monastery at Tashilunpo in 1774, referred to polyandry among the subjects of the monastic estate as a form of 'club[bing] together in matrimony as merchants do in trade'.[67] Engels too lauded these forms of political cooperation as representative of the 'mutual toleration among adult males' essential to the formation of permanent political groups.[68] Even the Bengali-speaking men who visited those societies in the late nineteenth century found these marriages praiseworthy, connected to the monastic arrangements of the same societies. Yet, when the first feminist histories of the subcontinent began from the 1980s, these patterns of marriages were acknowledged in all parts of the subcontinent *but* that of eastern India. For instance studies of northern India located fraternal levirate (*karewa*) in the labour-intensive agropastoralist work of women there.[69] But no study of eastern Indian historical practices tracked the persistence of such marriage patterns in terms of agropastoralist and labour-intensive work in the seventeenth or eighteenth centuries. Certainly no historian, including me, had previously tied these regimes of meritorious but monastic female subjects' labour to the very foundations of colonial or imperial political history.[70]

Had all of us postcolonial historians simply overlooked the evidence of the eighteenth-century 'colonial' archives? If we had, what were the reasons for such exclusion? After all, British officers who praised polyandry had also described landscapes of predominantly female cultivators. One who visited the winter capital of a Himalayan monastic lineage was struck by the women who cultivated the terraced corn fields; that it was mainly women who planted, weeded, harvested, and performed a 'thousand laborious offices, exposed themselves to hardships and inclement weather'.[71] Such officers noted the lack of a separation between 'domestic' and 'external' work and the absence of a sexual division of labour; women, like men, also worked as transporters or 'coolies'. In the 1780s, a Company official observed women in Sylhet carrying cloths, iron, cotton, and fruits 'from the mountains' of Assam for sale to the plains. These women carried back considerable quantities of salt, rice, dry fish, in extremely short supply in the Himalayan foothills. Colonial observers described the men of these groups accompanying the women 'with arms to defend them from insult.' These officers referred to such groups as 'my Tartar friends' while detailing the method of transportation: 'women in baskets supported by a belt across the forehead, the men walking by their side, protecting them with their arms'.[72] These colonial eighteenth-century descriptions of female labour did not disparage the labourers. But their encomia of such labour overlooked the twinned 'political–moral economy' within which such labour was transacted on estates owned by monastic lineages and in exchange for merit. Postcolonial feminist historians of eastern India appear to have mimicked these colonial observers twice over: first in overlooking the significance of monastic militias and men, and secondly in overlooking the predominantly female cultivators among

Tibetan-speaking people living on many of the hills and plains of Bangladesh-Bengal and Assam. Therefore a third area that this monograph engages is the persistent nature of labour-services and dues. These affiliated lay and monastic households to each other across different ecologies across different terrains. Legends collected in the early twentieth century from the same regions as earlier monastic histories called 'Buddhist lands' continued identifying adult women and female children at the literal centre of narratives of migration from the Tibetan highlands to the plains. As one account visualized it, 'the women and children were in the middle, before and behind [them were] the brave chieftains and warriors strong'.[73] The women carried the implements of cultivation—the short axes (*dah*s), hoes, the seeds and the brass cymbals, yak tails and harps; the men carried the implements of war—the swords and shields. These legends and accounts insisted that the women and children had been the main *producers* of the crops of consumption and exchange; males were soldiers who guarded cultivators. These accounts treated marriages of such productive females as acts of great political import, the substance of diplomacy, of 'friendships' between groups and collectives. They treated the theft of such cultivators as immoral. They even spelled out that transmissions of authority and property were mediated through daughters, sisters, and mothers: men accessed or managed authority and property by virtue of their relationships to women, not independently of them. And finally, these were *political* decisions taken in collective assembly, and therefore to be maintained as an expression of 'collective will'.

When postcolonial socialist feminist scholars of eastern India overlooked this particular mode of political cooperation routed through the household, they failed to value the 'protection of women' that reverberated in literati discourse from the nineteenth century. Postcolonial historians granted such affective investments only to the anti-colonial urbane literati nationalists. Partha Chatterjee, Tanika Sarkar, and Mrinalini Sinha highlight the ways in which nationalist 'Hindu' males responded to British colonialism by reconstituting the household and the family as the male's uncolonized 'sphere of sovereignty' in the late nineteenth and early twentieth century.[74] This position misrecognizes a common and central concern of males *dependent* on female producers for their food and their 'merit'. It rests on blindness towards the payments of labour-services as 'rent' or 'taxes', well-known everywhere in the lands flanked by the rivers Brahmaputra and the Ganges. As a result, monastic and lay communities' struggles to retain females and children as cultivators and transporters for their own monastic estates remains a curiously under-studied part of colonial economic and political history. By focusing on the political economy within which polymorphic households and friendships were re-constituted and labour-services 'freed' for colonially organized economic 'development', this study offers a new, culturally and historically specific way of conceiving gender and politics for a forgotten part of the subcontinent.

FORGETTING AND 'NORTHEAST INDIA': LAMENTABLE HISTORIOGRAPHICAL PRACTICE OR MONASTIC GOVERNMENTALITY RESTORED?

The causes for our common postcolonial historical refusal to name the political histories of eastern India correctly remain to be investigated. Had we never learnt or had we forgotten to look in the right places? Forgetting has been much lamented lately.[75] But not so in South Asia. In 1992, after mobs of Hindus destroyed a historic fifteenth-century mosque at Ayodhya in the name of an amoral certitude about the past, at least one scholar lauded the 'principled forgetfulness' located in the worldview of the victims.[76] Nandy celebrated those societies that refuse to remember the past either objectively or clearly or in its entirety. He argued that such forgetting was essential for maintaining the social fabric of the present and for defeating the amoral desires that drive post-Enlightenment historians.

This position puts historians of South Asian pasts in a dilemma: if forgetting is a value, then we are called upon to ensure its production and widespread distribution, rather than its amelioration. Yet, Nandy offers no guidelines by which political, economic and social institutions may create and transmit such forgetting. Moreover, he considerably mis-states the contrast between history and forgetting. A significant trend in modern South Asian history has been its sensitivity towards the malleability of memory.[77] Two studies of precolonial forgetting in particular have the potential to extend Nandy's argument regarding the objects and temporal rhythms of forgetting and remembering. The first is Sumit Guha's study of

Bhosle records between the seventeenth and nineteenth century. He finds that the Bhosles forgot the ancestral lands in the peninsula whence they came to prominence; instead, they laid their claims to authority in the region in political negotiations with a trans-regional Mughal administration.[78]

A similar process is found in Elliot Sperling's study of the migration of Tibetanized clans from Inner Asian (Tangut or Xi Xia, from around Lake Kokonor, in northeastern China) kingdoms to eastern and southeastern Tibet (Khams) and to the monastic centres of the Sa-skya lineage of Buddhists during and after the thirteenth century. Sperling argues that the migrants and their hosts in Khams integrated their historical memories to the extent that the link to an exalted past as rulers of the Xi Xia state became the common historical memory of the population in Khams as well.[79] Such deliberate amalgamation of memories binds both northern and eastern Tibetan clans (Tangut and Khams Mi Nyag) in narratives of the origin of Sikkimese 'kings' and clans, many of who held estates in eastern Nepal between the fifteenth and the eighteenth century.

Such purposive and precolonial acts of forgetting local particulars for more potent or illustrious pasts were also characteristic of early modern Buddhist 'pagoda histories' in Arakan. There the working of Time was denied altogether as an attempt to paper over the ruptures that Time imposed; stressing eternity was a method of reassurance to the community of followers.[80] This was especially true for histories of buildings or decoration of stupas, which constituted the highest kind of 'treasure' in Tibetan Buddhism: Buddha's mind-treasure.[81] Equally important, the calendar of 'decline' of the Buddhavacana (teachings of the Buddha) was a real concern among avowed Buddhists. Hence the stress on eternity, rather than the emphasis on change characteristic of European historical texts, was itself a sign of the composers' disciplinary location.

By reminding ourselves of the ways in which monastic governments shaped memory, this study historicises the forgetting of Himalayan pasts in the histories of 'Assam', 'Tripura', 'Northeast India', written in the twentieth century. For instance, an eminent Buddhist monastic complex such as Nako (in modern Himachal Pradesh, on the border with Tibet) lauded by seventeenth-century Tantric and Persian-writing historian, mystified a twentieth-century editor such as Suryya Kumar Bhuyan.[82] His omissions of particular Buddhist monastic sites in north-western parts of the subcontinent, while remaining aware of Saiva and Sufi actors in the same landscape, then generated an amnesiac colonial and postcolonial geography and history of a region called Assam. Post-colonial Indian historians of 'Assam', 'the Northeast' and of Bhuyan himself, remain unwilling to relocate the region in a broader trans-regional space that included Ladakh, Kashmir, Inner Asia and beyond.[83] In its place, a post-nationalist geographical sensibility attempts to come to terms with colonial policies towards forests, rivers, and environments shaped by animals.[84] Little in this scholarship re-imagines precolonial geographies shaped by monastic governments across dispersed sectarian traditions and ecological niches. Even less is said here about the ways in which the replacement of monastic government and geography substantially rewrote ideas of gender and rank for the 'Northeast'.

So, to return to the question posed by Nandy's argument, should modern historians of eastern India continue to emulate their predecessors in forgetting about the Buddhist centres in Ladakh and the Himalayan world altogether? Or are the histories they attempt to write meant to recover from such forgetting? The former is doubtless an easier option at present, especially since the histories one might recover potentially damage various kinds of nationalist and regionalist claims to land, dominance and dignity made by various politically active groups. Forgetting however is also a politically loaded action. One can illustrate the political costs of forgetting by alluding to the complex scribal cultures nurtured by monastic sites in the seventeenth and eighteenth century.[85] Such cultivation of scribal cultures, however, was conditioned by two factors: first, heteroglot languages and the second, a priority to oral transmission of core issues.

Ambiguous written language was especially part of Buddhist-Saiva Tantric cultivation.[86] In records generated within such epistemological traditions, twilight language was used to refer to three kinds of objects of knowledge—the manifest, the cognitive, and the realized—valued by non-dualist groups.[87] Such languages could only be deciphered by students formally trained by teachers empowered to explain such terminology. When the teachers lost their ability to teach, or the students disappeared, historians of the region failed to recognize the written record.

Furthermore, oral transmission enhanced this possibility. Turko-Mongols of the thirteenth–fifteenth centuries had relied on religious or clerical figures to perform the work of political ambassadors. Such clerical figures were charged with delivering the more important secret and oral message not trusted to a formal letter, while formal letters were produced collaboratively by a largely undifferentiated collective in the chancellery.[88] Cryptic letters from the chancellery of an Assamese heavenly lord (*svargadev*) to various hegemons in the vicinity similarly name priestly brahmans and scribes as conveyors of the much more important 'oral communication' to be delivered in secret. The high status of oral transmission, highlighted in writing itself, suggests the problems of interpretation that would arise in cases where sacred envoys—the 'brahmans', the teacher-monks, religious scholars and priests—were killed, persecuted, disappeared in the course of battle. The writing that they carried or created would become inexplicable without oral commentary. Something of this process occurred repeatedly between the seventeenth and the early twentieth century on the plains of eastern India. So that by the early twentieth-century, colonial literati failed to recognize their Himalayan and trans-regional pasts etched out in the records themselves.

Judging from the surviving diplomatic correspondence, Sanskritic Bengali was cultivated as a diplomatic language in eastern Himalayan centres in the eighteenth century. An Englishman who carried a Persian-language letter to a Bhutanese Buddhist monastic centre at the time found only Bengali in diplomatic use there.[89] This tradition remained vibrant well into the first half of the nineteenth century.[90] In the mid-nineteenth century, missionaries summoned to the hills of the east inhabited by Tibetan-speaking populations noted that the Bengali alphabet was adapted for expressing what missionaries called 'the sounds of Garo words'.[91] [The region constitutes modern Meghalaya in India]. Tibetan-inflected Bengali-language records abounded in other parts of eastern India as well. Even in mid-twentieth century, public intellectuals from Chittagong continued to use such Tibetan-Bengali unselfconsciously. For instance, two separate authors described historical texts as 'gojen-lama' books.[92] G*ojen* (written as `*kho.chen* in Tibetan and pronounced *gojen*) stands for a 'note written by a superior officer/official on a report submitted by a subordinate officer/official that indicates the superior's decision or answer'.[93] It exemplifies many such Tibetan phonemes and words used by Bengali speakers outside the metropolitan centre of Calcutta.[94]

Yet, in the same century as such Tibetan-inflected Bengali writers, Bhuyan collected written texts generated by locally settled scribes in the Brahmaputra valley and called them *buranji* without recognising the term's Tibetan and monastic connection at all. In Tibetan the term 'byas' (pronounced 'chi' and 'ji') means to say/tell. When added to the Tibetan verb 'phukhs.lon' (pronounced 'pulon' and 'bulon', meaning to know or understand the gist or essence of a matter) it suggests a synthetic narrative. Such syntheses, in addition to the difficulties of converting the Tibetan calendars (of sixty-year cycles) to Saka and Vikrama era dates, shaped major controversies about these chronicles and records, most of which were also editorially reconstituted and printed only after 1930.[95]

Postcolonial historians of 'modern' eastern and northeastern India have already mastered a particular kind of forgetfulness about their trans-regional, trans-sectarian and trans-national precolonial histories. In place of amnesia then, this monograph seeks to highlight its causes and its costs. In this it wishes to extend recent debates about historical thinking in another direction altogether.[96] While an earlier scholarship drew attention to the wealth and heterogeneity of communicative and commemorative technologies in prefiguring the constitution of historical records, it said little about the priority of monastic commitments in shaping the non-formation of 'historical records' or the non-transmission of scribal cultures. These issues have been especially significant wherever Vajrayana, Saiva, and Bon tantric lineages were collocated: their disciplinary regimens emphasize oral teaching, disciplined silence, institutions of social retreat and the determined maintenance of obscurity and secrecy.[97] Tantric Buddhist and Sakta emphases on oral modes of instruction and transmission of sacred knowledge made them particularly vulnerable to traditions of 'history-writing' that insisted on transparent and referential forms of writing. Forced to operate amidst groups with scribal cultures of the latter kind, many might have created written texts which appear as 'recovered treasures' only available to visionaries.

These conditions appear to have been shared by three verse narratives used in this monograph, all of which have been identified with a lineage of Himalayan-based Tantrics of 'Tippera'. One of these is *SriRajamala*, an annotated and revised verse narrative published in four volumes during 1927–30.[98] Others are *Krishnamala* and *Srenimala*: both were published only in 1995–6. However, the editor of the first claimed that he 'discovered' a manuscript copy of the poem which was originally written in the eighteenth century. In a similar vein, the published *SriRajamala* is offered *as* a continuous record from the fifteenth to the eighteenth centuries, but it was only finalized in its poetic form around 1840–4 by a Durgamani Wazir, composer of the *Srenimala,* a record of marriages in the same lineage. Moreover, the Bengali version was explicitly identified as a translation from an original 'Tripur bhasha', which has never been available in writing to any scholar till date. Admittedly, these verse narratives cannot be treated as accounts *from* the seventeenth-eighteenth century of which they speak, but they can be treated as local language historiographic narratives, parallel to and contemporaneous with histories written by men and women trained in colonial schools and universities of the nineteenth and twentieth centuries.

Only as contemporaneous texts can these records become meaningful as commentaries on colonial conditions. They are attempts to remember a precolonial past that was dominated by initiated monastic warriors. The opening segments of the first volume of the *SriRajamala*, for instance, encompasses all tantric traditions—the Saiva, Vaisnava, and Buddhist—by referring to 'root' texts such as the *Yogini tantra* and *Haragaurisamvada,* a composition by Hema Sarasvati, one of three poets patronized in fourteenth-century Kamatapura (northern Bengal-Assam) and dramatized at the court of the (eastern Nepali) Bhatgaon Mallas in the early seventeenth century as *Haragaurivivaha*.[99] Tantric composers of narratives of *SriRajamala, Krishnamala,* and *Srenimala* used explicitly non-dualist frame that united absolute (*paramartha*) and phenomenological (*vyavahar, laukika*) statements as 'truth'. Such non-dualist metaphysics emphasized dissolution of differences between subject and object, knowledge and knower, secular and sacred.

Earlier generations of historians of independent India were critical of such verses. Like Bhuyan who had ignored Buddhist-Sufi Nako, earlier critics of the mixed language verses of *SriRajamala* failed to notice the Himalayan and trans-national references in them. A few examples should suffice. The first volume refers to populations from 'Kaifeng', the metropolis of the northern Song Chinese empire, who accompanied others on their way to the Indo-Gangetic plains. Though the verses themselves provide no date for such an event, other sources mention gifts of cotton goods carried to the Song metropolis by Indian Jews in the eleventh century and the arrival of lay Buddhist associations in southern China in the fourteenth.[100] Read against these sources, the verses do not appear to 'falsify' the past so much as encode it in a non-European, monastic and itinerant hermeneutic. The geographical space encountered in these verses under the term 'trisrota' (or 'three rivers') was a reference in colloquial Sanskrit to the river Tista, which flowed from the eastern Himalaya through Sikkim-Nepal on to the plains of Bengal.[101] In the same vein, the verses speak of a mountain (*parbatiya*) king of 'Tripura', whose followers were knowledgeable in 'malla-vidya' (lit. wrestling, also hand-to-hand combat). However, since these verses were printed only after the circuits of a monastic geographic order were dissolved, many of the places named in such verses remained unrecognized by nationalist plainsmen of the twentieth century. 'Herambo' is a case in point: few Bengali readers after 1930 could translate the name as the district of Herombo in western Nepal, associated with an ancient (in Tibetan, the term is 'rNyingma', and represents an ordination lineage) Buddhist monastery. However, the verses that use such terms also specify the flora and fauna of the terrain. Animals referred to in the poem included mountain goats 'with extremely fine hair', horned goats of the high Himalayan and Tibetan plateaus.[102]

Such landscapes were eclipsed from view finally by the Second World War and its aftermath, the territorial Partitions of 1947. These were the second set of circumstances that shaped postcolonial historical imagination and methods of verification. As a result, the terracotta plaques, stone inscriptions, metal images and coins that corroborate names and dates mentioned in the verse-narratives and chronicles, which lie scattered across the monastic geographic order between western Tibet, Kashmir, Nepal, Burma, western and southern China, Assam, and Bengal, (many of which are in private collections across eastern India) were seldom studied at any length by professional Indian historians in the 1970s–90s.[103]

Place names on the coasts also hint at connections with foothills: for instance, a temple dedicated to the goddess Ambika, also called Tripurasundari, sits on a high hilltop outside the modern town of Agartala. A river that flows from Nepal into the Gangetic plains (of modern Uttar Pradesh in India) called the Gomti gives its name to a river in the southern part of modern Tripura. In the vicinity are Buddhist stupa sites such as Pilak and Baxanagar. Terracotta plaques found in the walls of the abandoned stupa at Pilak mirror the motifs of terracotta plaques found on the Buddhist stupa at Paharpur (presently in northern Bangladesh). The earliest plaque recovered from Pilak, sculpted with date Om Śakābda 1419 (1497 CE), in the same script and numbers used for medieval Bengali, puts the building, or at least embellishment, of the Buddhist stupa in the tenure of the Turko-Afghan Muslim Hussain Shahi (1494–1519 CE) governors in western Bengal.[104] Another terracotta plaque also recovered from Pilak is sculpted with the figure typical of Achaemenid Bactrian art: it is the mythical horned lion with a spearhead-ending tail, a long slim body shaped like an S and an open mouth.[105] The only difference between the older Bactrian motif and that of the Pilak terracotta and coins of the seventh-century Himalayan Buddhist-Vaisnava lords of Nepal (Manadeva and Sivadeva c 570s–605 CE) and those found in Kumilla/Tripura on the Bengal plains is that the horned lion of the latter has a raised right paw, and appears to be holding a plant in it.[106]

These objects, names, and practices resonate only when placed within the map of a monastic geographic order that connected the Himalayan and trans-Himalayan world with that of the coastal and riverine plains of eastern India. The 'Tipura' coinage, marked by the composite horned lion referred to above, had the same weight standards as the silver *tanka* of the Afghan sultans of Bengal.[107] The close economic relationship that is narrated by the *SriRajamala* between a lineage of monastic militants and a Turco-Afghan imperium appears plausible in the light of such external corroborative material.

Nor are these verses, chronicles, and correspondence limited to relations between men, women, deities, and spirits alone. They also treat all animals as wealth, given in payments of different kinds. Verses of *SriRajamala* aver that one of the scions of Tipura/Tripur, having presented the sultan, the supreme commander of Gauda (Gaudesvar), with elephants, was allowed to settle in 'Vanga' (eastern Bengal).[108] Buranjis refer to the number of elephants that were sent annually by monastic tenants, residents of Tipura and the Assam hills, to Mughal tax collectors well into the eighteenth century.[109] They refer to institutions of trapping and corralling elephants (*kheda*) established for such purposes. They document the many different lives that made up the monastic geographic order in the seventeenth and eighteenth century.

In addition, these heteroglot records alone allow us a vantage point from which to launch the interrogation of colonial categories of knowledge as well as colonial methods of recognition as the practices of distance. Viewed from the perspective of intimates—the perspective that this monograph adopts—the same groups that appear as 'Dafla tribes' in nineteenth-century English records reappear in chronicles and poems as seventeenth-century tenants (*bahatia*) of old monastic lineages of married abbots.[110] Other Vaisnava texts place names such as those of 'Govinda Garo', 'Paramananda Miri', 'Jayaram Bhutiya', a Nocte called Narottama, and a 'Jayahari Yavana' (literally 'Yavana' was Ionian or Greek, but in seventeenth-century usage referred to Muslims)—names taken as badges of subaltern and 'tribal' alterity in the colonial order—as fellows and members of ordination lineages.[111] Eventually, these heteroglot genealogies, poetry, and chronicles' insistent mapping of a relational universe commends them to every postcolonial historian as the starting point of a journey *out* of a fragmented landscape—that of a so-called 'Northeast India'—and into reviving a modicum of the friendships that have been valued in and among Buddhist communities.

ARCHITECTURE OF THE ARGUMENT

Chapter 1 surveys the ways in which monastic governments of collocated Buddhist, Saiva, Sufi, and Vaisnava guides, teachers, and their adherents shaped what van Spengen has called 'monastic geographicity'.[112] The term expresses the spatial extent of a cultural complex of establishments and movements, a conceptual map of dominant patterns of communication, lifeways, repertoires, and techniques, and a political complex of 'subjects' and 'sovereigns'. The chapter argues that exogamous marriages and polyandrous and polygynous unions were the fulcrum of such 'monastic geographicity'.

This chapter begins with the basic units of monastic geographicity—the monastic residence, established by adherent individuals and clans that focused pastoral networks, pilgrim itineraries, and trade routes, acted as local marketplaces and storehouses. By virtue of receiving the gift of donors in exchange for merit, individual monasteries came to possess extensive lands, livestock, trading goods, and capital on loan. This vast geographic order had been created by the establishment of monasteries at the crossroads of silk routes in the Himalayan domains, including Assam, as well as along the coasts of Bengal, Burma, and beyond.[113] At least one such silk road was called the Northern Route (*Uttarāpatha*).[114] There were others, either branching off from the Northern Route or entirely independent of it. Mobility between the Himalayan hills and coastal plains along routes dotted by such monastic establishments enabled the circulation of people, herds, and objects, as much as they led to the convergence of ideas, structures of lineage-making, rituals, and disciplines. Mahayana Buddhist manuscripts dated between the eleventh and fourteenth centuries circulated by many routes within this vast domain and were eventually found in Nepal.[115] Using similar routes and extending them further, men and animals from 'power' centres in Himalayan uplands settled the lowlands and swamps of the Indo-Gangetic and Irawati lowlands and swamps.[116]

Monastic centres, spread out across different environmental and resource niches, had to be connected to each other through other relationships, either of friendship or of marriage. Therefore alliances and marriages became the fulcrum of 'monastic geographicity' and the key to monastic governments. In the medieval Tibetan empire, these marriage alliances set up 'uncle–nephew' or 'father-in-law and son-in-law' relationships (*zhang dbon*) or 'elder brother–younger brother' relationships (*tschen-tschung*) between central governments and provincial powers. Similar marital relationships were recorded in genealogies that expressed the localization of Central Asian (Afghan) and West Asian (Arab) lineages of *ulema* and Sufi *pirs* in Bengal after the fifteenth century. In the late seventeenth century, Mughal attempts to reorganize monastic militias then created conditions in which descent from monastic men became important to remember.

Chapter 2 traces the early encounter between the English East India Company and the key figures of monastic geography and genealogical memory in the second half of the eighteenth century. Officers attempted to destroy monastic exemptions from taxes, and to tax lands held as service–wages by adherents in a temple–monastic economy. Female landholders, major donors and actors in the monastic economy, became particular targets of these policies. Twin dispossessions converged to create shifts of title in landed wealth within all groups with claims to collect payments in kind and services from people settled on such estates. At the same time, the legislative enactments also created conflicts of succession within the all-male lineages of teachers and gurus on the land.

Chapter 3 tracks the further diminution of authority of monastic leaders and their households of adherents across the early nineteenth-century network that encompassed lineages and families in Ava, Assam, Tripura, and Manipur. The East India Company's wars of the early nineteenth century, especially that with Burma and in the Brahmaputra and Barak river valleys, were crucial in the de facto delegitimation of a widow's rights of inheritance from a second husband. In highlighting this, the chapter links colonial land-revenue legislation from 1790–3 to the legal dispossession of daughters as well as widows much further eastwards than hitherto understood. This dispossession clarifies the ways in which 'Hinduism' itself was revised to keep it abreast of the expanding colonial military frontier. At the same time, this chapter attempts to fix the cause of such dispossession not in an idealized British law of coverture or married women's 'separate estate' but rather in military and economic concerns after the Anglo-Burmese War (1824–6). Such concerns, rather than abstract legal ideals, eventually eroded the political fraternities based in a common spouse, or polyandry and levirate, from eastern Indian history. Structural and discursive shifts occurred simultaneously to obliterate the marriages of daughters and sisters from the colonial archives and from the authority or dignity accorded to these households by subsequent historians.

Chapter 4 translates between metaphors and descriptions of adherence and the nineteenth-century Liberal and colonial Anglophone discourse of 'feudalism', 'slavery', and 'savagery'. In choosing linguistic and cultural translation as an interpretative stance towards both hybrid regional and English-language written sources, one of my goals is to reinstate translation to its intellectual dignity as a historically established scholarly activity. Translation had a hoary literary genealogy especially in the medieval and early modern periods during which texts and teachers from eastern India travelled and taught in Himalayan terrain; translations also engaged visiting Moroccan Muslim scholars and craftsmen at the same time.[117] In keeping with that past, I subject English-language colonial records to translation. On the one hand this renders coherent a great mass of descriptive terms and nomenclature found transcribed in the records of the East India Company between the eighteenth and twentieth centuries. It makes the hybridity of the colonial archives explicit. On the other hand, it allows us to read these terms against the shifting economies of land revenue and military service associated with the growing power of the East India Company. Finally, this method of reading also reveals the ways in which early nineteenth-century colonial Englishmen mimicked the very monastic political economies that their policies gradually, and selectively, overrode.

Chapter 5 analyses the implications of colonial mimicry of monastic politics. It traces the formation of two parallel and competing orders of 'friendship' in eastern India. While the conflicts over tea plantations have been hitherto studied as issues in European management of immigrant labour, this chapter tracks the politics of fraternity practiced by monastic subjects resident in places such as Kachar, Sylhet, Tripura, and Manipur when tea plantations arrived there. In particular, this chapter studies the confrontation that is known as the 'Lushai Expedition' of 1871 in the colonial records. This expedition inaugurated the territorial segregation of tea-growing regions by an imaginary 'Inner Line' and its administration by a Chief Commissionership of Assam set up in 1874. In effect this 'Inner Line' was aimed at keeping the visiting, non-residential, non-native monastic teacher, guru, and guide of yesteryear from acquiring lands, trade goods, and subjects in terrain and among 'labourers' coveted by European tea planters. An apparently political boundary was thus created to keep monastic subjects apart from their erstwhile 'friends'.

Chapter 6 studies the attempt led by women to restore older codes of friendship in the face of intensified militarization of colonial governance in southern Kachar, northern Chittagong, and the Arakan hills. British military policemen did not distinguish between male and female when using the term 'coolie'. Yet in at least a few instances, their demands for labour were also demands for sexual services from local wives. These demands were resisted by networks of intermarried clans. The resistance of 1890–1900 provided the background for the gradual turn to Christian healers who lived alongside the British Indian armies. I track the effects of events in the Himalayan monastic world of 1903–4 on a cluster of villages that had been affected by the exclusions of the Inner Line. The populations of these villages on the Indian side of the Inner Line followed older monastic ideas of debt and exchange and offered themselves to Christian missionaries. Elder women led this attempt to re-establish the merit-based monastic economy, only this time with a new kind of monk and teaching at its centre. The Inner Line had however cut off hillocks from flat lands. Therefore, Christianization of newly isolated societies also excluded such populations living on elevations from interactions with plainsmen. These circumstances finally and ironically led to the renunciation of collocated pasts in Bon, Tantric Buddhist, and Saiva communities as 'barbaric'. This simultaneously consolidated a social amnesia about the past within the new learning societies on the hills as well as on the plains. In postcolonial universities outside the Inner Line, scholars began to identify hitherto co-members of monastic discipleship as 'strangers of the mist'.[118]

NOTES

1. Eaton (1978, 1993); Digby (2001); Green (2006, 2008); White (2009: 198–254); Pinch (1996, 2006); Dube (2004); Chaturvedi (2007).

2. For studies of Arakanese Buddhist-Muslim kings between the fifteenth and eighteenth century, see Gommans and Leider (2002); Leider (2002); for Muslim–Mongol military commanders who protected Tibetan Buddhist texts and practices by compelling Jesuit missionaries to learn them in the eighteenth century, see Pomplun (2011).

3. For studies of monastic sites and assemblages excavated over easternmost India and Bangladesh, see Dikshit (1938); Das (1971); Mitra (1976); Mitra (1996); Gill (2002); Roy (2002); Das (2004); for a survey of all the sites in Bogra district, see Rahman (2000) and comments on the

co-existence of Buddhist and Brahmanic finds; for Avalokiteshvara and Akshobhya finds at Mainamati and Paharpur in Bangladesh, see Imam (2000a, 2000b); Bhattacharya (2000, 2003); for Jaina, Saiva and Buddhist finds, see all articles in Mevissen and Banerji (2009). For reports of Buddhist and Saiva finds at western and southern Tripura sites dateable to the sixth century by the Archaeological Survey of India, Gauhati Circle, visit http://asi.nic.in/asi_exca_2005_tripura.asp (last accessed on 15 June 2009). Compare standing Buddha figure of red standstone from Pilak, southern Tripura, dated to the tenth century by the Tripura Government Museum, http://tripura.nic.in/museum (last accessed on 15 June 2009), with red standstone standing Vishnu from Pilak at Tripurasociety.org/ photogallery (last accessed on 15 June 2009). The Tripura Government Museum has also collected miniature terracotta figures of Mukhalingam (Saiva) Avalokiteshvara, Tara, and Vishnu from various sites: for an analysis of these, see Sengupta (1986, 1993). Accidental excavations continue to yield paired Buddhist–Vishnu icons such as the pair found while excavating a pond at Taichama, western Tripura, for which see *The Telegraph*, 17 March 2006 at http://www.telegraphindia.com/1060317/asp/northeast/story_5976829. asp (last accessed on 15 June 2009). Some of these finds and sites have been read alongside Sanskrit and Bengali-language inscriptions, deciphered, and translated in Bhattacharya (1968); Das (1997); Bhowmik (2003); Palit (2004); Acharjee (2006); and Acharjee (2008); for descriptions of recent excavations, see Chauley (2009). For sites in modern Bengal and Assam such as Surya Pahar at Goalpara, see Kaushik Phukan, http://www.posoowa. org/2007/06/27/the-conditionof-surya-pahar-a-neglected-archaeological-site/ (last accessed on 15 June 2009) and http://explorenortheastindia.com/ assam.htm (last accessed on 20 June 2009); for the depiction of multiple deities at the Hayagriva Madhava temple at Hajo, see http://asi.nic.in/ images/epigraphy/008.jpg (last accessed on 15 June 2009). For reports that the Hajo temple is the site of the winter pilgrimage of thousand of Buddhist Tibetans and Bhutanese on the grounds that Shakyamuni attained Mahaparinirvana at Hajo, that the Vaisnava temple itself is a chortem called r-Tsa-mchg-gron (Tsamcho-dun), that a rocky area a few kilometres away is considered the site of the Buddha's cremation called Silwa tsal-gi tur do (the pyre of the cool grove), that Buddhists also consider sacred a Saiva Kedarnath temple on the shoulder of a hill nearby and call a lake beside the temple Tso-mani bhadra (the lake of the notable gem), see Ravi Deka's report filed in 2000 at http://www.geocities.com/ravideka/archaeology.htm (last accessed on 20 June 2009); for scholarly discussion of Hajo as well as the Tibet-Assam connections of the seventeenth century, see Huber (2008: 125–65); for other sites in modern Northeastern Indian states, see Dutta and Tripathy (2006, 2008).

4. For illustrative studies of the gradual discovery of Buddhism by the British, see Lopez (ed.) (1995a and 1995b); Leoshko (2003); De Filippis (2003 [1932]); and Harris (2006).

5. For representative illustration of such schema, see Verardi (2011).

6. For illustrative examples, see Niyogi (1980); Bhattacharya (2008).

7. For the fifteenth century, see Mckeown (2010); also Elverskog (2010); for translation activities of Indian pandits and Tibetan lo-tsa-ba between fourteenth and seventeenth centuries, see Shastri (2002).

8. Doctor (2005: 18); for a list of the epigraphs found in coastal Bengal, see Morrison (1970, 1974); updated lists and sites in Hussain *et al.* (1997); Banik (2009).

9. Tucci (1931: 697, 699).

10. *Taranatha's History of Buddhism in India* (1970: 330). Taranath, *b.* 1575, wrote this in 1608.

11. Hodge (2009: 171); Goldstein *et al.* (2001: 55).

12. Das (1990 [1902]: 10).

13. Sen (1942: 341–6).

14. Petech (1984: 66). Bhatgaon, in eastern Nepal, was also known as Bhaktapur in Sanskrit.

15. *Ibid.*, 107, 109. For earlier reports of worship of Tripuresvari alongside Bonpo and Buddhist practices in western Nepal (Jumla) and Tibet, see Tucci (1956: 17–62); for confusion about the status of Tripurasundari in late twentieth-century Bhaktapur, compare Levy (1987) with Gutschow and Basukala (1987); Vergati (2002 [1995]: 39, 110).

16. Gaenszle (2002).

17. Petech (1984: 124–9).

18. Dhungel (2002: 47–72).

19. For the Kagyupa, see Dargye (2001); for the Kadampa, see Rai (2006).

20. Pomplun (2010: 118).

21. *Jahangirnama* (1999: 142–3).

22. Huber (2008: 6); for different interpretations on both sacred geography of Tibetan Buddhists and of ethnic categories such as 'Mon-pa' in southern Bhutan, see Pommaret (1999) and Templeman (1999).

23. For debate on 'monastic' as a term, see Gellner (1987, 1992).

24. Amstutz (1998).

25. As Alexis Sanderson's studies of Pala disciples of particular Tantric teachers reveal, initiates were spoken of as 'kings': after initiation, these men rewarded their teachers with headships of monasteries and monastic estates. Though king, each Pala was also a 'subject' of a teacher; Sanderson (2009: 92–4) for Pāla-built monasteries for teachers; also see his lecture at the University of Toronto, February 2010.

26. Flood (2004). *Askesis* literally meant exercise or discipline, giving practical effect to a doctrine and continuous embodied practice. See Valantasi (1995); for the centrality of disciplinary practice, not doctrines, to the formation of all schools, sects and lineages in India, see Silk (2002).

27. Ingalls (1957); Pollock (1985); for *yogacara* as attempt to synthesize diverse contemplative, ruminant and renunciative practices or muni-yati cults, see Amstutz (1998); Bronkhorst (2011: 164–5 and passim).

28. For Theravada symbolism, see Kirsch (1996); Van Esterik (1996); Keyes (1984); for Mahayana gender, see Cabezón (1992); Gyatso (2003); Makley (2007); Cook (2009).

29. Silk (2008).

30. Among the earliest studies, see Schram (1957); R.J. Miller (1959, 1961); B.D. Miller (1961); Cassinelli and Ekvall (1969); Ellingson (1990); Mornang (1990). For elaborations of monastic governance and economy, see Schopen (1997, esp. 258–9), and idem (2005); Boulnois (2002); Nietupski (2011); for comparative medieval western instances, see Sliber (1993).

31. *The Blue Annals* 1996, 178–9.

32. *Ibid.*, 96.

33. Dotson (2007: 3–78).

34. Kane (1930, vol. 2: 321–61).

35. Orr (2005).

36. For a comprehensive account, see Davidson (2002).

37. See, for example, Subhanakarapataka Grant of Dharmapala, in Sharma (ed.) (1981 [1931]): 217–21.

38. Carl Shigeo Yamamoto (2008: Chapter 3).

39. This clause was the single common denominator of the grants: for which compare between the easternmost grant found in Tezpur, Darrang district of Assam, by Chaudhary and Sircar (1951, *EI* 29: 145–59), and the latest finds of 'Pala' epigraphs in western Bengal and south Bihar, such as reported by Furui (2008) and Fleming (2010).

40. See for example, Narendradeva inscription (641 or 643–79) found in Pasupati temple, Kathmandu, in Bajracharya (1998: 30–1, Appendix VI).

41. Sircar (1979: 30–1).

42. Bhattacharya (2007).

43. Sircar (1979: 31–2). For Khalji presence on the plains of Magadha, Gaur, and foothills of the Himalayas 1199–1227, see Sarkar (1973: 1–38).

44. Vergati (1987: 43–7); Vergati (2002 [1995]: 202–14).

45. For studies of inscriptions dateable between 1205 and 1707, see Siddiq (2009).

46. See Walsh (2007, 2010).

47. For example, an elder (Sthavira) Pindola Bharadvaja, deified as a 'Buddha of medicine' (*bhaisajyaguru*); Bhattasali (1929: 37–41).

48. For the donative declaration of 'de dharmoyang acaryya prathama ... bhadrasya' on a black stone lingam, see Bhattasali (1929: 143).

49. Huntington (1984: 65–6).

50. Bhattacharya (2000a: 373–83; 2000b).

51. See Kim (2010a: 269; 2010b). Among nine donors, three were female laity, named 'Queen Uddākā' and 'Hīrākā, wife of a *thakura*'; the third was unnamed.

52. Andaya (2006); Blackwood (2005); Peletz (2006); Loos (2009).

53. *Baharistan-i-Ghaybi*, II (1936: 669–672, 693, 736).

54. Mills (2000: 17–34).

55. Orr (2000).

56. Rangachari (2009: 432–6 and 435).

57. For records of sixteenth and seventeenth-century grants of tax-exempt lands to women, including a cluster of women led by a 'Musammat Raj Gosain', see Srivastava (1974: 19, 24, 29); Tirmizi (1979); Shakeb (ed.) (1982: 7–8).

58. Ahmad (1946). The document, dated 1783 CE, hands over a female donor's inheritance of slaves as a gift to a guru, Sarbananda Gosain in Kuch Behar, northern Bengal.

59. Dasgupta (1967).

60. Monghyr Copper-Plate in Mukherji and Maity (1967: 115–31); Sastri (1923, *EI*, 17: 310–27).

61. Sircar (1967: 128–33); for significance of Tara and other goddesses in inscriptions for eastern Assam and Manipur, see Bhattacharyya (1995).

62. Rangachari (2009: 410–14).

63. For levirate and widow marriages, and polyandry see Arti Dhand (2004); Sarva Daman Singh (1978); Meyer (1989 [1971]).

64. Sims-Williams (2000: 14).

65. Sahai (2007).

66. For comment on Bogle's notes on a 'modest and virtuous' wife of six of the lama's nephews, see Stewart and Lama (1777: 465–92).

67. Cited in Stewart (2009: 44).

68. Engels (2000 [1884]: Chapter II).

69. Chowdhury (1987, 1994); for studies of levirate and plural marriage from colonial peninsular India, see Poonacha (1996); for studies of shifting marital preferences and inheritance systems, see Arunima (2003); M. Srinivas (2008).

70. For example of oversight, see Chatterjee (2004); also Majumdar (2009).

71. Turner (2005 [1800]: 141, 180–1).

72. Robert Lindsay, Collector of Sylhet to Board of Revenue, 14 Dec 1787, *SDR*, 2, 205.
73. Rongmuti (1933: 54–60).
74. P. Chatterjee (1993); M. Sinha (1995, 2006); T. Sarkar (2002).
75. Bennett (2008); also Scott (2008).
76. Nandy (1995).
77. Novetzke (2008); in a similar vein, see Sreenivasan (2007).
78. Guha (2009).
79. Sperling (2011); Mullard (2011).
80. Leider (2009).
81. For discussions of such 'treasure literature', see among others, Vostrikov (1970 [1958]), Doctor (2005).
82. Bhuyan *Padshah Buranji* (1947: 62–3). For description of Nako, see Tucci (1988 [1935]: 3: 141–73).
83. Saikia (2008a); Purkayastha (2008).
84. Zou and Kumar (2011); Saikia (2005); Singh (2007); for political implications of such environmentalist histories, see Ludden (2003); Kar (2004); Baruah (2004); Pradhan (2007); Misra (2010); also Cederlof (2009); Suan (2011); Zou (2011).
85. D'Hubert and Leider (2011).
86. See surveys of the debate in Wayman (2005 [1973]: 128–35); Davidson (2002: 236–92); Kvaerne (2010 [1977]).
87. In addition to above, see Bhattacharya (1916); Thurman (1978, 1991); Lopez Jr. (1993 [1990]); reviews of Lopez in Griffiths (1990), Boucher (1990), Ruegg (1995); Cho (2002); Hershock (2003); Samuel (2008); Patil (2009); Urban (2001, 2010).
88. Broadbridge (2010: 17, 22–5).
89. Turner (2005 [1800]: 69); for another ordained monk who assumed the part of a 'buffoon' who hailed the Englishmen in 'bad Bengali', 151.
90. See Cooch Behar-Bhutan Diplomatic Correspondence in Biswas (1997: II, 923–40). A letter dated 1812 names 'Ramnath Kayeth' [member of a scribal community] as agent on behalf of the Buddhist monastic regime; the letter also names a polyglot Brahmana, Rammohun Roy, as Diwan of the British Collector of Rangpur, and emissary on behalf of the Company.
91. *Outline Grammar of the Garo Language* (1874: 2–3).
92. Karmi (comp) (1997 [1940]: 16); also Dasgupta (1997 [1372 B5]).
93. Goldstein, Shelling, and Surkhang (2001: 239).
94. For Kumilla, Sylhet, Chittagong, and Arakan, see Chatterjee (1993 [1926]: 108–9, 228–35); for its influence in shaping the study of Assamese and the lexical correspondence between Perso-Arabic, Burmese, Maithili, Malaya and Tibetan languages with Assamese, see Kakati (1962 [1941]:

xiii–xiv, 40–82, 263), and passim; for studies of subcontinental heteroglossia from the earliest period to the present, see Pollock (2000, 2005); Busch (2011); Guha (2004b, 2005).

95. Gogoi (1986), Tunga (1985).

96. For sample of debate on vernacular materials dateable to the seventeenth and eighteenth centuries from south India, see Rao, Shulman, and Subrahmanyam (2003, 2007); for east India, see Chatterjee (2008, 2009, 2010); Tony K. Stewart (2004, 2010); Curley (2008); Kar (2008) for west India, see O'Hanlon (2010); Guha (2004).

97. Among others, see Lopez (1995a); Davidson (2002).

98. For review, see Chatterjee (2002); Acharjee (2008, 2012); Deb Roy (2008).

99. Macdonald and Stahl (1979: 24).

100. Laufer (1930: 189–97), www.jstor.org, accessed 06/21/2010; for potential significance of the contemporary Buddhist-Taoist lineages of Song-Yuan deported to southern China, see Overmyer (1982).

101. Hossain et al. (1995: 10–11); for major Buddhist monastic complexes along this river-system, see Rahman (2000).

102. For a pictorial representation of the animals referred to, see Goldstein and Beall (1990: 96) and passim.

103. In addition to the government museums at Delhi, Calcutta, Gauhati, and Agartala, these include private collections such as those housed in Rajendra Kirtishala, Agartala.

104. The terracotta block is preserved in Rajendra Kirtishala; some of the numismatic collections can be found in the Indian Museum in Calcutta as well as Acharjee (2008).

105. Compare Aruz, Farkas, and Fino (eds) (2006, fig 16: 124), with a terracotta plaque of a horned lion and the same images on coins and seals associated with the Tripura Manikya, for which in addition to above, see Rhodes and Bose (2002).

106. For discussion of epigraphic and numismatic evidence on the Vaisnava-Buddhist genealogies of Jayadeva II, Manadeva, and other figures in the Himalayan foothills, see Bajracharya (1998: 18–35); Rhodes and Gabrisch et al. (1989); compare with Kuch Bihar in Bhattacharyya (1991); Mitchiner (2000); Rhodes and Bose (2003).

107. Rhodes and Bose (2002: 8–11); also A.C. Roy (1986: 259–318).

108. Kaliprasanna Sen, SriRajamala (1927, 1: 67–9).

109. S.K. Bhuyan Tripura Buranji (1938: 48-9). The text was written in 1724 and provided eye-witness accounts of routes between northern Bengal and the coastal plains of modern Bangladesh that passed through the Barak valley.

110. S.K.Bhuyan ed. Tungkhungia Buranji (1990a [1933]: 99–172).

111. Neog (1998 [1965]: 369).
112. Van Spengen (2000).
113. Luczanits (2004); also Luczanits (2011a, b: 13–24, 73–83); for archaeology of monastic sites along trade-routes, see Ray (2003, 2007); Neelis (2007); for an earlier study, see Dutt (1962).
114. Dar (2007); Neelis (2011: 186–204); for a later period, Sen (2003); Chakravarti, first 2002, revised 2007; Adhikary (1997 [1988]).
115. See Kim (2010a, 2010b).
116. Aung-Thwin (2005: 64 and passim).
117. For linguistic translations between Sanskrit and Tibetan, see among others Vostrikov (1970 [1958]); Van der Kuijp (1983); Eimer and Germano (2002); Gangopadhyay (2007); for Arabic translations of Sanskrit texts, see Pines and Gelblum (1989); Flood (2009); for other adaptations of literary forms and oral performances, see Guha (2004a).
118. The phrase is borrowed from Hazarika (1994).

1

Monastic Governance, 'Geographicity', and Gender

MONASTIC GOVERNMENTS WERE CRUCIAL in shaping human geographies across the greater Brahmaputra and Surma-Barak valleys (See Figure 1.1). This chapter argues that relationships between different kinds of monastic assemblages anchored discrete but intertwined geographies—one cosmographic and the other territorial, political, and socioeconomic. Residential monastic communities provided alternative ways of mapping the landscape that included the hills, rivers, and plains of eastern India. This monastic geographic order, while bestowing a great deal of commonality to life ways among people who lived in the entire region, also ensured the involvement of monastically related members in military conflicts there. Such conflicts intensified in the course of the sixteenth and seventeenth centuries, and made access to animals and labour power extremely valuable. A greater emphasis on diplomatic marriages resulted from this. These were intended to transfer animals and soldiers from one monastic's domain to another's in exchange. Thus political marriages, which had been important earlier, remained part of monastic politics and monastic geographies in subsequent centuries as well. The retention of the relationship between the two houses despite the death of one of the contracting parties remained critical to martial and monastic politics in the seventeenth and eighteenth centuries.

UNIT OF MONASTIC GEOGRAPHY: RESIDENCE
A variety of Sanskritic, Tibeto-Burmese, Bengali, Assamese, and other regional language terms refer to collective residential organizations

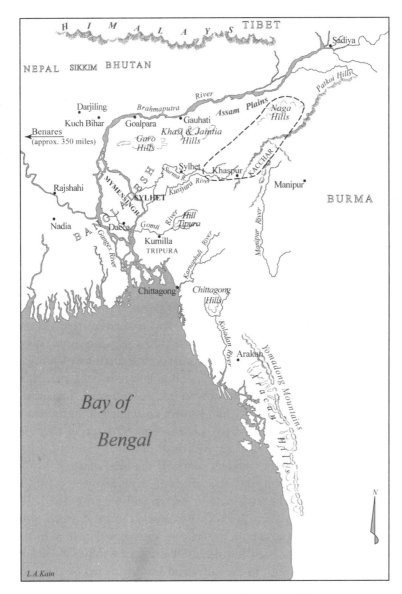

Fig. 1.1   Physical Contours of Eastern India.

of novice monks, the ordained, and dedicated lay disciples. These are *samgha, samhati, maṭha, akhāra, vihāra, sattra, khānqāh,* and *hkyaung.* All these refer to different sets of disciples' dormitories.

Many dormitories included women, since Tantric Buddhist ordination lineages, Vaisnavas and Saiva tantrics did not make celibacy mandatory. Sufi saints and blessed men also appeared to have had sons (*pirzada*). For want of a single word that can adequately comprehend the collective co-residential aspects of teachers and their male and female disciples, I use the term 'monastic'.

Most parts of the greater Brahmaputra River system were settled by such monastic assemblages.[1] Copperplate inscriptions dated between the ninth and twelfth centuries referred to the settlement of adepts and experts (*brahmans*), with all kinds of medical, technological, and ritual knowledge, in settlements along rivers such as the 'Lohitya' (another name for the Brahmaputra), and 'Kusiara' (a river east of Sylhet, northeastern Bangladesh) during the ninth and twelfth centuries.[2] Copperplates spelled out the knowledge and skill of the experts in *Charaka* a compilation of medical knowledge (Ayurveda), *Vyakarana* (grammar), *Mimamsa* (philosophy), *Nyaya* (justice-legality), and *Tantra* (ritual means) of the recipients of grants of land.[3]

Differences of forms of initiation and ordination that existed between different groups of Buddhists, Vaisnavas, Saktas, and Saivas paled before the commonality of organization of this form of political society.[4] The *samgha* or the assembly of Buddhist monks was paralleled by the *sattra*, an assembly of Vaisnava initiates of a guru. Each sattra had a political constituency and its own co-residential bureaucracy of the ordained, who governed a mass of subjects spread over the terrain. The sattra bureaucracy had three principal positions—that of the abbot or adept (master, *adhikar*), the heir apparent to the abbot (*deka adhikar*), and the adherents and devotees (*bhaktas*, alternate spellings in texts include *bhakats* and *bhagats*). The latter could number anywhere between two and a thousand. Succession to the position of *adhikar* in the celibate lineages was secured in the same way as in the highland Buddhist lineages: a follower's young son was sent as a 'gift' to the sattra and was instructed by the deka and the adhikar. The fourth and largest group was that of disciples (*sishyas*) who formed the 'mass of the Assamese people'. This group was also spoken of as 'subjects' (*praja*) of a monastic lord, or head of a monastery.[5]

Evidence provided in the *buranjis* (chronicle) about the nature of the 'headship' of particular monasteries and the relationship between such heads and the position of 'king' or *svargadeva* (literally, heavenly lord) in the Brahmaputra Valley has been extremely vague. One Assamese-language chronicle asserts that in the seventeenth century, the figure identified as the svargadeva was a lay Buddhist who hailed from the same patrilineage and clan as did the Himalayan Buddhist monk, the Bhutanese 'Deb raja' (*desi*).[6] Others assert that three seventeenth-century svargadevas were brothers or nephews from the same patriline. In effect, they imply that in the seventeenth century, the heavenly lord (of 'Assam') hailed from a clan of monastics or disciple–patrons of a Tantric Buddhist (Kagyupa) monastic lineage in the lower Himalayas. By the early and mid-eighteenth century, however, the svargadeva was an initiated disciple of a Vedic Hindu (*smarta*) teacher called Bhattacharyya Parbatiya Gosain; the disciple–initiant gave gifts of land and men to the son of his own guru/preceptor and dedicated these to the use of the Saiva–Sakta Banesvara temple built for the son by his father's disciple.[7]

Was the lay, ordained, or initiated status of the 'king' salient to the organization of cultivation, warfare, or diplomacy—the areas generally taken to be the province of all governments? I suggest not. For all these tasks were organized by the system of co-residential monastic and disciples' dormitories. The abbot, the heir apparent, and the devotees were often housed in a co-residential structure built around a shared tank or well. These structures may have arisen under similar conditions of monastic observance: Buddhist monks and Vaisnava novices and initiates (*bhakat*s) alike observed rain retreats and had to wait somewhere during the monsoon season before resuming begging for alms among disciples. However, there was a great variety of monastic residence. In the Brahmaputra Valley, the most common monastic structures were long houses or barracks divided into sets of rooms, one for each novice monk. But in the hills of Chittagong and Arakan, *hkyaung*s (or monasteries) were only 'wretched huts'; there were no brick buildings at all.[8] In modern southern Tripura, Buddhist monastic compounds entirely made of mud walls and thatched roofs are common: only the temple in which a Buddha statue resides may have a roof of metal (See Figure 1.2).

Since in Buddhist doctrine, human beings are transients who have no fixed or final resting place, the physical dwellings of people taught to live by those teachings often expressed such impermanence

Fig. 1.2   Sharecropper's Buddhist Temple, Pilak, Tripura.

Source: The Author.

by using makeshift local materials.[9] The thatched huts and bamboo dwellings, deliberately 'wretched', coded a discipline cultivated in especially rigorous forest and hill-based monastic lineages. Rather than construct typologies of monasteries and khanqahs, I suggest that the variety of residential lay and monastic dormitories found in any region signalled different moments in the life-cycle of the political community. Caves and thatched huts could evolve into a range of constructed buildings, depending on the numbers and wealth of subjects and adherents each lineage of teachers could attract. Each monastery set its own regimes of body–mind discipline: novices were required to perform ablutions and contemplations at regulated times of day, they also attended the mass assembly and devotional singing called *nam kirtan* three times in the day, in addition to giving personal service to the sattra. Novices were organized into different groups or *khels*. Some novices provided the labour of devotional singing (*gayans*), others were musicians (*bayans*), and yet others were readers (*pathaks*). From such groups came the manuscript copyists and artists, and the finer arts and craftsmen, such as those who carved ivory, horn, and bamboo.

All *sattras* had lands, whose management was entrusted to office-bearers elected from among the bhakats—one had charge of food, another of elephants and cattle, a third of entertaining guests, while a fourth ensured the regular supply of food grains, earthen pots, milk, ghee, and other necessaries from the *paiks*, peasants attached to particular monks, teachers and deities in each monastic community.

Paiks cultivated temple lands and rendered personal services. When they served as personal attendants of the officers, such paiks were called *likcau/lixoo;* when they remained liable for military services, they were *kari/kanri* paiks; when they prepared the ground for a ritual of a temple, they were referred to as *khalasara*. Exemptions from military service marked an elevated status (called *chamua*). Chronicles placed diviners and prophets (*bailung*) as well as brahman ritualists (*thakur*) serving at temples—as 'servants' of the deities—as *chamua* paiks.[10] The latter received seed or raw materials from those who settled them on their estates, the *kari* did not.

Cowherds (*gorakhiya*) and grass-cutters (*ghanhi*), washermen, guards, musicians and messengers, accountants and traders (*mudiar* and *bhandarkaystha*) were all attached to various temples and temple properties. Thus exemptions from the taxes of the land or the waterways, as well as actual relationships with lands or markets to be tilled or 'enjoyed' by the followers, drew all such groups into the ambit first of a brahman and then through that brahman to a superior human lord, his initiatic lineage, its deities and icons, and into bigger networks.

The labour of cultivators, artisans, fishermen, and herders living on and by the resources of some lands could be *both* objects of such 'gifts' to a teacher by a disciple and could themselves be subjects of a monastic order. Seldom in royal or lay donors' gifts to temples and monasteries were military servants (*kari* paiks) 'gifted' away: mostly other skilled craftsmen and cultivator paiks' services were gifted in permanent alienation of the donor's claims. In any case, paiks so gifted could *not* be resold or re-gifted or given away under ordinary conditions. Grants of paiks to *gosains* (colloquial term for Sanskrit term *goswami*, lit. owner of cattle-wealth, master of a particular Saiva or Vaisnava meditative or tantric lineage, also pronounced as *gohains* among many groups), temples, and monasteries (sattras) in perpetuity were inviolable and permanent in nature intended to secure 'merit' for the donors, rather than profit laymen.

Therefore, like other such 'gifted' paiks, initiated soldiers, craftsmen, boat builders, and ritualists were expected to accompany a guru as his 'subjects' to a gifted plot of land far away from their original homes and birthplaces as a form of devotion to their master.

LINKED LANDSCAPES OF MONASTIC GEOGRAPHICITY AND SHARED COSMOGRAPHIES

Monastic dormitories served as epicentres for a network of lay and ordained people. Although these centres were territorially scattered across vast distances, resident members and their affiliated tenants, traders, herders, and farmers were nonetheless connected by their common 'subjection' to the teaching–ritual lineage that formally owned the building.

Connections between monastic communities, residential dormitories, and laymen's associations and lineages between the Himalayan and the Gangetic worlds brought together three features of monastic geographicity. First, both donors and recipients originated from widely separated and varied territorial/geographical sites—or 'all four directions' (of an imaginary compass), as a favoured epigraphic phase put it; second, rather than personal biographies, they were tied together by a common tradition or name of teachers; and third, they were linked by monastically led, or monastically sponsored and authorized, militias.

Members of these communities came from all parts of Bengal, Assam, Tibet, Kashmir, Nepal, and Magadha. The presence of monks originating in 'other' lands was a well-known feature of Buddhist monastic settlements.[11] Geographic origins of particular monastic dormitories might be referred to by donors without necessarily discriminating between them in the kind and acreage of lands bestowed on them. Geographically distinct origins of monks were, however, subsumed to the common tradition or name of a teacher, or a ritual name given by the teacher to a disciple and initiate. For instance, the term *Pala* appeared to have represented something like this common bond of allegiance to a teacher. Tibetan-language chronicles described the Indian 'King Dharmapala' as the 'chief spiritual guide and minister' of the eighth-century Tibetan king, Khri sron lde'u btsan.[12] Tibetan histories outlined three lineages of ordination stemming from a 'celebrated Indian pandit Dharmapala from Magadha, who arrived at the Tibetan capital accompanied by three pupils, all of whom bore the surname of Pala.'[13] The three disciples of Dharmapala were referred to in a fifteenth-century text, *The Blue Annals*.[14] Another account named them as Siddhapāla, Gunapāla, and Prajñāpāla, 'from the eastern quarter of India'.[15] Clearly, the common name 'Pala' represented the membership of all thus-named individuals in an initiation-ordination relationship with teachers and disciples who came from different parts of eastern India and Tibet.

Monastic centres, spread across different geographies, were linked not merely by mobile monks and novices but also by monastically led, or monastically sponsored and authorized, militias. Thus, Inner Asian structures of military organization also shaped societies in the Indo-Gangetic plains and Brahmaputra-Surma valleys. For instance, after the eleventh century, Mongol commanders severed military labour from civilian services of herding and transportation of goods to market and divided the populations accordingly. Each part of the population was led by military or non-military commanders. Each leader recruited men for appropriate services. In order to do their work, these military and civilian commanders used two devices: the Tibetan histories called *khö* and *phalö*.[16] The first was something like a census, the second resembled an assembly. As soon as a khö was made, the domains became integral parts of the Tibetan empire. The empire itself was divided into four 'horns' (or divisions). Each horn in turn was divided into a few 'thousand-districts' (*chiliarchies*), which again were subdivided into smaller units for military and civil administration; a smaller unit of ten was called *pai*; members of it were *paitou*. Each horn's administration was organized in terms of 'upper' and 'lower' halves for military purposes; each half, in turn, was governed by its own commander.

Archaeologists in Central Asia have pieced together that Tibetan soldiers from different districts (*stong sde*) were brought together in units of four (*tshugs*); accompanied by their families, and carrying some of their own rations, these soldiers went off to serve in various desert and mountain posts.[17] An identical unit of four members was called *got* in medieval Kamrup-Assam; it replicated the Inner Asian world in the Brahmaputra Valley. It also explained the mixing of ideas and populations that was characteristic of the Inner Asian system. Drawn from widely dispersed landscapes, service in the tshugs mixed together social groups in turn, and varied their subsistence activities according to the season and terrain. Campaigns occurred in the autumn; when the campaigns ended, the men turned to the economy of livestock herding and farming that also needed them to keep working as watchmen and scouts of fields and herds. The identical mixed pattern of the Sino-Tibetan structures characterized medieval eastern Bengal, Burma, and Assam.[18]

Common co-residence and experience of military and civilian service, patterns of mobility interspersed with periodic settlement, histories of sponsored translation projects of Sanskritic texts as well as exchanges and travels—all generated a shared cosmography. All sites associated with the life of the Sakyamuni and his disciples were critical to Central and Inner Asian Buddhist identifications of themselves as residents of the cosmological map of 'Jambudvipa'. In this cosmological map were the towns on the Indo-Gangetic belt and the delta, such as Kausambi, Kapilavastu (Ser-skyahi-gnas), and Ayodhya (Mi-thub-pa); as also fortified monastic sites such as Pundravardhana (Li-kho-ri-sin-hphel-ba) of the eighth century (and Mahasthan in Bogra, Rajshahi subsequently).[19] These territories on the subcontinent were culturally significant to many different groups—Inner Asian Buddhists, Kashmiri Saivas, Southeast Asian Vaisnavas—at the same time; this common veneration of sites also explained the cultures of reuse found at such sites later.[20]

A shared cosmography of eastern India and Inner Asia was also manifested in a commonality of notions such as those of the venerability of mountains as well as deities and demons' 'ownership' of soil, water, trees, and rocks. In Tibetan, such 'masters of the land' (*gzhi bdag, yul lha* or *sa bdag*) were territorial deities. They had to be petitioned for protection from illness, plague, drought, storms, and other dangers. Rites conducted at particular sites, such as mountains and river banks, included offerings that obliged the local 'master' to favour the petitioner with timely rain, good pasture, or increase of human or animal herds sought.[21] A similar notion of ownership of soil was familiar from the northern bank of the Brahmaputra River, where lands in the gift of deities (Mahāgauri and Kāmesvara) had existed since the seventh century.[22] In the tenth-century epigraph found in Sylhet, lands were gifted to the deities (Mahākāla, Yogesvara, Vaisvanara, Jaimani) who were commonly venerated by Tantric Buddhist and Saiva Brahmans co-resident in regional monasteries (*matha*s).[23] Mahakala, an aspect of Siva, was a 'wrathful protector' in Tantric Buddhist ordination lineages.[24] The same deity was mentioned in documents pertaining to the Sakyapa Buddhist ordination lineage, whose members included the abbot of Vikramasila monastery in northern Bengal, a 'yogin' of Kamaru' (Kamarupa, western Assam), 'the old scribe of king Dharmapala' of Magadha.[25] The ownership of soil by such 'masters' was in turn related to the veneration of particular geological phenomena—such as mountains, rivers, forests, and especially trees—as either homes of the deities or as deities themselves.[26]

Medieval–early modern donors who endowed deities with 'owner-ship' of country shared the conceptual world in common with other Indo-Iranian and Central Asian populations. Mazda-ists in both societies endowed female goddesses with sovereignty: Nana/ Nanaia/ Anahita-Nahid, mentioned in the Rabatak (modern Afghanistan) Inscription, was an example of convergence, for she was worshipped as Mother of mankind, genius of cultivation, and mistress of animals.[27] These ideas overlapped with Bon and Tantric Buddhist and Tantric Hindu ideas of ownership of soil and water, recognized by scholars of the Inner Asian-Tibetan pasts.[28] Bon was believed to have risen in the region called Zhangzhung (between Central Asia or sTag-gzig/ Tajik and Tibet) with the teaching of sTon-pa-gShen-rab. R.A. Stein argued that Bon communities were themselves collocations of *non-Buddhist* and *Buddhist* specialists with shared veneration of territorial deities, beliefs in sacred mountains, sacrifices to tombs and on the occasion of oaths, and the taking of auguries and divinations.[29] Subsequently, other scholars have confirmed the picture of collocated Mazdaist–Bon–Nyingmapa (Tantric) Buddhist lineages and communities on the hills of Central and South Asia.[30]

The sacralization of hilltops and rivers was common to the northern Thai and Himalayan worlds; it made the landscape and the world of phenomena at large a source of 'truth' to the highly trained person, as well as of physical and spiritual health.[31] Such ideas of knowledge and health were also shared across the Brahmaputra River basin system as a whole. For instance, a list of eighty-four peaks was compiled for 'mountain pilgrimages' during the tenure of an eighteenth-century 'heavenly king' (svargadeva) in Assam.[32] Forests were worshipped as the home of *umanglai* (tree-dwelling deities) in the Manipur valleys.[33] Other chronicles compiled by members of the same monastic administration identified thirteenth-century dwellers in the Brahmaputra River valleys as *Tai 'Bouddha'* (Buddhist), and hill-dwellers (*kochari/ katsari*) as followers and 'subjects' of female territorial deities.[34] Thus another chronicler of Assam, referring to the numerous branches (*shakha*) of Buddhists laymen grouped together as 'Chutia Kochari, Borahi Kochari, Moran Motok' in the Brahmaputra valley in the seventeenth century, explained that this profusion of deities permitted each group to honor its own clan-deities, including goddesses such as 'Jayanti devi', alongside other clans' gods.[35]

MONASTIC GEOGRAPHICITY AND MILITARIES IN THE BENGALI-ASSAMESE LITERARY RECORD

From medieval times, monastic geographicity had set the terms for both military and economic movements of goods and herds between the Inner Asian plateaus and the South Asian deltas and plains. The struggle for control of the maritime trade of the coastline after the thirteenth century created the conditions for an escalation of ritual and military violence, as bands of armed men from a variety of ritual and geographical traditions were drawn into the armies led by Afghans, Mughals, Tibetan- and Nepali-speaking Tipura/Tripura,

Manipur, Rakhain, and Burmese-Pali–speaking groups in Pegu and Ava at the same time. Verses of the *Sri Rajamala* describe the immigration of monastic warriors from a Himalayan (*parbottiyo*) world and their resettlement in monastic dormitories around significant pilgrimage centres on the Indo-Gangetic plains. The second volume begins with a *sannyasi* (renunciant) named Dharma, who earned a great deal of merit by performing many pilgrimages and eventually came to rest at Varanasi.[36] There, he was befriended by a ritual-performing Kanaujiya brahman (named Koutuk) and his household. Headmen of Rangamati (a place in northern Bengal or Rangpur as well as the name of a place in Chittagong, southeastern Bengal) came to Varanasi, found the sannyasi, and took him and his entourage of eight ritual-performing Brahmans to Rangamati. This 'outsider'–sannyasi was then installed as 'king' in 1380 Saka (1458 CE, coinciding with the Turko-Afghan dominion in Bengal under Muhammad Shahi sultans during those years).[37] Just as digging of reservoirs, ponds, and tanks for supplying drinking water was considered a continuous charitable act (*sadiqah jariya*) in the Islamic code inscribed on the sultanate's fountains in southern Bengal, the *Sri Rajamala* recounts that the newly empowered sannyasi-king ordered the digging of a tank (Dharmasagar) and gave the lands on its banks to the brahmans in customary gift (*bhumi-dana*).[38] This simultaneously drained the water-logged land, rendering it cultivable and assigned responsibility for its cultivation on dependent settlers. Alongside the economic activity, the Bengali-language verses highlight the conditions of war under which young male monastics, already renouncers of natal identities, could be ritually inducted into other lineages and identities as warriors.

Manipuri chronicles outline a similar immigration of lineages of Vaisnava 'Brahmans' (goswamis/gosains) drawn from Benares (hence also called Kashi/ as well as 'Cassay', which in Tibetan-language records also referred to Kashmir), Bihar, Khardah, Gujarat, and Nadia (Bengal) at the same time in the fifteenth century.[39] Given titles (*Aribam*, Guru Aribam, *Gurumayum*, and *Manoharmayum* among the more prominent ones), many of these Vaisnava Brahmans were assimilated into the clan Meitei and married to local women. From the end of the sixteenth century, to these groups were added Muslim artillery and infantrymen, called Pāngons/Bongāls, who were also settled on the same monastic lands. Out of these multiple groups was born the 'ancestral' cult, a complex re-synthesis of Vaisnava, Bon-Buddhist, and Sufi Islamic concepts of *sunyata* (emptiness) as a Father Void (*Atingok*) and an alchemic pharmacopoeia of biomoral health. Documents pertaining to the late sixteenth century suggest identical movements and resettlements of monastic militias across eastern and northeastern India.[40]

The settlements of monastic militias became especially important from the early sixteenth century when contests between Afghan-Rajput soldiers and Mughal-Rajput commanders began to draw Tipura tantrics and Tibetan-speaking Rakhain Buddhist Tantric 'kings', and Portuguese sailors into tussles over trade routes, mints, and ports.[41] Disciplined and pious Afghan and Tantric warriors confronted Mughal commanders on the river Surma (Sylhet), especially under the leadership of the Afghan Bayazid Karrani, who prevailed there till the end of the sixteenth century.[42] Some of the warriors were Sufis: a Mughal commander recorded that he suspected his Afghan ally because the latter, the son of a *pir* (teacher-guide) of the Luhani Afghans, refused to fight against his own disciples.[43] At other times, these warriors, though also drawn from Inner Asia, were of other religious and ritual persuasions. For instance, Assamese chronicles refer to warriors from the Himalayan world living in the Surma Valley region in the plains. Letters from the north bank of the Brahmaputra address the fort holder on the river Surma (Sylhet) below as the 'Lāndā Sultān'.[44] Landa was the name of a river in northwest Afghanistan.[45] It was also the name of a 'clipped' script used exclusively by bankers, merchants, and shopkeepers from northwest Panjab, Sind, and Multan from the sixteenth century; it was critical in the spread and translations of Vaisnava and Buddhist doctrines and the creation of poetic classics in a distinctive form of Islam called Ismaili.[46] Yet as the letters preserved in the chronicles spell out, the same Central Asian 'Afghan' regions also sent forth groups who worshipped the female goddess Jayantia. Coins dated to 1590–1750 found in the same terrain, giving the name of the fort holder in each instance, also contained a tiny six-point star that suggested that fort holders along the Surma-Barak river systems were followers of a conjoined Judaism, Zoroastrianism, and Tantric Buddhism. The six-point star was simultaneously the symbol of a goddess Astlik (literally, 'little star'), consort of the Zoroastrian

Verathragna, one of the symbols of the Buddhist *dakini* (wrathful female deity), as well as the Judaic star of David.[47] Its presence on coins implies that Central Asian men practicing Tantric Buddhist, Jewish, and Zoroastrian rituals cohabited in and also commanded some of these forts in the eastern Indian highlands. This group of coins identified the fort-commanders as men who worshipped 'Haragauri' (Siva and Parvati); furthermore, the titles of the men identified them as belonging in the lineage of a 'Hachengsa' (*Hachengsa vamsaja*). Early twentieth-century numismatists averred that 'Hachengsa' stood for a 'mythical non-Hindu ancestry'.[48] What they did not allow for was the fact that the first part referred to the Tibetan name (lHa-chen, pronounced 'Hachen'), who was the king (shah) of Ladakh.[49]

The impression of ritual complexities of the militias is reinforced by the seventeenth-century Mughal commander fighting a 'Raja of Kachar' holding forts on the river Surma as an ally of Central Asian ('Afghan') forces.[50] The identity of the people called 'Kachar' is mystifying. Eighteenth-century English records treat 'Kachar' as a place somewhere in the foothills of Bhutan and Tibet; Assamese chronicles speak of 'Kotsar' and 'Kochar' in ways closer to the Tibetan term *katsar*, or fringe, perhaps intended to be used for the foothills of the Himalayas. The identities of populations living in these foothills were predictably hybrid. Modern Tibetan dictionaries put *kadzar* as people using both Nepali and Tibetan languages.

Such hybridity was born of the organization of military duties and responsibilities in the Tibetan and Mongol or Inner-Central Asian empires. This was a fact well established long before the arrival of Mughal forces in the region. The Mughal officer who defeated these forces in battle in the early seventeenth century discovered that the vanquished claimed to be the 'original Mughals' in that they had been stationed in this region by Amir Timur to protect the country when he returned to Samarqand.[51] Timur conducted three major invasions of Mamluk-held domains in Iran, Azerbaijan and Iraq during 1386–1404, and sacked parts of Tughlaq-governed Sultanate of Delhi.[52] Thus, by the mid-seventeenth century, it was already difficult to establish 'original' identities of the Tibeto-Mongol or Central Asian forces that the Mughal commander referred to as 'Khasa' or 'Khaza' and their contemporary Jesuits called 'Cathay or Tibetan' when referring to Kashmir-western Tibet.[53]

The Mughal commander had described the 'leaders' of these militia as 'white-skinned' and wearing 'large white turbans and big brass ear-rings' (*tankals*); these leaders were also found in the fort of Pratapgarh, in the domain of the 'Raja of Kachar'. The sartorial description corresponds closely with the identifying signs of a group of ritual specialists, mediums for oracles (*sungma*) found in Tibetan-speaking societies of the seventeenth–eighteenth centuries.[54] These fraternities of hereditary Tantric priests of the Nyingma-Bonpo and Vaisnava schools apparently wore white and were thus assimilated to two Tibetan terms simultaneously. One was '*gārru*' (which stood for both white and a herd of sheep and was written both as 'Garoo' and 'Garo' in the English records.[55] The other term was '*khasi*' (a single group made of both lay and ordained).

It is clear that the Mughal commander's descriptions of groups living in the Surma-Barak valley systems in the early seventeenth century were pregnant with meaning. As a rule, such commanders were sensitive to their rivals' manpower in these monastic militia dormitories: at least one platoon of four thousand men recruited by a commander from the hills (*koh-i-Garuwan*) had seven hundred recruits desert when asked to fight an Inner Asian Buddhist–Vaisnava alliance.[56]

Furthermore, these Mughal descriptions also suggest that tantric and magic-wielding monastics, favoured for being able to deliver psychological harm to an enemy as well as to cure, heal, and advise one's own troops and supporters, led initiated Vaisnava, Saiva, and Sakta Tantric male paik combatants. Rituals in the service of war were detailed by poets of the *SriRajamala*.[57] Verses describe the warrior's access to the *dakinis*. These wrathful female deities were summoned to cause delusions and hallucinations to the enemy's forces. The deities dammed the river Gomti (on the coastal plains) for seven days. At the end of the week, the dammed-up water was released and washed away the enemy; the stragglers were finished off with fire. Floods and arson were military tactics, but their use was controlled by ritual experts. The latter's military achievements, in turn, were sealed with the vision of another female deity, Chattesvari, who appeared in a dream and demanded the dedication of a monastery and icon of herself.[58] The *matha* (monastery) was suitably dedicated and presented to the deity in a Tantric rite. In the early seventeenth century, the poets recount, another imported Tantric sannyasi from Mithila (Tirhut, in plains Bihar) initiated (*dikshā*) a disciple in Sākta tantra (mother goddess) involving terrifying cemetry-based ritual cultivation (*smasān sādhanā*). But this initiation also brought precious firepower when two hundred and fifty similar tantric males from Mithila were added to the armies of the Tipra. The guru's icon then became the deity of the lineage (*kuladevata*) of the disciple.[59]

Mughal commanders thus confronted a conjoined ritual-military order that had been established for a long time. For one, the Tantric Buddhist lineages of the northern world such as the Kagyu and the Nyingma had coalesced by the mid-fifteenth century, as the career of the Drukpa Kagyu abbot, Drukpa Kuenley, shows.[60] Furthermore, the same pattern of ritual–military leadership also tied the labour and fortunes of another lineage of Saiva Tantrics to these Buddhist tantric teachers and their centres in the Himalayan foothills. The sixteenth-century tantric Buddhist adept of the Nyingma, Padma glingpa (or Pemalingpa, *c.* 1450–1521) was invited by a leader of 'eastern Monpas' on the northern bank of Brahmaputra (Assam), where he met a refugee, 'Raja of Kamata', Nilambar, ousted by the forces of the Sultan Hussain Shah (1501–5) in Bengal.[61] This 'Raja of Kamata' visited the Nyingmapa teacher and offered the usual homage of a scarf, touching the venerated figure's foot with his hand and then touching his own head in a typical gesture of devotional submission.[62] The devotional gesture was followed by a mid-sixteenth century restoration of sites and temples dedicated to tantric female deities in the highlands of western Assam, such as that dedicated to Kamakhya (1565) and the horse-faced Vaisnava deity, Hayagriva Madhava temple at Hajo (1583).

Gestures of ritual homage had economic implications. Those offered by Saiva–Vaisnava initiates to Tantric Buddhist ordination lineage heads implied that the services of the devotee or disciple were available to the guru in his intra-monastic conflicts of succession to headship, or for control of particular offices and lands. Thus discipleship went hand-in-hand with 'donations' or 'contributions' of human and animal labour, given towards building monastic residences and shelters, defensive or policing purposes, as well as for transporting goods to markets and other towns and monasteries. Sometimes, instead of their own labour, disciples created labour pools by 'gifting' labourers to a favoured deity, teacher, and temple. For instance, the Saiva disciple of the Nyingmapa Buddhist monk who sponsored the rebuilding of the temples also made large grants of labour to the restored temples.[63] 'Naranarayana', this rebuilder of Hajo and Kamakhya, was also a celebrated patron of poets: the career of a monastic warrior, disciple and patron were combined in a single individual and lineage.[64]

Monastic governments on both banks of the Brahmaputra behaved in a similar fashion. On the plains, one set of Saiva tanrics sought to recruit adherents: the 'Narayanas' established pilgrimage centres such as the Lolarka-kunda in Benares, one among many sites dedicated to the worship of the sun.[65] On the mountains, the Tantric Buddhist lineages of the Drukpa Kagyupa and Gelukpa centred on key fortress–warehouse-cum-monasteries and 'castles' (*dzongs*) at the mouth of valleys stretching between the lower Himalayas and the plains north of the Brahmaputra River. These fortified 'castles' which also held their own monasteries were the seats of lay governors (*dzongpen*) from social clans supportive of the spiritual-monastic ordination lineage, and often initiated in it. Each fortress contained within it an entire monastic administration whose ultimate head was an ordained Drukpa monk. The *Zhabs-drung* combined in himself the two branches of governance. For effective governance, matters ritual and spiritual were the jurisdiction of the *Je-khenpo*, and matters temporal of the *Desi*. Sponsored and rebuilt structures on the plains as well as in the mountains only enhanced the geographic, military, and cosmographic connections between apparently different theological units and monastic assemblages. For instance, the temple at Hajo attracted a Buddhist master of the Drukpa Kagyupa ordination lineage named Lama Tashi Wangyal, who went in the company of his Bhutanese patron, the head of the powerful Wangma clan, on a pilgrimage there.

Himalayan Bon-Buddhist authority over Saiva and Vaisnava disciples and supporters also involved the latter, the forces of the 'Kamta' raja, in a wider series of Inner Asian–Mughal conflicts in the seventeenth and eighteenth centuries. This conflict, too, was over trade routes and payments of dues. The lay governors of Ladakh were disciples-cum-protectors of the Drukpa Kagyupa ordination lineage, which had also consolidated itself in Bhutan. By 1646, this Ladakh–

Bhutan relationship coalesced in a larger series of confrontations between monastic ordination lineages for control or redirection of the long-distance trans-Himalayan trades and possibly the gold mines of the region. Right through the seventeenth century, this conflict drew onto the battlefield laymen supporters as well as 'homage-paying' patrons of each ordination lineage of Central Asian–Inner Asian forces.

Ritual and military means of combat flourished and explains the observations of the Mughal commander. The Assamese buranjis referred to ritual offerings to various territorial and river deities and spirits in the thick of battle. In 1615–6 ritual diviners (*deodhais*) 'offered oblations to the dead and the spirits' at the mouth of a river (Dikhau) and examined chicken entrails in order to predict the time for a successful attack on the Mughal forces.[66] In the same vein, another svargadeva ('heavenly king') in 1640 offered sacrifices to the goddess of river Taloi of 'many goats, ducks and buffaloes' to ensure that the Hajo branch of the river would dry up and the fleet of the enemy run aground.[67] The younger brother of this svargadeva, who succeeded him, was also described as having sat on a throne with the idol of Somdeva ('Chomdeu') on his neck, planting a banyan tree (for long life), and having arranged for a fight between three dangerous and destructive animals of the terrain—the elephant, the tiger, and the crocodile—in a ritual theatre of the destruction of evil.[68] The successor, another brother of this svargadeva, is said to have stepped up the ritual means of warfare against the Mughal forces by adding the propitiation of Indra and other gods to the offering of sacrifices to the forefathers.[69]

The more astute of Mughal and Rajput commanders entered this ritualized theatre of war well prepared. Letters from their chanceries, written in hybrid Persianate Bengali-Assamese, expressed personal tutelage (*shagird-gi*) to the monks they addressed as Chetiya Gohain, even as they asked them to fix the tolls on goods to be exchanged between Mughal merchants and others in their domains.[70] The impasse worsened only after 1679, when the Dzungari ('Mongol') commanders entrusted by the Fifth Dalai Lama, head of the Gelukpa ordination lineage, sought to occupy Leh–Ladakh. The governors of the latter, disciples and patron–protectors of the Bhutanese tantric lineage of Drukpa Kagyupa, appeared to have called upon other forces in the vicinity. Effectively, the tussle between two Himalayan and Inner Asian Buddhist lineages and their lay adherents drew the Hindustani forces commanded by Mughal–Rajput officers into the fight.[71]

Mughal–Rajput intervention exacerbated the ongoing tussle between forces and populations loyal to contending monastic centres across the Brahmaputra-Surma Valley. The Assamese chronicles touch upon two distinct sets of Himalayan Buddhist lords who fought against the Mughals. One was the 'Dharmaraja with his Khanglai Chetiya-ra' at the fortress of Taitagarh (in Sylhet); the second, the 'Lamaguru/lanmakhru of the Alchi monastery', who was appointed to the office of Baraphukan (at the head of the infantry).[72] Another chronicle, which referred to the Mughal forces as those of 'Mussalmans', noted that 'our Khunchang Lama Barua and Khunshai' died in battle.[73] References to Alchi Monastery and its lamaguru 'chetiya pandit' as the leader of anti-Mughal, anti-Mongol forces in the Brahmaputra Valley in the seventeenth century indicated widely separated geographical origins of the Kashmiri and western Tibetan troops fighting the Mughals in eastern India. The northwestern regions were referred to in both Bon and some Tantric Buddhist texts as Khyunglung: it was a magically manifested place in Bon ritual as well as a reference to Zhang Zhung in western Tibet; it was already a sacred site in Tibetan histories.[74]

In subsequent months, the chronicles state, Vaisnava tantrics from the plains—with names such as Dharmanarayana and Prananarayana, once allied with the Mughal commanders on the plains—either joined the conflict as partisans or sought refuge with the Buddhist Kagyupa lineage monasteries in Ladakh and Bhutan. Such sanctuaries were also referred to by a contemporary French physician in Mughal employ, who noted that when pressed by Mughal commanders on the plains, a Raja of Acham (Assam) retired to Garhgaon, and then further into the (increasingly Gelukpa-dominated) kingdom of Lassa.[75] Bernier's account confirms the picture of a relationship between monastic centres across the mountains and plains of the Brahmaputra as well as Kashmir.

In the later seventeenth century, the chronicles suggest, Mughal commanders intensified their attempts to wean away militias loyal to their Himalayan Buddhist monastic lords. For example, the Mughal emperor gave priests of the temple of Kamakhya and Umananda temples grants of lands and rights of fisheries in the river Brahmaputra.[76] Such gifts complicate the Tibetan-language historiography of the Mughal–Ladakh–Tibet peace treaties of 1684. The terms of the peace suggested that the Mughal emperor Aurangzeb had compelled the pro-Kagyupa Ladakhi governors to pay tribute to the Mughals, mint gold coins in the name of the emperor, build a mosque in Leh and have the *khutba* read, and establish trading privileges for wool trading Kashmiri merchants, had sought to further the cause of Islam in Kashmir.[77] A clause in one of the treaties even declared that there was nothing in common between Buddhism and Islam. Yet, the evidence from the temples of Assam for the same decade suggests greater sophistication on the part of the Mughal emperor in his attempts to control the routes through the mountains of the east. Aurangzeb's gifts, as well as those of his contemporary svargadeva, in fact suggested an intensification of war by ritual means. A Sunni Muslim, Aurangzeb did *not* demolish dormitories and temples wholesale, but sought to instate new men or wean away members of opposing groups by means of the gift of lands, labourers, and exemptions. Competitive gifting of lands and labourers to deities who 'owned' hills and rivers followed.[78]

In addition to the ritual military means commanded by various monastic–tantric ascetic leaders, their disciple–militias also had mundane means at their fingertips. Such were the 'bambos or canes made sharpe at both the endes and driven into the earth, and they can let in the water and drowne the ground above knee deepe, so that men nor horses can passe … poison the waters.'[79] These were famously used in flatland warfare. A Bengali Muslim poet, Shaykh Manuhar, eulogizing a warrior of the eighteenth century, described these pointed bamboos as *pui* inserted upright in a field to hurt the unshod feet of a pursuing enemy.[80] The Tibetan–English dictionary defined the same word as the very synonym for 'Tibetan'.

In addition to this technology, there were the famous poisoned arrows that almost decimated a large Mughal cavalry corps in the early seventeenth century.[81] This particular military technology persisted in the late eighteenth and early nineteenth centuries among groups on the Himalayan foothills and on the plains of Bengal and Assam. Samuel Turner, who witnessed a confrontation between the partisans of two monastic officers in the foothills, described these poisoned iron-tipped bamboo arrows. The poison, a black and gummy residue of some vegetable juice, in consistency and appearance resembling crude opium, was lodged in the grooved edges of the tip of the arrow.[82] At the turn of the century, the Scottish surgeon, Francis Buchanan (later Hamilton), was told of Bhutanese armies that visited the plains north of the Brahmaputra. They carried swords, battle-axes, and poisoned arrows, and surrounded their camp at night with 'poisoned arrowes stuck in the ground, so as to leave the points only projecting'.[83] A botanist by training, he had identified the source of the poison in a root found in the alpine Himalaya by 1810.[84]

Similarly, a Bengali-language prose chronicle, whose author was born in the late eighteenth century and had worked in the same region, characterized the militia that Fitch had described as that of the 'Bod/ Bhot', the very term that would emerge as 'Bodo' in English ethnonyms.[85] This chronicler referred to the seventeenth century as the origin of Tibetan dominance: when 'the Bhotiya extended their dominion from the mountains (*parbbat*) on to the plains (*samatalabhumi*) below'.[86] Describing the 'Bhot' armies stationed at outposts on the plains, this chronicler also described the equipage of the 'Bhot' soldier: 'each held a six-feet long bamboo cane sharpened at one end. When they stopped at night somewhere they dug those bamboos into the ground around them into a fort that was disassembled again the next morning.'[87] The eyewitness also described the method by which such poison-tipped bamboos (*bish painji*) laid in the ground trapped and killed an enemy. By the mid-nineteenth century, when British armies fought these monastic militias who were partisans of the Sikkimpati in regions east of the Tista river, guns reinforced the 'bows and poisoned arrows' wielded by several Himalayan soldiers.[88]

MARRIAGES AS ANCHORS OF MONASTIC GEOGRAPHICITY

If war could be conducted by ritual means as well as by more forceful ones, monastic diplomacy could also be conducted through the arrangement of marriages between clans of disciples loyal to a common teacher and spiritual-ritual lineage. Military and monastic geographicity was anchored by friendly compacts and often sealed by marriages. Poets who recorded the consecration of an immigrant monastic as 'king' also described the localization of this immigrant by marriage to a daughter of a lay disciple of the monastic's spiritual lineage.[89] The mobility and settlement of monastic militias were determined specifically by two different layers of marriages: one that occurred between lay disciples and clans who supported significant ordained monks and ascetics, and the second that incorporated tantric militants into households with daughters and sisters. The maintenance of affinity became a pressing monastic concern, because each monastic lineage and its lay patrons and supporters were caught up in contests and conflicts of their own which needed regular infusions of manpower, animals, and ritual 'firepower'. In particular, this meant that marriages among such monastic economies were entirely non-sectarian arrangements.

The Assamese chronicles portray systematic connubial transactions between families variously identified as Koch, Kotsari, or Kochari 'kings' of the Sylhet-northern Bengal foothills and speakers of hybrid Tibetan–Nepali, Bengali and Burmese languages and the Himalayan Buddhist clans. In 1575, one Nara Raja sent his 'grown-up sister' to the svargadeva also identified as 'Khora raja' (Tibetan *Khor ra* refers to the circumambulation of sacred mountain Kailash; Assamese *Khora* indicates the other bank of the river Brahmaputra): in response, the latter sent a horse, an elephant, and 120 servants to the bride.[90] Such exchanges of animal wealth for humans in the context of both intra-monastic conflicts and the conflict with Mughal armies from the plains redoubled the significance of marriages in strengthening monastic–disciple relationships across hills and riverine plains. Such relationships proved useful in battle, as the Mughal commander had noted of the 'Rajas of Kachar' aiding an Afghan corps on the river Surma.[91]

A well-established affinal relationship existed between the Afghans and the Assamese lords by the seventeenth century, when letter writers on behalf of the Afghan ('Landa Sultan') wrote to the heavenly lord (Jayadhvaja Simha, office holder 1648–63) lamenting the Mughal attack on the svargadeva's domains and expressed an intimacy of anguish at the event. Dateable to May 1663, the letter addressed the heavenly lord thus: 'Jayantia and Garhgaon [the svargadeva's center] are one. An attack upon you is an attack upon me. I am heart-sore (*bahut man dukkhi*) till I hear from you. The friendship (*prīti*) between us is old, and looks to be growing.... If I cannot stand by you in your hour of need, then what is the need for friendship?'[92]

Conjugal affinity (*kutumbitā*) strengthened military–political amity. Thus, the same letter writer, in the same year in which the Mughal commander Mir Jumla sickened and died while on campaign (1663), referred to a 'Bongāl' whose life-force (*prāna-shakti*) had been destroyed by divine justice in response to his own bad actions (*pratiphala*) earlier. In this second letter, the author spelled out the relationship between himself and the svargadeva: 'What worth is my valour (*subir*) if hearing of an attack on my affine (*kutumba*, in-law) I stay at home?'[93] Subsequent letters confirm this marital relationship between a southern and a northern clan. The same letter writer reminded the next svargadeva (Chakradhvaja Simha, 1663–9) that elephants and horses from the 'friend's' domains were in the letter writer's house, and maidens (*kunwari*) from the latter's house were in the svargadeva's. The new lord had apparently sought to renew the affinal relationship by securing another bride from the same clan. The letter writer (Jayantia) responded enthusiastically: 'growing affinity (*kutumbita*) is excellent. It strengthens friendship. The practice (*vyavahār*) has been for your side [grooms/ bride-seekers] to send the materials (*sāmagri*) with an agent to us for the maidens. We will observe that definitely (*nichoy*).'[94]

Though the exact goods contained in each bridal presentation are not listed, one of the later marital embassies sent by the svargadeva to the fort holder on the Surma brought from the grooms substantial amounts of gold jewellery (15 tola weight in bangles, a pearl-studded five-string necklace, different kinds of gold rings) along with various kinds of cloth, including a specific style of breast-cloth (*riha*) for young women.[95] Other goods mentioned in the diplomatic correspondence between the Himalayan lords and their plains disciples and donors hint that these marriages satisfied the military and diplomatic needs of both affines. Letters from one of the svargadevas to the Central Asian affine living on the Surma were accompanied with gifts of cloth, tents and shawls, yak tails (*chamar*), deer-musk (*kasturi*), daggers (*katari*), pieces of iron (*loha*), pepper (*marich*). In exchange, substantial militant manpower was sought in the battles of the seventeenth century. Clearly referring to the Mughal forces from

Dhaka, one of the officers on behalf of the svargadeva asked the Central Asian affine and ally to dispatch 20–30,000 (*trish bish hajaar lok*) men to fight on his behalf.[96] Marriages could only occur, however, when there were enough daughters, sisters, and nieces in the bride-giving (and troops-supplying) households and clans. In the absence of demographic details about sex ratios in seventeenth-century populations in the foothills and interiors of the valley systems, we are left with only fleeting glimpses of what might have occurred if such females in the 'blood-line' of a donor-disciple (referred to as *ji/beti* in the correspondence) were not available for the purposes of affinal diplomacy. In at least one such instance, a note from the svargadeva to his Central Asian disciple on the foothills below asserted that a daughter was equal to a nephew (sister's son, *bhaginā*). Hinting at a pattern of preference for daughters and sisters, characteristic of matrilateral lineages, a svargadeva assured a Central Asian follower that the old-established alliance (*sambandhagot*) could be maintained even 'if there is no daughter (*ji*) then you should send your bhagina. Do you not love him as much as your own daughter?'[97]

A sister's son sent in lieu of a daughter suggests that these relationships were less about establishment of sexual reproduction than they were about the participation of the senders in the administration organized by the recipients and vice versa. That is why the conduct of war by monastic governments depended on avoiding the kind of disputes that threatened the affinal relationships of the svargadeva and the Landa Sultan in the seventeenth century. Two different sets of chronicles refer to such disagreements. One refers to an event in 1632 when the svargadeva sent presents to the Saiva tantric Lakshminarayana as marriage presentation for the latter's daughter to be sent as a bride: by the time the gifts arrived, the father had died, and the brother of the bride refused. The chronicles state that a more devoted Biru Karji then offered his daughter and a granddaughter (daughter of his son) to the svargadeva and his son, Changidam, at Garhgaon, the capital.

Another episode occurred in the late seventeenth century. Correspondence between the clerical representatives of the svargadeva and the fort holder on the Surma Valley and hills reveals that conflict erupted when the latter, who had contributed labourers settled on his fields and estates to fight on behalf of the former, was denied his share of the prisoners of war, the *dimarua* (from the Tibetan term 'dim.bsekhs' or sedimentary deposit). The Himalayan bureaucracy believed that the prisoners of war were its own subjects and tenants. The Central Asian disciple–affine disagreed. A disruption of intimacy threatened in 1672–3. Both the svargadeva and his Central Asian disciple were done away with: the former was believed to have been poisoned, and his younger brother (Ramadhvaja Simh, 1673–4) installed in office. Meanwhile, the older Central Asian disciple was also replaced by his son-in-law (Lakshmi Simh); this younger male refused to implement his predecessor's promise to send one of his two daughters to the lord's clan in marriage. Suddenly, in 1673, after bridal goods had been brought to the disciple's house in the name of the older brother, the Central Asian disciple heard that the older brother (svargadeva) had been replaced by a younger brother; he decided to send the envoys back with the jewellery that they had brought for the bride. According to the buranji writer, the svargadeva's envoys insisted that it was the diplomatic affinal relationship (*kutumbita-shombondho*) that was serviced by the jewel-and-cloth bestowing ritual; it did not matter that the groom was a different man from the one who had dispatched the jewels. In the wake of the unresolved conflict about each side's claims on prisoners of war, the Central Asian lord, father of the bride-to-be, disagreed.[98]

Disagreements, however, suggest the outlines of a historical pattern of joint marriages (a daughter and granddaughter married at the same time to a father and a son) and plural marriages that would fall afoul of the Puritanical ethic of Dissenting churchmen as well as reform sensibilities of English-educated Bengali bureaucrats in the nineteenth century. This pattern will be discussed at greater length in Chapter 3. For the moment, however, I wish simply to highlight the practices of plural marriages in communities that were disciples and adherents of important monastic lineages. For example, the *Ahom Buranji* suggested that in 1643, the eldest brother of a svargadeva lived with his stepmother as man and honoured wife: after being anointed as svargadeva, this man brought another maiden, renamed her, and made her queen. This consort, in turn, had been married previously: she adopted a boy of her former husband's elder brother.[99] The younger brother of this svargadeva (known in the chronicles as

Udayaditya) was similarly described as having made the chief consort of his deceased brother also his chief queen.[100]

Therefore, the episode of 1673 recounted in the *Jayantia Buranji* was not exceptional in a political context where a maiden affianced to one brother would have been implicitly or overtly also been understood to become the wife of a younger brother of the husband. It belonged in a pattern of political associations which had to be sustained for military–ritual and economic reasons. It was the marital pattern that twentieth-century social scientist would name 'levirate' and when one sister of a wife was wed after another by the same groom, was 'sororate'. Both patterns were part of a larger labour-pooling, resource-sharing, and child-sharing set of household arrangements. But as the chronicles insist, they were also fundamentally political institutions. Rather than collective contracts stated explicitly to be between all brothers in one generation and a common wife, the narratives of the chronicles suggest that each generation of brothers (who became 'svargadeva' in the seventeenth century) had one formally, ritually accepted wife from the household of the Central Asian follower on the Surma-Barak Valley below. Such a practice—of an exogamous marriage that constituted the core of a stem family in each generation—was also noticed in the early eighteenth century by a Jesuit missionary, Ippolito Desideri, who had lived in Tibetan towns and monasteries for four years. Describing the ritual of smearing butter on the forehead of the bride, the missionary wrote that though it was the elder brother who put the butter, he performed this rite 'for all his brothers, big or little, men or boys, and she is recognised and regards herself as the legitimate wife of them all.'[101] Furthermore, he had also observed that the stem family was preserved across generations: speaking of a 'principal family' and a high official at Lhasa who had a son by his first wife, married a second, and was then posted away from his home permanently, the son 'married his step-mother without a word of reproval from anyone.' This pattern of marriage continued the transmission of the relationship between affinal households rather than ensuring sexual reproduction in all instances. It was political—and economic—because of the presentations of animals and skilled experts that accompanied such alliances. Therefore, marriage negotiations became economic as well as environmental issues.

Bride-wealth arrangements and 'gifts' mentioned in the records were related to the increased militarization of eastern Indian societies during the seventeenth century. Negotiations over animals became part of bride-wealth negotiations at the same time that certain skills—of trapping and hunting—became extremely valuable in many terrains at once. The most reliable of Manipuri chronicles, the *Cheitharon Kumpapa*, records a series of marriages revolving around the flows of animal wealth in bride-wealth payments resembling those mentioned for the svargadeva and his allies holding forts in the region of Sylhet and the Surma-Barak Valley. This record of the marriages between the governors of the Vaisnava-initiated Meetei (Manipur) and those of surrounding militias of Takhen (colonial 'hill' Tippera), Mayang (colonial Kachar-Sylhet), Tekhao (colonial Assam), and Aawaa (colonial Ava, capital of Burma) early suggests the flow of skills, technologies, and livestock that came in the form of bride-wealth given by grooms' households to those of the brides' parents and relatives. The Meetei bride affianced to an Assamese man left for her husband's place only after a 'road to Tekhao was opened … Elephant Tekhao Ngampa arrived. They began to make Tekhao Lu from that time. Aniseed was also introduced.'[102] A pathway, an animal transport fitted to the terrain, a fishing trap of bamboo, and an aromatic cultivar were all part of the transfers necessary to the completion of the betrothal.

Shortly thereafter, negotiations regarding bride wealth narrowed down to an almost singular focus on elephants. This dramatic emphasis on elephants as part of bride-wealth payments appears to make little sense unless one can relate it to the transportation and war needs of plains-based Mughal provincial administration and armies from the seventeenth century. Horses had been successfully imported into the plains of Hindustan by a pattern of trade involving many intermediaries between the plains and Chinese partners on the Yunnan plateau after the thirteenth century.[103] These horses were the 'hill ponies' or 'tanguns' found in stables of the mighty in lower Tibet, Assam, and Pegu. But the forests of the same regions also hosted the pachyderm. In the region east of Dhaka, where water framed the land, all dry land was high land. These high lands were home to both bamboo forests in the lower elevations and pine, sal, and teak at higher. These forested elevations were often the hinterlands of forts on rivers. As one can infer from the *Baharistan-i-Ghaybi*, Mughal policy from the seventeenth century had focused on these riverine forts. While Mughals depended on fleet of boats and oarsmen, artillery, and cavalry, almost all the work of battering down forts and entering them was done by elephants. These elephants worked as ultimate all-purpose all-terrain vehicles in the armies.

Such transportation animals were valued in every monastic domain of the seventeenth and eighteenth centuries. It was not just the Landa Sultans off the river Surma who spoke of elephants sent from forests of the Himalayan foothills. The poets of the *Krishnamala* suggest that disciples often brought valuable animal wealth and trade goods to the treasuries of their revered monastic leaders and commanders. Referring to a corporate Himalayan community (*khuchung samaj*), it listed the gifts of animals that such a corps made to its guru (72), one of the peripatetic monastic-warriors identified as the Tipura Manikya, and enabled him to turn the tables on his rivals. The allegiance of such militia and animal power was secured through personal initiation and rituals intended to bring these corps directly into relations of 'obedience' and 'service' to their monastic leader (99–114). At the same time, the goods that they brought enabled the leader to hire (on money wages, *chakar*) other mercenary soldiers and commanders from the hills around Panduah (northwest Sylhet, 115). Together, these sannyasi-led forces are described as driving back the usurpers and *ijaradars* who had contracted with Mughal governors and brought men of the Company into the fray. Translated into familiar terms, the poets seem to be saying that upland populations, tied by monastic and military affiliations to particular monks and gurus, had come right into Company and Mughal-held terrain to drive them out.

However, the payment of such animals to others also represented the giver's acknowledgement of respect for the recipient. That is what the numbers of elephants given from these forest-based monastic communities to Mughal commanders represented. Assamese buranjis carry letters from commanders of Mughal armies to the svargadeva reminding the latter about unpaid installments of elephants: these demands grew with growing warfare in eastern India.[104] Given the status and value of these animals, their presence in bride-wealth transactions that the Meitei conducted with neighbouring groups established a barometer of value for the brides hailing from an especially significant lineage or household. Only elephants in a transaction distinguished a high-status marriage from others. Each groom's status and command over resources was displayed in the number, size, sex, age, and tusks of the animal paid. Whereas the principality of Kapo (Kabo, currently in valleys between upper Burma and Assam) sent 'many elephants' in the bride wealth it transferred in exchange for its aristocratic Meitei bride, Sna (golden) Langmeirempi,[105] such animals had to be literally forced out of other potential affines in the course of the century. When the Meitei conquered a flourishing metallurgical and manufacturing economy in and around an Islamized Sylhet, among their gains were 'thirty elephants' and their caretakers (along with thousands of skilled Muslim craftsmen).[106] In the mid-seventeenth century, when a potential groom's household (from 'Mayang' or another term for 'Morang', the foothills and plains between modern Nepal and Bengal) sent ox-drawn palanquins as bride wealth for the Meitei maiden, the mother of the bride 'regarded the price as too little and sent them back. An elephant and other items were sent.'[107] The ability to demand an elephant in bride-wealth denoted the high value that either the person of the bride or an association with her lineage had in the seventeenth and eighteenth centuries. At the very least, such brides appeared to have come from lineages with well-established reputations in two domains: in knowledge of physical environments and the ability to tame them through hunting and trapping as well as in ritual and clerical administrative skills. Such skills, moreover, were not the sole preserve of men. Female clan-members of the Meitei were dispatched to highlands of the Takhen (or 'hill' Tipra) to bargain for elephants. By the 1670s, a full-fledged transfer of elephants was established from these hills to the people of the Meitei in the valley below. Most of these animals were young pairs, as evident from the description 'one male and one female elephant which had not yet grown tusks'.[108] These transfers of animal wealth further consolidated the status of the lineages receiving them: they became militarily powerful as well as secured the animal widely venerated by Buddhist populations in the vicinity as the ultimate royal animal. So as Mughal armies moved further north and east in the terrain, their relationships with lineages in command of forests

and animals also deepened the network-like effect of the monastic geographic order.
Curiously, they also appear to have deepened ties that prevented sectarianism. For instance, the Tibetan-speaking Buddhist laylord of Ladakh who had allied with a Mughal commander in the seventeenth century had married the sister of the Shia Muhammad Ali Khan. Even in the early nineteenth century, a more orthoprax observer from the plains who was revolted by fraternal polyandry among western Tibetan Buddhists nevertheless praised them for 'they marry their daughters to the Muhammadans and do not object to their adopting the faith of their husbands.'[109]

A MUGHAL INHERITANCE

Mughal imperial grants of subsistence to sacred and learned figures distinguished their recipients by stating that they were exempt from yearly renewals; the lesser recipients were vulnerable to such yearly renewals. During the sixteenth and seventeenth centuries, such renewals were often the occasion for reductions of the grants: if the lands in the original grants had been uncultivated, and in the interim had become arable, the area of tax-exempt land granted might then be reduced. Such reductions also occurred at the death of the original grantee and the renewal of the grants to the heirs. But reductions and cancellations of tax-exempt grants were also sensitive to political and military trends. Thus, both Akbar and Aurangzeb used resumption of revenue-free grants in a pointed fashion—Akbar against the overweening Afghan lords of the sixteenth century, and Aurangzeb against all rebellious grant holders in the latter half of the seventeenth century. It was in the course of such resumptions that the Mughal emperor laid down the principles by which exemptions as well as the objects of such gifts could be inherited. In 1690, Aurangzeb decreed that the land of the grantees (*aima-i-uzzam*) 'confirmed by valid farman old and new would be retained completely and fully *without loss or reduction* by the heirs of deceased grantees generation after generation.'[110] Though genealogical descent from the prophet had historically made Sayyids eminent among Muslims, and descent from Sufi pirs favoured Shaikhzadas from the seventeenth century on, descent from sacred teachers, holy men, erstwhile gurus and gosain recipients of gifts became especially significant after 1690.[111] Thus, this order became important to the consolidation of exemption-based genealogies of sanctity, as well as for ordinary histories of family and of gender in the subcontinent.

Even as it specified that inheritance of exemption was governed by imperial order, not by Islamic law (*shari'a*), the farman simultaneously spelled out the lines of inheritance from such *madad-i-ma'ash* grantees that adhered to Islamic, namely sunni, principles. It allowed a direct share to the male heir of a male grantee; it did not allow the same privileges to a married daughter. However, it did lay down that a widow might keep her husband's grant for life before it passed to her husband's heirs. If the husband had no heirs, the grant would be assigned to the relatives of the widow. If a male grantee died leaving behind his daughter as heir and agnatic heirs (related on or descended from the father's or male side or *asbat*), then the daughter was to be the entire recipient of the renewed *madad-i-ma'ash* grant. If a grantee left his mother, grandmother, and other ladies whose maintenance was to be made by him according to the Quran (*sahib-i-farza*), the land was to be divided among them according to the Islamic code (*mulabi-i-share-i-sharif*). If a grantee left a nephew or cousin as heir, his land was to be granted according to prescribed rules of shari'a. If a man died without leaving behind any heirs, his *madad-i-ma'ash* grant was to be resumed as imperial property (*bait-ul-mal*). Under such conditions, the matter of genealogical reckoning from sacred figures became especially important in the transmission of moral and social capital. Men and women who could remember and transmit genealogies were favoured with authority. At the same time, the farman's provisions indicated the extent to which women's kin-relationships (sisterhood, unmarried daughterhood, motherhood, grandmotherhood, and consortship) with male sacred figures was critical to their ability to function as economically independent agents in the landscape. The political and economic weight of kinship was laid bare in such an order.

The historic value of such a decree can only be appreciated in the context of the contemporary stabilization of monastic governments and geographies everywhere in the seventeenth and early eighteenth century. Even the most exacting of Mughal tax-collectors in Bengal could thereafter make 'no retrenchments in any royal grants, or in those of former *Soobahdar*s, for charitable purposes; but, on the contrary, increased them.'[112] Many Mughal *faujdars* and zamindars in eastern Bengal, across the Tibetan–Burman–Bengali speaking worlds of eastern Bengal and Assam, gave plots of land and income from markets, from among their own allotments of income from lands and shops (jagir) as 'gifts' to sacred figures, thereby extending the network of *mathas*, *akharas*, *masjids*, and *khanqahs* between one Mughal province and the next.[113] The grants typically stipulated that their holders were exempt from all calls upon their labour, and from search and seizure of all kinds; that 'no yearly demand' would be made of such revered grantees. Equally important, such lands could not be measured, nor the persons of such sacred beings searched or treated with any sign of contempt.

As in earlier centuries, so in the eighteenth, cultivation expanded, and was organized by 'Brahman' recipients of grants of income from lands and markets (*brahmottar*).[114] Some documents even spelt out that the brahman was to cultivate with his own hands (*nij haste hal chash koraiya paramsukhe bhog korouk*). But as with previous centuries, recipients of such grants were not limited to a particular sect or lineage. For instance, the particular Tipra donor appears to have been especially generous to Vaisnava 'brahmans'.[115] Similarly, a Vaisnava Hindu zamindar (Baidyanath, Raja of Dinajpur) gave the income from a market (*hat/bazaar*) in western Bengal (Dinajpur) to a Sayyid Pir Ali; the latter in turn dedicated the income—and the deed—to the *khadim* (literally, servant, but effective custodian and steward) of the shrine of Hazrat Shah Jellal (in Sylhet).[116] Between the 1740s and 1760, another zamindari in Rajshahi issued sanads granting amounts varying from three to five rupees annually to a wide variety of such monastic–ascetic figures.[117] Other distant Mughal governors, such as the Nawab Asad al-daulah of Awadh, granted charters to Sufi males to 'clear and cultivate' and hence re-populate erstwhile arable land that had turned to scrub in Sylhet. These charters were called (*abadi sanads*).[118]

The responsibility for collecting the sums given in such charitable donations also strengthened governance by monastic lineages especially in those geographical contexts in which the source of dedicated income—such as a piece of land or a market or a custom-booth—was distant from the residence of the donee. Thus, militant and mercantile monastic lineages and teachers remained active in parts of north and western Bengal estates (Purneah) as well as riverine and coastal ports (Dhaka, Chittagong, Kumilla).[119] A French private trader, Jean-Baptiste Chevalier, who sought to use the services of these men in 1756–7, called these tax-exempt figures 'bairagis' (renunciants) and 'fakirs allowed to do business in the kingdom of Assem without paying any duty'.[120] The special status of such renunciant–traders arose from their status as monastics in their own right, as well as subjects of even more accomplished monastic figures also exempt from search and seizure. Their connections with other monastic centres up and down the rivers of Assam and Bengal made these mercantile monastic subjects the ideal trading partners for many aspiring households. From Chevalier's account, we learn of a vibrant network of trade in goods such as wax, lacquer, gold, tea, silk, eaglewood, porcelain, saffron, and saltpeter. Various networks of faqirs–sannyasis were involved in these trades all over the hills and plains of Hindustan right up to the borders of Sichuan and Yunnan. Such bairagis or faqirs had enormous wealth of information about market conditions in a variety of domains, as Chevalier found out from one who offered to take him directly to the presence of the lord of Gherghong (the royal capital of Assam). The connections of the sannyasi network extended deep into the Sylhet-Cachar region and into Burma. Among merchants and traders Chevalier saw in Gauhati in the 1750s were those from Pandua and 'Silot region', who brought 'copper, toutenague [alloy of copper and zinc], and other goods' obtained from Europeans there to Gauhati. Their modes of operating commercially across this entire terrain rested on personal adherence and attachment to a raja at Gherghong, a steward or boatman elsewhere. Chevalier had witnessed this face-to-face commercial system: none of the bairagis he partnered with asked for any gift or advances, but insisted on prompt and full payments on completion of the job of selling and buying.

Bairagi traders operated and extended monastic geographicity, but many of them also cultivated a suppleness of ritual and political identity as a result. For instance, the agent of a Vaisnava grain merchant (Doulut Das) was a man called Radharam, a sannyasi/ faqir who owned a shop in Sylhet. A Bengali-language biography of Radharam, written by a descendant of one of the zamindars of Sylhet, says that Radharam was a sickly child in a locally eminent Vaisnava lineage (Dattas) but had been cured by an itinerant sannyasi who brought him in turn to the grain centre (*chargola*) of Pratapgarh, itself the domain of a pir called Sahija Badshah. Here, Radharam was initiated as a devotee of the pir and gained access to other followers of the pir as well as the latter's biological kinsmen. One of these was Ghulam Ali Chowdhury, a shareholder in the estate of Pratapgarh. As Radharam supplied the Chowdhury with necessaries of life on credit, he slowly acquired portions of the Chowdhury's estates in the region. His proximity to sacred and temporal authority made his writ supreme; eventually he claimed to be a nawab and established his own court, fort, and militia.[121] This sannyasi/faqir Radharam ensured that the grain harvests were readily brought to the granary (*gola*) established for the Vaisnava temple and fort stronghold of the Tipura raj.[122] At the same time, this network of shopkeeper and trader, Sufi and Vaisnava connected Kumilla and Sylhet to the very well-established trading houses of Unao district of Awadh.[123] The implications for monastic subjecthood were that pockets of attached adherents could be found geographically distant from the objects of their devotion, as well as the buildings and sites considered to be sacred to them. Tenants living in the hills of easternmost Sylhet as headmen (*chaudhris*), managing tenants and/or cultivating a sannyasi's tax-exempt grant, could quite coherently claim that they were adherents or 'dependents' of the lord who lived far away in Nurnagar, on the coastal plains of Kumilla.[124]

SHIFTING GROUND UNDER THE ENGLISH EAST INDIA COMPANY?

In what ways did this complex of monastic governments, militias, and marriages become the inheritance of the English East India Company? Descriptions of militarized conflicts almost inevitably raise the spectre of comparison with European histories of the same period. However, through none of this evidence does there arise a single structure of command such as that of a papacy in Rome, directing its forces against this or that 'infidel'. Nor, as we have seen above and as scholars of South and Southeast Asian histories argue, was there a wholesale sack of all monasteries of the kind that occurred in Reformation-era England.[125] But these conflicts do suggest that each monastic and military group sought greater and greater advantage, often by inviting outsiders endowed with skills or technologies not common to the locality, to break an impasse. Each local attempt that looked like the installation of a new 'orthodoxy' at the centre was actually therefore an attempt to expand the networks of potential adherents and disciples from which a monastic lineage could expect cash, goods, and labour services, while maintaining the older exemptions from taxation of the monks and tantric or visionary teachers themselves.[126] Thus, the Buddhist ordination lineage conflicts in the seventeenth century brought the intervention of ever-distant sets of disciples (such as the Qosot Mongol armies, disciple–protectors of the Gelukpa). Conflict within and between lineages went 'global' across networks of adherents and land masses because these conflicts occurred within the order identified here as monastic geographicity. As is well known, the Zunghari invasion of Central Tibet from the northwest in 1717 meant the persecution and destruction of all Nyingma-Kagyu texts and images in the region, and the flight of the persecuted to a variety of 'hidden sanctuaries' to the south and east.[127] This pattern would help to explain how and why in the late eighteenth century, similar conflicts between lineages drew the East India Company's military forces into the terrain.

Nothing about this was revolutionary. It was both old and shared across the area of monastic governance. It became significant in the eighteenth century because conflict appeared to have erupted everywhere in the Brahmaputra Valley system simultaneously at the time. In the early eighteenth century, the power of the 'ancestral' cult in Manipur Valley was threatened by the import of another lineage of Gaudiya (that is, from western Bengal) Vaisnava gurus from Sylhet (the teaching lineage of Shanti Das Gosain).[128] This imported lineage of intensely emotive teachers and interpreters of Vaisnava doctrines burned the older texts (*puyas*), changed the mythology/history of the valley by making Manipur part of an anecdote in the epic Mahabharata and by representing the Meitei prince–patron as the Krishna incarnation of the deity Visnu in place of the earlier Rama incarnation.

An identical occurrence was noted in the disestablishment of older (*puraniya*) monastic lineages in Assam at the same time.[129] Inmates and adherents of a 'Dihingia Sattra' (monastery on the Dihing River) opposed the ritual and disciplinary innovations supported by an eighteenth-century svargadeva, who was the disciple and patron of a Bhattacharyya Brahman.[130] These tussles remained violent, since heads of monasteries commanded huge numbers of male disciples to put in the field: thus an abbot (*mahanta*) of a 'reformist' monastery 'collected all the disciples he could lay his hands on' to put a 2000-strong army in the field.[131] Similarly, in Burma, 'hat-wearing' and village-living (*gamavasi*) monks had set up *pwegaing* schools where training in martial arts and special sciences enabled disciples to earn a living in the lay world. But in the eighteenth century, these householder–monastics were disestablished by the import of Vaisnava 'Brahmans' from Manipur.[132]

Were these 'Brahmans' militants too? Oral histories provided by teachers and genealogists to the author confirm that they were. Coins from the fortresses of the Surma Valley support this interpretation. The star-studded coins of the earlier centuries gave way in the eighteenth to coins bearing the legend that the entire country was dedicated to the deity Siva, the 'illustrious lord of Jayantapur'.[133]

Obviously, these conflicts were not between 'Hindu' and 'Muslim', but between one group of allied and intermarried Tantric Buddhist, Saiva, Vaisnava, Jewish–Zoroastrian, and Muslim lineages against an identically heterogeneous alliance and network. Marriages were not only exogamous but also plural. Monastic governments and communities related to each other in the latter context through ritualized activities, in peace and in war, and above all, in the maintenance of marital–political alliances during the seventh–seventeenth century. These interlocking politics produced and reproduced monastic codes of gender which valourized youthful monastic militancy on behalf of disciples, and of polyandrous and plural marriages for women of eminent lay clans on the other. This was the context for the equation of marriages, or 'gifts' of favoured daughters and sisters to military–monastic clans of the Himalayan world and the gift of a favoured nephew to the monastic lineage itself. In subsequent centuries, ways of accumulating such male followers were patterned on the Buddhist vihara and the Brahman's sattra. Bengali Muslim poets of the eighteenth century, too, measured the moral worth of a warrior in terms of the markets and free schools (*tols* and *maqtabs*) established.[134] It was notable that the poet's free school was envisaged as meeting ground of different skills and experts: a *hafez* from a coastal island, a *maulvi* from a distant land, and a *munshi* from the provincial capital were all appointed at the same time to work and live alongside each other. The poet describes Quranic and Shastric recitation and Arabic and Bangla writing at the same time as war and elephant trapping. The trapper's skills as well as the scribe's, learned through the establishment of a workshop-style teaching-learning lineage, remained important in the eighteenth century.

Control of such workshops therefore made the change of heads of such teaching institutions, as well as their affiliations, of concern to erstwhile patrons. Disputed successions to headship of monasteries and estates attached to them always operated as the thin edge of a wedge for the induction of 'outsider' militias, and the subdivision of the lands and tenants belonging to a monastic estate. It was one such disputed succession in the spiritual lineage of Ramdev, the Vaisnava mahant of Borduar favoured by the Ahom 'king' Laksmisingh (1769–80), that led the English Company–supported rival king Kamalesvar Singh (1795–1811) to split the original endowment of Borduar into two separate segments, Norua and Hologuri, and to endow the latter with 101 *bhakat*s separately. Perhaps it was as such newly endowed monastic 'subjects' that several thousand Sikh, Muslim, and Hindustani faqirs were brought to Assam in the late eighteenth century, when the English East India Company's officers were also invited to intervene in a conflict between two orders of monastic lineages.[135] Certainly, efforts to arrange for similar infusions of fighting men had led to priestly embassies between Tipura and the lords on the north bank of the Brahmaputra between 1711 and 1724 as well.[136] Therefore, the arrival of 'outsiders', including English officers and Indian soldiers in the late eighteenth century, confirmed the persistence of monastic geographicity, even as individual lineages moved in and out of control of vast estates and people. It was for such reasons that the colonial officer who did the most to change the inner workings of this monastic geographic order across greater Brahmaputra–Meghna River valley noted that 'long before the Ahom Rajahs were converted to Hindooism or Brahmanism, the temples were established in Lower Assam, having large establishments of priests who read and taught the Hindoo sacred books in Sanskrit; and immediately after their conversion, the Rajahs brought in

Kanouge and Santipore Brahmins for whom they instituted immense establishments and them they invested with so much rank and power that gradually *the greater part of the authority of Government fell into their hands*' [emphasis added].[137]

The colonial officer's comments reveal the strengthened cross-regional links of monastic governments in the eighteenth century. What they do not reveal is that the Englishmen had come up from the plains of Bengal, where they had already initiated measures intended to shrink the power of monastic militias from the 1760s. Before we can understand how this might have affected the monastic geographic order in the Brahmaputra-Surma valleys after the 1830s, we will have to glance over the shifts in the monastic governmental order on the Company-held plains of Bengal. The next chapter will do just that.

NOTES

1. Lahiri (1991, 2011); also K.L. Barua (1933, 1935); for a similar argument about the lands given by the Nidhanpur Grant, *see* Bhattacharya (1936); rejoinder to N. Bhattasali by Barua (1936); for the reference to the 'garland of peacock-trees' in the grant, see Nath (1937); for a broad view, see Chakravarti (2010).

2. Nath and Vidyavinode (1938); for commentary on this, see Bhattacharya 1938.

3. First Copperplate of Indrapala, in Sharma (ed.) (1981 [1931]), *Kama-rupasasanavali*, 199–202.

4. Colonial Assamese bureaucrats, too, remembered the similiarities of Buddhist and Vaisnava structures in the Brahmaputra Valley. See Goswami (1933).

5. Barua Sadaramin (1990 [1930]), *Assam Buranji*, 76, for the coupling of *sisya-proja* (disciple-subject) or followers of the Moamara Mahanta, and construction of prayer halls and monasteries (*sattra*) by such subjects.

6. *Ibid.*, 48–59. The man, identified as 'grandson of Debraja', Chupangmung with the Hindu name of Chakradhvaj Simha, held the office during 1663–70. His two brothers held it in succession during 1670–9.

7. Adhikary (2001: 76). Lands and cultivators granted to this temple appeared to have linked to both a village called Jayantipur and a village, Pachim Khandik in the Kacharimahal pargana. Seven gots of Brahmans and forty-five gots of Sudra and Ganak paiks were granted to the temple, appearing to link in one circuit people and places that surfaced in English records as Jaintea and Kachar with the histories of Kamrup or western Assam.

8. Malcolm (1839: 146).
9. I draw upon MacWilliams (2000); Ashraf (2012).
10. Tamuli (2005 [c.1904]), *Naobaisha Phukanar Asom Buranji*, 228–314.
11. Hirananda Sastri (1923).
12. Das (1970 [1881–2]), *Contributions*, 61.
13. *Ibid.*, 50.
14. *The Blue Annals*, I, (1996a [1949]): 34.
15. Das (1970 [1881–2]): 70.
16. Uebach (2003: 21–7).
17. Takeuchi (2003: 43–55).
18. Ostrowski (1998). The word *tamma*, derived from Chinese *tanma*, initially meant a mounted scout, and from the time of the Chin emperors represented the military vanguard of a military governor of a province; his parallel in a dual system of government was the civilian governor in each province, also permitted to recruit forces.
19. Thomas (1935: 262–3).
20. For sixteenth-century Buddhist reuse of a twelfth-century Khmer Vaisnava site, see Kim 2010a; for Islamic reuse of Jaina-Saiva monastic complex, see Patel (2004).
21. Sneath (2007).
22. Guakuchi Grant of Indrapalavarmadeva in Sharma (1981 [1931]), *Kamarupasasanavali*, 203–6.
23. Paschimbhag Plate of Sricandra in D.C. Sircar 1973, 27; Imam 1999; Chowdhury 1999.
24. Linrothe (1999: 22 and passim).
25. Vitali (2001: 24–5, n. 13).
26. Boyce (1979: 46, 164); Russell (1987: 26–7); Nebesky-Wojkowitz (1956); another and fuller translation is that of Per Kvaerne (1975 [1958]).
27. Azarpay (1976).
28. Ruegg (2004, 2008); Kapstein (2009).
29. Stein (2010: 231–72); Stein had however insisted that non-Buddhist aspects of Tibetan practice did not have a particular name.
30. For combination of Iranian and Central Asian systems, see Reynolds (2005); for Bon Tantra common to Tibetan and Indian Himalaya, see Bellezza (2008); Karmay and Watt (2007); Huber (1998); Martin (1994, 2007); also Templeman (2002); Snellgrove (1967).
31. For northern Thailand, see Swearer, Premchit, and Dokbuakaew (2004); for Himalayan Nepal, see Tautscher (2007) and McKay (2007a, 2007b); for southeastern Tibetan plateau, whose southern end includes the northern ends of modern Assam and Burma, see Gardner (2006: 12–53).

32. See list prepared under Rudrasimha Svargadeva, *c.* 1714 CE, in Bhuyan (1987 [1930]), *Kamrupar Buranji*, Appendix A, pp. 105–10.

33. Parratt and Parratt (1997).

34. Tamuli (ed.) (2005 [1904]), *Naobaisha Phukanar Asom Buranji*, 16–17.

35. *Ibid.*, 16.

36. Sen (1930), *SriRajamala*, II, 2–7.

37. For Khalji and Tughlaq travails in Kamrup or western Assam in thirteenth and fourteenth centuries, see Karim (1992: 95–7); for fifteenth-century Sultanate, see Karim (1992: 98) and passim.

38. *SriRajamala* II, 5.

39. Singh and Ray (2007: 25–6).

40. See, for example, sanad of Sher Shah, dated 18 Sha'ban AH/19 December 1540 in Srivastava (1974: I, 1). This was two years after the Sur conquest of the sultanate of Bengal, with its capital at Gaur-Jannatabad, in which canon was also important; for which see Karim (1992: 383–424); especially 386 for involvement of 'Taraf' in southern Sylhet in these battles.

41. See, for a report on such a struggle, Ralph Fitch in Foster (1999: 26).

42. Inscription of edifice mentioning city of Sylhet, of date 1588, followed by inscription from Kumilla mentioning the Mughal Emperor Akbar, of 1591, in Siddiq (2009: 192–7).

43. Borah (1936: I, 179).

44. Correspondence between Svargadeva Jayadhvajasimha and Jasmattarai, 1655–63, in Dutta (1937: 18–22).

45. Moonshee (1868–9: 130–3); also Moonshee (1870: 35–9).

46. Asani (1987: 439–49).

47. Rhodes and Bose (2006, 2010); for the same symbol in Himalayan Buddhism, see Tournadre and Dorje (2009: 486).

48. Botham (1912: 556–7).

49. For three patrons of Buddhists with the same name between the twelfth and the mid-fourteenth century, see Shakspo (1988: 5–7); for two of them, also see Vitali (2005: 119).

50. Borah (1936: 208).

51. *Ibid.*, 166, 325–6.

52. Broadbridge (2010: 168–97).

53. See Introduction by C. Wessels in De Filippi (1932: 13); for 'Khasa' used for western Nepal and Tibet, see Tucci (1956); for 'Khaza' as also a potential term of reference to Khazaria or northern tip of Persian Central Asia, from where Sogdian traders had traded to Kashmir and Ladakh, see Beckwith (1987: 180, n 11); for Tibetan term 'khache' as reference to Kashmir, see Goldstein, Shelling, and Surkhang (2001).

54. Aris (1992: 107–17).

55. For description of 'Garo' in the eighteenth century, see Chevalier (2008); for description of 'Garoo' as short for Gartop, a major Himalayan market for goat-hair shawls, see Gerard (1824 [1818]): 42–3; for Gartok as 'Gerduk' in a contemporary Indian account of the shawl-wool trade-mart owned by Gelukpa lineage at Lhasa, see Izzet Ullah (1843 [1812]: 283–342).

56. Borah (1936: 528–32).

57. SriRajamala II, 23–4 for an account of a ritual that 'tied up' the river Gomti and then released to drown the troops of the enemy; as well as for a destructive tantric ritual with decapitated heads which was intended to terrify the remaining enemy soldiers into flight.

58. SriRajamala II, 30–1.

59. Ibid., II, pp. 35–7, 101.

60. Dargye (2001: 95–6).

61. Aris (1988: 76).

62. Aris (1979: 104–5); for three Shabsdrungs of the nineteenth century, all hailing from the Drametse Ogyenchoeling of eastern Bhutan, see Pommaret (2007: 260).

63. Adhikary (2001: 60).

64. For the example of Ananta Kandali, the son of a Ratan Pathak, reader of Bhagvata Purana, and hailing from a lineage of tantrics (tantri-kula) in the vicinity of the mountain-pilgrimage site of Hajo, see Chaliha (2000 [1949]: 128–9, 164–7). Before completing his translation and commentary, the poet was named Haricharan; the successful translation secured for him the name Srichandra Bharati. For skill in doctrinal debate, he was named Ananta Kandali, and he also held the title Bhāgavatāchāryya.

65. For two inscriptions at Lolarka-kunda, Benares, see Ghosh (1937a, 1937b).

66. Barua (1985 [1930]: 98, 99).

67. Ibid., 118.

68. Ibid., 130.

69. Ibid., 195–6.

70. Bhuyan (1987 [1930]: 42–3), Letter of Allah Yar Khan to 'Chetiya Gohain' [Baraphukan], c. 1638 CE. The phrase is 'aami tomaar chaagir hoilon, tumi aamar salaahkaar'.

71. Emmer (2007: 81–108); Elverskog (2010: 220–3).

72. Kamarupar Buranji, 35. Since this chronicle history compiled at least four others on the same theme, the variant spellings of Alchi as 'Allachi' also exist in the current buranji at 85,101. The reference to this monastic centre and community as having provided one of the administrators of the Ahom administration is also confirmed in other chronicles of the war such as those in Bhuyan (1951 [1936]: 56 (for Lanmakhru), 71–2) (for Alchi

Rajkhowa). The founders of Alchi, a ninth-century monastery in the western Himalayas, belonged in the prominent 'Bro clan that was active in Central Asia and Tibet, for which see Papa-Kalantari (2007: 167–228). A variant reading of the *Kamrupa buranji* may, however, yield the word 'Lamayuru', also a monastery belonging to the Drukpa Kargyupa in Ladakh. According to Fernanda Pirie, after the Ladakhi-Tibetan war of 1680s, the Gelukpa domination of Ladakh's monasteries was replaced by Kargyupa authority, for which see Pirie (2006: 173–90).

73. For the battle at Bharali fort in 1616, see Barua (trans. and ed.) (1985: 99–100). The preface identifies the manuscript found on oblong strips of bark, in the possession of a Deodhai Pandit in Sibsagar District in 1894, as the main source for Edward Gait's *A History of Assam*. The editor also admits to breaking the narrative up according to modern conventions.

74. Ramble (1999) and Martin (1999). Such names as Khyunglung are also found in *Ahom Buranji from Khunlung and Khunlai, Assam Buranji from Khunlung to Gadadhar Singh* but were overlooked by scholars such as S.N. Bhattacharyya (1929).

75. Bernier (1999 [1934]: 172); also see Mohammed (2005: 147–60).

76. Adhikary (2001: 60).

77. For an eyewitness account of the Kagyupa ('Red-Cap') monastic ambassador and entourage who negotiated with the Mughal emperor, see Bernier (1999 [1934]: 423–5). The date of the treaty does not correspond to the date provided in Bernier. For statement on retreat of Raja of Acham, see 172.

78. See petition of Bhutan's ambassadors in Bhuyan (1990a [1933]: 152–5).

79. Ralph Fitch in Foster (1999 [1921]: 25).

80. Barman (1998: 51).

81. Borah (1936: 317, 398) for the guns and poisoned arrows of the Ahom forces who corralled the Mughal-Afghan-Rajput forces as though in a hunting enclosure and nearly extirpated the entire force.

82. Turner (2005 [1800]: 119).

83. Hamilton (formerly Buchanan) (1963 [1940]: 73).

84. Hamilton (1824–5: 249–51).

85. Munshi (1985). The editor's preface identifies the chronicler as an eyewitness to the English East India Company's annexation of Kuch Bihar, as well as one who had read the report submitted by Mercer and Chauvet in 1788. Seven years later, in 1795, the author was appointed tutor to the young prince. He began the chronicle sometime during 1823–33 and completed it in 1845. His erstwhile ward, then zamindar of Kuch Bihar, read the completed chronicle and rewarded him with a grant of rent-free lands (*lakhiraj*). For the description of 'forts' with bamboo fences and timber thickly set with spikes 'in the usual porcupine fashion of these structures' in

nineteenth-century Arakan, see Lt Henry Yule, Engineer on Duty to Offg Secy GOI, Military, 5 July 1853, FPP, 28 April 1854, nos 125–7, f. 14.
86. Munshi (1985: 41).
87. *Ibid.*, 55–6.
88. Col J.C. Gawler to QMG of Army, 24 December 1860, in Gawler (1987 [1873]: 9).
89. For the marriage of a tantric monastic in the sixteenth century, see *Sri Rajamala* II, 9.
90. Barua (1985 [1930]: 92–3). See 94, 97 for other exchanges.
91. R.C. Majumdar cited in Ali (1965: 90).
92. Datta (1937: 22–3). Three letters of the same import and written by the same authors to the same recipients were copied into a manuscript, which in turn was secured from another member of the polyglot Assamese literati of the twentieth century.
93. *Ibid.*, Letter dated 10 Jaith 1585 saka (end May 1663), 24–5.
94. *Ibid.*, Letter dated 9 Karttik 1589 saka (end October 1667), 35. The month is considered very auspicious in the Vaisnava calendar.
95. *Ibid.*, Letter dated 24 Magh 1594 saka (mid-February 1672), 42.
96. *Ibid.*, Letter from Svargadeva, dated 4 Pous, 1590 saka (mid-December 1668), 37.
97. *Ibid.*, 36–7.
98. *Ibid.*, 43.
99. Barua (ed.) (1985 [1930]): 127.
100. *Ibid.*, 212.
101. De Filippi (1932: 193, 195).
102. Parratt (2005: 49), entry for Sakabada 1458 (using the older calendar which equated the start of the Saka era with 78 CE, the translator renders this date 1536 CE).
103. Ray (2003: 9) (for horse market in China to which the Jurched and Mongols brought horses for exchange with textile, grains, satins), 95 (for Hajo, Assam, as exchange point for Tibeto-Indian and Bhutan-Indian trades).
104. Bhuyan (1987 [1930]): 66–8 (for 1662–3 CE), 87–9 for correspondence between Shaista Khan and Burogohain about a far greater number of elephants delivered than agreed to by treaty.
105. Parratt (2005: 57), entry for Saka 1491 (translated as 1569 CE).
106. *Ibid.*, 67, entry for Saka 1528 (translated as 1606 CE).
107. *Ibid.*, 89, entry for Saka 1592 (translated as 1670 CE). Only after the arrival of the elephant did the bride leave for the husband's house.
108. *Ibid.*, pp. 100–1, entry for 1691 CE.
109. Izzet Ullah (1843 [1812]: 283–342).
110. Mohammed (2002: 37).

111. *Ibid.*, 34–8.

112. Salimallah (1788: 115).

113. See, for example, a grant from Alivardi Khan 'Translate of Sunnud under Seal of Nawab Mahabit Jang Bahadur, Subahdar of Bengal, dated 24 Zikadah and Jalouce', in J. Willes to John Shore and BOR, 19 October 1789, *SDR*, 3, 174–5.

114. Brahmottar Sanad on Copperplate, J.G. Cummings 1899, *Settlement Report*, Appendix IV.

115. Gosvami (1994: 58–9).

116. Petition of 'Ally Mohlah, Khadeim of the Dorga of Hazrut Shah Jellal', in BOR (Misc), 16 March 1791.

117. Note of Collr. Rajshahi, n.d. in BOR (Misc), 6 August 1792.

118. Translation of Potta Abadi, encl. in Willes to BOR, 23 November 1789, *SDR*, 3, 185–6.

119. Lt Bentley, 7th Battalion sepoys at Kumillah to Chief of Chittagong, 8 July 1773, *BDR, C* 1, 103–4.

120. Chevalier (2008: 145–6). See also the accounts of other bairagis and fakirs going between Rangamati and Gauhati in Assam and another to 'kingdom of Catta' towards the south of Assem, on 150–1.

121. Hosena (1990: 370–3).

122. Enclosed Petition of Doolut Das, in J. Shakespear et al. to Mr. Lindsay, 20 April 1778, *SDR* 1, 27–8.

123. Cummings (1899: 21).

124. Wazeeb ul Arz of the Choudrees of the Pergannah Koylashahr dependent on the Chucklah Roshnabad, Tipperah, enclosed in Letter from Resident, Commillah, to Collr Sylhet, 26 May 1789, *SDR*, 4, 78.

125. Huxley (1996, 1997, 2001, 2002); Huxley and Okudaira (2001).

126. See discussion of the expanded connections in the late seventeenth century between the Vaisnava monastery (Auniati sattra) on Majuli Island in the river Brahmaputra with other Vaisnava centres on the plains of western Bengal such as Nadia, Santipur, and Simlagrama in Barua (1990 [1930]: 65–6).

127. Pomplun (2010: 104-30).

128. Brara (1998: 105–11), supported by numismatic and epigraphic evidence for the region in Devi (2003); and M.K. Singh (1998: 122–89, 236–71).

129. Barua (1990 [1930]: 68–74).

130. Barua (1985 [1930]): 318–19.

131. Bhuyan (1990a [1933]: 105).

132. Charney (2006: 45); Charney (2011).

133. Rhodes and Bose (2006, 2010).

134. Barman (1998: 67–8).

135.   Francis Jenkins to Secy GOB, 7 December 1854 in Bengal General Progs. 3 July, no. 85 in Accounts and Papers of the House of Commons 1859, Session 2, Correspondence relating to the Education Despatch dated 22 June 1858, vol. 10, part 1, 21–2.

136.   Bhuyan (1990b [1938]).

137.   Jenkins to Secy GOB, 7 Dec. 1854, Accounts and Papers, 22.

2

Eighteenth-Century Shifts of Monastic Governments

AT THE END OF THE EIGHTEENTH CENTURY, when the East India Company's armed forces were sought by the monastic governments in the Brahmaputra and Surma valleys, the Company had already developed three decades' worth of experience in the military-led reorganization of monastic governments in eastern Bengal. This chapter surveys the tripartite aspect of such reorganization. The foremost effect was the erosion and realignment of political and economic exemptions and privileges of the monastic 'lords' ('rajas', 'kings') that involved the Company in direct confrontation with monastic armies, their commanders, and monastic merchants. Of the more representative confrontations, one involved a Sufi–Vaisnava lineage in Sylhet and the other a Muslim lineage. Such confrontations, in turn, shaped the growing Company official sociology of knowledge. As warfare segmented hitherto connected groups, Company personnel picked out newly disaggregated groups for ethnologizing. Company officials observed, but could not understand, the complex and collocated Buddhist and Muslim groups living in southern Bengal. Most dramatic, however, were the effects of both Company-driven policies and systems of knowledge on households containing either female donors or female relatives of monastic militants and merchants.

COMPANY REALIGNMENTS OF MONASTIC NETWORKS AGAINST RIVAL EUROPEANS

The intersecting network of monastic governance, geography, and gender began to shift shape well before the formal grant of the

Diwani to the East India Company. In 1757, the British East India Company sent troops to the aid of a Mughal commander, Mir Jafar, and was allowed to recover the costs from the taxes collected from Chittagong.[1] The earliest figures suggest that the Company hoped to collect a minimum of 5 lakhs of rupees annually, since that was the sum erstwhile Mughal governors of the region had collected.[2] But the Company officials were also confident they could do better: they would eliminate all the expenses that the Mughal governors had supported from the income of these lands. One such expense was the sum used to maintain those 'Christians' (Roman Catholic Portuguese, Greek Orthodox, or Nestorian Christians) who protected the different forts (qilahs) of the region. These Catholic troops were dismissed from the employ of the Bengal Nawabs, and the money was paid to the British Company for providing the same services.

A second step was to 'reduce the immense number of collectors', many of who were recipients of the 'charity' grants of older regimes. That was the context in which Company servants first complained of the considerable quantity of lands held 'free of rent, having been lands formerly given in charity'.[3] The servants of the Company were fully aware that lands once given in charity in these parts were held to be sacred and inviolable. But from 1761 on, military officers on behalf of the Company collectors complained about the ways in which these rent-free tenures 'alienated' the best and most productive lands. In Chittagong, one complained that 'two-thirds of the best of the cultivated lands in this province are held by charity sunnuds … the major part possessed by a set of drones who wallow in wealth and luxury'.[4] In Sylhet, another collector a decade later complained that only one-eighth of the entire arable was held by Mughal zamindars, paying taxes that the Company was authorized to collect after the Diwani; seven-eighths of the land was held in tax-exempt 'charity tenures'.[5] Yet another of his successors heard that there were at least five or six hundred deeds (sanads) under which lands were held rent-free or tax-exempt in that province.[6]

As valuable as arable land were forests on the uplands which, in addition to timber, were also home to the most important cash crop of the eighteenth century—raw cotton. Thus, interest in the control of those cotton-growing elevations was foremost among the impulses behind another official lament about the holders of tenures in the uplands north of Sylhet: 'Waste and jungle lands were in the most profuse manner bestowed in charity or given up on a kharidge jumma by the Phozedar (*faujdar*) to his priest and menial servants, nor was any register kept of such gifts. In consequence of this liberality, there is not a person, even of the most inferior rank in Sylhet, who is not possessed of Lackerage [*la-khiraj*, tax-exempt] land of some denomination or other, and the best richest lands in the province are exempt from the revenues.'[7]

Initially, Company officials informed holders of these tenures that they endured only for the lifetime of their present possessors. At their death, these lands would be annexed by the Company.[8] This acquired a graver aspect, however, because it involved surveying and measuring of the extent of lands that would be affected. Advertisements were published asking all zamindars and holders of grants 'whether *jaghir Uttumgha, Firman, Sunnud, Perwannah,* Deed of gift, or Bill of sale, whether *Khiraut, Bumooter, Devooter, Cunnea Dawn, Mohataran, Muddud Maush, Khusbassan Haut, Serai* & ca' to appear in person 'within a month' at the collector's office with vouchers they possessed.[9] As the term '*haut*' (local market) above also indicates, the examination of all charitable gifts extended to an interrogation of the various imposts and tolls taken at markets from which the pious 'gifts' were then deducted and sent to intended recipients. *Khush-bash* referred to privileged immigrant settlers—presumably these were favoured leaders of caravans, merchants, and businessmen at a smaller market (haut) who enjoyed particular exemptions for residence and business there.

TAMING TRANS-LOCAL MILITANT AND MERCANTILE MONASTIC NETWORKS

Sannyasi/bairagi and faqir-held lands, settled by many different kinds of under-tenants, were spread between the plains of Kumilla and Chittagong at one end and the Himalayan foothills on the other. Tax-collectors from the Company tried to collect taxes from the coastal plains but it was really access to the intercontinental land traffic that they sought in the highlands. Aware of the vibrant trade between the trans-Himalayan and oceanic centres and ports, officials of the Company hoped that a region they identified as 'Tippera' (and that Taranath and Nepal historians had identified as 'Tipura') would provide a passage through the mountains of 'Couke [Ko-ki?] into Thibet and the Norther [*sic*] parts of Cochin China. … [Such a passage would] redound greatly to the state of the Europe imports, besides what benefits may be reaped by the natural pro[d]uce of those parts'.[10] Setting out to control these estates on behalf of the Company required that the early British officers come to a direct arrangement with the holder or holders of such lands as intervened. To this end, Verelst sent a 200-strong force led by Lt John Matthews to establish direct contact with the Raja of Tipura and collect whatever dues had been promised in 1761.

Similar forces had been sent to Burdwan, where the Vaisnava zamindar, Tilakchandra, enlisted at least 15,000 peons and paiks, led by a body of faqirs, to attack the Company's battalions in 1760. The confrontation cost the peasants dearly in life and in punitive taxation subsequently: the net demand (Rs 30 lakhs for 1761–2) was enhanced by Rs 2,50,000 by the Company to compensate itself for the military expenses of 'putting down' the peons and paiks the previous year.[11] The officer sent to collect the sum from Burdwan on behalf of the Company began by dismissing over 4,000 of the 10,363 land-servants and resuming their *chakaran* or rent-free support lands. By 1765, the Raja's military payroll was pared down to half its size; two years later, the 1,487-strong household guard (*naqdi*) was reduced to 839 men. In all instances, chakaran lands, used to support these paiks, soldiers, and guardsmen, were resumed and additional lakhs of rupees brought to Company government's account.

News of these processes, one can assume, would have spread fast among the networks of Vaisnava akharas. The arrival of British-officered armies on the coasts of Tripura at this point appears to have alerted the initiated monastic warrior 'Raja Krishnamanikya' that a similar process was to unfold against him. He abandoned the coastal estates for the hills to the north. Matthews followed the Raja, lamenting that this 'cunning, rascally and Iell man' had the mountains to retreat to where the Devil would not catch him.[12] Similarly, the sannyasi's chief lay support, Abdul Razak, who the poets of the *Krishnamala* suggest hailed from Bhojpur (Bihar), found that his wife, children, and family were imprisoned by the Naib Nazim at Murshidabad: once the 'principal zamindar' of the Tripura Rajah succumbed, so did the Raj. Matthews claimed that the Raja was relieved at this denouement and looked forward to paying his tribute to the Company as 'he is the true Rajah of this country'.[13]

Unlike Matthews's report on the positive attitude of Krishnamanik towards the Company in 1761, the poets of *Krishnamala* narrate the events after 1761 as a downward spiral fed partly by the Company's own commercial interests and partly by its readiness to use cannon and troops to extract every advantage. For instance, the poets corroborate Verelst's attempts to establish a route to Tibet through Tripura domains almost immediately after taking office. But they describe the traversing by Verelst's entourage of eight European officers and horses as a form of trespass (*lekhajokha naai*) (148). Similarly, the poets evince dismay at the repeated display of Company arms, mentioning a 'Captain Kinlakh' (Kinloch) who arrived with canon at a settlement on the plains called Mirzapur.[14]

As the poets suggest, disciples of the Tripura sannyasis were not limited to the coastal plains but were also found on the Himalayan foothills, along riverine ports and spurs of hills. Given the Himalayan pasts of which the poets sang when they sang of these sannyasis, it is quite likely that the 'Mirzapur' that the poets referred to was the well-known market and quarry on the river Ganga, adjacent to old pilgrimage town, Varanasi and an eminent centre of many gosain establishments. In the early nineteenth century, on the eve of the Anglo-Nepal war, the British officers would record that numerous faqirs and mahanta establishments constituted the 'frontiers'.[15] But in the mid-eighteenth century, British officers were only determined to find routes to the bullion trade of the Himalayan world. They were less concerned with conciliating the disciples and followers of such mahants and faqirs standing in their way.

The Company had even appointed an official surveyor for tracing these routes in 1764.[16] That surveyor, James Rennell, already surveying the Brahmaputra in the region north of Dacca—'in sight of Tartarian mountains', as he put it—was travelling considerable distances into estates held by monastic/faqiri orders. In February 1766, he had travelled 300-odd miles north of Dacca, the Mughal provincial capital, and was on the frontiers of 'Boutan or Thibet, the southern part of great Tartary', when he was confronted by 'a tribe of facquirs (kind of sturdy beggars)' drawn up in two lines, with sabres out, in the marketplace of a village he was reconnoitering without permission.[17] Rennell was oblivious of his transgression of monastic governance, the exemptions stated in donor's charters. Unaware of the protections against trespass by armed forces of another power that was promised to all bairagis, the surveyor killed one of these sannyasis, and was wounded in return. This hostile encounter further impeded the surveyor's recognition of his opponents as monastic figures.

In this, he was aided by the logic of Puritan history in England. Rennell, like other eighteenth-century Englishmen, took as his 'tests' of religiosity the sincerity of belief and interiority of faith common among English gentry of his own church. The Vaisnava–Buddhist and Muslim monastic governance rested on the performance of obligatory duties. Puritan thinkers had criticized such performances as 'externals'. Such Puritanism predisposed Rennell to censure that which was obligatory for Muslims to perform or the rules that orthodox Vaisnavas, Jains, and Sanatan Hindus committed to live by. For instance, Rennell wrote to his clergyman about the norms (presumably of *zakat*, or charitable giving) by which Muslims in Bengal were expected to act: 'with these people, a rich man is expected to be more religious than a poor man and very justly I think when Religion consists in *outward ceremony only*, for it is easy to determine which of the two has most time to spare. If I remember right *our* rich Folks are the least religious of any among us.'[18] Similarly, he queried the rationality of the desperately ill soldier in his entourage who, unable to keep any food down, nevertheless refused to swallow the chicken broth Rennell prescribed for him, 'because his sect never eat anything that had life in it.'[19] Many Vaisnava, Theravada Buddhist, and Jain groups shared the Upanisadic view of the continuum of life and the codes by which humans were expected to organize the accumulation of *karma*; the same groups were also equally clear-sighted about the ways in which the generation of commerce and profit as well as its appropriate expenditure accumulated moral–social capital as *punya* ('merit'). Their organization of monastic estates and endowments were the continuum of their commercial networks. It was this social and economic interdependence that Rennell did not understand, even though he saw the remains of the mud fort of the 'Sanashy Facquirs' at a place called Sanyashigotta (Sannyasi-ghat or landing piers reserved for their boats) on the river, and knew that they had had taken over the market town of Balarampur.[20]

Despite being physically stopped in his encroachment on monastic domains, Rennell returned the next year to the same region and was again obliged to retreat forthwith by the 'Boutese' [Bhutanese] who had drawn up an army to oppose him and seriously harried the retreating party.[21] Calling these men 'the banditti that commonly enter the northern provinces once a year, and after collecting from 5 to 6000 pounds sterling retire to neighboring provinces', Rennell devised a plan to destroy these groups and avenge himself. His plan was approved for implementation as the horrific famine of 1770–1 hit the plains; Rennell himself led the expedition that marched 320 miles north of Dacca in February 1771 to deliver the 'drubbing' he felt he had owed the monastic militias since 1766.[22]

Such incursions by armed British surveyors, engineers, and administrators played into ongoing crises and conflicts in the clans and households that managed or leased such estates. One of these families happened to be that of the descendants of seventeenth-century Mughal mansabdars or 'rajas' of Kuch Bihar and their paternal cousins, brothers, and half-brothers who held offices such as that of military commander (Nazir Deo) or manager (Diwan Deo). By the eighteenth century, the tensions within the Kuch Bihar lineages had reached a crescendo, aided by different segments of gosains battling for control of markets and trades.

Already divided among cousins and collaterals, each with its own sannyasi/bairagi entourage, the household at Kuch Bihar was also caught up in the political drama of the rise of the city and lordship of Gurkha in the valley of Kathmandu and over various western and central Nepali hills. The lords of Gurkha attempted to insert themselves into the ongoing pattern of Indo-Sino-Tibetan trade and in the process threatened the older Malla–Narayana lineages into which members of the household controlling Kuch Bihar were also married. The double set of conflicts led to the murder in 1772 of the infant raja of Kuch Bihar by a brahman adherent of a Vaisnava guru who enjoyed the confidence of both the woman (Maharani) who headed the lay household called the Kuch Bihara Raj and the Bhutanese monastic authority identified as Deb Raja. In the struggle that followed, one party secured military assistance from the Company's tax collector at Rangpur by promising to pay half the collections of his jurisdiction to the Company if the Bhutanese monastic protectorate could be removed. In 1771–2, when promised payments for military intervention did not materialize, the Council at Calcutta dispatched its troops to the town of Kuch Bihar guarded by militias serving the Bhutanese monastic government.[23] News of this reached the court of the Gelugpa ordination lineage and its government in Lhasa. On behalf of the infant Dalai Lama, the regent, Tayshoo Lama, intervened to reestablish peace between the East India Company and the forces of the Desi (Deb Raja, Drukpa monk). An infant was put on the seat of Kuch Bihar—and would henceforth be guarded only by the Company's armies.[24] This also brought the Company closer to participating in an immense trade in woollens, silks, black pepper, and bullion and other metals between Bhutan, Assam, and other countries adjacent to the British post. Parliament instructed the servants of the Company to establish a direct trade with these places.[25] The Council at Fort William complied. Captain Bogle and Alexander Hamilton were dispatched to Bhutan in 1774, Captains Samuel Davis and Samuel Turner to the Tibetan capital at Lhasa in 1783.[26]

Bogle's despatches came from Bhot domains (stretching over the Bengal and Assam plains) under the authority of a Drukpa Buddhist monastic called 'Deb Raja'. These observations may not have been those of an initiated 'insider', but they certainly invoked the sense of monastic governmentality originating with an ordained monastic teacher (Tibetan *bla.ma*, pronounced *lama*/ translation of Sanskrit *guru*). The teacher's corporeal death inaugurated a rule by reincarnation—of a child with the lama's 'spirit'. 'Upon the death of these holy men their souls pass into the bodies of children, who after a strict examination, are recognized and thus a *succession of saints under various forms but animated by the same spirit* have continued at different intervals to enlighten this corner of the world'.[27] Calling it an Order that 'never dies', Bogle outlined a government in which the lamas (gurus) stood 'first in rank and power', but whose authority was delegated to others. Such executors either came from the groups of the ordained or, if lay, were immediately received into the monastic order. It was clear that this governmental order was effective. 'As the priests are taken from among the subjects at large, and keep an intercourse with their respective families they naturally retain an influence in every part of the country and in all their measure are sure to be supported by the People'.[28] There was no specialization of labour in this administration, nor a standing army. The same populations that were farmers today would take up arms on the morrow: as Bogle put it in the same account, 'the same arrow which has killed the wild goat or the musk deer is now pointed against the Breast of an enemy'.

Furthermore, Bogle knew the routes that connected Tibetan monastic entrepots and the Indo-Gangetic plains. One road from Bengal lay through 'Bukshadwar' (Baxa duar, one of many gateways or duars between the plains and the Himalayan foothills). Merchandise on this path moved on the backs of people, hired for that purpose. Bogle, who had seen this human transport, noted that 'neither sex nor youth nor age' mattered in this labour service. He had marvelled at a young girl who had travelled 15 or 18 miles on the steepest roads with a burden of 70–5 lbs weight strapped to her back while he had not been able to move half that distance unencumbered.[29] A second route went through the 'Morung'—the plains and foothills of the Nepal–Sikkim Himalayas. Animal transport was used on this route, since the elevations were gradual. But it also took longer to reach Lhasa. Female transportation workers were quicker than animal-laden caravans: females fed themselves, while animals had to be fed and watered by others. Both had to be guarded against others, and that was why armed militias accompanied mercantile and monastic deliveries.

While the French Chevalier had noted the command of waterborne traffic by the sannyasi/faqirs, the Englishman Bogle commented on land routes controlled by the gosains, the 'trading pilgrims of India'. While both appeared to be revered by many different populations, the former carried bulk goods, while the latter confined their trade to high-value, low-bulk articles and to mountainous paths and routes unfrequented by other merchants.[30] The writ of this monastic trading network ranged over various parts of Bengal–Assam–Burma. For instance, the ascetic (sannyasi) warrior-trader or gosain Purnagiri, who had accompanied Bogle to Bhutan, told him that in the 1771 war the Deb Raja (Desi) had applied to his neighbours for assistance. Among those who responded were the 'Naphaul Rajah' (Nepal, a reference to either Lalit-Patan or Bhatgaon) who had sent 7,000 men. The 'king of Assam' (*svargadeva*) also promised to contribute his aid and a 'Rajah near Sylhet, at the instigation of the Deb

Rajah actually commenced hostilities'.[31] Likely, this was the lineage of Central Asian ('Landa Sultan') fortholders whose letters to the svargadeva in the seventeenth century had established that strong marital and military–diplomatic bonds (Chapter 1) committed the two geographically separate units to each other. The presence of plainsmen from the lowlands of eastern Bengal in the service of the Himalayan lords of hidden valleys and the pre-eminence of Bengali (alongside Tibetan) in commercial and business correspondence of the monastic governments of hills and plains were born of such relationships.[32]

In 1771, following Rennell's lead, the Council at Calcutta called these armed militant monastics from a variety of centres in Bengal-Nepal and Assam a 'lawless banditti'.[33] A multipronged policy was devised to curb their power and rein in the competitive edge of this network. Since many of these monastic lineages had enjoyed receipts of ready cash or a percentage of goods from the revenues of markets and fairs, withholding these cash sums fulfilled both political-economic and military ends of the Company. For instance, in 1772, investigations into the revenues of Rangpur revealed that substantial portions of the revenues were given as stipend (*vrtti*) to the brahmans of Kashi (Varanasi)—small charitable gifts to various poor brahmans, as well as a substantial charitable gift to a Ramshah Bairagi. But more important, these allocations implied that these donees had claims to lands in the region: one set of brahmans held lands separately from those held by their assistants in the business of worship. The Committee of Circuit instructed the Collector of revenue in the district to discontinue any further payment of allowance to these brahmans under the article of 'ready money bertie'.[34] Stopping the transfers of money to these figures or their deputed agents stationed on their behalf at various toll booths on riverine trade routes became one of the many strands in the process of Company-led restructuring of the monastic political economy.

A second strand was directly military. In the context of the Anglo-Bhutan skirmish in 1772–3, the Company's officers issued dire warnings against the sannyasi/ faqir lineages ('lawless banditti').[35] This was followed up with a military attempt to pursue and expel them by force from all the regions claimed by the Company. But as the military officers learned soon enough, such sannyasi/ faqirs were so firmly ensconced in the veneration of their subjects that they could not be got at. Officials referred to such devoted adherents as 'bigotted' men for screening these sanyasi/ faqirs from arrest on every occasion that the Company officers ordered their apprehension.[36]

In these decades, these obdurate attachments were gradually prised apart by Company strategies focusing simultaneously on the persons of these venerated beings and on the lands and incomes these revered beings enjoyed. The investigations that preceded these as well as these attempts do not corroborate the facile assumption of a 'liberal compact' that was said to have been made by a Company state and so-called 'religious' communities in 1771–2. Given the centrality of charity as the core of monastic subjecthood and disciplined personhood across Buddhist, Saiva, Vaisnava, and all Muslim households in eastern India, the Company's gradual encroachment on 'charity' lands as well as on the income from markets made it clear that the maintenance of the 'religious laws' of the Hindus and Muslims was far from the intended effect of Company legislation.[37]

Attempts at resuming tax-exempt grants humiliated their holders twice over: first by interrogation and measurements that they had been exempt from earlier, and second, by loss of tax-exempt status in a new Company-held managerial system. Older Mughal recipients and donors alike objected. One argued that the erstwhile Mughal provincial administration had allowed holders of taxable lands to donate in charity (*khairat*) lands and incomes from their *own* zamindaris; this right to donate was never made over to the Company.[38] Some of the donor zamindars as well as the recipients of tax-exempt gifts pointed out that attaching the several petty bazaars whose profits maintained the different *masjid*s and *thakurbari*s as well as individual ritualists and rituals constituted a double infringement— of 'rights of property' as well as of the 'fundamental principles of their religion'.[39] Descendants of original donees also objected. A 'Cutubudeen' (Qutbuddin) reported that his ancestors had been given such lands for religious purposes by a 'subah of Chittagong'; but the grant was in a region over which 'the Muggs [the Arakanese] the Original Masters of the Province retook possession and held it till the last conquest made by the Bengal Subah'.[40] Apparently, the descendants of the original recipient had deserted or abandoned the region for other parts, and the lands returned to secondary forest.

By the 1770s, the descendants of the original grantee could produce neither the original deed of gift, nor a single man who could give the smallest information validating the history of his ancestors.

Others, who had received too small a grant to be recorded on paper, could not produce any documents—perhaps because these did not exist. This appeared to have been the fate of those who were granted small amounts of produce from some shops as the entirety of the 'gift'. Lal Maham and Navazish Khan, who had been gifted the produce of lands in Mahmudabad by one Rajeh Beeby, found this produce assessed for taxes. Unable to pay, they borrowed money against their holdings and lost them.[41] Yet others, who could produce deeds and documents, such as the erstwhile zamindar of Dhaka, explicated that it was 'a disgrace to a man of my rank' to have to give accounts of his donations and gifts in this way. Nevertheless, it was evident that income from the major markets of the town of Dhaka went to maintain the 'mullahs or priests' attendant at the tomb of Burhanuddin Khan, his ancestor, also buried at a tomb in Imamganj.[42]

By 1782, those who resisted the Company's encroachments in the hills of Sylhet, for instance, found themselves staring down the barrel of an order to sequester all their 'Milky [malki or owned] and Lackerage [la-khiraj, tax-exempt] lands'.[43] Such sequestration was not directly implemented in all instances by individual British Collectors, but by their Indian subordinates, both Hindu and Muslim. In Rangpur, the implementation was left to the devices of the Rajput revenue farmer Raja Devi Singh. The stringency with which this revenue farmer collected taxes on behalf of the East India Company included the seizure and sale of cattle as well as lands hitherto allocated to the maintenance of the schools, mosques, and temples in Rangpur.[44] As Wilson notes, these bodies had provided a local social and political order that incorporated peasants and herders into a set of hierarchical but inclusive political communities and allowed a degree of local redistribution of income, cooked food for the indigent, and a basic literacy for the poor. But Devi Singh's stringent measures did not merely affect local political community formation but also cut at the translocal connections of the monastic geographic order. Thus a note from a Vaisnava abbot (mahanta) in an adjacent province complained that the revenue farmer had stopped sending the stipulated sum that an earlier Zamindar of Dinajpur had fixed as a charitable donation for the maintenance and worship of the deity in his care.[45] When the peasants in Rangpur protested in 1783, troops mowed down sixty men, and arrested their leader.

Newly ascendant men such as Devi Singh who associated themselves with the Company accumulated social prestige and its correlated political and economic power from their connections with the British. But these groups only repeated the pattern, by sponsoring their own rounds of temple building and elaborate performances of rituals and festivals. These 'new' men, associated with the rising power of the Company, whittled away some of the older sannyasi trading networks and Sufi establishments in eastern India.[46] This too came to a head dramatically in 1782, in the town of Sylhet. The majority of the town's population was Muslim. But the Company's banker, a Diwan Manikchand, also lived in Sylhet town, an administrative centre. In December 1782, the month of Muharram, the Shià period of mourning for the martyrdom of Hussain and Hasan, coincided with a festival that the Diwan celebrated with gusto at his private temple or 'house of worship'. What followed is only available from the pen of Lindsay, who suggests that, led by a 'priest of considerable rank' (presumably a Pirzada), a group of 300 armed men attacked those who entered the temple set up by the Diwan, the representative of the Company's economic policies. The victims complained to Lindsay. At the head of 50 armed guards, the Company's tax collector marched up a hill to confront the 'old man' (the Pirzada). Instead of laying down arms, the old man drew his sword, aimed at the Collector's head and exclaimed, 'This is the day to kill or to die: the reign of the English is at an end.' The Collector then shot the 'old man' dead, and his troops charged the rest. When the attackers retreated, Lindsay wrote that 'the high priest and his two brothers were lying dead on the ground, and many of his dependents were wounded'.[47]

Killing a 'high priest' was bad enough, given that such figures were considered inviolable in their persons. Lindsay would not even allow the devotional public to pay their last honours to the revered monastic leader. That night, as members of that public gathered up the corpses and set off in a solemn procession lit with torches to the burial grounds, other fear-mongering Europeans ran to the magistrate's office, charging that a torch-bearing army was on the move. One of them, Beck, even assured the Collector that the 'mob' was on its way to burn the Collectorate. Another military force was assembled and sent out with the message that no public honours would be allowed to 'those who had rebelled against the existing governments'. A steady trickle of the dispossessed began to appear on the global labour market, both within the subcontinent and beyond it, from this moment.

REDIRECTED SUBJECTS: COTTON SUPPLYING HILL-PLAINS NETWORKS

The effort to maximize and monetize tax collection required an intense scrutiny of the rights in forests that were held in gift by certain monastic figures in regions such as Kumilla/ Tripura and Chittagong, and led directly to confrontations with hill–fort commanders and members of the Mughal sub-imperial administration. These hills too grew cotton, a crop that could not withstand water pooled at its roots and preferred elevations above low-lying deltaic plains and marshes. Cotton grown on these hills had brought them under the jurisdiction of 'Kapas mahal' in Mughal accounts. Cultivators had paid their taxes to all overlords in raw cotton. The *sayrmahal* (customs collections) were entirely based on the cotton that was brought down from the hills. In addition, cotton also contributed to the majority of the ordinary tax-collections (*jamma*) from this hilly region. Besides, as Company officers knew too well, there was precious little money to be made from the internal trade of Sylhet, dominated only by the exchange of sticks of lac, wax, coarse cloth, and rice. Every object of valuable commerce was commanded by 'the hill people'. In 1786, however, the company's resident at Nurnagar (a plains centre commanded by Tripura Sanyasis) complained that the merchants on behalf of the English company were not being allowed to collect the cotton and bring it down from the hills of Tripura.[48]

At least one of the men involved in stopping the Company's collection of cotton from the hills was the Vaisnava–Sufi trader 'Radharam of Pratapgarh'. By 1786, the Company records state, 'Radharam of Pratapgarh', erstwhile overseer of estates loyal to the lineage of the Tipura, 'joined with a large party of mountaineers' to attack the Company's fort (at Chargola) on the border of the Kachar country.[49] Another note shortly thereafter identified Radharam acting along with 'a considerable number of Cosseahs or mountaineers' in the same districts.[50] Another report identified these men as 'cookies of the Tipperah mountains' who along with Radharam had begun to collect the crop from five or six parganas in the hills 'northeast of Jytner' (Jaintia) in the direction of the foothills of Bhutanese Assam.[51] Unaware, perhaps, of the intersecting monastic networks between all parts of the Himalayan world, the Company's troops set off to chase Radharam from hill to hill; shortly thereafter, the collector at Sylhet found that a separate 'tribe of hill people from the western part of the district' surprised the sub-imperial Mughal *thanedar* at Laour, killed him and his men, and retreated to the mountains just as suddenly as they had come.[52] Apparently, older military–diplomatic alliances continued to act on behalf of a lowlands and junior partner in crisis.

Company and sub-imperial Mughal officers' attempts to capture Radharam and his allies were ill-timed. The floods of 1787 drowned all the cattle on the lowlands, swept away entire villages, and made boat-dwellers out of the remaining peasant-cultivators. As a hapless collector described the 'extensive sea' that developed on the lowlands of Sylhet, whoever could do so had climbed to the higher elevations of the hills.[53] The impoverishment and famine in the lowlands left most with no food: the only food anybody on the lowlands could get was a small root procured by diving in the middle of the ponds and marshes in six or seven feet of water.[54] With all his adherents on the hills, Radharam, the sannyasi/ faqir agent of a lord of the Tripura, set up a parallel government with enough guns and manpower to collect the grain from five or six districts of the region.[55] In 1787, a corps of *khasi* (Tibetan for 'a group made up of priests and laity') inspired by him plundered the Company's granaries over six districts of Sylhet.[56] Then another group on the plains, 'living immediately under the mountains', were joined by the first group and together they prevented the Company's agents from collecting taxes from tax-exempt villages in Sylhet and Dacca.[57] The Calcutta Council ordered troops to march to Sylhet to cut the standing grain, and prevent Radharam and his forces from harvesting it and carrying it to their own villages. These troops were ordered to distress Radharam's forces by burning the villages and driving away their cattle.

A set of clans and households came together to preserve Radharam and his authority. Like Radharam's own dual identity—of a Vaisnava and a Sufi—the movement that he led was of ritually heterodox platoons. The officers of the Company referred to the leaders and headmen as the 'Cosseah/ Cusseah' but a closer look at the names of the individual 'headmen' reveals both a relationship with ongoing monastic and temple-based economies and a pluralist bias among Radharam's followers. Names such as Hurry Dully (Doloi), Nusser Sustee, Hurree Sustee, Currin Kawn (Karim Khan), Nubbe Sirdar (Nabi Sardar), Anoupram (Anupram), Sam Ram (Shyam Ram), and Manickram (Manikram) can be found in the records of this resistance.

All these headmen were figures authorized to conduct potent rituals of their own. Though British tax collectors referred to them as 'Cosseah/Cusseah' their descriptions suggested great power over cultivators on the plains. As one put it

A Cosseah never cultivates the soil; he employs Bengali ryotts, he comes down at the time of harvest and carries off the produce. ... all the merchants, whether Europeans, Armenians or Bengallees, though living under the Company's protection, have looked up to the Cosseahs, have courted them by presents of guns etc, etc, etc and from this intercourse, the Cosseahs have learnt an idea of their own strength, and these, particularly Armenians and Bengallees, have frequently been their guides and instructors in their attacks on the Company's lands.[58]

In sum, all manner of Central Asian and coastal plains populations had collaborated with each other in a network of trade and piety.

British collectors responded by arresting headmen with various kinds of sacralized authority and potency—men from the networks of temple managers, shamans, diviners, oracles called dolois, sannyasi/ faqirs, and sastris.[59] This was a clear departure from a system in which monastic figures had been exempt from search and seizure, an exemption that had allowed such figures to monopolize the tasks of envoys and diplomats between different political centres. Eventually, Radharam too was arrested—with two small guns and 200 stand of matchlocks and small cannon. Radharam and a follower (called a son in the English records) were brought to Sylhet township.[60] The 'criminals' were lodged in a mosque used as a jailhouse.[61] From there, Radharam was sent to Calcutta to stand trial.[62] After that his trail runs cold in the archives. His later biographers allege that he committed suicide by poison.

But simple arrests did not immediately put out the rebellion. Other leaders came to the fore from within the subject–adherent communities attached to such monastic figures—men with names such as Ganga Singh, Oboosing (Abu or Abhay Singh), Soobasing (Shobha or Subha Singh), Raj Singh (zamindar of Susung, Maimensingh).[63] As in the past, these men too sought out alternative suppliers of arms and ammunition in exchange for the high-value goods available in the hills—cotton, limestone, timber, elephants. The French company, arch rivals of the English since the 1740s, was located nearby in Chandannagar; one of the leaders, Subha Singh, allied with the agent of the French company, Champigny. This ratcheted up the conflict with the British Company immediately. The British Collectors feared that a French 'colony' would form on the hills, and build up another network of arms and adherents that would bring armed 'Cosseahs' and European forces (French, Greek, Armenian) to attack the English markets and warehouses on the plains. Anxious officers of the British Company complained about the hill-top commanders who 'afforded protection to Europeans (Greek-Armenian, French) who had taken refuge among them.'[64]

Moreover, many of the populations from the cotton-growing and fruit-cultivating hills had been courted by Mughal zamindars such as Omaid Errezah (Umaid Reza, or Ahmad Mirza or even the Jewish 'Umaid Ezra') who held rent-free estates on the Sylhet plains.[65] These Mughal holders offered extremely favourable rates of rent to the 'hill people' to cultivate lands on the plains for them. At least one of the most enterprising and successful of such hill 'Cosseahs', a man called Ganga Singh, had become both rentier and possessor of villages on the plains, some of which were in the jurisdiction of the English Company, and simultaneously owned villages in the hills where he was titled 'Raja of Barakwa Hills'. Men such as this successful rentier-owner had in turn recreated hybrid and fluid networks between hills and plains that British collectors knew as volatile groups—of 'Bengali Cosseahs'.

Again, the Company officers adopted a two-pronged military and legislative attempt to quash the military and monastic networks that operated across the hills and plains. On the one hand, the officers of the Company elected to supply arms to one of the headmen and use his services and labour to establish the dominance of the Company on the hills. This was how Oboosing was weaned away from the rest of the Cosseah confederation and sent to put down his rival for leadership of the confederation, Ganga Singh. On the other hand, and simultaneously, legislative devices were put in place to segregate the hill-dwelling leaders and their adherents from their grain-supplying supporters on the plains and coastal port cities. In 1788, the river Titas was chosen as the limit of the Company's tax-collecting authority in Sylhet.[66] By 1790, the jurisdiction was extended to the river Surma, northwest of which no trade or intercourse was to be carried on by persons living in British Company jurisdiction (limited to the west of the river). Regulation I of 1790 forbade all 'Cosseahs' (ritually empowered headmen) and 'other mountaineers' from purchasing lands or residing within the Company's jurisdiction.[67] It directed that all Armenians, Greeks, and those who were not British-born subjects (such as the French) seek British Company's licences for living in Sylhet and for trading with the hill-dwellers. Finally, it absolutely forbade such non-British traders from supplying 'the Cosseahs or other hill people' with arms, ammunition, saltpeter, sulphur, and military articles.[68]

FROM CONTAINMENT TO REVERSAL: RESISTANT MEN, AUTHORITATIVE WOMEN, AND THE COMPANY

Tanika Sarkar has argued that since 1772, a compact between the liberal Company state and religiously defined communities of colonized people guaranteed 'sovereignty' to the latter in marriage and gender relations in such a way that all women were subsumed to a community in which their individuality became inseparable from that of their family and kin.[69] Viewed from the perspective of the Mughal farman of 1690, this was far from the truth of the experiences of women related to the monastic males discussed above.

Jigar Muhammad's study of the grantees of Awadh during 1658–1750 substantiates this. His study found at least twenty-nine women among those holding revenue-free lands in the province. One group was made up of daughters of substantial male holders who had died sonless. The other was made up of widowed wives and mothers who had no other sources of income. The former may have inherited substantial portions of their father's estates; the latter the smaller holdings that were also given in 'charity' to destitute women. While at least six or seven women held very substantial plots (200 bighas or 66-odd acres of land) in Awadh, most of the other women held smaller holdings (between 10 bighas or 3 acres to 150 bighas or 50 acres) of cultivable wastes.[70] In either instance, Muhammad finds, the female holders had the responsibility for securing and organizing the labour necessary for turning wastes into arable land, collecting their share from these tenants, encouraging production, and organizing reliable witnesses regarding their claim at the time of renewals.

This Mughal pattern of female holding and inheritance of monastic estates was gradually reversed under the East India Company's direction. Studying the records of the Banaras region, Rochisha Narayan found evidence of networks of gosain traders who had enjoyed tax-free rights to quarry, shape, and transport limestone from Mirzapur.[71] These traders, closely associated with the rajas of Banaras and various locally dominant clans of Rajputs and Afghans, also confronted the officers of the Company in the 1770s–80s in the Indo-Gangetic belt. Confrontations with gosain-manned forces led not only to the destruction of the men's exemptions and privileges but also to the destruction of the rights of their female supporters, such as the Shia Begams of Awadh, or Rajput female supporters and adherents of the gosains such as Panna, the mother of Chait Singh, the Raja of Banaras until 1781. Having tangled with these forces and confronted the power and resources of senior secluded (*pardanashin*) women who could not be physically coerced, officers serving the Company began the task of dismantling women's titles in land. In Bengal, too, by the 1770s–80s, Company officials had developed an aversion to permitting widowed *rani*s to manage the zamindaris for their minor sons. For instance, in Burdwan, a widowed dowager zamindar held 780 villages as *deori mahal*s (income from which was directed by the females of the holding household) and bestowed 'large sums of money' on a vast concourse of 'vagrant Hindoo facqueers'. The Company appeared to have had both financial and military objections to these titleholders' methods and objects of expenditure: these women could raise alternative militias with such gifts. Yet, curiously, one of the main objections of the Company officials was that these women knew no unrelated males except 'family priests', who along with other estate servants, subverted the Company's interests.[72]

Muhammad's, Narayan's, and McLane's findings are confirmed by the epigraphic evidence from northeastern Bengal (Sylhet, Tripura, and the hills in between), which argues for an identical pattern of women's authority, expressed by their donations to initiated Sakta tantric males (for example, Jayantipura Purandhara) in hills north of Sylhet; the title of the fort-holder was BaraGosain.[73] This fort holder was ordained as a sannyasi in 1770; his chief consort (Mahadevi Kasasati) gifted her own claims in a village ('22 halas of Govindapur village with its tenants') to the fierce goddess (Kalikadevi) established in Sri Lilapuri Sannyasi's monastery and temple (*mathamandir*) at Jayantiapur in 1788. The consort granted the most important gift in an agro-pastoralist economy—the pastures (*gochar*) and water-tank (*jalashaya*) of the village—to the female deity, Kalika. Smaller quantities of land were donated to the writer of the copperplate, and the least bits of land to the Brahmana and the oil-presser attending the goddess. Even when this donor was widowed, she continued her gift-giving activity. In 1801, she gave smaller portions of another village (and its people) to the same female deity. In 1803, she gave smaller gifts of land and people for the divine couple Radha–Krishna adored by Vaisnava lineages, for the ceremony of *doljatra* (procession on the occasion of the spring equinox) of the two cradles (*manchas*) lying at the Kalikamatha and at Ujaninagar. The implication of these grants was that men initiated in the Sakta tantric lineages held the fort on the basis of the support extended to them by adherent women, some of whom were their wives as well. These women's adherence, as well as catholicity, was important to the subsistence of both Sakta tantric warrior ritualists and Vaisnava scribes, deities, and subjects in the same domain. Verses describing Vaisnava strongholds in Kumilla similarly name 'queen-consorts' who sponsored the excavation of two tanks at Kumilla, one named after her husband and another named after herself.[74] Moreover, widows remained in authority at such forts—just as the ranis had remained in authority in Kuch Bihara at the same time.

It is important, then, to understand that the resistance of such bairagi/faqir males to the Company's policies also affected their female adherents and kin. The effort to reduce the exemptions and privileges of the monastic males led inexorably to the delegitimation of women's titles to land (which they could also use to sponsor militant monks). The Decennial and Permanent Settlements (Regulations XIX and XXXVII of 1793) consolidated hitherto piecemeal orders that had passed (since the 1760s) regarding the resumption of Mughal imperial (*badshahi*) and sub-imperial (*subahdari* and zamindari) grants of lands to various revered figures. Along with the reductions of tax-exempt holdings, the Decennial Settlement and the subsequent Permanent Settlement also established that only 'actual proprietors' of lands were to be held responsible for revenue payment; Clause 20 established that females, minors, idiots, lunatics, and others rendered incapable of managing their lands by 'natural defects or infirmities' were excluded from the category of actual proprietors.[75]

REMADE RENUNCIANTS, MARRIAGES, AND THE COMPANY COURTS

These legislative enactments simultaneously brought the claims of gosain lineages of men and the claims of laywomen living in parallel households to the Company's courts. Lineages of gosains were established by spiritual succession to a teacher, a discipline, a style of worship, a particular image, a monastic dormitory. One could be a synecdoche for the whole. Conflicts about succession to lands within such lineages appeared immediately after 1790–1 as conflicts over stolen images. In 1790, for instance, a Nitaichand Gosain, the guru of a lay trader, inherited the house, idol (referred to as Thakur, literally, Lord, in the records) and lands of a celibate disciple, who had separated from his brothers and lived apart from them. The guru appointed a ritualist brahman and another junior gosain to conduct the worship at the inherited house.[76] The dead disciple's creditors secured the house, however, and exiled the priest and junior gosain. The latter brought the image to the main akhara of Nitaichand Gosain in Dacca, where the junior attempted to establish an independent income and estate by taking the image door to door, to 'the houses of the Thakur's *raiyat*s' (subjects of the Lord), obtaining alms from them. This incensed the senior gosain, who sent a group of his loyalists. They physically restrained the junior gosain and brought the fought-over image to the main monastic centre. On investigation, it transpired that the control of the image gave the holder control over the lands with which the image had been endowed, and nobody wished to keep the idol without access to those lands. Eventually, neither gosain gained either land or image. Both were awarded to the dead man's brothers, presumably on the understanding that they would pay taxes on them.

Such disputes had more complex results in monastic lineages where celibacy was not required, and social reproduction and spiritual succession pulled the identical and extremely remunerative lands and households in opposite directions. This was most obvious among a group of Vaisnava gosains at Nadia, an eminent centre of Vaisnava assemblies in Bengal.[77] Here, a Vaisnava female guru, Damayanti Devi, was the centre from which social and spiritual lineages radiated outwards. She had married an Amritachand, a polygynous Vaisnava gosain who had hitherto held tax-exempt land (*brahmottar*).[78] Her co-wife had a daughter, and this daughter's descendants included three gosain brothers related to each other by blood. But the female guru also had male disciples and 'foster' sons of her own. All of them were included in the minute distribution of cash incomes and estates when her husband died.

The centrality of women to both social and disciplinary lineages also characterized the various Muslim sites and centres. In Chittagong, a Mir Hayat built a mosque and established a madrassah, endowed with lands from which income was stipulated for its maintenance as well as for charity (*khairat*).[79] Upon his death, the maulvis distributed the properties to the widow, to each of the two daughters, and to the dead man's mother as well as his sister. Each of the daughters and the dead man's sister, in turn, had daughters who inherited from their mothers.

The provisions of the Decennial Settlement in 1790 (which became permanent in 1793) may have been thinking of dowager women when conceived, but in effect they aimed straight at the heart of daughters' and granddaughters' inheritance rights from their fathers and mothers. One of the main lines of criticism of these legislative enactments was enunciated in the early nineteenth century by Rammohan Roy, who knew firsthand the way in which the order of 1790 had reduced at least two hundred widows to penury in the Burdwan estate.[80] Yet, instead of being critical of the colonial army or commercial establishment, Roy directed his anguish at the court pandits, his contemporaries, who worked for the colonial judiciaries. Through *their* interpretation, he said, these men whittled down the provisions of inheritance (*dāyabhāga/dāyatattva*) to a point where only if a husband divided his property during his lifetime between all his heirs and included the childless widow would the latter receive an inheritance at all. He blamed the lawmakers for making no provision for stepmothers, who according to his reading of the complexities of polygynous households, had 'less hope of support from their stepsons than mothers can expect from their own children'.[81] These childless 'Hindu' widows, disinherited, were those who committed suicide at an alarming rate.

In focusing critique from the perspective of childless 'Hindu' co-wives and widows, Rammohan Roy eclipsed a larger set of concerns—the many female–male relationships that tied together monastic recipients of tax-exempt lands and gifts, with female patrons, teachers, consorts, daughters, sisters, mothers, and others for whom they assumed responsibility. One of the latter kind of women were the wives and mothers of teachers (*gurus*) towards whom many young disciples assumed lifelong obligation. The nine-year-old boy who became zamindar of Dinajpur in early 1790s, for example, had an obligation to maintain the mother of his guru by sending her money every month from the revenue of his estates.[82] Another significant group of women were the daughters who, as in the instances touched on above, inherited from their fathers' tax-exempt lands (either brahmottar or pirpal), as well as from their mothers and grandmothers.

Furthermore, in focusing the discussion on the operation of 'Hindu' law, Rammohan also appeared to have ignored the near synchronicity of Vaisnava brahman and Muslim households in the region who responded to the Regulations in identical fashion. In both groups after 1790–3, adult males were acquired as in-marrying grooms for daughters who might have otherwise inherited the lands directly from their brahman, alim, and sufi fathers. A deed of gift (*hibbah-nama*) filed by a widow of a brahman male who had held such brahmottar lands but had died leaving an infant daughter spoke to such devices. The brahman's widow secured an in-marrying groom many years the daughter's senior as a live-in manager of the daughter's estates. Only by registering the lands in the name of the son-in-law could this widow secure the release of the estates from the Company's tax sequestration.[83] But the exemptions from revenue were not restored on those brahmottar lands and tanks. Hitherto, they were only to be held as tax-paying lands.

An identical pattern appeared in the substantial Bengali Muslim households in Chittagong in response to the same legislation of 1790–1. As a petition from Musammat Nur Chumna, a widow of a substantial revenue-paying estate observed, the land had been given to her in a marriage settlement or *moranna* by her dead husband and registered in the joint names of the widow and her daughter. But the widow had found a native of Allahabad to marry her daughter. The son-in-law promised that he would maintain both his wife and his wife's mother for the rest of their lives and would pay the government revenues punctually: in exchange, the mother-in-law nominated the son-in-law as the zamindar and proprietor of the estate.[84] A document of 1793 from the collectorate of Tipperah showed a similar trend. Among the fifteen estates where women had been 'disqualified' from holding or managing lands, the greatest number were managed by inmarrying husband–managers.[85]

Obviously, responses to the Decennial and Permanent Settlement Regulations varied by region and group, and affected different age-grades of women differently. Daughters of monastic and militant men were differently affected from the same men's consorts, mothers, and grandmothers. But everywhere on such estates after 1790, the tilt to the masculinization of all landholding was obvious. The most obvious face of such masculine authority was based on marriage: the son-in-law was the favoured male figure for this pattern of management. The difference in ages of spouses was implicit in such arrangements, and they did not make for wedded bliss. For example, one of the disqualified landholders in 1793 was a four-year-old girl Mymuna Bibi; her husband-manager, a Mirza Ghazi, was found to be embezzling from his spouse by 1795.[86] In the same region, another husband–manager of the estate failed to pay maintenance to his wife, Roshanara Khanum, and found himself both imprisoned and divorced.[87]

More ominously for the late eighteenth-century environment of eastern Bengal and Assam, where multiple ritual groups had coexisted since the earliest records available, the Regulation XI of 1793 had validated only the operation of 'Hindu' and 'Muslim' laws of 'succession, marriage, and inheritance' to landed wealth. The conditions were ripe for another kind of dispossession—and that was of the hybrid and complex Bon-Buddhist, Jaina, Catholic, and other groups that had also coexisted in all the districts of eastern India, and especially in districts such as Sylhet, Tippera, Chittagong, and Arakan. I have tried to touch on this complexity in discussing Sylhet ('Cosseah', 'Kochari'); but the same cosmopolitanism can be inferred from a page out of one year of a British tax-collector's file in Chittagong.[88] On one page are listed big landed estates, with substantial payments of taxes to the British Company's Collectorate. Some of these estates belonged to Zabardast Khan and the Portuguese-Danish, Aura De Borros. Alongside these were estates with smaller tax payments such as those of Sarmad Khan, Tita Tavares, and a Madhuram Bhattacharjee. Alongside all the young boys, girls, and women listed as 'disqualified' holders in each of these estates was also an 'Endoo Bootea' (Indu Bhutia, from the Himalayan north) who had had a share in the estate of a Brahman Bhattacharjee in Chittagong. Neither the Regulations of 1772 nor those of 1790–3 had said a word about the preservation of Buddhist, Sikh, Armenian, Catholic, or Jain 'laws'. It appears that the resumption of all 'charitable' lands for revenue-paying purposes also affected the holdings of all these groups in eastern Bengal (and later Assam). But more important, the very drive to gather revenue blinded the most scientific of revenue collectors to the very presence of Buddhists in eighteenth-century Chittagong and Tripura.

COLONIAL INFORMATION GATHERING AND THE CONSTITUTION OF IGNORANCE FROM THE LATE EIGHTEENTH CENTURY

At almost the same time as the rebellion of Radharam's complex sannyasi–Sufi forces was brewing in centres spread across Sylhet and Assam, another Tantric Buddhist-Sufi society had resisted the demands made by the Konbaung dynastic and monastic lineage. In 1783–4, both the lord at Mrauk-U (Arakan) and the source of his moral and political authority, a colossal image of the Mahamuni (great contemplative, the Buddha), were captured and relocated to Amarapura.[89] Muslim–Buddhist societies, organized like the Burmese and the Assamese ones, on the basis of a tenurial system that committed particular households to deliver military labour service, or to pay dues in grain, or be exempt altogether by becoming permanently attached servants of monasteries and temples, were expected to serve in Amarapura's wars with Siam in 1785. Large numbers of Arakanese who did not wish to serve in the Burmese armies fled their homelands for nearby regions, such as Chittagong, Kumilla, and Noakhali (coastal and deltaic Bengal). Resistance to Burmese occupation occurred from these bases, where there were thriving Buddhist populations to give sanctuary and support to the Arakanese. In turn, this brought Burmese retaliation, and disrupted both trade and revenue collection organized by the East India Company in the region. Captain Michael Symes was sent to negotiate a truce on behalf of the Company. Accompanying him was a man born in 1763 in Edinburgh and trained as a doctor, Francis Buchanan (later Hamilton).

Buchanan was ideally suited for the mission. His enthusiasm for botany, geology, and geography was evident in his own journal of his trip to Rangoon, Pegu, and Ava in 1795.[90]. His acute absorption with things botanical allows us to infer the continued vitality and inseparability of monasteries ('convents') from the economic and social life of the communities in their vicinity. His journal also allows us to see what the late eighteenth-century officers could not, perhaps because they had no concept for organizing such data. Take the instance of a thriving granary town in the late eighteenth century named Myaunaung (entry for June 8, f. 42). Situated on a green bank sloping towards the river, to Buchanan's eyes the houses appeared 'nearly as mean as the common Bengal huts, yet the Town looks well being adorned with little gilded Temples, the convents or *Kiaung*s of the priests with their long cylindrical flags, and many stately and beautiful trees particularly the *Ficus Religiosa*, Mango, and Palmira. Near the convents are also many cocoa and betelnut palms ... at the town, a great many/ not less than 200/ large and good boats on an average you may say of sixty tons burthen each' for transporting rice from granaries here to Amarapura. Further upriver, Buchanan stopped at another town, around which were 'handsome kiaungs, or convents', ornamented with carved work, and surrounded by level areas inclosed by neat fences'.[91] Buchanan noted the presence of fields around monasteries, of boats docked at towns over which monasteries predominated, but said nothing of how the fields were cultivated or the relationship between the granaries, boats, and monasteries. With minor differences in pronunciation and hence orthography, other servants of the East India Company in the late eighteenth century identified similar architectural marvels without in any way being able to place the relationship of a building with people or fields and herds in its vicinity. Like Buchanan, they overlooked the interrelationship between the ecological, economic, and ritual–spiritual aspects of such monastic communities and subjects.[92]

Missing from the conceptual lexicon of these eighteenth-century officers was the concept of monastic governmentality and subjecthood—the relationships that were established prior to the donation of lands, labourers, buildings, and incomes from markets. As a result, many could not understand the ways in which human populations attached to, or occupants of, lands and buildings owned by the monastery or monastic lineage were the *kiaung-sa* (in Burman,[93] *khongjai* in Anglicized Tibetan, *khangtsen* in southwestern Chinese).[94] This showed up particularly when Buchanan was sent to survey the geological and mineral resources of Chittagong, Kumilla, and Noakhali in 1797–8. In his keenness to count potential taxpayers after the Permanent Settlement of 1793, Buchanan described various 'kiaung-sa' in the vicinity who neither he nor his subsequent interpreters have understood as political monastic dormitories.[95]

Unlike his knowledge of botany, Buchanan's knowledge of Theravada Buddhist monastic life and organization was derived from Sangermano, the French Jesuit who had lived for a decade or more in Ava by the end of the eighteenth century. This did not prepare Buchanan for the complex Tantric Buddhist–Saiva and Muslim power-sharing arrangements he found in easternmost Bengal.[96] Here, Vajrayana Buddhists, Muslims, Sakta, and Saiva refugees all lived together, confirming the observer in his opinion that the 'religion of Arakan differs a great deal from that of the orthodox Burma' (60). But Buchanan, like most Englishmen of his time, did not know the hybrid languages being spoken—least of all the Tibetan-inflected Bengali and Maithili. Thus, when he arrived at the mouth of the river Ramu in Arakan in 1798 (59), he described a tribe of 'Kiaung-sa', even providing an elaborate etymology for this term, making them the 'sons of the rivulet' as 'all the nations of the Burm[a] race call the Ramoo River' (59). Apparently this 'tribe' had a 'chief' who, attended by two Bengali speakers, visited Buchanan and described the cotton in which he and his co-villagers paid the English Company's taxes. This 'chief of the cotton-growing Kiaung-sa' provided a glimpse of the relationship between the cultivators and the monks: he told Buchanan that he had 'poun-gres, or priests, who are men of learning and have many books and that like the Rakhain, he worships Ma-ha Moon[ny]' (59). When Buchanan enquired about the language of this tribe, he found it was 'the same with the dialect of Arakan, and their writing differs very little from that of the Burmas'. When Buchanan in turn visited the villages of this 'chief' he found the huts of the 'kiaung-sa' to be 'tolerably comfortable, raised on posts like those of the Burmas, and swarming with people' (62). Translated, Buchanan's description outlined merely a community of cotton growers who were attached subjects and participants in a larger monastic Buddhist political economy. It was a political economy that rested on close territorial relationships between distinct groups of monastics and their initiates and a rhizomic network of relationships between spatially separated monastic dormitories, sanctuaries, and shelters.

A perfect embodiment of Enlightenment science and empiricism, Buchanan stood inside the monastic geographic order and did not know it. Arriving at a cluster of huts in the valley of a tributary of the Karnaphuli River, he found a man 'dressed in yellow habit' who was reading a book in Bengali characters and confessed to understanding no other. This man, apparently in temporary retreat of a monastic sort, explained that the people in the huts called themselves in Bengali 'Sagma or Chakma'. Of these people, Buchanan would say 'Their religion is that of Godama, *corrupted* by their having adopted many Brahminical superstitions, and especially bloody sacrifices to the Devtas' (104). At the same time, they worshipped a spirit named the Prince of the Mountains (*Taung-Mang*). Like the Mughal emperor before him, Buchanan too would note with horror that these Chakma, whose huts were surrounded by an abundant poultry and hogs, practiced universal commensality: they ate everything and ate with everybody.

Similarly, the greater standing of the married monk among the Vajrayana Buddhist orders in the terrain, rather than that of the renunciant ascetic figure familiar from Theravada lineages, eluded Buchanan. He was told by at least one Buddhist monk ('priest' in his account) in Chittagong in the 1790s of the two ranks of priests—'the Samona and Moishang, the latter of whom are the superiors and by the Bengalese are called Raulims' (108). If 'Samona' is Buchanan's peculiar rendition of *sramana* or novice monk, then the Moishang were householder Buddhists, akin to the northern *vajracharya*, erudite and strict disciplinarians who officiated at rituals in the 'inner core' of Tantric Buddhist worship. That such Moishang among the Rakhain and Chakma in Chittagong were equally valuable repositories of literary cultures was evident in Buchanan's own descriptions of one group of Moishangs 'having books in the Ra-kain language and character' while the community around them only read and spoke Bengali (112). Yet so firmly did the Theravada monastic order at Ava overdetermine the surgeon's vision that he was impelled to note that 'these Moishangs however appear to be not so much respected among the Chakmas as the Rahans are among the Burmas'.

As a result of his experience of the grandeur of the Burmese Theravada Buddhist architecture, Buchanan was plainly unimpressed with the impoverished, plainer buildings of the Vajrayana Buddhist lineages that he found among the refuge seekers in Chittagong. Walking up to a building with a plain roof, which he noted was 'not ornamented like the convents of the Burma Rahans' (91), Buchanan found within it three rooms, two ordained monks, one novice who was six years old, and what appeared to be destitute families and debtors seeking sanctuary within its walls. Noting that the boy of six had not yet been ordained, he asserted that this two-step ordination was contrary to the Burma custom and to the precepts of their book of ordinations. Furthermore, he noted with disapproval that these monks did not go begging for alms, as did the Burmese monks. Instead, the pious made contributions to them at their convents.

Second, the Rakhain Buddhist monk spoke of Brahma, a Supreme Being, 'who had given a different religion to each of the one hundred and one Nations with which he had peopled the Earth'. Instead of recognizing the potential of this idea for promoting the coexistence of multiple faiths, Buchanan judged the idea in terms of its deviation from some pure ideal; on behalf of the Burmese arahats, he declared that such ideas were 'very unsound'.

Third, the Scotsman heard the Rakhain monk-teacher name five mortal *bodhisattvas* venerated by his order. They were 'Chaucasam [Chakrasamvara?], Gonagom [Kanakamuni?], Gaspa [Kashyapa?] and Godama [Gautama?]; but to these they add a fifth named Mahamoony' (92).[97] This was the Mahamuni that Arakan had only recently lost to the Burmese. Clearly, Mahamuni was the ultimate hope of a Buddhist futurity, Maitreya. That was exactly how the monk–teacher had tried to analogize it for Buchanan's easy comprehension—he had compared Gautama to himself and Mahamuni to his young disciple. Face-to-face with a tradition of teachers for whom students represented the future, Buchanan excluded himself from the status of the potential initiate. In keeping with the Buddhist pedagogic traditions in which students and novices initiated learning and hosted eminent teachers at residences built for them, the Rakhain monk asked Buchanan whether he wished to take him, the monk–teacher, to Europe (93). Buchanan answered that he wished to take the monk to Luckipour and learn 'Arakan or Burma language' from him. The monk replied that some time in the future he 'would be happy to live with me' but that he could not do so immediately due to his current teaching commitment to a son of his patron (Kaung lha-pru). This, the Scotsman thought, was an 'impudent assumption of gratitude on the monk's part' to hide his unwillingness to go to Luckipour, rather than Europe.

Unaware also of the ontological nature of Buddhist chants and texts, Buchanan enquired whether the 'priest' would sell him a copy of the kamma-wa. The monk replied that he could not sell the book but offered instead that if ever Buchanan lived in Chittagong, and furnished the materials, he would 'make for me whatever Books I wanted.' Though the monk had kept the hope of future interactions alive, Buchanan appears to have shut the door firmly on him.

Missed opportunities sum up Francis Buchanan's presence in the subcontinent. Perhaps alone in his generation, he visited the various cardinal points of the monastic geographical order between the hills and the coasts—Ava, Chittagong, Kathmandu (Nepal), Goalpara (North Bengal), Purnea (Bihar)—between the late eighteenth and early nineteenth centuries. All his journals record face-to-face encounters with Buddhist monks, monastic subjects, monastic routes and itineraries, conversations with Vaisnava Assamese literati bureaucrats and with Muslims of various persuasions, all of which the observer noted copiously but failed to synthesize. Such synthesis is left for the later reader of his journals to attempt, and it is imperative for those who wish to understand the ways in which Himalayan social, political, and economic orders and events could reach deep into the coastal plains and establish networks of monastic communities and shelters all over the terrain of Bengal, Assam, and Nepal.

This extensive network was important because various kinds of military labour corps accompanied Buddhist monks in the lowlands of the eighteenth century. A term for a military detachment that all the plainsmen used to Buchanan was 'Bonjoogies' (86–7). The root Tibetan term was *buŋ*. It referred to a military force. Marching troops were *buŋjuu*; troops marching and giving battle were *buŋjuugi*. So when refugee Rakhain men in Chittagong referred to the 'Bonzu' (87), they confirmed their retention of at least some of the Tibetan languages that a seventeenth-century Mughal emperor had identified with the 'Muggs.' Other key terms used by his informants and transcribed by the surgeon appear to gain new meaning in this context. For instance, Buchanan had referred to the 'Moroo' as 'inter-mixed' with the Ra-kain but speaking a 'language totally different from the Burma' (33). The Chinese accounts of Tibet of the eighteenth century also refer to a Muru-ussu country north of Ts'ang, the central Tibetan province, home to Lhasa.[98] Translated into the late eighteenth-century context of Buchanan's informants in Chittagong, the Moroo were speakers of northern Tibetan dialects and could thus live alongside the Rakhain.

Though there are obvious limits to what can be gleaned from Buchanan's records, some words that came to have 'ethnologized' meanings in the nineteenth century deserve special pause. For instance, a term Buchanan used, '*koongkies*' (16), had at its root the Tibetan form for referring to the self in the most humble situation, *kuŋ*; paying respect was *kuŋgur*. Since his informants used the term as a synonym for Ling-ta and Lang-ga (86, 87), both in turn described as 'tributary to the Raja Tauboka in Runganea' (107), the implication was that these were people who paid respect to—were subjects of— the Muslim Chakma overlord called Tabbar Khan.

In such words used by local Rakhain-language users lies the key that unlocks the ways in which Himalayan and sub-Himalayan confrontations of the Qing regime as it expanded into eastern Tibet as well as with Nepal in the long eighteenth century may have also shaped social worlds of Chittagong, Arakan, Tripura, and its vicinity. Once more, the word 'Bonjoogies' can open the door to such histories. Its use referred to Nepali-Sikkimi-Sino-Tibetan confrontations since the 1760s.[99] These had escalated with the growth of the Gurkhali in 1790–4 over currency issues, command of trade routes, and of monastic centres. Chakma Muslims or Buddhists told Buchanan that bonjoogis dwelling in their fortifications on hills between the Karnaphuli and Sankar rivers had 'three years ago' (circa 1794–5) penetrated through the hills and descending by the rivers, caused 'great devastation on the Bengalese of Runganeea' (104). This military attachment was described as having 'muskets, swords and other Arms and are subject to a Chief named Ta-kang' (87), an officer also referred to as Tai-biak (116) or Tai-koup (117); all these terms were localizations of the Chinese *amban* or *ta ch'en*.[100]

The Chakmas told Buchanan that this 'chief of Bonjoogis' had two kinds of subjects under his command, one Bon-zu and the other Loo-sai. From the head of every family in his dominions this head of a military corps received 'an annual tribute of one basket of rice and one piece of cotton cloth' (110). But, the Chakma informants went on, the Loo-sai or Loo-shee subjects formed a plundering band and came down the river, Kassalong, from a place in the vicinity of 'Kundal' (Khandal, in Noakhali district). The Chakmas pursued these parties for eight days but found none of their houses. 'They are supposed to live near Kundal' (112–13).

More important were the historical and temporal conditions of northern conflict under which Buchanan had found members of the Sino-Tibetan complex on the plains of Chittagong. One of the more easily identifiable names from the Himalayan world representative of this monastic mercantilism was Aung-ghio-se Tam-mang. The surgeon referred to him as a 'Chief of the Kiaung-sa' in the neighbourhood (68). Not even when he visited this Tamang in his home by the stream and found a 'Kiaung or convent of Poungres' on a hill to its west (68), nor even when the Tamang was joined by 'a Priest who was in the same dress used by the Burma Rahans, and who said that they belonged to the same order' did Buchanan figure out the significance of the many layers of monastic subjecthood in the social formations around him. Modern ethnographers such as David Holmberg have described Tamang as the demographically predominant population in large areas of east-central Nepal around Kathmandu who sought their cultural inspiration from Tibet and spoke a Tibeto-Burman language.[101] But their presence in eighteenth-century Chittagong was as lower-level monastics who, moreover, set out sums of money on loan to people from his vicinity living on the plains. These people in turn pledged their daughters with him as security (77).

In order to understand the groups who were the Tibetan monk's clients or subjects, we will trace his footsteps in Buchanan's work. On a particularly significant day in the ritual calendar, the Tamang offered the Scottish surgeon two gifts. One was a pig. The second was a written itinerary. This gave a glimpse of the north–south routes travelled between the Chittagong plains and the foothills of the Himalayas. The itinerary began with the Tamang's village on the Yaung-sa (Rong River?), identified places according to the monastic rest stops or *kiaungs* along the way, and offered a classic map of relational identities inhabiting the same space in the late eighteenth century (72–3). The map showed a valley cultivated by Muslims, abandoned monasteries ('Rauk kiaung, no inhabitants'), headmen (*rua-sa*) of cultivators attached to a monastery (Ku-like Ruasa, a *joomea* or Kiaung-sa). The particular people who were assigned the responsibility of maintenance of these rest houses were identified by ecological terms—the 'Mo-roong that have their hair tied behind' at the Tuin-kiaung, the Tiperah at the Prein-kiaung. The Tibetan Buddhist Tamang portrayed the Morung and the Tiperah as similar people. They 'dress alike, and speak the same language', he said. (74). Only the methods of paying their taxes led to some Mroung being called Wa-the Mroo.

This was remarkable information, and was corroborated repeatedly by other local worthies who knew such details in the late eighteenth century. Local leaders, such as the man Buchanan called variously the Pow-mang-gre (34) and Pomang (87), or 'Great Captain' and Kiaung-lha-pru (depending on the tone, the Lord-Protector of the Deity in the Monastery or Lord-Protector of the River-Deity), confirmed the Tamang's words. He too asserted that 'the Sak are the same people with those who in the Northern parts of the province are called Sakma or Chakmas; that the Mroung and Tiperah dress in the same manner and speak Dialects of the same language having to each other as great an affinity as the Burmas and the Rakhain have' (87).

While a military commander stressed relational similarities between two groups, the Tibetan Buddhist monastic emphasized the terms of the political, not moral, economy within which each group was located. The two groups arose in the same territorial context—the lower Himalayan foothills and riverine lowlands that in late eighteenth century was shared between lords in eastern Nepal, northeast Bihar, extreme northwestern Bengal, and the Drukpa lineages of Sikkim and Bhutan. This was the terrain called the Morang. Members from there were clearly in the cultural ambit of the Tibetan Buddhist monastic order on the coastal plains of Chittagong. So groups that lived on the plains of Chittagong and Arakan in the late eighteenth century hailed from mutually recognizable worlds.

Furthermore, as with a cosmopolitan monastic order, origin in one geographical or cultural location did not confine individuals to a particular role. Buchanan had found a Tippera lad in the entourage of another Rakhain Buddhist monk (104). Yet, this Tippera lad told Buchanan that his own community lived near the Barak River, or was 'Borooksa'. Buchanan wrote the sounds of the language this Tippera lad spoke and compared them later to the sounds of the Tippera spoken near the Feni River, and found them identical.

Not all groups that rose in the Morang, and appeared to have been active in the coastal plains of the eighteenth century, were subjects of Buddhist monks or of the Chinese *amban*. Buchanan found a Muslim guide and another man to take him on a ride up the river Mahamuri. The Muslim distinguished between different groups of people from the Morang by faith. He referred to a category called the Deinea Moroong, whose root was a Persian term, *dīn*, or Islam (75). Clearly there were many different communities living in the Morang, but they were all mutually recognizable at the same time that they were also aware of the distinctions. These distinctions were of faith—the Tantric Buddhist, the Islamic, and the Sakta or female shamanic traditions—as well as juridical, such as the terms on which one worked for a military commander. By no means was this world bereft of engagement with such distinctions and differences.

Buchanan's statements such as those which postulated that vast numbers of 'Moroong' and 'Tipra' were 'subjects' of a Po-mang-gri or a 'Tabbo-ka' resident within fortified enclosures on the plains, translated correctly, indicated that substantial numbers of people from the Himalayan foothills and plains owed labour services, goods, and crops to either Buddhist or Muslim fort-commanders. The former were represented by the 'Great Captain'. The latter included men with professional military standing, such as an Alichan Lascar (Ali Jan Lashkar) or with Turko-Mongol titles of Khan, such as Tabbar Khan and Jabbar Khan (107–8), were described as administrators of clusters of villages containing syncretic Buddhist–Saiva communities, alongside Muslims and others. Neither violence nor hierarchical relationships were absent from such a cosmopolitan order, even though syncretism was its political condition of existence.

The surgeon, however, thought that this monastic and militarized cosmopolitanism was a sign of 'degradation'. This was especially true of the many small translations and adaptations across different cosmological and symbolic systems, concepts, institutions, and practices that enabled the collocation of Buddhist, Saiva, and Islamic communities. At a place called Sitamoora (currently in Rangamati district, Chittagong Hill tracts) was a rock pilgrimage site that was called Rampahar. Here the Hindus offered grain, flowers, and eggs to the gods of the place, Ram and Sita, as did the Muslims. Similarly, at a short distance from the sacred site of Sitakundu (Chittagong) with its Saiva Buddhist symbols, Buchanan visited the Kadam Rasul in Jaffarabad, a pilgrimage that devout Muslims of the province believed was to the 'Prophet's Foot'. Of course, theologically puritan Islamic doctrine made no allowance to such corporealization of sanctity; such corporealization was specific to Buddhist and especially Tantric practices and communities of adherence. For Buchanan, the convergence of Muslim populations to the non-dualist notion of corporeality, to what Fabio Rambelli has called a non-hermeneutic relationship between object, body, and performance, represented a failure, a fall from pristine principle. Surmising that the 'Rakhains had one of these stones, which among the followers of Godoma are in great veneration, as representing the foot of that personage', he characterized the local Muslim translation of such a metaphysics of presence as an adoption of superstition by the ignorant.[102] He was hostile to the many gestures of translation and adaptation that enabled Muslims to cohabit the terrain inhabited by Buddhists and Tantrics. 'Foolish Mohammedans of this province, who have adapted some fable to almost every place esteemed holy by the Gentoos: probably thinking that it would be disgraceful for their religion, were it not provided with as many ceremonies, and holy places as that of their neighbours'.[103] In the same vein, a full twenty years later, he would find in the vast region of northern Bengal–Assam called Kamrup many Muslims similarly 'degenerated into heathen superstition'.[104]

The vituperation of cultural translation and incorporation fundamental to the creation of a cosmopolitan order appeared in Buchanan's case to be directed at other flexible communities, as well. Thus, an identical disdain towards the many collaborations of Bhutanese–Sikkimese–Tibetan Buddhist and Ahom Vaisnava monastic governmentality and lifeways was manifested in Buchanan's attitudes towards the Bhot–Ahom formations in northern Bengal by the turn of the nineteenth century. Writing from Goalpara, in a terrain freshly annexed by the Company, Buchanan wrote of the monastic 'Dharmaraja' as one who 'lives after the usual silly manner of such persons' and Tibetan Buddhists as an undiscerning group who 'eat everything that is considered horrid or impure by the followers of Vyas.'[105] Such attitudes were salient in historical as well as in historiographical terms.

THE SEGREGATION OF ONCE-LINKED MONASTIC GEOGRAPHIES

In terms of their reflection on monastic geographicity, both the military and legal confrontations were extended in the later eighteenth and early nineteenth centuries by the Company's involvement in affairs in Assam. Buchanan's information on this head was thus especially significant. He was told of a late eighteenth-century (Assamese) Bura Gohain who had 'procured soldiers from the west of India' (11), appointed a boy-king named Kinaram/ Kamalesvar (Singh) (12), and forbidden intercourse with all those who supported the rival claimant, Gaurinatha (80) favoured by the Company's forces. In addition to this Bura Gohain, there was the Ahom office of the Wazir Borua, who had hereditary charge of the intercourse with Bhutan. All the servants of the 'Deva Raja', whether messengers or traders of Bhutan, repaired to him, gave him 'presents' and then took their goods to Hajo (north from Gauhati) (48).

In 1808, long after the formal relationships between the Kuch Bihar and the Tibetan Buddhist order of the Shabsdrung (in Bhutan) had been reshaped by Company arms, other fortress holders in the plains north of the Brahmaputra River continued to fulfil the obligations of their inherited subjecthood to northern Buddhist monasteries. The fortress holders at Sidli and Bijni, both men with titles of Narayana, and both claiming to be descendants of seventeenth-century Saiva initiants, sent annual 'homage' contributions to their Bhutanese Buddhist overlords. Sidli sent 500 rupees, oil, dried fish, and coarse cotton cloth. Bijni sent dry fish, cloth, and other articles (72–3).

Regardless of personal ritual or worship practices, similar groups of non-Tibetan adherents of Himalayan lordships lived in the low hilly country at the foot of the plains and paid tribute and labour services to officers of the Shabsdrung political monastic order—the Katmas (or Laskar) appointed by the Desi and answerable to the various fortress commanders (*dzongpen*) and *Penlops* in turn.

After the conflicts with the Burmese forces from 1812–15, however, these entanglements, imbrications, and attachments undergirding monastic geographicity bore the full brunt of Company attempts to segregate groups by treating various deified mountains, hills, and rivers as 'natural' boundaries. Partly this was in response to the ways in which hilltops and mountains, the home of the gods and deities, also provided sanctuary to groups of monastic subjects. During the resistance led by Chin Byan (and his allies Dadan Sahib and Sadruddin Chaudhuri) to Burmese occupation of the Arakanese–Chittagong plains during the early nineteenth century, many Vajrayana Buddhist and Muslim Rakhain together fled to 'the wild and uninhabited mountains between the Burmah and Assam country'.[106] Hundreds of 'Mugs and Mussulman' brought over cattle, families, and effects to the jungles and hills.[107] Just after the war, when officers of the Company tried to occupy hills at elevations between 1,000 and 1,500 feet, Company officers were shot at by hidden monastic armies using arrows with poisoned tips.[108]

Colonial officers were also invested commercial actors, participants in a fairly extensive network of traders, mindful of rival networks and routes from which they were excluded. Speaking of a district

at the extreme east of Sylhet, for instance, flanked by the branches
of the Barak River called the Dhaleswari and the Sonai, the British
Baptist missionary's son Felix Carey pointed to the 'Kachar trade
in elephants, Ivory, Wax, "Jowall Timber" of the best quality and
several other kinds of valuable wood' which came from the nearly
inexhaustible forests through which these rivers flowed.[109] All the
articles, he pointed out, came down these rivers to the Sylhet markets.
Those on the hills who controlled the mouth of the rivers controlled
the goods and markets below. These mountaineers, said Carey, were
the 'Khangchai Kukis'. The term *khangchai* was a reference to the
dormitory-like structures or exclusively male organizations which
were the equivalent of the Burmese-style *hkyaung-sa* that Buchanan
had seen in the plains in 1798. It was of such groups that Carey spoke
when he used the term 'Khongchai Kukis', governed, he believed, by
four independent 'rajas'.[110]

After 1826, colonial officials were particularly keen to extend
British commercial and political control over specific territories in
regions won from the Burmese armies. This enhanced their attempts
to segregate territories that were 'Burmese' from 'British Indian'
markets and rivers. Officers sent to survey the regions in question
picked on the mountains and rivers as 'natural' divisions, thus
overriding the political–social relationships that connected different
groups of monastic subjects to market towns, lands, and plots
of ground. War and a creeping territorialism then pushed British
commissioners to ignore both the evidence of the epigraphs (see
Chapter 1) and the evidence of their own partisan informants. Their
arguments regarding the valley of Kubo are illustrative in this regard.
The Burmese (Buddhist) representatives considered only permanent
Buddhist structures as proof of possession; they produced an old
inscription on a stone in the 'pagoda of Koungmhoodan' to show
that domains east of the river Khyndwyn (Chindwin) had been in
the gift of Buddhist monks and monasteries.[111] The military officer
sent by the Company government to negotiate the matter added only
that there were also other buildings in the valley, such as Vaisnava
temples built by Shans and Manipuris, of which some twenty or thirty
ancient edifices were still standing. Such collocations of Vaisnavas
and Buddhists and tantrics in the valley of Kubo had also allowed
for an avowal of spirits of place and of strategies of possession. So,

another officer noted that 'the religion of the Kubo is the same as that of the Burmese, Bhoodism' even though he insisted that 'witchcraft and gross superstition' was the core of such societies.[112] The ways in which the Burmese Buddhist commissioners mapped the valley in terms of monastic assemblages, however, undid the divisions of hill versus plains that the British commissioners regarded as 'natural distinctions'.[113] The propensity to follow geographical divisions as 'natural' mocked the language of centuries old land grants (Chapter 1). The latter had mixed uncultivated or forested land with grants of arable precisely so that monastic subjects would go where others might fear to tread—the hitherto uncultivated 'wild', forests, or plateaus at high elevations.

Like the Buddhists arguing about the possession of Kubo Valley, Vaisnava hegemons too claimed certain pieces of land on the basis of two related but discrete relational registers. The first was a descent-based claim in which the speaker placed himself in a patrilineal relationship with a generous ancestor. The second claim was made as an inheritance to the original ancestor's 'charitable' gift. Much more than Burmese Buddhists, Vaisnava initiants staked their relationships to land on marriages to monastic figures in the past and descent from them. Although the next chapter will trace the ways in which these relationships were reformulated by the Company officials after 1826, for the moment we should emphasize merely the persistence of the monastic geography's relational aspects in the thinking of early nineteenth-century men in eastern India. Thus, though Gambhir Singh had allied with the Company in its war against Burma, he too claimed a hilly tract of land (Chandrapur) in one of the bends of the river Barak (modern Sylhet) by referring to an eighteenth-century Gharibnawaz ('my great grandfather') who had bestowed a daughter in marriage to a figure named alternately (in the English records) as 'Santhi Giri', 'Sunthee Karee', and 'Santi kari', the then Raja of Kachar'[114] (see Chapter 3). By this reckoning, Gharibnawaz had 'gifted' a daughter to an initiated Saiva monk, who either worshipped mountains (Sanskrit *giri* is mountain) or was located on mountains. Moreover, Gambhir Singh claimed that 'Santigiri' had in turn (as bride wealth?) gifted '200 hals of jungle land on the hills' to Bhagyachandra (also known as Jaisimha, initiated Vaisnava lord at Manipur, father of Gambhir Singh and his half-brothers). From this land grant on the hills in the eighteenth century had grown a way station for pilgrims 'when going to teerut [*tirtha*, pilgrimage] people might put up after descending from the hills'. The name of the place (Chandrapur), too, was a happy etymological derivation from the two last syllables (Chandra) of a donee's name—'my father Bakyo-Chunder' (Bhagyachandra). Most important, said Gambhir Singh, there were forty or fifty families from Manipur settled there, cattle and all. The labours of these families did not yield a single farthing of cash; instead they provided the whole of Manipur with betel nuts; alongside this, they paid in raw cotton which was woven into cloth and then sold in Sylhet. 'In this way the people of Chandrapur were found useful.'

Since people organized in overlapping small and large clusters (*gots* and *khels*) had always been part of 'charitable' gifts and settlements, claims to the lordship or 'rule' over human subjects were prior to claims over lands. Both Burmese Buddhist and Manipuri Vaisnava claimants to spots of mountain passes and valley lands foregrounded pious labourers 'attached' to those sacred sites. Moreover, their production of betel nuts and cloth referred to a system of taxation in kind, and rendered tax payment itself a form of homage paying or *seva*. Monastic geographicity's imprint in cosmography and vernacular thought had remained strong till the nineteenth century. What changed then? It would appear that only the women related to such monastic communities experienced dissolution of authority. The next chapter will focus on one particular aspect of women's authority—that resting on marriage and sponsored motherhood—to highlight this.

NOTES

1. J. Irwin to John Shore, Acting President and Committee of Revenue, 5 May (no year mentioned), in *Islam BDR*, 168. The letter mentions the date of the sanad given by Qasim Khan as Kartick 1167 in the Bengal year or 'Muggy 1122 being the year of our Lord 1760'; that Mr. Verelst took charge on 2 January 1761.

2. Harry Verelst, Randolph Marriott, and Thomas Rumbold from Islamabad [Chittagong] to Henry Vansittart and Council at Fort William, 16 February 1761, in *Islam BDR* 1, 119–25.

3. Verelst, Marriott, and Rumbuld from Islamabad [Chittagong] to Vansittart and Council at Fort William, 16 Febuary 1761, *BDRC* 1, 148–53.

4. Note to Claud Russell, *ibid.*, 261–2.

5. Robert J. Lindsay to Provincial Council of Revenue at Dacca, 1 October 1779, *SDR* (1: 75–7).

6. Willes to Shore, 25 October 1788, *SDR* 3, 78–9.

7. Lindsay to Shore, Committee of Revenue, 18 July 1782, *SDR* (1: 114–15).

8. Council of Fort William to Verelst, 24 June 1761, *BDRC* 1, 20.

9. See advertisement in *Islam BDR*, 168–9.

10. Verelst, Marriott and Rumbold at Islamabad to Vansittart and Council at Fort William, 16 February 1761, *BDRC* 1, 155.

11. McLane (1993: 183–4).

12. Letter of Matthews, 28 February 1761, OIOC, Mss Eur F 218/1, f. 16b.

13. Letter of Matthews, 18 [March] 1761, ibid., f. 22a.

14. A Captain Kinlock of the Tenth Battalion commanded troops in the region in 1766/7, for which see Collector to GG and Council of Revenue, 28 December 1778, in *Islam BDR*, 80–1; revenue collectors of nonmilitary service, such as a 'Mr. Campbell' and a 'Mr. Leeke', also appear in this correspondence, for which see 82–3. For the role of the same Captain Kinlock in Nepal, see Chaudhuri (1960: 13–33).

15. Secretary to Government Fort William, On the Ganges, to Major Bradshaw, 30 September 1814, OIOC, H. 644, ff. 417–18.

16. James Rennell to Reverend Gilbert Burrington, 1 September 1764, OIOC, H. 765, ff. 24, 145–6.

17. Rennell to Burrington, 30 August 1766, *ibid.*, ff. 29–30, 156–66.

18. Rennell to Burrington, 1 July 1768, *ibid.*, f. 189. Underline in original. Italics added.

19. *Ibid.*, f. 191.

20. La Touche (1910: 72).

21. Rennell to Burrington, 20 January 1768, OIOC H. Misc 765, ff. 34, 181.

22. For famine prices and numbers dead, see Rennell to Burrington, 1 September 1770, *ibid.*, ff. 38, 203–9; for discussion of vengeance on the Bhut sannyasi/faqirs, see letter of 31 March 1771, *ibid.*, ff. 220–1.

23. Stewart and Tayshoo Lama (1777: 465–92).

24. President and Council of Fort William, Secret Dept, 15 January 1773; for clauses of the treaty of 1772 signed between the representatives of the East India Company and the Gosain on behalf of the infant Raja of Kuch Bihar, see OIOC H. Misc 108, ff. 33–6, 227–9.

25. Extract Company's General Letter to Bengal, dated 7 January 1774, in OIOC H. Misc 219, 327.

26. Teltscher (2006); Stewart (2009).

27. Mss Eur E 226 (47): Notebook Containing an Account of Bogle's Conversations with the Deb Raja of Bhutan and Account of Journey from Cooch Behar to Trashi Chodion, Letter to Governor 17 July 1774, OIOC ff. 11a–12b.

28. *Ibid.*, f. 13a.

29. Mss Eur E 226 (47): Notebook Containing Account of Bogle's Journey from Beyhar to Tasseessudden in Letter to Governor 17 July 1774, f. 2a.

30. Bogle to Warren Hastings, 5 December 1774, Extract Bengal Secret Consultations, 24 February 1775, OIOC H. Misc 219, f. 358.

31. Mss Eur E 226 (47), f. 16a.

32. Turner (2005 [1800]: 69). The polyglot Purnagiri Gosain continued to interpret and act as mediator for Turner's mission. For the continued presence of 'Bengal mohurirs' in the Tibetan Buddhist dzong at Punakha in the mid-nineteenth century, see W. Griffith's 'Journal' in Eden (1865: 146).

33. Council of Fort William, Secret Dept, 15 January 1773, OIOC H. Misc 108, ff. 38–9.

34. Committee of Circuit to Collr. Rungpore, 16 December 1772, BRC 30 December 1772.

35. Secretary Fort William to Collr. Chittagong, 21 January 1773, *ibid.*, 71–2. For the information that 800–900 sannyasis remained on the Bhowal side (near Dhaka) and another body of the like number about three or four days' march from Chittagong in the region of the river Fenny, see Acting Chief Dacca to Acting Chief Chittagong, 20 February 1773, *ibid.*, 74.

36. President and Council Fort William, Secret Dept, 31 March 1773, OIOC H. Misc 108, f. 242.

37. Council at Fort William to Walter Wilkins, Collr. Chittagong, 25 June 1771, *BDRC* 53–4. This note repeats that whenever any of those to whom monthly charity is allowed dies, their name and allowance be immediately struck off the list.

38. Enclosures to nos 3 and 6: Remarks on the Statement of Zemindars Complaints, in *Islam BDR*, 210–11.

39. Letter of Collr. Dhaka to BOR, 7 May 1790, in BOR (Misc) 13 May 1790.

40. Collr. Chittagong to Supt Khalsa Records at Calcutta, 14 March 1775, *Islam BDR*, I, 228–30.

41. Translation of Durkhaust of Gomani Mall, 20 June 1771, Enclosed in Docket of Letter from Council Fort William to Collr. Chittagong, *ibid.*

42. Translation of letter addressed by Nawab of Dhaka 'Entizamut Douwlah Nussurut Jang Syed Ali Khan Behader', in Douglass to BOR, 11 May 1790, in BOR (Misc) 21 May 1790.

43. Warren Hastings and Council to Robert Lindsay, 24 December 1782, *SDR* (1: 126).

44. Wilson (2005: 81–109).

45. Translation of Petition from Sundar Das Mahanta to Goodlad Sahib, n.d., *RDR* 1: 292–3.

46. Lindsay to Warren Hastings, GG and Members of the Supreme Council, 14 December 1782, *SDR* (1: 123–4); Lindsay to John Shore, Acting President, Committee of Revenue, 16 December 1782, *SDR* (1: 124–5).

47. Lindsay (1849, vol. 3: 183–4). This account was dictated to his daughters in 1821, when he was quite blind with age, and was reproduced in *SDR* (1: 127).

48. Resident Tipperah to Collr. Sylhet, 1 December 1786, *SDR* (2: 78).

49. R. Lindsay to Lieutenant James Davidson, 3 November 1786, and Lindsay to Davidson, n.d., *SDR* (2: 71–2).

50. W. Hyndman to BOR, 2 December 1786, *SDR* (2: 80).

51. Lindsay to BOR, 30 March 1787, *SDR* (2: 105–6).

52. *Ibid.*

53. Acting Collr Sylhet to President and Members of BOR, 11 July 1787, *SDR* (2: 143–4).

54. Lindsay to John Shore, BOR, 23 October 1787, *SDR* (2: 181–2).

55. Lindsay to John Shore, BOR, 30 March 1787, *SDR* (2: 105).

56. Lindsay to John Shore, 26 October 1787, *SDR* (2: 184–5).

57. Lindsay to Liuetenant James Davidson, 18 November 1787, *SDR* (2: 188).

58. Willes to Corwallis, 15 September 1789, *SDR* (3: 165).

59. Willes to Cornwallis, 22 April 1790, *SDR* (3: 225–6); Willes to Cornwallis, 29 April 1790, *ibid.*, 231.

60. J. Willes, Collr Sylhet to John Shore and BOR, 11 February 1788, *SDR* (3: 6–7).

61. Willes to Cornwallis, 14 March 1788, *SDR* (3: 19). The letter says that no Mughal governor had hitherto stationed a superintendent of police (Darogha) to Sylhet, and so there was no jail for 'those convicted capitally or under sentences of perpetual imprisonment'. At hand was a mosque 'excessively unhealthy and damp'.

62. J.W. to G.C. Meyer, Acting Preparer of Reports, Revenue, 10 July 1789, *SDR* (3: 153).

63. John Willes to Governor General at Fort William, Cornwallis, 26 July 1788, *SDR* (3: 58–67).

64. Willes to Cornwallis, 26 July 1788, *SDR* (3: 62).

65. Willes to Shore, 18 December 1788, *SDR* (3: 86–7).

66. Enclosures in letter from Willes to Cornwallis, 27 December 1788, *SDR* (3: 91–3). To 'correct' this intermixture, Willes established the Titas

River, an affluent of the Meghna, as the southern boundary for 'Company's lands' in the region of Sylhet.

67. Great Britain, House of Commons, 1872.

68. This regulation was rescinded only in 1828, for which see *ibid.*, 2, 808.

69. Sarkar (2002: 227–32).

70. Mohammed (2002: 73, 85–7, Appendix III).

71. Narayan (2011: Chapter 3).

72. McLane (1993: 224–5).

73. Gupta (1933); Ali (1954: 33–4).

74. *Srenimala* (1996: 14). The consort's name was Subhadra, and she sponsored Dharmasagar at Kumilla and another reservoir called Nanuar Dighi.

75. Regulations of 1793, Government of India Legislative Department (1897: 25).

76. Judge of Diwani Adalat Dacca to Register, Sadr Diwani Adalat, Calcutta, on Case of Nitaichand Gosain, Proceedings of the Sadr Diwani Adalat, 19 September 1793, OIOC, P/152/40.

77. For the place of modern Nadia, or medieval Nabadvip, as a gathering of different schools of Vaisnava logicians, see De (1961: 29–33); also see Stewart (2011: 300–36).

78. Petition of Ramjoy Sarma, in Sadr Diwani Adalat, Progs, 10 October 1793, P/152/40.

79. Judge of Islamabad (Chittagong) to Register of Sadr Diwani Adalat, Progs, 19 September 1793, P/152/40.

80. See petition of the widows of Chitrasen in McLane (1993: 262).

81. Roy (1822: 5 and passim).

82. Abstract of Establishment for Rajbari and Household for 1201 BS [1794 CE] in Collr. Dinajpur to BOR, 11 July 1794, Proceedings of Court of Wards 25 July 1794, P/89/60.

83. Translation of Hibbahnama dated 11 Poose, 1201 BS [1794 CE], in Letter from Collr. Dinajpur, to BOR, 13 May 1795, in Court of Wards, 5 June 1795, P/89/61.

84. Petition forwarded by Collr. Chittagong to BOR, 1 August 1796, Court of Wards, 19 August 1796, P/89/62; for actual transfer deed to the son-in-law, a native of Allahabad, see Collr. Chittagong to BOR, 15 June 1797, in Court of Wards, 11 July 1797, P/89/63.

85. Collr. Tippera to BOR, 8 August 1793, in Court of Wards, 3 July 1793, P/89/57.

86. Collr. Tippera to BOR, 19 May 1795, in Court of Wards, 5 June 1795, P/89/61.

87. Collr. Tippera to BOR, 15 November 1793, Court of Wards, 8 January 1794, P/89/59.

88. Collr. Chittagong to BOR, 30 April 1793, in Court of Wards, 4 September 1793, P/89/58.

89. See synthesis of extensive literature on this event and its aftereffects in Arakan in Leider (2008: 409–59); for translation of a nearly contemporary chronicle of Badon's tenure, see Pranke (2004).

90. Buchanan's Burmah Journal, OIOC, H 687, Bengal Political Consultation of 17 April 1798, no. 1.

91. *Ibid.*, entry for 10 July, f. 99.

92. Kirkpatrick (1969 [1811]: 307).

93. Leider (2008: 426), suggests *kyaung* be understood as both monastery and school.

94. Hillman (2005: 29–51). Hillman defines the *khangtsen* as a residential unit of monks organized along geographical lines. Some large villages may have their own khangtsen in a monastery, but a khangtsen could also represent a township-sized area. The khangtsens funded themselves through donations from pilgrims and benefactors from their home regions, but they also competed over access to the larger monastery's resources by seeking to place lamas in the monastery management committee and in the coveted positions.

95. Van Schendel (1992b: 95–128, 2005); for the journal of Buchanan's visit, see Van Schendel (1992a); for extracts of his travels published in the nineteenth century, see Hamilton (1825a, 1825b, 1825c, and 1826).

96. Buchanan (1799: 166–308, esp. 255); for a description of Sangermano as a 'most worthy intelligent man', see Buchanan's Burmah Journal, OIOC, H 687, entry for 3 May, f. 22; for information on 'Karayn', the history of bad blood between Manipur and Amarapur gleaned from Sangermano, see *ibid.*, entry for 7 May, ff. 23–4.

97. The five mortal Buddhas were distinct from the five transcendental Buddhas named Aksobhya, Ratnasambhava, Vairocana, Amoghasiddhi, and Amitabha, always iconographically represented along with distinctive female deities. For the simultaneous meditation on mortal and transcendental buddhas, signifying the attempt to make present the different temporal-spatial orders of the Vajrayana Buddhist cosmology in the eleventh to thirteenth-century Indo-Nepali monastic geography, see Kim (2010a: 273–4, 2010b).

98. Rockhill (1891, esp. 127).

99. See Dai (2004:145–89 and 2009).

100. See the eighteenth-century Chinese accounts of the duties that ambans had taken upon themselves to regulate Tibet's relations with its neighbours along the Nepal, Sikkim, and Bhutan borders in Rockhill (1891).

101. Holmberg (2000: 927–94). Holmberg notes that along with Buddhist lamas, such groups also adhered to shamans and sacrificial practices of various sorts.

102. Van Schendel (1992a: 124).

103. *Ibid.*, 103.

104. Hamilton (1963 [1940]: 55).

105. *Ibid.*, 68.

106. Extract from Captain Canning's Dispatch of 29 February 1812, in Bengal Political Consultation of 25 April 1812, no. 2, F/4/375/9265.

107. Translation of Report from the Daroga at Teknaaf, 5 January 1812, Encl. 2 in Extract Progs of GG in Council in Judicial Department, 21 January 1812, *ibid.*

108. David Scott at Myrung to Lamb, 6 May, 21 May 1831, 60–2.

109. Felix Carey to Mr. Ewing, 15 October 1817, NAI, FPP, 30 June 1830, no. 60 B.

110. Carey to Ewing, *ibid.*

111. See queries 2, 7 in queries referred to Captain Pemberton by Major Burney Resident at Ava, 13 August 1830, Encls in Note by Secy, 21 July 1832, *ibid.*

112. Capt. Grant's Journal of a Route from Langthabal to Ningthee etc, entries for 17 and 18 February 1832, NAI, FPP, 14 May 1832, no. 123.

113. R.B. Pemberton to Dy Secy to Govt of Fort William, n.d., Enclosure in Resident at Ava to Secy GOB 22 January 1834, and Political Letter to India 3 December 1834, BC, OIOC F/4/1548/61874.

114. Enclosed Translation of Statement Received from Raja Gumbheer Singh, 4 October 1832, Extract BPC 31 December 1832, no. 91, OIOC, BC F/4/1447/56959.

3

Political Ecology and Reconstituted 'Hindu' Marriage

AFTER 1826, COLONIAL KEENNESS to convert newly acquired lands for aggressive commercial and defensive military ends had the effect of devaluing the marriages of the daughters and sisters of men initiated in the spiritual lineages of gurus and monks. This devaluation simultaneously narrowed the socially inclusive possibilities of Vaisnava 'Hinduism'—its ability to incorporate groups from various geographical origins—at the same time that it weakened the claims of married daughters and widowed wives to property and title in the estates enjoyed or managed by fathers and husbands. These twin processes, devised by a cash-strapped Company government to control regions only recently annexed from Burmese (and Buddhist) governments, also consolidated the colonial order's blindness towards the marital politics that undergirded the relationships between Buddhist and Vaisnava lineages, the backbone of the monastic political system of the area. The same relational politics had been seen in the plains of Bengal as well in the 1760s–90s. But further east of Dhaka, as the Company's officers began to redistribute grants of land to men from lineages they favoured, they shifted authority away from women both as daughters and as wives and widows. In addition, relationships that had even in the late eighteenth century yoked together the fortunes of households and lineages across the monastic geographic order (of Burma, Bengal, Nepal, and Tibet) became officially 'disreputable'.

In the Burmese–Buddhist clan that held power in Ava and Amarapura, marriage preferences between close kin were sufficiently important in the seventeenth century to merit a decree that legalized the union of same-generation siblings born of the same father but by different mothers.[1] By the late eighteenth century, when a Burmese prince ordered the marriage of his son (the prince of Pakhan) to his half-sister (princess Shwegu), such unions were given a Buddhist gloss in keeping with the enhanced Theravada influence on Burmese polities in those years. The royal order proclaimed that a marriage between a half-brother and half-sister had been the custom among Siddhartha's patrilineage.[2] By the late eighteenth century and the turn of the nineteenth, such matches were expressed as patrilateral cross-cousin marriages. An English visitor to the palace at Ava reported one that was arranged between the daughter of one prince and the son of another prince, both princes being sons of Bodhawhpaya, the sovereign Lord of White Elephants in 1802.[3]

But alongside this, there existed a parallel pattern of marriages, with brides representing various social and economic forces in the kingdom. Konbaung dynasts since 1750 secured 'daughters of the blood' from Manipur and Khaspur (centre of 'Kachar') as 'devotees' of the person of the Buddhist occupant of the palace. The lord of the 'Cassayers' (Kashmir *and* Kashi-based Vaisnava) resident at Manipur delivered a young man and woman 'of the kindred of the raja' to the palace.[4] In 1774, in response to an appeal from the maternal uncles of the fort holder at Langthabal (Manipur), a formidable force under three Burmese generals compelled the latter to retreat to the hills to the northwest, the domain of the Raja of Kachar. The latter allied with the fort holder on the river Surma, also referred to as prince of Jayantia, and negotiated a truce with the Burmese generals which included sending 'a maiden of the royal blood' to Ava. As another letter in the British colonial archives puts it, the Buddhist occupant of the palace at Amarapura was represented as sovereign because he was both 'unequalled by any king in the world by his piety and boundless charity', and because he had received a daughter from a 'king in the Chinese empire' along with eighty field-guns.[5] These marriages confirmed the claims of the Buddhist lord to be a 'world ruler' (*chakravartin*), with dependent allies from among formally different ritual practice groups in four different corners of the Buddhist cosmological world. These marriages extended the claims of the Burmese house to the territorial doorstep of the East India Company's domains in the plains west of the Brahmaputra.

It is important to keep in mind that many of the cohabitations established as 'marriage' were *not* directed at the generation of children. Nor were they to be viewed as contracts established to secure the 'paternity' of such beings: there were plenty of rituals available by which individuals could be attached to particular groups and rendered into sons or daughters for reasons of property management and inheritance. That is how favoured disciples succeeded to the headship of a particular abbot's monastery and its attached estates, adherents and subjects. Instead of biological or social reproduction, marriage was one among many strategies available to ambitious individuals and lineages to simultaneously generate and accumulate prestige. The use of marriage as a form of diplomacy as well a measure of value tied together dispersed households in a Buddhist–Bon–Vaisnava–Sufi order in the eastern part of South Asia. In the conflicts around ritual and disciplinary practices that set one ordination lineage against another, households participating in these plural marriages changed, but the principles undergirding these marital diplomatics remained fairly constant—and visible in the records as well.

This was important because of the diverse worship communities that were yoked together by means of affinal relationships (see Chapter 1) in the seventeenth and eighteenth century. A representative example was the man, Jaisimha, whose original name was said to have been Chin-thang-khomba, literally, 'hugger of the hilly land'.[6] If this original name suggested his social origins in populations residing in the hills surrounding the little valley of Manipur, a wide variety of traditions also characterize this hill man as a revered member of one or the other of Vaisnava monastic lineages contending for power in the eighteenth century. According to a literary–oral tradition, Jaisimha was trained and educated by a Ramgopal Bairagi and initiated by the Vaisnava Gosvami Paramananda, who in turn belonged to the initiatic lineage of Narottamdasa, hailing from a Bengali Kayastha zamindari family in the village of Khetturi in Rajshahi in the late sixteenth century. Narottamdasa's monastic centre (*akhara*) was in Vrindavana. According to a very different tradition engraved on a brass plate (locally called a *khunti* or permission) preserved in the sanctum of the monastic site at Navadvip (in modern western Bengal, India), Jaisimha was initiated (*diksha*) as a disciple (*shishya*) of yet another Vaisnava guru, Ganganarayan Chakrabarti in 1760

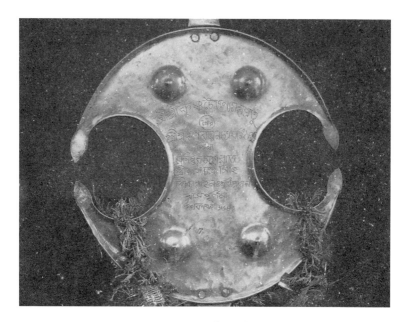

Fig. 3.1   Navadvip Khunti.
Source: The Author.

CE[7] (See Figure 3.1) and its location as an object of worship alongside a portrait and a modern marble icon of the Vaisnava guru (See Figure 3.2) This initiation in turn allowed him to establish a diksha-centred lineage of his own disciples.

Whichever tradition one follows, the conclusion is inescapable that Jaisimha's initiation from a Vaisnava guru placed him as an intimate in a larger network of monastic-ascetic communities beyond the valley of Manipur. It connected him to particular sacred sites and pilgrimage centres everywhere in the plains of Bengal, Assam, and Hindustan. It is this tradition that Vaisnava historians celebrate in the sacred biography of Jaisimha, who is remembered as the Royal Saint, or Royal Ascetic (*Raja-rsi*). Initiation also endowed him with another name, Bhagyachandra, the name by which his grandsons claimed social precedence as well as property (see Chapter 2). Such property included the lands and images associated with the temple of Govindaji in Manipur, which the initiate is said to have completed in 1779; he also organized and trained lineages of male and female *rasa* dancers in the valley.

Fig. 3.2   Follower of the Khunti, Portrait and Image of Jaisimha
at Navadvip.

Source: The Author.

A militant tradition also links Jaisimha, like other eighteenth-century
monastic figures, with histories of war and the attempts to secure
military assistance from the courts and militias to his west and north,
namely, from the heavenly king (*svargadeva*) and from Tripura.[8] This
tradition asserts that his maternal uncle, the holder of Mairang, came
to power in Manipur in 1760–2 with the support of the Burmese lord.
Jaisimha believed that it was his inheritance, and sought armed assistance
from others in the vicinity. A gosain intermediary was dispatched to
the English factor at Chittagong, Henry Verelst. This mission having
failed, Jaisimha sought refuge with the 'Kochari Raja', a devotee of Siva.
The latter brought his guest and a favoured Saiva idol to the sanctuary
offered by the Himalayan heavenly king (svargadeva) in the north.

One *Ahom Buranji* uses the language of elaborate ritualized
subjecthood to express the events that followed after Jaisimha
'prostrated at the feet of the heavenly king' and begged for the latter's
militias to drive back the Burmese.[9] In return for the help of the

heavenly king, Jaisimha sent his niece Kuranganayani, an only child of his brother, as a bride to the heavenly king.[10] By other accounts, she was a daughter of Jaisimha, who was sent in 1768 CE along with an elephant, a horse, two hundred male and female servants, and many other 'gifts' for a different heavenly king (named Shutenpha/ Pramatta Simha).[11] Most chroniclers agree that this princess was anointed as 'chief consort' of the Himalayan svargadeva, having been ceremonially bathed with turmeric and water from the Brahmaputra.

Marriage across religious communitarian boundaries both underscored the nonsectarian political alliances of Tantric Buddhist and Vaisnava households in eastern India at the same time that it suggested that their impermanence was also taken for granted. For instance, shortly after the ceremonial mentioned above, the groom died, and his successor (named Shunyeupha/Lakshmi Simha) imprisoned the sons, grandchildren, and the chief consort of his predecessor. Kuranganayani apparently went to live in the house of another man, a commander of Vaisnava forces who mustered in opposition to the new svargadeva; for the new svargadeva had set about changing established practices—such as mortuary rituals, from burials of corpses to cremations. This ritually Vedicizing svargadeva also had his co-consecrated and renamed consort (Phulesvari) given the title of 'senior governor' (*bodoraja*); when she died, her sister (Ambika) was given the office and seal. A 'sororate' followed.[12]

But these ritual, political, and marital innovations within the regime were resented by another lineage of monastics led by an abbot who claimed to be able to decipher the will of Tara, the female deity adored and visualized in Vajrayana or Tantric Buddhist lineages: this was the 'Moamaria Mahanta'.[13] The Moamaria Mahanta's son was appointed as the spiritual–political leader (*adhikari gosain*) as well as military commander. He led the Moamaria's disciples (*bhakat*s) in their secession from the new ritual political authority established by the Smarta Hindu svargadeva (Lakshmi Simha). The field commander of these Moamaria disciples, a man called Ragha, took Kuranganayani (niece of Jaisimha and recent widow of one svargadeva) as his consort. In addition to this widow, Ragha also kept the wife of a key administrator of the opposition, and 'divided the daughters-in-law and granddaughters-in-law' between his own forces and those of his allies. Subsequently, the victorious Ragha 'and the daughter of Maglau king' negotiated with the deposed Lakshmi Simha, who offered his daughter to the rebel commander in exchange for his life. Later historians characterize Kuranganayani as the widow of one lord (Rajesvar Simha or Pramatta Simha), who was taken into the household of the leader of the Tantric Buddhist–Vaisnava rebels, a Ramakanta Moran, in 1769.[14] They also hint that having lost the Manipuri princess–widow to the Moamaria, the ritually innovating 'Smarta Hindu' svargadeva sought to renew his affinal compact with the Manipuri Vaisnava lineage that had earlier sent a bride to the Himalayan lords. A second round of marriages between clans of Himalayan lords and those from which the Manipuri lords hailed took a niece of the much-married Kuranganayani ('daughter of the elder brother of Kuranganayani') as bride to the northern Tantric Buddhist lineage.[15] This marriage was accompanied by a ritual reinforcement of the worship of the deities—Kalika, Mahesvar, and Lakshmi—associated with the Saiva pantheon. Along with this, the offering of dedicated animals ('white cow' for Indra, buffaloes), the planting of banyan trees on significant occasions, and many of the older rituals were restored in the once innovating household by the late eighteenth century. This second marriage also secured military assistance from the Manipuri affines and estates against the Tantric Buddhist–Vaisnava monastic (Moamaria Mahanta) forces. The Manipuri lord Jaisimh is said to have marched with a huge army to Naogaon and then to Rangpur against the Moamaria Mahanta's forces.[16]

The power of inherited consorts of previous svargadevas, evident in this tangled history, perhaps lay with her seniority as much as in her direct descent from a lineage of revered gurus. Such patterns of authority were also evident in less obviously well-known households, such as those on the hills north of Sylhet, where a colonial tax collector experienced such authority in a deliberative assembly that he attended after Radharam's resistance had been quelled. Elliott noted 'some of the chiefs wished to pay an inadequate sum, when Momee, wife to the principal chief rose, and spoke for some minutes, after which she asked me I declared the truth to them, and on my replying in the affirmative, they agreed to the revenue I demanded.'[17] Public authority of women-as-wives, as well as their control of cattle-wealth, was further deepened by the practice of in-marrying grooms that

Elliott also reported. He had witnessed the nuptials of a seven-year-old girl to a twenty-three-year-old youth (Buglun) and noted that the groom was slated to succeed to his father-in-law's headmanship and estate; but had also learnt that 'if Buglun were to die, Lungree would marry one of his brothers; and if all his brothers were dead, she would then marry the father; and, if the father afterwards should prove too old, she would put him aside, and take any one else, whom she might choose.'

Thus, everywhere in the hills of eastern India, there were a variety of connubial arrangements all of which acknowledged the power of women who had once been married by a brother in a lineage; his death would not end the relationship between the two households but would extend it. However, at the end of the eighteenth century, north of the Brahmaputra River, this pattern was apparently suddenly disrupted by a changed order of succession. Instead of brothers succeeding each other in the office, a son (Gaurinath Simha) succeeded a father (Lakshmi Simha) to the office of the svargadeva. The predecessor's chief consort and her daughter were driven away. Entirely novel affinal politics and rituals were arranged in 1782: the bride of the new svargadeva was to be a young daughter of one Phutak Deka, living in Garhgaon. The water of the Brahmaputra was used to bathe the couple ceremonially: 'bodies of both the king and the girl were anointed with turmeric and oil, and washed with water fetched from the Dikhau River in a procession ... For nine days this washing ceremony was continued. Then on Hindu Brihaspathibar [Thursday] the marriage ceremony was performed. People were entertained with soft-rice and curds etc. The [man who] acted the part of the parents of the bride, offered innumerable dowry.'[18]

Different rituals—bathing, maiden-marriages, dowry—were directed at securing the social and political alliances of a group that remains largely invisible in the same records. But these shifts also occurred in the midst of a renewed conflict with the Tantric Buddhist disciples and clans supporting the Moamaria Mahanta. From the very next year after this altered ritual, war between the Moamaria and the forces loyal to the neo-Brahmanized svargadeva was renewed. Shortly thereafter, bodies of men from different parts of eastern India—including Manipur—joined in the forces of the svargadeva at Jorhat. So fierce was the fighting that the idols and deities and temples of all sides were destroyed; many died and fled. One of the councils advising the svargadeva, Gaurinath Simha urged him to seek aid from the governor general in Calcutta and acquire a thousand armed soldiers (*sipahi*s or *sepoy*s) from him. Troops trained by the East India Company entered Gauhati in 1791 by invitation—as other troops before them had done. While one svargadeva allied with the English, his opponents and rivals sought the aid of the Burmese lord at Ava. The officers of the East India Company had intervened on behalf of Gaurinath Simha in order to install him as svargadeva. His rival's partisans and adherents then sought Burmese assistance in order to depose Gaurinath. The English official, Cox, arrived in 1793 at Amarapura, when a marriage had been negotiated between Bodhawpaya and a daughter of one of the contenders for power at Gherghong (capital on the north bank of the Brahmaputra). As a representative of the Company, Cox vehemently opposed the diplomatic–marital pact that unfolded in front of his eyes. Cox was shown a map painted on cloth of this Vizaddee or Vizallee (mis-transcription of Vaisali).[19] It turned out to be another name for Ghergong, the capital of Assam. The ruler that the Burmese were being asked to proceed against was the svargadeva (Gaurinath Simha) installed by sepoys of the English Company in 1792.[20]

None of the Assamese buranjis refer to the marital–political relationship between one of the lineages of Assam and that of the Buddhist house at Amarapura. Even though hostile witness to the theatre of marital diplomacy, Cox alone reported the elaborate preparations made for the reception of an Assamese princess as bride for the elderly Burmese monarch. These ceremonies clearly suggest the seriousness with which both lineages had entered the relationship. A Burmese royal escort was sent off by water to accompany the Assamese bride. The fronts of all the houses on the main street through which her procession was to pass were ornamented with verandahs of bamboos and mats and brightly painted. Shops fronting on the street were filled with their best goods, to be sold to the princess's retinue at reduced rates. Plantain trees, sugar cane, and cannon at appropriate intervals were planted on each side of the street, the street swept clean.[21] When she arrived (24 June 1796), she was lodged in a temporary bungalow erected for her on the banks of the river. On 26 June, the queen mother's majestic entourage went out to greet the princess and bring her into the capital. In the bridal entourage were men carrying 'huge tusks of ivory, Assamese arms, chests of clothes, bedding'—and of course the necessary 'Assamese Brahmins, with white turbans, and long white jammahs' (suggesting both Vaisnava and tantric Buddhist initiation). The march into Assam by Burmese troops from 1795 onwards was related to the prior marital compact between the two houses. When the affine was threatened by a rival faction, it was to his Burmese son-in-law that the Ahom father-in-law turned for military help (see below).

As Chapter 1 has also suggested, securing such militias was the very heart of the political obligations created by the betrothal of the daughters and sisters in any lineage in the region. The political need for labour-power amidst intramonastic conflicts determined the shifting direction of marital alliances, ritualized practices, and the fates of widowed women and their daughters and sisters. Its most obvious manifestation was in those prestations called bride wealth in English and a variety of terms in local languages. In the eighteenth century, this form of politics was especially acute in eastern India.

BRIDES AND BRIDE WEALTH IN THE
EIGHTEENTH CENTURY

The buranji writers excised the memory of the Assamese–Burmese marriage of 1793–6 perhaps in an attempt to shield their own patrons from the wrath of the Company administration that took over from 1833. If daughters and sisters had been given as 'gifts' to Buddhist lords, it made little sense in terms of the merit economy or in terms of political and moral capital to have erased these gifts. Indeed, such gifts of daughters in marriages to significant Vaisnava lineages were minutely recorded by other households and lineages in the vicinity, further testimony to the politics of value that linked marriage to wealth and security. If daughters and sisters were simply to be 'given away'— and their children and grandchildren to be excised by the fathers and brothers' scribes—then the labour invested in recording lineages descended from such daughters' children (called *dauhitra*) would have been superfluous. But they were not. Daughters' marriages were as politically significant as those of sons in the monastic geographic order. A typical instance was that of the lineage of the lords of Tipura. Here, the daughter of the lord Durgamanikya had a daughter called Urmila with her husband. This granddaughter of Durgamanikya, Urmila, was married with a Manipuri Vaisnava called Tilak Simha.[22] For this reason, perhaps as well as for establishing the generational extent within which 'endogamous' relationships may have been arranged, the *Srenimala* gave greater lyric space to these dauhitra lineage marriages and births than it did even to the sons. These genealogists recorded the inmarrying husband's sister's wedding to another man and the children she had with him. Similarly, the absence of the marital relationship through such daughters and granddaughters were also recorded by these genealogists.[23]

The only absence from the detailed record keeping of daughters' marriages is the nature of bride-wealth transfers in such marriages. One has to take some of these transfers for granted on the basis of observers' descriptions. Thus, the presence of 'ivory tusks' in the Assamese bride's dower that accompanied her to Amarapura suggested that control over elephants and their habitat had continued to be important in at least some of forested regions of the subcontinent. But this was not the case in areas such as Company-governed regions such as Sylhet, Chittagong, and Kumilla, where the value of bride wealth in the late eighteenth or nineteenth centuries no longer included an elephant. Instead, a rich man in search of a wife paid bride wealth in heads of cattle.[24] An Arakanese Hindu in the later eighteenth century lamented an instance when such cattle wealth was not transferred: the Burmese armies, he complained to the visiting botanist that Buchanan Hamilton, had taken away 'the young Girls without giving any consideration to their parents, and thus deprived these poor people of the property by which in eastern India, the aged most commonly support their infirmities.'[25] Obviously, this man was referring to a system reminiscent of other bride-wealth paying systems of the more northerly hills, in which young men, unable to make transfers of commodities paid with labour, often a more precious commodity to an elderly farmer. The parents of a daughter, especially if she was the youngest, might acquire an in-marrying son-in-law as a permanent member of the household. Taking away the daughter, the Arakanese Hindu implied, removed all resources from a household which could otherwise have hoped to have secured either cattle or male labourers as support for themselves. Complaints about unpaid bride wealth and abducted daughters pointed to a crisis in the late eighteenth century in daughter-rich households east of Dhaka that had expected to acquire labour servants, ascetic soldiers, itinerant craftsmen, and traders as in-marrying husbands of these daughters, and found they were unable to do so.

The resumption of 'charity lands', as well as of lands hitherto held by under-servants in lieu of wages (*chākarān, nānkār*) may also have reduced the eligibility of many males vis-à-vis negotiations regarding bride-wealth payments and household formations. This was true of the households of the lords of Meitei and others in the vicinity of Sylhet and the foothills. So dependent had these households become on persistent injections of human and animal wealth from others that economic failures to gather bride-wealth payments in animals sharply impacted the affinal, diplomatic, and military arrangements of the other. For instance, Jaisimha aka Bhagyachandra, Vaisnava guru and fort holder in Manipur in the mid-eighteenth century, was unable to exercise his right to corral elephants (*kheda*), was further despoiled of the horses and elephants of his estate by his Burmese protector, and then found his subjects deserting him for the domains of his grandson-in-law the raja of Kachar, Krishnachandranarayan.

According to the poets, the lord of the Kachar household had taken to wife a daughter in the gosain or sannyasi/faqir lineage led by Krishnamanikya 'raja'. The leader of the house that the poets referred to as Herombo (and the English called 'Kachar') came from a combined Tibetan–Nepali past and had married Krishnamanikya's sister's daughter. The sister, in turn, was married to a man whose second name was stated to be *kobra*.[26] In other words, Krishnamanikya's niece combined in one person different lineages, one from the Tibeto-Nepali gosains and another from Central Asian Sufis. This marriage, represented by the Vaisnava poets as an alliance sought by the lord of Herombo, was lauded by the poets for having expanded the bridal kinsmen's ritual repertoire, their access to territorially powerful deities. The bride's maternal uncle, Krishnamanikya, is described as having added to his daily worship that of the territorial deity of the Kachar—a 'sword-carrying female deity called Rana-chandi' (goddess of war).[27] Since deities 'owned' the land, and cultivators and craftsmen were their subjects first and monastic subjects by extension, the addition of deities to one's ritual repertoire implicitly added the deity's followers to the entourage of an expansive lordship such as that of the sannyasi, Krishnamanikya. Affinal relationships with the Herombo entailed participation in his worship community. But the lord of Herombo also gained monastic and military manpower by this marriage, as well as sanctuary in times of crisis. One of the significant political gains of such a widely dispersed network of marriages was the diversity of refuges that any one group could seek in times of trouble. Such trouble was fairly common in lineages where a sister's daughters or sons were expected to inherit either equally with others or wholly from the female member. In such institutions, the relationship between men and their paternal uncles could be extremely hostile. Such hostility is referred to often in genealogical segments of lyric records such as the *Rajamala* (4, 38) as a tale of conflict between paternal uncle and nephew who either tried to capture or kill each other; the uncle even succeeding at one stage in getting the nephew (Indramanikya) trapped and sent to the Mughal faujdar. Each faction promised the representatives of Mughal governors that they would secure the remaining elephants and pay Mughal revenues (with each elephant valued at one thousand rupees). This situation persisted unresolved until the time of Muhammad Jang (Alivardi Khan, *c.* 1740s). He is said to have devised a third option: he gave the contract for the collection of revenues to two local Muslims, who chose to ally themselves with yet another of the many contenders for the Tipra zamindari. This third man also brought Mughal forces to the region to catch elephants. This force removed one of the contending nephew lines out from the capital altogether and pushed the entourage into the woods and hills beyond the capital. The entourage of the deposed Indramanikya retreated northwards.

According to the poets of the *Sri Rajamala,* this refuge was no more than a return. Both Indramani and his rival, Krishnamani, were born to a woman from the lineage that dominated the fort of Jayantia/Jointah. This was significant for two reasons. In the eighteenth century, the Raj of Jayantia was held by men who succeeded their maternal uncles (avunculineal succession). Men succeeded to rights and dues through their mothers' brothers, and bequeathed their own wealth or sources thereof to their sisters' sons. As an English record put it, the Raj of Jayantia was given to a man who was born of a marriage of the preceding ruler's sister with a 'Cossye' man.[28]

Similarly, the adjoining raja of Cherra (*panji*, currently in Meghalaya) in the eighteenth century was succeeded by his sister's son, Subha Singh.[29]

Second, it was from this region that the epigraphic evidence of Sakta Tantric sannyasis called BarGosain have been found for the late eighteenth and early nineteenth centuries. The evidence of the *SriRajamala* for the same period asserted that a Vaisnava Mukundamanikya had married a woman from the Sakta Tantric (and woman-headed) lineage that dominated the fort of Jayantia. She was his senior consort. Her sons were Indramoni and Krishnamoni (4, 32). The poets of *Krishnamala* and *Srenimala* insist that Ramchandra Dhvaja Narayan, the lord of Hirimbo, who worshipped a female deity called Jayantia, had married a niece from the Tipra lineage. This niece was the daughter of a sister of Krishnamanikya. The colonial English records do have a Ramsingh (1790–1833) as a Jayantiapur fort holder during the period. So the poets may be referring to this person.

Regardless of the differences between the poets, they suggest that some households were favoured over others because of a prior marital relationship. When the marriage had occurred in an earlier generation, the relationship was inherited by the sons and daughters born of that marriage. When the marriage occurred between an erstwhile follower's lineage and that of a guru, such as that between Herombo Raja and the niece of a Tipra lord, it consolidated the obligations of followership with the obligations of labour services and goods in kind paid as bride wealth. From the perspective of a refugee household, it made ample political sense to place a daughter or a sister as the bride of a male hailing from a resource-rich, manpower-rich household. From the perspective of the resource-rich household, taking a bride from the lineage of a guru-teacher, or a militant warrior, enhanced its own standing vis-à-vis others in terms of its access to skills and manpower. When the groom's household was that of a militant warrior, taking a bride from a guru-teacher's household enhanced the former's status as exemplary devotee, especially if the groom were required to provide labour services, manpower, cloth, food, or other goods in homage.

These relationships spread the risks of political crisis and military conflict around. For example, due to the dissolution of the payments of elephants and the *kheda*, a lord of Kachar (Krishnachandra) might withdraw from his relationship with his father-in-law, the Manipuri Vaisnava guru Jaisimha, but an indirect relationship remained between the two houses. For both Krishnachandra and Jaisimha had *taken* and *given* a daughter from and to a Tripura sannyasi's lineage in the eighteenth century, as well. So, an indirect relationship continued between them. All three lineages were entangled in each other's domestic and diplomatic affairs. A nephew Rajdhar, son of a step-brother of Krishnamanikya, was married to a daughter of Jaisimha.[30] Thus, when the Kachar affine attacked two messengers sent from his father-in-law, the latter, Jaisimha, had another road cut by the 700-odd labourers in his entourage. This road, as one of the Vaisnavas ('priests') in the Manipuri entourage confirmed to Buchanan, was passable for elephants, horses, and bullocks. It brought an immense entourage to Kailashahar in the east of Sylhet, for the protection offered by another son-in-law, Krishnamanikya, and his household among the Tipra.

Buchanan, on his way back from Ava and Amarapura in 1798, landed at Kumilla (currently part of Bangladesh), and learned all this from the agent of Rajdhar Manikya (r. 1785–1804), nephew of Krishnamanikya.[31] An addition of 700 people to Rajdhar's forces was a very good reason to welcome the refugee in the region. Though these were technically disciples ('subjects') of Jaisimha, their immediate lord had cast himself on the protection of his junior affine. This gave Rajdhar Manikya claims upon these disciples in Jaisimha's entourage. Such transfers of human populations and resettlements as part of marital and affinal relationships between lineages set the pattern for what unfolded in the early nineteenth century. Marital imbrications brought the political fortunes of one household directly into the shaping of another.

MARITAL DIVERSITY, POLYGYNY, AND MULTIPLE PARTNERSHIPS

Risk-sharing, while conducive to nonsectarian marital arrangements, suffered from the volatility of the new military arrangements made by the East India Company. In 1807, two of the many sons of Jaisimha attempted to secure the aid of the Burmese against each other's affines and factions. One of these sons was Marjit. The other was Chourjit. The Burmese records represent them as the 'Cassay Sawbwa' or tribute-paying governors of 'Cossay' (since *kache* was the term used by Tibetan speakers to refer to Kashmir, the term encapsulated both geographical and ritual identities of the people referred to as Vaisnava contingents from Kashmir). The *Srenimala* records the many marital diplomatic relationships that these two men had set up with other Vaisnava networks and lineages: as 'ruler' at Manipur, Chourjit had given in marriage a daughter to the neighbouring lord at Kumilla, Kashichandra Manikya (son of Rajdhar), and yet another daughter to Kashimanikya's rival and male cousin in a collateral line, Krishnakishore Manikya.[32] However, the latter had also received a bride from Marjit.[33] The poetic record thus corroborates the sense that the Burmese orders of these years give—of an escalated competitiveness among step- and half-brothers among themselves which involved using marital compacts to acquire human, animal, and technological resources. Thus the Cassay Sawbwa, at this point Chourjit, reported to Amarapura that his junior and brother had betrothed one of his four daughters to the Angun Sawbwa, and asked the Burmese lord to send the affianced daughter as well as her father back to Manipur.

Aware that the two brothers were quarrelling, the Burmese court agreed but demanded that one of Marjit's three remaining daughters be sent to Amarapura as a royal bride.[34] Marjit, the Yuvaraja, was given a ceremonial departure, complete with homage to the white elephant (representative of the Buddha Sakyamuni, the 'real' ruler of the land) and an escort of a hundred gunners and sent back to Manipur. Remarkably, it was the Burmese lord who sought to mediate between the two brothers, sending a message to the elder to forgive his junior, arranging for the representatives of the elder brother to visit the sister of Chourjit who had been married into the Burmese household earlier, and taking two brides now from the two brothers into the Burmese household.

This did not assuage the rivalry, but only intensified it. This is the message of the intricate ceremonial choreography that followed, establishing precedence between the brides and their entourages. For example, the bride sent from the junior (Marjit) was presented *before* the bride sent by the Maharaja (Mahayaza). The officers sent with the latter were also required to visit the Yuvaraja under Burmese supervision. Men from the central administration were sent along as observers to this meeting between rival groups. They were to report all discussions to the Burmese crown. Such investments in the Manipuri and Assam courts worked well for the Burmese court at Amarapura. In 1808, when it went to war with Pegu, all the Manipuri (Vaisnava) and Kachari (Muslim) cavalry and others identified as 'Cassay Thatch makers, salt producers and time keepers, Indian Muslim tailors' and similar groups were organized in fighting corps in the service of Konbaung hierarchs.[35] One of these corps, of 202 men raised by Marjit and provisioned by the Burmese rulers, also joined Burmese forces in 1810.[36] By 1811, these forces had also helped Marjit depose his elder brother (Chourjit) from the valley of of Manipur itself (and forced him to seek refuge with the Company's government in western Bengal). By 1814, the ambitions of the combined Burmese-Marjit alliance had fixed on the house of Kachar, where one brother died and was succeeded by his younger brother (Govindachandra). In October 1816, when a rebellion in Jorhat and Gauhati deposed Chandrakanta Simha, once more it was the Burmese-Marjit alliance that took the field along with other forces raised from other townships and jurisdictions.[37] Having established Burmese authority in Assam, and secured yet another young Assamese daughter as 'bride' in the Burmese household, the Burmese–Marjit alliance looked to clear a swathe of territory from Chittagong and Kumilla in the south to Sylhet and the Himalayan foothills in the north of the East India Company.[38] By 1817, the Marjit-Burmese alliance was headed for the fort of Khaspur, whose holder had been allied with the East India Company since 1809. An Englishman who passed the joint Manipuri–Burmese force on his way to Sylhet wrote that he knew this was a joint Manipuri–Burmese force, for he had counted the seven or eight elephants. 'There are no elephants in Munneepore. Their umbrellas and equipage ... denote that most of them are Burmans ... they have a vast number of musquets which the Munnepooreans have not.'[39]

When the Collector of Sylhet remonstrated with Marjit, the latter confirmed that negotiations around livestock had been uppermost in his considerations. The elder and deceased Raja of 'Herrum' [Kachar], he claimed, had preferred Marjit's elder brother as governor of Manipur. 'I agreed to give four horses annually to the late Raja of Hurrum and afterwards to the present Raja his brother for aid. But in addition to these four, seven horses have been taken from me by violence, this has placed me under the necessity of resorting to hostilities, the above is the true cause of the quarrel.'[40] If one did not know the history of the shifting monopoly of elephant trades and livestock trades in the region prior to the nineteenth century, one could easily dismiss such an argument as an attempt to dissimulate. But offering livestock in exchange for political preferment was itself a declaration of ambition. Marjit attempted to barter in the same vein with the Company's officials. He offered the Collector the revenues of the entire village of Hylakandi (easternmost edge of Sylhet) in exchange for the stationing of a 'Feringi thanadar' in the Kachar Raj.

WHITHER 'FAMILY'? THE SOLIDITY OF 'GIFTS'
The curious detail about Marjit's march on Kachar in 1817 was not that it happened for the reasons that it did, but that it happened at all. Indraprabha, the woman married to the Raja of Kachar, was a daughter of Marjit's eldest half-brother, Madhuchandra. In relational terms, she was Marjit's niece; he was her paternal uncle. Her elder brother, Pabitra Simha and her elder sister lived with her; both received stipends from the estates on the foothills (Kachar).[41]

If uncles such as Marjit thought little of attacking their niece's husband's estates, the curious additional detail in this relationship was that one of the uncles in the Manipuri lineage in the mid-nineteenth century claimed an ancestral control upon the foothills (Kachar) based on an original 'gift' of a daughter to an ascetic-warrior saint. Marjit's junior (Gambhir Simha) referred to an eighteenth-century Gharibnawaz ('my great-grandfather') who had bestowed a daughter called Lakkhiprabha in marriage to a figure named alternately (in the English records) as Santhi Giri, Sunthee Karee, and Santi kari, the then 'Raja of Kachar.'[42] 'Giri' meant mountain; a man whose name ended with Giri was likely to have been a man initiated into an order that worshipped mountains or worshipped on mountains. 'Kanri/ Kari' stood for the soldier-cultivator (*paik*) who bore arms. Both meanings could be combined in the same person, especially where an initiated Tantric militant was concerned. In any case, from this marriage had been born a son, Kirtichandra; from this son, two grandsons called Krishnachandra and Govindachandra, both of who held the fort at Khaspur, and were spoken of by the English as 'rulers' of Kachar. The former composed many hymns to the Tantric goddess early in his life, though he became a Vaisnava subsequently; the younger brother, Govindachandra, had composed many devotional songs on Radha-Krishna, collected under titles such as *Rāslilāmrita*, *Vasanta Vihār*, *Sri Govinda Kirtan*.[43] It was their terrain that was under attack by the Manipuri Vaisnava–Burmese Buddhist alliance.

The Manipuri men claimed to be descended through the sons of Gharibnawaz, founder of the fort and lineage from the early eighteenth century. So their relationship with men in Kachar was consistently stated as mediated by marriage of a female of their line to a male of the Kachari line—once through a marriage of a grandaunt, Lakkhiprabha in an older generation, and in their lifetime, through the marriage of a niece (brother's daughter). Or, if one wished to state the relationship from the perspective of the Kachari men of the nineteenth century, the men in Manipur were their uncles once through a grandmother's brother's line, and also affines by marriage. Yet since 1809 their relationship had been tense. A brief note in the records suggests that the ruler at Khaspur, Krishnachandranarayan, already feared his affines or was suspicious of them, for he requested a British battalion to prevent a takeover of his capital during his absence from it while on a pilgrimage.[44] He was refused. Krishnachandranarayan died in 1814.

Political marriages did not appear to have calmed either side. Nor did blood-based relationships work to smooth conflicts. Neither nieces and uncles, nor nephews and uncles, nor step-brothers and half-brothers fared well at each other's hands since all were expected to compete with each other to establish their precedence in each generation. Each constituted independent factions of their own. Just as the lineage members of the Tipra fought savagely against each other since the seventeenth century and well into the nineteenth century, the scions of the Manipuri lineage went to war against each other in the nineteenth century. By virtue of the marital relationships created with other Buddhist or Tantric or Vaisnava or Sufi lineages in the monastic geographic order, these dissensions inevitably involved entire social networks in resolving their and each other's fortunes.

However, the involvement of Ava-Amarapura monastic authorities with the lineage politics of Assam, Kachar, and Manipur also drew the government of the East India Company into these wars. In 1811–16, the Company fought with the Gurkhali regime in Nepal; by a treaty of 1817, it established a fence around Gurkhali domains which involved the Company with Buddhist lineages in Sikkim. By 1823–4, the Company was involved in war with Burma. One of the contenders for the office of svargadeva, Purandhar Simha, ousted by the Burmese forces, persuaded the English East India Company to intercede militarily on his behalf. Unfortunately, this meant that all those Manipuri, Ahom, Kachari, and Tipra men allied with the Burmese or living in domains attached to them became 'enemies' of the Company at once—and are so recorded in the archives of the period.

Initially, the men of the Company were not hostile to Govindachandra Narayan, the commander of the fort at Khaspur, even though Felix Carey, a Baptist missionary stationed at the fort thought he was a 'poor and weak-minded Raja'.[45] Partly because of Govindachandra's own need for protection from his Manipuri affines, and partly because the Company needed to establish a direct route from Sylhet to the Ava frontier that passed through the foothills (Kachar), a treaty was signed in 1824. Under its terms, Govindachandra was to pay 10,000 rupees yearly for the maintenance of Company-trained troops at Khaspur (this was the Sylhet Light Infantry).[46] Having signed this treaty, the Company's officers began to plan ways to increase the earnings from the region, to 'develop' its resources. Since 1822, military officers had been surveying the hills east of British-held Sylhet.[47] They reported that the plains and the low hillocks of Kachar were all 'lying waste', having been abandoned by people with the onset of war in 1817.[48] By 1827, seniormost officials of the Company had decided that the 'plains of Kachar which have so long run to waste ... would under British management yield a considerable Revenue and facilitate the means of communication with Manipur'.[49] Company officials calculated that an addition of 3 lakhs of rupees could be raised from taxes if the 'waste lands' of the province of Kachar could be settled by loyal tax-payers.[50] Colonial surveyors recommended that 'settlers possessed of capital' should be encouraged from other districts to migrate to these regions. These could neither be the people of Sylhet, who appeared unwilling to emigrate, nor the 'hill tribes' who were considered too poor and savage for the purpose.[51]

A hurdle in their path was the Vaisnava king, Govindachandra, himself, who by the reckoning of his hostile Manipuri affines, was a lineal descendant of an ascetic 'Santi Giri'. He was not particularly old in 1829. But either because of his severe attacks of asthma or because of his 'corpulence', he did not come across as an active military figure to the English official sent to negotiate a transfer of Kachar with him.[52] Mrinalini Sinha has suggested that the British colonial valourization of a hyper-masculine ideal led to the representation of educated Indian males from the latter half of the nineteenth century as effeminate. The treatment of Radharam in the late eighteenth century and of Govindachandra in the early nineteenth century suggests that such dismissals happened much earlier in the century; furthermore, those who were so dismissed were ascetic–monastic military commanders who appeared to be obstacles to the advance of commercial capital in the region.

After the Anglo-Burmese treaty of Yandabo in 1826, the Regulation II of 1828 enlarged the freedom of Englishmen to trade in limestone and other articles on the frontier of Sylhet, and had specifically 'opened' the country lying northwest of the Surma River to traders resident in the Company's provinces (and paying taxes to the Company).[53] This economic–political conjuncture proved opportune for a colonial official investigation of Govindachandra's income in 1828–9. It also explained the reason that the Englishman who went to survey Govindachandra's estate did not recognize it as a typical sannyasi–gosain estate. The latter had allowed various corporate bodies (khel) living on the land to pay their dues in kind and with labour-services. Those who grew betel-nuts paid in nuts, those of another place in wood. Collections from various khels were in turn devoted to deities and gurus.[54]

As with other estates in the plains in the eighteenth century, this early nineteenth-century official also complained about Govindachandra's management of the fort and estates of Khaspur. His protectionist policies hindered the Company's aims. Govindachandra had forbidden cultivators of grain to export their surpluses to British-controlled markets in Sylhet, but induced them to sell to him. This kept prices of paddy low in the vicinity, and prevented traders of the Company from profiting from sales in the vicinity. Govindachandra had also not expanded a trade in ivory or wax from the forests in his estates, even though he gave a gift of two small elephants to the official who visited him. The official envied Kachar's 'inexhaustible supply of valuable timber for purposes of boat building', but Govindachandra's high tariff on timber cut from the forests hobbled the timber trade. Equally, Govindachandra allowed the cultivation and consumption of opium by his adherents, making the Company fearful about the preservation of its own monopoly of the opium trade.

As far as the Company officials were concerned, Govindachandra's estate was a classic 'waste' of resources. All the earnings from agriculture and forests were assigned to Govindachandra's two wives, his mother, and four daughters. The elephants collected by one khel were reserved for the eldest daughter, the collections by a 'Nokte Lama' for his fourth daughter. Individual spokespersons of khels also seemed to hold bits of rent-free lands. Such rent-free lands, under investigation and resumption proceedings in lower Bengal since 1760, assumed even greater significance to the East India Company officials in the early nineteenth century. These lands paid nothing to the Company treasury. They only participated in what officials thought was the general abandonment of cultivation altogether after the arrival of Manipuri-Burmese armies in 1817. They were convinced that many of these rent-free lands (one estimate puts them at 200 kulbahs or 660-odd acres) were 'wastelands'.[55]

The investigations of income also extended to the personnel of the household of Govindachandra. There were many women involved: the household commanded the loyalty of some khels whose labour services and goods were dedicated to a younger brother and a junior male who would succeed to Govindachandra's status. But there was no son. Aware that the Company's administration was keen to annex the lands in the valley (that the Company was referring to as Kachar), the Commissioner of Sylhet pressed Govindachandra to adopt a male child and name him as successor.[56] Initially, Govindachandra responded coolly that it was none of the Company's business. In 1828, however, an ambitious khel of 40 sipahis or *sempung* (in Tibetan, an honorific term for male servants) claimed to be the real king-makers of Kachar.[57] They took over one of the fortifications and outposts claimed by Govindachandra as his. Unable to get a sympathetic ear from the Company, and perhaps suspicious that the Company officials were colluding with his rivals to partition the estate, in 1829 Govindachandra declared that he would adopt a child from one of the families of 'reigning rajas of the neighbouring states'. Despite this, the Agent of the Governor General (AGG) of a newly established North-East Frontier, David Scott, needled him by asking him to lease a spot of land—the Ilaka of Chandrapur—to a disliked Manipuri affine, Gambhir Simha; Govindachandra tried to compromise by offering to lease the terrain to the Company instead.[58]

All these compromises meant little to the officers of the Company after 1828. Its military men wished to establish a military cordon against Burma in the region. Its tax-collecting machinery needed to minimize the cost of such militarization to the Company and to Parliament of the cordon. Scott, the AGG, urged that Kachar under a better rule would become the granary of the surrounding regions, afford adequate supplies to the Manipuri country *and* enable the latter to resist future Burmese invasions. In sum, Kachar needed to be annexed in order to establish the security and tranquillity of the Company's holdings in Bengal. The annexation of Kachar was necessary for the Company to *have* a 'North-East Frontier'.[59] By 1830, the Company's chosen man and a Vaisnava initiate, Gambhir Singh of Manipur, had secured what the Company officers had desired for a while. Govindachandra was murdered—by Vaisnava initiates chanting 'Haribol' (a name of Krishna)—while in his fort, surrounded by Company-trained soldiers for whose protection he had paid annual subsidies.[60]

THE DEFEAT OF 'HINDU' WIDOWS

The murdered man's widow, Indraprabha, claimed to succeed her husband and continue to collect labour services, dues, and cash in the estates governed by Govindachandra. This was completely in keeping with the provisions of the Dayabhaga school of Hindu law that prevailed in Bengal, even though Rammohan Roy had recently claimed that the English-allied 'modern' interpreters of these texts who worked in the new colonial courts had considerably shrunk the capacity of widows. Nevertheless, this version of inheritance law had provided that in the absence of a son, grandson, or great-grandson, a wife had rights in joint family property, as well as in her husband's self-acquired assets.

Regulations of 1790–3 had guaranteed the adjudication of inheritance disputes by the terms of 'Hindu law'. By Regulation III of 1828–9, the governor general had further declared that though he was keen to 'recover' revenue-exempt lands for 'public revenue', the authority to investigate tax-exempt lands was vested in the Company's revenue-collecting officers alone. Legality required that no grants be resumed until the titles to such were adjudged invalid by a judicial decree from a Company magistrate. This was the context in which an elaborate investigation of the 'Hindu' nature of the widow's cohabitation with her first husband's brother unfolded in Kachar.

The local colonial tax collectors in this region, military officers fresh from the Anglo-Burmese war of 1824–6, quickly narrowed the investigation down to the actual performance of a contracted ceremonial marriage between Indraprabha and her two husbands. She had been originally married to the elder brother, Krishnachandranarayan. After his death in 1814, she had resided with Govindachandra as his consort, although 'no ceremony passed at their union except the replacing of the Seal on her forehead by some Brahmin women at the Raja's command'.[61] These military officials wanted documentary evidence of precedents and textual treatises. A Lieutenant Gordon was sent off to consult 'many Brahmins' residing in Kachar and the various Vaisnava Manipuris. According to Fisher, they had all declared that the marriage was unlawful and that the levirate 'greatly scandalized the people of the plains'. As a ground on which to deny the claims of a widow to govern, it proved sufficient.

It did not matter that this determination was entirely inaccurate in textual Hindu terms as well as in historical practice all over the monastic geographic order (see Chapter 1, and above). Explicit identification of the levirate as the central relationship between households of Vaisnava Manipuri lineages and those of the Himalayan-originated order of the Tipra was articulated in the nineteenth-century poem, Srenimala.[62] This record of polyandry was also known among other Tibetan–Buddhist aristocratic families from the southernmost ends of the Himalayan foothills, Arakan. Nor had the Vaisnava poets singing praise of particular gurus forgotten this Himalayan world. The poet-narrator of Krishnamala, who signed himself as Dvija Ramganga ('Dvija' indicates initiated Vaisnava monastic authority) also associated levirate unions with a particular kind of female potency and household structure to which it was considered appropriate (64–6). The poets narrate a 'history' of levirate as part of a larger narrative of military science and technology that gave the warriors of the 'khu-chung society' of the hills their peculiar advantage over armies drawn from the plains. The poets refer to a daughter of a 'khu-chung' general married to an eminent 'kuki' husband. Instead of consummating the marriage, the husband died on the nuptial bed. Six of the husband's brothers claimed the bride in succession and paid with their lives. Only the youngest brother remained awake on the night of his wedding, saw a serpent emerge from the nostril of the sleeping bride and not finding its usual human meal, returned to its home in the woman's body. The watchful husband understood that the serpent had consumed his six elder brothers. Resolved to avenge their death, he lured his bride to a desolate part of the woods, killed her, buried the corpse under a tree on the banks of a river, returned to his father-in-law's home and lamented that the wife was lost. The father of the bride searched high and low for his daughter but could not find her. When overwhelmed by his loss and grief, the father was visited in a dream by his daughter. She informed him of what had transpired, but assured him that she now existed as a tree with deadly leaves. In this form she could remain useful to all her people who lived north of the Chatheng River and would not grow south of it.

In its mention of Chatheng, the poet of *Krishnamala* suggested a Himalayan context whose political borders were still unspecified in their time. There are two possibilities for identifying the region. In the eighteenth century, an Italian Jesuit missionary had identified a town located on the southern bend of the Brahmaputra River east of Lhasa as Če-thang (modern spelling Tsethang).[63] The southern ends of the town abutted on the provinces of Pari and Mon (currently northwest Bhutan). He had located this stretch of terrain extending to 'Kieerong on the border of the kingdom of Nepal' as the region where a poisonous plant, aconite, was found. A second possibility was the 'Chatheng' located between 10,000 and 12,000 feet above the sea in the Sikkim-Darjeeling Himalayas.[64] Similar aconitum palmatum (from whose root the deadly poison was extracted) was located at this elevation.

As a history of aconite or any other herbal poison available to highland archers, the poetic narrative *Krishnamala* simply wove a commonplace of successive fraternal widow marriage, that is levirate, into the terrain of female-centred societies in the Himalayan foothills marked by 'Chatheng'. The poets localized these marriages as specific to communities of 'mlecchha' (of indistinct speech), those 'khu-chung' and their affines, the 'kukis', all of who were devotionally subject (*proja*) to individual ascetic–warrior lordships. Conflicts within both the family-clan and ordination lineages of a guru (46–7) turned deadly when members of the conflicted guru lineage mustered and recruited especially fierce militia described under the category 'Khu-chung samaj' (53–5). The poets also described this latter as a corps of helmeted archers who used poison-tipped arrows (*bishe-maakha tir*) for long-distance attacks, sharp blades and swords for close combat, and shielded themselves with enormous leather shields across the back. Obviously these were the Bhot militia (see Chapter 1), a broadly Tibetan-speaking Inner and Central Asian polyglot army—in the following of a Manikya.

The poetic compass of the *Krishnamala* was reinforced from all corners of the older monastic geographic world between the Himalayan and the coastal societies. In 1783, Samuel Turner had described the system as a positive one thus:

> To the privileges of unbounded liberty, the wife here adds the character of mistress of the family, and companion of her husbands. The company of all, indeed, she is not at all times entitled to expect. Different pursuits, either agricultural employments or mercantile speculation, may occasionally cause the temporary absence of each; yet whatever be the result, the profit of the labourer flows into the common store, and when he returns, whatever may have been his fortune, he is secure of a grateful welcome to a social home. … [The custom] operates against superabundant population, tends also to prevent domestic discords arising from a division of family interests and to concentrate all the spirit and all the virtues inherent in illustrious blood.[65]

In a similar vein, in the 1790s from the hills where he had been sent to subdue Radharam's Vaisnava–Sufi resistance, Elliott had found, along with the public authority of wives in councils, the presence of inmarrying son-in-law and the possibility of levirate among cattle-herding communities. Similar patterns of household formations had been found among the Tibetan–Bengali-speaking populations fleeing from Arakan into Chittagong and coastal Bengal in the period between 1783 and 1790.[66]

In 1815, travelling among the subjects of the Tibetan Buddhist monasteries called 'Bootea' by the British, Krishna Kanta Bose had written about marriages that needed no ceremonies as well as the synchronicity of plural marriages (both polygyny and polyandry) with uxorilocality. He explained,

'for the most part the husbands live in the houses of their wives, the latter seldom going to their husband's house. A rich man may keep as many wives as he can maintain, and when poor, three or four brothers club together and keep one wife amongst them. The children of such a connection call the eldest husband father and the others uncles. It is not considered as a crime for a man to have connections with any of his female relations except his mother; but it is looked upon as discreditable in the case of a [biological] sister or daughter. Older women are frequently united in marriage to boys, in which case the husband usually takes the daughter of his older wife after her demise.'[67]

Furthermore, the colonial search for a 'ceremonial' contract for a once-married widow explicitly militated against the Sastric textual provision by which once-married widows were to be given to second husbands *without* ceremony.[68] Not having found a ceremonial of a second marriage, Fisher declared the union of Indraprabha and Govindachandra 'utterly profane, incestuous and by consequence invalid'.[69] In this sweeping judgement, Fisher took on a much more authoritarian stance than the Vaisnava *pandit* poets of the *Srenimala* and *Krishnamala*. The latter granted that this form existed among specific groups. Fisher would not grant its legitimacy at all.

On the face of it, this was peculiar. Indraprabha was both a daughter of a 'Hindu' Vaisnava–Manipuri man, Madhuchandra, and a widow of another Tantric, Govindachandra. Yet she was not allowed to inherit from her husband by the standards of a 'Hindu Shastra' that she was doubly compliant with. She was also the youngest of her siblings: her elder brothers, elder sister, and mother lived with her in one house.[70] These brothers (Pabitra Simha and Nilambar Singh) and elder sister (Bhabanipuri Rajkoowuri) and mother (Mahadebi Rani) were both Manipuri and Vaisnava. Although the women were not called to provide evidence of the marriage, the brothers were. Investigations into the murder of Govindachandra in 1830 had thrown up the name of Pabitra Simha as a host to the assassins: one man named the assassin Hiranand as having come to the house of Pabitra Simha (the family house as well) for a 'religious feast' (Vaisnava commensality indicated in the term *bhandara*), though

Pabitra Simha of course denied it in his own testimony.[71] Their complicity in the removal of Govindachandra suggests that as far as the Manipuri affines were concerned, their sister's husbands, the two brothers, Krishnachandranarayan and Govindachandranarayan were males brought in to manage estates 'gifted' by the Vaisnava house of Jaisimha. The two brothers had risen to the status of *mukhtar* or spokesperson from among the khels and had been treated as 'raja' by the East India Company. But real power lay with their wives' relatives. Nevertheless, the English officers did not examine Indraprabha's mother (and the dead man's mother-in-law). Given the ways in which senior women were significant decision makers, this omission was telling. Women such as a 'Chandraprabha, the widow of a Raja Tamradhvaj' had had a hand in selecting a Kirtichandra for the governance of the estate in the distant past, about 150 years previously.[72] Where widows and elder women had been important, it was hardly likely that the mother of Indraprabha was a mere spectator in the matter of her youngest daughter's multiple marriages. It was likely that the widow's matrilateral kin were invested in these marriages.

Fisher also overlooked key parts of the evidence that emerged in the course of the murder investigations of Govindachandra. According to his own officials, Govindachandra had 'built a separate house at Latu for the security of his Ranee and himself'.[73] The rani in question was not Indraprabha at all, for there is absolutely no record of her having cohabited with the dead man. On the night that he was killed, the dead man was awakened from sleep and with a 'slave-girl and two or three servants attempted to escape'.[74] He may even have been living in a dormitory (*akhara*) of sorts. In 1832, daughters of other paiks—Chandrakala, daughter of Nandaram Bormon; Joobandi, daughter of Rajaram Bormon; Lakkhidi, daughter of Galoo Dev; Jayanti, daughter of Mohyn dev—were also found to be consorts of the 'raja'. At any rate, Indraprabha's was a characteristic form of a polygynandrous levirate: the relationship with a daughter from a substantial household was inherited by males, who were brothers. The widow-wife, in turn, expected to inherit from her husbands' self-acquired assets and thus consolidate her household's eminence.

Instead of granting her status as daughter of a Vaisnava and the widow of another Hindu, Fisher arrogated to himself the right to pronounce upon the 'un-Hindu' past of the husbands. Or at least, in his search for the 'ceremonials' of marriage—in fact considered unnecessary for second marriages of widows even in 'Hindu' classical texts—Fisher secured the right to pronounce upon the nature of the recent 'conversion' of the two brothers, erstwhile husbands of Indraprabha, to Hinduism. Speaking of 'Kacharis' (of Lower Tibet–Bhutan) descended from 'Kamrup', the officer referred to a religion that still prevailed over parts of Sylhet, Dharampur, Tripura, and the mountains thereof. It was not a religion he knew much about. It consisted, he wrote, of the worship of an 'immortal and supreme being called Aloo Raja and his wife Delo-jio and under these were various inferior deities each in his turn charged with the Government of the spiritual world for a certain number of weeks annually'.[75] Buffaloes, fowl, pigs were offered to these gods in propitiation. But there was no priesthood to perform these rituals, the ceremonies being performed by the eldest or most respectable person in the assembly. The moral codes, so far as Fisher could figure out, appeared 'conducive to virtue and restrictive of vice and the laws regulating social intercourse peculiar but not apparently noxious'. However, about thirty years previously (circa 1790s–1800), Krishnachandranarayan and his brother Govindachandranarayan had been initiated by 'Brahmans' and 'received with many ceremonies within the pale of the Hindu faith'. By which set of laws should one judge the marriages of these neo-Hindus?

In shifting the discussion of levirate onto ideals of textual law—or 'Hindu Shastra'—that his interlocutors apparently had never referred to, Fisher at one and the same time bypassed all textual precedents in 'Hindu Shastra' as well as historical referents. As we have seen in Chapter 1, laymen who were disciples of Buddhist monastic lineages as well as some Buddhist Tantric male lineages had married or consorted with women from other lineages. Classical epics revered by most 'Hindu' courts had illustrations of honourable levirates.[76] Fisher had apparently not been told of either. Nor had he been given the meanings of the terms of reference: 'Aloo' was also polite *dzongkha* for a male infant, the figure in which reincarnated Himalayan Buddhist hierarchs were found, recognized, addressed, and installed as supreme spiritual lords. *Doloi* were the regents and managers of the temporal concerns of such potent infants. Fisher had described a society he did not know at all: it was a world of Tibetan–Tantric–Buddhist lords and their Saiva–Sakta disciples, a world as dependent on sacrifices of animals as on the propitiation of mountains and river spirits and magical medicine. Which group of 'Hindus' had Gordon and Fisher consulted in their haste to pronounce on the 'incestuous' and 'un-Hindu' nature of Indraprabha's affinity? Or was this also a meaningless quest, given the East India Company officials' foregone conclusion about the change of regime needed in the fort of Khaspur and the readiness of intra-lineal rivals to stand forth as Company men?

Disallowing Indraprabha's rights as a widow to the management of the estates in the Barak–Surma River valley on the grounds of a levirate union simultaneously delegitimated the property and status inheritance patterns of widows, delegitimated an honourable and widely accepted practice of polyandry and levirate, and wiped out the traces of many daughters and sisters, the main diplomatic links between their brothers', mother's brothers', and husbands' lineages from the colonial archive. This was quite an impressive achievement for one political decision to manage. Each deserves separate attention.

The widow, Indraprabha was the youngest daughter of her mother. In the 1790s, John Elliott had noted the practice of female ultimogeniture and its association with the public authority of women-as-wives in hill-worshipping communities. While Bengali-language verse chronicles of the region (*Srenimala*, for instance) had attended to daughter's marriages, and recorded the ways in which inmarrying sons-in-law constituted local bureaucracies and administrative personnel of monastic-ascetic estates such as those of the Tipura/ Tipra, colonial records of the same estates failed to count various daughters' khels as significant political actors in the terrain. Company officials and law-courts thus fashioned the idea that in regions east of Dhaka, daughters did not count at all, when in fact, what happened to daughters and especially daughters' marriages continued to be an ongoing concern till well into the early twentieth century.

At the same time, delegitimation of levirate as 'incestuous' diluted the validity of institutionalized practices by which different ritual orders pooled political capital and manpower resources under one roof as affinal relationships. Households in which authority descended to females had incorporated men from other clans and corporations (khel) by establishing unions with the latter. As we have seen in the case of Assam, Manipur, Tipura, Ava, and Jayantia earlier, the heads of the women's households had attached and retained the services of inmarrying husbands and their clansmen and dependents. Both 'Brahman' and non-Brahman males were incorporated in the same ways. Newly arrived English officers, though unaware of co-residence of Buddhist Tantrics and Vaisnavas in the terrain since the seventh century, nevertheless noted that it was very usual for 'Bramins of high caste from various parts of Bengal to come for religious purposes to Jynteahpoor, the Bramin of which, being of an inferior order, consider it an honour to be allied to the Bengalees and frequently give their daughters in marriage but with this provision that neither the women nor the offspring of such marriages were to quit the country of Jyntea.'[77]

There were long-settled Bengali Brahmans in the terrain who had married into local Vaisnava, Buddhist, and Sakta households, and had daughters with these wives who were not affiliated to the 'Brahman' fathers but to their mothers. The decision regarding Indraprabha's marriage and widowhood jeopardized such daughters' claims on their mothers' estates as well as their claims on visiting husbands, and on sibling solidarities. Expansive Buddhist–Vaisnava alliances centred on households where daughters and mothers were stable and brothers, husbands, and fathers roved as monks, herdsmen, and traders-soldiers. After the annexation of Kachar, all these alliances were suddenly and simultaneously rendered both unhistorical and 'un-Hindu'.

REVENUE IN RESTRUCTURED HINDU LAW

Rather than recognize the claims to land that were generated by the relationship between people, relationships that had to be repaired repeatedly, Company officials in the newly annexed regions zeroed in on the land itself. Already in 1831, Fisher, the superintendent in Kachar, had written about the vast lands in the command of Khaspur (Kachar): there were about '1,800,000 kulbahs [about 60 million acres] of excellent land lying waste to which there are no claimants, respecting which therefore there would be no disputes in making grants from them to Europeans'.[78] Why Europeans specifically? Because apparently Fisher knew the nature of land tenures were 'heritable' in Kachar. Imposing an indigenous superior, such as one of the soldiers like Tula Ram or Gambhir Singh, would 'result in insurrection or failure of cultivation'. Claims to the same lands by widows from their first or subsequently married husbands fell directly in this category. The disqualification of widows' titles to lands begun in the 1790s on the grounds that such widows were females, continued in the period after the Anglo-Burmese war as part of a broader political liberal economy.

Initially, the Company partitioned the lands, giving control of the northern half to a soldier from the household while keeping the southern half for itself. In Langthabal (capital of Manipur), it installed its favoured agent, Gambhir Simha, another Vaisnava faithful who upon his installation as 'Raja' of Manipur, immediately dispatched a lakh of rupees for 'the construction of a temple at Brindabund' (Vrindavana, in the Gangetic plains, centre of Krishna worship).[79] He then proceeded to give similar gifts to other 'Brahmans' in the locality—probably other gosains or 'gooheins and priests', whom more than one officer described as 'the idle retinue that surround him'.[80] As an army officer observed, all of this Vaisnava male's earnings were in kind: the villages paid annual tribute to the Raja in greater or lesser qualities of raw cotton and woven cloths. He also provided for most of the influential men, civil as well as military, by placing two or three of the hill villages under their authority.[81] Many of these 'influential men' about the Manipuri power holder were also either initiated Tantric and other Vaisnava gosains (Assamese 'gohains').The populations who made up the 'hill villages' that colonial officials commented on had been tenants of monastics of an older Vaisnava–Buddhist lineage. The Company's decision replaced that lineage with one amenable to their bidding. Or so they hoped.

However, Vaisnava men such as Gambhir Singh simply repeated older patterns of gift-giving and settlement. To the colonial officials, these gifts alienated wealth because their recipients were the 'idle' priests and gosains (recipients of *brahmottar* and *devottar)*. Charges of idleness against priests, monastics, and their adherents ('retainers') resonated with anti-Catholic and anti-feudal histories that had elevated many yeomen farmers into the propertied backbone of a largely Puritan English and Scottish middle class by the mid-nineteenth century. The successes of this British yeomanry in turn inspired the distaste that early nineteenth century colonial military officers, their social peers (the merchants), and their social subordinates and junior partners in the empire (the missionaries), all felt for the 'idle' landholders in lower Bengal and Assam.

But this elevation of industriousness in the hands of a colonial English middle class also placed the division of labour by sex—the horizon of an aspirational middle class itself—on moral high ground. From this vantage point, the absence of a division of labour by sex, the absence of the divisions of 'public' field and factory versus the 'private' home, taken for granted by the British in the 1830s, diminished the moral and social standing of those groups in which such divisions did not apply. Unsurprisingly, the absence of the 'angel in the house' worked against all the laywomen who worked in the fields or as transport workers ('coolies'). In the eighteenth century, officials in the hills to the north of Sylhet (modern Bangladesh) thought the ubiquity of labouring women made them 'drudges', and their hard work was characteristic of 'savage nations'.[82] In 1827, another official observed of the cotton cultivation in the hills between Sylhet and Arakan that women sowed, weeded, and tended the cotton crops while the men cut heavy timber, built fences, and took materials to market.[83] Another officer in 1830 passed through Manipur and remarked upon the exclusively female shopkeepers at a bazaar, and then noticed how everywhere else women remained 'eternally busy picking cotton, weaving cloth, husking rice'.[84] When he walked up to a 'Kuki' hamlet, and found the exhausted men resting with their immense baskets, having brought in grain and cotton from the hills, he again commented on the *women* 'husking rice and weaving ... [who] appeared to be overworked—for they carry just equal burdens with their lords'. In the hills of southern Assam and northern Arakan, the earliest published reports by Bengali-speaking plainsmen, commenting on seven different cycles of rice-growing in the swiddens, also described the centrality of women's labour during the sowing and harvesting seasons, and the constant weeding necessary to keep the crop from being choked off.[85] A little later, another colonial officer noticed that the women were the 'hardest workers, the chief toilers'.[86]

What these colonial officers had not recognized was that such labour and its fruits were objects of exchange in a monastic economy. Male renunciants, warrior-ascetics, and celibate monks all depended on the work of the laywomen who fed them. In the early nineteenth century, an officer had described in very precise terms the institution of monastic Buddhist alms-begging in easternmost Assam (Sadiya), a region which overlapped with the sites considered sacred by Tibetan-speaking populations of the southeast corner of the Tibetan plateau or Khams.[87] Early in the morning, three or four of the monks from the temple hurried through the streets of the fortified town, preceded by a boy with a little bell, each holding a lacquered box in which he collects the offerings of the people, 'presented generally by the women, who stand waiting at their doors with a portion of their ready cooked meal'.[88] He had witnessed the classic institution of merit exchange that tied monastic men to multiple generations of women and children. The latter's work of provisioning monks, moreover, was comparable to the offerings of cash, grain, animals, products, and lands made by lay and initiated or ordained males—the various warriors, landlords, and kings whose donations were inscribed on copperplates and paper between the second and the eighteenth centuries.

A second epistemological absence shaped colonial official observations of 'merit-making' work among male and female subjects and tenants of monastic teachers and lineages. They lacked the linguistic category for disciples' dormitories. Instead, many officials referred to such disciples' dormitories as those of slaves and savage 'tribes'. This was as true for Vaisnava ('Hindu') groups as it was for tenants of Buddhist monasteries. An officer thus counted the Vaisnava political community of the elderly ascetic Moamaria monk (gosain) as a 'tribe'.[89] If one looks beyond the terms of colonial agnosia, one can, however, see that officials had suggested merit-making economics when they described hospitality as 'one of the virtues of this tribe, any number of strangers who take up their abode in a village or in the chief's house, have food and lodging so long as they remain and on such occasions the pounding out of the rice occupies the attention of the whole female community.'[90] This was how in Kachar–Manipur, Indraprabha hired a 'band of assassin Kukis' who went up the Dhaleswari River to do away with the man favoured by the Company (Tularam 'Senapati') in northern parts of the estate. The superior official (AGG) Francis Jenkins advised that she should be deported to Dhaka.[91] Only after that was Kachar formally annexed in March 1833.[92]

If the Company officers in the 1830s rode roughshod over widows' and daughters' claims in lands in eastern India, their decision also managed to hide from view the remarkably nuanced ways in which earlier monastic estates had accommodated and settled non-sectarian others in the same terrain. In actual fact, the greater part of the population living and cultivating lands on the estates of Govindachandra and others were already descendants of Afghan–Rajput cultivators and craftsmen, soldiers and traders organized as extended clans (khels). Like Buchanan earlier, Fisher had not understood the practice of animal sacrifices (common in both devotional Islamic festivals as well as in Tibetan Buddhist and Sakta–Saiva ones) as part of an ongoing cosmopolitan order of assimilation and translation. Yet, he had himself presided over Muslim 'Kacharis' such as Jharu Meah, a man who held a sanad from Raja Krishna Chandra of Kachar from the year 1217.[93] Another English officer, Francis Jenkins, had found in the newly acquired Kachar in 1831 at a very extensive village of Sonabari at the foothills of the mountains, headmen or Chaudhuris, who were both 'Mussulman' and self-identified as 'Kachari'.[94] In 1834, having annexed the region, another officer would find that the 'Muhammadan portion of the populace was the most numerous in the state' of Kachar, as in the adjacent province of Sylhet'.[95] In both there were only a few 'Brahmans and Kayasthas' mainly invited from the Gangetic plains or elsewhere. These had been assimilated into societies where Muslims predominated. In other words, it was Afghan Muslims who were the dominant groups, but they had given lands to Vaisnava, Tantric Buddhists, and Saivas in the region.

The thoroughgoing overhaul that colonial officials wished to implement after 1833 aimed simultaneously at maximizing the cutting of timber from the forests that earlier fort holders had not permitted. Such 'clearance' work, the officers calculated would make available at least 1,000 square miles of excellent land in southern Kachar and it was hoped, the work would be performed by the poorest Muslims from Sylhet attracted to Kachar. These cleared lands would then be given over to the exertions of British capital to develop.[96] These arrangements of land and labouring populations met with the approval of the Liberal Governor General, William Bentinck, presiding over a cash-starved Company treasury. Bentinck thought that the fertile soils of Kachar could be given in family-friendly plots to veteran

Company sepoys instead of the promised cash pensions. But shortly afterwards, he realized that these lands and labouring populations were suited especially for European development. What stood in the way of European colonization of these lands was a Regulation II of 1793 that forbade European land-revenue collectors and military officers from holding lands in any province from which such taxes were collected. This was intended to prevent the development of the settler-style colonialism that had led to revolutions such as in America and in Haiti. Clauses that prevented such colonization were henceforth identified as unnecessary restrictions on Englishmen. Bentinck, keen to encourage 'European enterprise, capital and skill in Kachar', urged that the district be treated as legally separate from the geographical and social continuity that was Sylhet district.[97]

In particular, Bentinck wished to protect Englishmen in the newly annexed and segregated Kachar district from the hybrid Mughal patterns of cultivation that had evolved in permanently settled Bengal. Cultivation of an uncultivated piece of land began with a grant of land that allowed the holder three years of rent-free holding. Liability to taxation began after that; if the holder could not pay the taxes, the land was sold at auction and could be bought by another. Apparently, or so Bentinck thought, the taxes demanded could be arbitrary; and when auctions occurred, there might be no reference to the initial investments of the original grantee. All these were 'evils' from which British capitalists needed protection. Thus, began the treatment of a region that, though annexed by the East India Company, was to be treated differently. Instead of the Permanent Settlement of revenue that prevailed in Bengal, lands annexed after the Anglo-Burmese wars would be settled on the Ryotwari pattern. Kachar, culturally and geographically continuous with Bengali-speaking Muslim Sylhet, would become segregated from it as a 'Scheduled District' of Assam thirty years later.

THE AFTERMATH OF NON-RECOGNITION: AUTHORITY WITHIN FAMILIES, LINEAGES, AND LANDSCAPE

A threefold transformation occurred across the eastern settlements of the erstwhile monastic geographic order. The first and most important was that of the transformation of authority within the household and lineage which, given its monastic and political networks, would rebound on the Company and imperial governments. In addition to sending her entourage to assassinate rivals, the widowed Indraprabha tried to recover her authority through peaceful means, as well. Having learned that the Company would only allow a son to succeed to Govindachandra's estate, she put forth the claims of a young man called Govindram Barmanya, born of a daughter of a Dolai Dev Naskar, said to be a slave girl of Krishnachandranarayan, as the next heir and successor to the Raja of Kachar.[98] No official was willing to believe this claim of paternity, especially after Govindram, who lived with the widows at Kaatigora, was involved in leading the 'Kuki attack' on the man the Company officials favoured at the moment, Tularam.[99]

The Company officials preferred to install the widow's elder brother, Pabitra Simha, as a successor to his dead brother-in-law's estates. Apparently mimicking ancient and pious 'kings' of the past, colonial officials gave Pabitra Simha a plot of 'forested' land in southern Kachar along with an advance first of 600 and then another 400 rupees. With these advances, he established either 80 or 100 families about four miles above the mouth of the river Sonai (a tributary of the Barak). Many of the men in this settlement were given muskets from the armoury and stores of the dead Raja of Kachar.

Company officers thought they had secured two things for the price of one. They praised the neatness with which the needs of revenue and military 'security' had both been fulfilled by the Pabitra Simha settlement. Eager to gain guards for the region annexed to Company-held domains, while unaware of Tibetan linguistic references to Buddhist reincarnation, a colonial officer thus praised Indraprabha's brother for having 'established a friendly intercourse with the Tang-coking Kookies who reside on the Sonai'.[100] Various other men in the entourage of the dead Govindachandra also secured tax-free estates in Kachar as part of this colonial order of provisioning a military cheaply. Some of them merely exchanged their tax-free claims upon the revenues of one place for landholding in another—such as Dharampur (in the bend of the Brahmaputra) for another estate in 'jungle-land'.[101] These grants suggested in turn that the officers of the Company had not demolished the revenue-exempt grant entirely, but had reserved it for their own purposes, allies, and favoured ones.

This is important to recognize in order to pinpoint the specific political, rather than ideological circumstances, under which the Company officials reshaped the nature of 'charity' and its relationships with landholding. Scrutinized for purposes of permanent taxation in Company-administered Bengal since the 1760s, these holdings might have appeared especially irrational to Company officers after 1830s. But instead of dispensing with such holdings altogether, officers of the Company simply reallocated the tax-free grants to Vaisnava men of their own choosing who would support particular kinds of anti-Burmese politics. Far from establishing 'peace' in the region, however, these arrangements continued the conflicts between lineages from the late eighteenth century into the mid-nineteenth.

A second process was locked into place thereafter. This was the intensification of violent confrontations between sets of uncles and nephews and their entourages and disciples both in the capitals and in distant lands. The extension of Manipuri-Burmese (and Vaisnava-Buddhist alliance) and lineage politics over Ahom, Kachar, Sylhet, and Bengal (especially Nadia, the centre of Vaisnava learning and worship) dragged out and reignited a dormant fraternal conflict along various guru-shishya lineages. Groups of men from similar Buddhist–Vaisnava lineages contended with each other for the recapture of the valley and temples of Manipur from what they considered Company-nominated place-holders. British officials were aware that there were many different contenders for Manipur spread out all over Bengal, Burma, and Kachar, 'all of who probably secretly cherish hopes of one day or other being Raja'.[102] Chief among contenders was Pitambar Simha, who had continued to live in Ava.

From 1834, when Gambhir Simha suddenly died, leaving a minor son, Chandrakirti Simha, as successor with the aid of a regent called Narsingh, all of Gambhir Simha remaining brothers and nephews (cousins to each other through their fathers, and uncle to the minor on the throne) began to make lightning dashes from wherever they were, with a few followers and guns, in an attempt to 'recover' the throne of Manipur. First to go was Jogendrojit, already rumoured to have 'volunteered' his service against his uncle, Gambhir; in 1835, he was arrested in Sylhet as he gathered guns to make a dash on Manipur.[103] Others followed, with varying degrees of success.

Obdurate in upholding their nominated male authority in Manipur and Kachar, Company officials appear not to have recognized the nature of age-based seniority to which ideas of gender, rank, and status were linked. While motherhood certainly bestowed status on a woman, the significance of the seniormost female presence in the household was lost on Company officials. This only further alienated senior women of Manipuri lineages. Unable to act as regent for her son, the mother of Chandrakirti arrived in Kachar, where the Manipuri princes waited in 1844. Like Indraprabha's presence in the vicinity, hers too inspired these Manipuri men: 'these enterprises have been revived only on the Maharani's coming to Kachar, since when she has sent people and remitted considerable sums of money to Calcutta'.[104] The official response, once more, was to relocate her physically as far away as possible from Kachar.[105]

The third process was tied up with the first two. Not until the annexation of Kachar and the allocation of individual plots of land to various Kachari–Manipuri men and their lightning raids on Manipur did the records show entire collectives of guerrilla fighters, forest guards, warrior-traders coming forth under names of Lushei-Kuki and Nagas. Only after parts of southern Kachar were given out in land grants to this or that member of the Vaisnava–Manipuri household did the records begin to describe groups such as the 'Taling Kookies on the banks of the Pakoochera [who], using arrows, attacked a Company outpost guarded by the Sylhet Light Infantry at Jaffirabad.'[106] Likewise, after one member of the Vaisnava–Buddhist Manipuri lineage failed to secure power in Manipur, he disappeared amongst men called 'Chakma Kookies'.[107] Or a Manipuri landholder who had 'cultivated the jungles situated on the south of perganah Haliakandy in Kachar' boasted of having subdued 'the Kookies who infest the Hills and forest' and asked for more funds to 'keep up a body of armed men to defend the country from the eruptions of the savage Kookies'.[108]

What appeared on the surface to be three distinct processes were all part of the same process, as the colonial records themselves reveal. Each of the Manipuri men was a Vaisnava guru either in office or in waiting. Each could command the loyalties of at least a 100 to 150 armed men at any time. As would be repeatedly admitted by frustrated colonial administrators, 'princes' such as a Nawal Singh (sometimes also referred to as Nil or Nal Simha) of the Manipuris, were wandering monastics and ascetics. Nal Simha in particular was a 'Fakeer and a Priest or Gooroo of the Munnypoories, and lives by charity, and is constantly moving about amongst the Munnypoories' of Kachar and Sylhet.[109] One of his disciples was a Kanai Simha, who in 1850 was wounded in a skirmish with the lord in power at Manipur (for more on this man, see Chapter 5). If such men roamed around collecting food, goods, and services from populations whom colonial officers understood as 'tribals', it implied that these men were roaming among groups they called *praja* (subjects). This is exactly what the poets said the Buddhist monks and Vaisnava lords did among their 'monastic subjects', which we will study at greater length in Chapter 4. Vaisnava lords and Buddhist monks who emerged as leaders of groups that colonial officials identified as 'savages', 'Kukis', 'Luchayes', etc. The next chapter will track the imprint of these male–male relationships as well as tease out increasingly fugitive male–female relationships from the colonial archive.

NOTES

1. Andaya (2006: 181) and for the Ayutthia chroniclers' discussions of incest that might have been the cumulative result of marriages over two generations, see 192–5.

2. Tun (1986, vol. 5: 116), entry for 23 January 1798.

3. For the marriage arranged 'with great pomp' between a figure called 'King's grandson', the eighteen-year-old eldest son of Bodhawpaya's eldest son, and a 'daughter of the Prince of Prome', which was to occur in early March 1803, see Hall (1955: 198), entry for 2 December 1802.

4. See for instance Symes (1800, vol. 1: 35–6 and passim).

5. Translation of letter from Moha Silwa, a Burmese military officer stationed at Assam, addressed to Rangpore Saheb, recd 24 December 1821, BPC, 11 January 1822, no. 22.

6. Gosvami (2002: 17); Singh (1980: 143–53); Mukhopadhyaya (1975); Roy (1958: 66–106); Simha (1916: 51–5).

7. Personal visit to Manipur Math, Navadvip, 23 December 2011. I thank Probir Bhattacharjee, the descendant of the *kulacharya* of the lineage, for his detailed oral narrative explaining the signs and symbols of Buddhist Awakening at the Vaisnava site; and Rajkumar Tikendra Singh, the lineal descendant of Bhagyachandra and current *sebait* of the temple, for permissions to photograph all the images within.

8. Cited in Singh (1980: 63–4).
9. Barua (1985 [1930]: 286–90).
10. Gosvami (2002: 18, 27–8).
11. Bhuyan (1990a [1933]: 55).
12. Barua Sadaramin (1990 [1930]: 71–4).
13. Barua (1985 [1930]: 301) for invocation of Tara, 302–3 for the retention and distribution of wives; 304 for subsequent joint authority of the widow-consort and rebel-commander.
14. Barpujari (1994: 295); for date of Rajesvar Simha's death in 1769, see 303.
15. *Ibid.*, 314.
16. *Ibid.*, 293.
17. Eliott (1792: 17–37).
18. Barpujari (1994: 339).
19. Cox (1971 [1821]: 70 and passim).
20. *Ibid.*, 138–9.
21. *Ibid.*, 276–8.
22. *Srenimala of Ujir Durgamani* (1996: 15, 25).
23. *Ibid.*, 42.
24. Rawlins (1790: 188).
25. Van Schendel (1992a: 82).
26. *Krishnamala of Dvija Ramaganga* (1995: 16–17).
27. *Ibid.* The lines are '*khadgaakaar devi ek aachhoye she deshe/ rono-chondi naam taan shorboloke ghoshe/ boroi probhav debi shuni juboraja/nana upahaar diya korilek puja*'.
28. Pemberton (1865: 228).
29. *Ibid.*, 247.
30. *Srenimala of Ujir Durgamani* (1996: 19).
31. Van Schendel (1992a: 130–8).
32. *Srenimala of Ujir Durgamani* (1996: 21–2). The relevant lines are '*Kashi manikya patni Kutilaksha jeno/Chourjit Mekhol nripa pita je tahan*'.
33. *Ibid.*, p. 22. The relevant lines are '*Krishnakishor manikyer modhyoma je rani/ naamete akhilesvari eimatro jaani/ marjit name hoiye mekhol nripoti/ tahan duhita rani bolilam iti*'... '*aarek madhyama rani marjit suta/sanatoni naam jeno tahan akhyata.*' The word *madhyama* in this usage should be read as a reference to 'middling rank' and status.
34. Tun (1986, vol. 6: 31–2), Order of 25 March 1807.
35. *Ibid.*, 207–8, Order of 14 March 1810.
36. *Ibid.*, 218–19, 222–4, 234–5, Orders of 31 March, 8 April, 10 April, 27 April 1810.
37. *Ibid.*, 97, Order of 28 October 1816.

38. For the details of the Assamese bride's entry into the Burmese household, her title as the Swargadev's/Sakkadeva's princess, for the ceremonial and ritual aspects of her ear-piercing, bathing rituals, see ROB, vol. 7, Orders of August, September–December 1817, 103–53.

39. Note from F[elix] Carey, 20 December 1817, encl BJC, Criminal Lower Provinces, 6 January 1818, no. 5. The writer, son of the Baptist missionary, Reverend Carey of Serampore, lived at the court of Govindachandra in Khaspur, Kachar but travelled as a missionary through various parts of the region; for vivid depiction of the takeover of Kachar by forces from Manipur and Burma, see his correspondence to his father and to the magistrate of Sylhet in 1817, in extracts from his letters in NAI, FPP, 18 June 1830, no. 60B.

40. Translation of letter from Raja of Manipur to Mgte. Sylhet, 12 Poos 1739 (December 1817), encl Mgte Sylhet to Judicial Department, 28 December 1817, BJC, 6 January 1818, no. 19.

41. Statement of Purbitter Sing [Pabitra Simha], 4 May 1830, NAI, FPP, 4 June 1830, no. 30.

42. Enclosed Translation of Statement Received from Raja Gumbheer Singh, 4 October 1832, Extract BPC 31 December 1832, no. 91, OIOC, BC F/4/ 1447/56959.

43. Barpujari (1994, vol. 3: 294–6).

44. Translation of a Bengali Letter from Krishnachandra dated 13 June 1809, BPC, 29 Aug. 1809, no. 60, OIOC, F/4/312/ 7123. The letter states that the Vaisnava was on a 'pilrimage to the places of Hindu worship' when he began to worry about the estate left behind.

45. Letter of Felix Carey to Mr. Ewing, 25 June 1817, in NAI, FPP, 18 June 1830, no. 60 B.

46. Reference to treaty, and the regular payments of sums by Govindachandra, in David Scott to Commr. Sylhet, 17 November 1825, FPP, 14 May 1832, encls. 1 and 2 in no. 78.

47. Lieutenant Thomas Fisher to Acting Judge and Mgte. Sylhet, 18 May 1822 in *Tripura Historical Documents* (1994: 20–30) for 'A Report on the Boundary between British Frontier of District Sylhet and Independent Territory of Tipperah'.

48. Extract from Fisher's Memoir on Kachar, 24 November 1824, A, in Note by the Secretary to Govt, 17 June 1830, NAI, FPP, 18 June 1830, no. 59.

49. Chief Secy to Govt to Commr Sylhet, 23 Nov 1827, in FPP 14 May 1832, no. 79.

50. Scott's dispatch of 20 July 1829 referenced in GG in Council, Fort William to AGG, NEF (T. C. Robertson) 17 December 1832, NAI, FPP, 17 December 1832, no. 40. The estimate had been provided by Fisher.

51. Memorandum of Extent and Revenue of Kachar by Thos. Fisher, n.d., NAI, FPP, 14 May 1832, no. 89.

52. Commr. Sylhet to Chief Secy. to Govt., 18 February 1829, FPP, 14 May 1832, no. 81.

53. Great Britain, House of Common, 1872.

54. For the list of khels, see Report of the Annual Revenue Administration of the district of Kachar, 1871–2, Assam Secretariat Proceedings, File 636C.O. of 1872.

55. Thos. Fisher, In Charge of Kachar, to T.C. Robertson, October 1832, NAI, FPP, 29 October 1832, no. 142.

56. Translation of letter to Raja Govindachandra by Commr. Sylhet, 24 December 1827, NAI, FPP, *ibid.*, no. 83.

57. Translation of Arzee of Forty Sepoys to AGG (24 Kartick 1749 si), Arzee of Tularama to Mr. Tucker, Commr. (5 Falgun 1749), FPP, 14 May 1832, no 82.

58. AGG, NEF to Chief Secy., Fort William, 17 July 1829, *ibid.*, no. 87, and Accompanying Agreement of Govindachandra Narayan, dated 30 Asarh San 1236 and 1751 sakh, for 50 koolbahs of land leased to the Company for fifteen years at Chandrapur north of the Barabakra River. This, it appears, was the vicinity of the 'Chandrapur visaya' mentioned in the Srichandra inscription found in Paschimbhag, see Introduction.

59. David Scott, AGG, NEF, to Chief Secy, Fort William, 30 July 1829, *ibid.*, no. 84.

60. Mgte. Sylhet to Chief Secy. to Govt., Secret and Political, 17 May 1830, NAI, FPP, 4 June 1830, no. 29; for sworn depositions on Gambhir Singh's complicity in the murder, see *ibid.*, no. 30, and FPP, 18 June 1830, nos 53–62. The involvement of men from the Sylhet Light Infantry, first raised by Lindsay in 1780s, is clearly suggested here.

61. Thomas Fisher to AGG, NEF (Jenkins), 28 September 1830, NAI, FPP, no. 103.

62. *Srenimala of Ujir Durgamani* (1996: 22).

63. De Filippi (1932: 140–1); for aconite, see 123, 129.

64. See Key on Map of British Sikkim Comprising the Darjeeling Hill Territory and two Morung Pergunnahs Surveyed in 1852, OIOC, Map Collections X/1280/1. A note at the bottom of the key cites Joseph Dalton Hooker, the British plant-collector, as the source for the information. For poisonous rhododendron species in the vicinity of Chatheng (Sikkim), see Hooker (1969 [1854]: 376–7).

65. Turner (2005 [1800]: 350).

66. See, for example, Captain Hill to Lt. Col. William Kirkpatrick, Secy to Govt, Secret, Political and Foreign, 15 February 1800, in BPC 27 February 1800, OIOC, BC, F/4/72/1593.

67. 'Account of Bootan by Kishen Kant Bose' (1815), translated by D. Scott, in Eden (1865: 200). For placing these observations within patterns of fraternal and maternal multi-marriage systems, see Singh (2002).

68. Kane (1930, vol. 2: 554–6); for the case of a once-married widow who is given by her family without any ceremony to a male relative (*sapinda*) of deceased husband on failure of brother-in-law, see 599–608; for other widow remarriages, see provisions of texts, 609–19.

69. Thos. Fisher, In Charge of Kachar, to T. C. Robertson, 1 October 1832, NAI, FPP, 29 October 1832, no. 142.

70. 'Statement Showing Annual Allowance Received by Ranis of Kachar', encl 1, NAI, FPP, 29 October 1832, no. 142.

71. Statement of Hidy Mia, Kooby Mia, Saloo Manji, 2 May 1830; and Statement of Purbittur Singh, 4 May 1830, NAI, FPP, 4 June 1830, no. 30 encl; for testimony that the assassins had been men loyal to 'Purbittur Singh the Raj Coomar', see depositions of Bishun Ram Brahman Kachari, and Santa Ram Brahmin, 7 May 1830, Letter from Mgte. Sylhet to AGG, NEF, 30 May 1830, NAI, FPP, 18 June 1830, no. 54.

72. Fisher to AGG, NEF, 27 September 1830, NAI, FPP, 14 May 1832, no. 100.

73. Deposition of Myib Singh, Nazir of Raja, 1 May 1830; evidence of Khamar Mea Choudhuri of parganah Chabghat, same date, NAI, FPP, 4 June 1830, no. 30, encl; and deposition of Pabitra above.

74. Abstract of evidence of Kachar Dow, servant of Raja, 1 May 1830, *ibid*.

75. Thos. Fisher to T.C. Robertson, 1 October 1832, NAI, FPP 29 October 1832, no.142.

76. For the birth of Dhritarashtra from the levirate union of Bharata's widow, Ambika and the sage Vyasa, see Dhand (2004); for the early studies of this, see Hopkins (1889).

77. Supt. Kachar to Commr. Dacca Division, 11 December 1836, *CDR*, 1, 32.

78. Encl copy of letter from Fisher at Kachar, 3 March 1832, entry for 7 December 1831, Private Journal of F.W. Jenkins, OIOC, Mss Eur/F 257/2.

79. R.B. Pemberton on Special Survey Duty to Chief Secy to Govt, 16 April 1832, NAI, FPP, 14 May 1832, no.109.

80. Off AGG W. Cracroft to Chief Secy Govt of Fort William, 22 March 1832, FPP, 14 May 1832, no. 98.

81. R.B. Pemberton on Special Survey Duty to Chief Secy Govt Fort William, 16 April 1832, FPP, 14 May 1832, no. 109.

82. Lindsay, Collr Sylhet to BOR, 14 December 1787, *SDR* (2: 205).

83. David Scott to Mr. Fenwick, 18 August 1827, in White (1888 [1831]: 79–80).

84. Private journal of Francis W. Jenkins on his trip from Calcutta to Chundrapoor in Kachar in 1831, OIOC, Eur F 257/2, entry under 8 December 1831, unpaginated.

85. 'Shubhokori' in *Dacca Prokash*, 18 August 1864 (3 Bhadra 1271 BE).

86. Lewin (1996 [1869]: 36).

87. For a study of the post-seventeenth-century Khams in which both Qing and Lhasa governments were invested, see Gardner (2006).

88. Wilcox (1855 [1825–28]), *Selections from Records*, no. 23, 113.

89. Letter from GOB to Court of Directors, 14 December 1832, OIOC, BC F/4/1505/59025.

90. Hannay (1847: 11–12).

91. Private note of Jenkins to Swinton, 22 April 1832, NAI, FPP, 14 May 1832.

92. Extract Minute of GG on Reports of Capt. Jenkins and Lt. Pemberton, 25 March 1833, in OIOC F/4/1447/56959.

93. Petition of Jharu Meah, in AGG, NEF to Off. Secy. Judicial, 23 October 1832, BPC, 26 November 1832, no. 194.

94. Private Journal of F.W. Jenkins, IOR Mss Eur/F 257/2, entry for 5 December 1831, no pagination.

95. Supt. T. Fisher to Commr Dacca Division, (blank) June 1834, *CDR* 2007, 1, 17.

96. Fisher to T.C. Robertson, 11 February 1833, BPC 16 January 1834, no. 2, OIOC F/4/1447/56959.

97. Minute of GG in Political Dept, 29 March 1833, OIOC F/4/1447/56959.

98. Abstract translation of Bengali petitions of Maharani Indra Prabhau of Kachar, and Koonwur Govind Chunder to Bentinck, GG in Council, recd 9 March 1833, BPC, 19 March 1833, no. 85. In another copy of the petition, the name of the father of the woman reads as 'Debendu Nushkur', the latter name suggesting a connection with an army or 'lashkar'.

99. AGG Cracroft to Chief Secy., 22 March 1832, NAI, FPP, 14 May 1832, no. 98.

100. Fisher, Asst in Charge of Kachar Affairs to AGG, NEF, 18 December 1832, BPC, 28 January 1833, no. 106, encl.

101. AGG, NEF to Secy GOI, 21 October 1833, BPC, 7 November 1833, no. 127.

102. Memorial of Tribhuvanjit Singh to C.T. Metcalfe, Dy. Gov. in Council, n.d. in NAI, FPP, 16 December 1831, nos. 91–2.

103. Commr. Manipur (Capt. Grant) to AGG, NEF, 4 December 1832, BPC 7 January 1833, no. 89; AGG, NEF to Secy Govt, 18 October 1833,

BPC 7 November 1833, no. 123; for Marjit Singh, see Urzee to the GG along with that of his son Jogendrajit Singh in NAI, FPP, 20 March 1834, nos 38–9; re Pitambar Singh, see Resident at Ava to Secy GOI (W.H. Mcnaghten), 1 September 1836, BPC 7 November 1836, no. 48, and Jaibir Singh Jubaraj to AGG, 30 March 1844, NAI, FPP, 13 April 1844; Jogendrajit Singh to GG in Council, 15 April 1836, BPC, 6 June 1836, no. 176; for his arrest and escape with armed band of 20–30 followers, see Political Agent Manipur to Mgte Sylhet, 2 December 1837, NAI, FPP, 3 January 1838, no. 83; for advances of cash to clear 400 bighas of jungle in Kachar made to Tribhuvanjit Singh, see correspondence in OIOC, BC F/4/1874/79717, and Tribhuvanjit Singh to Dy Govr of Bengal in Political Letter from India, 3 July 1840, no. 49, F/4/1869/79498; for the attempt of Purbitter Singh, Khairaba and a brother of Tribhuvanjit Singh coming from Kachar to drive out regent in Manipur and their removal to a place beyond Dhaka, see FPP, 18 October 1841, no. 58, and 25 October 1841, nos 84–85; for Tribhuvanjit Singh's murder of the Regent at Manipur, see Political Letter from India 12 October 1841, no. 53, and Political Letter to India, 26 January 1842, no. 2.

104. For description of Kumudini, mother of Chandrakirti, as 'intriguing with the four princes in Kachar named as Nug-thaw-ma-cha alias Gunadhorjo, Me-hi-khomba, Purno Singh, and Surturtha Singh commonly called Sa-Chaw-ba', see Supt Kachar to Secy GOI Foreign, 7 October and 15 October 1844, NAI, FPP, 9 November 1844, no. 121.

105. Commr Dacca to Secy GOI, Foreign, 29 October 1844, *ibid.*, no. 120.

106. Fisher to AGG, NEF, 13 January 1834, BPC 20 February 1834, no. 25.

107. Commr 16th Div to Secy GOB Judicial, 4 February 1837, BPC 27 February 1837, no. 6, encl.

108. Tribhuvanjit Singh to Dy Govr of Bengal, in Political Letter from India 3 July 1840, no. 49.

109. Supt Kachar to Political Agent Manipur (McCullock), 31 May 1852, *CDR*, 1, 214.

4

Translations of Adherence
From 'Feudalism' and 'Slavery' to 'Savagery'

THE COMPANY'S ATTEMPT TO RESHAPE monastic governmentality in the wake of its military victory over Burmese armies had the contrary effect of reinforcing it in the Brahmaputra–Meghna Valley as well in the ravines and on the plains of Chittagong and Arakan, regions gained for the Company from hitherto conjoined Burmese–Buddhist and Vaisnava administrations. Regimes in this domain were all alike in that most 'revenues' were realized in goods, produce, and labour services; no more than a third was realized in cash. All payments of administrators (doubling as members of a monastic or ritual lineage) also occurred in terms of allotments of labour services of a specific number of *paik*s and an allotment of rent-exempt land. The dilemma of the Company officials rose from the fact that they had to take over the tasks of the lay members of a hitherto monastic governmental order when they were not themselves initiated or ordained disciples of any *gosain* or monk. A series of contradictions followed that became fundamental to the establishment of colonialism as the prefiguring context for 'freedom' or liberalism.

Some of these tensions have been explored by Jayeeta Sharma for the period after 1841.[1] She argues that the East India Company government did not destroy or confiscate the land or authority of the Vaisnava gosains in Assam till the aftermath of the rebellion of 1857. This chapter places events in the Brahmaputra–Meghna Valley in an older history. It argues for a subtle and selective destruction of two aspects of monastic governments in the first half of the nineteenth century. On the one hand, Company officials sought to tax hitherto tax-exempt and military service-exempt lands and their attached labourers; they monetized the labour services and dues in kind that had hitherto made up the monastic subjects' payments to the person of their gurus, deities, and lay lords who patronized those gurus and deities. At the same time, Company officials' attempts to regulate and use hitherto monastic tenants, personal disciples, and temple servants for lay military purposes of the Company-state led to a colonial mimicry of the 'special estates' that it had sought to tame in the plains of Bengal since the mid-eighteenth century. Since 1827, Christian missionaries were invited by colonial officers to settle on some of the most productive hillsides of Assam and Bengal. These settlements were exact replicas of the endowments that Indian lay disciples had earlier made to favoured teachers and ritual experts. Alongside these missionary estates, colonial officers reinforced the rhizomic aspects of monastic geographicity when they favoured one lineage of monks over another in intra-lineage disputes: as we have seen already, since the 1830s, colonial officers decided which Manipuri Vaisnava lineage would reside in the lands around the valley, and which would be dispatched to distant Navadvip or Dhaka or Benares. After 1835, colonial governors annexed the hillside (currently Darjeeling) that had been gifted by a Sikkimese monastic lineage to the East India Company for a sanitarium to 'British territory'. Tea plantations arrived there from 1840. All lands where hitherto Bengali, Assamese, and Himalayan Buddhist and Vaisnava lineages overlapped then experienced rapid dissolution of older resource-sharing arrangements. These structural processes left their imprint in colonial languages which established the values of adherence as morally reprehensible and deplorable. Anglophone terms such as 'feudalism', 'slavery', and 'savagery' were signposts of these transformations.

A POETICS OF ADHERENCE

Chroniclers using heteroglot Bengali and Assamese had used the term *praja* for disciple-subjects of monastics (see Chapter 1). Outlines of such a politics of followership emerged in the poetic record under other terms, such as those revealed in the Bengali poem *Krishnamala* around *luchi*. In Chinese, the term *lu shih* stood for a Buddhist monk who taught monastic rules (*vinaya*) to novices. In Tibetan, however, the words *lug gnyi*s stood for 'subjects' of such teachers and gurus.

Mullard argues that the term expressed the institutionalization of the moral-political sponsorship performed by lay subjects who provided the goods and services that collectively unified and expressed the ethical and temporal authority of the guru-preceptor, his monastery and his teaching lineage.[2]

It is likely that the groups referred to in the Bengali poem under the term *luchi* also referred to the lay subjects of a monastic teacher and lineage. For *lus-sbyin* (pronounced lu-ji or lu-chi) stood for meditators who visualized the sacrifice of the body and *lus-gzhi* (pronounced lu-shi) also stood for body, and from it body-consciousness. All these were references to Tantric meditational practices. However, the poets of the *Krishnamala* also used the term *luchi* to identify a group organized as a corps (*dafa*, originally Persian for cavalry, in Nepali also known as *dapha*, a corp of singers, drummers and dancing men); the same term was also used as well as in the title of Buddhist leaders (*borua senapati*) of such devoted labour corps, such as in the title Luchidorpo Narayan.[3] This particular title was received as a reward by the commander after he had defeated the troops of another Tipra rival. This titled Buddhist warrior subsequently defeated forces loyal to a Mir Ata at a place called Dakkhinshik (in the parganah of Khandal, Kumilla) in 1760.[4] The usage suggests that the term was associated with a single person, also singular in his skill and valour. However, since the word luchi is used in this way, the entire title Luchidorpo is also liable to a literal interpretation. It means 'the Narayana [name of the god Visnu] who was the pride (*dorpo*) of the lay Tantric meditators and subjects of a Tantric leader'.

When they used luchi in a title, the poets apparently referred to a Vaisnava or Buddhist male who commanded a corps of followers. When they used Luchi dafa/*dapha* or 'corps', the same poets located them among a broad worship collective called the *Kuki-gana*, living in various parts of the bank of the Barak River. The poets identify 'Kuki-gana' in turn as a composite of fourteen clans (named Chhakaccheb, Khaamachheb, Charai, Rang, Rung, Ranghkhol, Chaibem, Chhatoi, Chhaimaar, Vanga, Langai Rufani Telpoi, Kung) of devout worshippers of the river Rufali. Equally significant for the poets was these clans' daily and periodic worship of a stone image of a ten-armed goddess riding on a lion (*Krishnamala*, 24). Four of these clans were responsible for the worship of the deity, with each clan collectively hosting the icon in their midst for three years. Should the deity wish to relocate before the requisite period of her visit was complete, she appeared in a dream to a particular member of the chosen clan. Her annual worship coincided with, but was distinct from, the poets' recognizably Sastric Hindu 'Durga worship' performed by Brahmans (39) as much as it is distinct from the Tipra's own worship of Fourteen Deities (38). The Kuki-gana's female goddess required the sacrifice of mountain cattle (*goboy*, called *goyal* in English). Many auguries and omens could be taken during such worship, said the poets.

Second, the poets placed such a collective worship community (kuki-gana) of the early 1760s as generationally related 'subjects' (praja) of the Tipra lord whose biography unfolded in subsequent verses (*Krishnamala*, 25). In a poetic move that paralleled the worship community's hospitality towards an icon, the Tipra 'lord' was described as being removed from his location north of the Barak River to the retreats of his subjects 'eastwards' whenever crisis threatened. There they offered the core of devotional subjecthood—food and service—to this Tipra lord as they did to their deity (26). However, the very substance of these relationships was translated in English under three terms in the course of the nineteenth century. The first was 'feudalism'.

ADHERENCE AS FEUDALISM

The *feodum* was a Latin legal concept for a fief, first used in English in 1776.[5] It described a system in which principal families conducted all government as lords and granted tenures to vassals which allowed them to levy militias. From the outset, such usage characterized a society of the past, especially those associated with Catholicism. The use of 'feudalism' by English speakers to describe other monastic and adherent relationships—such as the wide range of Buddhist, Sufi, Vaisnava, and other lineages and networks in a vast terrain covering Mughal Bengal and Assam—was persuasive and popular. Francis Buchanan, writing of early nineteenth-century Assamese society, in which descendants of first settlers retained 'ancient dignities, likened this to medieval Europe's "feudal government"'.[6] The term 'feudalism' thus yoked in one and the same politics of periodization the trounced religious cultures of medieval Europe with those of non-Europe. It robbed both of the potential of modernity. At least thirty years before Marx conceived of a 'feudal mode of production', therefore, officials of the English East India Company had articulated ideas of temporal and territorial supremacy over non-European cultures, using ideas of linear time and implicitly Anglican Christian lay ideas of modernity as the basis for English dominance. In early nineteenth-century southeastern Bengal, the term enhanced the politics of dispossession developed since the 1760s, for it stripped all dignity and ethics from social groups organized by monastic commitments and vows. An Anglophone translation of the poets' vision of followership and refuge, the term 'feudalism' emptied the relationship of responsibility and protection that tied disciples and gurus to each other, while simultaneously dismissing the value of the gift of sons given to a monastic order by women, or the gift of labour given by men and women of humble countenance.

As Francis Buchanan's comments revealed, Company officials used the term 'feudal' in the course of Anglo-Burmese confrontations in Chittagong–Arakan and Assam to describe the prestige of individual men in a social order shaped by the superiority of the monk. Speaking of seven classes of Rakhain (Arakanese) refugees lately arrived in Chittagong region, an official noted that the highest in rank were the 'Raowleys or Priests, second, the relations and descendants of the Royal family called rajbungshee. ... The office of washerman is always performed by a Mussulman and that of a barber by a Hindoo of which there are numbers in every Mug village both in the country and in Arracan. The Mugs divide themselves into parties, each of which is headed by a sirdar elected by themselves and whose orders are always obeyed by those contained in his party. ... In Arracan the sirdar is always of the highest rank'.[7] The social influence of the latter (*sardars*) in resolving disputes among the refugees apparently to the satisfaction of all parties made the Company's judicial structures, fees, and fines redundant at the same time that they appeared to the officers of the Company as a 'feudal system'.[8]

'Feudal' thus emerged as a label of scorn aimed at the highest social rank available in southeastern Bengal, that of the ordained monk-householder, said to be spiritually descended from the social lineage of Rahul, the son born to Siddhartha Gautama before the prince became a renunciant and achieved enlightenment (*bouddha*). Followers of this householder-prince were generally Vajrayana Buddhists: their monks were called rahulis or 'raolis'.[9] Lineages from which men were ordained or 'given' to the monastic order were believed to have earned great merit. As a result, lay members from such lineages also earned great esteem. It was as lay members that they performed critical services for the monastic lineage, both earning and donating to it cash, animals, goods, lands, and cultivators and craftsmen. Most 'kings' in the region began careers as lay members of such lineages, and reinforced their social standing and authority by further gifts to the monastic lineage after assuming high office. Descent from such kings and sardars became in turn important to recognize and remember. The groups that could claim such descent were the *rajavamsi* or ancestors, descendants, and co-parceners forming the clans and households from which both kings and rahuli monks were drawn. Sardars were influential because of this doubled connection—one with the spiritual monastic lineage and another with a network of households.

The term 'feudal' expressed colonial officials' ire at such men's social authority. These officials were responsible particularly for arresting and removing from Company lands those rebels and refugees from Arakan who were legally referred to as 'immigrants from foreign countries and their descendants', but colloquially called 'Muggs settled in Chittagong'.[10] It was the operation of this feudal system alone, an official claimed, that was responsible for the successes that the Rakhain 'rebels' had in procuring people to join them in their 'unwarrantable schemes'. It was necessary, the officer continued, to detach such emigrants from their sardars in order to break 'the bonds of feudal influence' by which they lived. These bonds allowed these hybrid Rakhain refugee clusters to be secreted as labourers on estates of landlords (zamindars) in Company-governed provinces. Yet the latter paid no taxes for the enhanced area of cultivation. Referring to the 'wilful concealment of the number of Mugs on their estates who have cleared and pay them revenue for land which they do not pay Government for', this Magistrate of Chittagong asked that such refugee 'mugs' be separated from their sardars and sanctuaries, that they be rendered into individual tax-paying units.

As with Buchanan, who had not comprehended the Tibetan-inflected languages he had heard in the same terrain a decade before, this official too did not know that the Tibetan term *muggu* stood for the occupant of a tenure specifically reserved for refugees from famine.[11] The English collector failed to appreciate the version of compassionate economics at work in the 'secrecy' and labour services he described. Significant among the names that he presented as evidence of the combination of secrecy and refuge-taking were those of Buddhist Rakhain sardars. One of these was Ishanchandra, who became a tenant in the zamindari of Krishnadas Kanungo (in thana Chakarea). He in turn settled 184 houses of 'mugs' (a total of 631 men, women and children) with fifteen sardars on these estates. A far greater numbers of households (630, with a total of 2,264 men, women, and children) with forty sardars were settled on estates that Ishanchandra held along with others in the zamindaris of 'Gourishankar and Baidyanath' at Ramu. These were Saiva sannyasi lords Gourishankar Gupta and Baidyanath Sarma, themselves recipients of gifted lands from their Tipra lay disciples. The administrators of the Company were right in suspecting that refugee Buddhist, Hindu, and Muslim clusters had found sanctuary amidst groups to which they were already affiliated by marriage and by common services and goods delivery. More important, however, was the Company official's insistence that these resettled populations, and their sardars, were tax-evaders. 'Feudal' bonds, or the relationships of monks and their protectors–disciples, hurt Company collections.

The sardars were drawn from a variety of religious backgrounds, both in Chittagong and in other places touched by Burmese armies and tribute-gathering systems (such as Manipur, Assam, Tripura, and hills of north Bengal). For instance, in the course of the Anglo-Burman war in the southern Bengal area, a magistrate of Tipperah reported that he had transported for life a 'Shambhu Thakur' who, with his brothers Kanu Thakur and Kashi Thakur, had hoisted the flag of a Balaram Deb at a market and inaugurated a new 'Raj' or government.[12] Balaram, elder brother of the deity Krishna, was also venerated by one lineage of Vaisnavas whose major centre was the Jagannath temple in Orissa. A copperplate inscription, only recently discovered in the house of ritualists in Puri, Orissa, shows that in the 1770s, a Tipura lord called Krishnamanikya had brought these priests and their icon to the capital 'Udaipur' in the coastal plains.[13] The worship of Balaram by Oriya Vaisnavas in distant Kumilla only reconfirmed monastic geographicity.

The males named—the thirty-ish Shambhu Thakur, his father, Ramchandra Thakur, and his step-brothers, Kashi and Kanu—were all members of a lineage of initiated Vaisnava monks who had contended for dominance with another lineage of initiates since the seventeenth and eighteenth centuries, ever since Mughal armies had established contracts with one group and secured tributes of elephants from it. The *Krishnamala* had gestured at this conflict by referring to the setting up of alternate centres of power with claims over proximate monastic subjects and worship communities. Their conflicts had ranged over markets and populations spread among British Sylhet, the hills that made up the not-yet-British province called Kachar, and the hills and valleys of Chittagong—and by virtue of marital contracts, with individual members and clans of power holders at Langthibal (medieval capital of modern Manipur).

A fresh set of conflicts had erupted in 1813, after a Vaisnava guru-cum-zamindar (Durgamani/Durgamanikya) died while on pilgrimage to Varanasi; he had nominated Shambhu Thakur, grandson of an earlier Vaisnava place holder to succeed to the zamindari, but had not ritually or publicly anointed the latter.[14] In the late eighteenth century, when taxes from this zamindari to the Mughal governors in Dhaka had been paid in elephants, Shambhu Thakur had been in charge of the elephant-catching operation (*kheda*) and had command of the skilled trackers and hunters trained to survive in forest and upland terrain. In 1813, unable to produce proof of the kind that would stand up to the Company court's judicial process of investigation of his title to collect goods and money from his adherents, Shambhu Thakur retreated to the shelter of his subjects in the hills of Chittagong. From there, he periodically swooped down with his adherents (named 'kukis' in the English records) on those markets which paid tolls to his rival whom the British collectors had deemed the legitimate 'raja' of Tipperah, a man called Ramganga.

In 1824, Ramganga was allied with the Company's troops in the Anglo-Burmese war. His rival, Shambhu Thakur, seized this opportunity to divert the collection of taxes and tolls from his rival to his own toll booth. Nevertheless, asked to respond to the allegation that he had proclaimed a new Raj, all that Shambhu Thakur would point to was the presence of a 'faqir' of the 'Phadung dafa' at the village of Kunchun near the hill of Sitakunda (Chittagong). He had acquired great influence 'by his religious exercises as a dervish and ... many people of the Chuckma, Mug and Tippera tribes as well as Bengalees both Moosulmans and Hindoos in the villages of Goozkhola, Nizampoor, Khundul, and other places in Zillah Tippera were in the habit of resorting to him with offering of curds and milk and fruits of every kind and that Raja Ramganga Manik of Tippera had sent him a present of Rupees 5. On hearing this I said ... I too [must] go and see what sort of Fakir he is who gives himself out under the immediate protection of the Deity'.[15]

In Shambhu Thakur's view of his actions, he was marking the terrain ruled by Krishna and Balaram, guarding it against the inroads of another potential monastic government in the making. Claims by men to be favoured by a local deity were claims to authority over the terrain and people resident there. Phadung was a monastic centre south of Prome, in mountains that separated the provinces of Ava and Arakan; military forces that took one of these routes in 1826 would report on the 'pagodas and keouns' scattered along the way.[16] A faqir and 850 disciples-followers and connections belonging to such a Buddhist centre (Phadung dafa) and led by several village headmen (such as Ram Jai Roaja, Kanta Ram Roaja) could have immediately established a monastic government, a 'Raj', elsewhere. This was not impossible. The followers had already established themselves at a fort at Oota Teela (Uttar Tila, northern hill) and received the homage of a British ally. Shambhu Thakur was carving out a terrain where such rule could not extend. The Company's collector identified this largely defensive action as an infringement of the Company-backed authority of Ramganga Manik.

Many of the suggestions in Shambhu Thakur's statement rang true to the ways in which monastic subjects were gathered and 'states' established on the basis of such monastic gatherings, on the plains as well as in hills nearby. For around the same time as Shambhu Thakur's arrest on charges of setting up a different Raj, another monk, referred to as *phoongee* (correctly *hpongyi*) by an officer in Arakan, very nearly established one near Sandoway. The effort began when the monk's adherents and followers, having developed an idea of his superhuman abilities to metamorphose 'trees and twigs into fighting men', declared the hpongyi a Raja and 'made their obeisance, and took oaths of fidelity to his cause.'[17] Only this monk's inability to magically produce the boats necessary to cross the river led his followers to desert.

Monks, sannyasis, gosains, and sufi faqirs who hailed from eminent social lineages and clans combined the power of two systems in one. Many, by virtue of being simultaneously linked to wider groups through relationships of marriage and descent, could materialize men and goods in ways that no simple individual renunciant could. Shambhu Thakur's rival, Kashi Thakur, was successful vis-à-vis the Company's tax-collecting machinery partly because of the manpower he could assemble with his marriages (first to Kutilaakhi, a daughter of the 'raja' of Manipur, subsequently also to the daughters of other Manipuri Vaisnava refugees on the plains of Bengal).[18]

Therefore, it was not ignorance of monastic politics but political and military antagonism that was evinced in comments made about such figures and their entourages from the late eighteenth until the mid-nineteenth century. The Frenchman Chevalier had reviled as impostors the monastic community that owned a temple to the goddess Durga on the river Manas: 'credulous people reward them abundantly with their copious donations. Hence they look rich', he complained in 1755.[19] On visiting a Buddhist monastery in either eastern Nepal or Sikkim a little later, he wrote indignantly of the lethargy and dissoluteness of the monastics that allowed them to accept 'donations' of rice, wheat, fruits, sugar, sheep, chicken, kids from their subjects.[20] A similar attitude was evinced by British colonial officers in the 1830s. The military officer, Lieutenant Robert B. Pemberton, dispatched to the Tibetan Buddhist *geloŋ* (pronounced *gelong*) in Bhutan in 1837–8, characterized the entire monastic order itself as a 'privileged class, whose numbers, avowed celibacy and utter idleness constitute a mass of evil under which a country of far greater natural capabilities would materially suffer'. Pemberton railed against the monasteries for having occupied all the best lands and all the resources of the country, giving nothing back in exchange. 'The time of the priests is divided between the mummery of religious worship morning and evening and occasional celebration of festivals, eating and sleeping.'[21] His companion, a Dr W. Griffiths, echoed these views completely. The 'priests or gylongs' (ordained Buddhist monks of the highest vows), he animadverted, had no other duty except to 'be idle, to feast at the expense of the country and at most to tell their beads and recite mutterings'.[22]

A mid-nineteenth-century colonial critique of monastic 'idleness' had not merely forgotten its own predecessors' praise of the educational, medical, bureaucratic, economic, and aesthetic services provided by individual monks–ascetics and priests for their subjects. It also completely ignored the physical evidence around them—the bridges and buildings built and maintained by such monastic orders, the constant trades and traffic between places and people centred on fortified monasteries (*dzongs*) in which they lived, the diplomatic, peacekeeping and information-gathering services that many married and celibate lamas and gosains had done for the colonial bureaucrats.[23]

In reality, the mid-nineteenth-century official disdain for idle feudal lords was a discussion about the constitution of a market in land and waged labour that was impeded by the monastic estates and the strength of their adherents' attachments. Colonial English discussion about the monastic economy and politics was focused on two separate parts of the same polity—people's adherence to their superiors and the latter's attachment to given pieces of land and people. The refashioning of the second had already begun in the eighteenth century and would proceed through the nineteenth. For this reason, the worship communities that heteroglot poets identified as subjects (proja) of initiated monks and guru 'lordships' were identified as 'hill savages', 'slaves' and 'tribals' by colonial officials in the nineteenth century.[24] Using a wide variety of criteria from among food-habits, sartorial styles, and above all, ritual performances, nineteenth-century British officials evinced a growing distaste for the collocated Tantric Buddhist–Saiva–Vaisnava–Islamic populations in all the terrains through which they passed. Echoing something of the Mughal emperor Jahangir's dismissal of the Tibetan-speaking Rakhain 'Mugs', the Company official in 1812 had described hybrid Arakanese refugees in Chittagong as 'in the scale of civilization but little beyond the rank of savages'. Their qualification for such status rested almost entirely on their foodways: 'they live partly on rice, but chiefly on putrid fish, pigs, alligators, snakes & in short anything they can find. The immense tracts of jungle about that part of the country furnish them with wild animals in abundance for their subsistence and with materials for building their huts, boats and making implements of all sorts.'[25] These observations created the impression of stasis for subsistence patterns that James Scott has argued were contingent responses to crises.[26]

However, rather than emphasize the contingent character of such groups, I argue that in times of crisis, subjects, and adherents of monastic orders on the plains fled to the hills *because* they had prior relationships with establishments located there. Gods, temples, and mosques were always located on elevated ground in such terrain. It was for such reasons that during 1812–15, many Buddhist and Muslim Rakhain together fled to 'the wild and uninhabited mountains between the Burmah and Assam country'.[27]

Older relationships of refuge and homage remained visible even in the comment of the nineteenth-century military officer who described villages of 'Nagas' who were 'formerly tributaries to the possessors of Kubo and who have changed masters as Manipuri or Burma influence might preponderate in the valley below'.[28] There were two possible ways of deciphering the term. One was as 'Nāga'. In Buddhist–Saiva and Vaisnava cosmologies, the term referred to serpents who guarded rivers and subterranean waters. As Willis argues, the iconographic imagination of Vaisnava kingship and ritual made the body of the Eternal Serpent (Anantanāga) a place for Visnu's cosmic rest.[29] The cosmic body of the serpent, Nāga, rested on cosmic waters, and represented them simultaneously. The agricultural calendar of humans, which began with the sowing of seed after the rains, corresponded with the awakening of the deity from his cosmic sleep, with his ability to control the waters, 'rescue' earth (imagined as a female) from those waters, and distribute uncultivated lands to those in need of maintenance. So the control of waters and the 'gift' to Brahmins (noted in Gambhir Simha's gift upon his assumption of 'kingship' in Manipur) were intimately tied to each other in the patron-protector's ability to place his adherents in the vicinity of the headwaters—on the hills.

But the term 'nāga' also referred to Tibetan words: one, naga, stood for 'yoke' and another, noga, indicated a junior member of a lord's entourage. In a context where 'dependence' upon a teacher was a value in and of itself, such usage did not imply disrespect for the persons thus described but its absolute opposite. Thus, the awe in an eighteenth-century Assamese chronicle for the 'naga' populations settled on hillsides overlooking river valleys.[30] Or the tenderness of the nineteenth-century Assamese chronicler towards the 'nogamajumdar' descended from a Brahman astrologer from Kanauj from whom the chronicler traced his own genealogy.[31] The same tenderness was thus found in the Manipuri Vaisnava Gambhir Simha's argument with a British official in 1830: the Vaisnava argued that in previous regimes (of his half-brother and predecessor Chourajit), such populations were excused all other labour tributes if they gave their labour for building roads. These rules had been common to the Tibeto-Burman world. Those who paid their dues in cash or kind did not pay in labour. Those who paid in labour did not pay in any other form.

Colonial officials too in the early 1830s knew this: thus one wrote of a group of 'Nagas' who acknowledged 'themselves exempt from tribute on condition of personal service'.[32] But it was the *personal attachment* that Gambhir Simha referred to in his advice to the colonial officers: 'the only way to discover to whom the country belongs is to ascertain who has exercised authority over or received tribute from these Nagahs; from this it will be seen whose tributaries they are'.[33] As Gambhir Simha's emphasis revealed, it was not a case of *who* the Naga were, but a case of *whose* Noga they were. The two different spellings here are deliberate. For both meanings—the adherents of a king, and the guardians of earth from water—converged in Gambhir Simha's claims.

A language of 'attached' labours, payments in kind, and exemptions therefrom was well-established language among inhabitants of the monastic geographic order of donors, donees, protectors, and subjects. Indeed, it was exactly the language that men such as the dead raja of Kachar, Govindachandra, had also used to refer to the monastic warriors or *sempung* (*dpung* was Tibetan for soldier) named Tularam, Govindram, and Durgacharan, who had led a 1,000-strong 'body of mountaineers' at Dharmapur, on the northern banks of the Kopili (a branch of the Brahmaputra) River.[34] Dharmapur was the hub of small-scale traders from Gauhati, Goalpara (westernmost Assam, geographically northern Bengal), and Dhaka (modern Bangladesh).[35] It was the market town to which many prosperous cotton-growing communities from the hills in its hinterlands repaired with their cotton. When officials went to investigate the hills and mountains of Dharmapur, they met nephews of a man called Sanandram: the latter 'has long embraced a religious life, but his nephews appear to be considered the chiefs of Hajaee.' Suggesting the identical connection between social clanship and spiritual lineage described as 'feudal' by a Chittagong official, officials in the hills of Kachar noted that the influence of the nephews was based partly on 'respect borne to Sanandram and partly to the long connexion of his family with this part of the country'.[36]

Groups that nineteenth-century British officers called Angami Naga, viewed from the perspective of a Tibetan-speaking Vaisnava lord (such as Gambhir Simha), dissolved into Tibetan *ŋogä + mi* or 'men who constituted the retinue of' a lord. From a Vaisnava lord's perspective, claiming men in one's entourage acknowledged the lord's dependence on its members. The effort by particular gurus to retain such regiments and regional dormitories often pitted one temple or monastery against another. Such disputes had been a staple of the eighteenth-century political economy (Chapter 1). In the nineteenth century, similar disputes about the ownership of paiks and areas of land persisted in the same context. These contested attachments surfaced in the poetic literature referred to already, as well as in the early colonial records. Some lords tried to lure other lords' subjects away and retain them on their own estates as cultivators, herdsmen, trappers, and craftsmen for the holder's own ordination or domestic lineage and khel. For such reasons, groups descended from eighteenth-century Tipra forces who had invaded Manipur 'upward of a hundred years ago', were found in the 1830s in distant villages, between the hillock called Langthabal (Manipur) and regions further to the east bound by the Ningthi River (Burma).[37]

Colonial decisions in the nineteenth century continued these conflicts within and between the same households and patron-protector clans. For instance, there was a dormitory of people officials identified as 'Kuki' but who were otherwise 'known under the general name of Tunghum' (a place-name), originally dependents of a raja of Tippera.[38] These service providers were lured away by an affine from Manipur. The raja of Tippera could provide no written documents but asked the Company officials to ask living witnesses and to refer to the neighbours—the rajas of Kachar and Jayantia. The last-named, Raja Ram Singh of Jayantia, agreed, saying that he always understood Tanghum to be 'included in the Raj of Tippera'.[39] However, Tungum was in a region (foothills of mountains, or 'Kachar') which colonial officers had handed over to the administration of the Vaisnava Gambhir Singh in the 1830s. Thereafter, officials found, their nominee had driven a group of Tipra subjects—a 'body of Kookies consisting of 250 families', or a group of a 1,000-odd souls, from 'Tanghum' farther northwards.[40] These clusters had been settled, under Gambhir Singh's 'protection' at Chandrapur, at the place in the hills that he claimed was a sacred 'gift' estate that descended to him patrilineally. Officials of the Company referred to these resettled subjects as *khonjai*.[41] Therefore, it was said of these Khonjais at Chandrapur that among this group was a 'traditionary report of these people having been at one time tributary to the Raja of Tipperah—they are now so to the Rajah of Manipur ... despite the much greater distance of these villages from Tipperah than Munnipore.'

Gambhir Singh's relocation of particular dormitories from their southern locations to northern ones in the foothills (Kachar) in the 1830s outlined a pattern in which the mobility of particular clusters of households was tied to the biographies of their monastic leaders. A local informant spoke of the corps thus relocated as the Thadoi Khyong (Thado hkyaung), whose labours belonged to the Vaisnava monasteries at Majuli/ Mayuli, a famous island in the Brahmaputra River, home to many Vaisnava establishments. This cluster of monastic subjects, said one informant, during 'the reign of Raja Gambhir Singh came up from the south and settled within the Manipur boundary, that it had then given annually a gong and an elephant's tusk as tribute to the Raja, that it had removed from the Manipur territory to the western side of the Barak and settled on the Bhobun Hills.'[42]

The second move of this labour corps, however, was part of what appears to be a Manipuri clan effort to unseat Tularam Senapati, the man selected by the Company to administer the northern hills and resented by the household of Indraprabha (see Chapter 3). A corps that owed loyalty and labour to Buddhist–Vaisnava men such as Gambhir Simha, Pabitra Simha, and others was not the band of simple 'savages' that official language might mislead some into thinking. Yet as this evidence also revealed, conflicts between different members of the same monastic ordination lineage, or between different groups of lay subjects of such monastic lords and establishments, were also historical features of the landscape of monastic subjecthood.

Company officials, put in the position of deciding such disputes in the aftermath of the Burmese war, increasingly based their decisions on fiscal grounds, rather than on any great principle of either propriety or precedent. Thus, in keeping with the growth of Company-held and sponsored estates in the Brahmaputra–Meghna Valley after 1827, it was no surprise that one of the great goals of the Company regime was to wean away labour-service providers from their monastic lords to service in the Company's estates and armies.

DISCIPLES AND ADHERENTS AS 'TRIBES', 'RACES', AND 'SLAVES'

The journals of a Captain (later Colonel) Francis Jenkins travelling between Bengal and Assam in 1831 provide a glimpse into colonial officials' ambitions. The officer had been carried on the backs of porters (*coolies*) delivering labour services to local lords. But in Jenkins' diary, they are described as 'tribes of Kukis'. He found them 'really most willing and good tempered … part of a race that inhabit all the immense tracts between Arakan and this and from numbers, courage and superior skill in weapons of war they are a formidable nation—now divided unfortunately and nearly useless to mankind.'[43] Like the Company's tax-collecting officials in Chittagong who had seen the need to disrupt the 'feudal bonds' of Rakhain refugees and their leaders, Jenkins too was irritated to find these groups attached to a small boy—'a little scabby dirty ill-fed and ill clad child of 5 or 6 years'—as their 'sardar'. He also found these transport labourers 'miserably enslaved to the Munnipuris' (that is, Vaisnava men) and hoped they would escape from their present masters. 'They would be most useful men for cutting timbers-bamboos-grass etc and invaluable porters', Jenkins confided to his journal in 1831.[44]

He had the identical characterization of groups he called 'races' of 'Nagas'. Referring to the fertile and well-drained lands of Kachar, he urged that the establishment of total 'command over these races' was essential to the conversion of the rich resources of its forests by capitalists.[45] Instead of providing labour services to others, Jenkins thought, the Nagas, who were 'an invaluable race of porters' needed to be secured to the British Government. The redirection of labour services of adherents away from monastic leaders (*gosains*, *gohains*, *sardars*, etc.) to British colonial military and economic enterprise was therefore implicit in the discourse of liberty and freedom that such officers articulated. Attempts to liberate the 'enslaved' families of such adults from their infantile attachments as well as from their 'feudal' masters led to humiliating encounters between British colonial officers and erstwhile monastic lords in the 1840s.

Some of these encounters occurred particularly in the Brahmaputra Valley after 1838 and involved groups of monastic estate workers identified as 'hill tribes' by officials confronting a thriving monastic economic network across the hills around Gauhati, crowned with one or two little temples, all still well-endowed and in good repair and inhabited by Vaisnava ministers and mahantas.[46] The populations who lived on the hills that ringed the valleys were people the officers called 'hill tribes'. These hill tribes, one wrote, occupied a prominent place in all statistics of the province, either due to their 'contribution largely to population and *tillage* of the valley, from the *trade* they maintain with the Assamese, the hostile incursions they still make upon their unsuspecting neighbours, the treaties of *tribute* and *alliance* that unite their interests with Government, the stern neutrality of their policy towards strangers or the determined resistance to all ingress into the interiors of their country.'[47] As my emphasis highlights, this surgeon had identified these groups as economic and military actors.

Most important among these had been the group this officer, the surgeon John M'Cosh, called 'Booteas' (Bhutanese), groups famous for their terraced cultivation, and allied with the ancient Assam government to secure rice by irrigation on the plains. These allotments were called *dvars*; sovereignty over these allotments was shared, with the Bhutanese holding them for the greater part of the cultivating cycle of eight months, and the Assamese holding it for the remaining four months. The surgeon granted that those who grew opium on the strip of alluvial land along the northern banks of the Brahmaputra and bartered it for grain with the Assamese were '*Miris*' (another Tibetan term of reference to a generic hillmen's collective).[48] He called traders from northern Tibet *Abors*. This was an abbreviation of *a.bod.hor*, a term in Tibetan that was always used to refer to nomadic populations from northern Tibet, and sometimes euphemistically referred to as 'older relatives from the north' or Mongolia. They brought musk,

musk deer skins, vegetable dyes and poisons, ivory and copper pots obtained from the 'lama country', and descended from the south face of the Himalayan mountains to Sadiya every winter and departed in spring ('when the Simula tree blossoms').[49] The trade mart of Sadiya was the main revenue-generating centre, surrounded by a people called the 'Kangtis'(correctly Khams-te, or people from eastern Tibet). In the surgeon's account these were the most 'civilized of all these mountain tribes'; they were all Buddhists, though 'Hinduism was gaining ground'.[50] Even the so-called 'barbaric' Mattak Raja, who had the office of Bara Senapati, was a 'Hindoo'.[51]

M'Cosh had no problem in identifying the 'hill tribes' as Buddhists; the largest proportion of their populations was 'gelums in monkish celibacy'. He understood clearly that the 'Dharmaraja' was both a sovereign of the people and a spiritual guide and worshipped as a 'god who never died', that all his subjects were also his disciples.[52] Therefore, colonial official deployment of the term 'tribes', especially after the dissolution of Company monopolies of trade in 1833, coded a discussion of the most cost-effective ways of managing colonial gains of authority over populations hitherto structured by relationships of adherence. The coded nature of the discussion can be understood best if one places such discourse in the context of the official attempts in the same years to mimic the very monastic estates that they had sought to tax on the plains of Bengal in the late eighteenth century.

The white-wearing peoples of the hills (*koh-i-Garuwan*) north of Sylhet who had fought Mughal armies in the seventeenth and eighteenth century (Chapter 1) illustrated this process well. These hills were flourishing cotton-growing areas in addition to providing very good serge cloth for cold weather from the huge herds of sheep that the Frenchman Chevalier noticed in the mid-eighteenth century.[53] In the Frenchman's estimation, the wool was a lot finer and of better quality than the wool found in Europe. But the people who made it refused to compete with each other or to trade with the Frenchman. Frustrated by the refusal of a man he called 'king of Assam' but who was more likely a Buddhist monk of a Tibeto-Sikkimese lineage, the Frenchman went on a killing spree against peacocks and found instead, a people he called 'the Garo'; these people were 'formerly part of the kingdom of Assem and are now dependent on Rangamatty, their caste is unique in itself. ... They are very gentle and humane ... they came and guided me in groups and showed the ways in the mountain.'[54] Under the *pax Mughalica*, these gentle and humane people were settled on a tax-exempt ('rent-free') estate of Soondakhoollee, and were attached to a 'Mahindra Narain Choudhuri, who they hailed as their Raja and zamindar'.[55] As one of his tenants put it to a British revenue officer in the early nineteenth century, they had been subjects of the Kuribari lords since the time of the lord's grandfather; his son had induced groups of cotton growers to sell their wares at the markets established and controlled by the Choudhuris.[56] By this tenant's reckoning, the relationship between the subjects and the lord did not yield a fixed sum of money as tribute, but varied from Rs 20–400 in a year. The present lord, Mahindra Narain, had similarly asserted that the sum was a matter of annual negotiations with the six hundred houses in the estate, and such negotiations depended on the state of the crops.[57]

In the late eighteenth century, Company regulations against the movement of Catholic Portuguese and Frenchmen, Greek Orthodox, and Armenians in the most productive areas of the erstwhile Mughal domain had enabled the Company to establish a strong hold over these cotton-growing populations north of Sylhet. After the Permanent Settlement of revenue in 1793, the Choudhuris, unable to pay the cash demanded by the Company, found these lands put up for auction. By 1809, the lands were bought by a new zamindar who found the attachments of local cultivators to their old landlord an impediment to his collection of taxes. He is said to have organized a fatal attack on the house (or Rajbari/ mansion) of Mahindra Narain and wiped out all the members of the family.[58] Presuming that the murderers were a platoon of 'savages' collectively called Garos, the officers of the Company devised a punitive measure to bring these cotton cultivators to heel. They were barred from bringing their cotton to markets such as at Singimari on the river below, where they had earlier bartered it for grain and salt. By 1822, a Regulation X had separated the dwellers of cotton-growing uplands from their acknowledged but distant lords.[59] The 'Garrow Mountaineers and other rude tribes', said the legislation, were to be liberated from their dependence on the zamindars of British provinces and to be governed by a 'special system' of government with no reference to the Regulations of the Company's government.

The 'special system' was nothing other than a colonial mimicry of an Indic and Asian pattern of monastic governments that Company officials knew only too well. David Scott, the administrator at Rangamati (Goalpara), knew the economic value of these hills: the high land was much richer, 'if we may judge from the colour, than is usual in Bengal'.[60] In 1827, just after the end of the Burmese war, he had settled 500 households of Tibetan-Burman prisoners of war in Singimari on the hills north of Sylhet with advances of a few agricultural tools. He had then asked the Church Missionary Society for a clergyman. In his letter to the missionary society, Scott asked that this clergyman be given a house and a school where weekly markets were held for the exchange of cotton brought down from the hills. The main qualifications that were sought in the missionary were neither moral nor theological achievements but mechanical and agricultural expertise.[61] These, hoped Scott, would enable the missionary to point out to these cotton growers such obvious 'improvements and simple mechanical inventions' that would stabilize the cotton production of these hills. Currently, this cotton was grown in two-year swidden fields on hill slopes whose inclines ensured that rains washed away fertile top soils and forced cultivators to open new fields, leaving old ones fallow. If the missionary could develop a system of damming up the hill-streams and rivulets where required, and cut the sides of the hills into steps, then such losses could be avoided and good crops ensured, independently of the vicissitudes of season.

In the 1820s, the Company's officers had not directly supplanted the Buddhist–Vaisnava monastic estates as replicated it on these hills, with only one difference: instead of favouring all groups, as previous lay sponsors had done, colonial officials only sponsored clerics they could control. These happened to be from working-class populations from whose ranks were drawn British and American Baptist missionaries. Such deployment of dissenters by Company administrators had been sanctioned in 1793, when the charter of the Company had called for the advance of 'useful knowledge' and 'religious and moral improvement' of the inhabitants of British dominions in India. As Powell puts it, even the prohibition on missionizing activity till the 1790s had been ineffective on the ground, since chaplains were 'embedded' in all Company military battalions from the outset and had been actively disseminating copies of the gospels. By the 1820s, a generation of civil and military officers sympathetic to evangelicalism were in positions of authority across northern India.[62] There was substantial continuity then in the 1830s–50s when colonial officials invited Dissenting churchmen to especially productive zones gained from the Burmese monastic governments. A note from the 1830s in the American Baptist offices made the same point: it referred to the same populations ('Garo' hillmen) as the most important economic producers of the region.[63] The hills, said this note, bore the burden of one-tenth of the whole revenue collected from British Assam or an annual sum of Rs 50,000. The products that came from the hills were precious: naming the great revenue earners of Company trade, the lac, cotton, madder for dyeing red, ivory, skins, and timber as 'products raised by the rude tribes', this officer calculated that at least a fifth of the revenue was therefore dependent on the 'rude tribes'. Contrary to all the precolonial and eighteenth-century notices of the same populations—such as evinced in the poetry and the chronicles—from 1833 on, officers such as Jenkins claimed that these populations had neither caste nor Brahmans. Of Tantric–Vaisnava and Bon-Buddhist groups, officers wrote: 'the Nagas like the Garrows … have no priesthood and nothing like a received religion and there are consequently no religious prejudices to oppose or offend'.[64] Since Vaisnava and other 'priests' elsewhere had resisted colonial-style 'improvements', their presumed absence from the hills brought great hope to newly arrived colonial officers. The patronage of American Baptist missionaries coincided with their hopes for the expanding empire.[65] Such patronage also extended to the grant of land: in 1840, American Baptist missionaries N. Brown and Miles Bronson were granted a 100-pura land grant on a gently sloping hill on the north bank of the Buri Dihing River for the cultivation of tea.[66]

CONTRADICTIONS OF CALLING ADHERENCE 'SLAVERY': INVERSION OF SACRAL MANUMISSION IN ASSAM

Official attempts to replicate Indic monastic governmentality on the ground also conduced to the convergence of Christian missionary and lay British official discourse which classified disciples of Buddhist monks and Vaisnava gurus as 'slaves'. Such a characterization was not new. Chevalier had referred to the subjects of a Bijni raja, himself a disciple of Bhutanese monks, as 'slaves'; he had complained that the policies of these Buddhist–Vaisnava governments made their subjects loath to labour.[67] The reorganization of the economy on the south bank of the Brahmaputra River in 1833–8, however, brought the colonial administrative officers into a head-on confrontation with a dual structure of labour services that the Company did not have sufficient familiarity with. This was a structure in which servants were either attached to the person of a lay lord or to the lands held by monasteries, temples, and icons themselves.

As scholars of both medieval Burma and southern India have found, the slaves of the temples were especially exempt from labouring for lay lords, either king or commoner.[68] In eighteenth-century Burmese regimes as well as under the Ahom, exemption from labour service for military purposes was a significant privilege permanently available to the slaves of the monasteries (*hpaya-kyun*). In Assamese societies, cultivators, artisans, and merchants who were exempt from military service were *chamua,* identified as a 'more respectable class of the population'; those who remained liable to military labour services were the *kanri/ kari*.[69] Furthermore, the system favoured exemptions as a whole by a system of cash commutations of labour obligations. In some parts of Assam (such as the very prosperous Kamrup), even those paiks attached to temples may have commuted military obligations at the rate of Rs 1 per man per year, or Rs 5 per *got* of four paiks; of this sum Rs 2 were said to be received by the governor of the province, while Rs 3 went to the service of the temple.[70] The same kind of commutation may have been available to those who were obliged to provide military labour to lay lords. Those kari paiks who belonged in prosperous khels could secure exemptions from labour services by offering cash. Workers in brass and bell-metal were said to have commuted for cash at the rate of Rs 5 per head. Gold-washers (*sonwals*), even more prosperous and spread out across many rivers and working in three or four types of gold, commuted their liability at Rs 7 per head or half a tola of gold in lieu of money. Colonial officers called such commutations 'poll tax' or 'capitation tax'.

Some of the British colonial officers knew that paiks gifted in perpetuity to temples, gosains, spiritual advisers, sattras (monasteries), and brahmans were exempt from both military or other labour services to laymen. In lands north of the Brahmaputra, paiks attached to temples, gosains, or spiritual teachers and 'brahmans' were designated *bhugguts* (*bhakta* in Sanskrit); when attached to individual nobles, themselves disciples of monks and gurus, they were called *laguah* or *likshoo/ lickchoo/ likchau*.[71] In 1825–6, in the course of a famine generated by the Anglo-Burman conflict, the Company's administrator at Goalpara, David Scott, had allowed individual kari paiks to offer themselves as personal attendants (*laguah/ likshu*) to eminent individuals fleeing from Burmese-held Assam to Company-held Bengal.[72] Even after Assam and Arakan were transformed from being juridically 'Burmese' to British terrain after 1826, the Company administrators in Goalpara did not respond with any degree of alarm. In 1828–9, colonial officials in Calcutta were prepared to forego claims to erstwhile labour-liable men who had become exempt from military labour by virtue of offering themselves for the rest of their lives to eminent individuals.[73] But the Court of Directors in London objected to this proceeding because they thought Scott had allowed men to become 'slaves': it was 'revolting to moral feelings of Englishmen'. Henceforth, the Directors asked the Company officials to investigate all such 'self-sales' to pay arrears of revenue. Thereafter, all arrangements involving the payment of personalized labour services by tenants and under-tenants were described as forms of either slavery or bondage. The labour-service regime devised by Gambhir Singh became part of such colonial enquiries into the 'slavery' of all Manipuris who performed military service in the Arakanese ('Mug') corps.[74]

Metropolitan sensitivities to trans-Atlantic discourses of abolition especially impinged on the provisioning of the monastic lineages spread all over the Brahmaputra and related river valleys of Assam and Manipur after 1833. Noticeably, Englishmen called the military labour corps constituted of monastic subjects 'slaves' labour; their movements across various territorial units was then described as criminal activity, either that of piracy or as 'slave-trade'.[75] In Kamrup, an administrative division containing at least thirty-seven well-endowed temples and a minimum of 386 monasteries, the officer who was in charge of the census referred to the paiks as 'servants' of the deities': they held rent-exempt lands (*devottar* and *brahmottar*) scattered over the entire province, but he referred to them as 'Sudras' and 'virtually the slaves of the temple'.[76]

Baptist missionary encounters with monastic disciples and adherents both echoed and strengthened official discourse on slavery all over the Brahmaputra–Meghna river system. American Baptist missionaries passing through Company-governed Akyab and Arakan in 1836 characterized the 150 families attached to the monastery lands the 'slaves of the pagoda' Shwedagon, but noted that they had become such 'chiefly by being given to some pagoda by a great man, as a *meritorious offering*. Sometimes they are malefactors whose punishment is thus commuted. More generally they are unoffending inhabitants of some district, whose prince or ruler, for any cause, chooses to make such a donation.'[77] If their descriptions remind us of the persistence of patterns of antiquity spoken of in the epigraphs and charter of the eighteenth century, these descriptions also establish the fact that these consecrations were grants of permanent manumission, of permanent 'freedom' from punishment and debt or whatever other obligations they owed to laymen.[78] The 'meritorious' nature of the donor's deed lay in this very gift of freedom. In keeping with such patterns of sacral manumission, the oblates thus given to the temples and monasteries of Assam were neither poor nor despised, nor were the localities in which they lived segregated. Besides these 'gifts', there were others around the temples and residential complexes who performed various services for the monastic order within and without the temples. In the case of particularly orthodox lineages whose monks did not touch money, these non-ordained and lay servants—'retainers'—received the money offerings of followers, went to market, and exchanged surplus gifts of clothing, mats, boxes, and so forth, for other necessities.

But many of the missionaries, unaware of the sacral and permanent nature of manumission they had observed, proceeded to demand freedom for these 'slaves' from their gods and monasteries. In 1836, Nathaniel Brown, an American Baptist missionary stationed at the easternmost market town of Assam on the Brahmaputra River (Sadiya), reported on men from northern hills (that is, eastern Tibet) who came to the British cantonment to demand the return of 'two slaves, an Assamese father and a son' who had escaped to the British. Lauding the refusal of the British to give them up, Brown likened the caps, feathers, skins, long spears, and knives carried by the Bhutanese militia as those of 'savages much resembling the North American

Indians'. Yet these groups lived in the vicinity of the monasteries, from where a young monk had recently laid aside his 'yellow cloth' in order to learn English from the missionaries; this monk had been renamed Elijah.[79]

Missionary Baptist accounts in particular converged with the liberal economic ideals espoused by their colonial military patrons in the later 1830s and 1840s. Speaking of the 800 disciples (bhaktas/ bhokots) of a Vaisnava abbot (*mahanta*), such a missionary noted that these disciples had originated from all sorts of caste and occupational backgrounds, but considered themselves bound to the establishment for life, with their wives and children, in 'the capacity of slaves and bondsmen'. What really irked the reverend was that, unlike the African slaves that they were familiar with, these adherent estate workers did *not* work round the clock but only when the monastic lords required their services. This system, he declared, was made possible by the structure of endowed lands. Referring particularly to the Vaisnava monastic estate's 'whole thousands of poorahs of land … a waste jungle', this missionary charged that the endowments had 'encouraged a great body of people in idleness'.[80]

Convergences of discourse notwithstanding, only military official governors were accountable to their superiors in London for generating cash surpluses from newly annexed social groups in the vast Assam of 1833–8. This was a difficult task in a terrain in which most transactions did not involve substantial movements of bullion. Additionally, all the colonial administrators of Assam after 1833–8 were military officers. Military concerns about the absence of standing professionalized armies in the newly annexed regions, the absence of a structure of cash wages and salaries, and the absence of intensive cultivation of the soil emerged in these officers' correspondence on the many 'failures' of a monastic government resting on labour dues and labour exemptions, corporate liabilities, and corporate delivery systems. From the outset of colonial annexation of the Brahmaputra Valley, the basis of taxation was changed from labour service to cash taxes, from maximalist units of the corporate occupational and clan groups (khels) to minimalist units (households) and clusters of households ('villages').

As on the plains of Bengal, the first to be destroyed were exemptions from labour. Post-annexation colonial officials were especially keen to attach all military service–provider kari paiks to the military service of the Company. Many monastics, oblates, and novices were exempt from military labour (as *chamua* paiks) when they were permanently attached to temples and gosains. In Upper Assam, home to the erstwhile raja of Assam Purandhar Simha, substantial exemptions were offered to such paiks.[81] The soil here was very rich, and grew sugarcane, cotton, and rice, but all cultivators were organized in clusters (khels), some of which contained between 500 to 2,000 people, with their own officers (*boras*, *sykias*, *hazaris*, under a senior or *kheldar* who was generally a nobleman related to the royal family). Formally, every paik assessed at Rs 3 per head was said to hold a basic unit of land with which he raised the sum; if he failed, he delivered labour service. The kheldar of the khel he belonged in collected the goods or services and delivered it to the Treasury.

Colonial officers were concerned by the social and political effects of exemptions that allowed members of such bodies (*ryots*) to be distinguished from the mass of other workers. Their earlier attachments to monastic estates had secured them remissions during distress and commutations of receipts in kind for money payments. Such remissions were not given to cultivators on tax-paying estates (*khiraji*) held by the colonial government. Colonial officers feared that people would desert tax-paying government estates to tax-exempt monastic estates. Something like this had already happened in 1826 to Purandhar Simha, who the Company had selected to be 'king' of Assam on the basis of his willingness to pay Rs 50,000 annually to the Company's government in cash. But the pressure to monetize older attachments translated badly in domains with abundant arable land, many of which were owned and managed by the clerical administration of particular monasteries. The transition from one regime to another proved unworkable for Purandhar Simha, from whose estates large numbers of erstwhile paiks migrated to lands held by the elderly ascetic Vaisnava Bara Senapati.[82] The latter had a large following that the colonial records refer to as 'Moamaria'.

Neufville, the military officer who had arrived among such a population living on the banks of the Brahmaputra near the famous Majuli Island, had simultaneously referred to them as 'Hindus worshippers exclusively of Vishnu' and as 'negligent of the proper observances and religious opinions of their faith … nearly as much addicted to plunder as the wild tribes surrounding them'.[83] This confused description obscured the relationship of subsistence and protection that tied the Vaisnava lords to a dependence on their military and other service providers. Some among these populations were also listed as Miri battalions of archers, using the well-known 'vegetable poison to tip their arrows' that grew in the northern hillsides, living in clusters ('villages') headed by particular clan-heads or elders. The relationship between the military service corps, their clan heads, and either the Vaisnava lord on the plains or the Buddhist monk of the mountains allowed for a range of hierarchical positions. As some colonial observers knew, there was a species of service offered by 'the poorer and more destitute individuals … who when reduced to want were in the habit of selling themselves into bondage and either temporarily or for life to their chiefs or more prosperous neighbours. They sometimes resorted to this step in order to obtain wives from the daughters and in either case, were incorporated with the family performing domestic and agricultural service but under no degradation.'[84] These bonded members of the population, often junior males in their own patrilineages or orphans, married to women of the landholders in uxorilocal marriages, were *gumlao*.

Turning away the destitute constituted an ethical breach in a domain governed by Buddhist and Vaisnava strictures regarding the sustenance of the weak. Such strictures also bound the lords living in proximity to groups rooted in this ethic. The Bara Senapati was a leader committed to this ethic. In the late eighteenth century, ancestors of some of his disciples had successfully resisted paying double duties to their own Vaisnava leader as well as the Sakta Ahom Raja. When Company rule began in these regions, they paid tribute to their Vaisnava leader alone. The latter received 'presents in lieu of his settling their dispute and some portion of their labour … but little direct money taxation'.[85] The only people who paid him anything in cash were those prosperous refugees from another man's estate; yet even of these men, he asked only a third of what they would have paid in their older domains.

During the Anglo-Burmese war, British officers had asked various abbots in charge of monastic estates to supply men to the British war effort. All the estates between western Assam and northern Bengal had been asked for contributions in manpower of this kind.[86] So had the Bara Senapati. There is confusion in the records about the numbers of men he was asked to provide: one account from 1835 says 300 men, while a later account suggests that it was 300 gots or 900 individual paiks out of the 1,260 paiks over whom he had any authority. Other gosains were those who held the office and title of Sadiyakhowa (literally, the gosain who 'ate' from the earnings of the market town of Sadiya). This was a flourishing township, from where it was estimated that the quantity of tea taken away by the Chinese amounted to 40,000 maunds a year.[87] Revenues from that trade should have generated enormous sums and could raise troops and men. Other monks enjoyed the allegiance of yet others in the same vicinity. Yet, all of them received only presents in goods and occasional labour services from their devoted subjects. Colonial officers asked them to contribute military contingents of 100 men or so from among their attached subjects and tenants.

Many Gohains were unable or unwilling to supply the full labour corps they had been asked for. The Bara Senapati was one of these: he was compelled to commute for a cash payment of Rs 1,800 per year to the Company.[88] Despite this commutation of labour services into cash dues, the old Vaisnava leader did not cash in his attachments. When he died in 1838, it was discovered that there were 9,301 grown males in the area called 'lower Muttuck' in his jurisdiction, whom he had not volunteered for war. After commutation, the Bara Senapati had been expected to extract Rs 2 per head per year from these men. Instead of demanding cash from each, he had kept his adherents close to his household and its constituent members ('family'), and he had allowed various paiks to serve four months each year as personal attendants (*lixoos*) for any of the ten sons, five daughters, three widows, one brother, or other relations.[89] These were the households that were also most often accused by the colonial officers of being 'slave holders' and from whom such dependants were compulsorily 'liberated'. The substance of these liberations, as in the instance of the men attached to the Bara Senapati, was a monetary payment to the Company's bureaucracy instead of labour services to an individual Vaisnava male or his household. In 1838, when Upper Assam was annexed to British-held 'lower' Assam, southern Kachar, and Bengal, erstwhile attached paiks (such as those of the Bara Senapati's household) were commanded to pay not 'poll taxes' to the Bara

Senapati or his descendants but to pay a land tax to the Company.[90] The sons of the Bara Senapati were not amused.

In Sadiya itself, Tibetan-speaking Buddhist monastic lords and their lay subjects identified in the English records as 'Singfo/ Chinpha chiefs' were (*shing.pha*, a Tibetan term for wet-rice-farmer). They had responded to the Company's presence by offering to clear, fence, and guard tracts of forests for tea cultivation, in exchange for guarantees that the Company would not molest their adherents or seek to drive away these adherents and refugee-settlers.[91] Many of these adherents were also refugees of the kind seen in Arakan-Chittagong in the early nineteenth century. These resettled clusters of families owed either goods in kind ('tribute') or labour services ('feudal service') to their hosts, some of whom were the zhing.pha sardars, as well as to the Sadiyakhowa Gohain. The latter was a more austere monastic and literary figure who knew Bengali and had abjured the tantric customs of meat-eating and alcohol for a purist Vaisnava discipline.[92]

Having defined all forms of attachment as 'slavery' per se, the colonial officers found they were trapped. They could not offer the guarantees sought by the heads of clans and monastic adherents. The strength of the anti-slavery movement in Britain was great, the numbers of abolitionist members of the English middle classes growing, and their views vociferously expressed in the British and British Indian press and pulpit of the 1830s. Besides, the Company itself needed freely available labourers. So an officer of the Company refused to return those refugees when some of them drifted into the British cantonment at Sadiya in 1836. Their resettlement under Company governance was to be hailed as 'freedom'. By 1836, one estimate put the numbers of 'slaves' freed among the shing.pha (in English 'Singhpho' and Khangtis) at 10,000.[93]

The guarantees sought by their monastic leaders were not offered. All these groups—the lineal descendants of the Vaisnava Bara Senapati as well as of particular orders and estates—had the identical relationships with 'wealth'. Their wealth lay in the numbers and depths of attachments and adherence, not lands per se. Company-led attempts to detach adherents of such households resurrected the spectre of despoiling and impoverishment that, under earlier dispensations, had led to serious disputes between different ordination lineages, monastic and temple lords, and their military supporters-patrons. In 1838–9, the greater part of the populace from Kham and their lay lords attacked the buildings of the Company's military outpost and killed the political agent stationed there.[94] This inaugurated a movement by northern sardars which continued through the 1840s.[95]

As the repetitious discourse on slavery and feudal idleness revealed, colonial administrators were faced with a determined monastic geographic order. Even when colonial governors co-opted dissenting missionaries as junior partners in colonial governance of Assam, the results were no more amenable to the establishment of a capitalist Eden than they had been in pre-1826 Assam. For after two decades of declaiming Christ, a missionary lamented that the same populations he called Miri were so attached 'to the priests who have made them disciples' that they refused to convert.[96]

THE LURE OF FREEHOLDING AND THE EROSION OF MONASTIC TENANCY

After 1838, as in Bengal so in the greater Brahmaputra Valley system, hitherto tax-exempt lands held by monastic estates and bodies became gradually liable to direct taxation by the Company's government. Officials hoped that in the process, erstwhile adherents, ordained junior monks and their disciples (*shishya*), and kinsmen would become expected to become 'owners of the lands in full proprietary rights' and would pay to the Brahmans and Buddhist lords only miniscule sums. The government was willing to sanction these.[97]

Colonial taxation policies set about creating a market in land. This in turn impinged on the different groups of ordained-lay relationships that made up the community around each temple and monastic lineage. We can appreciate this by understanding the way that the sattras functioned in Kamrup in the early 1830s. It was usual, said the officer in charge, to find on one spot 'a noble house of vast dimensions erected for the accommodation of travellers and the poor, and where worship is daily performed, and alms daily distributed'.[98] The bhaktas (junior disciples and ordained monks of Vaisnava orders) lived close by. These men were individually exempt from capitation taxes, but each paid a little something as 'house tax', and together with others assumed responsibility for the cultivation of dharmottar lands. Similar collectives (khels) worked sattra-held but otherwise tax-exempt boats, markets, looms, and so on, and were thus similarly attached to distant monastic centres and lords, even as they were managed by a representative appointed by a temple or lineage. This was also common to the Tibetan Buddhist orders, in which monastics managed, and the clans from which such monks emanated farmed, deity-held lands, paying rents for such farms to the temple or monastery treasuries. It was this structure that now had to be reorganized in favour of a Company that was neither a Buddhist nor a Vaisnava lord.

As in the plains of Bengal, exemptions were the first to be diminished. Colonial officers believed that the Burmese interregnum had completely destroyed all exemptions operable under Ahom kings.[99] Pending a fuller enquiry, Scott had already begun taxing gosain-held lands at 5 annas per plot (*poorah*).[100] The process of doing away with monastic exemptions altogether was speeded up in Kamrup and Nowgong after 1833. Acreage enjoying tax-exempt status amounted to half the cultivated area in the former and was almost the whole arable in the latter division in 1833–5. Large acreages of tax-exempt lands did not fit the new administration's goal of establishing saleable property in land so that the industrious would gradually acquire larger possessions and raise themselves in society, while the less industrious and their progeny would become labourers or emigrate to the 'waste tracts'.

The earliest region to be reorganized was called Darrang, on the northern bank of the Brahmaputra. The largest division in this, Desh Darrang, had been home to members of the same lineage that held Kuch Bihar and Bijni Raj in the seventeenth and eighteenth centuries. Under the Ahom lords, these rajas had continued to exercise some jurisdiction here and enjoyed rent-exempt tenures in exchange. In addition to this, 'some hundred years ago', said the Company officer, 'the Ahom Rajas had granted the entire tract of territory to the Bhutan Raja' (a monastic called Desi 'Deb Raja'; see Chapter 2) to enable his subjects to cultivate rice and other necessities which could not be produced in the mountains, in consideration of which the Bhutias would pay an annual tribute of mountain products to the Assam Raja, such as horses, gold, and cloth. From 15 June to 15 October, the Assam Raj held the lands, but for the majority of the cultivating year of eight months, the land was held and cultivated by the Himalayan lords.

These lands, also spoken of as the dvars or gateways, were broadly 220 miles in length between the Dhansiri River on the east and the Tista River on the west. They made up the richest and most fertile plains of Bengal and Assam. The lands were particularly well suited for irrigated rice cultivation, and the most common kind was a coarse (red) kind, not favoured by the urbane Bengali. Alongside rice, there were valuable other products such as cotton, opium, tobacco, sugarcane, raw (*munga*) silk, and lac produced in Darrang.

Under agreements made in the eighteenth century, soldiers attached to the Himalayan monastic forts had been allowed to collect small sums in kind from the cultivators on estates on the Assam plains. Detachments of males from Himalayan societies had provided military assistance to Ahom lords and been awarded the right to provision themselves also with goods from subject villages attached to the Ahom lords. These hill-based detachments, like the monastic representative and zinkaf, also came to the plains each February and collected the articles (produce, rice, sugar, cloths) to which they were entitled. This is what Company officers called 'blackmail' (*posa*). In the official records of the time, their collectors were referred to as 'Bhutias, Akas, Dufflas'. But such arrangements were common everywhere along the Brahmaputra Valley system. Moreover, under the Ahom compromise, the Himalayan lords' subjects also brought down gold, musk, blankets, rock salt, and ponies to barter for the products of the plains—such as rice, broadcloth, liquor, and dried fish. So the goods in kind that were collected from populations on the plains estates were hardly the unjust taxation that the Company's officers believed they were. These arrangements were part of older diplomatic as well as ongoing monastic diplomacies and governmental arrangements. The process of reformulating these total relationships that tied together plains and Himalayan monastics also occurred as a discursive tussle about subjecthood.

FOREGROUNDING TERRITORIAL FRONTIERS: MAKING MONASTIC SUBJECTS 'BRITISH'

The attempt to collect taxes from cultivators on the Brahmaputra plains necessitated that the region be first rendered into an exclusive domain for the operation of British laws. In 1833, 'frontier making' began in earnest along the long strip of lands lying between the

Brahmaputra River and the Himalayan foothills, called Upper Assam at its eastern end and Kamrup at its western. This world, of which at least something had been known in the late eighteenth century, had been entirely eclipsed in the intervening decades. Colonial officials such as Jenkins had forgotten that in 1785 and later, their predecessors had acknowledged the claims of an entwined regime of Bon-Buddhist lordships and Vaisnava and Sakta groups arranged in minute detail all along the riverine plains of Assam and Bengal. Here, lay the estates of Ambari Falakata, in the heart of a Company-taxed zamindari of Baikunthapur, in the gift of the Deb Raja; revenues of the estate had been collected and transmitted northwards. There were other older estates such as Guma, admitted even by the records of the colonial regime to have been an estate gifted to the Drukpa Kargyupa by one Balramchand Baruah in the time of the Mughals (1159 BS or 1752 CE).

There were eleven towns or customs outposts in this strip governed by authorities in Bengal and seven outposts administered by authorities resident in Gauhati. Although all the administrators of such outposts were 'Kacharis, Assamese, Bengalees', these men owed their appointment to their intimacy with, discipleship of, the Buddhist Trongsa or Paro Penlops. These nominations were confirmed by a sanad from their Tibetan Buddhist monastic lord in charge of temporal matters, the desi (Deb Raja) who governed on behalf of the Drukpa Kargyupa hierarch (Dharmaraja).[101] Men such as the Narayans holding Sidli and Bijni estates on the Bengal plains (Goalpara especially, westernmost Kamrupa), held such sanads of appointment from the desi (Deb Raja) and exercised magisterial and judicial authority on behalf of the Himalayan Buddhist monks among their subjects living on the plains.[102] Others, such as Shib Gosain, claimed to hold a piece of land rent free under a grant of the Dharmaraja. Other deeds proved that the Bhutan authorities had leased the Cherung Forests to representatives of Bijni Raj.[103] There were three estates designated Kulling dvar, Buri Gumah dvar, and Koreapara dvar here that were especially significant. Each had a civil administrator appointed by the desi (Deb Raja).

These monastic appointees lived on the plains, collected 'tribute' in kind (rice, butter, betel-nut, cloths, dried fish, etc.) from the tenants and cultivators on the plains, and arranged for their delivery and transportation to the particular forts (dzongs) authorized to warehouse them. The Himalayan Buddhist lordships appeared to have no problems with sharing and exchanges of resources from the outset: the desi had written to the Company's governor general in 1785 that 'the zemindars of Byjumee [Bijni] make kheddas for elephants for your government and give to me cloths, oil and dried fish'. These goods were carried up to the Himalayan kingdom by men and women paying labour services to the Bhut authorities; they also brought goods back from the mountain kingdom on their backs.

Such tribute-sending and goods-receiving relationships rested on power-sharing and resource-sharing arrangements that tied many populations on the plains of Bengal and Assam to monastic orders of the Himalayan world. The produce-tribute from these monastic subjects—a majority of whom were described as 'Kachari tribes', or 'Kachari subjects' of Bhutia lords, or 'Mechis'—was realized in kind during February to March by a visiting monastic official.

Revenues in kind went northwards—on people's backs—and sustained particular members of the monastic governmental order in the Himalayan federation.[104] The revenues from Dalimkot went to the Dharmaraja, by whom it was assigned to the Kulling governor. Goods that came from other dvars were meant for other members of the monastic administration (Chamurchi and Bala was kept for Paro Penlop, Buxa was the estate of Tashichu Dzongpen, Haldibari of the Daga Penlop).[105] The Company's tax collectors calculated that these collections amounted to Rs 2,000 each year. Now that the Company's armies had proven their worth, such military assistance did not need to be paid for. They were dismissed now for being puny: 'They had no fire-arms, but occasionally use poisoned arrows … their whole numerical strength not exceeding 3000 or 4000; they are armed with a dow or long sword and bows; they are extremely poor and dependent on the plains for food. … They are said not to be renowned for feats of courage'.[106]

After 1833, colonial intransigence towards people-sharing and resource-sharing arrangements became policy. Senior officials of the Company administration objected to the obligations of maintenance (posa), which they called blackmail, that had allowed Himalayan militias to deliver military aid to particular svargadeva lineages.

Though aware that the man they called Dharmaraja was the supreme spiritual authority throughout 'the vast realms of Tartary', that Bhutan was one of the residences of the Dharmaraja, and that a conflict with authorities in Bhutan would involve the Company with nothing less than an eventual war with China, Company administrators thought that the lack of a professional Bhutanese army and the general Tibetan dependence on the products of the Bengal and Assam plains would ensure the upper hand for the Company's troops.[107]

Furthermore, the remissions and exemptions that all monastic holders of estates in the plains offered to their subjects (also noted in Assam in the 1830s) made the Vaisnava–Buddhist–Muslim dvars especially hospitable to hard-pressed peasants who found themselves at the receiving end of suddenly monetized tax-payment regimes of the Company in Bengal and post-1826 Assam. A colonial survey of population in the three estates of Darrang in 1835 suggested as much, counting a population of 23,000 in 5,800 houses. 'Most of the Kacharees who have deserted from Assam have settled in it,' complained a colonial tax-collector.[108] So populous were these districts that the Deb Raja had organized the houses into 'villages' each with its own headman (*thakur*) who received a small portion of land rent-free and a commission on his collections.

The greater populousness of monastic estates on the Brahmaputra Valley plains held by the Buddhist lords compared badly with the thinness of the Company-taxed lands in the same region. An officer in the Darrang division calculated that there were only sixty-nine persons to the square mile in his jurisdiction. Among the four factors held responsible for this miserably underpopulated condition of the region were: emigration of families to 'foreign states' (such as Nepal, Sikkim, Bhutan), disease, and the system of early marriages. Most important, however, in this official's eyes, was the extensive 'kidnapping' practised particularly by 'surrounding mountaineers', that is, the various groups of Sino-Tibetan and Tibeto-Burmese–speaking groups, named as Singphos/Shinpha and Bhutiahs, Akhas, Dafflas.

The unwillingness of the Company state to continue to honour the obligations that had kept preceding Vaisnava regimes closely entwined with their Buddhist and Bon partners grew out of this situation. A monastic economic system resting on exemptions for the sacred and the most potent, that treated the inheritance of sacrality as a claim to veneration and tribute payments by others, sat badly with a regime intent on private freeholding of land as the basis of taxation, and treated the amount one paid in taxes as the very basis of civic personhood, legal status, and moral worth. Rather than sharing, colonial officers began to plan the separation of the conjoined Vaisnava-Buddhist worlds. Their ire was first directed at the administrative appointees of monastic lordships, those governors (zinkafs and dzongpens) of dvars and loyalists of Himalayan lay and monastic lordships, or those who moved between the hills and plains as traders during the colder months of the year. 'Mountaineers'— with names such as Afsar, Dharma, Madhuram, and Bholanath Bura Talukdar—described as 'Kachari' in the colonial records— were admitted to be in the 'constant habit of going backwards and forwards' between the Himalayan valleys and the British territories as petty traders bartering grain and other produce for articles that were produced in Bhutan. An administrator (zinkaf), resident of the monastic stronghold Punakha, Bhutan, had also told an English administrator of the plains of 'Mongol Khasees [who] trade a good deal in Hassa [Lhasa] they occasionally go to Rungpore in Bengal by the Paree and Parogong route for the purchase of otter skins.'[109]

These movements were seasonal as well as functional. Herds of *mithan* (Asian ox), goats, and other cattle were brought down to the plains in winter and returned in spring. Trader-pilgrims and monks followed similar rhythms of movement between hills and plains, based on their commercial and ritual calendars. The same traffic continued between subjects of the Nyingmapa lineage that governed Sikkim and the market it had long handed over to the British. John Ware Edgar, on a visit to eastern Sikkim to negotiate duty-free markets for British manufactures there, noticed that there was not a day that he did not see people 'either coming from or on their way to, Darjeeling with goods, the value of which at first sight seemed quite disproportioned to the labour that had to be undergone in taking them to market'.[110]

But such going and coming irked the military administrators who administered colonial legal procedures. From the end of the 1830s, officers such as Jenkins accused the nominees and appointees of Himalayan Buddhist monks of kidnapping and enslaving (newly annexed) 'British subjects'. These appear to have been fugitives from Company tax-regimes of the plains, identified as 'criminals' in colonial law, who were sheltered in estates governed by monastic lords and their appointees. For instance, in 1835, servants from an estate hitherto taxed by the East India Company (Raja Premnarain of Kuch Bihar) took away goods from the household of one of its officers and escaped to the valley of Kalling dvar, whose governor was a subject of the Tibetan Buddhist Dharmaraja. Colonial officers demanded the return of the 'criminals' but were ignored. In an attempt to exercise colonial authority and colonial laws, the Agent of the Governor General in the North-East Frontier (AGG NEF), Jenkins, collected the dues of the Buxadvar and refused to send them on northwards.[111] In response, one of the preeminent officers of the monastic order in the mountains, the Trongsa Penlop, articulated the relational and monastic logic that constituted the antithesis of the liberal colonial market in land and people. Referring to the Ahom 'Gohayns and Gallung [*gelong*, ordained Buddhist] Brahmans', the monastic administrator asked Jenkins to release the revenues of the dvars. 'By means of that Dooar I am enabled to help and serve the Gohayns with fish, oil, tobacco &ca. By serving the Gohayns much good will result.'[112]

Tibetan Buddhist monks who articulated claims upon cultivators and traders on the plains in order to 'serve' gosains (gohayns) with consumables had acted completely in keeping with Bodhisattva ideals of the Jataka, and the Mahayana codes of maternal masculinity. The commitment to 'feed' the non-ordained, non-Buddhist 'other' was a critical part of monastic politics in the subcontinent since at least the period for which there are epigraphs. A ninth-century inscription record of a monastic (Narayanpala's) gift of a rent-free village in Tirabhukti (Tirhut, northern Bihar) to the Saiva temple at Pasupatinath (Kathmandu) for the performance of *puja, bali, charu*, and sattra of the congregation of Pasupata Saivacharyas speaks of such nurturant relationships between a Bouddha abbot and Saiva ascetics.[113] The grant to the temple was to enable it to *feed* all visible and invisible creatures: puja fed the divinities, sattra fed brahmans.[114] The life of all creatures was sustained in this elaborate fashion *because* there were ritual obligations and commitments to do so.

Moreover, such feeding extended a code of 'mothering' by male monks to nonsectarian others. As Anne Klein explains it, ordained

Tibetan Buddhist (Mahayana and Vajrayana) monks in particular were adepts in the cultivation of compassionate relationships modelled on motherhood.[115] In the Himalayan monastic universities, where mothers and women were nearly absent, the work of the ordinary mother (*ma*) and the high (*bla*) mother or lama, were united in the cultivation practices of monks. Klein argues that these practices and acts that cultivated compassionate relationships to others cut through three sets of oppositions taken for granted in post-Cartesian philosophies: they cut through ideas of male and female, they devalued ontologies of autonomy and submission, and they destroyed conceptions of dominance and subordination. These were the terms in which the monk wrote about the provision of consumables as 'service' to theologically distinct 'gohain' others—presumably the Saiva, Tantric, or Vaisnava figures well known in the foothills.

These monastic ideas of compassionate 'service' (*seva*) to others interfered, however, with the ability of colonial administrators to extend their jurisdiction over the same peoples, lands, and markets that were connected to these lords. Pemberton had been dispatched to Bhutan for precisely this reason—he was supposed to renegotiate older monastic arrangements.[116] Pemberton's mission did not secure a promise from the Himalayan Buddhists that they would refuse sanctuary to those the Company's courts sought as criminals. So the Company turned to an Ahom manager of the Koonyapara dvar (called Madhu Saikia) to get him to give up 'dacoits' rather than shelter them in the valley. The Saikia paid for this with his life.

Officers of the Company, already chafing at the payment of posa, took the opportunity of the murder of the Saikia to suspend the payment of the posa. Finding it impossible to collect and store the cloth, grain, and perishable goods given in dana to monastic lords in the Himalayan north and their disciples and agents, the military officers administering these tracts commuted dana into cash taxes.[117] Instead of the monastic regime in which collections differed by house and in quantities proportionate to the means of the owner, whether of rice or of pigs or liquor, under the new military regime of the 1840s, all inhabitants in the dvars were required to pay a flat rate of taxes in cash—Rs 1 per hearth and Rs 3 per plough.[118] Flat rates and cash taxes injured the poorer of the monastic subjects, some of who physically repaired to their lords. Shortly thereafter, 'Booteah outrages' were reported on village Darrang (in the dvars). Nobody was injured, but a few pieces of cloth went missing. Fumed the AGG, Jenkins, 'it is impossible to make these savages comprehend that their systems of maintaining themselves by rapine and plunder are not estimable nor honourable.'[119]

What had changed? From 1833, colonial British officials, both Protestants and liberals committed to expanding sales of British-manufactured goods and maximizing collections of taxes, could neither allow nor implement an economic policy whose goals were so dramatically different. For instance, when the officers of the Company levied cash taxes on monastic subjects living in eastern Bhutan in 1840, the monastic head of all spiritual matters in the domain, the Dharmaraja, expressed his disapproval succinctly. Referring to the Company's sequestration of the dvars of Barreegooma (Buri Guma) and Kalling (in eastern Bhutan), he wrote, 'it is not correct that country given me for worship should be attached'.[120]

Another letter from a senior monk, the desi (Deb Raja) spelled out the differences in attitudes between a monastic administration and the British commercial interests of the government in Calcutta. This letter suggests that the Company's officials, who had always sold the elephants and horses they had received as revenue payments in the eighteenth century, had offended the monastics by selling at auction horses and goods that the monks identified as being part of a *dana-prasad* cluster of objects, beyond market-values. The letter remonstrated: 'You say that the Korun/ Blackmail consisting of horses, gold, musk &ca was formerly paid in articles of a better quality and that now the horses are shamefully bad and fetch no price. … Formerly the Assam Rajah exacted from the Dharma Raja for the country given him for the performance of Seeba Poojah [Seva-puja/Siva puja?] only one good horse and a number of inferior ones as a nominal tribute and the other articles without reference to price or quality and they were never put up to auction as is now the case. The number of horses and the amount of the different articles have been regularly sent, and it is only from a fixed price being put upon them and their being put to auction that arrears have accrued … you say… I have to pay rent.'[121]

Monastic disquiet at the erosion of tax-exempt status and the devaluation of monastic gifts was reinforced by the growing distance between the particularist vision that the monastic lords had of their subjects and the view the colonial regime had of a liberal subject, a generic 'human being' who was the bearer of British 'rights'. Like the Vaisnava Gambhir Simha or Tribhuvanjit Simha on the plains, the Himalayan Buddhist lords paid close attention to the adherent status of the person from whom they received, or expected to receive, material objects and services. Thus, when British colonial officers complained that a man from Gooma Dvar (a monastic estate) living in 'British territory' had been 'forcibly carried away by a party of armed Bhutias from Bhulka dvar headed by a Bhutan officer', the desi (Deb Raja) responded, 'The Zamindar has all along been a servant of mine. ... I have not done an injury to any subject of your territory'.[122] Mid-nineteenth-century British liberal ideals could not accommodate the monastic's particularist definitions of subjecthood.

Such entanglements also shaped the geographical connections of regions that the Company officers had annexed as 'Bengal' and after 1838, 'Assam'. For instance, there was Baikunthapur (en route to and from Darjiling), erstwhile estate in the 'gift' of a northern monastic Buddhist order. From 1841, the Bengal zamindar, confronted by the Company's tax regime in Bengal, claimed that he held the 'devottar lands direct from the Dharma Raja'.[123] Rather than arrange for the title of these estates to be formally restored to their older monastic owners, the Company's officers asked such men to pay taxes directly to the British colonial regime. In the same vein, from 1841, the Company continued to hold the Buxa Dvar (Baksha dvar) that the Tibetan Buddhist monastic lineage claimed as their gift from the Ahom monarchs.

The contest over the dvars came to a head after 1842, when private British merchants, such as William Becher, took on the responsibility of collecting the goods from monastic adherents and sold them for cash, a portion of which was to be handed over by British officials to agents of the monastic governments in the hills. But as tea plantations inched across Darjeeling and the northern Bengal valleys, these collections in turn were used to chip away at the bonds that tied adherents to their lords. By 1851, the colonial administrator on the plains was willing to offer the Buddhist lords in Bhutan only a third of the revenue collections of the dvars. In exchange, the lords in Bhutan were to give up all administrative claims over populations and valleys that the British government in India claimed as its own.[124] The resumption of tax-exempt lands begun in plains Bengal in 1760s, extended in Assam in 1830s, and was completed here by 1853. Between estates lost by Tantric Buddhist monastic lineages and Vaisnava sattras alike, the gains of the British Government in India equalled a total of 1,32,282 acres (3,96,846 bighas).[125] Of these, the greatest share of resumed estates lay in Darrang (on the north bank of the Brahmaputra) and Kamrup (all of modern western Assam).

RECONSTITUTED SUBJECTS AND LANDSCAPES OF 'KACHAR' AND MANIPUR

An equally critical attempt to redirect labour-service obligations away from monastic lordships to the Company's military officers and their appointees occurred in the context of engineering projects in other river valleys east of Dhaka. Keen to bring agrarian capitalism to Kachar and Assam, and arsenals to Manipur, the first engineering projects associated with Company administration everywhere east of Dhaka were roads. The road that would connect Sylhet to Manipur required construction labour to be supplied for such road-building activities. Part of the Company officials' understanding with Gambhir Simha in 1833 had been that he would supply his labour corps periodically to the British Government. This contract was inherited by his successor, the Regent of Manipur, who governed on behalf of the infant son of Gambhir Simha. However, the supply of 400 labourers by the Regent to the road-construction project also ran into trouble when local British officers sought to keep able-bodied male labourers (of such leased contingents) away from the fields beyond April, when the agricultural sowing season started in the region.

Trouble erupted in 1840 when the Regent of Manipur supplied 400 of his 'Nogas' for the construction of the road across the hills from Kachar to Manipur. According to one account, also from a colonial officer, the gradation of dues changed against the labourer. Villages that provided one man for four houses were not supposed to pay other tolls, either in goods or grain or anything else. It was a rule that no road village gave tribute (in goods such as rice, cotton, or eggs) in addition to labour service.[126] Demanding both from one village or set of houses amounted to punishment. Additionally, there were implicit conditions under which labour services could or could not be demanded: there were those who could legitimately ask for labour services of a group to which the demander was tied by ancestral or generational obligations and relationships, and there were others who could not.

After 1841, military officers of the Company who gained the upper hand vis-à-vis the civilians were simply uninterested in preserving such fine distinctions. In 1841, the same village of Tunghum referred to earlier, that had been relocated twice over and was now found on the banks of the Jiri and Barak rivers and cultivating territory on both banks, refused to provide labour service for building the Sylhet–Manipur road.[127] The villagers ('Khangjais' or dormitories of Vaisnava followers) could only have been asked to provide labour and goods by Gambhir Simha and his direct descendants, such as Gambhir's son, on whose behalf an adult regent ruled in Manipur.[128] Under the old order, they owed nothing to anybody else, and certainly not to the colonial English engineer in charge of getting the road constructed. This was a Lieutenant Guthrie, who sought to enforce the regent's contract for supplying adherents (noga) as 'Nagas' in 1840–1.

Liberal Whig members of both London and Calcutta bureaucracies could not understand the graded nature of labour services as part of a monastic government's arrangements of dues. One Secretary of State for India even demanded that such labour services be performed for the colonial government gratis by such dormitories. As he said to the Governor General of British India, if the 'Nagas' owed their own government a contribution in labour, the Regent of Manipur particularly was obligated to make over a 'reasonable number of labourers free of any payment by our government' from among these men, since the British armies had secured the regent's control of Manipur in the first place.[129] The alternative was to induce these men to work for the road by offering money wages. The Government of India authorized the latter system.[130] But this authorization was also founded on misperception.

As seen under Govindachandra's khel system, which paid its dues through one spokesperson (*mukhtear*), *khangjai*s paid their labour dues too under a headman of some kind, who resided 'within the Manipur territory'.[131] When such khel leaders deployed them in ways that were contrary to the needs of the colonial regime, these corps themselves appeared as savages, barbarians, 'coolies'. In Manipur and southern Kachar during the 1840s–50s, this was exactly what had occurred. The British colonial government upheld the authority of a line of men in Manipur whose claims to rule were constantly challenged by their patrilineal cousins, uncles, and others. These men, buoyed by the attachments of disciples and labour corps of their own, redeployed these men as soldiers in a partisan contest. Hence, such attached labour corps were not available to work in ways the colonial state or its puppet regent demanded of them.

Their refusals in turn earned them the anger of individual military officers serving as indirect rulers of such regimes. The latter's responses were representative of official pique and incomprehension of the relationships that made followers into an entourage. Tribhuvanjit Simha, the Manipuri scion who held a rent-free grant of 400 bighas (about 100 acres) in Kachar, provided the perfect illustration of such official unease. Describing the fifty or sixty armed followers who had accompanied Tribhuvanjit Simha from his grant at Jaffeeraband, through the forests of Kachar, until they arrived at the fort of Manipur, an official at Kachar noted that 'not more than 9 or 10 were the prince's own people, the rest are his coolies and men who gave him house.'[132] Men who provided porterage as well as shelter for a revered lord appeared as coolies or labourers to British officials. But they had been drawn from the very groups of adherents and subjects that paid their obligations of attachment as seva to the ascetic-monastic lord. Since Tribhuvanjit at the time was intent on destroying the British-backed regime of the Regent (Narsingh) at Manipur, the former's adherents, organized as dormitories (*khangjai*) harassed the loyalists of the latter—also called 'Naga' (clan Kampooi/Kabui?) in the English records. At this point, the colonial government determined to punish Tribhuvanjit's 'Khangjai' villages with a military expedition.

Though the regent at Manipur was completely unwilling to participate in this venture, he was pressed by the British military officer at Sylhet (Colonel Lister) to send a 600-man army headed by Lister himself on a notorious expedition against what he called the 'khangjai tribe in the habit of committing aggressions in Kachar'. The expedition is said to have succeeded in effecting the submission of the wrongdoers, but the regent at Manipur, on whose behalf the expedition was apparently undertaken, showed little desire to 'retain the Khangjai village'.[133] Surely the regent needed labourers, but he needed labourers attached to him or his clan, not those who would attack him on behalf of their own leaders, 'sardars' or 'chiefs'—many of whom were in fact ranged against him in the 1840s. Sending an armed expedition (peopled by his partisans) against his rivals' armed partisans preserved the conflict, to be fought on another day and perhaps at another venue. This group split off in two directions. One, led by the powerful 'chief' Shekapas, went with his partisans and followers in a 'southeasterly direction towards the Mug [Arakan] country', while the remainder moved to the west of the Sonai River.[134] The former would return with a replenished labour corps from a segment of a Tipra lineage at war with other segments. That is how in 1847 'subjects of the Raja of Tipperah' attacked raiyats serving the regent at Manipur in territories far away from both—in a Sylhet district claimed by the raja of Tipperah. The second branch appeared to have merged into the estates of other Kachar-based Manipuri rivals; these rivals returned to attack the Company-backed regent's government at Manipur between 1848 and 1852 repeatedly. One even joined the mutineers of the 34th Native Infantry 'with his followers', in January 1858.[135]

MONASTIC ADHERENTS, MILITARY LABOURERS, MALE 'SAVAGES'

Let me pause here briefly to dispel two aspects of British military officer's mystification of 'khongjai' (khangjai) methods of warfare in the domains east of Dhaka. Since Company military officials did not know the histories of Afghan-Mughal-Ahom warfare in the region in the seventeenth and eighteenth centuries, or the histories of personalized attachments and labour dues, they tended to read practices established as part of warfare in culturalist terms, as emblems of 'savagery'. Colonial officials never failed to mention the numbers of heads taken and bodies kidnapped in their descriptions of 'Kuki attacks'. Referring to the political warfare of the Manipuri nephews' factions in Kachar and their raids on Manipur in this period, one agent described how in 1840, 'a party of Kookees from the hills to the south of the plains of Kachar and west of the Barak attacked the Nagas tributary to Manipur carried off upwards of 200 and took off the heads of 103'.[136]

This theme of head-taking and captivity became such a well-rehearsed feature of all the colonial records in the 1850s–90s that it seems necessary to point out the long histories of Mughal and Central Asian warfare as precedents important in this region. Moreover, such kinds of combat were not beyond the 'Brahmanic', Sufi, or other scruples of monastic leaders or guru-figures. For instance, in 1830, a man called Hurnea, who also had an initiatic name Ganga Das and was a personal attendant of Pobittro Singh Rajkumar (brother of Indraprabha), and also a guard in the colonially sponsored Sylhet Light Infantry, struck the fatal blow that decapitated the Kachari lord, Govindachandra.[137] Whether this made him a less authentic Vaisnava or Brahman is to ask a question about 'interiority' that cannot be historically resolved. The question may itself betray our incomprehension of the ways in which commitment to the person of the guru, or to a promise made to him, may have superseded other obligations of such a Vaisnava peasant-soldier. But the more important point that I would like to establish from this is that the very people referred to as 'head-hunting savages' in the colonial records were members of devoted corps.

It was as devoted warriors, inhabitants of military tenures, that such collective of men such as '30 kookies headed by a chief from the villages of Thadoi and Kyong', loyal subjects of the lineage holding power in the Manipur Valley, killed a group of eight female cultivators from their own community who had resettled in Kachar.[138] Similarly, in 1849, after another group of monastic subjects (kukis) was attacked by a 'tribe of Luchaye-Kookies', the investigating officer had to report that though the attackers came from very far away, near Chittagong, the two groups knew each other. Many 'were on friendly terms with them formerly and they lived near to one another and … enmity now shown is owing to their having left them and taken up their abode' in Company territory, that is, Kachar.[139] When fellow subjects owing labour services left or deserted a commonly cultivated set of fields, those left behind were often pressed to work harder. Collectively given labour dues needed stabilization of the collective; flights and desertions, especially of the most important female members on whom the entire collective depended, were especially damaging. They also betrayed the community left behind. Since the eighteenth century, temples and lords had fought over such flights of labour servants.

A second aspect of such warfare was hostage taking, sometimes as security for the maintenance of a truce and at other times to force an enemy to come to a peace negotiation. An identical series of hostage taking was reported by a local informant who had lived among the Thadoi as a hostage himself: alongside him was the son of a Wa-heng-ba, the Ahul-lup lakpa (the head of one of the four working groups established in Manipur) who had been carried off when a boy. But when the father sent two large gongs to the Thadoi, the son was released and allowed to return. Reports about 'Kuki kidnapping' by colonial officers betrayed a fundamental incomprehension about the historical nature of warfare conducted by attached monastic subjects.

These methods of warfare, used by groups which had not established themselves as a professional army but came out of and merged back into monastic-ascetic militias attached to monastic lineages and forts, were also well-known features of the Himalayan-plains landscapes. Tibetan Buddhist texts and traditions, as much as the Sakta Tantric on the plains below, had valourized the 'war' with forces of evil, desire, and grief as the core of masculinity in monastic-ascetic disciplines. As Charlene Makley argues, non-Gelukpa lamas in eastern Tibetan regions were particularly keen to delink tantric tropes of cultivated strength, fearlessness, ferocity, and intelligence from contemplative monastic lineages.[140] These tropes were especially significant in bringing together the lay and ordained males in alternative non-contemplative lineages of militant skills, reconstituting them in communities of warrior monks and monastic subjects. But colonial governors, especially in the course of the 1850s, referred to such monks as savages and their adherents as dacoits in a growing confrontation between colonial liberal economics and Buddhist-Vaisnava monastic economies and militias.[141] Thus, the same thing happened to the Buddhist administrator-monk who lived at Dewangiri inside the fortified monastery. He was an uncle of the ordained monk who was supreme head of spiritual and textual affairs, the Dharmaraja. In addition to his genealogical claim to sacrality, he held monastic and administrative officers and was also the brother of the Trongsa Penlop, the main temporal authority in the district. As he put it to the AGG NEF in 1855, 'in my family there have been 3 or 4 Dhurm Rajahs born and I have descended from 7 generations of nobles.'[142] Nevertheless, colonial officers referred to this monastic's entourage—twenty sardars on ponies, 600 followers armed with matchlocks, bows and arrows, swords, spears and shields, with helmets of brass and iron—as a 'rabble array of some hundreds of rude and lawless followers'.[143]

A charge that was repeatedly made against all monastic lords whether in the Himalayan world or in the plains was that these figures 'kidnapped' men and women, cattle, and elephants from the tea plantations.[144] Such charges of kidnaps and dacoities legitimated the expansion of liberal law, British markets, and imperial territorialism. But they also delegitimized the attempts by monastic men and supportive lay women who sought to provide sanctuary to those who sought it, or 'liberate' them from distress.

CRIMINAL MONKS, DISPERSED ADHERENTS, AND DISPOSSESSED WIDOWS

Although we will study monastic attempts at such 'liberation' in greater detail in the next chapter, for the moment I want to return to exploring the implications of criminalized monastic governments for the reconstitution of household-based social reproduction, that is, the nature of marriage and household-based authority in the 1830s–50s. The vast terrain that officials called 'Kachar'—or all hills east of Dhaka and Sylhet—after 1855 provided exemplary evidence of simultaneous displacements as the tea plant was discovered growing on many slopes east of Sylhet township in 1855.[145] European tea planters rushed to grab land here, just as soldiers serving the East India Company's government rebelled everywhere. During the Mutiny of 1857–8, the 34th battalion of the Native Infantry stationed at Chittagong and Dhaka made directly for 'the jungles at the foot of the Bhuban mountains', the terrain called Kachar in Company records of this period. Managers of the European tea plantations armed local groups, and used the forces and scouts loyal to the current raja of Manipur (Chandrakirti Simha) to hunt down and kill rebel soldiers in these forests.[146] On the other side, though, there were reports that some of the Kachar-based Vaisnava Manipuri gurus or 'princes' were either leading the soldiers or sheltering them. Though awards were announced for their capture, none of the leaders were caught. But the effort to catch them led the Company officers into a minutely detailed compilation of the wider network of relationships within which each contender for power in Manipur was inserted. In addition to recording the names of the father and grandfather of each man, the officials started noting the names of the father-in-law of each and the number of marriages established by each. One such list gives us the names and terse descriptions of thirty-two men (and two women) living in Kachar in the 1850s.[147]

While nineteen of the men and both the women—this includes Indraprabha—were described as 'petty landholders', three of these men were described as 'princes' who lived by begging. They had no means of subsistence, except what they 'receive from their countrymen in the way of charity'.[148] Another official described most of these men as 'miserably poor, living chiefly on the charity of their countrymen or on the families of those whom they honour with their alliances'.[149] Why, despite their apparent material poverty, had these men been given wives?

Colonial officials, exasperated by the attitudes of commoners towards these apparently poor 'princes', suggested that commoners 'deified' these men, 'so great is their respect for Royal blood that [it] leads them into mischief'.[150] As with the English official despairing of the 'feudal system' and sardari influence in early nineteenth-century Chittagong, this comment on the nature of adherence offered by the followers-disciples of Manipuri Vaisnava males who were spiritually and biologically descended from deified Vaisnava guru Bhagyachandra/Jaisimha suggests the substantial continuities of characteristics in the monastic geographic order even in the mid-nineteenth century. As in Chittagong earlier, descent from guru-lords (*raja*) made men 'of the royal clan' (*rajavamsi/ rajbongshi*, a title taken by some of the men on this list as well). This was dual descent of prestige: descent by blood from men of spiritual accomplishments (*siddhapurush*) presumably also conveyed the same capacity for ritual perfection, as well as the symbolic capital of ties to a relational network of adherents and disciples. The colonial list of Indraprabha's male relatives thus clarifies that the relationships described by the poets of *Krishnamala* and *Srenimala* for the eighteenth century had continued into the mid-nineteenth century.

Even in 1857–8, some of these men continued to be affiliated with other equally widespread lineages, such as those of the Tipra.

One figure (Shambhu Chandra, the thirty-year-old son of Nal Singh Rajkumar) lived with a father-in-law, who was caught up in a monastic lineage and succession dispute in one of the Tipra households at the same time. Another man (Debendro Simha, the brother of a regent of Manipur and holder of the throne for a few weeks in 1850) wrote from Sylhet to say that as a Manipuri he wished to live in the district of Tipra—by which he meant Kumilla on the plains—where he would get his sons married in an appropriate Vaisnava household.[151]

Perhaps the officers had begun to suspect what the Burmese Buddhist, the Manipuri Vaisnava, and Sufi Mughal had long known—that marital relationships were significant routes through which ambitious men could bring other men's armies to shore up their plans. But their fear of biologically descended claimants to authority made such officials ignore the claims shored up by spiritual authority, as is revealed in their handling of Debendro Simha's request. This man was the son of a Burmese appointee (Kabo Simha) at Manipur in the early nineteenth century. His presence in Kumilla would have placed him in greater proximity to groups coming through the southern routes from Burma. His marital relationships with other Vaisnavas would have further strengthened this man's access to men and arms. So instead of allowing him to live at Kumilla, they sent Debendro— and a thirty-two-member household—from Sylhet to Nadia (present Navadvip in West Bengal), an even more prominent centre of Vaisnava cultic gatherings which brought together large numbers of Vaisnava men and women in regular pilgrimages. Apparently these mid-nineteenth century officials did not understand that going to an eminent pilgrimage centre enhanced, rather than diminished, a Vaisnava man's social and spiritual capital.

Such capital made these Manipuri Vaisnava men acceptable as sons-in-law or brothers-in-law to men of lesser genealogies, including those who served in petty capacities in the colonial bureaucracy. Though the contemporary reform Bengali press did not name these poor Vaisnava males as superior (*kulina*) in dignified and generous behaviours, their marital patterns were identical with their contemporary kulina brahmans in western Bengal.[152] Like the latter, Manipuri Vaisnava men descended from eminent gurus also lived with their wives in the wives' fathers' homes. Like them, these men too had plural wives, and depended upon the 'gifts' that their wives' natal kin made to their subsistence. Like them, these Manipuri Vaisnava men also happened to be uxorilocal: just as Pabitra Simha had lived with his sister and been maintained by stipends from his sister's husband, six of his nephews (Pabitra's father was their paternal grandfather) and three other male cousins of the nephews lived in the homes of their wives. This included sons and grandsons of former rulers or holders of the golden umbrella—such as Marjit's son, Kanai Simha, who lived with his father-in-law, Pooran Singh Soobadar, and from there joined the mutineers in 1857. After the Mutiny, this Pooran Singh was commended for being one of the Manipuri scouts who led the private militias maintained by tea planters to one group of rebel soldiers in the jungles.[153] Had a father-in-law actually turned against his son-in-law in the course of the rebellion? He had, in the service of a greater loyalty to his employer, the Company officer. The implication was that as in the late eighteenth century, when monastic lords and subjects had been found on both anti- and pro-government armies, in the mid-nineteenth century as well, descendants of monastic lords and their affines continued to be on both ends of the anti-colonial and pro-colonial armies.

However, in the immediate aftermath of the Mutiny, colonial official decisions about the relocation of pro-Burmese Buddhist men in regions apparently remote from the Burmese–Bengal border only reinforced the trans-local aspects of a persistent monastic geographicity. This can be established by looking at the fortunes of those who the officials described as 'petty landholders' in 1858. All the men were related to Indraprabha, then only sixty years old. Her siblings, it appears from this list, had continued to live with her in Kachar. Her elder sister, the seniormost lineal descendant of an erstwhile raja of Manipur, was seventy years old in 1858, and she lived with her two sons and one daughter—nothing is said of her husband at all—with her sixty-year-old widowed sister (Indraprabha), her sixty-eight-year-old brother Pabitra Simha, the latter's six sons ranging between the ages of twenty-five and thirty-five years old, and their various younger children; they all shared the same address. It was a place called Barkhola. In stark contrast to the men described as 'desperately poor', Indraprabha—the youngest of her siblings—owned a market (*hāt*). Apparently there was enough money or goods available at this market for revolutionaries of 1857–8 from her own household—her brother's sons, her nephews—to plot to raid that market in preparation for an attack on Manipur. In terms of both lineal descent and wealth of relationships and income, Indraprabha was the last surviving Manipuri aristocrat in Kachar. But she had been denied her claims to Kachar. Then her household, too, was shorn of its members: all six of her nephews were given small pensions (Rs 8 a month) and deported to Nadia, the famous pilgrimage centre.[154]

In conclusion, it was obvious that colonial military governors, even while trying to reorganize monastic economies based on adherence of disciples and labour dues, had replicated the monastic estate when they installed Christian missionaries in some special estates, repeated the patterns of 'kidnapping' valued members of lineages in a pattern that they accused monks and their adherents of doing, while strengthening the monastic geographicity of the Manipuri Vaisnava males with the western Bengali order of pilgrimage town and estates. It is impossible to establish and, perhaps even beside the point, to wonder whether these effects were indeed intended by colonial officers. More significant were the short-term consequences of their policies, as well as the long-term effects these policies had on those who inherited such colonial bureaucracies as their own after 1947. It is to these that we will now turn our attention in the next chapter.

NOTES

1. Sharma (2011:121–46).
2. Mullard (2011: 25).
3. *Krishnamala of Dvija Ramaganga* (1995: 107). The verses are '*narayana padavi dile jone jon/ pandav borua naam aachhilo jaahaar/ luchidorpo narayan naam hoilo taahaar; jonardon naame ek chhilo senapoti/ khuchungadorpo narayan hoilo taar khyati*'.
4. *Krishnamala of Dvija Ramaganga* (1995: 130). The date mentioned in the verse is 1682 saka or 1760 CE.
5. Planta (1776).
6. Hamilton (1963 [1990]: 4).
7. Mgte Chittagong to Secy to Govt, 12 November 1812, Extract Bengal Secret Consultations 25 November 1812, no. 76, OIOC, F/4/ 404/ 10130.
8. Mgte Chittagong to Secy to Govt, Secret 9 December 1812, in Letter of GOI to Board of Control, 5 February 1813, no. 2, OIOC, F/4/404/10130.
9. Choudhury (1973: 19–25).
10. For Bengal Regulation XI of 1812 to this effect, see GOI Legislative Department (1897: 48–50).

11. Goldstein *et al.* (2001: 814).

12. Mgte Tipperah to Secy to Govt Fort William, 15 September 1824, OIOC, F/4/404/10130.

13. Acharjee (2008: 73–9).

14. Singha (1984 [1896], vol. 1: 139–51). Singha (1851–1914) had been an intimate of the households and lineages involved in the struggles, and had inherited a great many documents and much oral information from his ancestors who had worked in the same zamindari. His 'history' of the lineages and households is simultaneously a primary and a secondary source.

15. Translation of Reply of Sumbhoo Thakoor, in Mgte Tipperah to Secy to Govt Fort William, 15 September 1824, OIOC, F/4/404/10130.

16. Capt. in Charge of Surveyor General's Office, to Secy to Govt Military, 23 June 1826, Extract Bengal Military Consultation, 30 June 1826, no. 56, OIOC, F/4/1017/27955.

17. Sr Asst Supt Arakan to Capt. Dickinson, 3 May 1831, in BPC, 24 June 1831, no. 61, OIOC, BC F/4/ 1450/56967.

18. Singha (1984 [1896], vol. 1: 151). The son born of the first Manipuri marriage died. However, the place-holder after Kashichandra Manikya (formerly Kashi Thakur) was a man with the title Krishnakishor Manikya (r. 1829–1849); he married three daughters from the Manipuri household of Marjit; cf. Singha (1984, vol. 1: 153–5); this tradition is supported by Manipuri commentators from the early twentieth century cited in Singh and Ray (2007: 88–98).

19. Chevalier (2008: 120).

20. *Ibid.*, 87–8, 90.

21. Pemberton (1865: 50).

22. Griffiths (1865: 162).

23. *Ibid.*, 128.

24. GG in Council to Court of Directors, 5 February 1813, OIOC, BC, F/4/404/10129.

25. Mgte Chittagong to Secy to Govt, Secret 9 December 1812, in Letter of GOI to Board of Control, 5 February 1813, no. 2, OIOC, F/4/404/10130.

26. Scott (2010).

27. Extract from Captain Canning's Dispatch of 29 February 1812, in BPC of 25 April 1812, no. 2, OIOC, F/4/375/9265.

28. Private letter from Lt Pemberton to Secy of Govt, 9 September 1828, in Note by Secy, 21 July 1832, NAI, Foreign Secret Progs., 23 July 1832, no. 16.

29. Willis (2009: 36, 65–70).

30. For instance, a Vaisnava ambassador from the svargadeva to the Tipra capital of Udaipur on the plains below passed through the Barak River valley early in the eighteenth century and wrote 'mountains (*parbat*) flank the valley. On the mountains live about three hundred people like our

noga doffla but who are called kuki [by the Tipra court]', Bhuyan (1990b [1938]: 21). The observer noted that some of these men were given arms by the Tipra court and were organized under the term 'Halamcha'. This term is the closest these records get to the Jewish code 'Halacha' said to be established since 70 CE, for which see Katz and Goldberg (2004[1995]: 18).

31. Barua (1990 [1930]: 2).

32. Jenkins to G. Swinton, n.d., in Gauhati Archives, Assam Sectt, Letters Recd from Govt, vol. 8, 1832, 298–9.

33. Translated letter from Gumbheer Singh to Capt. Grant, 7 February 1829, OIOC, BC, F/4/1447/56959.

34. Arzee of Raja Govinda Chandra, in FPP, 14 May 1832, no. 83, encl.

35. Minute by GG in Political, 25 March 1833, NAI, FPP, 30 May 1833, no. 99.

36. Captain Jenkins and Fisher on the Kopili River to AGG, NEF, 5 January 1833, FPP, 30 May 1833, no. 98.

37. Capt. Grant's Journal of a Route from Langthabal capital of Munneepore to the Ningthee, entries for 13 and 16 January 1832, NAI, FPP, 14 May 1832, no. 123.

38. Commr Sylhet to Chief Secy Govt, n.d., Assam Sectt, Letters Recd from Government, vol. 6 a, 87–106; for report on Tipra Raja assembling forces at Budderpore/ Bhadrapur, see Capt. Grant to Commr Sylhet, 11 June 1828, ibid., 81.

39. For report that this village lay in hills southwest of the fort of Manipur, see ibid., 157; for the relationship of tribute that this village gave in goats, cloth, and 'sellongs' to a Sikkim ['Succum'] family, despite being the cultivators of the 'finest description of rice grown in Manipur', see Capt. Grant to Commr Sylhet, 5 August 1828, ibid., 107–13.

40. Thos Fisher to AGG, NEF, 3 March 1831, NAI, FPP, 14 May 1832, no. 105.

41. Capt. F.J. Grant, Commr Manipur to AGG, NEF (T. C. Robertson), 26 October 1832, OIOC, BPC, 31 December 1832, no. 91.

42. Evidence of 'Thok-chow' in Political Agent Manipur to Sessions Judge of Zillah Sylhet, 29 August 1844, NAI, FPP, 7 September 1844, no. 111.

43. Entry for 12 December, Private journal of F. W. Jenkins, OIOC, Mss Eur/F 257/2.

44. Entry for 16 December, ibid.

45. Capt. Jenkins to Chief Secy to Govt, 21 April 1832, NAI, FPP, 14 May 1832, no. 110.

46. M'Cosh (1837: 21).

47. Ibid., 131.

48. Ibid., 141.

49. Ibid., 144–5.

50. *Ibid.*, 145.

51. *Ibid.*, 155.

52. *Ibid.*, 136, 139.

53. Chevalier (2008: 142).

54. *Ibid.*, 138.

55. Mgte Zillah Rangpur to Secy Judicial Dept, 30 June 1813, Gauhati, Assam Sectt, BG File 349, serial nos 1–10, 1812–16, no. 2.

56. Extract from Joint Mgte Rangpur, David Scott, to Secy Govt, 15 August 1818, OIOC, BJCC, 28 December 1821, no. 88.

57. *Ibid.*

58. David Scott to Acting Secy to Govt, Judicial, 17 January 1815, *ibid.*, no. 4.

59. Government of Bengal (1854, vol. 2: 659–63).

60. David Scott to Mr. Lamb, 18 July 1827, cited in White (1857: 53).

61. David Scott to C.A. Fenwick, Register to the Local Record Committee, Sylhet, 7 March 1827, in White (1857: 77–9).

62. Powell (1993: 80).

63. Capt. Francis Jenkins to Secy of General Committee of Public Instruction, n.d., Miles Bronson Papers, Official Correspondence with Rev. Lucius Bolliz of 13 May 13 1837, American Baptist Historical Society, Valley Forge, Pennsylvania.

64. Capt. Jenkins to Secy GOI, 14 April 1840, *ibid.*

65. Mabie (1901).

66. Letter from C.A. Bruce, A. Brown, M. Bronson, and J. Cutter to Capt. H. Vetch, 10 March 1840, and Letter from M. Bronson to Capt. F. Jenkins, n.d., OIOC, BPC 13 April 1840, nos 129–31.

67. Chevalier (2008: 141).

68. Aung-Thwin (1983) and Daud Ali (2006).

69. Lt James Mathie Offg. Mgte and Collr Darrang to Capt. F. Jenkins, Commr Assam, 15 February 1835, Gauhati Archives, Assam Sectt Progs General Dept, File 298 Bengal G, 1836, serial 1, 29.

70. Offg Collr Kamrup to Commr Assam, 1 September 1835, Report on Judicial and Revenue Administration of Assam, Assam Sectt Progs, General Dept, File 298 Bengal G, 1836, serial 1, 102–7.

71. Mathie to Jenkins, File 298 Bengal G, 1836, serial 1, 30.

72. David Scott, Commr Rangpur Division to Judicial Secy GOB, 25 September 1830, OIOC, BC F/4/1454/57705.

73. Letter from Court of Directors to Bengal Political, 10 March 1830, OIOC, BC F/4/ 1371/54510.

74. Progs Relating to the Mug Corps in Arracan-Sylhet Local Corps, and Political Letter from Fort William to Court of Directors, 15 December 1831, OIOC, BC F/4/1449/56966.

75. See correspondence between C.A. Bruce, Commr of Gun Boats at Sadiya and Major White, Political Agent, 1833–4 on the Sadiya 'chiefs' kidnapping people, in OIOC, BC F/4/1505/59030, a file cover that also reads 'Rude Tribes on Frontier of Upper Assam'.

76. Collr Kamrup to Commr Assam, 1 September 1835, Report, 103.

77. Malcolm (1839: 80 and 274).

78. See Patterson (1982: 237).

79. Journal of Nathan Brown, Sadiya, entries for 2 April 183[6?], 19 May [year not mentioned], ABHS, Official Correspondence, ff. 5a, 8a–b.

80. Miles Bronson, February 1843, in Barpujari (1986: 197).

81. Political Agent Lakhimpur to Commr Assam, 10 January 1835, Report on Judicial and Revenue Administration of Assam, Gauhati Archives, Assam Sectt Progs General Dept 1836, file 298 Bengal G, serial 1, 62.

82. Jenkins to Mcnaghten, 1 July 1836, Gauhati Archives, Assam Sectt: Letters Issued to Govt, vol. 4, no 46.

83. Neufville (1855 in Selections).

84. *Ibid.*, 8.

85. Political Agent Lakhimpur to Commr Assam, 10 January 1835, Gauhati Archives, file 298 Bengal G, 62–3.

86. Letter from GOB to Court of Directors, 14 December 1832, OIOC, BC F/4/1505/59025, esp. 32–4 on Bara Senapati and his control of the Vaisnava 'Moamaria'.

87. AGG, NEF to Secy GOI, 2 July 1836, *ibid.*, no. 47. It was in this region that C.A. Bruce set up his own tea plantations. For acquisition of 3,000–4,000 young plants from their native soil in the 'Muttuck country' and planting of 17,000 young plants in these pieces of ground that he held along a section of the river Kahong, see Bruce (1838: 10–11 and passim).

88. AGG, NEF to Dy Secy GOI, 6 July 1838, Gauhati Archives, Assam Sectt: Letters Issued to Govt, vol. 7, no. 80.

89. Political Asst Vetch to AGG, NEF, 21 March 1840, Gauhati Archives, Assam Sectt: Letters Recd from District Officers, Series VII, vol. 15, no. 314.

90. Political Agent Vetch to AGG,NEF, 14 October 1841, and AGG, NEF to Secy GOI, 6 November 1841, OIOC, BC, F/4/1969/86427.

91. Political Agents' Office NEF to Secy GOI, 29 June 1836, Gauhati Archives, Assam Sectt, Letters Issued to Govt, vol. 4, no. 44.

92. Letter of GOB to Court of Directors, 14 December 1832, OIOC, BC, F/4/1505/59025, f. 33.

93. AGG, NEF to Secy GOB, 16 January 1836, Gauhati Archives, Assam Sectt, Letters Issued to Govt, vol. 4, no. 4.

94. India Political Letter, 5 September 1838, no. 45, para. 27, 205–6, NAI, Political Progs, 1 April, no. 12 of 1840.

95. For a 1,000-men force of zhing.pha 'chiefs' and 'hill tribes' in the vicinity of Tibet, see Commanding Officer at Ningrew to Capt. Vetch, n.d. [circa 1843] in Gauhati Archives, Assam Sectt, Letters Recd from District Officers, vol. 22, 17–19; for orders from Vetch to Commanding Officer, 27 January 1843 and for argument that zhing.pha attacks were related to 'desertion of their doanneah slaves', see AGG, NEF to Secy GOI, 15 February 1844 with encls 1–7 in Gauhati Archives, Assam Sectt, Letters Issued to Govt, vol. 13, no. 12; also Note to Secy GOI, 10 February 1848, Gauhati Archives, Assam Sectt, Letters Issued to Govt, vol. 14, no.13.

96. Miles Bronson to Ruth Bronson, 23 July 1854, in Miles Bronson Letters Recd (1849–57), Special Collections, Rutgers University, New Brunswick, New Jersey.

97. Report on the Judicial and Revenue Administration of Assam 1835, Gauhati Archives, Assam Sectt Progs General Dept 1835.

98. Offg Collr Kamrup Division to Commr Assam, 1 September 1835, Report on the Judicial and Revenue Administration of Assam 1835, Assam Sectt Progs 36, file 298 Bengal G.

99. *Ibid.*, 104.

100. Lt James Mathie, Offg Mgte and Collr Darrang to Capt. F. Jenkins, Commr Assam, 15 February 1835, Assam Sectt Progs, *ibid.*, serial 1, 9.

101. Pemberton (1865: 12).

102. Translated petitions of Sidlee Raja Gouri Narain to Commr Assam dated 3 Falgun 1271 (1864 CE), July 1865, December 1865, and Sanads I–V, Appendix to Letter 71S of 17 April 1866, in Commr Cooch Bihar to Secy GOB 8 April 1867, BG 10G of 1864–74, Gauhati Archives, Assam Sectt.

103. Commr Cooch Bihar Division to Secy to GOB, 3 April 1867, *ibid.*

104. Foreign Political Progs, Gauhati Archives, Assam Sectt, BG 10 G of 1874, 1864–74.

105. Offg Secy BOR, Lower Provinces to Secy GOB, Revenue, 22 June 1869, *ibid.*

106. Offg. Mgte and Collr Darrang to Commr Assam 15 February 1835, Report on Judicial and Revenue Administration of Assam 1835, Assam Sectt Progs General Dept 1836, file 298 Bengal G.

107. AGG, NEF (Robertson) to Secy Govt, Political, 6 December 1833, NAI, FPP, 12 December 1833, no.75.

108. Offg. Mgte and Collr Darrang to Commr Assam, 15 February 1835, Report on Judicial and Revenue Administration of Assam 1835, Gauhati Archives, Assam Sectt Progs, General Dept, serial 1, 12.

109. Memo of Conversation with Cheetey Zeenkaff, by Lt H. Inglis, SLI, *ibid.*, no. 76. According to a note by the superior attached to this file, Lt Inglis was 'master of the Assamese dialect which the Zeenkaff speaks with fluency, their communications were carried on without interpreter'.

110. Edgar (1969 [1874]: 32).

111. Governor General in Council, Political Dept, to Court of Directors, 16 January 1837, and correspondence between AGG, Lt James Mathie, 21–4 December 1835, OIOC, BC F/4/1657/66312.

112. Translation of a Letter from the Tongso Pillo to AGG dated 1st Bysack [1243/1836 CE], in Pemberton (1865), 104–5.

113. Bhagalpur Copper-Plate in Sircar (1983, vol. 2: 80–6).

114. Deva (1983); also see Willis (2009).

115. Klein (1995: 106–22).

116. AGG, NEF, F. W. Jenkins to H.T. Prinsep, Secy GOI Political, 19 April 1839, NAI, FPP, 22 May 1839, no. 120.

117. Lt A.A. Sturt to Capt. James Mathie, 13 January 1840; Capt. Mathie to Lt Sturt, 5 January 1840; and Lt Mathie to Capt. Jenkins, 4 February 1840, OIOC, BC, F/4/1874/797.

118. Extract Political Letter from the Board of Control to GOI, 11 May 1841, no. 12, OIOC, BC, F/4/1948/84651.

119. AGG, NEF to GOI Political, 14 May 1840, OIOC, BC, F/4/1874/797.

120. Translated Letter of the Dharma Raja to the AGG (Jenkins), 12th Agrou[agrahayan], encl., ibid.

121. Translated Letter from the Deb Raja to the AGG, encl., ibid.

122. Cited in Eden (1865: 31).

123. AGG (Jenkins) to Secy GOI, 21 May 1841, OIOC, BC, F/4/1874/797

124. AGG, NEF (Major Jenkins) to Offg Under Secy GOI, Foreign, 31 October 1851, NAI, FPP, 5 December 1851, no. 8; also see Bengali-language letter from Dharma Raja to AGG complaining of the resumption of 6 villages in Assam enclosed in Secy GOI to Offg Secy GOI, Foreign, 4 October 1851, in NAI, FPP, 15 October 1851, no. 5.

125. Report of Special Commissioner of Assam 1853 in Goswami (1986: 290–1, Appendix D).

126. Political Agent Capt. Gordon to Capt. Guthrie, Supt Manipur Road and Engineer of Public Works, 6 April 1841, OIOC, F/4/ 1874/79715.

127. Capt Guthrie, Supt Manipur Road to Capt. Gordon 1 April 1841, F/4/1874/79715.

128. Political Agent in Manipur to Secy GOI Political, 3 March 1841, OIOC, F/4/1948/84654.

129. Extract Political Letter to India, 2 June 1841, no 7, OIOC, F/4/1948/84654.

130. Superintending Engineer Lower Provinces to Offg Secy Military Board, Barrackpur, 28 April 1840, in OIOC, F/4/1874/79717.

131. Political Agent Manipur to Capt. Guthrie, Supt Manipur Road, 23 February 1842, and Political Agent to Secy GOI, 8 March 1842, in OIOC, F/4/1989/88090.

132. Supt Kachar to Commr 15 Division (Dacca), 4 May 1841, OIOC, BPC, 12 October 1841, no. 53, encl. Among his entourage, however, was also found 'head bramin of the prince'.

133. Para 45, Political Letter from India, 12 October 1841, no. 53, OIOC, F/4/1948/84654.

134. Evidence of Thok-Chow, in Political Agent to Sessions Judge, 29 August 1844, NAI, FPP, 7 September 1844, no. 111.

135. For report on Norendrojit Simha, the son of a Raja of Manipur, Chourjit Simha, see Commr of Circuit (W.J. Allen) to Secy GOB, 27 March 1858, NAI, Delhi, GOB, General Political Proceedings, 22 April 1858, no 95. But correspondence in the same file, no. 96, gives a list of raids led by other lineage members from Kachar and Sylhet between 1848 and 1852. The list suggests the possibility that such labour groups were merged with households and entourages of all these men.

136. Political Agent to Sessions Judge of Zillah Sylhet, 29 August 1844, NAI, FPP, 7 September 1844, no. 111.

137. Deposition of Bishnu Ram Brahman Kachari, in Mgte Sylhet to AGG, NEF, 30 May 1830, NAI, FPP, 18 June 1830, no. 54.

138. Supt Kachar to Commr 15th Division, Dacca, 5 July 1844, *CDR* I, 137–8; same to Sessions Judge Sylhet, 9 January, 1845, 142–3.

139. Offg Supt to Sessions Judge Sylhet, 20 November 1849, *CDR*, I, pp. 173–5.

140. Makley (2007: 238–84).

141. Under Secy GOB to Under Secy GOI, Foreign, 17 July 1855, BFP, 22 February 1856, 78.

142. Dewangiri Rajah to Capt. Rowlatt, 2nd Chait, encl in BJP, 10 May 1855, no. 222, NAI, Delhi.

143. Major Hamilton Vetch, AGG Lower Assam at Gauhati to Secy GOB, Judcl, 12 January 1856, NAI, FPP, 14 March 1856, nos 35–7 and k.w.

144. Rennie (1970 [1866]: 43–59).

145. *Selections from Records of the Government of Bengal* No. 25E, 1857.

146. Offg Supt Kachar to Secy GOB, 23 January 1858, Gauhati Archives, Assam Governor's Sectt, Military Secretary Officer, BOR, file 109, sl.1–8 of 1858.

147. List of Manipur Princes & Ca Resident in Kachar 23 January 1858, NAI, Delhi, GOB, Political Progs, 22 April 1858, no. 98.

148. Supt Kachar to Secy GOI, Fort William, 19 November 1852, *CDR*, I, 215–17.

149. Lt R. Stewart, Offg Supt Kachar to Commr Circuit Sylhet, 26 January 1858, NAI, GOB Politicial Progs, 22 April 1858, no. 97.

150. Offg Supt Kachar to Commr Circuit Sylhet, 26 January 1858, *ibid.*, no. 98.

151. Debendro Singh to W. J. Allen, Member of BOR, 3 July 1858, NAI, GOB General Progs 29 July 1858, no. 186.

152. See Karlekar (1996).

153. Secy GOB to Offg Member BOR on Deputation (W.J. Allen), 13 January 1858, Assam Sectt. Governor's Sectt Military Secy's Office, BOR (Sylhet), file 110, serial numbers 1–20, 1858, no. 133. This file contains reports from a 'Gurkha' native officer, Jamadar Ganga Ram Bist of the Sylhet Light Infantry to his commanding officer about the number of mutineers he shot dead, the valuables in cash and weapons (guns, bayonets, etc.) taken from them, and all the names of the Hindu and Muslim headmen (*chaudhuri*s) and police chiefs (*darogah*s) of the region who aided him.

154. Off Supt Kachar to Commr of Circuit, 9 March 1858, GOB Political Progs, 22 April 1858, no. 99, encl. 2.

5

A Fraternity of Tea and the Politics of Monastic Friendship

FROM 1840, TEA PLANTATIONS BEGAN to dissolve the monastic geographic order of the seventeenth century; they especially reconstituted the landscape of memory across all lands north and east of Dhaka. Initially, the Company's administration in Calcutta was reluctant to lease or grant lands in a 'frontier province like Assam, surrounded by barbarous and hostile Tribes'. But it had already been overtaken by privately capitalized joint-stock companies such as the United Assam Association or the Assam Company.[1] From 1840, this latter company was given the right to cultivate existing 'indigenous Tea Tracts' or *baris* in lands that were 'British Territory'.[2] The total acreage under tea in Assam went from 2,311 acres in 1841 to 8,000 acres in 1859; until 1850, the only company in the field was the Assam Company.[3]

Scholars who have studied the extension of tea cultivation in both Assam and northern Bengal (Darjeeling) have focused on two different parts of the system. One has been the partnership between British private capital and nascent Indian capitalists such as Maniram Dewan (the minister of a deposed svargadeva) and Dwarkanath Tagore (grandfather of Rabindranath) in raising some of the 500,000 pounds sterling in the Assam Company.[4] These scholars refer to nascent Indian capital in tea as an Indian subsidy to English colonial industry, which enabled the creation of an 'enclave economy' with an outflow of capital and profit from the region, but one in which colonial planters remained dependent on social and economic brokerage of local suppliers for goods, labour, and funds.[5] A second group of scholars has studied the labour relations on tea-plantations from the 1860s till the end of the nineteenth century.[6]

Both sets of scholars overlooked three crucial aspects of the landscape: first, the extent to which the advance of tea cultivation rested on the defeat of older Buddhist–Vaisnava monastic governments all over the Brahmaputra and Barak valleys. As we have seen, during 1838 to 1853 substantial lands held and cultivated by different groups of monastics and subjects had been resumed by the British government of India. Tea spread to all those places.[7] Second, labour historians overlooked the extent to which disciples and tenants of monastic estates in the region were being lured towards colonial estates and monetized taxation regimes after 1840. Labour historians, thus, unwittingly overlook the simultaneously material and ethical–political wellsprings of the resistance to the advancing tea plantations that monastic lords, the gosains, as well as their clerical bureaucracies, their tenants, under-tenants, and farmers organized during the 1860–90s. And third, in ignoring these monastic assemblages, holdings, and settlements prior to tea, post-colonial historians underappreciated the nature of militarized colonial fraternities that evolved around the advance of tea plantations. In turn, this enabled the deliberate oversight of the fact that much of 'British northeast India' was created by guns and bayonets and would be maintained by it well into the present millennium.

Monastic and 'ancestral' lands were the grounds on which the plantations of tea took root and from which they grew out. In 1838, after the svargadeva Purandhar Simha was pensioned off by the colonial government, all the lands on the northern bank of the Brahmaputra were annexed. In 1840, the Assam Company was allotted lands on this bank for tea cultivation. Within a month of the formation of the company, the pensioned-off svargadeva reported that the Assam Company was digging up all parts of the old royal capital for tea, including the tombs of his ancestors. Purandhar Simha explained that the custom of the Ahom royals was not cremation but burial; when any royal person died, all the ornaments and golden plates to the value of from Rs 50 to 25,000 were buried with him. The body was buried at Charaideo and a mound raised over it, called a *maidam*. These tombs, he explained 'are in a manner holy with us and the cultivating of Tea or anything on them would much affect me'.[8] Besides this, he pointed out that building tea factories over and around the royal palace at Ghergong was also destroying the royal capital. At the dawn of the age of colonial capital, neither the Agent of the Governor General (AGG), Francis Jenkins, nor the government in Calcutta or London was enthusiastic about ideas of conservation or preservation of 'heritage'.[9] But the space that the tombs took up was small. So they were prepared to be magnanimous, and ordered a halt to the cultivation of tea around it. Not so the brick-built buildings on the site. It was advantageous to 'all parties if the jungles were cleared and the materials of the ruined buildings converted to any useful purpose'. Factories were built with such bricks, relocated to sites in adjoining valleys such as Sibsagar. It was to these lands that a grandson of the deposed Purandhar Simha referred in 1856, when he wrote that the Company had 'derived revenue from lands that had not previously been liable to assessment'.[10] When he asked for the return of these lands permanently to him (as a *zamindari*) a colonial official responded that this demand 'would place all the Tea planters under him as Tenants'.[11] The grandson's pleader in this instance was the very diwan, Maniram Datta Baruah, who though a 'nascent capitalist', was executed for his part in the rebellion of 1856.

The militarized aspect of colonial liberalism rested on the comity of private English planters and managers and British military officers as investors in tea. Dissenting missionaries were junior members of this militarized fraternity. Curiously, the earliest gifts that were given by members of these new fraternities to their native allies in the Brahmaputra region were also symbolic of this militarization. One of the earliest such gifts was a cache of abandoned Mughal canon— eighteen large brass guns—found in the jungles of Namrup.[12] The military officer who discovered them found that the name of the eighteenth-century Ahom lord, Gadadhar Simha, had been inscribed on most of the guns, over Persian inscriptions. All the guns appeared to have been manufactures of the Hindustan plains. He speculated that these had been abandoned by Mughal armies as they retreated from Gherghong in the late seventeenth century and had been brought up by Gadadhar Simha in the eighteenth century. His senior officer and administrator ordered that the guns be broken up and sold, and the sum given as a gift to the man who had advanced the colonial investments in tea in the region, a man they called Ningrew-la.[13]

Disappearing objects may have produced historical amnesia and non-recognition of the communities in the vicinity. On the other hand, reused as 'gifts', they were expected to produce new solidarities. Such gifts were supposed to attach the loyalties of local men to the dispenser of such gifts, the colonial official. The gift of found canon to Ningrew-la was motivated by the fact that he was a man who had 'great influence' among the followers of the Bara Senapati's descendants.[14] He was also described as a man 'chief among the Singhphos in Ava'. In other words, he was an intimate of both worlds—the Vaisnava estates in the vicinity of the Brahmaputra and the Theravada Buddhist orders in the Burmese capital—even though he lived in the hills far to its north and west.

In early March 1840, Captain Vetch gave this man an advance of Rs 200 to clear the tea baris near his village. Without his active cooperation, and a superb plantation that he cultivated, there would have been no tea culture. Charles Bruce, the Superintendent of the Government Tea Culture, also dispatched expert cultivators of green tea and a group of transportation workers. According to the government's final orders on Ningrew-la, Bruce and Vetch were to agree on a fair rate and monthly stipend to be paid to Ningrew-la, and similar arrangements were to be forwarded to other Singhpho chiefs and Assamese Gohains. So the attachment of a powerful local man to the support of an agro-military combine was no small return for 'gifts' of reused objects.

In presenting the work of the tea companies in this light, this chapter unpacks the conditions under which the very ideas of friendship were contested in eastern India. On the one hand, the vaunted goals of the liberal 'bourgeois' democratic revolutions in Europe from the 1830s to 1848—including fraternity—were closely tied to emergent codes of consumption, such as those of respectable English middle classes gathering at tea shops in metropolitan centres such as London or Edinburgh after the 1840s.[15] Consumption of colonially grown agricultural produce such as tea from Assam (and thereafter Sikkimese monastic estates of Darjeeling and Kalimpong) produced metropolitan 'ethnicity'—the consciousness of being akin in class and culture in British society in the second half of the nineteenth century. But this emergent metropolitan sociality and ethnic consciousness overrode the coded socialities of monastic

subjects in the colony. The code by which many groups of Buddhist–
Vaisnava and Jaina subjects organized their fraternities was called
'universal compassion' (*maitri*), or the extension of kindness to all. It
was a code of conduct which did not discriminate between a 'self' and
a discrete Other, but saw all living beings as interdependent, in need
of compassionate action.[16] The militarized cultivation of tea tested
these ideals of universal compassionate friendship and eventually
defeated them. In the process, a permanent militarization resulted in
entrenching ideas of economic 'development' as intimately wedded
to a 'security state'. This then was the poison in the 'gift' bestowed
by colonial state of the late nineteenth century to the postcolonial
nation-state that followed it.

TEA AND THE TRANSFORMATION OF KACHAR, NORTHERN ARAKAN, AND HILLS OF CHITTAGONG

Within four months of the foundation of the Assam Company,
the hills of northern Kachar were also administratively corralled by
colonial administrators. Remember that English 'Cachar' or 'Kachar'
was a mangled form of the Tibetan word *katsar* or fringe; and the
Kadzari/Katsari were speakers of mixed Tibetan and Nepali languages.
The replacement of *dz/ts* by *ch* by local speakers thus obscured from
view the process by which mixed Central Asian ('Afghan' and
'Kashmiri') Tibetan–Nepali communities living on both banks of the
Brahmaputra, on estates in the gift of particular Buddhist, Bon, and
Vaisnava monastic lineages came to be identified as either living in
'northern Kachar' or 'southern Kachar', respectively. From 1841 on,
officers such as the military official who was also civil administrator
of the newly annexed Assam, the AGG Jenkins, began calling for
the outright annexation of the hills of North Kachar (until then
governed by Tularam Senapati, the nephew of the religious figure
Sanundaram).[17]

Many of the British local officers (and their relatives) were
themselves investors in tea plantations. This was well enough known
for the matter to be touched upon—but apparently not explicitly
outlawed—by the Assam Wastelands Regulations of 1842.[18] In all
parts of British 'Kachar' after 1843–4, but especially in lands in
the Surma-Barak Valley extending into the northernmost tip of
Arakan province and called southern Kachar, the British colonial

government acted as zamindar. Initially, it offered fifteen-year leases at differential rates: arable lands were taxed at a rate higher than the lands that had fallen 'waste' or were still forested but cultivable. The latter, referred to as 'jungle' lands, initially appeared to have attracted many smallholders, including Muslim headmen from Sylhet and others from Jaintea and Kachar, who wished to trade in the thatch and grass markets in Sylhet.[19] Some of these leases were held by collectives sometimes made of fifty to sixty members. Ghosts of many *khels* past had continued to thrive, even though British officials apparently never connected the strong family and descent structures of mountainous Central Asia (including northern Afghanistan) with such continued corporatized groups in the terrain. As a result, modern historians of the economy, too, have tended to see the khel as 'voluntary associations for economic purposes'.[20] Whatever its roots, there were many such khel groups on record, as khel Kukis, khel Mikir, khel Naga, khel Kachari, even in 1840s northern Kachar.[21]

After 1848–9, all khels were required to pay taxes to the colonial treasury at the higher rates at which cultivated lands were assessed. Many defaulted. Customarily, defaulters' lands could not be sold by public auction if there was another person willing to pay the arrears of the defaulter. The defaulter only had to repay within the next two years, failing which, the holding became permanently that of the person who had paid the arrears. But some of these defaulting 'jungle grants' had been acquired by European private capitalists, especially after southern Burma had been annexed to the British Empire in 1852. Tea was discovered on the slopes of Kachar and Sylhet in 1855.[22] Overnight, both British venture capitalists and erstwhile Company and Crown military officers were added to those scrambling for all the low-lying hills of Kachar.[23]

As capital flowed into tea plantations, the latter moved from the northern hills of Kachar to the south and further east. Major (later Colonel) McCulloch, Resident and Political Agent at Manipur in 1850–61 and 1864–7, was an outstanding example of military capital in tea. During the early part of his career as a civil servant, McCulloch had never heard that officials were prohibited from investing in private businesses in the colony. Only after British Parliament took responsibility for the administration of India in 1861 was he explicitly asked to give up his active investments in tea plantations in the region. As he put it, 'I cleared in Kachar some land to plant tea … upon His Excellency the Governor General in Council appointing me to be Political Agent, I at once sold the land I had cleared.'[24]

Military officers did not always invest on their own, but through agents. In some instances, their brothers and other male and female relatives acted on their behalf. An Appendix in the 1859 report on tea grants in Kachar provides a clue to these critical fusions of private capital and public office everywhere in the region. Josiah Patrick Wise, a British moneylender and businessman living in Dacca, held two separate grants—one for 1,000 acres and another for 4,000 acres—in Kachar in his own name. The latter was even more substantial than the 1,500 acres held by the Assam Company, or the 3,000 acres held by the Assam Tea Company in Kachar. Such a private venture would not have been important except that this man was also the brother and business agent of a Captain William Wise, whose moneys he allegedly used to make usurious (and illegal) loans in the 1830s, against which he also acquired estates in various zamindaris.[25] Long before the formalized stages of 'finance capital' described by Lenin, the colonial military pattern of financing tea plantations took military earnings and savings into regions quite far afield from where the officer himself worked or lived.

Ordinarily, the Company's military officers held relatively small plots: a Serjeant Fitzgerald held 500 acres, a Major Graham held 800 acres, and the man who led the first military and punitive expedition against the 'Nagas' in North Kachar in 1849–50, a Lieutenant Vincent, held 1,000 acres of land in Kachar.[26] Such holdings by military officers grounded their discursive and manifest militarism towards populations who paid labour services and 'tribute' to Vaisnava estates in Manipur, and Buddhist estates in eastern Assam and lower Bengal. American Baptist missionaries at Nowgong reported that the first of Vincent's 'expeditions' was a 'failure'.[27] Yet such a judgement was hasty: the gains of these British military expeditions were both indirect and deferred. By leading to the permanent appointment of military officers and outposts in once venerated hilltops and mountain peaks, they reproduced militarism as the foundation of imperial cultivation. Following close on Vincent's expedition of 1849–50 came the expedition of a Lieutenant

Colonel Lister against 'Kookies of the independent Luchye tribe' in the same vicinity in 1850–1.[28] Lister's attempt to destroy villages inhabited by Tantric Buddhist males proved difficult because his opponents had substantial numbers willing to defend them. Lister called for more troops. Four companies of corps arrived. Military posts were established all along the 'southern frontier' of Kachar, and recruitment for local paramilitary 'levies' began in earnest.

Furthermore, reports of such expeditions were often replete with a theme that would be picked up and elaborated in the next decade. This was the theme of rescue of little girls from this or that 'savage' labour corps. Military official discourse of 'liberation' from slavery of such girls presented these girls as 'scapegoats' for sacrifice, who had been redeemed by the military ventures of young British soldiers.[29] Thus, from 1849–50, a masculinist abolitionist discourse was harnessed to the expansion of tea cultivation in Assam. More materially, such expeditions created their own rewards: Vincent's expedition found a seam of coal of very large dimensions on the banks of the Buri Dihing and Dhansiri rivers. Immediately after this discovery, the British Government of India formally annexed North Kachar in 1853.[30]

Apparently, an armed expedition by a local military officer, tacitly supported by his superiors, could force the hand of the government at Calcutta into annexing regions and making them part of 'British territory'. Such expeditions set governmental precedents that allowed administrators in Calcutta and London to turn a blind eye to the nature of 'gentleman' capitalism in the empire. This creeping territorial expansion then allowed managers of the tea companies and other agents to finance and equip individual forays into domains that they then reported as inhabited by 'savage tribes'. Yet who were these people?

Vincent's expedition against the 'Nagas' had found the latter exactly where such groups had been at the turn of the century—in the vicinity of rivers and mountain streams. Irony-free official memos of this period locate these 'savage and rude Nagas' alongside the former capital of the Kochari kingdom, Dimapur, on the same Dhansiri River, a little below Ghoraghat. While the 'Nagas' were presented to the public officials in Calcutta and London as bloodthirsty, no one paused to wonder those whose labour had built the 'three noble tanks still in good condition' in the former capital of the now extinct polity.[31] Predictably, once a fort was annexed and its female holders scattered, it was impossible to represent a household's former *proja* or adherents as loyal and ethical corps on their own terms. Even after the annexation of North Kachar, the old order's jagged edges remained visible like the archaeological ruins on the site. Mr. Browne Wood, a private capitalist, leased the rights to mine the coal beds and cut timber from people called 'naga chiefs' of Namsang and Kungan: these 'naga chiefs' turned out to be the relics of the old Ahom monastic bureaucracy, in an area henceforth called Naga Hills.[32]

The same picture can be pieced together from the descriptions of Lister's expedition to a region south of the Barak River, where he destroyed a large village belonging to a 'Mullah', a village that contained 800–1,000 houses. Yet, these populations had sent representative spokespersons and arbitrators—a 'mantri and four Luchyes, deputed by the five principal chiefs of the tribe'—to the Superintendant of Kachar, bearing elephant tusks as 'tribute' to government, and seeking to have markets established closer to their villages.[33] In a note that surfaced a decade later, Lister had noted of the people he had attacked that the group he had called Looshai were made up of three segments: 'first of Looshais who appear to be a cross between Kookis and Burmese; secondly, of a certain number of true Burmese entertained for the purposes of warfare and thirdly, of refugees and outlaws from Manipur.'[34] In other words, a Tibeto-Burman Buddhist, Bon, and Vaisnava Ahom order—marked by a corporate social and military existence and characterized by codes and expectations—had remained on the ground.

Nor did these groups shrink from market forces. Bengali-speaking traders regularly visited these groups who were adept at buying, selling, and gifting the proceeds of markets and toll booths all along the hills from easternmost Sylhet outwards. Envoys from these communities also asked for more markets in proximity to their villages.[35] It may well have been that the desire for more and closer markets was rooted in a greater dependence on cash payments than ever before. As the headmen (*gaon bura*, literally, village elder) from the Darrang (*dvars*) told a British collector, 'in the reign of the Assam Rajahs the revenue was realized according to the khelwari system, afterwards in the time of the Company's rule the above methods was done away with and the mouzawary system with survey introduced, by which many of the ryots have been put to great distress of their unable to pay up their revenue'.[36] Khelwari referred to the cluster of people or khel who were assessed as a collective, while mouzawary referred to taxation calculated on the acreage of land one held or cultivated. These difficulties had only extended to populations all over lower Burma after its incorporation into the British Empire after 1852. Correspondence in the files of the first British commissioners of revenue show that households such as those of the poorest working groups—such as *bhisti* or water-supplier attached to the British army—had begun to feel the erosion of the older system of calculating dues to the government.[37] With the monetization of all dues, many found themselves unable to pay taxes under the new dispensation; they had even tried to hawk their children and failed. Others, such as a subahdar who worked for cash wages in the colonial army, managed to buy a fourteen-year-old boy from some people 'living in the jungles to enable them to pay their tax'. As the records of the depositions reveal, all the buyers of the children were sworn in as lay 'Buddhists'. Surely, such laymen were not unheeding about altruistic and ethical action. Their participation in the buying or mortgaging of children must have logic anterior to the moral horror expressed by the colonial officers.

In Arakan province, an American Baptist missionary had noted that people had not reconciled to the imposition of Company taxes. 'Though the Burman government … took from them more than they pay now, yet it was occasional; consisted chiefly in labour, and they were not under the necessity of saving' in cash to pay the annual sums demanded of every single household.[38] Yet another missionary recorded that the monetization of the house tax had established an extraordinary level of taxation: Rs 4 per annum on all married people, and Rs 2 per annum to be paid by widowers, a group hitherto exempt from money taxes. Members of 'hill tribes'—populations identified as Mrung, Khyen, and Areng—were liable to pay half that rate in money and commute for the rest with labour in road-building.[39]

Complaints from colonial tax collectors support missionary evidence.[40] A similar process had unfolded since 1850 in the forested lands in the uplands of Chittagong and Arakan, which were held at lower rates than the same kinds of lands in Kachar.[41] Leases in Chittagong and Arakan remained rent-free for much longer periods than they did in Kachar. After 1852, many Britons hastened to buy land in an enlarged 'Arakan division', made up of broadly four districts of Akyab, Aeng, Ramri, Sandoway. By 1861, Arakan division had the greatest number of tea plantations and the largest acreage of 'wastelands' sold under the new rules: 16,425 acres, holding twenty-eight plantations.[42] These purchases took European companies directly into areas where refugee Rakhains had resettled since the eighteenth century.[43]

These refugees and their flocks had all headed towards settlements in the hills exactly where older Buddhist structures had been established since the end of the sixteenth century. For example, there was the 'Kon-dan Pagoda', five miles below a town called Dalekmay, built by a Burmese princess said to have hailed from a dynasty that had once governed Pegu/Bago.[44] Many of the inhabitants of the region claimed descent from the followers of the princess even in the nineteenth century. In 1851, a military official, Captain Tickell, had visited Talek-me, a village on the Koladyn inhabited by 'Khyongthas lately immigrated from Chittagong.'[45] Many of these immigrants were indeed beleaguered tax refugees of the plains. But that was not all they were. They also had ethical and moral resources that they had taken with them.

ETHICAL COMMERCE AND MONASTIC SUBJECTS

The corporate relationships among these inhabitants were visible in the interstices between 'northern Kachar' and the Himalayan Bon-Buddhist lineages, as well. Even in 1854, groups of subjects of Tibetan Buddhist monasteries described as the 'Bhutea and Kookies' in North Kachar collaborated with each other.[46] They provided sanctuary for the rebels of 1857, as shown in the records of both song and official reports. Their motivations for doing so have seldom been probed, but it appears that Mahayana, Vaisnava, and Sufi Central Asian codes all came together in this context. In Mahayana ethics, the saving of all beings was an important aspect of a virtuous life, one of the four bodhisattva vows first developed in China in the sixth century: 'Beings are infinite in number, I vow to save them all'.[47] Particularly directed at laymen, the transformation of such ethics into practice—such as learning medicine, maintaining canals, protecting animals, consoling the grieving—had been reported by both colonial officers and missionaries among the societies in the hills.

In 1851, an English officer had found a village (Ruproa) in the northernmost reaches of the Arakan division, just beyond the mouth of the Kaladan River. Here he encountered the ethics of compassion for all living things in the context of pastoralist culture. In the village, goats were plentiful and poultry and pigs abundant, but rice cultivation minimal and horticulture paltry. Most of the rice the humans consumed came from the lowlands, and was carried in by Muslim Rakhain. This officer was not merely surprised by this lack of 'good husbandry' when such a plenitude of soil and water existed in the vicinity but he was also deeply shocked by the regime of care in this pastoralist culture. In the evenings, the pigs were loosed from the sties and fed with 'rice, milk and vegetables'.[48] Such a regimen made the 'pork of this part of the world free from the odium' of Indian pork, but these villagers did not appear to have indulged in a great deal of meat eating. Though they lived on a river teeming with fish, they did not catch any. These abstemious measures baffled British colonial officers, who could not fathom the pluralism of values simultaneously at work. The logic of the market was apparently transparent to such officials, but the command of compassion towards living things was not. Mid-nineteenth-century British military officers therefore could not fathom how feeding rice to pigs could be a 'gift' of life, though it maintained the Upanisadic continuum between human and animal, asserted the status of the *jiva* (life-consciousness) as indivisible particle (*amsa*) of an absolute (*paramatma*), and expressed the nuanced relationships between the preservation of animal and bird wealth and its deification. One of the important deities of northern Buddhists was Vajravarahi, the female deity with the face of a sow, while Vaisnava iconography rendered the boar as an incarnation of the deity, in addition to the fish and the turtle; and Varathregna's favoured animal was the pig.

In these contexts, the spilling of animal or human blood had always had grave consequences. To a monastic subject, with an eye to a future or hereafter, such consequences might have been better shared as a collective. British officers may have been unaware of how seriously this idea created notions of 'debt' and energized mechanisms of corporate responsibility for repayments of loans, payment of revenue, and the return of stolen goods. They had even fewer concepts to understand how their own participation in an animal bloodletting ritual implied a political compact by which they implicitly shared in the crime of causing suffering to an animal and the animal's owner, and therefore shared liability for redress. Unaware of the many judicial and political aspects of such rituals, military officers such as Captain S.R. Tickell, and later other officers, participated in a ritual in the hills of North Arakan that involved the killing of a chicken, and the putting of the chicken's blood on Tickell's feet. The colonial officer put the same blood on the forehead—as a *tika*—for the local man who had killed the chicken. Such joint performances of ritual sacrifices of wealth from animal or poultry stocks were not mere exotica; these were condensed compacts that local performers may have seen as the equivalent of an IOU from a colonial official of a debt of 'blood' to the second party if the contract to which they had sworn was not fulfilled.[49] Such an unawareness of the political nature of government by ritual thus made many such military officers cavalier in their commitments to the sponsors and audiences of such rituals.

Cavalier disregard for ritual also hid from the perceptions of such officers the nature of collocation that enabled Muslim Rakhain to live alongside Buddhist Rakhain in the same societies. Travelling on the Kaladan River, one of them described villages on the banks of the river peopled with 'Mug Mussalmans' (Rakhain Muslims), speaking 'indiscriminately Arakanese or Bengali to each other'.[50] He had even hunted in the jungles behind their villages and found, in the heart of woods in which he went hunting with his Muslim hosts, 'a statue of Gaudama, in his usual squatting posture, of colossal size, for he was full 7 feet high; and here had he remained, solemn and alone, so long that a tree had grown up behind him, and cast its gnarled roots round his body.'[51] If such officers could not recognize, as Buchanan had not, the cosmopolitan character of both Islamic communities and Bon-Vajrayana Buddhists in the region, it was entirely because such mid-nineteenth century British officers only had models of the absolutist state and monotheist interiority with which to gauge tests of either political sovereignty or the cultivation of sanctuary and of pluralism of practice. To them, as to Buchanan, pluralism was akin to degradation or dilution of sincerity. Thus, as one census taker later in the nineteenth century put it, these tribes indulged in a 'spirit worship of the lowest kind, and the principal mode of appeasing the spirits is by killing and eating the flesh of animals'.[52]

TEA AND THE POLITICS OF COMPASSION

All these aspects of agnosia—the unknowing or deliberate ignorance of the political and legal effects of rituals by representing them as 'savage' performances, the denial of moral and legal authority to the performers of the compacts—were enhanced by the extension of empire by the Crown and Parliament after 1860–1. Despite knowing the difficulties of privatized and perpetual ownership of land for the cultivation of tea, officials of the British Government of India between 1856 and 1861 preferred to trust their own abilities to tame the beast rather than diminish the spirit of enterprise. Only the 'penniless adventurer' and the 'bubble Company' needed to be kept out, they thought. Canning's tenure as a governor general liberated European tea planters and managers of tea companies from all state or governmental controls. In 1862, even though the secretary of state did not formally approve the plan, the Government of Bengal passed a piece of legislation that allowed tea planters or their managers to transform hitherto leasehold land into freehold (or absolute private property in land) on paying certain amounts ranging from 2 to 8 rupees per acre upwards.[53] Existing planters who wished to acquire wastelands from that date paid a price of 5 shillings per acre. Possession was granted on the payment of 10 per cent of the total cost into local treasuries. These rules enlarged the territorial scope for the freedom of British capitalists in the buying and selling of 'waste lands' in Assam and Kachar.

Some of the best lands—lands which had earlier had thick undercover and especially bamboo forests at elevations between 500 and 1,500 feet above sea level—were acquired by the tea companies. By 1859, about 91,000 acres of land in southern Kachar alone had been given to tea cultivation; most were held by European companies and officials. Most of these lands lay in low hills, some of which had been previously cultivated with varieties of hill rice, mixed with broadcast cotton. In fact, most of these plantations were opened in terrain that continued to produce grain, vegetable, and cotton crops for local Buddhist and Muslim populations called Kukis.[54] These people, a colonial official's note to the manager of the Equitable Tea Company acknowledged, persisted in *jhuming* (slash-and-burn cultivation) in the land claimed by the Tea Company, and disregarded the manager's order to stop.[55]

Moreover, many of the plantations appeared to have annexed the very homesteads and lands of these peasant-cultivators or 'hill tribes'.[56] Conflicts brewed. As some officials recognized,

the neighbouring ryots consider these Tea plantations a grievance because from time immemorial they have been in the habit of supplying themselves, free of cost, from these jungles with timber, firewood, bamboos, cane &ca. A considerable portion of these forest lands has now been taken up by the Tea Planters, and in consequence the neighbouring ryots are put to some expense and inconvenience for firewood and other jungle articles.[57]

The very collectives (khels) that had claims to use the forests for their livelihood—collecting fodder, timber, beeswax, lac—defaulted as taxpayers as European private capitalists moved into the same regions on which they depended. A very large estate of Gangapur, for instance, was acquired by a European-owned, privately funded, Kachar Company in this manner.[58]

The commission that inquired into the expansion of tea in Assam and Kachar and Sylhet in the course of the 1860s found that the Assam gardens were on flat land, while those of Kachar and Sylhet were on *teela* or small hillocks with greater variety of soils. The Kachar hills had all been occupied, though not all cleared for cultivation. The Commission thought the expansion of tea cultivation had been so sudden that it had placed a premium on inexperience. 'Young men fresh from England, who had no knowledge whatever of the business in which they were engaged, of the habits and language of the people who were under their control or of the difficulties to be met and overcome' had taken up management of tea plantations.[59] In the process, they had made many mistakes. Most important, they had put on the market, tea that was worth little or nothing in order to keep production levels per acre very high, and suggest a flourishing economy. Even the official commission was constrained to admit that their care of labourers was 'very defective'. All of this had led to a crisis in 1866, which lowered the prices of tea and wiped out profits from tea plantation for a short while.

British army officers with shares in such tea plantations suffered from the crisis of 1866. One of these was a Captain (later Colonel) Thomas Herbert Lewin. Hailing from three generations in the Company's service, Lewin had an 'India uncle' who secured him a cadetship in the East India Company's army. Lewin arrived in India in the thick of the rebellion of 1857.[60] Taken to Kanpur and shown a well, he apparently never forgot the horror of seeing the mass of 'bodies of my countrymen and women' there. In his memoirs, he even recalled having picked up at the spot a dirty and blood-stained Bible, a token of the savagery of humans towards each other.[61] Having served in Hazaribagh as a senior police officer just after the 1858 peasant resistance against growing indigo, Lewin was in Chittagong by 1864. At some time during his term at Hazaribagh and then Chittagong, as we find from his letters about his various 'tea speculations', he had invested in something he referred to as a 'Hazaribagh concern'. He hoped for only a 'moderate return. The Chittagong estate will I hope be a real success'.[62] By 1866, he had placed his younger brother, William, as a manager and apprentice with a 'Mr. Sinclair Tea Planter'.[63] But the crash of 1866–7 began to eat away his dreams of a quick and sizeable fortune. In September 1867, Lewin explained to his mother that he could not leave India yet because in addition to valuable share in a tea garden in Chittagong, which would bring him something like 150 pounds sterling a year in two years' time, he also had money invested in the Bengal and Nahor Habi (Sylhet) Tea Companies. Their shares, owing to the panic in the money market on the score of tea, were currently unsaleable.[64] In 1868, the Nahor Habi and Hazareebagh Tea Companies were talking of winding up; the shareholders won't get a penny, he wrote to his mother. Besides which, the Bengal Tea Company had paid no dividends. Tea speculation appeared a losing investment.[65]

Such British official investment portfolios suggest the ways in which problems of global markets came to intersect directly with the shaping of a colonial public discourse in the foothills of Bengal and Burma. These portfolios also reflect some of the ways in which global market fluctuations shaped colonial military policies in the region. Though the falling market for tea in 1866–7 was not the handiwork of a single group of men in the plantations of Kachar, it was so perceived by shareholders in tea companies, by men such as Lewin. Completely in keeping with the actions of military officers before him such as Vincent and Lister, unauthorized by Fort William but with a nod and a wink from local administrators, Lewin led his own 'expedition' from Chittagong against a group he called Lushai and Shendu.

The region that Lewin called Lushei country was within 100 miles east of Chittagong town on the Karnaphuli River, 110 miles south of Tipaimukh in Kachar, and 50 miles within the border of British-held north Arakan. Plantations had extended themselves into this region without formal sanctions of British governments in either India or Burma. Once confined to the northern Kachar, tea plantations had of late years swept farther and farther. As the cultivated frontier expanded south, populations living in those parts appeared to be withdrawing even farther, 'keeping the boundary line of their villages and cultivation nearly parallel to that of ours, a belt of impenetrable jungle intervening'.[66] Withdrawal from the British government-sponsored tea and military also pushed some of the same populations to climb higher up the hillsides, abandoning the lowlands to the plantations.

This withdrawal did not suit the gentleman capitalists of tea. As the Secretary of the Tea Association put it, no crop was more dependent on an adequate supply of labour than tea.[67] On the basis of his calculation, prior to the coming of the bush into tea, labour at the rate of 1 man to every 2 acres of land was needed; once the leaf appeared, labour was needed at man for each acre. The provision of cheap labour was the 'sole question to look to in the future'. Such gentlemen capitalists looked to the British Government of India to secure labour for them cheaply.

Administrators on the ground found ready-made answers. Some colonial officers expected that revenue-related stresses would induce affected populations to seek employment in 'European-owned' plantations and other concerns, and that this labour would be both 'cheap' and 'free'.[68] Therefore, no administrative officer took it amiss when managers of tea plantations such as James Davidson (of the Kachar Company) began to report that they had got 'considerable numbers of Kookies and Nagas' to work on daily and monthly wages on lands owned by his Company. This was the sort of use that military men turned provincial administrators (see Chapter 4) had long considered the correct use of land and labour. It was especially important, one wrote, to convert these forests into fertile fields while simultaneously having a large number of labourers available for tea cultivation.[69]

The problem of labour scarcity was particular to Kachar for the additional reason that this was the very terrain in which members of the Manipuri-Kachari-Tipra 'princely' (*guru*) lineages had been settled on 'rent-free' grants in the 1830s–60s. These, and their entourages, were some of the 'local labour' available. They were men who occupied a position more resembling in its independence that of small landed proprietors than of ordinary cultivators. Others were the Muslim smallholders from Sylhet. They were not expected to leave their own fields to work regularly on the tea gardens.

The import of lowland labourers to southern and eastern Assam tea plantations had begun in 1863. Although subsequent events would force the admission that the majority of these transported workers were females and children, none of the contemporary official records spelled out sex ratios of this labouring population in the 1860s. The contemporary Bengali-language press did not, either. Instead, novellas like *Kulikahini* made clear that a majority of tea-plantation 'labourers' were women. The protagonist of this novella was a mother who brought her two young daughters with her to an Assam plantation. The language put in the mouth of a labour recruiter clarified that the labourer was female (*māgī, betī*).[70]

The predominantly female nature of this labour force perhaps explains the minimal transactional and transportation costs of moving these workers. The conditions in which they arrived and worked on the plantations were dire. During 1863–7, Kachar received 52,155 'imported labourers', just a little behind Assam, which received 54,352 emigrant labourers. Most of these had been shipped from Lower Bengal, Bihar, the southeastern part of Northwestern Provinces, and districts of Chhota Nagpur. Mortality rates were shockingly high: in Assam 1,712 'labourers' died in one month, and almost half as many again, 2,456, died in the Kachar plantations.[71] By the terms of their appointment, managers of the companies were required to clear and cultivate a minimum of one-eighth of the acreage of every plantation. This encouraged managers to flog 'labourers' to force them to keep working in order to meet those goals. Nor did the promised wages materialize. 'Labourers' sought to escape. Between July 1865 and June 1866, 9,147 died and 3,187 deserted.[72]

Female fugitives added another layer of besieged populations to the ghosts of runaway sipahi males (and their families) from 1857–8 in the same area.[73] Some of these mutineers had been killed by villagers (Kuki) employed by the Kachar Tea Company, which paid spies reporting on the rebels.[74] Some other rebels had survived because monastic lineages in the vicinity sheltered them. These sanctuary givers included the Vaisnava–Buddhist and Tantric Buddhist ordination-based lineages of Manipur, the Tipra, and the women-headed Vaisnava households in Kachar. Among the retinue of men from the exiled Manipuri princely lineage of Kanai Singh in early 1860, for instance, were men identified as 'Looshai, some Munipuri, and a few Hindustani, the latter most likely old mutiny sepoys'.[75]

A range of factors may have been at work in the sanctuary given to male soldiers who rebelled or deserted. Sardari refuge expanded followership, and potentially enhanced human following and resources. Individual monastic leaders were also caught up in intra-lineage or 'household' contests over authority and access to the rights of tribute collection in regions such as Kumilla, Dacca, Manipur, and Agartala. Expanding the numbers of male followers in the 1850s and 60s could not have hurt. However, given the intimate imbrications of such figures with their own adherents (praja) and the difficulties such adherents had already experienced in the 1840s and 50s with colonial road-building projects in the region, it is more likely that these individuals had an intimate understanding of the labour demands of the plantation economies that were spreading around them.[76]

Demands for transportation labour for colonial armies and engineers added to the grief of hill cultivators when the latter were asked to supply *rasad* (rations) for the soldiers of colonial armies sent in to 'protect' them.[77] However, all too often, such armies were requested by one set of hegemons of a dominant lineage to uphold their claims against those of rival lineages. This had happened in Kuch Bihar, Kachar, Assam, and Tipura and early nineteenth-century Manipur. The same conflicts had simmered into the mid-nineteenth century. In 1860–1, a conflict in the Tipra–Manipuri alliance led to an attack by followers of one set of contenders on the tenants and adherents of the other, resident at Khandal, Noakhali. Since followership in each instance extended considerable distances from the headquarters of each lineage, the conflicts spread out over vast distances. As in 1860s, the conflict within the Tipura lineage of Vaisnava–Buddhist lords then encompassed Muslim men from Sylhet and Kachar, such as the zamindar Ismail Ali Khan of Lungla, who had a 275-strong entourage and tenantry.[78]

Though there were good material reasons for all such lineages to absorb runaways from the plantations, there was significant risk in doing so. Since Act XIII of 1859, any flight by 'workmen, artificers, labourers' could be construed as a breach of contract by the runaway. Despite this, one Joomun Mea, who began as a labour recruiter for a plantation, induced the labourers he had recruited to break the contract and flee.[79] An Act VI of 1865 addressed this recurrent problem of desertion on the plantations. Under this legislation, any person who 'harboured' or 'employed' a labourer from a tea plantation was liable to a fine of Rs 500.[80] Notwithstanding such laws, in the same year, a 150-strong collective (which included Muslims) was led by another Vaisnava guru-in-training, Kanai Singh, and his son in attacking the police posted by the colonial government and the tea planter Mr. Eagleton at Jhiri, Kalla Naga, Khoboom.[81] British military men, posted as political agents to these frontiers of tea cultivation, called these 'raids by a Loosai tribe of Nagas' and represented the Loosai as 'intractable set of savages … plentifully supplied with firearms procured from Chittagong, Kachar & ca'.[82] Lewin, too, referred to Kanai Singh's attack on Khoboom in 1865 as the entry of '1500 Lhoosai Kookies' into British territory, and blamed it for his terrible economic fortunes.[83]

He set off on another unofficial expedition in November–December 1865, with the blessings of the commissioner of British Burma. Though it misfired, Lewin was given the office of the Superintendent of Hill Tribes in Chittagong Hill Tracts. By April 1866, he had assumed office.[84] By September–October 1866, Lewin set off, again unofficially, to the village of a man called Rutton Puia, who in turn summoned other local headmen to a ritualized political assembly to deal with Lewin. According to Lewin's letters home, he is said to have offered the 'chief' in a conclave an oath of friendship. 'Swear now to be friends with me', he reportedly said, 'and your enemies shall be mine your welfare my interest—but if you turn your faces away from the oath—then most surely you will be destroyed by the power of the great sirkar'.[85] The chief apparently agreed to take the oath of friendship. So to the sounds of guns and the Burmese war gong, Lewin and the 'chief' grasped one spear and 'invoking the spirit of the Hills and of the fountains', thrust the weapon slowly into the body of a hog which had been bound for the purpose.

But Lewin's knowledge of the social and political economy of the groups he had been sent to govern was guided by his investments in tea. Besides, like Lister and others in the 1840s and 50s, his unofficial visits to those he called 'savages' in his letters home were never referred to in either of the two books he authored as the Superintendent of the Hill Tribes of Chittagong.[86] The first book was far closer to Buchanan's work in spirit than to any other. Like Buchanan in the eighteenth century, Lewin knew that khiongs were temples, that each village had its own bamboo khiong, the great resort of all bachelors of the village most of who were required to sleep in it at night. Like Buchanan, he had no appreciation of the delicate and institutionalized political social norms that tied together the hill-based Buddhist populations with plains-dwelling Bengali-speaking Muslims and Hindus. So, like Buchanan, he tried to segregate them from each other. Writing from a Muslim-majority Chittagong to his sister, he confided that every effort of his was directed at the 'elimination of even the slightest touch of the Bengallee element from among the Hill people and strengthening and stabilation [sic] of their own nationality'.[87] Since many of these 'Bengalis' were also elderly lay women such as the Rani Kalindi, widow of a Rakhain Muslim soldier-governor and patron to many local Buddhist monks for whom she had constructed monasteries, Lewin's ambition to segregate hill men from their plains relatives, friends, and patrons was not a little ominous. It was matched by his desire to Christianize the segregated populations, just as Scott and Jenkins had wished in the earlier decades. If his mother could not find a Protestant missionary, a Roman Catholic would do for uncivilized people such as the hill-dwellers, he wrote her. 'Catholicism was preeminently the faith for minds of the weaker sort that required an infallible guide and a supporting helper. It is the religion for children, women (as a class) and barbarians,' he granted.[88]

Unlike all of his predecessors, Lewin knew that the Arakanese language had strong affinities with the Himalayan and Tibetan dialects, but he did not learn any of the Tibetan languages until 1878.[89] A Bengali-speaking man from Chittagong, Sarat Chandra Das, was a teacher of English in a boarding school in Darjeeling when Lewin was appointed deputy commissioner of the region. Das, who eventually learned classical Tibetan and two related dialects, remembered Lewin's hostility towards Tibet as a 'wild country' that rejected European commerce, soldiers, and merchants, and especially Lewin's personal disdain for him, another of those 'Bengalis' he loathed. As a result of such classic disdain of Tibet and of the literary ambitions of the Bengali male, the British military officer apparently never understood that the people he referred to in ethnic terms as 'Howlongs' were better understood as a regional cluster of households or one of the six major proto-clans of ancient Tibet (*a'o ldong*), whose leaders were all related to each others as brothers and cousins.[90] Regionally, they hailed from a part of east and southeast Tibet, where a river called Hualong was known of in the nineteenth century as flowing north of the Brahmaputra. A region further north of this river was also called Hualong.

Part of Lewin's deafness to the meanings of his informants was explained in terms of the very recent humiliations that officers such as he had either experienced or heard of in the humiliation of the British embassy in Bhutan in 1864–5. So when, about the same period, Lewin was told by 'one of the principal karbaris (officers) of the Sylu tribe' about the first chief Tlandrukpa who came 'out of a cave in the hills',[91] he remained oblivious to this explicit reference to the devotional adherents of the monastery of Druk or 'Thunder-Dragon', associated with a southwards transmission of Tibetan Mahayana teachings. Deeply contemptuous of a Government of Bengal that had been shocked into accepting the tributary payments (*posa*) after the Anglo-Bhutanese war of 1865–6, Lewin declared that posa was 'blackmail to a set of savages who I could rout with a hundred men. I shall not write this to Government but shall quietly go on my own course in which I have the Commissioner's full approval.'[92]

Finally, for an Englishman who wrote so regularly to his mother and sister, Lewin remained singularly unappreciative of the social and cultural networks of the men he took the blood-oath with such as Rutton Puia (or Pooeia). The term *poo* itself stood for all things Tibetan; that this man's sister was also married into a chain of families that hailed from Hualong escaped Lewin. Rutton's sister was married to a man called Sungboonga, the son of a Lal-poitang and nephew once-removed to two brothers, the elder of who was called Vandula and his junior, Sipuia (alternately Seipooeya).[93] They were part of an intricate network of brothers, cousins, nephews, half-brothers, and uncles, each in turn commanding between 100 to 360 households ('villages') with significant populations varying between 1,000 to 4,000 people who lived in the hills in this period. In a pattern that was typical of many Himalayan societies, men from these lineages, such as the brothers Vandula and Sipuia, were married to at least one woman in common, Ropuiliani, daughter in a Hakka (Burmese) clan of equal social status. This woman, not the men, was the real authority within the villages or labour-teams led by the men. Through their wives, men such as Vandula and Sipuia were in turn related to other lineages of brothers and half-brothers, cousins, and uncles. Neither Lewin's published books nor his private correspondence betrays a glimmer of these complex inter-relationships of followership, descent, and marriage.

In the first published account of his encounter with Rutton Puia's patrilineal kinsmen, Lewin omitted the details of the blood-oath.[94] He replaced it with an account of his own performance of Houdini's bullet-trick to convince his audience of the invincibility of the white man's person, the effect of this performance on his audience, and the long speech made by one man, 'a big fellow, Vanlula'. The sacrificed animal too was different—a far bigger and more valuable animal, the hill cow or gayal. There are so many discrepancies between Lewin's private letters immediately after the blood-oath and his published account of it thirty years later that readers can legitimately wonder whether Lewin's memory of the compact had completely failed him over time. Yet, at least Sipuia and Vandula's names match closely enough for us to believe that some version of a blood-compact had occurred between the two groups.

In any case, Lewin appears not to have set great store by the political compact of 'friendship' that he had accepted. Within a month of his return from the hills, he was pressing the Lieutenant Governor of Bengal to authorize a 'hostile expedition' into the very region from which he had returned. Calling it the 'Kookie meeting' in a mail to his mother in December 1866, he wrote that the Government did not like the idea—but 'in /68 I hope something will be done.' Where did this eagerness for blood come from? For one thing, as the same letter suggests, all Lewin's savings, amounting to 1,000 pounds sterling by his own estimate, were wiped out with the failure of the Bank of Hindostan. This included his tea shares.[95] A secondary charge came from science: his dream was to provide for the 'Ethnological Committee of the Asiatic Society certain Loosai crania and pelves for which they are enrage at present.'[96]

The political compact that had meant so little to Lewin was followed to the letter by the very men he had called the savage Lushai. During the intervening period between the compact and the expedition he hoped for, when many Buddhist–Muslim Rakhain and Bengali subjects of the region tried to petition against him to his superiors, Lewin recalled that the 'Lushai chief Rutton Poia' offered not merely sanctuary but material support of cultivators or 'houses' from each of their villages. 'Come to us brother, You will be a great chief,' Rutton Puia is said to have offered. Other headmen, such as a man called (Lal) Savunga, 'the head chief of the great Sylu clan of the Lushais', acknowledged to be a great influence in Kachar and Chittagong, sent emissaries.[97]

LINEAGES: THE LOCALIZATION OF COSMOPOLITANISM

The evidence since the fifteenth century in eastern India shows that the ability of an immigrant to localize rested on the successful ability to insert either the self or a kin-member into criss-crossing networks of monastic ordination lineages, marital affiliations, and friendship pacts through the performance of oaths and other rituals. This kind of open-border policy in terms of social adherence and community had made many Vaisnava–Buddhist men from the Manipuri lineages cooperate with their northern Buddhist partners, especially after the Anglo-Bhutanese war broke out in 1865. Shortly thereafter, Gokul Simha, the younger son of Debendro Simha, erstwhile Burmese appointee to the management of the Manipuri valleys, tried to regain the Manipuri capital for himself; he had travelled to Kuch Bihar, that in-between place where Himalayan and plains lords and their subjects met to recoup forces, but he was arrested there.[98]

The administrative reorganization that followed the Anglo-Bhutanese war may have affected the related or affiliated monastic estates and lineages in the Bengal-Assam plains as well. Such annexation may have had some impact on the intermarried lineages of the Tipra-Manipuri Vaisnava lords. At the heart of such networks, we find figures of Vaisnava Manipuris, such as Kanai Simha, a son of

Marjit, the man who had long sought to be ruler in Manipur. Kanai Simha's sister or half-sister had been married to a Tipra zamindar; her son had contended for and lost the zamindari title in the Tipra household to a paternal uncle, Bir Chandra. The latter, having secured his own zamindari title after having put his predecessors' Vaisnava guru in prison, then moved against his remaining male kinsmen and their adherents by reporting a 'sudden outbreak of Kookie tribes near Koilashahar'.[99] These were merely the adherents of the opposite faction. As yet another early twentieth-century Bengali-language record of the Vaisnava Manipuri lineages puts it, there were many such praja of the Vaisnava gurus on all sides.[100]

These 'Kukis' (Buddhists) were the monastic subjects of the Vaisnava initiates Nilkrishna and Kanhai Simha (nephew and maternal uncle), who surrounded the partisans and adherents of Bir Chandra. The latter included Muslim landholders and tenants such as Ismail Ali Khan of Lungla, Sylhet, and his ally, a man called Hrangbhum, who lived off the edge of Sylhet. Lest it be concluded that these conflicts were between 'Hindu' and 'Muslim', let me emphasize that this was not so. Even in the mid-nineteenth century, Muslim landlords in the region, such as the famous Sona Mian Chaudhuri, had sought to influence the succession to particular emoluments (tolis, income from markets, ports) amongst lineages of Vaisnava bairagis in Sylhet and Kachar by favouring one over the other.[101] Sona Mian favoured a Kachari lineage over a Sylheti Vaisnava lineage, and had ordered a change of tilaks (mark made of sandalwood, turmeric or vermilion on the forehead of initiated members). The latter had complained to the colonial officer, who had promptly imprisoned the chaudhuri. Either a continuation of this struggle, or a similar kind of struggle, erupted in the 1860s involving the Tipra set of Vaisnava 'seat-holders'. One set of Vaisnava monastic subjects (which included a Muslim tenant and a Buddhist 'Kuki' Hrangbhum) confronted another set of monastic subjects of the other Vaisnava lineage.

Leading the group on behalf of Kanai Simha and Nilkrishna was a man called Sukpilall, organizer of three other labour corps (khels). One of these had attacked a British outpost at Adhampur guarded by British Indian Sikh soldiers. The latter testified that they had 'exchanged Hindustani abuse' with men who they believed were mutineers escaped from the fight at Latu in 1857.[102] All the witnesses said there was a 'Manipuri Raja' riding a pony alongside the attackers, who appeared to be cultivators on rent-free tenures in villages in Sylhet. These were adherents of Kanai Simha, of the 'exiled Rajah family of Manipur'. Such adherents were intimately related with each other as well as with Kanai Simha. Sukpilall's daughter was married to him. Kanai Simha, while a 'prince' and potential Vaisnava guru and ruler at Manipur, was thus a son-in-law of one of the five significant heads of villages living between Kachar and Sylhet.[103] Given the strength of relationships mediated through women in the entire community, this affinal relationship was an enormous resource to the 'prince'. Sukpilall's sister had been married to a Murshchoi Lall *luce* (alternately *lu shih* or Buddhist vinaya master), the son of a man who had been treacherously trapped and deported in 1847 by a British military officer.[104] Sukpilall would not let Murshchoi and his half-brother (Docompo) settle among people other than his own kinsmen; even when his sister separated from her husband in 1862, many of the vinaya master's adherents, also her 'father-in-law's villagers', accompanied her to live in a separate but neighbouring village with her brother's.[105] Complex relationships through Sukpilall's mother and her kin tied him to the loyalties of many other villages.

The effects of tea plantations on the social networks as well as the lands claimed by such networks for their cultivation, grazing, and foraging grounds were obvious only if one could read the evidence of the lineages correctly. For instance, villagers on the highlands on the banks of the rivers (such as the Dhalesvari) who said they belonged in the lineage of a senior matriarch—Sukpuilall's mother—had been forced to move into North Kachar once these tracts were sold to the tea companies. Apart from the obligations of kinship, men from these villages joined the entourage of Kanai Simha for explicitly economic reasons—objections to the extension of tea planting in the direction of Kachar.[106]

So though English-speaking officials used the term 'Lushei' as an ethnonym of warriors or 'savages', their own evidence reveals that the term encompassed bands of militant ascetics and bairagis, fused through marriages and rituals of feasting and blood-oaths in a complex and cosmopolitan coalition that pooled technological skills and cultural competencies. By the 1860s, the more appropriate sense of 'Lushei' was the Tibetan term *loshee*, meaning 'courageous, bold'. They were not merely followers of a single Buddhist master or *lu shih*. Nor were they all runaways and refuge-seekers. They had become a major network of followers, each node of that network its own moral and ethical authority. In such a band, therefore, there was place for the 'tall and stout Hindustanee, wearing a full white beard' who led the 'Loosais' in challenging the planters and the British Indian armies sent to the hills in 1869.[107]

A mass of poor Muslims supported them. These were smallholders in Hylakandy who were also in the entourage of Kanhai Simha and supplied its arms.[108] Officials especially commented on those Muslim zamindars in Sylhet, who despite 'holding considerable settlements of hill-men' would supply neither the men nor arms to British Indian troops. The English-language press of the mid-nineteenth century also weighed in against hybrid Muslim populations living and working alongside Buddhist-Vaisnava groups in the region. Referring to the events in Kachar of January 1869, a leading English-language paper fulminated, 'The village Moslems of Sylhet are low enough to be reckoned among the barbarians; those of Kachar, both in the villages and in the civil station, are but the dregs of the latter. To call them simply illiterate would be to offer them a compliment; the amount of decency and common sense usually in exercise cannot save them from the term *savage*.'[109] These were indeed the terms that an officer such as Lewin would use for the group: these were the 'barbarians [who] dared to disturb Englishmen in making money.'[110]

From January 1869, this complex of hybrid marital, martial, and moral authorities marched from Sylhet through two major plantations of Kachar eastwards towards Manipur.[111] One of the plantations, called Monaikhal (variously Monierkhall) at the junction of two rivers (Sonai and Rukni), was owned by Jardine, Skinner and Company. The second was the garden of Dwarband, owned by the British India Tea Company. Monaikhal was completely sacked, and its buildings burned; its entire labouring population ('coolies') as well as most of the European administrators were allowed to flee.[112] Yet other large tracts of land had been bought up by the tea companies but not yet commenced cultivation; some such as the one identified as 'Telinagar to Looshaipara (an unopened tea grant)' were waiting, while others such as the one marked Pollicherra, an inhabited tea plantation with a police post, are not mentioned in the reports of 1869 as damaged.[113] In the winter months of 1870–1, another set of six or seven plantations were stormed by similar hybrid corps of monastic subjects. These plantations were spread between south of Chittagong Hill Tracts (Golangiya), extreme east of Sylhet (Alexanderpur in Chargola district), Kachar (Monierkhal again, Jhalnacherra, Katlicherra, Dhurmikhal), and Hill Tippera (near Adampur).[114] In the course of one of these marches, a plantation at Alexanderpur experienced one fatality. A friend of the plantation manager, a Mr. Winchester, was killed; his six-year-old daughter Mary, born of a local unnamed woman, was taken away, along with many of the labourers on the plantation. Colonial officials subsequently narrated the events of 1869–71 as a kidnapping narrative of a little white girl called Mary Winchester.

CAPTIVITY AND THE PROBLEM OF ETHICAL ACTION

The seduction of the figure of the captive for historians of empire, race, and gender is well established.[115] When the captives have been adult women, narrations of captivity have suggested the multiplication and fracturing of the 'possibilities for identification and alliance' in the founding of states and communities.[116] When the victims have been white males—as for instance in the Barbary narratives of the eighteenth century, or in the British soldiers taken hostage by eighteenth-century Indian potentates—then they called attention to the incompleteness of the political community in the making (as in northern America where black slaves had been retained as captives),[117] or to the characteristics of a citizen (in the French Enlightenment),[118] or to the misplacement of imperialist power.[119]

Since the English-language records only talk of the Lushai armies as 'slave-catchers' or 'slave-raiders', historians of the region who have encountered these records can be very easily seduced by the false universalism of the captivity narrative. Like all those narratives familiar to historians of Euro-American colonization, this one in the heart of Kachar has also been presented by colonial officials as the victimhood of white females. In myriad ways, such narratives were constitutional charters for the founding of trans-colonial 'community'. In late nineteenth-century British tea-planting Kachar and Chittagong, narratives about the captivity of females came to play a dominant role in the expansion of colonial frontiers. They also invited and created a community of sentiment around the unlikely figure of a female European infant. But did such narratives have equal valence in South or Southeast Asian politics? In his study of medieval India, Daud Ali refers to a profusion of female captives of military campaigns in the inscriptions, architecture, and poetry of the Cholas.[120] He finds that 'seizing women' formed a conventional boast in the royal eulogies that cover the walls of temples. The prevalence and style of early modern warfare (with women, servants, and children in the auxiliary corps and trains of battle-ready soldiers) across the early medieval and modern periods made such boasts meaningful in particular narrative traditions. Is this what caused initiated or ordained Vaisnava–Buddhist men, aspiring to 'rule' in Manipur, to also lead their Muslim, Bon-Buddhist, and Vaisnava tenants and followers in repeated marches through the plantations in 1869–71?

The narrative and rituals of Vaisnava kingship that associated the god-king with 'seizing' the earth-as-female and rescuing her from the floods certainly provides a clue to an alternative ritual and political tradition. The image of 'rescuing' female earth from the rains as an act of royal aspirants connects at least some of the monastic lords of this terrain with elaborate rituals of liberating trapped and caged birds, as well as dedicated cattle and horses, which had also been reported from a wide set of Rakhain, Jain, and Himalayan–Buddhist contexts since the seventeenth and eighteenth centuries.[121] These rituals had been observed by eminent disciples—temporal authorities—on the advice of Buddhist 'Raulins' in Arakan in the seventeenth century.[122] Such rituals of liberation were also observed in Mahayana Buddhist Tibet on regular occasions.[123]

The ethos of 'kind-ness' that rested on the admission of all sentient creatures as beings 'of the same kind' had been the basis of governmental decrees and arrangements in nearby Amarapura since 1795. Though much has been made of Bodhawpaya's early efforts to impose a Theravada Buddhist protocol among his subjects, by the end of his tenure he had given up the attempt and allowed all other practices of Buddhists, whether living in the forests or in the villages, to flourish.[124] Bodhawpaya, who was a relative through marriage of many of the Manipuri and Ahom Vaisnava males living in British Bengal, had declared the list of Buddhist Jatakas as the basis of his government.[125] The legal implications of governance by Jataka were milder punitive regimes. Pardons for thieves and robbers were regularly decreed, severe punishments commuted into milder forms of labour services. Among the three guiding principles laid out for the administration of a town officer, the reminder of the hereafter verged close to the Mahayana concern for the liberation of all beings from the fetters of samsara: 'he is expected to know what good deeds should be done in this life and what good deeds should be done for benefit in lives hereafter.'[126]

So seriously did most ordained monks take their vows that capital punishment, a signal aspect of criminal justice in the British legal order of the nineteenth century, was waning when many of the Burmese domains were annexed to the British Empire. As an English officer who served as an agent at Bhamo in the 1870s reported, two Burmese caught stealing cloth from a Chinaman's boat were executed at night 'in order to evade the hpoongyees who would of course have made an attempt to rescue the unfortunate men.'[127] Not only was this behaviour expected of ordained monks, but the same order of behaviours was also certified as 'royal' in the decrees of the nineteenth century for laymen: charity came first, but restraint, moderation, and forgiveness were close behind. In such a context, small and large gestures of *karuna* (compassion) and *dana*—the gift of life, not merely freedom—were internalized as part of a diffused 'governmentalized' subjectivity because it had been part of a monastic governmental system. The same order extended to the Himalayan Buddhist societies, as well. In 1862–3, Ashley Eden had encountered the same compassion in the attempt of a Bhutanese dzongpen who 'insisted on the release of coolies who were being flogged by the English officers', even to the extent of drawing his knife and rushing into the ring with his followers.[128] Eden had simply ordered his soldiers to draw their guns up and prepare to shoot the monk instead.

Was it possible, then, that the grant of life and 'freedom' came together in the attempts of these lineages and brotherhoods in their march through the plantations of Kachar in the 1860s? Testimony from two different groups of female labourers suggests that this was a plausible interpretation of the events that unfolded in the hillsides. The marchers removed whole corps of female and child labourers from the plantations. One woman, a tea labourer removed from Alexanderpur tea plantation, remembered the names of at least twenty-one removed with her, including the 'illegitimate daughter of Mr. Winchester'.[129] Though this woman, called Shabitri Culini (an attempt to feminize the term *coolie*), gave confusing testimony regarding the care of the child Mary—at one place saying she was fed thrice a day with boiled rice and molasses and at another place saying the child was given an egg to eat each day they were on the road— the impression the testimony left was not that of a vengeful and hostile group of men, but the reverse. A tiny piece of her testimony, examined in great detail subsequently for the House of Commons, recorded that some of the men in the group that marched through the Alexanderpur plantation said 'droo droo' to her and those twenty-one tea workers with her.[130] Depending upon the tone used, 'droo' in standard Tibetan meant 'going' and 'trotting'. Used as an imperative to someone by a speaker of Tibetan languages, it would only have meant that the speaker was urging the audience to trot, to run. The records suggest that this was a command directed at the labourers on the plantations, urging the women to flee.

Most of these were young women, girls, and young boys. In one of the tea plantations in Kachar, most of those who fled ('kidnapped' in the records) were ten women, sixteen girls, eight boys: there were only three adult men in the lot.[131] This age and sex differential reflected the nature of the labour profile that had been amassed on the tea plantations of the nineteenth century. Yet, many of these 'labourers' were not even kept on by the so-called raiders. At least another fifty-one women and children, described in police records as 'captured' by 'hillmen from Manipur territory' (also called Looshai), noted that of these, fifteen adult women with their children had been 'allowed to escape' by their captors.[132]

Such enforced acts of forceful and compassionate liberation of labourers trapped in suffering on the plantations hurt the capitalist fraternity that had organized the import of such labour. Tea planters of Kachar and Sylhet were especially vehement on this head. A twenty-member delegation met the Lieutenant Governor of Bengal, Ashley Eden, who had been at the centre of the Anglo-Bhutanese war of

1864–5. On Eden's urging, the delegation drafted a petition to the Governor General of India which pointed to the 'very large number of labourers coming from all parts of India who are now resident upon tea estates and upon whose labour the very existence of tea-planting on this frontier depends.'[133] Indirectly admitting that the lineage networks' march through the plantations had successfully stopped cultivation for some months, the petition clarified that the flight of 'imported labourers' not only removed capital from the land but threatened to destroy it permanently, as those who remained 'absolutely refuse to remain beyond the term of their existing legal engagements.'

Such refusals were significant precisely because, as the memorialists admitted, the majority of the labourers were women and children. Instead of being compliant, these female labourers were turning out to be recalcitrant. The risk of collapse of property values and of tea plantation was imminent. As the planters saw it, the task of the British Government of India was to keep labourers tied to the tea-plantation lands: it was required to send out a punitive military expedition to the 'enemies' country, those tribes who have raided upon us', to recapture and restore fugitive labourers.

This was the context in which the great flurry around the victimhood of Mary Winchester in the English-language press was generated.[134] By presenting the work that the monastic–military lineages had done in liberating female and child workers as 'kidnapping' that threatened all fair white maidens as well as all European planters, the English-language press deflected attention from a colossal irony of nineteenth-century Liberalism. This was the spectacle of a colonial British government and an abolitionist middle-class metropolitan public that had cooperated in the re-enslaving of females and children and in re-bonding of their bodies to lands possessed by European capitalists. For those who had fulminated against 'slavery' and 'feudalism' practiced by Indians in an earlier decade, such ironies of British governments acting as slave owners on the Atlantic model did not invite comment in the Anglophone public sphere. A campaign to push down 'the Lushai' began.[135] An entire phalanx of managers of tea gardens, Indian petty clerks, and traders who supplied the commissariat of the British Indian army, as well as various branches of the British Indian and Burmese military and police officers, closed ranks.

Lewin was on leave in England in 1870. He hurried back to participate in the military expedition. His desire was finally going to be realized: besides, 'he had eaten much dirt at the hands of the Lushais for some time past.'[136] To the more astute of the participants, it was clear that the expedition was about making southern Kachar safe for tea, perhaps annexing more territories for the plant in Chittagong and Arakan. But for the greater English public, all that was said to justify the expedition had to do with the rescue and liberation of 'slaves', a standard justification in the 1870s for another round of imperial annexations in the African continent and the Indian subcontinent. To others, the expedition was to save a little white girl, an unwitting icon at a besieged intersection of gender, class, and ethnicity.

All military reports of that expedition refer to her rescue directly as the crowning success of the expedition. Lewin's records are overwhelmed by this figure of Mary Winchester. He was confident that the 'Howlongs', governed by two brothers, had her. They lived on the highest elevations of the hills. One arm of the British army started from Chittagong on 8 October 1871 for the hills. Another arm began the march from Kachar. Rutton Puia, even at this difficult moment, attempted to keep to the unwritten compact of blood that he had performed with Lewin. With money from the Chittagong officers, he offered his sister's affines Rs 400 as ransom for Mary.[137] But these groups did not want money. They wanted five sets of gongs, each set consisting of three gongs, of different tones, flat and about fifty inches in diameter. These gongs 'are supposed to be made by the gods and goddesses' and were greatly prized by these communities. For all the fire power that was amassed at the headwaters of three rivers—the Dhalesvari, Barak, Kaladan—apparently to rescue one little girl, it was not the armies that secured Mary Winchester's release. If anything, the men refused to offer violence in exchange for violence. They preferred to retreat, as Lewin's letters in the thick of the expedition suggested of Savunga's villagers.[138]

But as an editorial in the *Friend of India* announced, an undeclared 'war' existed on the ground. It involved the colonial fraternity's destruction of food stores of the 'enemy'.[139] While the British Indian army destroyed at least ninety granaries in the hills of Chittagong and captured, killed, and ate large numbers of the bigger bovids, the gayal, Rutton Puia went by another route with a Subahdar Mohamed

Azim to effect the release of Mary Winchester (see Figure 5.1). He secured Mary and brought her to his own village, asking the officer commanding at Demagiri to fetch her. Lewin, the author of a newspaper account on the expedition under the title 'Correspondent

Fig. 5.1   Mary Winchester in 1871.

Source: Mss Eur E361/7, 04E00302, OIOC. By permission of British Library, London.

with the Right Column' (the precursor of the 'embedded' journalist of our times), did not even see her, let alone participate in her rescue.[140]

Rutton Puia's role as intermediary and peacemaker, though seldom lauded by colonial officials, was replicated by other peacemakers who intervened to stop further bloodshed, especially destruction of animal wealth. These figures only appear in individual autobiographies of military officers marching through Kachar. A military engineer left a vivid account of a colonial Indian army (made up of 'Gurkhali' soldiers and Sikh sappers) killing men and burning granaries, stopped in their tracks by a man 'wearing a yellow cloak and waving a red puggree'.[141] Englishmen called this man Darpong or Dorpong. According to another account, this was a 'Looshai clothed in an orange coloured garment ... who now appeared with a flag of truce.'[142] When the British commander agreed to a temporary cease-fire, Darpong climbed up into a dead tree, 'sounded the cry of peace to the invisible foes in the jungle and from that moment all firing ceased.' Darpong promised that all firing would stop and that all communications would be kept open thereafter. It was a promise that even the British officer agreed was religiously kept. From that moment, the roads became perfectly safe for dak-runners, coolies bringing up supplies, and so on. Darpong, according to Roberts, was also the man who secured the release of another Manipuri woman, except that the woman begged not to be separated from her local spouse and so was allowed to go.[143]

Who was this yellow-robed or orange-robed figure waving a red turban? Why did his voice silence the guns so completely and effectively? Was he the same man who was identified as 'Durpun Raja' deputed by the monastic order in Bhutan to the colonial governors in 1860–1 to receive the annual rents of the Ambari Falakata estates?[144] Or was he just an ordinary Sino-Tibetan general used to giving commands and being obeyed? Did such generals wear saffron-coloured robes? If they did in the Sino-Tibetan world, yellow-orange or ochre-coloured robes were never associated with anything other than ordained monastics in the South and Southeast Asian world. The colour of the robe alone places this peacemaker as a member of one of the many monastic lineages in the terrain. However, it was the 'red' turban that suggested his membership in one of the older

Tibetan sects—Nyingmapa, Kagyupa, and Sakyapa—all of who were spoken of as 'red hats'.[145] The red turban may have been the particular badge of one of these lineages. The Nyingmapa were a strong lineage, especially in Bhutan, Sikkim, and eastern Tibet, the very 'Hualong' that the British military men ethnologised as 'a tribe of Howlongs'. Perhaps the colour of the robe should have told the British officers everything necessary about this figure and his commitments. Perhaps that alone ensured his authority among his invisible subjects.

Darpong, however, did not take the ethical or ritual literacy of the British military officers for granted. He brought three young men as pledges to one of the British camps. One of these pledges, a man called Santong, was shown a sketch of Darpong and another fugitive plantation worker living among them called Rutton Singh.[146] He responded with what appears to be an unrecognized reverence. 'He sat on the floor of the hut, looking at them, laughing occasionally, and gently repeating their names at intervals as if he expected to be answered. This he continued doing for about half an hour, and when asked to give back the sketches and portraits, could not be prevailed on to do so till he had called in a sepoy who was passing to share his satisfaction.'[147]

As labour was pooled, so was delight. It too was soon communicated to the collective. Several others, having heard of a coloured sketch of Darpong, visited the Englishman requesting to see his sketch-book. It contained largely black and white pencil sketches, but suddenly, on turning a page, a coloured picture appeared to their delighted eyes. 'Darpong', they all cried at once. The officer believed the spectators had made a mistake: they had named a landscape of a north Indian place of pilgrimage, Hurdwar, as Darpong. But was it really a question of mistaken identity? In Tibetan the term 'dar.phung' referred to a heap of prayer flags, of the kind found at mountain passes and certainly found at pilgrimage sites. The officer did not know Tibetan. Nor did he recognize the monastic subjects' attempts to 'see' the picture of the monk as an attempt at securing liberation of the Saiva-Buddhist kind. In both Buddhist and Saiva-Sakta worlds, gazing upon (*darsan*) a deified place, person, or syllable had the capacity to 'liberate' the devotee from suffering. There was even a term in Tibetan for an object that when viewed offered deliverance, like the sketch of an eminent lama. It was *toŋdree*. Local men's reverential responses to a painting—of a place or person—that could not be correctly identified by military officers suggested an unbridgeable and widening gulf by 1871.

Such colonial agnosia about the Bon, Tantric Buddhist, Islamic, and other collocated communities in these hills followed the besieged sardars into death and beyond. Officers of the British military wing that went southwards from Kachar towards North Arakan in 1871–2 arrived at a cluster of 500 huts at 6,000 feet elevation. In the centre of this settlement they found the tomb of Vonolel, one of the two allies of the Vaisnava Manipuri 'princes'. Its base was a platform of stone about thirty feet square. Around it was a high paling of timber, chiefly posts on which were suspended numerous skulls 'of every animal in the country, elephants, metnas, tigers, bears, deer etc'.[148] A very similar tomb was seen by another officer in the same detachment. This was the tomb of Vonpilall, who had died aged twenty, leaving behind an infant son.[149] Visible for miles around, it too was made up of a platform of rough flagstones and wood, about seventeen feet square and three feet high. In the centre grew a young banyan tree, brought from the plains, which seemed to be flourishing in its elevated home. The branches of the tree were crowned with the skulls of animals such as elephants, tigers, hill-cattle, wild boar, and deer, as well as the head of a Manipuri pony.[150] Standing around the platform were ten-foot-high Y-shaped posts, the sacrificial posts on which hill-cattle and other animals were sacrificed at the death of a significant figure. This eyewitness added that Vonolel's tomb was similar to his cousin's, but in a better state of preservation. Inside the tomb, said the same eyewitness, a 'broken Burmese idol was placed in state, and in the centre was a post bearing a very large metua skull'.[151] From one of the horns of this cattle head hung a human skull that had been smashed. If it had not been so smashed, the doctors accompanying this expedition would have collected it for a museum, mused the military officer who witnessed the removal of the skull. The dismantling of other peoples' sacred sites was not new. It had happened in Assam already. It was now happening in Kachar, Arakan hills, and Chittagong.

Since such military men did not identify the 'idol' in question, we have to fall back on a constructive risk—by referring to the old cosmopolitics that had constituted the everyday of the colonized.

The grave's multiple markers were the clue. All the elements of sacrality—the tree of life, the symbol of plenty, the assurance of animal wealth, and an icon—in the same monument both addressed the heteropraxy of visitors to the grave and suggested a community such as the Bon-Buddhist one, whose adherents had built these graves in the course of 1869–71. These were the monastic subjects or members of Bon-Buddhist communities that the British military machines had sought to destroy.

Like the skulls of the animals on the graves of valiant war heroes, there were other signs of the collocation of a cosmopolitan order strewn around these hills, such as the small pagodas at elevations between 3,000 and 4,500 feet, many of which were still surrounded by old fruit, palm, and cinnamon trees that one observer found. This was a newly appointed superintendent of 'Hill Tribes in Arakan', and he suggested that not very long ago, 'judging from the freshness of the inscription on a stone found on the top and from the well preserved state of a small pagoda discovered there in 1872' there were people living here.[152]

At least one of the generals who had climbed up to the elevations between 3,500 and 5,000 feet above sea level from the Chittagong end was surprised enough by the abundant and certain crops, the houses surrounded by pigs, poultry, goats, and gayal at 5,000 feet to grant that these 'so-called tribes … appear to me … very far removed from the savages they are supposed to be.'[153] Yet another, a transferee from a military career to the position of superintendent of the North Arakan Hills, found his contemporaries—the people who were now British subjects—as Buddhist as other Arakanese elsewhere. Less prone to find savages among such men, he was even prepared to liken the male hairstyle (a knot at the back of the head) as emulation of the terracotta images found on the walls of the Thatone 'pagoda'.[154] In other words, he was prepared to concede that so rigorous was the discipline of the monastic subject that even his body had been remade in the image of sacred figures of long ago. The same superintendent would also note that languages spoken in these hills north of Dalekmay were hybrid: there was a dialect here associated with the *hkhongtso* which 'contains many words and expressions intelligible to the Munnipooreans'. In other words, there may have been regional monastic dormitories of Manipuris in the Chittagong-Arakan region.

STRATEGIES OF EXCLUSION

Individual military officers' reports and files suggested that the monastic subjects were everywhere in the region, but that administrative policies after 1871–2 sought to destroy them altogether. Immediately after the expedition roads were planned to connect each of the tea plantations that had been attacked in southern Kachar and northern Chittagong to one another.[155] The extension of roads further eroded the exemptions from labour services and dues of certain groups of monastic subjects of the old monastic-ascetic lordships of the Tipra-Rakhain. For instance, reporting on the strong resistance to the road-surveying party in the aftermath of the expedition, a colonial magistrate reported that the traditions of the Tipra Raj family were that 'all the hills up to Burma' had been held for many generations by the Raj.[156] These were the 'eastern provinces' claimed in the poems of the Tipra estates. Though there were still some men alive who remembered that past, they were in no position to claim it.

Everywhere after 1871, the military-planter-missionary brotherhood put its fences more securely around hillsides and peoples growing high-value global cash crops. Tea was only one of these. An identical story unfolded around the cotton-growing hills of northern Mymensingh, Goalpara, and northeast Rangpur. These had been in the property of the zamindar of Shushung since at least the eighteenth century. But by 1871, his older relationships with his tenants, hill-dwellers only some of whose names ended with 'Garo', were ended by the British Government of India for a one-time payment.[157] And just as administrators in the 1830s and 40s had secured lands and labour for Baptist missionaries among populations described as the godless 'Naga' and 'Garrow', so in 1871 the Welsh Presbyterian Mission was given rent-free grants in the 'Khasi and Jynteah Hills' (that is, north of Sylhet and northern Kachar) by a commissioner of Assam.[158]

Most important was the implementation of a suggestion made since the crisis of 1866–7: the establishment of separate tea districts as a 'distinct province with a separate government'.[159] A colonial administration formally implemented the Inner Line Regulation of 1871, subsequently called the Regulation V of 1873.[160] Its clauses ensured that monastic heads or even gurus-in-waiting, men like Darpong and Kanai Simha—participants in monastic geographicity rather than men of permanently fixed abodes—were to be successfully shut out from their adherents and families in the terrain acquired by the colonial fraternity of military and tea planter. Such men, who were 'not natives' of resource-rich, plantation-filled districts of colonial Assam (Kachar, Lakhimpur, Sibsagar, Kamrupa, Darrang, Nowgong, and Goalpara) or tea-growing Sylhet, or the hills of eastern India (Garo, Khasi, Jaintia, Naga, and Chittagong), were forbidden to acquire any interest in land or products of the lands (such as rubber, wax, ivory, or forest produce) thereof.[161]

While such male monastic leaders and guardians of female cultivators and tea labourers were to be excluded from such terrain, this regulation also ensured that British Indian civil administration—the domain of penal codes, civil and criminal procedures and courts, hospitals, schools, and banks—lagged a considerable territorial distance behind the advanced military posts of the British Empire. The intermediate country, full of timber and rubber, cotton, petroleum, and 'tribes', was to be governed 'on a less strict system'.[162] Perhaps missionary administration constituted an alibi for colonial administration itself. But the tea planters and investors secured much greater freedoms in the flurry of legislation that followed.

In 1874–5, Acts VIII and XII of 1874 removed all the commercially valuable hills and dales from the administrative remit of a lieutenant governor of Bengal, and gave them instead to a chief commissioner of Assam appointed by the Governor General of India, and indirectly that of the secretary of state for India and British Parliament. Act XIV of 1874 (also called Scheduled Districts Act) formally excluded valuable tea-growing districts in the Jalpaiguri and Darjeeling districts in northern Bengal, as well as in the hill-tracts of Chittagong in southern Bengal, from the operations of criminal and civil judicial procedures operable elsewhere.[163] The very next year, another act provided for the whipping of labourers in all the scheduled districts and those incorporated into the Assam Hills districts.[164] This was ominous, not only because the same 'scheduled districts' and 'hill districts' were then identified as the 'labour districts of Assam'.[165] It was ominous because so many of the 'labourers' were young girls and women; though the clauses of the Act of 1882 required that each labourer have reached the minimum age of sixteen years, there were no penalties for planters who recruited under that age. Authorized whipping of such 'labourers' in order to season them to the rhythms of plantation life was hardly good advertisement for British liberalism and ideologies of freedom, 'equality' of gender, and fraternity.

But such legislation towards labourers also amplified the politics of dispossession of householder women in these hills of southern Kachar–northern Arakan and Chittagong begun long before. Administrators levied fines on all the householder women who had opposed the advance of tea-cultivating regimes. For instance, in the hills of Chittagong and Kachar in 1871, the widow of Vonolel was fined '4 gayal, 10 goats, 50 fowl, 20 maunds of husked rice [approximately 180 lbs of value-added rice]', all of which was delivered to the British army general within the space of four days.[166] These material aspects of male military and colonial appropriations from women of agro-pastoralist communities continued under the sign of the liberation of 'captives'.

WHITHER FRATERNITY, FRIENDSHIP, AND KINSHIP?

The fraternity around tea plantations had comprised men who had travelled across the seas, secured the cultivation of lands which they thought was 'waste', and tied women and girls to it in forms of labour contracts that needed a security apparatus to enforce. Ranged against them was a collective of monastic males leading a bunch of adherents, who had forced the liberation of women and girls from the plantations. If judged by the criteria of the kinds of borders each crossed in the course of their actions, whose cosmopolitanism was greater? The military-planter-missionary men had crossed geographical boundaries, and built up their own brotherhood around the profits of a drug for the global economy. These men entertained no ethical doubts about their own actions. As their orders and rules reveal, they delivered violence in astonishingly new ways. From the same region in which Tickell had seen pigs being fed with rice and milk, two decades later we can find colonial militaries destroying the animal wealth of a monastic subject's estate: lines such as 'all the pigs were burnt, to the number of 60, 20 goats and numerous foul killed—they will have no livestock left' are a commonplace of such records.[167]

The Vaisnava-led hybrid Bon-Buddhist and Muslim networks on the land crossed fewer geographical distances in one generation, but their ethical universe extended to include immigrants from elsewhere, a large number of who were female. Their social boundaries admitted these immigrant women's parity with themselves in ways that Lewin's attitudes towards the recovered Eurasian child and later adult Mary Winchester would not. The Vaisnava-led network's gestures extended a quality of 'kind-ness' to these populations that Buddhist and Bon agro-pastoralists had extended to birds, pigs, and cows: they had 'liberated' them. To the military-planter brotherhood, no doubt, these forced liberations appeared to have transgressed orders of capitalist and colonial legality, propriety, and property. But the Vaisnava-led network's extension of 'kind-ness' to those *not like themselves* was actually remembered long afterwards by one of its recipients as the very substance of love.

This was the once-victim Mary Winchester. In 1912, having read the second edition of Lewin's autobiography, she recalled the year that she had spent as a six-year-old in the hills. Now married and a mother of three, Mary wrote to Lewin relishing his mention of the moment of her recovery, but sounding a completely surprising note of warmth for the household from which she had been 'rescued'. She wrote that though she had a mixed recall of the journey into Lushai country, she did remember

'a dear old motherly woman who was so good and kind to me. There was a younger man of whom I was afraid as he threatened to kill me but the old woman would not let him have anything to do with me. … she wove me garments, a blue striped skirt and a red tartan shawl made of silk, which I treasure not only as a relic of my life there, but of the *love, Divine given,* that prompted the weaving of them. Then came troublous times. I was threatened to be killed as being the cause of it all, but the old woman shielded me. One could see villages being burnt lower down the slopes and a general uneasiness prevailed where I was. Then I was fetched and *with grief I left my friends.* … I was given up on the 21st of January, 1872 one year except six days after my being taken prisoner.'[168]

This remembered kindness of an elder woman in a household of the hills may offer us a partial answer to the question both of memory and of the little-understood cosmopolitics of Vaisnava-Buddhist-Bon communities. Some friendships it appears *were* remembered long afterwards.

But such remembered friendships also offended the military bosses. According to the military-planter brotherhood that had gone to war holding up the unlikely icon of a white girl-child's victimhood, Mary's testimony as an adult woman appeared as the gravest treachery. When Lewin met Mary as an adult, he could neither overcome his own racism nor overlook her stance towards the remembered village. He commented to another military officer that she was 'a stuck up conceited little *half-caste* woman.'[169] A Eurasian woman's memory of a remembered village matron and the latter's gift of cloth has seldom been set up as a measure of European male military bonds, European male middle-class standards of civility, fraternity, or cosmopolitanism. Nor is an enduring memory of a piece of cloth gifted to a child ever offered as a counterpoint to an adult colonial officer's spoilia of a bloody Bible.

Histories are seldom written from the perspective of the fleeting friendship of a child and an elder woman. Yet, everything about Mary's memories was verifiable in terms of the experiences of other individuals put in her place for a brief while. They illuminate the affective authority of older women in all decision making. If one reads Mary's memories carefully, what emerges is the affective control that an elder woman exercised in bringing about 'restraint' in a young man, a restraint that had been treated as a laudable behavioural goal by the Burmese governmental and monastic decrees. It was such women who had ensured the stability of the cosmopolitic order. Military officers had also met many such older women in the hills. Even in 1871, when various local Bengali-speaking Kachari traders were going back and forth among the hills of Kachar, Arakan, and Chittagong, it was of old women they had spoken. Sukpilall's mother, Pibuk, and his sister were said to be the 'heads' of villages located on peaks called Dartlang and Motitlang.[170] Further south was a village headed by Vonpilall's mother, Impanu, a widow and a mother who had outlived her son. For the sake of her grandson, Lalhi, she had invited Sukpilall's son, a man called Khalkhom, to settle with his villagers in her vicinity.[171] Even in 1871, such officers knew that Mary was living in the 'village of Bhenkui's mother, the widow of Lalpitang, and to be treated with some kindness.'[172]

Nor was such 'kind-ness' limited to a flaxen-haired little girl, shown by a matronly figure. Officially anointed as saviours and liberators of female 'captives', at least three colonial military officers recorded separate instances in which other adult non-European women shared

Mary's grief at having to return. Older female 'captives' expressed an unwillingness to be rescued and repatriated. Woodthorpe and Roberts recorded the tears of an adult 'captive' woman, sometime of Manipuri origin, who had married a man in the hills and refused to return. A decade later, another officer sent to the same hills on an identical errand, found people of Arakanese origin ('all Mughs'), namely, two old men and two old women, none of who remembered how long ago they had settled in the hills. One old man said he had married a Lo'kha wife and did not want to move. Another old lady said she did not care to return.[173]

Mary's memories, arranged against Vonolel's grave, illuminate the distinct possibility that none of the actions that the various men had taken in marching through the plantations had been done without the consent of the elder women. Vonolel was not even alive in 1870 when the march through the plantations occurred. Was it his mother who had sent these forces? Or was it his widow? Were these matrons the secret authors of the liberations of 'labourers' from the plantations? Evidence from women suggests that was the case. Something of Mary's memory of the authority of the older woman was corroborated by the memories of the labouring women. Puran Chang, one of those women plantation labourers, reported that when she heard her captors talking about a 'rani' she recognized this woman as being Rani Banye Thung, wife of Moorchoylall, who with the 'Umbry Daffa' and the 'Dartong Kuki' went and built a home near her brother Sukpilall's homes and fields. The woman was confident that it was men attached to this rani who were the 'raiders', that indeed, it was she who had put men in the field and not her husband or son.[174]

A similar account was given of a woman called Ropuiliani, who was the wife of Vandula, believed to be the head of Hualong/ Wallong groups in the vicinity; her father was Lalsavunga, against whom the Kachar column had proceded in 1871–2. Her youngest son was Lalthuama, who would organize another group of tenants (villagers) against another British officer, a Lieutenant Stewart, near Rangamati in the Chittagong Hill Tracts—and set off the next military expedition in the region.[175]

The memories of adult women, once supposed to have been victims of 'kidnap' and subjects of rescue, finally illuminate the ways in which a colonial government had successfully turned itself into a machine for the destruction of monastic political communities. In 1871–2, colonial armies brought down from the hills of Kachar '56 men, 52 women and 99 children'.[176] Many of the adults had lived for thirty or more years in those same societies. But by drawing away ninety-nine children, the expedition benefited European male plantation owners, rather than the women or the children themselves. One of these children had been Mary. Her memory of a matron in a remembered village must then stand as the final word on the kind of brotherhood with which we began this chapter.

Compassionate friendship, not a masculine militarist fraternity, Mary's testimony suggests, was created, maintained, and transmitted within the household and by elderly women, who were mothers of sons. The household, not the monastery of either bamboo or stone, or the flourishing tea factories, constituted the heart of monastic cosmopolitanism. The household was the heart of the cosmos because women married an entire lineage of brothers. The household was its heart because women had given birth to sons and given them away. Motherhood had continued to be idealized by monastic men. Colonial military-planter brotherhoods had called some of these sons, brothers, and husbands 'savages' until the latter joined them. But in calling these men savages, all that the colonial military-planter brothers had achieved was to first obscure, and then ensure the forgetting of, the woman-headed households that had centred the local cosmopolitics of both monk and layman. By driving this cosmopolitics from the picture, it had become easy to paint the monastic lineages left behind as mere savages, rather than as men trying to emulate a stance of 'motherhood' towards the world. It was also easy to overlook elder women who sustained the laymen, the monks, and the maidens. The British general whose garrisons occupied monasteries during the annexation of Burma (1886–8) was thus surprised to find that the 'chief monk' (Thathanabaing) remonstrated with him not about the destruction of the monasteries, but about the 'sufferings caused to the monks by the removal of the inhabitants from the walled city, which was being converted into a cantonment'.[177] Monks suffered when householder women moved away. Who would feed them? Only the next chapter can answer that question.

NOTES

1. Fielder (1869: 29–37). Fielder was the Secretary to the Lower and Northern Assam Tea Companies and Honourary Secretary to the Tea Planters' Association.

2. India Revenue Progs, 19 February 1840, no. 2, 852–70.

3. Guha (1997: 158 and passim).

4. *Ibid.*, 171–3, 207–13.

5. Chatterjee (2001: 84–114).

6. For examples of this scholarship, see Behal (2006); Sen (2009); Sharma (2009, 2011).

7. See *Taylor's Maps* (1910).

8. Representation of Raja Purandhar Simha, encl in letter from AGG Jenkins to Secy GOI, Political, 6 April 1840, BPC 20 April 1840, no. 12.

9. Secy to Govt at Fort William to Capt. Jenkins, 20 April 1840, *ibid.*, no. 13.

10. Representation of Kanderpesvar Simha, grandson of Raja Purandhar Simha, to GOB, encl in BFP, 26 December 1856, no. 73.

11. Extract Foreign Letter from Fort William, 3 June 1857, no. 41, OIOC, BC F/4/ 2688/187932.

12. Capt. Vetch to AGG, NEF, 24 March 1840, BPC, 20 April 1840, nos 87–8.

13. AGG, NEF to Secy GOI, 2 April 1840, OIOC, BC, F/4/1874/79712.

14. Jenkins to Secy GOI, 2 April 1840, BPC, 20 April 1840, nos 87–8.

15. For a selection see Graham (2008) and Whitlock (2005).

16. Discussions of Mahayana doctrines are as numerous as they are sophisticated. Representative examples are C. H. Hamilton (1950), and more recently, Gray (2007); for a larger discussion on the relationship between Buddhist doctrine of liberation and war, see Jerryson and Juergensmeyer (2010); for accounts of war in Inner Asia, Elverskog (2010).

17. For Jenkins's recommendations to government to negotiate with Tularam for the lands between the Dhunsiri River and the Dooyang (identified as 'Naga hills') for disposal to private capitalists, see F. Jenkins AGG at Assam to Secy GOB, Revenue, 4 May 1840, BRP, 26 May 1840, no. 84, negatived in 1841, see Extract Revenue Letter from Bengal 20 March 1841, no. 5, OIOC, BC, F/4/1985/87508.

18. See correspondence in BRP, 28 February 1842, nos 58–103; and India Revenue Letter to Bengal, 21 June 1842, no. 7.

19. Supt Kachar to Offg Commr Dacca Division, Sylhet, 11 February 1850, in Gauhati Archives Dacca Commr's Files, Kachar Papers, File No. 17, 1–26, 1850–1, no. 1.

20. Bhattacharjee (1977); Suparna Roy (2007: 11–17), and Kumar *et al.* (1982–3: 92). These authors also fail to note the significance of the

survival of the Kabuli measure of land, *kulba*, in Kachar-Sylhet until the mid-nineteenth century. One Kachar kulba was 23,313.89 square yards or very nearly 5 acres of land in this period, for which see Supt Kachar to Offg Commr of Revenue, 12 April 1850, Gauhati Archives, Dacca Commr's Files, Kachar Papers, File No. 17, 1–26, 1850–1, no. 5.

21. Lt Bigg's Report, 17 October 1840, encl, BPC, 16 March 1841, no. 13.

22. For reports of tea trees found in several forests in the region, see Supt Kachar to Secy GOB, Fort William, 10 July 1855, *CDR*, II, 308–9. This note specified that the tree was recognized by a man who had worked on a tea-plantation in Assam, and was found on 'low hills' to the south and southwest of Silchar. For identical reports of tea trees on several low hillsides of Sylhet and Tipra, amidst revenue-paying estates of what had once been tax-exempt service lands (*sega*) held by Hindu and Muslim zamindars, see letters from Mgte Sylhet to Secy GOB Judicial, 4 January 1856, 19 February 1856, and 6 May 1856, in *Selections from Records of the Government of Bengal*, no. 25E, 1857, 292–305.

23. For letters to individuals applying for grants of 'waste' land for tea cultivation in Kachar between July 1855 and 10 January 1857, see Supt Kachar correspondence, *CDR*, II, 317–35. One of the lists includes an agent who applied for 1,000 acres of land on behalf of Lt Vincent, 30 N.I. Kachar, cf. 321.

24. Political Agent at Manipur to Secy GOI, Foreign, 10 October 1864, FPP (A), November 1864, no. 7. This note throws light on McCulloch's aggressive politics vis-à-vis people he had been sending 'expeditions' against—the so-called Kukis and Nagas. There are two McCullochs in the records of tea-plantations: one held 515 acres, but cultivated only 20 acres, in Ramsaypore Kachar; the other is an I.B. McCulloch, who held a plot in Jaggerbund.

25. See Wise v. Juggubundhoo Bose, XII Moore, Indian Appeals, 1869, 479–94 in *The English Reports of the Privy Council* 1902, vol. 20, 419–26. For favourable comments on Wise's fiscal arrangements with a native 'front', see Collr Tipra to Secy BOR, 13 April 1836, in *Select Records on Agriculture and Economy of Comilla District 1782–1867* (1989: 163–71). By 1860–1, J. P. Wise also held other substantial tea grants of 1,204 acres in Moirapur, employing 150 labourers, for which see *Report on Annual Administration of Bengal 1860–61* (1863: 118–24). A son of William Wise, Thomas Alexander Wise, who brought the suit for the recovery of his father's moneys, was also an author; see Wise (1845, 1867).

26. See Appendix A, dated 9 July 1857, Allen (1859: 13); for Lt G.F.F. Vincent's diary of the expedition to the Angami Naga in 1849, see East Bengal and Assam Sectt, File no. 639 of 1850, Assam State Archives,

Dispur, Gauhati. From Vincent's correspondence in this diary, it appears that McCulloch, then Captain, was already serving as Political Agent of Manipur, and had also joined the expedition.

27. Ira J. Stoddard to Miles Bronson, 20 January 1851, Miles Bronson Letters Received, Rutgers University, Special Collections.

28. India Political Progs, 5 November 1851, 252–63, para. 34.

29. For Vincent's recovery of 'little Mikir girl' from 'Lhota Nagas', see AGG, NEF to Secy GOB, Judicial, 21 September 1850, Letters Issued to Govt., vol. 15, no. 111; for descriptions of Lt Vincent's attacks on other groups described as 'Angami Nagas', see other correspondence in this file.

30. AGG, NEF to Secy GOI , 28 January 1851, *ibid.*, no. 4 of 1851.

31. AGG, NEF to Secy GOI, 2 January 1851, *ibid.*, no. 2 of 1851.

32. AGG, NEF (Jenkins) to Secy GOB, 2 October 1853 in GOB Judicial Progs 26 July 1854, no. 56. The so-called Naga chiefs whose names are attached to the agreement with Wood, dated 2 March 1850, appear to be those of functionaries of Ahom governments with titles such as Sondeekye and Gaon Bura (village elder), and witnessed by men with 'priestly' titles such as gohain, for which see *ibid.*, no. 57A.

33. *Ibid.*, para 38.

34. Col Lister's Report of Expedition vs. Looshai in Memorandum of 22 February 1861, endnote on p. 7, encl. in NAI, FPP, A, March 1869, no. 319.

35. Lt R. Stewart, Offg Supt to Secy GOB, 28 November 1857, Extract Bengal Political (General) Progs, 24 December 1857, no. 83, BC.

36. Petition from Durrung of Bhaboorker Bhossorah Gaon Bura, Galoo Koteah, Dabondo Deka, Nathoo Chowdhree, and others, encl. in Secy BOR, Lower Provinces to Commr Revenue for Division of Assam, 23 April 1858, Gauhati Archives, AC 446, March 1858–65. This was with reference to a tax called *gurkatti* imposed on jungle grass and reed since 1841/42, which yielded only trifling amounts, 340–60 rupees annually.

37. Major Nuthall Commanding Pegu Light Infantry to A.P. Phayre, Commr Pegu, 4 January 1856, in India Revenue Dept Collection 13, OIOC, BC F/4/2713/195418.

38. Malcolm (1839: 74).

39. Comstock (1847). Comstock's tenure in Arakan was 1834–44.

40. Supt Kachar to Offg Commr Revenue, 12 April 1850, Gauhati Archives, Dacca Commr Files, Kachar Papers, File 17, 1–26, 1850–1, no. 5.

41. Minute recorded by H. Ricketts, 5 March 1850, Gauhati Archives, Dacca Commr's Files, Kachar Papers, File 17, 1–26, 1850–1, no. 4.

42. *Report on the Annual Administration of Bengal for 1860–61* (1863: 22).

43. Joint Mgte Chittagong to Mgte Chittagong, 16 December 1850, encl., BJP, 29 January 1851, no. 163.

44. Offg Supt of Hill Tribes, Northern Arakan, to Lt Col J.F.J. Stevenson, Commr Arakan, Akyab, 10 May 1870, and correspondence, FPP, A, May 1870, nos 123–9.

45. Tickell (1854: 108).

46. Note by AGG, NEF, 19 April 1854, no. 35 re 'despatch of arms and armour used by the Bhutiahs and Kookies in North Kachar' in NAI, Foreign, Political Despatch to Court of Directors, 28 February 1856, no. 26.

47. Cited in Chappell (1996: 352).

48. Tickell (1854: 104).

49. *Ibid.*, 107.

50. *Ibid.*, 92.

51. *Ibid.*, 95.

52. Offg Supt of Hill Tribes, Northern Arakan to Stevenson, 10 May 1870, FPP A, May 1870; for comment on the labourers, see Offg Secy Chief Commr British Burma to Offg Secy GOI, 22 July 1870.

53. These were the 'Fee Simple' rules. According to Behal (2006), these rules allowed the number of registered tea companies in Assam to boom from 6 in 1860 to 86 in 1865.

54. For short-staple cotton grown in soil of Kachar by 'Nagas', 'Hookies', and Manipuris, see C.B. Stewart to Tea Committee of Landholders, 10 November 1862, and for similar descriptions for cotton grown on the hills of Chittagong and Arakan until 1861, see correspondence of Commr Chittagong Division to Secy, BOR, Lower Provinces, 26 July 1848, Commr of Arakan to Secy GOB in Great Britain, PP House of Commons, (1863: vol 44, 107–22, 156, 251–2).

55. Offg Supt Kachar to I. Sandeman, 25 May 1860, *CDR*, II, 411–12.

56. Statement showing sums refunded to Hill Tribes Settled on the Tea Plantations of Kachar being the Collections Made on Account of Their House Tax, in Dacca Commr Files, Kachar Papers, File 37, 1–3, 1862.

57. Allen (1859: 12).

58. *Ibid.*, 15.

59. *Report of the Commissioners* (1868: 14).

60. Statement of Service of Lt T.H. Lewin of the 104 Regiment, dated 1859, Mss 811/II/4/1, LP.

61. Lewin (1912 [1884]: 1–6).

62. Letter of 15 January 1866, OIOC, Mss Eur C. 79, Letters from Thomas Lewin to his Mother and his Kind Elder Cousin, Jane Lewin, f. 231.

63. Letter to Aunt, 6 May 1866, *ibid.*, f. 262.

64. Letter to Mother, 1 September 1867, 6 September 1867, OIOC, Mss Eur C 80, ff. 139–40.

65. Letter to Mother, 26 February 1868, *ibid.*, f. 155.

66. Woodthorpe (1978 [1873]: 8, 123).

67. Fielder (1869: 31).

68. Commr of Revenue to BOR, n.d, Board of Revenue Papers, files 109–110, no. 6, Assam Secretariat, Gauhati, Assam.

69. AGG, NEF to Secy GOB, 5 April 1860, Gauhati Archives, Assam Sectt: Letters Issued to Government, vol. 23, no. 40.

70. Bidyaratna (1999).

71. *Report of the Commissioners* (1868: 52).

72. *Report of the Assam Labour Enquiry Committee* (1906: 136–9).

73. See correspondence about mutineers from 34 Native Infantry in Sylhet and Kachar, BOR Papers, files 109–110, nos 1–8, and 1–20, respectively, 1858, Assam Sectt, Gauhati.

74. Stewart to Secy GOB, 22–24 December 1857, in Sujit Choudhury (1981: 6–8). These lay out the pay and arming of 40 employees, men who lived in villages owned by the Kachar Tea Company.

75. Private letter from Earl of Mayo to Duke of Argyll, 18 January 1869, OIOC, Mss Eur. B 380/1, ff. 28–9.

76. See letter of G. Verner Offg Supt Kachar to Political Agent at Manipur, 3 May 1848 re local protests about supplying '80 coolies to carry 30 boxes and two bags of ammunition' to Manipur in Datta (2007: 147).

77. G. Verner to Sessions Judge, Sylhet, 20 November 1849, in Datta (2007: 157–9).

78. Offg Commr. Dacca to Secy GOB, 6 January 1869, NAI, Foreign Political A, 1869, February, no. 73, encl.

79. Offg Supt to A.I. Tydd, Buggliat ghat estate, 23 August 1860; same to A.L.Webster, 4 December 1860, *CDR*, II, pp. 413, 415.

80. *Report of the Assam Labour Enquiry Committee* (1906: 137).

81. See correspondence in NAI, FPP, A, February 1865, no. 116; November 1866, no. 25; December 1866, nos 27–31; January 1867, nos 99–100.

82. Political Agent (R. Brown) to Asst Secy to GOI, Foreign, 9 November 1868, FPP, A, December 1868, no. 418; see also nos 421–4; also see R. Brown to Secy to GOI, Foreign, 24 December 1868, FPP, A, February 1869, nos 66 and 69, 72–73; and Secy GOI to Secy GOB, 22 January 1869, *ibid.*, no. 79.

83. Letter to Aunt, Kassalong, 10 January 1867, OIOC, Mss Eur C 80, f. 123.

84. From Offg Junior Secy GOB to Lt. Lewin, Dist Superintendent of Police, Chittagong, 6 April 1866, Mss 811/II/5, LP; for appointment as

Dy Commr of Hill Tracts of Chittagong alongside his police duties from August that year, see Offg Under Secy GOB to Capt Lewin, 17 August 1866, Mss 811/II/7, LP; and for official approval of his various unofficial expeditions till this date, see Resolution, Judicial Fort William, 14 October 1868, on Annual Report of Administration in Chittagong Hill Tracts for 1867–8, Mss 811/II/8, LP.

85. Extract from Letter to sister Harriet, 15 October 1866, OIOC, Mss Eur C 79, f. 290.

86. *The Hill Tribes of Chittagong and the Dwellers Within*, first published London 1869; for the approving adoption of Maine's *Ancient Law* into Lewin's classification of the 'Khyoungtha' and 'Toungtha', see 41, 49.

87. Letter to Jenny, April 30, 1867, OIOC, Mss Eur C 80, f. 133.

88. Letter to Jenny, January 10, 1867, *ibid.*, f. 124.

89. Das (1969: 18–19). Das's account of Lewin is as unsympathetic as Lewin's views on 'Bengalis' expressed in his personal letters.

90. Smith (2001: 320); also Mullard (2011: 69–75).

91. Lewin (2005: 242).

92. Letter to Jenny, April 30, 1867, OIOC, Mss Eur C 80, f. 133.

93. See three lists on the brotherhoods enclosed in Offg Dy Commr Chittagong Hill Tracts to Secy GOB, 5 February 1871, NAI, FPP, A, May 1871, nos. 303–6.

94. Lewin (2005: 202–4).

95. Letter to Mother, Chittagong, 11 December 1866, OIOC, Mss Eur C 79, f. 295.

96. Letter to Aunt, 10 January 1867, OIOC, Mss Eur C 80, f. 123.

97. Lewin (2005: 218, also 241, 250).

98. Notes by E.W.C., 16 March 1881, NAI, Political A, May 1881, k.w. 197–8; also August 1868, no. 35; for Kanhai Simha, see Political A, March 1866, 105–7, November 1866, 25–6.

99. Beer Chunder Deb Burmoon [Barman], Joobraj of Tipperah to Commr Dacca, 3 January 1869, encl. in Offg Commr Dacca to GOB, 6 January 1869, and Offg Dist Supt of Police to Mgte Sylhet, 2 January 1869, in India Military Progs, January 1869, no. 246.

100. M. Chaudhuri (n.d.: 17, 46–8). Internal evidence suggests the author wrote sometime after the publication of the 1901 census but before the 1911 census.

101. Supt Kachar (E.R. Lyons) to Sessions Judge, Sylhet 10 May and 2 July 1845, *CDR* 1, 149–53.

102. Offg Mgte and Collr Adhumpore to Commr of Revenue Dacca, 9 January 1869, India Political Progs L/PS/6/562, Military Letter of 26 January 1869, no. 35.

103. The evidence of the intersecting relationships was secured by Edgar in April 1869 in the course of many interviews; see Offg Dy Commr Kachar to Offg Commr Dacca Division, 3 April 1869, encl. in FPP, A, December 1869, nos 235–40; the reference to Kanai Simha's marriage is in Offg Mgte Sylhet to Commr Dacca, 16 April 1869, encl. *ibid.*, nos 245–6.

104. This man, whose name is variously spelled in the English records as Mischoey Looy/ Marchoy lall/ Gnoshae Lall, was said to be the son of Lallchoogla/ variously Lall chukla, captured and transported in 1846–7, for which see Memorandum of Col Raban, 11 February 1869, FPP, A, March 1869, no. 319. The same note comments on the great deal of 'confusion' among English officials caused by 'different pronunciations of the names of several chiefs in Chittagong and in Kachar,' aggravated by mistakes and alterations in writing and spelling.

105. Diary of Offg Mgte Sylhet, entry for 19 February 1869, in Offg Mgte Sylhet to Commr Dacca 16 April 1869, FPP, A, December 1869, nos 245–6.

106. Offg Commr Dacca Division to Secy GOB, 19 February 1869, FPP, A, *ibid.*, no. 322. See also *Relations between Looshais and Munnipoorees* 1979 (Foreign Dept, Political A, 1870, nos 271–7), 11.

107. Dy IG of Police, to PA of IG Police, Lower Provinces, 24 March 1869, FPP, A, December 1869, nos. 232–3 and k.w., encl.

108. Offg Dy Commr Kachar to Offg Commr Dacca Division, 14 April 1869, encl. FPP, A, December 1869, nos 245–6.

109. *The Friend of India*, 28 January 1869, 93.

110. [Lewin's] Letter to Jeanie, 15 June 1871, OIOC, Mss Eur. C 80, f. 166.

111. P.A. Manipur to Secy GOI, Foreign, 27 January 1869, FPP, A, March 1869, no. 309. For the list of the plantations on rivulets off Sonai and Dhaleswar tributaries of the Barak that were passed by 'Kanai Singh and the Loosais', see Dy Commr Kachar (Edgar) to Offg Commr Circuit Dacca Division, 4 February 1869, encl., *ibid.*, no. 311.

112. A. Olding, Manager at Dwarbund, to Messrs. Balmer, Lawrie and Company, Agents of British India Tea Company, 14 January 1869; Percival Bury to Messrs. Balmer, Lawrie and Company, 18 January 1869, reporting attack on Monaikhal on 15 January in *Correspondence between the Landholders' and Commercial Association* (1871: 4–5); a third plantation, Woodlands, is mentioned in the weekly paper *The Friend of India* (later *The Stateman*), Serampore, 21 January 1869.

113. Capt. Stewart, Dy Commr Kachar to Commr Dacca Division, 2 May 1866, Appendix A, Memorandum by Colonel Raban, 11 February 1869, FPP, A, March 1869, no. 319.

114. Secy. GOI, Foreign, to Secy. GOB, 12 May 1871, Confidential, FPP, A, May 1871, no. 636.

115. Socolow (1992); Ghermain (1975); Derounian-Stodea and Levernier (1993); also Burnham (1997); for reviews of the latter, see Logan (1998: 398–9), and Singh (1999: 442–4).

116. Marez (2001); and Macneil (2005).

117. Montgomery (1994).

118. Weiss (2005).

119. Colley (2002).

120. Ali (2006).

121. For modern lay Jain ethics, see Laidlaw (2010).

122. Luard (1926: 141 n10).

123. Holler (2002).

124. Tun (1986, vol. 7: 118–20). Bodhawpaya was king of Burma 1762–1814.

125. *Ibid.*, xxviii.

126. *Ibid.*, 21 April 1813, 74.

127. Resident Mandalay to Offg Secy GOI, Foreign, 29 March 1877, Bhamo Diary, in OIOC, L/PS/7/14.

128. Eden (1865: 60).

129. Statement of Shalutri Culini, Alexanderpur Garden, 9 Feb 1871, NAI, FPP, A, March 1871, no. 527.

130. Statement of Shalutri Culini, *ibid.* Emphasis added.

131. Commr Dacca Division to Secy GOB, 16 March 1871, and Appendix, FPP, A, May 1871, nos 599, 601.

132. Political Agent at Manipur to Secy GOI, Foreign, 5 March 1871, FPP, A, May 1871, no. 576.

133. 'Memorial of Tea Planters and other European Residents in the Districts of Kachar and Sylhet to the Earl of Mayo, 17 April 1871', in *Correspondence between the Landholders* (1871: 300–3).

134. See *Friend of India/ The Statesman 1869–1872*; this episode was subsequently offered in many missionary biographies and autobiographies as the starting point of missionary careers.

135. Offg Dy Commr Kachar (Edgar) to Offg Commr Circuit Dacca Division, 18 February 1869, FPP, A, March 1869, no. 328.

136. Lewin (2005: 257).

137. Asst Supt Police Chittagong Hill Tracts to Commr Chittagong, 6 June 1871, NAI, Foreign Secret, July 1871, no. 462; *PP* (1872, vol. 45: 205–6).

138. Letter to Mother, 18 January 1872, OIOC, Mss Eur C 80, f. 171.

139. *Friend of India*, 4 January 1872.

140. Extract from Printed Diary of 1871–2, 26 February 1872, Mss 811/ II/29, LP.

141. Woodthorpe (1978 [1873]: 141).

142. Roberts (1878: 1).

143. *Ibid.*, 8.

144. *Report on Annual Administration of Bengal for 1861–62* (1863: 73).

145. For these lineages in the eighteenth to nineteenth centuries, see Sardar (2007); for illustrations of turban-like head-cover worn by Nyingmapa, see Olschak (1979: 110).

146. For presence of Rutton Singh in the party that liberated workers at Monierkhal, see Note by Offg Dy Commr, *PP* (1872, vol. 45: 84).

147. Woodthorpe (1978 [1873]: 177–8).

148. Roberts (1878: 11).

149. Dy Commr Kachar on Special Duty to Commr of Circuit, Dacca Division, 13 March 1871, *PP* (1872, vol. 45: 122–3).

150. Woodthorpe(1978 [1873]: 172–3).

151. *Ibid.*, 267–8.

152. Hughes (1881: 4).

153. Despatches of Brigadier General C.H. Brownlow, Calcutta 1872, 28.

154. Report on the Administration of the Hill Tracts of Northern Arakan for 1870–1, 22.

155. For roads between the plantations of Nagdigram, Monierkhal, Mynadhur, Jalnacherra, and Noarband, all of which had been attacked in the previous years, see Offg Commr Dacca to Offg Secy GOB, 24 November 1872, FPP, March 1874, no. 40. For comment that these roads benefited the plantations and should be paid for by local government and not from imperial funds, see Quarter-Master General to Military Secy GOI, 6 February 1873, *ibid.*, no. 42.

156. Mgte Tipperah to Secy GOB, Judicial Dept, 26 May 1873, *ibid.*, no. 29.

157. Resolution in Judicial Dept, 17 August 1872, Gauhati Archives, B.G. File 300, 1–76, 1868–9; for contemporaneous boundary claiming in the region, see Memorandum on Khasia and Garo Boundary Settlement carried out by Colonel Bivar, and Capt. Williamson, March 1873, in Gauhati Archives, Assam Commr's File 635, 1871–3.

158. Offg Under Secy GOB to Commr Assam, 29 November 1871, Gauhati Archives, Assam Commr's Sectt, 668, no. 1 of 1871.

159. Lees (1867: 26).

160. Gazetteer of India, Military Dept, 30 April 1872, no. 480 of 1872.

161. Regulation V of 1873, GOI Legislative Department 1897, 215–17.

162. Notes on the Chittagong Frontier, GOI, FPP, A, May 1871, k.w. 295–335, see note signed by H. LeP[oer]. W[ynne]., dated 6 March 1871, confirmed by signatures of M[ayo] and C.U. A[itchison] alongside.

163. Wigley (1905, vol. 5: 85 and passim).

164. See Appendix, GOI Legislative Department 1897, 773.

165. See Assam Labour and Emigration Act 1882, GOI Legislative Department 1897, 121–89. This was subsequently renamed the Inland Emigration Act (VII of 1893).

166. Roberts (1878: 12).

167. Diary of Offg Supt Hill Tracts Arakan, entry for 4 December 1876 in Commr Arakan to Chief Commr British Burma, 5 February 1877.

168. Letter to Col Lewin, in Ms 811/II/54, LP; also quoted, though with an additional paragraph that is absent in the letter to Lewin, in Mary Winchester to D.E. Jones, cited in Lloyd (1991: 6–7).

169. Letter from T.H. Lewin to Daughter, 7 November 1912, in LP, Ms 811/IV/57.

170. Dy Commr Kachar (Edgar) to Commr Dacca Division, 6 March 1871, PP (1872, vol. 45: 88).

171. Edgar, PP (1872, vol. 45: 123).

172. Ibid., 93.

173. Diary of 16 February 1891, OIOC, Mss Eur/ Photo Eur/89/1 f. 45.

174. Enclosed Deposition of Puran Chang, wife of Beng Taung They Ouzir, in Raja Birchandra Manik Bahadur, maharaja of Independent Tipperah to Offg Commr Chittagong Division, 6 March 1871, FPP, A, May 1871, no. 593.

175. Sangkima (2004: 137–44).

176. *The Friend of India*, 1 February 1872.

177. Crosthwaite (1968 [1912]: 38–9).

6

Undoing Gender?

Restoring Motherhood and Merit

MONASTIC CODES OF GENDER had long elevated the cultivation of transcendence. But the policies of undoing gender that appeared as part of British Indian military governments of the entire region between the Brahmaputra and the Kaladan rivers finally sealed off women's worth in the merit-based economies of the region. From the late nineteenth century, the preambles of almost all economic legislation (land revenue collection, municipal administration of inns and gambling houses, and so on) in the region warned that 'words denoting masculine gender include females.'[1] This folding of laywomen into men had its own political–economic basis in revenue extraction, rather than a reference to local linguistic or ascetic codes. This chapter surveys the culmination of a colonial military politics of the attempt to undo Buddhist, Vaisnava, and Sufi codes of transcendence of gender, as well as of Inner Asian structures of household formations in the eastern parts of the expanded British empire. It was the final act of erasure that had begun in the late eighteenth century against disciples and adherents of Bon-Buddhist, Vaisnava, and Sufi teachers.

Such erasures in turn impeded historians who began in the twentieth century to wonder at the Christianization among the same populations.[2] Missiological sources generated only celebratory histories of such processes. In response, postcolonial historiographies equated Christianization with 'denationalization', an alienation from kith and kin.[3] This chapter will demonstrate that both views misunderstand the continuities between the older Mahayana Buddhist idealization of compassionate care—the education of the young and the delivery of health care to lay subjects by monastic lineages—and the successful planting of missionary schools and hospitals in the same region once inhabited by Bon-Buddhist subjects.[4] By foregrounding lay subjects' attitudes to suffering and non-selfhood, and its translation to other contexts, we can understand Christianization as a political response specific to a particular time and context, rather than a process amenable to interiorist explanations of various sorts.[5] To help initiate this process, I begin by replacing the term 'conversion' with a term more suited to the historical institutions of initiation-ordination summed up in local Bengali and Assamese as 'seeking refuge' (*saran neoa*). Viewed as a 'seeking refuge', the resort of some men and women to Christian medical missionaries, I argue, was not a rupture of monastic politics but a restoration of an older form of monastic government organized around learned monastic teachers, novices, and their disciples. Such processes of restoration were also known in colonial Sri Lanka after the 1840s. Lay and clerical Lankan Buddhists sought to revitalize Buddhist polities after British colonial rules disestablished state support to the Buddhist samgha.[6] Pious lay women emerged as especially significant leaders of such revitalization. This chapter will argue for a similar process in eastern India from the end of the nineteenth century into the early twentieth.

MARKETS, LABOUR MARKETS, AND
SOCIAL STRUCTURES, 1871–91

Since 1865, colonially licensed male traders had been buying rubber, timber, bamboo, and so on, from men on the hills and exchanging them at markets at the junctions of rivers and roads between hills and plains. At markets like Sonai Bazar and Tipaimukh, rice was bartered against brass vessels, red cloths, and useable goods. At other markets, between the hills of Tipra and the plains of Chittagong, cotton was bartered for salt, cloth and poultry. Colonial officers regulating these markets understood that the value of hill-produced cotton far exceeded that of the manufactured goods these producers—the so called 'nine tribes of Kukis in the hills'—acquired in exchange.[7] But tax collection had to occur in money, and colonial metal currency was introduced into these transactions in the hills. In South Kachar, sellers initially used the coins not as final payment but as tokens of future payments.[8] From 1869, the exchange in India rubber, a valuable staple, picked up dramatically in and around Kachar. Edgar noticed what he called a 'paltry 1,300 maunds' of India rubber had been extracted in one year from amidst the vast untapped forests in the vicinity. The amount extracted was worth only 65,000 rupees in Calcutta. This could not have amounted to even a tenth of the output possible from Kachar, Manipur, and the hills tracts. The forests near the villages of 'the Howlongs and Sylhoos' were far greater than those in the north; there were great forests of caoutchouc trees east of the Tipai. On-the-spot officials secured promises from various men that they would 'plant suitable portion of their jhum [swidden] lands, as they abandon them, with caoutchouc trees'.[9] The Inner Line Administration of 1871 then moved British military guards out over those trees, and annexed the trees to colonial programs of 'forest conservation'.

But this extension affected local societies adversely. In the forested hills of late nineteenth-century Arakan and Kachar, women were active as cultivators and were understood by colonial revenue authorities to be so. That was the reason that, while folding women into men, regulations for the Arakan Hills Districts in 1875 had established that a tax of one rupee be paid by 'each family of cultivator' for each swidden field (*taungya* in Tibetan, *jhum* in Hindustani Bengali) cultivated every year along with a 'tribute' of one rupee per year per family.[10] 'Families' of cultivators implied women. Apparently, it was taken for granted that male cultivators with access to cultivator-wives were richer and able to pay greater amounts in tax. Thus, the Burma Land Revenue Act of 1876 had levied a higher capitation tax on married men (5 rupees per year) and only half that sum on the single males.[11]

More important still, the shifting nature of land use during the late nineteenth century affected women's grain and fruit cultivation vis-à-vis cash-crop cultivation. Such shifts also heightened vulnerability to periodic food shortages especially if they could not replenish food stocks by resort to forests 'reserved' for colonial governmental use. In 1881, when the bamboo flowered and encouraged rats that ate right through the standing rice crop, the final chapters in the story of women's wealth was written on these hills.[12] Famine broke out in 1882. Tenants and subjects of hill-based monasteries avoided violent seizures of other people's grain stores; they tried to barter their belongings for food instead. Encountering some of these people on the plains of Chittagong, for instance, a German ethnologist called them 'the Tangloa, Haulong, and Pakhoa Lushai tribes', whose famine-struck members sought to trade their textiles, head-dresses, wickerwork baskets, weaving implements, and funerary objects—contributing directly to his stunning and colourful collections of photographic plates—for his stores of rice. Yet, the ethnologist was peeved that these men accepted his rice 'as a gift' but would not give him porterage-labour 'as a return'. He complained, not too differently from the British military men who governed the same populations, that these famine-struck 'Lushei' would not lend a hand in improving the roads leading to their villages. 'Troops had to open up the routes themselves through the impenetrable bamboo thickets.'[13]

These populations, increasingly dependent on trade for cash incomes, had also lost their conflict-resolution mechanisms. In 1884, an innocuous dispute over market shares that began at Tipaimukh blew up into a bigger conflict. Each shopkeeper at that conjuncture of many rivers was to bring goods from the plains and exchange it for rubber and forest produce. Each shop paid a yearly rent in cash and salt, which was divided among different 'chiefs' and constituted something like a rental income for all. Unable to stabilize a rent-sharing dispute, one of the sons of Vonolel invited the deputy commissioner of Kachar to come and settle the dispute in person. When the British administrator arrived, he was fired upon, presumably by the other party in the conflict.[14] The dispute about profit-sharing of the other markets in the vicinity escalated. But the mechanisms by which earlier disputes were resolved were no longer working. For one thing, Sukpilall had died in the interim and his sons fell out over the rents and profit-sharing of the Sonai Bazar market with the sons of Vonolel and Vonpilall. After decades of plague, pestilence, and flight from these hills, 'Bengalis no longer [kept] up the bazaars, nor do wood-cutters go and fell timber in Lushai land, and even the rubber, which once afforded ample means of subsistence, is failing'.[15] Men and women living in the same households which had been drawn into a dependence on failing markets for generating cash became ever more vulnerable to both colonial tax regimes and the market.

These vulnerabilities were exacerbated by the annexation of Upper Burma to British rule in 1885, which was fiercely resisted by many. British imperial dominance over this resistance took many forms;

road building was one of them, and from 1891 railway building was added. Roads were to be constructed to link Chittagong directly to parts of Upper Burma, and they would pass through the hills and valleys of the regions to the west of Burma. These hills of northern Arakan and parts of Akyab were administratively reorganized with parts of the southern Kachar hills, and called Lushai Hills. Populations on these hillsides became especially vulnerable to labour demands for road building in the aftermath of the annexation.

Older calibrated scales for the extraction of labour disappeared rapidly in this context. Colonial regimes established no grounds on which remissions of labour payments could be secured. Jenkins had spelled the rates out in Assam in the 1830s–40s. His successors in the southern hills followed his precedent in removing all remissions and exemptions. All households alike were to provide taxes at the same rates. The superintendent and his assistants were authorized to collect taxes at given annual rates: Rs 2 in cash, or twenty seers of cleaned rice, or one maund of unhusked rice per house, *in addition* to each house supplying one coolie's services for carriage and transportation or road construction for ten days each year.[16] This additional taxation (in labour service) destroyed older grids of merit-based and gift-giving social respectability.

Labour services had been given by men and women under precolonial regimes as well. But these labour services were either paid as commutations of fines, or as direct tax payable by ordinary indigent folks *in lieu of* cash or grain taxes or as 'donations' to lords. Those to whom the indigent labourer paid such personal services were also well-known figures in the local community—the local monastery's head monk, ascetic warrior, teacher, lay lord. Face-to-face relationships existed between those who were waited upon and those who performed the labour service. Labour services, redolent of co-dependence of payee and recipient, could always be commuted against other kinds of payments—in grain, cattle, trade-goods, and cash.[17] By demanding that every household supply both cash or grain *and* labour service, colonial rulers collapsed these distinctions of status and intimacy.

LEVIRATE'S SPECTRE AND COLONIAL CONSCRIPTION

The collapsed distinctions of status and the shrinking sources of cash with which to meet the incoming colonial presence proved especially dangerous to younger able-bodied women among all social clusters in the hills. The generation of military officers who were given the task of adjudicating issues of property, law, and order were no better trained in Buddhist legalities than their predecessors had been. Nor did they have the language to describe the institutions they presided over. For instance, in 1882, a fairly long-serving officer reported of societies in the hills of northern Arakan that post-pubertal marriages were the norm in those parts (a girl at 17 and a man at 20–1), but he described the payments made by the male suitor to the woman's parents as 'dowry' instead of bride wealth. Another military officer, and one who would have as much power in defining the public impression of these groups as Lewin had had in the sixties and seventies, referred to the payments that grooms were expected to make as those of bride 'purchase'.[18]

One has to translate nomenclature rooted in late Victorian and Edwardian sensibilities into modern English academic usage to understand that the institution that both officials described had existed in the region for a long time as bride wealth. These payments were not fixed. They depended entirely on the local status of the woman. If the betrothed was the daughter of a powerful household, as much as Rs 600, or the equivalent in bullocks, *gayal*s, and spears was expected; while the form and amount demanded for daughters of commoner men might be different. Even though officials did not have the right language for it, their halting and confused references allow us to suggest that the potential for accumulating a herd of animal wealth was greater for a household with daughters than for households without them. At the same time, these officials recognized implicitly that the fact of the payments by a groom to many different members of the bride's lineage—her nearest male relative, her aunt, her elder sister, her maternal uncle, and elective male and female guardians—also meant that in case of a dissolution of the marriage, all the maternal and paternal relatives had to return the sums or gifts to the groom.

This feature of household formation, intimately related with the persistence of descent considerations and high bride wealth paid for a woman of a great lineage—discussed in Chapter 3—reappears in the reports of the late nineteenth-century officials in Arakan and Chittagong, or what these officials called Lushai Hills. Unknown to themselves, they echoed descriptions of the Himalayan Buddhists (called Bhutia) in 1837, which had found it no 'uncommon thing for two or three brothers to club together and share one woman between them. The eldest brother is considered the father of what offspring may take place and the younger as uncles.'[19] The same patterns were now reported among the many groups living in the hills, where officers discovered a 'custom for the widow to become the wife of her late husband's brothers.'[20] Describing what modern scholars call uni-generational and bi-generational patterns of implicit or successive polyandry, the officer referred to a code that had been devised to keep the patterns of marriage in place. This code said,

'if a man die leaving a son (whether a minor or not) and a brother, the brother succeeds to the exclusion of the son, marries his brother's widows, administers the property pays his brother's debts, and as soon as the son has arrived at puberty provides for his marriage. If a man die leaving a son of age and no brother, the former inherits directly and marries his father's widow unless she is his own mother [This is another provision for keeping the dowry in the family].'[21]

Nor were such formulations merely hypothetical. Many women who had been fugitives from the plains and plantations and had remained in these hills had done so on the basis of such household maintenance patterns. One such woman was described in southern Kachar, as first married to a man in Tetua Punji, and on his death, married to his brother. He too died and so she was asked to live at another man's house. Her son with the first husband was assimilated in the first husband's lineage.[22] Such expectations of widows presumed that entire lineages of males, related to each other as brother, half-brothers, cousins, nephews, and uncles lived in sufficient community with each other to have made the death of one communicable and important in the life of the others. This pattern of 'brotherhood' had been found in the same hills in the 1830s–60s, but had been discredited (see Chapter 3). I refer to these codes of household constitution—the bride-wealth payments in cattle wealth, the implicit polyandry, and the institutions of levirate that sons and brothers in a lineage would expect to maintain with the spouses of a brother and father—in order to establish spatial–cultural continuities with the worlds of pastoralist societies in the Himalayas as well as temporal continuities with the Vaisnava–Manipuri–Kochari world described earlier. I wish to suggest that the practices of bride wealth and implicit polyandry brought all generations of men on both sides of a man and a woman's lineages to be equally concerned in each other's marriages, the clans married into, and the wealth promised, paid, withheld, and circulated. In other words, the operability of such codes made the conduct of a heterosexual marriage between two households or lineages of collective import on both sides, and its dissolution of equally significant collective impact.

Collective responsibility was spoken of, for instance, in the methods by which a groom had to transfer bride wealth to two parties before his marriage was considered binding: the first was the nearest male relative on the bride's father's side (*amanpui*), and the second was the nearest male relative on the bride's mother's side (*pumamana* or the 'debt to the womb'). The former sum, in the late nineteenth century, depended entirely on the status and achievements of the father and therefore varied considerably. The latter was much more consistent, and only varied according to whether the male in question was an ordinary person or an extraordinary one.

Collective brotherhood and clan responsibility was implicitly assumed for the maintenance of a woman by a husband's male kinsmen. Not only was this principle of collective responsibility ignored by colonial military officers after the 1880s but its operation has evaded the studies of historians of anti-imperialist resistance of the late nineteenth century in eastern India and Burma.[23] For the same reasons, such an act of collective resistance also escaped other postcolonial historians of colonial violence.[24] We can extend both historiographies if we add the events after 1885 to the political histories of the variously intermarried lineages that we have traced in earlier chapters.

Since 1888, these intermarried lineages had resisted the land-survey operations conducted by the colonial military in the hills that were continuous with northern Akyab, Tipura, Arakan, and Chittagong hills. An officer of the colonial police, C.S. Murray, who had participated in snuffing out Santhal rebellions in western Bengal and Bihar in 1880 and in Darjeeling in 1885, was now appointed to cow the opposition in the hills of Chittagong and Kachar: he was given the post of assistant political officer in 1891.[25] He arrived at the southern end of these hills at a place called Lungleh and consulted with another military officer, John Shakespear, about the terms on which labour services and house taxes were to be extracted from resident populations. Every house, he was told, was to pay tribute of one basket of rice each year. In addition to that, each able-bodied man was to give ten days' labour *free* in the year.[26] Murray interpreted this directive to immediately demand sexual corvee from women in the villages.

This was symbolic of both the discursive un-gendering of women under the sign of 'labourer' or 'coolie' and the simultaneous structural shift that debased women's sexual and social work for a lineage and an entire household by the mechanism of colonial 'development', that is, road building for marching colonial armies and tanks to the top of the mountains. Both discursive and structural shifts were felt within the smallest unit of the taxpaying order, the household; and it was felt especially by different generations of women, whose participation in the monastic economy through the gift of labour as well as fruits of labour—sons—also earned these women prestige.

Not surprisingly, the imprint of this profound shift is barely visible in the jottings of the officials at the heart of the event. The entry for C.S. Murray's diary for 8 February 1891 shows that he had marched to Jacopa's (aka Zakapa) village and secured an agreement from him to provide 'coolies' to go on to Lallbuta's village. Jacopa, the diary notes, was very friendly but he did not sleep in the village that night. Next morning, when Murray sent for Jacopa, the latter refused to attend. On 10 February, Murray set off to 'burn the rice stored 2½ miles off. 13 rice houses burnt,' notes the diary.[27] This is followed by a series of official one-line reports about the punitive expedition sent against Jacopa's village, with lists of how many granaries of rice were burned in a month. His fellow officer, Shakespear, also recorded having received a note from a Captain F.F. Hutchinson that Murray had set off to burn Jacopa's 'jooms' because the chief refused to give him coolies, and that he had been attacked and had lost two men and all his baggage.[28]

On the face of it, 'coolie' (like 'labourer') said nothing about the sex of the person involved. Its use could have signalled either men or women who performed such labour. However, all colonial observers of transportation workers since the late eighteenth century had noticed the presence of women alongside men in virtually all

hill societies in the region. In 1832, an army officer convalescing at
the colonial sanatorium in Cherrapunji (northwest of Sylhet) had
observed both women and men carrying loads between 80 and 120
pounds in split bamboos carried tied by slings which passed across
their foreheads.[29] Identical modes of carrying loads by women had
continued in the hills east of Chittagong and were described by at
least one missionary observer in the early twentieth century.[30] So
which sort of 'coolie' had Murray demanded, and been refused? What
sort of repercussions did such demands have on local households and
intermarried clans?

In order to answer this question and elaborate on the larger
politics of representation and monastic community, we turn to a ten-
page note entitled 'Autobiography of Dara, Chief of Pukpui' tucked
away inside another colonial officer's records in the British Library
collections.[31] Though called an autobiography, it does not appear to
have been written directly by the narrator of the life. Nor is it an
entire life that is narrated in this brief document. It does not even
have a date to authenticate the moment in which the narration was
recorded. Nor are there dates within the narration of this terse little
document that would pinpoint the year in which the narrator was
born. Yet, the document uses 'I' to indicate that Dara is the speaker.
He identifies himself as belonging in the 'clan Ralte', and that his
father's name was Darsuakvunga, and that he, Dara, 'often used to
go to Sylhet to sell rubber'.

Despite the abridged biography of the narrator, Dara appears
as a polyglot in the narration. He had learned Hindustani on his
sojourn at Sylhet. When he heard at Silchar (erstwhile Kachar) that
the government needed men who could speak 'Lushai' (a particular
Sino-Tibetan or Tibeto-Burmese or Tibeto-Bengali dialect?), he
arrived at the British camp to teach the language to the officers, a
task he performed for the next three years. Perhaps due to the high-
handedness of Murray, who gave Dara a 'language test' and failed
him for being an ignoramus, Dara went off to Rangoon and served
in the police force there for the next three years. While at Rangoon,
he heard that the Government was going to the region that he
called home. He returned to Chittagong, staying in one 'Betalram
Acchhami's [Assamese] house', and returned to the British Indian
military camp he had left. There he found John Shakespear in charge,

became his 'interpreter', and thereafter was made into a 'Lushai chaprasi'. Albeit the occupant of the lowliest rung of a colonial bureaucracy, a subaltern in the broader pattern of military-planter brotherhoods, Dara was no ordinary person. As the biography suggests, he had moved between a fairly diverse group of people and places. Presumably along with Hindustani, Dara knew Assamese, and at least one Sino-Tibetan or Tibeto-Burman language. Given the strength of polyglossia among mercantile and monastic communities and lineages in the late eighteenth-century world of Chittagong and Arakan, is it likely that Dara was himself a lower-level monastic figure of some particular disciplinary lineage?

There is little in his own account of any ordination or teacher or lineage. Since teaching or lineage assertions acted as authenticating devices for the validity or verity of the speaker or orator, the cumulative weight of all the absences from Dara's 'autobiography' would have been troubling if it were not for Shakespear's own descriptions of Dara. According to the British officer, Dara was a godsend: 'He had the very valuable quality of not being afraid to tell me what he really thought and expressing his opinion very clearly if he thought I was in the wrong and he was never afraid of giving a message or an order however unpalatable to the recipient'.[32] Such force of character and moral authority, rare at all times, may have been the product of cultivation that we are not privileged to learn about. Unless, that is, we place a second trait that the British officer praised in Dara at the centre of our investigation. That trait was Dara's 'capacity for carrying large quantities of zu [grain-based alcohol] without becoming drunk. So that he could sit late with chiefs and drink fair and yet not babble out secrets.' This rendered Dara valuable to the British officer in a purely functional capacity—as a secret-keeper.

But how had this human being come by such ability? Was it acquired as a form of cultivation? In the 1870s, a Bengali Tibetologist from Chittagong, Sarat Chandra Das, had seen such drinking in a Sherpa village attached to the tantric Buddhist Nyingmapa monastery at Tashichoding, one of the finest and richest in Sikkim and eastern Nepal in 1878–9. The village had hosted Das and his travelling monastic companion (Ugyen Gyatso) to dinner and provided large jugs of *murwa* (millet-based beer) in large jugs. As Shakespear did with Dara, Das remarked of his hosts that 'even after emptying two or three murwa bottles our friends preserved their usual temper. No one was drunk, although there were warm discussions, everyone speaking in vociferous tones'.[33]

Apart from these teasing hints at Dara's own past—his ability to hold alcohol without being vanquished by it, his ability to maintain silence when necessary and speak truthfully when necessary—there is one other aspect of Dara's biography that suggests great self-discipline and cultivation of fortitude. Only Shakespear, not Dara, tells us that the British military had burned Dara's home on the hills. If there were women or children in Dara's life in that home, there is no mention of it in Dara's own account of his past. This does not rule out the possibility that he subsequently lived the life of a householder. In 2005, when I went looking for his traces in the hills of the modern postcolonial state of Mizoram, my hosts took me to the home of a locally significant person called R. Lalthangvunga, who introduced himself as the youngest grandson of Dara. This descendant in turn allowed me to read in his house many of the letters that Shakespear had written to Dara in the 1920s–30s. In one of these letters, which is undated, Shakespear asks about Dara's son's name and even supposes that he has by now many grandchildren whereas he, Shakespear, has not yet had any.[34]

There is not even a whisper of these relational bonds and affective ties in Dara's own autobiography. Nor is there even a hint of a memory of a burned home in the account. It would appear that it was not only alcohol that Dara had mastered but also grief or *dukkha*, that most unruly of entities, the quintessential starting point of Buddhist disciplines in mindfulness. The fact that Dara's 'autobiography'—with a largely absent 'self' in its centre—betrayed not a word of grief or loss on his own account was the final mark of a training in the ideals of mindfulness and selflessness (*anatta*) at the same time. Stephen Collins has showed the extent to which the textual canon banished the 'ultimate' validity, solidity, or permanence of the self as an object of analytic or speculative philosophy. A 'doctrine of the self' (*attavada*) was one of the four forms of 'grasping' behaviours (the others were sense-pleasures, mere rules-and-rituals, and 'views') that were to be rejected at all times, especially for the cultivation of the monk.[35] Thus, a refusal to speak of a 'self' and its past suffering constituted the final claim for the authority of Dara's account of what transpired in the village in 1891. And it is this valued selflessness that should be understood as an illumination on the absolute non-I in Dara's 'autobiography'. His—and other hill men's—testaments would suggest that the Tantric Buddhist male monastic subject cultivated a particular mode of address based on the non-self. If subaltern females did not speak, neither did subaltern males speak of a suffering self.[36]

They spoke instead of the suffering of others. Dara's testimony focused entirely on reproducing the voices of others in what appears as a form of compassionate ventriloquism. It went:

There were two Paihte young women in Khawhri and Mr Murray asked for them for himself and Mr Taylor as soon as they arrived at the village. The two young women fled into the jungle and the chief and his elders could not find them. Mr Murray was very angry and said to the chief, 'If you do not give them to me I shall demand your wife.' As they could not be found, Mr Murray demanded the wives of the chief and his brother, respectively. The Chief replied, 'I send coolies when he demands them and have supplied everything he has required. Now that he asks for my wife, I know he is seeking a quarrel with me. I will not give him my wife, let him do as he likes.' This made Mr Murray very angry and he threatened to burn their rice.

The chief Zakapa then secretly planned to attack him with his young men if he did so and also to attack the signalers and the sentries guarding the cash box outside the zawlbuk in the village [cf. Khawhri]. He said, 'even if he destroys our rice we will divide the money and will not starve.' Mr Murray had only time to burn a part of the rice when he was attacked and surprised ... This was the time of year when the jungle is cut for jhums and Mr Murray and his party fled through the cut down jungle ... Finally taking Zakapa with us, Shakespear and I proceeded to Chittagong—(Murray was officer at Rangamati)—Shakespear asked Zakapa in front of Murray why he had shot Murray and got the answer. ... 'Why should I not, he asked for two young women and when they fled he demanded my wife. I refused so he went to burn our rice. Seeing he was going to destroy that on which we depended for life, I could do no other than shoot him.' Murray however maintained that he had asked for coolies and been refused. The chaprasis were called and questioned. They replied, 'What Zakapa says is true. He did ask for the woman and on being refused he set out to destroy the rice.' We took Zakapa on to Chittagong and the Chief Commissioner investigated the case. On finding that Mr Murray was guilty of the first offence he put Zakapa in prison for three months only. We returned to Lungleh.

Dara's formal location as a male subaltern in one of the more brutal colonial machineries in the late nineteenth century did not prevent him speaking 'truth' to power. Yet this speech-act does not offer any explanation of the speaker's motives for doing so. Moreover, instead of 'his own voice', Dara's testimony attempts to incorporate the voice of the injured other. Thus, in the testimony, it is the second man whose voice comes through. This is Zakapa. Giving place to the injured was an enactment of ethical priority on the part of the one giving witness. It speaks not of the speaker's heroic deeds or inner states, but of the injuries of the other and demands attention on behalf of that other. Dara's testimony foregrounds Zakapa/Jacopa's truthfulness and courage. The husband of the woman is represented as declaring the grounds on which he had shot at the British superintendent. Zakapa's voice, too, lays little claim to representing an interiority or individual subjectivity.

Down in the plains of Bengal and Assam, as Tanika Sarkar urges, the Bengali-speaking intelligentsia had attempted to create the domestic sphere as the only autonomous space that the colonized male subject could defend vis-à-vis colonial legislation of conjugality.[37] Here on the hills, Zakapa's defence for shooting Murray offered no claims regarding the *autonomy* or *sovereignty* of his home. Zakapa's defence—as refracted through Dara's testimony—was not framed in the discourse of conjugal rights and enjoyments of one husband in the person of his wife. It had been articulated as an attempt at the preservation of food—sources of a *community's* life: 'that on which we depended for life.' Women were the growers of all food, its major preparers, and therefore key pillars on which the political community rested. Defending the cultivator in order to preserve the life of the political community was the task to which inmarrying husbands had long been called in many societies from the Himalayan foothills. It was not a defence based on the individual 'native' male's patriarchal and proprietary right in the body of a spouse but a defence based on some larger collective beyond a 'self'.

If this was not articulated as a defence of the sovereignty of the nationalist male and his household, it was perhaps because sovereignty was not the desired object of men and women who had been trained as *subjects* of monastic lords and deities. Nor might they have desired sovereignty over wives, who were implicitly the concern of an entire lineage of brothers, not of the singular monogamous husband alone. The 'villagers' of Khawhri resisted, not the individual husband on behalf of a wife.[38] Did this absence of claim-making indicate a different order of conjugal inter-dependence of political partners towards each other? Perhaps. Training instilled greater concern for 'merit positions' and social statuses than ascriptive kin-based ties alone.

Furthermore, even if the individual women never spoke their own testimony, their refusals to serve colonial commanders came through loudly enough. Panjiham Tipperah, also referred to as a *dubashi* or interpreter who worked for Shakespear for a while, told the enquiry that Murray had dispatched him to 'get two girls for himself and the Chhota Saheb (Mr. Taylor)'.[39] Confirming Dara's narrative, the interpreter reported that he negotiated with two girls who, when told that they 'would sleep with the Saheb, they said "No we won't" and run away'. In sharp contrast to the courtly Sanskritic discourse on the female subject as an always 'desiring' beloved, these male witnesses remembered women as noncompliant colonial subjects, unwilling to service the sexual appetites and greed of colonial military–police officials.

Just as the refusals of female 'labourers' to serve a day beyond their stipulated contracts in 1871 had been *heard* by tea planters in Kachar as a threat to the survival of the plantation structure as a whole, the military and colonial bureaucracy in the 1890s heard these women's voices as refusals to provide 'coolie' labour. Murray had not paid bride wealth for these women; he had simply commanded the women's presence. Murray's official 'brothers', colonial bureaucrats in Bengal, *heard* these women's refusals albeit refracted through the voices of men, and air-brushed it as 'opinion in the hills'.[40] They preserved their own official camaraderie and brotherhood by reporting to their superiors an echo of Murray's own exculpatory rhetoric. Murray, they said, had merely 'demanded coolies'.[41] This allowed senior colonial officials to attribute the civil resistance around them to a simple-minded individual ('Zakapa's rebellion') and the slothfulness of native males. 'The rising was caused by objection to give labour but not by objection to pay tribute'.[42] It cast the men and women who refused to serve in the light of the 'lazy' poor.

Such aspersions were commensurate with the logic of a militarized colonial economy in the late nineteenth century. They valued all human relationships merely in terms of the market, of labour-worthiness, of the maximization of profit. Military men, supreme governors of such domains, readily abstracted female bodies from their place at the centre of networks of ongoing social and political relationships. As 'coolies', women were not recognized to have other relational status vis-à-vis lineages of monks, brothers and sisters, ancestors and descendants. At the same time, such representation of all women as 'workers' equally with different age-grades of men liable to the same kinds of work emptied sexual labour of its value and old age of its authority and dignity. Devaluing female sexuality had the effect of devaluing local sexual divisions of labour on which the dignities of daughters, sisters, and mothers and their male associates and affines had depended.

After Murray burned thirteen granaries ('rice-houses') in an attempt to bring the intermarried lineages to their knees, and the standing crop was devastated, the cultivating households ('villagers of Khawhri') led by Zakapa/Jacopa shot at and wounded the British officer and his entourage. In response, a colonial army descended on Zakapa's village to destroy all 100 maunds of rice. The next day, the entire village was destroyed, and twenty-nine large cattle (gayal) brought to the colonial stockade.[43] Already violent in its demands on women's bodies, the imperial regime then rapidly set about reducing the besieged political society to the debris that Agamben calls *homo sacer* or 'bare life', as distinct from the 'good life'.[44] Appropriately, it happened in a domain that for at least two decades had been 'British territory'.

In response, labour services and grain were denied to colonial officers and armies all over southern Kachar, northern Arakan, and Chittagong hills. Officers named these villages according to the names of men, such as 'Daokoma', 'Doponga' (Darpong?), 'Jaduna', and so on. A closer look at these villages and men's names reveals an altogether different structure of authority within them. The real authorities here were the mothers of men named as the 'chiefs'. Many of these mothers had survived 1871–2. There was the woman called Darbilhi, who in 1889 was forced to supply guides from her village to her own dead relative's grave so that it could be dug up for proof. When the punitive expedition of 1892 arrived in the same hills, the widow of Vonolel/Van nhoi-lien, referred to in an official report as 'Rani of Maite', was located in a Maite (Manipuri) village; among her sons were Lalbura, Bungteya, and Lengkam. Since Zakapa had refused to supply 'coolies' for officials, officials began taking draconian measures for extracting labour from these resistant British subjects. They were authorized to burn all food stocks of resistant villages.[45] The burning of rice made the women and their sons even less willing to hand over their adherents as porters for the work of the colonial armies.[46] By March 1892, Lalbura had attacked McCabe and his battalion. A savage reprisal by the British Indian armies began with the destruction of thirty granaries (and 2,000 maunds or 180,000 lbs) of rice.[47]

Military superintendents' strategies to cow the opposition should be read in the light of the nature of the opposition. Women had been the 'rice-growers' as well as the 'rice-givers' in the terrain. Thus, official military eloquence about creating man-made shortages of rice was also specifically targeted at women's work and merit-generating actions: rice would have to be imported from the plains, and the cost of this realized from the starving in labour, also performed by women.[48] Exposure and starvation were praised as the 'strongest allies of the empire'.[49] Others espoused the alchemy of fire and famine to achieve desired ends. To burn the village was no punishment, one argued, as villages with ample able-bodied young men could be rebuilt elsewhere in three months. A third alternative was 'to establish oneself in a village in sufficient force and with ample supplies, and regularly hunt them down until the terms offered are agreed to, and then repeat the operation at the next village.'[50]

Such strategies cratered the thriving social relations of the cultivating villages. Younger men like Lalbura, instead of caving in, moved their adherent households southwards to find food and sanctuary.[51] Some of these communities were reported in the contiguous valleys, such as those of the Tipra. 'From the time of the Lushai disturbances', a Bengali administrator of the Tipra-Kumilla and Noakhali domains reported, 'about 160 houses of Chakmas, Mugs and Riangs' had moved from the Chittagong hill tracts and the Feni Valley to establish swiddens (*jhums*) for growing cotton and oilseed.[52] These cash crops could generate adequate cash returns if the refugees could be forgiven the high export duties on cotton and oilseeds, such as would have been forgiven such refugees on erstwhile monastic estates.[53]

The people left behind on the older sites on the hills, having had their granaries destroyed, were reduced to eating whatever roots and leaves they could scrounge from the forests. Though lured by military officers in a typical 'food-for-work' programme, they would not give in to the labour demands of the colonial officers. Their resistance was bolstered by the proximity of the old woman, the mother of Lalbura. Even in 1896, she was reported to be living, the chief authority in a village in which her son-in-law, Lalthangvunga, also lived. Though her son had moved away, this old woman had remained where she was. When asked if Lalbura ever came to visit her, she said it was not the custom for a Lushai chief to visit his mother, but she said her grandsons had each been once to see her.[54]

In the hills of the late nineteenth century, then, elderly women waged a desperate struggle against the British Indian army. A woman identified only as 'Vansanga's mother', head of the Zote village, summoned the English officer Shakespear to her village for talks, and then ensured that he was attacked on his way there. The officer returned with greater force to find his path blocked by four stockades and barred by fifty to sixty armed men, and turned back, aware that his guns could not prevail over the Zote village.[55] Ropuiliani's role was found to be both subtler and more all-encompassing. Military superintendents found villages loyal to her exercising a form of 'passive obstruction' that they could not break. In 1892, they arrested her with her son Lalthuama and deported them to Chittagong, where she died.[56] But Ropuiliani's grandson, Dokhama, picked up the resistance where his grandmother had left off, until the very granaries were sacked and the livestock taken away by the British Indian armies.

Given that these were the years during which a serious anti-imperialist resistance tore through southern Kachar (1890), the valley of Manipur (1891), the hills of west Burma (1888–92), and hills of Arunachal Pradesh (1890–4), it is no small measure of colonial military anxieties that all military records paid great attention to the various mothers who commanded the societies of the hills during 1892–1900. One, described only as 'mother of Kairuma' (Nepuitangi), was an old woman of about 65 to 70 years of age, with considerable natural dignity and self-possession. She exercised full authority over her people, presiding over a village of

293 households, wrote one officer.[57] Officials watched over this elder woman in the hopes of catching out her son, Kairuma, said to have authorized the resistance of Zakapa and his brother. They were not wrong in suspecting this woman of staunch anti-imperialist views. A list of 1895–6 showed that the households loyal to Nepuitangi, the mother, allied with 455 households loyal to her son, Kairuma, along with four other clusters of households in their resistance to colonial rule in the hills.[58]

Yet, this last round of resistance, and retaliation by a British Indian army, came on top of four or more decades of militarized colonial governance. The cumulative arc of impoverishment, isolation, and indignity desolated the political communities. First, the young men—the grandsons, sons, the able-bodied warriors—who resisted physically were seized and deported. No old 'friendships' were respected: the sons of one-time colonial allies were also deported.[59] And second, the colonial plunder of food extended to its creators, collectors, and givers—to the capture and redistribution of the women, children, and stock animals themselves. Such officially conducted rituals of captive-taking systematically robbed the basic units of the monastic political society of its members and its wealth.

Colonial military strategy aimed at just such a result. Senior colonial bureaucrats lauded the 'clever capture of Jacopa by Major Shakespear and complete success of operations undertaken against Kairuma'.[60] However, Shakespeare's private correspondence with Dara suggests that this could not have been done without Dara's knowledge of the real authority structures in the locality. Two of the notes in the personal collection of Dara's descendants even suggest that among the hill cattle (gayal) taken from Zaduna, two were given to Dara as a reward for his services.[61] Another note signed by Shakespeare explicitly said of Dara 'He was largely responsible for the successful captures of Lalthuama Vansanga, Zakapa and Zaduna and in fact for all the successes which had attended my efforts.'[62]

And what Dara had known was that the most 'powerful force in the South' was the sister of Vanhnuailiana (Vanhoilien), while the 'biggest chief in the North' was Ropuiliani, then an 'old woman'. These women were central to the anti-imperialist resistance that had unfolded in the hills. Fire, famine, and deportation of the young men was apparently intended to reduce these old women's—or mothers' and grandmothers'—centrality to the political order, and wipe out their 'merit' accounts in the hereafter.

Having destroyed the granaries and barns through which women's merit-making activities had long been sustained, it was only the treatment of eminent women's corpses that remained of the vestiges of reverence paid to local women. In a village off Lungleh, Shakespear recorded having visited a man called Lalruma who had lost his mother. When he visited, he found the corpse in the room in a hollowed-out log plastered up with mud, a bamboo leading through the floor into the ground. It was explained to him that the coffin would stay thus for the next three months, after which the coffin will be opened and the bones buried with great ceremony. 'It is only chiefs and their families that are honoured with this lengthy funeral' the officer noted.[63]

Identical burials had been noted among Buddhist societies in Chittagong and Arakan in the early nineteenth century.[64] But in the late nineteenth century in the hills, the military officers were most concerned not with the state of the Buddhist dead but with the spectre of the 'violent savage'. Having carved Kachar and Sylhet out of the Presidency of Bengal and attached it to the Chief Commissionership of Assam, the land rules of Assam had been applied to these regions. Tea had boomed. By 1893, Kachar sent to market 30.7 per cent of all the tea grown in India.[65] In Sylhet, the area of land under tea cultivation had exploded from 2,050 acres in 1868 to 71,940 acres in 1900. A proportionate number of 'labourers' were brought in: a total of 71,950 'labourers' between 1891 and 1901 from places such as Bihar, Orissa, and Uttar Pradesh worked on the plantations of Sylhet.[66] This influx of labourers, combined with a particular set of management styles on the plantations of Kachar and Sylhet, caused repeated protests from the workers. The issues varied from the matter of wearing wide-brimmed hats (*jhampis*) or the use of plantation tools for workers' own small-scale agriculture, to the speeded-up production rhythms used by managers in Sylhet and Kachar.[67] But most often the issue of the honour (*izzat*) of the female plantation worker was the object of collective action: the physical abuse of young women workers by managers was resented fiercely in many plantations. The violent articulation of dissent extended to the murder of a tea planter, Cockburn, on the Baladhun tea estate.[68] The flight of 'coolies' did not stop, either. In 1899, another official of the Indian Tea Association complained that fifty plantation workers from the Amo tea plantation and fifty-four from the Jeliapara plantation had fled to shelters in the monastic estates of the Tipra lords.[69]

Murray's system of demanding sexual corvee in a para-military system of sexual conscription spread across many hill-based cultivating groups in such a context. In the region called Lushai Hills in the late nineteenth century, military police outnumbered civilian policemen ten to one. In 1897–8, two of these military (British) policemen raped a 'Lushai' girl, and in a prehistory of postcolonial courts, the accused were acquitted because they could not be identified 'satisfactorily'.[70] Where sexual corvee remained a viable form of expropriation, its parallel—the governmentally sanctioned forms of corvee for building roads, bridges, and huts called 'labour taxes' in the colonial archive—also remained alive in the form of enormous amounts of pitifully underpaid labour time for colonial projects of public engineering.

Even those officers who had to extract it were a little embarrassed to pay the pittance (4 annas a day in 1894, 8 annas a day in 1895–6) for something like ten days' labour per able-bodied man per year. The sums paid out did not approximate a living wage; for out of the accumulated 4 rupees from such work, each house had to hand over half in the form of a house tax of Rs 2 per house per annum. Moreover, the figures of the collections of such house taxes between 1893–4 and 1899–1900 showed that though the number of houses being taxed remained largely constant, the amounts actually collected in cash from these houses doubled or trebled over six years.[71] The military superintendent, Shakespear, had described the region that he administered as 'not a country … for old men and fixed notions acquired elsewhere.'[72] In keeping with this, he simply exhausted the population of able-bodied males with his impressments of corvee. When the men protested, Shakespear, having either never learned, or having forgotten about, the tea-plantation-led histories of the region, told the exhausted men 'You forced us to occupy your hills … and so now you have got to bear as much of the cost of the occupation as possible: you cannot expect us to spend the money of the people of the plains on importing coolies to do the work that you are too lazy to do except under compulsion.'[73] It was against such a method of government by terror that Curzon, in 1901, attempted to control the officers 'acting beyond the border' and to prevent the conversion of small police trans-border excursions into expeditions that were in effect small military campaigns. However, like other ameliorative colonial gestures, it was too little, too late, and came with many more strings attached.[74]

'MOTHERS' OF REPAIR: MISSIONARIES, NATIVE COMPOUNDERS, AND HEALTH

War, the accompanying destruction of grain and livestock, corvee, famine, and the rigours of plantation labour all took their toll of the physical health of affected populations. Those who had only their own bodies left as their means of survival in the world were further impoverished by a fall from a tree, a fractured hip, immobilization, and bed sores such as those that brought a young man's wife to the missionary, J.H. Lorrain, living in the colonial fort Aijal.[75] For others, decades of burned grain, stopped salt, killed-off animal wealth, and stopped access to forests affected their ability to recover from illnesses, such as those that afflicted the large numbers of 'Hindustani', Oriya- and Bengali-speaking 'labourers' on the tea plantations of Silchar and Kachar.[76]

The severity of such effects, coupled with malaria, smallpox, and cholera epidemics that frequently accompanied famine, defeated the pitifully small skills and resources of the early Welsh missionaries. Despite having held grants of land in the hills of Kachar and Sylhet since 1871, two decades later these missionaries remained entirely dependent on the goodwill of local men and women. Welsh Presbyterian missionaries accepted as much when one of them admitted his own 'medical incompetency', his linguistic inability and financial distress, and the cumulative effect that these had in turning away scores of people from the dispensary.[77]

While Buddhist and Bon monastic leaders were becoming rapidly unrecognizable to colonial militias, impoverished Christian missionaries also became powerless before these military machines. From 1890, two Baptist missionaries (Frederick W. Savidge and J. Herbert Lorrain) had been working in Brahmanbaria mission set up in the western lands taken from the old Tipura lords in the eighteenth century.[78] They had begun to learn Bengali when the post-annexation Burmese and Manipuri resistance (1885–92) occurred everywhere in the hills, merging with that among groups in the British-governed regions called Chin-Lushai Hills. News of such resistance relayed to the metropolitan orders redoubled the energies and funds of many small evangelical bodies. One of these was the Arthington Trust at Leeds, which began to sponsor specifically hill-focused missionary work.[79] This trust sponsored Lorrain and Savidge's establishment in the newly established British province called Lushai Hills, where they were sent in 1894.

The poverty of these early generations of missionaries constituted their saving grace. It put them at a disadvantage with their middle-class social superiors, the Anglican officers of the British Indian army. American Baptist missionaries in the 1850s had spoken of spending a few days in the local military officer's home as a 'vacation': 'They live so differently from us missionaries that going there was about as much as of change' as a missionary could afford.[80] Like the earliest of the Baptist missionaries, the majority of the early Welsh missionaries also originated from the working poor of the late nineteenth century. Documents in the keeping of descendants of one of the missionary Lorrain brothers include a seventeen-year-old boy's indenture bond from 1897.[81] According to this bond, the youth Reginald Lorrain was apprenticed to a female greengrocer in the county of Surrey. The unpublished diary of the same man lists his travels from 1899 to 1902 working at a variety of agricultural and ranching jobs between Manitoba and Houston, Texas. In the course of four years, this one man had held a variety of hard labouring jobs ploughing, harrowing, haymaking, building sod-stables, tending stock, laying rails on the Canadian Pacific Railway, building roads, cutting wood in lumber camps in the backwoods of Ontario, and sorting timber for saw mills.

This biographic profile is important both for the mechanical skills such missionaries brought to their work and also for explaining the missionaries' lack of educational resources. In 1905–6, when this junior Lorrain brother, Reginald, wished to join his elder brother in the northern Arakan hills, he knew he needed to complete a course of medical training at Livingstone College: the problem was to find the 45 pounds fee for the course.[82] In contrast, Lorrain's counterpart, the

American Baptist missionary Frederic Harding, who also apprenticed at thirteen to an electrician, had a college degree before he arrived in 1907 as a missionary at Tura (present-day Meghalaya).[83]

In functional terms, however, whether American Baptist or English Baptist or Welsh Calvinist, these late nineteenth- and early twentieth-century missionaries remained equally unable to identify correctly the collocated Tantric Buddhist-Bon, Vaisnava, and Sufi ritual practices of people around them. For example, Harding believed he was coming out to meet the 'semi-savage tribe of Garos'.[84] Yet, an American Baptist missionary history noted of these hills that a young 'Garo' man called Ramke Momin, 'proficient in Bengali'—one of the three clearly defined language groups in the area (the others being Hindustani and Assamese)—had learned to read the *Mahabharata* and *Ramayana* from 'monks living in secluded *akra*s (shelters of reeds)' before joining the Baptist congregation.[85] More singularly, such a Bengali-speaking 'Garo' youth had worked in the colonial army in some menial capacity and had been a devoted Vaisnava for a while before his baptism in 1863.[86] Another American Baptist in the western hills of Burma in the late nineteenth century (contiguous to the Indian region known as Lushai Hills) failed to identify the Buddhist icon (of alabaster, eighteen inches long, very heavy and very white) that a local man said he had been worshipping in the forks of a tree every day of his life. Instead she used it as a 'door stop' in the Thayetmo Mission until she overheard someone identify the mission as Buddhist on the basis of that icon.[87]

Missionaries, untrained to recognize the particular traditions of Bon-Buddhist and Vaisnava collaborations that had lodged among a range of Tai, Sino-Tibetan, Tibeto-Burman, and Bengali-Assamese–speaking groups in the hills, remained dependent on local lay adepts and adherents of older-established monastic lineages and communities for their own linguistic training—and for their missionizing. Lorrain the elder gathered around the same *zawlbuk* as did the youngest fourteen-year-old boy every evening in order to learn the language, and to hear the stories and the daily news. From such endeavours emerged two distinctive texts, one called the 'Abor' Bible, and the other a dictionary of the Lushai language.[88] Both were results of many years of talking-work. It was hard labour because the Tibeto-Burman language groups are tonal: the same word has several wholly different meanings if the pitch or length of tone is varied in uttering it.[89]

By virtue of their proximity to these groups, missionaries reported at great length about the sensitivity to health evinced by them. Though early missionaries for the Welsh Calvinists or the Baptists (James Lorrain and J.H. Savidge, Edwin Rowlands, and David Evan Jones) had no medical skills when they arrived in the southernmost hills in 1897–8, all of them were struck by the ways in which very young and very old alike sought them out for bodily health. In the very first year that Jones lived in the hills, he noted that 'great and many are the calls to heal all kinds of diseases, and they expect to be healed at once'.[90] A similar eagerness for health was reported by the younger missionary, Edwin Rowlands. In his first year in the region, he noted the ways in which news of efficacious medicine was shared among the locals: 'they tell each other of the cures effected.'[91] Most vociferous in their concern for efficacious medicines were young men and women who had come from village-clusters recently ravaged by the imperialist armies. For instance, Rowlands reported on Dokhama, a twenty-year-old who had been hospitalized for many months, had lost his strength, and was 'no longer wanted in the house where he stayed previously'.[92] A missionary obituary to Dokhama (the grandson of Ropuiliani) referred to him as 'one of our first evangelists'.[93]

These missionaries did not connect the decayed health or the physical disabilities and impairments of local populations with processes in the vicinity. But the same processes also brought in young women from the same sorts of villages at the same time. The same missionary who described Dokhama reported that three adolescent girls (between twelve and fourteen years) had fled from the village of Zote, a village that had recently endured severe colonial military assaults.[94] One of these girls was afflicted with 'facial paralysis'.[95] Another three-year-old child was brought to the missionary by villagers the morning after her ailing grandmother died.[96] From these missiological reports emerge the social profile of those who sought refuge. They were the bruised survivors of the elder women's war. It is these figures and names that help us to understand the exact temporal and political contexts in which Christianization occurred in south and southeast Bengal-Assam.

Until 1905, most of the effective 'care' was provided by local intermediaries, most of who were males of the older Vaisnava and Tantric orders. Most of these men appear to have hailed from Vaisnava and Sufi Muslim communities. In Muslim-majority Sylhet, a man called Gour Charan Dass pushed for the reopening of the mission school in 1886. At Maulvi Bazar, a town south of Sylhet, the Welsh missionary depended on Abdul Hamid, a Muslim man from Silchar who, after formal baptism as a Christian, set up a school near Sunaibari for the surrounding populations living in the hills.[97] Such dual-identity figures appear to have been especially popular with audiences who were themselves drawn from diverse ritual and social groups. Thus, we find that a 'Brahman' (Prem Ronjon Upadhya), baptized in 1895, preached at Silchar among 'the large numbers of Khasis' who lived there; his colleagues in this work were Hemronjon Sirkar, Anoda Ghose, and Abdul Hamid. The latter was especially popular with a group of Tipra who built a residential hut and an assembly room and then requested the Welsh missionaries to send him as a teacher.[98]

Similarly, in Karimganj, a town that developed once the Bengal-Assam rail line was laid, a Welsh missionary with a bachelor's degree in science, remained dependent on the aid of Rajkumar Sarma, a 'Brahman of high caste and of some influence' to work with him in the dispensary.[99] The work of such 'native' assistants baptized or otherwise, appears in the same light as the work that Dara performed in a military context once and would later perform again for a trained Welsh doctor. Sarma, like Dara, appeared to have a monastic-ascetic background. The Welsh superior at Karimganj observed of Sarma that he was often found in the dispensary with 'a group of Hindus, some of them perhaps former disciples, sitting around him and receiving instruction from his lips.' Within a short while, other 'natives' were found assisting at these dispensaries: Babu Heraball Biswas and a 'Khasi compounder' worked at Karimganj.[100] By 1903, when the entire 600 miles of the Bengal-Assam rail line was thrown open, Karimganj had several 'Khasi compounders' working at the Welsh mission dispensary and several others visiting the mission compound regularly.

The effective delivery of care—either in the shape of talking cures or in the form of tablets and pills and other pharmacological interventions—made these indigenous male nurses and compounders significant for two reasons. None of these 'native' care-workers appeared in the formal employ or on the payroll of Christian missions for these years. So no historian of either missionary histories or of subalterns has speculated about the inspirations and goals of these men in their participation in the work of Christian missions. Was it likely that these men had simply taken on the codes of transcending gender that had been recommended by Mahayana Buddhist teachers earlier?

Scholars of medieval Mahayana Buddhist texts establish that laymen were encouraged to become 'maternal' nurturers as part of the discipline of universal compassion (*maitri*).[101] As Cabezon puts it, the two most important concepts of Mahayana Buddhism, wisdom (*prajñā*)—gnosis (*jñāna*), and method (*upāya*)—compassion (*karunā*) were gendered female and male, respectively. Wisdom was 'female'. All behaviours to do with love and altruism were identified as 'male'. A similar idealization of compassionate and emotive masculinity was enunciated in contemporary Bengali-language tracts. Chandrasekhar Mukhopadhyaya's *Udbhranto Prem* outlined this ethic as emotive, empathic, and relational: 'a person is divine (*devata*) when he knows to weep with others (unrelated, *anya*), to experience (*anubhav*) the others' pain in their own soul (*hrdaya*), to discern (*jnan*) the difficulties (*apad*) of others as endangering one's self. Humans cry for the self, gods weep for others. The day the human being learns to weep with others is the day he attains divinity (*devatta*).'[102] Equalizing the figure of Buddha and Jesus Christ, this tract deified both as venerable humans who had perfected the cultivation of empathy, the suffering *with* others. Such historic articulations of the priority of the suffering of others over the suffering self united Dara's testimony with the ethics suggested by Bengali-speaking, Assamese-speaking 'native' compounders and dispensers of care.

All these men shared in the same ethic of daily and small-scale acts of care. Their remedies and strategies of seeking relief from distress thus remained those of the older Tibetan Buddhist and Vaisnava pharmacopoeia. In a context where many Bonpo lineages had mixed in with the Kagyupa and other Buddhist schools, there existed an understanding of the body as pervaded by breath (*dbugs*).[103] These ideas combined with both Mazdeist ideas of two or three souls and

Mahayana Buddhist ideas of *dharmakaya* and *rupakaya* in rituals that treated illness as caused by transactions between various souls and sentient beings ('spirits'). Rituals for the restoration of health were based on ideas such as that of one soul selling the second one to the *preta* (malevolent spirits). The rituals of cure mimicked ransoming (Tib. *bla glud*), summoning the soul (*bla bod*, Tai *khwan*), and shepherding it back to the place from where it had wandered. These rituals involved placating the sentient beings of the cosmos with food, drink, and cloth, as well as what all British sources called animal 'sacrifice'.[104]

In most Vedantic doctrine, animals were proximate to humans, serving out their own particular karmic obligations. The ritual of offering an animal could not have effected a cure without this prior valuation of life-forms. Thus, the ritual's transactional symbols mimicked the Vedic doctrine by which all human beings were born as a debt to Yama, the lord of death, who loaned them their bodies; once born, they had to repay him. An individual was released from such debt only by dying; freeing oneself from such debt required that the lord of Death be convinced of the value of the substitute for what was owed him. The 'giving up' or payment of animal wealth to ransom an ailing human spirit-body encoded and expressed many simultaneous values in the same transaction.

This vibrant Tibetan Buddhist, Bonpo, and Vedantic order clearly sufficed most members of local societies until 1905. That is why so few asked for ritual baths of baptism from the Christian missionaries resident in the same region. At Aijal in 1899, only four adults and a child were baptized; by 1905, there were a total of 58 males and 28 females. In the same year, Sylhet had 71 males and 100 females; the 'home' mission in the hills (Khasi-Jaintia or modern Meghalaya) had 226 males and 292 females. Similarly, in 1905, Karimganj had only one man and five women listed as Christians; Maulvi Bazar had 58 men and 28 women. These numbers did not suggest rapid Christianizing. Far greater numbers were baptized members at places such as Shillong (2,164 males and 2,259 women), where the American Baptist mission had long had medically trained doctors attached to the Church and delivering health care. Thus, if the numbers of baptisms were to be explained by the presence of caregivers in the region, then the majority of the populations tended by 'native' health-care workers in the Surma-Barak Valley and its vicinity remained Buddhist-Vaisnava-Sufi subjects, as they had long been.

RESTORING MONASTIC DORMITORIES IN THE MISSION SCHOOLS

The restoration of monastic dormitories in mission schools was manifested also in the ways the people responded to the building of mission schools, huts, and medical compounds. Though lately arrived Welsh missionaries did not see themselves as parallel with the 'native' healers around them, locals built 'mission schools' that were replicas of Buddhist and Vaisnava monastic schools in the vicinity. The mission school set up in 1898–9 in the hills, for instance, was as impermanent as the best monastic school might have been earlier—'a building with poles of solid trees, walls of bamboo, a thatch of leaves'.[105] The ghosts of the old monastic estates hovered over such schools: young boys came from distant villages and stayed on the compound, as any novice and monastic subject might have earlier, and paid for his keep by exchanging labour service for food and board. All such young men wished to live on 'mission land'—perhaps because they had once lived on monastic estates of this or that Buddhist, Tantric, Vaisnava, or Bon transmission lineage.

Some paid for their education in grain. Others paid by cleaning the colonial Indian army sepoys' utensils, working as government messengers, road makers, blacksmiths, and carpenters; the wages earned from such services were given to the missionaries as payment for education, board, and lodging.[106] Some of this labour was onerous, especially in those tea plantation and 'scheduled' districts marked off as beyond the pale of criminal and civil procedures. For though the Assam Labour and Emigration Act of 1882 had declared that 'no labourer shall be bound to labour more than six days in one week', few military superintendents who governed these Scheduled Districts were bound to follow such laws. Some male labourers tried to implement such laws by invoking the biblical command of rest on the Sabbath.[107] Such porters pushed the missionaries to plead on their behalf with local military bosses. The British Superintendent in Aijal recalled an incident in 1899 when he dismissed a group of missionaries who had appealed to him on behalf of Christian coolie-porters to lay off 'Sunday labour'. The Superintendent exulted that he had 'defeated them by saying that ... the Sabbath was made for man and not man for the Sabbath'.[108]

Some of the labour servants who attached themselves to the Christian mission, refusing to work on a Sunday, set up a separate 'Christian' village (near Lungleh).[109] But military officers generally refused to give any credence to the attempts of baptized youths to stop work on Sundays. They justified this denial of rest on the grounds that this constituted a 'special consideration' to one religion. Missionaries who converted 'slaves' to Christianity, one argued, should be fully apprised of the impossibility of preferential treatment to any one religion as a special 'favour'.[110] Despite the failures of the missionaries to win exemptions for their disciples from onerous labour payments, the fact that they had tried to speak on behalf of their disciples was only further proof of their ability to spiritually 'befriend' their students and disciples.

The final imprint of older monastic patterns among those who sought education from the newly established missionary schools and health from the same men was the memorization of texts, a characteristic of monastic education to which lay people also adhered.[111] As Georges Dreyfuss observes, the process of memorization was aural. Monks did not rely on visual mnemonic devices to memorize texts but on a musical tune to support their vocalization of the texts. Students concentrated entirely on the text's sonic patterns, ignoring other associations. These patterns of memorization were common across populations of both hills and plains in the early twentieth century. For instance, in 1900–1, a Welsh Calvinist missionary reported that all the three young men who had joined him on tour 'commit verses to memory for Sunday and lately they have begun to learn the Gospel of St John by heart.'[112] In 1908–9, another remarked on the sonic regime as a whole in two closely related hill-dwelling populations ('Khasi' and 'Lushai'): both were eloquent speakers, fond of singing, and were especially tuneful congregational singers. There was great talent among these people, he noted, especially for memorization. He had offered a prize for learning the fourth chapter of John's Gospel. Several of the women 'learnt it all through.'[113] In 1910–11, another young woman was reported as having memorized most scriptures—over a thousand verses.[114]

Memorization itself had a curative place in most Bonpo-Buddhist societies. Selected verses had long been learned and chanted by monks as *paritta*.[115] The word itself meant protection or safeguarding, and could sometimes be extended to medical prophylaxis and cure (*bhaisajya*). The verses could be recited in groups or individually for the benefit of the chanters, those who listened to the chanting, and others. Paritta was also chanted to help recovery from illness, and to exorcize danger and possession by harmful spirits.

CARE, CURE, AND POSSESSIONS: 1905 AS REVIVAL

The need for collective prayer and the exorcism of demons arose dramatically in 1905. Welsh missionary sources imply that the origins of this lay in a movement in the Welsh church. What they did not mention were the dire events that had shaken all monastic subjects of Tibetan-speaking Buddhists and Bonpo the previous year. In June 1903, the Younghusband expedition had set off from Darjeeling on its invasion of Lhasa. In its military encounter with Tibetan subjects in March 1904, the British Indian army slaughtered 1,500 monastic subjects, and looted all the dead men's amulets, images, and substantial wealth from the monasteries.[116] Vajrayana Buddhist amulets, prayers, and rituals seemed to have lost their potency against British Indian guns.

The turmoil generated by this became part of a mystic political movement on the Bengal plains and hills that was identified in Calvinist Church reports as a 'revival'. By the second Sunday in March of 1905, sermons by local preachers in a church were suddenly followed by 'men and women *crying* and confessing their sins, others *shouting* for joy, others *confessing their love* for Jesus; shy timid women and some who could not read, getting up to confess their love for Jesus, and as they did so tears streamed down their cheeks.' The wave spread to Cherra, then Shillong, and then onwards; women's prayer meetings were held daily. The Rajah of Mairang, a baptized Christian, hosted and fed a 4,000-strong congregational assembly. But when Christian missionaries tried to address the Mairang assembly, they were drowned out by a collective wave of emotional praying, singing, shouting, and weeping at the same time. Many were in a trance, and received messages to the congregation direct from God. Quiet and reserved women were described as 'praying with overpowering effect'. Four sermons were delivered during the day, but it was the singing, the praying and the direct message which most deeply moved the people.[117] At this assembly were visitors from the southern or 'Lushai' hills—three males, one of who was accepted as a great 'healer' by his adherents, and two women. These visitors were also touched: 'heavenly fire descended upon them with remarkable power, causing each one of them to weep aloud. One of them rose to pray … *his* body meanwhile trembling violently under the influence of the spirit. One or two men had to support *him* to prevent *him* falling to the ground.'[118]

In other historical contexts, such movements have been referred to as millenarian movements. But as a rich and layered South Asian historiography has lately suggested, there is better cause to understand these movements within the rubric of collective rites and sites of possession. When the body was possessed by non-human beings, the possessed 'became' the deity.[119] Such outwardly directed forms of possession involved the intentional, and ritually conducted, introduction of a spirit or deity into a visionary (*sramana* or monk) for generally curative purposes. The possessed person was supposed to deploy the cosmic being, spirit, or deity, to outward ends. The shouting, singing, crying noted in the missionary reports of the hills in southern Assam-eastern Bengal were curative possessions of the same kind. Moreover, such possessions were simultaneously claims to 'empowerment' by divine force itself. Possession trancers among Sufis were thought to ascend ('soul flight') to the realms of the gods, to access special knowledge and transmit it to an enculturated and ritually constituted group. But what happened here was the reverse. As a local teacher told a missionary in 1905 in the hills, 'heaven had come down to earth. We feel that the world and its pleasures are as nothing compared with the love of Jesus. Nothing else is talked about in the house, on the roads, in the market place and everywhere but the love of Jesus to us sinners: we are drunk with the Holy Spirit'.[120]

By entering into the body of these men, the deity—in this case Jesus—reconstituted and re-empowered broken and injured limbs, healing and transforming battered bodies into heroic ones. As the missionary reports of 1888 had suggested, local men did not revere Christ as a deity but as a 'great man'. Emasculated young men and broken others were especially taken with the notion of Jesus as soldier-commander whose resurrection meant that he had beaten Death; he was especially manly in this victory over Yama.[121] In a conceptual world where reincarnation was well known, and names such as Maitreya and offices such as that of a Mahdi symbolized a hopeful futurity, ideas of a Christian Second Coming were entirely translatable in terms of futurescapes.

Moreover, these were populations that had venerated militant monks and served as warriors in the following of monastic lineages even in the nineteenth century. Biblical teaching about 'love' of a heroic man such as Jesus towards his followers had the potential of inspiring such congregations to renew their own heroism. The conditions of 1905 were ripe for such renewal of hope and heroic masculinity. It began when young men from distant villages formed a band called Kraws Sipahi (Soldiers of the Cross), established a swidden field for growing rice for themselves, and set up an other-directed programme of 'salvation of their fellow-men ... go[ing] out to the villages far and near'.[122]

British military superintendents saw in such movements a potential danger. Like David Scott and Francis Jenkins before him in the 1830s, Major G.H. Cole wrote a strictly confidential unofficial note to the directors of the Welsh Presbyterian mission in 1906. He asked that the mission improve its services in three ways immediately. First, that it build permanent buildings as homes for the missionaries. Currently, he complained, the Welsh missionaries lived in the same bamboo and grass structures as did their flock; they fell ill and suffered in the same ways and also nearly died without medical attention.[123] 'Savages', he argued, could not help but be influenced by appearances; they judged Europeans by their surroundings rather than by their intrinsic merits. Substantial buildings had political value for empire. Their absence brought the flock too close to their lords.

Cole also asked the directors to increase the stipends of the missionaries, because each missionary appeared to have to maintain out of his own funds the various boys who came to read with them. 'Your workers' he wrote, are 'very charitable and maintain many persons out of their private pockets whose maintenance should, I venture to think, rightly fall on the mission.'[124] Finally, he pleaded for the mission to send out a trained doctor. 'One of the greatest needs of the Lushai is proper medical treatment. ... I have little doubt of the good work that a medical missionary would be capable of performing among them or of the ultimate religious value of his efforts.' Statistical details about the pay of the missionaries are impossible to glean from the reports before us. But Cole's directive yielded results forthwith. A qualified doctor, long requested by the early missionaries from their directors to no avail, was promptly secured and dispatched to the hills.

This medically trained missionary, Peter Fraser, arrived in the hills to which he was summoned in 1908.[125] With him were his wife, Mary Catherine, and another young man, J. Watkins Roberts. Though it might have been an unconventional threesome by Christian models of conjugality, it was not out of place in a context where elder and junior brother might expect to live conjointly with the same woman. His arrival, probably combined with the news of Swadeshi, was electric. Almost immediately on arrival, the doctor was summoned to meet a man called Hrangvunga, who lived over sixty miles away. Two men had come from him to Aijal, asking for a doctor 'as Hrangvunga was in a dangerous state, bringing up large quantities of blood'. Fraser reported having treated this man and staunched the vomiting of blood. What Fraser did not know was the intimacy of this man with the Tripura Rajas and zamindars of Sylhet. One of the famous adherents referred to in the correspondence of the Tripura Raja was Sardar Hrang Bhunga, placed on the same honourable rank as the Raja Daikoma who had settled in the Jampui Hills in the jurisdiction of the Tripura raj.[126]

Within six months of having been treated by Fraser, Hrangvunga called on the medical missionary and his wife and told them that he 'intended to set his slaves free'. Citing Luke 4:18, Fraser wrote, 'He came to proclaim release to the captives and to set at liberty those who are bruised.' By October 1909, as the result of yet another medical intervention, another young man called Khawvelthanga had issued a free pardon to many of his subjects (the doctor called them 'slaves' or *bawi*). Apparently referring to the new sources of law and obligation (*dharma*) stemming from the 'names of King Edward and Jesus Christ', Khawvelthanga issued a public pardon to his debtors, refuge-seekers, and under-tenants: 'From this time no one will be able to make you a slave', said the proclamation.[127] Like Hrangvunga, Khawvelthanga (1884–1971) too was connected to locally eminent and revered figures: he was married to a daughter of one of the men involved in anti-imperialist struggle in 1890–1902.[128]

But these men's pardons sparked off a bitter struggle *within* the colonial administration, dividing the missionary fraternity and hardening the stance of the military governors even more.

Fraser, the newly arrived medical missionary, was appalled at finding 'slaves' all over the hills, while his military sponsors—the very men who had ensured his arrival here—objected to his setting up little manumission courts of his own, and eventually secured his extradition from the hills.[129] Although Cole would eventually accuse the doctor of having usurped the military superintendent's political authority, Fraser was only another missionary who was unaware of the rituals that governed Bon-Buddhist practices of compassion by all lay and ordained alike. Like Baptist missionaries before him in Assam, Fraser also made the classic mistake of defining as 'slaves' entire families of under-tenants who, unable to pay various monetized fines and taxes, repay loans, or make alimony, child-support, and marriage payments, had joined the households of eminent individuals and offered them labour services in exchange for their subsistence. The hosts were expected to meet the fiscal obligations of their adherents who had turned themselves into bondsmen, women, and children.

Fraser was also unaware of the long-established rituals by which suffering beings—such as trapped animals, birds, humans—were liberated on significant occasions. As a recently arrived medical missionary, Fraser had probably not heard of the recent events in which ideals of compassionate solidarity had led some men to liberate 'trapped' labourers from the plantations. Though he witnessed such acts of solidarity on a daily basis, Fraser did not question his own notions of 'freedom' as he battled the military administration on their condoning of 'slavery'. Having lost a male patient to death, the doctor described how a small body of men 'intended to run all night to carry the dead body home as quickly as possible'. He marvelled at 'the sympathy and kindness of these poor heathen shown at a time of sorrow and need.'[130] Though appreciative, Fraser could not see how the same kind of 'kind-ness' could be extended by elder men (headmen, 'chiefs') to the sustenance of the indigent, refugee, famine-struck.

The doctor thus misunderstood the ethical and economic implications of the gestures of liberation made by Hrangvunga and Khawvelthanga of their under-tenants. These were completely consonant with Buddhist ethics, but were also harbingers of economic distress among the better-connected headmen in the hills. In 1897, a colonial officer, writing about a 'singularly intelligent hill people' in the North Lushai Hills, had described only large villages.[131] But by 1909, the date of the liberations practiced by the local headmen, large villages had turned into small vulnerable communities and households on the same lands. Mass liberations indicated that men such as Hrangvunga and Khawvelthanga, earlier able to offer sanctuary to the indigent and the disabled, had renounced their responsibilities. Famine was on its way. The very next year, 1910, the bamboo flowered again. Rats appeared to feed off the bamboo flower and continued to eat their way through the rice crops in the swiddens.

The indigent sought refuge elsewhere: several of the former 'slaves' offered themselves to the doctor, asking him to take them on as 'schoolboys'. Unable to refuse, Fraser began to build a house for about twelve boys; by October, he had admitted forty-nine boys in the same schoolhouse or dormitory. Since Fraser had no more idea of old-established Buddhist doctrines of debt and obligation than any other missionary of his generation, he had no inkling that debts prevented novices from becoming ordained monks, and that released from such debts and contracts, many former debtors headed straight for the nearest approximation to the monastic infirmary and school they could find, the church and the doctor's domestic establishment. By early 1911, a full-fledged famine had erupted in the hills and completely disabled older patterns of compassion and sanctuary. 'From one village 4 decrepit persons were brought to Aijal by the chief as they could not be supported by him.'[132] Hrangvunga and Khawvelthunga had been significant bellwethers of the dissolution of lay and monastic sanctuaries.

While the compassionate masculinity of the hills wavered, the wisdom and heroism of the elderly women did not. Like the men who had paid for the return of their own lives and health by releasing their own under-tenants and labour servants from their obligations, elderly women too paid for the doctor's gift of 'life' by becoming his 'disciples.' On his way to treat Hrangvunga, Fraser went past the house of a woman suffering from advanced dropsy, who was 'tapped' to relieve congestion. She, not Hrangvunga, was Fraser's 'first Christian convert'. Immediately after the operation, she had asked to be placed among the followers of Christ. In terms exactly translatable between Buddhist-Vaisnava and evangelical Christian monastic disciplinary and initiation structures, Fraser wrote, 'she has since been a consistent follower of the master'.[133]

But in so doing, this woman remained completely faithful to the ideas of 'debt' and repayment that animated the poorest of the poor in these societies. American Baptist medical missionaries had observed this behaviour on the part of poor women whose daughters had been healed by some medicine given by the doctor.[134] On the other side of the same hills in the second decade of the twentieth century, the Welsh doctor's wife observed an identical ethical pattern of behaviour among the very poor, who insisted on paying for everything they received in some way or the other. She spoke of these hill-dwelling societies around her thus:

for any kindness and if we do ever so little, they bring us eggs and often a hen or bananas and sometimes they bring a big vegetable called a pumpkin. …The people are very poor, nearly all of them and even some of the poorest will bring a live hen, which costs 8 annas, 8 dimes of your money and that is a big sum for a Lushai, so you see that they give the 'widow's mite' and they even apologise for giving so little.[135]

Those who had nothing else to give offered themselves, their labour, as labour servants and disciples.

The doctor's dispensary case load for the same period showed the extent of such self-gifting that might have occurred in payment for medical treatment. In one month alone in 1909, Fraser had treated 1,666 patients out of a makeshift tent. Ailments ranged from pneumonia, tuberculosis, severe bleeding, to severe dysentery, and in periods of acute crisis such as in 1911–12, cholera. The medical work in the hill post was heavy, with the mission dispensary alone treating over 20,000 cases of illness in 1911. Though the doctor did not keep statistics by sex and age, it was clear from accompanying notes that a large number of his patients were female. For instance, speaking of patients he had to visit in their homes because they were immobilized, he mentioned alongside a young Santhal male labourer whose foot was crushed by a falling stone, two women 'badly burnt while burning their jhum.'[136] Describing dysentery that commenced after the heavy rains of early May brought the debris of plantations and cantonments into the water sources, Fraser described two little girls called Fibi (Phoebe?) and her cousin Hawtinthangi dying from it.[137]

Fibi was the daughter of Vanchhunga and granddaughter of the matron who had been so kind to Mary Winchester. Did two little girls compare in any way to one grown male labourer? Perhaps not from the perspective of those invested only in labour extraction, such as colonial administrators and tea planters. But those men and women who invested in 'futures' through the acquisition of networks of kin by the marriages of their daughters and sisters might have regarded the doctor's care for their daughters differently. As in 1890, so during Fraser's tenure in the hills, yet another father was asked to send his daughter to 'serve' yet another government official; when the father refused, he was beaten with heavy pieces of wood until almost dead. Fraser had been summoned to revive the father.[138] His complaint against the government official was ignored by the civilian and military bureaucracy alike.

FEMALE ORACLES, SONIC REGIMES, AND THE LINEAGE OF FEMALE ORDINATION

Despite Fraser's heroism, and in ways not recognized by eyewitness reporting at the time, many of the populations appear to have valued the doctor's wife more even than they did him. At least some of the fruit and vegetables that were brought to the mission were not payments, but 'offerings' directed towards Mary Catherine. For example, in the midst of the bruising confrontation between the doctor and the administrators about the 'slave question', the doctor's wife noticed that a crowd of local hill-dwellers from ten miles away came to comfort her with 'potatoes, cucumbers, tomatoes and big fruits'.[139] These were all very high-value crops in the hills, where fruits were a specialty. Moreover, even though their main staple had been entirely destroyed by February-March 1911, in mid-August the same year these populations bore precious fruit to the home of the missionary's wife.

Why? A conversation with one of the elders still living in the vicinity, the Reverend Zairema, one of the 'boys' trained by Mrs Fraser, allowed me to understand the distinctiveness of her presence in the hills at this time, and the fruit bearers' visit to her house from another distant village. Almost entirely unrecorded in almost all the missionary and colonial correspondence was the fact that Mary

Catherine was a trained singer. She played a harmonium, taught piano to all the 'boys' of the mission school, and provided musical accompaniment to church prayers.[140] Song was her great contribution to the Christian missionary presence in the region.

Local populations had long been accustomed to women oracles as expert communicants with the deities.[141] In the seventeenth century, the Jesuit monk Manrique had described Buddhist monks (*raulins*) attempting to heal the sick by appeasing their 'god Char-Baos' with 'sacrifices' of the very best and fattest of animals. Manrique called these rituals 'Caloucos' (*Kalika*), but his descriptions reveal that the central figures in these healing rituals were neither Buddhist male monk nor patient, but females who danced in the presence of the 'idol' in expiation of a vow. Dancing till exhausted, the dancer falls on the ground, 'all present express their delight and congratulate each other, holding that the god had come and inspired or talked with the exhausted vow-maker'. Manrique's descriptions suggested that the 'Calouco' was the female who danced her way into special communication between different realms.[142]

Female mediums had remained very significant through the nineteenth century in all the Mahayana Buddhist and tantric communities. Buchanan had reported them in the Chittagong hills as women called 'Deearee'. In all crises of sickness and health, the Chakma applied to these dearees, who 'are supposed also to be able to render a joom [*jhum*] inaccessible to tigers and wild elephants.'[143] Identical female mediums and oracles had been found in the same hills in the mid-to-late nineteenth century. Reporting on what appeared to be a combination of visual and sonic perfection that combined a diagnostic vision (or 'insight') with a prophetic communicative skill ('foresight'), military officers such as Lewin and Shakespear had referred to this highly valued skill as *zawl*. Individuals possessed by the benevolent deity were *khuavang zawl*, 'subject to long trances or ecstasies when they are thought to be present only in body, the soul (*thlarao*) having gone to visit'; this power, however, was associated with an inherent knowledge of medicines. Noticeably, Shakespear's informants named women (Lianthangi, Thang-tei-nu) as the superior communicators or *zawlnei*.[144]

In crisis, then, the people had brought the highly valued fruit to Mary Fraser, the expert of the kind of sonic regime that was considered more efficacious among many Mahayana Buddhists and Tantric Bon. Their arrival forced the host to get out of bed, thank them, and then hold a prayer meeting on the verandah. Though Mary Catherine did not say exactly what they prayed about that evening, she did note the preponderance of women at these prayer meetings and their concerns. Quite a few women attended women's meetings 'in order to pray to the One who provides for His children. There was a ring of deep earnestness in all the prayers—several spoke too of their distress'.[145] It is hard to know from the records whether this was a prayer of last resort of the kind that people had turned to when male monastic medicine failed, or whether this was in some way to initiate the female 'consort's' obligation to care for the male monastic's flock.

But other missionary wives had noted that by November all the hens in the village had died from want of food, and the widows with children, left in desperate traits, asked to be taken on.[146] By early 1912, Mary Catherine, too, was describing in great detail the ways in which famine affected women more than it did men. A large number of men, it appears, went to the plains to search for food and work. The women stayed behind. But they did not beg. They came with sticks of kindling gathered from the forest, and only asked others to buy 'a penny worth or two and that is how we help a great many, by buying sticks but it is little after all'.[147]

The doctor's official accounts of expenses for the same period (the first quarter of 1912) shows that the directors of the mission spent a pitiful 35 pounds sterling on the seventy to eighty persons on the mission compound who, with others living elsewhere, were fed entirely or partially by the Frasers.[148] Mary Catherine specified that many of those who had sheltered in the compound were female. She spoke of old women who held her to their hearts and said 'you love us as if you were our Mother: you are like our real Mother.'[149] The childless Mary Catherine reported being ashamed of her poor kind of love. She tried to rise to the occasion by organizing the care of nine or ten little babies, many more toddlers, and the forty to fifty widows and temporarily abandoned wives who sheltered in the compound. By end of June 1912, the doctor's domestic establishment and mission compound contained a 'family of from 60 to 100 of our own to feed and clothe … 8 seers of milk a day for the babies alone, indeed more and it comes to one rupee two annas a day'.[150] Mary

Fraser spoke of 'our little family', but it was a largely female one.[151] She might as well have called it her own 'tribe'.

She also tried to change uninformed 'public opinion' in Wales about the people among whom she lived and worked. In a note to the mission Directors in Aberstywyth, she referred to the idea common there that 'we are among savages here, whereas really we are surrounded by some of the wisest of men and the "Guprassies" [Government Servants] are among them'.[152] Like local men who had given testimony about *others* suffering, Mary too referred to others, specially a Dara-like figure. Possibly it was Dara she was referring to. For in the records of this missionary couple, a polyglot man called 'Dala' appears repeatedly, interpreting between local patients and English military superintendents, teaching languages to the missionary and his wife.[153] Their notes describe this polyglot and teacher of languages as one who 'gave up a good berth in the Government service in order to serve Jesus. ... [He] has only been a Christian about two years'. Perhaps the experience of having served a colonial military regime had convinced Dara about joining the following of a Christian doctor. But it was noticeable that he did not seek to live on the mission compound even in 1911–12.

It was the women who did. They 'took refuge' in the Frasers' home, the mission compound. Mary Fraser also described the 'first' Christians in 1912 as female. The sister of Khawvelthanga named Huangi, a former wife of another 'chief' deserted by her partner, also joined the mission house and gave her 'name to be a Christian'.[154] Even if brief, we have an account of this woman's ritual and spiritual relocation within a Christian world: every morning she attended mission school and then helped Mary Fraser with chores around the mission and orphanage, and sometimes in the evening, she and the doctor's wife attended women's meetings. Mary Fraser described one such meeting to which the two travelled in the dark: Huangi carried the lantern and 'took the greatest care of me—we had a splendid meeting and Huangi took part in prayer and gave out a hymn, "I am coming to the Cross."'[155] The expert female singer had transmitted some of her oral efficacy in a female transmission line. Albeit never studied as an aspect of monastic transmission lineage, this female-to-female lineage of sonic skill also evokes a parallel and gendered monastic subjectivity in the making.

The impact of such a female lineage appeared in the unlikeliest of places—the statistics of the Welsh Presbyterian Church.[156] These statistics were organized by gender-neutral categories of communicants, candidates for communion, the baptized, the dead, and the transferred. However, the total membership in the Church was counted by sex. A comparison of these numbers suggests that even though most of the formally accepted deacons, preachers, and ministers of the missionary churches were male, a larger majority of their 'hearers' were women. For instance, in Shillong in 1899–1900, there were 633 female members of the church and 525 male. In the same year, the southernmost Lushai centre showed a majority of males to females, 13 to 2. But by the end of year 1913–14, the number of females in Shillong had grown to 3,278 over 3,151 males, and in Lushai Hills there were 3,141 female churchgoers to 2,698 males.

The completion of Fraser's dispensary at Aijal and the outbreak of the famine of 1911 may have had a great deal to do with the numbers who sought medical assistance, refuge, and sustenance from the Frasers, and the latter's ability to offer shelter. The dispensary had only just been completed in November 1911—a building of corrugated iron and lime-plastered walls containing four rooms and two bathrooms—when people flocked there from great distances, some even ninety miles away, to seek medical attention. In that year alone, 24,000 cases were treated there.[157] The following year, Fraser reported that the number of the ailing who required hospitalization was greater than could be accommodated at the dispensary, so that some had to be admitted into orphans' and schoolboys' houses for a while, especially since several had come from great distances. So great was the demand for health care that the Mission had to expand accommodation in a new hospital block. But even with this expanded facility, only fourteen inmates could be admitted in the two buildings. Though there is no way of reckoning the numbers of women who either consulted the doctor or were admitted, the doctor noted that most of the in-patients, after a stay in the hospital, 'have willingly given their names as believers in Christ and also tried to lead others to Him.'

Such declarations of adherence to the Church that accompanied the consumption of missionary medicine or food were completely consonant with Buddhist-Vaisnava traditions of debt and the terms of dignified personhood at the heart of gender-generation codes. All records after 1912–13 noted that most church membership was of 'older women'.[158] These groups had already proven to be the real powers in the organization of young males and militias in the 1860s–90s. Had these women merely sought refuge in ways similar to those associated with the famous Vaisnava akharas and shelters for the destitute at pilgrimage sites such as Vrindavan and Mathura? Or was their preponderance in Church membership from 1914 to the 1940s indicative of an attempt to restore their authority as actors in the monastic economy of 'merit-making'? Is that the reason for the ritual declarations of 'discipleship' that baptism implied?

Historians of both celibate Burmese–Buddhist and Vaisnava monastic lineages in the eighteenth and nineteenth century highlight the differences regarding women's ordination and leadership roles that set apart the austere monastic lineages from the esoteric ones. For example, among the austere Vaisnava lineages centred on the Mayamara/Moamaria *sattra*, women were not central to key rituals of initiation, collective prayer-song, and worship (*nama prasanga*). Leaders of such ordination lineages refused to acknowledge the guruship *by* women and recognized only husbands as gurus *of* wives.[159] In the same vein, Sthaviravada Buddhist monastic lineages in Burma did not enrol or ordain women as nuns. The exclusion of women from ritualized membership in such lineages, their exclusion from leadership roles and responsibilities in clerical administrations, suggests that like indebted males formally excluded from ordination, many female lay disciples of male monastic ordination lineages experienced membership in the Tantric Buddhist, Sahajiya Vaisnava, and the Christian communities as more satisfying alternatives to discipleship of orthodox celibate monastic lineages. Moreover, in the ritual bath of baptism, the Christian church in general and the Welsh Methodists in particular, did offer the hope of 'universal salvation' that, like its Tibetan-Tai Mahayana counterparts, did not discriminate by sex, caste, or class. The real significance of the membership of elderly women in the Christian church after 1912–13 was therefore to restore the possibility of transcending the physical body of gender for a transcendent, meritorious, and cultivated personhood. Women's direct membership in the Methodist Church thus restored gendered and generational patterns of an older monastic governmental order. Furthermore, it restored laywomen's claims to 'merit-making': everywhere that begging monks and lay households had been fed by women, one could find male deacons and pastors of the Christian church restoring their dependence on these women's tithe-paying capacities.

However, the famine that had brought local elder women to the Christian doctors drove a wedge, as we have noted, between the latter and the military officer who had done the most to secure his services. Infuriated by the non-conformism of Peter Fraser, the military superintendent pressed the directors of the Welsh mission at Aberstywyth to muzzle the doctor. The directors asked Fraser to leave the region and work in some other hillside.[160] An ill and tormented Fraser refused, and left for Wales to face an enquiry.[161] His agitation did lead in 1915 to the first (and last, and pitifully flawed) official census of labour servants (*boi*) in the region, a disproportionate number of who were women and children. Among the limited number of villages that were surveyed, census takers found 119 indwelling labour servants, of whom 96 were women and children, while only 23 were males between the ages of sixteen and sixty. Extrapolating from the overall census figures for the hills (a total population of 91,204), administrators then estimated that the total number of the indwelling labour servants in the district approximated to 550, of whom 101 would have been males, and 440 women and children.[162]

Fraser never returned to the hills, and died in 1919.[163] A song, said to have been composed by (Upa) Thanga in 1913, commemorating the 'abolition of slavery' due to Fraser's work, survived him.[164] If there was such an abolition decree, there is no material record of it in the colonial archives. The paper trail actually suggests the opposite. Nevertheless, in a largely rebuilt landscape of the same hills in postcolonial India, Fraser's name has been given to an institution to which every young woman living in and around Aizawl comes at some point. This is the main obstetric and paediatric clinic in Aizawl, the 'Fraser Clinic'. Harried local female nurses within, distracted by clamorous mothers and wailing infants, nevertheless take time out to politely instruct curious (and female) visitors in the achievements of Peter Fraser. The clinic is the closest a Christianized community can come to building a *stupa* for a revered man whose bones are not available for veneration and proper burial. The doctor's name, along with two of the first missionaries, J.H. Lorrain and Savidge, figures in the nave of the largest church that exists in the modern acropolis of Aijal. Both the clinic in his name and the plaque in the church are memorials to a caregiver, to his daily and small acts of care, and to local perceptions of his heroism in having argued with armed fellow Christians, the military superintendents.

But like all other rock-and-stone memorials in the landscape, these too remain silent about the doctor's wife who continued to live and work in the hills after his death—as a widow and as a teacher of music. There is neither a commemorative plaque nor song that celebrates her lineage or work. Nor for all the other senior women whose work sustained and built the communities and relationships torn apart by guns and military demands. Was it that they had already been dismissed as unmemorable because they were not 'ordained' nuns but laywomen of no proven or visibly efficacious credentials? Or was it that in being anti-colonial women, they had offended the record keepers of the archives and tablets twice over—once for being recalcitrant British subjects and second, for being women who had outsmarted Death and outlived warrior males? Or was it that those who might have remembered these women—the professional historians of the region—had themselves fallen under the spell of a colonial legal discourse that effaced gender altogether, implying 'women' while writing about the memories of 'men'? None of these questions could be answered without understanding the conditions in which remembering and forgetting became political and socially constitutive acts—the context of nationalism, Christianity, memory, and history writing in the colony in the early twentieth century. In order to understand the final acts of excluding and marginalizing women's lineages of labour and song, the suppression of the monastic codes of gender that made men mother and women soldier on, we will have to return to those Anglican British officials who wrote the first 'histories' of Assam. Somewhere in *their* politics of memory perhaps lies the key to unlocking the silence of the stones.

NOTES

1. See Act III of 1867 (Public Gambling), Arakan Hills Civil Justice Regulation of 1874 in *British Burma Code*, Government of Burma (1875: 26, 165).

2. Among others, see Dena (1988); Lhuna (1992); Downs (1994); Debbarma (1996); Studdert-Kennedy (2005); Cox (2002); Howarth (2010); Thong (2011).

3. For similar positions, see Viswanathan (1998); Johnston (2003); and Palsetia (2006).

4. For the early centuries, see Zysk (1991); for seventeenth-century Gelukpa emphasis on the Bodhisattva ideal as related to medicine, see Schaeffer (2003); for study of fourteenth to seventeenth century texts, see Emmerick (2001) and Garrett (2008).

5. Hefner (1993a, 1993b).

6. Bartholomeusz (1992).

7. Smart (1866: 2–3).

8. Dy Commr Cachar to Commr Dacca, 6 March 1871, *PP*, 1872, 89.

9. *Ibid.*, 130.

10. Government of Burma (1875: 179–81).

11. *Ibid.*, 142–62.

12. Different varieties of bamboo flower in cycles of different lengths— most in 20- to 80-year cycles.

13. Riebeck 1885, 5. For the objects traded, see plates 1–15.

14. NAI, FPP, E, March 1883, nos 47–8.

15. Dy Commr Kachar to Secy Chief Commr Assam, 10 June 1884, NAI External A, October 1884, no. 379.

16. Assam Regulation of 1 October 1897, quoted in Lalrimawia (1995: 91–2).

17. Davis (1894: 8–12).

18. Shakespear (1909: 381).

19. M'Cosh (1837: 140).

20. Hughes (1881: 25).

21. *Ibid.*, 30.

22. Offg Dy Commr Kachar to Secy Chief Commr Assam 10 March 1884, NAI, External A, October 1884, no. 377.

23. See Myint (1983: 123–54) for Kachin and Chin Hills, until 1894; also Adas (1982); Maung Maung (1990); for the ethics informing resistance, see Gravers (1999: 10–30); P. Ghosh (2000: 83–101); Callahan (2003: 26–7); Myint-U (2002: 198–254).

24. Kolsky (2010).

25. Lalthlangiena (2004: 38).

26. Diary from 7 to 25 December 1890 in Memo of Commr Chittagong 12 January 1891, OIOC Mss Eur/Photo Eur/89/1: Official Tour Diaries of Shakespear, 1st Battalion, Leinster Regiment, f. 30.

27. Diaries of C.S. Murray, Asst Political Officer, Lushai Hills from 1 to 18 February in Memo of Commr Chittagong Div, *ibid.*, ff. 54–8.

28. Diary for 16 February 1891 in Memo by Offg Commr of Chittagong Div 16 March 1891, *ibid.*, f. 45.

29. Murphy (1832).

30. Lorrain (1988 [1912]: 50, 90, 129, 134–8).

31. 'Autobiography: The Story of Dara, Chief of Pukpui', OIOC, Mss Eur E 361/4, f. 2.

32. Shakespear to McCall, 29 March 1934, OIOC, Mss Eur E 361/5, f 4b.

33. Das (1903: 314–15, Appendix C).

34. Letter signed John Shakespear to Ka Thian Dara, 16 April, year unavailable. The letter refers to 'Parry Sahib', Col N.J. Parry, who was Superintendent of these hills in the 1920s–31. I am grateful to R. Lalthangvunga for sharing these documents in his private collection with me.

35. Collins (1990: 71 and passim).

36. Compare with Spivak (1999: 255–69).

37. Sarkar (2002: 197–9).

38. Compare with another enraged husband who killed his wife, conscripted by the Mahanta of Tarakesvar; for this murder, see *ibid.*, 53–94.

39. Statement of Panjiham Tipperah, in Lalthlangiena (2004: 90).

40. Secy GOI Home to Chief Secy GOB, 13 July 1896, in BPP, September 1896, no. 1, and from H.J.S. Cotton, Offg Secy GOI Home to Chief Secy GOB, 18 August 1896, BPP, September 1896, no. 4.

41. W.B. Oldham, Commr Bhagalpur Div, to Chief Secy GOB, 23 July 1896, in OIOC, IOR, BPP, September 1896, no. 2.

42. Notes by 'L' [Landsdowne, the Viceroy], 26 October 1892, and by 'W.J.C.' in the Military Dept, 27 October 1892, NAI, Foreign External A, February 1893, k.w. 1, of nos 45–105.

43. Diary from 7 to 16 May 1891, Memo by Commr Chittagong, 24 May 1891, Mss Eur/Photo Eur 89/1, ff. 79–80. It was after this date that Dara's name appears in the records of Shakespear's journals. This suggests that Dara's village had been in the vicinity of those destroyed, or in Zakapa's village itself.

44. I draw on the critical discussion of Agamben in Ziarek (2008).

45. Letter of R.B. McCabe, Political Officer North Lushai Hills, to Chief Commr Assam, 2 March 1892, OIOC, Mss Eur/Photo Eur 108, entry for March 1892.

46. Diary of R. B. McCabe, Political Officer, North Lushai Hills, 2–13 February 1892, OIOC, Mss Eur/Photo Eur 108, entry for February 6.

47. McCabe's entry for 2 March 1892, *ibid.*

48. *Ibid.*, 23 January–1 February, 1892.

49. *Ibid.*, entry for 8 May 1892.

50.   Note by Captain Shakespear, South Lushai Hills, 5 September 1892, NAI, Foreign External, A, February 1893, 45–105.

51.   Diary of A.W. Davis, Political Officer, North Lushai Hills, 5–22 December 1892, OIOC, Mss Eur/Photo Eur 89.

52.   Das (2004: 6).

53.   *Ibid.*, 16.

54.   Diary of Porteous, North Lushai Hills, for March 1896, entry for 8 March, OIOC, Mss Eur/Photo Eur 89.

55.   Lalthlenglieana (2004: 95).

56.   *Ibid.*, 107.

57.   Diary of McCabe, 2 February 1892, OIOC, Mss Eur/Photo Eur 108.

58.   Lalthlenglieana (2004: 112).

59.   See, for example, *Administrative Report of North Lushai Hills* (1896: 9).

60.   Secy GOI to Chief Secy GOB, 8 September 1896, encl in Curzon's note to Secy of State for India, 21 September 1899, OIOC, L/PS/ 7/116, no 930. This note also outlines the imperialist strategy of isolating the government of 'native-ruled' Manipur ,'the Alsatia for troublesome Chins and Lushais', from the groups of intermarried lineages in all adjacent hillsides.

61.   Notes by R.S. Hutchinson, 26 February 1895, by Major Shakespear, 21 March 1896, personal collection of Mr. Lalthangvunga, Lungleh. I am extremely grateful to Mr. Lalthangvunga for his permission to read and cite this material.

62.   Note of 20 March 1896, *ibid.*

63.   Diary for week ending 17 October 1891 in Memo Offg Commr, 26 October 1891,OIOC Mss Eur/Photo Eur 89, f. 112.

64.   See, for example, Malcolm (1839: 234–5); for the post-mortem treatment of the body of a venerated hpongyi, 316–7. For the continuation of such practices in the late twentieth century, see Khan (1999: 163–4).

65.   Secy Indian Tea Association to Secy Chief Commr Assam, 20 June 1893, OIOC, L/PJ/6/256.

66.   Rahman (1999).

67.   Varma (2011).

68.   Telegram to Viceroy 3 July 1894 re Baladhaun Murder and Robbery Case, and correspondence, OIOC, L/PJ/6/376.

69.   Acting Secy Indian Tea Association to Chief Secy GOB, 15 May 1899, BPP, September 1899, no. 41, Dhaka, National Archives of Bangladesh, Sylhet Judicial Progs, Branch D, Bundle 1.

70.   *Administrative Report of North Lushai Hills* (1898: 7).

71.   *Administrative Report of North Lushai Hills* (1899: 4).

72.   Demi-official from Capt J. Shakespear to J.A. Crawford, 5 September 1892, NAI, Foreign External A, February 1893, k.w. 2, nos 45–105.

73.   *Ibid.*, 4.

74. Confidential Summary of the Principal Events and Measures of the Viceroyalty of Lord Curzon in the Foreign Dept 1899–1905, OIOC, V, 1.

75. Kyles (1944: 15–17).

76. One such plantation called Rampur, and another, Duldelly, were regularly mentioned in the missionary reports. Vanlalchhunga (2003: 25–31).

77. Report by Rev. T.W. Reese for 1898 for Sylhet, *ibid.*, 61.

78. Kyles (1944: 9–10).

79. For a background of the Quaker response to another Bengal missionary, St. John Dalmas, see Chirgwin (1935).

80. Ellen Stoddard to 'Sister Bronson', 5 July 1855, Miles Bronson, Letters Received, Rutgers University Special collections. I am grateful to Geraldine Forbes for sharing this document.

81. Apprenticeship indenture dated 8 February 1897 between James Lorrain, father of Reginald Lorrain, in unpublished diary of Reginald Lorrain in the keeping of Reverend Mark Lha Pi and Mrs Violet Lha Pi, Serkawr. I am grateful to the entire Lha Pi family for allowing me to read the diary.

82. Lorrain (1988 [1912]: 6–7).

83. Harding (1974).

84. *Ibid.*, 55.

85. Carey (1919: 43).

86. *Ibid.*, 45–6; see also Bangla-Garo dictionary of Ramkhe (1887).

87. Carson (1997 [1927]: 126–7).

88. Lorrain (1908).

89. Lorrain and Savidge (1898). The younger Lorrain brother's grammar and dictionary was only published posthumously, after the formal end of empire: Lorrain (1951).

90. D.E. Jones, *Report of Lushai Hills 1898–9*, in Thanzauva (1997: 4).

91. Edwin Rowlands, *Report of Lushai Hills 1899–1900*, *ibid.*, 9.

92. Edwin Rowlands, *Report of Lushai Hills 1901–2*, *ibid*, 14–15.

93. D.E. Jones, *Report of Lushai Hills 1916–17*, *ibid.*, 60–1.

94. Edwin Rowlands in Report of the Foreign Missions of the Welsh Calvinist Methodists for the Year ending December 1901, Presented by the Executive Committee to the General Assembly held at Liverpool, 1902, NLW, CMA, GZ/84–8, 56.

95. Edwin Rowlands to Reverend Williams, 10 December 1907, NLW, CMA 5, file no. 27, 314.

96. *Ibid.*

97. Report by Rev. T.J. Jones for 1901 for Silchar, in Thanzauva (1997: 93).

98. Report by Rev. T.W. Reese for 1902 for Sylhet, *ibid.*, 97–8.

99. Report by Rev. O.O. Williams for 1896 for Karimganj, *ibid.*, 49.

100. Report by Rev. O.O. Williams for 1899, Sylhet-Kachar Reports, 68.

101. Richman (1992) and Cabezón (1992).

102. Basu (1992: 359–413, especially 366).

103. Gyatso (1998: 153).

104. See, for example, Lorrain (1988 [1912]: 96).

105. Report of Lushai Hills in Thanzauva (1997: 3).

106. David E. Jones and Edwin Rowlands, *Report of the Lushai Hills for 1902–4, ibid.*, 18–20.

107. Morris (1939: 159).

108. John Shakespeare to McCall, 25 June 1934, OIOC, Mss Eur. E 361/5, f. 5a.

109. *Report of Lushai Hills, 1901–2* in Thanzauva (1997: 16).

110. Note by R.W. von Morde, Asst Supt Lushai Hills 23 December 1909, on Case no. 4, Lalbuta Chief against Tekawla and others, NLW, CMA 5, no. 27, 318, unpaginated.

111. Dreyfus (2003: 79–97).

112. *Report of Lushai Hills, 1900–1*, in Thanzauva (1997: 9, 11).

113. *Report of Lushai Hills, 1908–9, ibid.*, 38.

114. *Report of Lushai Hills, 1910–11, ibid.*, 42.

115. Harvey (1993).

116. See Dalton (2011: 148–9); Carrington (2003); for suppression of such details, see Younghusband (1905).

117. *Report of Lushai Hills, 1905–6*, in Thanzauva (1997: 29).

118. *Ibid.*, 34.

119. Smith (2006: 60–75 and passim).

120. Report by Miss Thomas on Khasia and Jaintia for 1905, in Thanzauva (1997: 23–4).

121. Troughton (2006).

122. Though this group existed from about 1905, it is mentioned only in the reports of 1911–12, see Thanzauva (1997: 48).

123. Major H.W.G. Cole to 'Dear Sir', 21 September 1906, CMA 27315, ff. 1–24, esp. f. 12.

124. *Ibid.*, f. 20.

125. Peter Fraser to Rev. Williams, 13 November 1908, from Goalundo on the Ganges, CMA 5, 27315, no. 247.

126. Birendra Kishor Manikya to Govr Assam, 25 July 1909, *Tripura Historical Documents* (1994: 136–8).

127. Khawvelthanga cited in Peter Fraser to Rev R.J. Williams, 29 October 1909, CMA 27, 315.

128. Personal letter by son of Khawvelthanga, Lalsanga Sailo, 1 March 2006. The letter provides names of the persons liberated, and biography of Khawvelthanga, who was 26 years old in 1910.

129. Chatterjee (2006).
130. P. Fraser to Rev. R.J. Williams, 29 April 1909, CMA 27315, no. 99.
131. A. Porteous, Political Officer North Lushai Hills, to Secy Chief Commr Assam, 19 January 1897, encl 3 in L/PS/7/116, no. 930.
132. *Report of Lushai Hills 1911–12*, Thanzauva (1997: 48).
133. Peter Fraser to Williams, 26 January 1909, CMA 27315, no. 99.
134. Carson (1901).
135. Mary Catherine Fraser to Rev. Williams, n.d., CMA 27315, no. 100.
136. P. Fraser to Rev. Williams, 10 March 1909, *ibid.*, no. 53.
137. P. Fraser to Williams, 4 June 1909, *ibid.*, no. 130.
138. Peter Fraser to Rev. T.W. Reese at Haflong, 3 November 1911, CMA 27318, unnumbered.
139. Mary C. Fraser to Mr. Williams, 12 August 1911, CMA 27318, unnumbered.
140. Mary C. Fraser to Mr. Williams, 8 August 1912, *ibid.*, no. 228. This is the only mention of her harmonium, a wind instrument, 'which attracts many people' to the doctor and her when they went on the road with it.
141. For the special place of female practitioners in Tibetan medicine, see 'Introduction' in Gyatso and Havnevik (2005); Diemberger (2005); and Tsering (2005).
142. Luard (1926: 225–7); Luard cites later reports and eyewitness accounts of the early twentieth century for interpreting Manrique in n. 9, 225.
143. Van Schendel (1992a: 112).
144. Shakespear (1912: 111).
145. Mary C. Fraser to Mr. Williams, 22 September 1911, CMA 27318, no. 279.
146. Katie G. Jones, North Lushai Hills, 12 November 1911, CMA 27318, unnumbered. She was the wife of the missionary David E. Jones.
147. Mary Fraser to unavailable addressee, CMA 27318, eight-page letter from which front page is missing. Presumably this is dated prior to 28 March 1912, because the subsequent letter from the author thanks the directors for some money sent in response to the earlier appeal.
148. Peter Fraser to Rev. Williams, 17 May 1912, *ibid.*, no. 140.
149. Mary C. Fraser to Williams, 14 May 1912, *ibid.*, no. 139.
150. Mary C. Fraser to Williams, 21 June 1912, *ibid.*, no. 192.
151. Mary C. Fraser to Mr. Williams, 25 November 1911, *ibid.*, no. 337.
152. *Ibid.*
153. P. Fraser to Rev. Williams, 1 April 1909, CMA 27315, no. 81; for Dala as the teacher who came after dark to the house, see undated letter from Mary Fraser to Rev. Williams, *ibid.*, no. 100.
154. Mary C. Fraser to Williams, 14 May 1912, CMA 27318, no. 139.
155. Mary C. Fraser to Williams, *ibid.*

156. Thanzauva (1997: ix–lx).

157. *Report of Lushai Hills 1910–11, ibid.*, 45.

158. *Report of Lushai Hills 1914–15*, *ibid.*, 55. This feature is noted in all missionary records and newsletters of the 1930s–50s, but remains unexplained in the historiography of Christianization in India. This is in sharp contrast to studies in African histories such as Hodgson (2005).

159. Mahanta (1936).

160. Letter from Rev. R.J. Williams, 3 February 1911, CMA 27314.

161. E. Williams to Rev. Williams, 29 October 1912, CMA 27314.

162. B.C. Allen, Chief Secy Chief Commr Assam to Secy to GOI, Foreign and Political, 23 June 1915, OIOC, L/PS/11/95, P 2973/15.

163. Last Will and Testament of Peter Fraser, probated 9 April 1920, in St Asaph's Diocese, NLW, *Wills of 1920*, 132.

164. This song is now published in Khiangte (2002: 11–12).

Conclusion
Rule by Ethnology—Forgetting Histories and Households

BY THE MID-TWENTIETH CENTURY, various itineraries had been developed all of which ended in the misrecognition and forgetting of friendship between the hills and the plains. One of these paths had been mapped out since the eighteenth century by surgeons and botanists such as Buchanan (Hamilton) who met and spoke with monastic subjects but recognized neither them nor the larger political economy within which monastic teachers related to their disciples and dormitories or had dependent under-tenants. Their oblivion was significant in enabling their followers among the Bengali-speaking literati to also misrecognize their linguistic and social ties with their Tibetan, Uighur, Burmese, and Newari-speaking neighbours and relatives living alongside them. Colonial scientific knowledge schemes were particularly unable to comprehend the legal and political status of the intermarried clan-dormitories of laymen and laywomen, adherents of Tantric Bon and Buddhist teachers, some of whom were also patronized by Central Asian Afghans and plains-dwelling Mughal and Vaisnava laylords. Colonial policies that aimed at reducing the coherence of such clan-dormitories thus nibbled away at the authority of women, holders of real estate, who were patrons–donors of the monastic-ascetic lords and temples in the eighteenth and early nineteenth centuries. The erosion of various kinds of monastic exemptions of revenue payments and labour obligations that began in the 1760s, intended to diminish the authority of competitive lineages of monk-traders and priests, thus ended up whittling down the status of elderly women as well. Instead of recognizing the 'merit' economy within which many women had offered their services, labour, and hospitality, including systems of polyandrous unions and levirate, officials were increasingly quick to dub such women either drudges or prostitutes. As colonially sponsored agriculture expanded in the 1830s–50s through all parts of Assam, Kachar, Manipur, and Arakan, so too did colonial ignorance of the collocated monastic dormitories.

A second kind of colonial knowledge formation occurred at the same time and recognized monastic subjects for who they were. However, this branch was steadily eroded by the weight of colonial economics, and then entirely snuffed out with the intensification of commercial agriculture between 1833 and 1900 in all regions north and east of Dhaka. The ecology of plantations, stock exchanges, Crown and Parliamentary government buildings—all provided conditions in which ignorance flourished. This ignorance too was directed at resident elderly women and at female 'labourers' brought to the tea plantations from the plains. From the mid-nineteenth century, European tea planters and their friends among the military officers, some of who were also colonial administrators and ethnologists, scientists, and scholars, strengthened the general non-recognition of monastic subjects further. Therefore, one of the most important military expeditions in the mid-nineteenth century, the so-called Lushai Expedition of 1871, remained largely understudied by those who were interested in labour and land legislation. After this expedition, most 'tea districts' were made inaccessible to monastic itinerants.

It is not a mere coincidence that colonial census and military ethnological reports were consolidated at exactly the same time in the second half of the nineteenth century, from 1871 onwards. These ossified a decades-long pattern of official Anglophone descriptions of dormitories of the disciples and lay servants of monasteries as 'tribes'. Both sets of reports were produced by colonial officers, and both came together at the end of the nineteenth century in the figure of Edward A. Gait, the superintendent of the census operations in Bengal since 1891. In 1901, Gait sent out a circular dated 6 September asking all the local officers in the province to cause enquiries to be made in each district 'on the traces of Buddhism in Bengal'.[1] Answers had to be returned within a month—by 1 November at the latest. An interesting dichotomy emerged in what the scientists thought was a 'trace' and the extent to which the Assamese and Bengali literati, among whom many had continued to be monastic subjects themselves, saw the living organism called 'Buddhism'.

Men such as Sarat Chandra Das in Darjeeling—living in a house called 'Lhassa Villa' that kept alive the memory of a visit to a sacred centre—and his guide and companion on those trips, Ugyen Gyatso, were now authoritative but unofficial members of the colonial bureaucracy. From their humble position, they nevertheless proceeded to gently mock the colonial scientists. Gyatso referred to the complex of *practices*, not beliefs, that included the propitiation of 'fever-demons', the adoration of the Buddha and Bodhisattva, the rituals involving earthly gods such as Mahakala, Isvara, Visnu, Brahma, Indra, Seridebi (Sridevi, a form of Durga), and Saraswati. It was not Buddhist practice that was the 'relic' but the reverse: from his vantage point in Kalimpong, once part of Sikkimese terrain and then part of British North Bengal, Gyatso found 'All that is peculiar and interesting here is the traces of Hinduism in the religious services of the Buddhists'.[2] Das wrote, 'Almost all the tribes who worship demons honour Buddhist and the Buddhist deities' and proceeded to list all the groups living in the district: the Newars, the Kiranti, the Limbu, the Khambo, Lepchas, and so on.[3]

A minister of the Tippera State suggested that this held true for many populations of his region, as well. Speaking of the Mrungs and Chakmas, immigrants who had brought their Buddhism with them into the country adjoining the Chittagong Hill tracts, he pointed out that alongside the worship of an image of the Sakyamuni, they combined it with local forms of disease-dispelling deities, such as the small round stone that was said to drive out smallpox, along with the ever-present Kali, Siva, and other Hindu gods and goddesses.[4] This was fairly consistent with the stance that most educated Indian respondents took to the issue. Each wrote at length describing the particular forms of recombinant practice that brought together Buddhist, Vaisnava, Saiva, and other groups in the same villages and centres we have been tracing.

Literati descriptions of these practices suggested that in the early twentieth century, the clusters of monastic subjects had gone into hibernation, but had not been extinguished altogether. The accounts of village shrines revealed the extent to which each resident on village lands had continued to consider himself as this or that deity's tax-paying 'subject'. For instance, in the northeast corner of Murshidabad, the seat of a hegemonic Shia Muslim lineage of Mughal governors (Nawabs) since the late eighteenth century, a learned Vedic scholar (Ramendra Sundar Trivedi) spoke of Dharmaraja, the god of the village community.[5] There was scarcely an important village in the district that did not have its own Dharmaraj, he said; like every local tax-collector's office-building, all business of the village was also conducted at the temple and precincts of the Dharmaraj. Unlike the local lay lord's (*zamindar's*) mansion, however, the temple of the Dharmaraj was a mud-hut, which was occupied by a wooden human figure called Banesvar or Ban Gosain for the better part of the year. This wooden icon was the 'agent' of the superior lord; on annual festivals, it was this icon who went begging for alms on his lord's behalf from household to household. Furthermore, regardless of whatever personal attitudes upper-caste men had towards the village lord, they 'high or low, are bound to make contributions to the fund raised for his worship.'

This collocation, translation, and reuse made it impossible to categorize human subjects of deities and lords in terms appropriate to the British liberal imperialist's categories of the voting political subject or the Christian church's model of the sincere, textually aware, and contemplative religious subject. The vernacular literati respondents identified themselves and their *practices* as those of political subjection. Furthermore, rather than a purist form of 'Buddhism', 'Hinduism', 'Islam'—each held in some sort of box of its own—local literati had continued to record obviously mixed practices as the core of political organization. Therefore, an erudite Sanskritist respondent to Gait's circular referred to commentarial textual traditions only to legitimate hybrid practice. A professor of Sanskrit College in Calcutta, he considered the 'custom of erecting monuments on funeral grounds prevalent specially in East Bengal' as the main identifying behaviour that marked Buddhist life in eastern and southern Bengal.[6] Clearly, he was thinking of votive and monumental stupa-architecture as he looked at a landscape dotted with tombs.

DEBATING TRANSLATIONS, DEFLECTING COLONIAL TRANSMISSION

Gait had combined his role of electoral officer and census taker with that of a historian of Assam. Despite being told repeatedly by experienced laymen such as Sarat Das and Ugyen Gyatso that there was no 'tribe' that was not also a monastic subject of one sort or another in the late nineteenth century, Gait had not allowed such knowledge to tamper with his *History of Assam* published in 1906. His condescension towards such subjects, especially the ambiguously located Buddhist–Vaisnava initiatic lineages of gurus and followers, was amplified in his treatment of the vernacular-language sources that he used to craft a history of 'savages' in Assam. One of these was a poetic narrative very similar to the poetic narratives studied in this monograph. The verses of the *Darrang Raj Vamsavali* had recorded and eulogized the mundane gifting or consecration (*utsarga*) of animal and human wealth to a monastic order (*matha*) by two brothers: *saat kuri paik dila kori taamrafali* (literally, 'a copperplate charter recorded the grant of 140 labourers or paiks for service in the monastery'). The subsequent stanzas mentioned that the *paiks* included men from different occupational groups—Brahmans, dancers, singers, weavers, garland makers, blacksmiths, carpenters, washermen, sweetmeat makers, oil-pressers, goldsmiths, potters, fishermen, the skinner of dead animals or the leather worker, scavengers. But in 1898, Gait translated these verses for an article 'Human Sacrifices in Ancient Assam' for the *Journal of the Asiatic Society of Bengal*. Describing King Naranarayan's restoration of the temple of Kamakhya in 1565, Gait went on to translate key verses thus: the king 'celebrated the occasion by the sacrifice of no less than a hundred and forty men whose heads he offered to the goddess on salvers made of copper.'[7] Unchecked, he repeated the same translation as his argument about the historical past in all editions of his *History of Assam* after 1905.[8] The force of such translations lingered far beyond his time and into the present: Gait's authority continues to be cited for the practice of human sacrifice amongst various 'primitive' and 'tribal' groups in Assam in contemporary studies on Sakta Hinduism among Tipra and Jaintia.[9]

Such translations from Ahom Bengali verse to English-language prose history disabled a historical understanding of monastic subject-making and the processes and institutions that had led to the convergence of Tantric Sakta and Bouddha groups, the collocation of both subaltern low-ranked and high-ranked persons in the same entourages of monastic lineages and estates. Yet, these structures and practices had continued to function as crucial frameworks for the 'histories' that Gait's contemporaneous Ahom-Bengali literati chronicled. None of these literati were trained as 'professional' historians; yet their commitment to materialist methods was complete. Such commitments lay in their initiatic and monastic knowledge traditions, not necessarily or wholly learned from colonial schools and universities.

Two clear trajectories of thinking and writing about the past thus parted ways at this moment. One was Gait's own. This colonial version rested on distance between, and affective detachment of, the observer and the observed; it also rested on absolutist and purist rejections of the plural Buddhist, Sufi, and Hindu timetables by which monastic subjects recorded and remembered events, people, and places. This colonial and largely military version, strengthened by rearrangements of Parliamentary governance after 1861, was manifested in a profusion of ethnological tracts produced by military officers during 1905–19. These tracts mirrored the extra-textual fragmentation of the monastic geographic order that had emerged after commercial cultivation of the hills in eastern India. As the hillsides were carved into 'hill states' and 'excluded' territories, and erstwhile monastic subjects were described as savages and prostitutes, the military officers made them 'subjects' of new kind of colonial histories. Each of these publications had either forewords or introductory commendations by eminent colonial scholar-officials. Each of these sought to pinpoint the exact territorial and biological origins of the groups' resident in the particular regions concerned. In sharp contrast to the *kavya*-writing poets, who had swept diverse groups into broad categories of worshipful, tax-paying, service-performing devotional 'subjects' of this or that deity and monastic lord, the early twentieth-century colonial ethnologists set about marking differences between each such group in terms of their territorial origins, migration stories, food, clothes, hair styles—as though none of these could be, or had ever, changed!

Two years after Gait's *History*, Thomas C. Hodson, the political agent appointed to Manipur after a serious and bloody resistance to colonial governance (1891–1904), published *The Meitheis*.[10] In this compilation, Hodson reinforced the negative judgements on the 'authenticity' and 'purity' of Manipuri adherence to Vaisnava doctrines passed half a century previously by Colonel McCulloch.

The tea-planting military superintendent had said that Manipuri observances were 'for appearance' sake, not the promptings of the heart'. In his ethnology, Hodson also declared that Manipuri adherence was, 'without any of the subtle metaphysical doctrines which have been elaborated by the masters of esoteric Hinduism ... unmindful of its spirit and inward essentials.'[11] Regardless of the connections of these Manipuri Vaisnava with eminent monastic schools and centres in Nadia, Rajshahi, or Benares, Hodson advised his readers, it was never safe to rely on what the residents of the valley said of their religion. The only test was to 'ascertain what they do, and by this test we are justified in holding them to be still animists', following a 'mass of animistic Deities' of field and forest, households and 'tribal ancestors', whose worship was a strange compound of magic and 'Nature-worship.' These were the groups I referred to in Chapters 3, 5, and 6.

A similar account appeared the next year from the pen of another military officer who had administered another scheduled district as its deputy commissioner and judge all in one. As a Captain Alan Playfair, this officer had successfully prosecuted and imprisoned the leaders of a local movement that demanded wages for the labour services that they had to perform gratis for British officers.[12] But by 1909, this officer had been promoted and also published an account of diverse Tibetan-speaking Vaisnava and Muslim populations clubbed together as 'Garo'.[13] Playfair drew up a list of 50-odd words that people around him used every day and compared it with words from Charles Bell's *Manual of Colloquial Tibetan* published in 1905.[14] Gone from Playfair's account were references to Tantric Buddhist, Bon, or Mazdaist practices.

An identical politics animated Lieutenant-Colonel John Shakespear's monograph on the 'Lushei-Kuki' clans. It too was published on the orders of the Government of Eastern Bengal and Assam. It too paid elaborate homage to other military ethnographers in the region, tea-planting military men such as Thomas H. Lewin and Colonel McCulloch. Since the Census of 1901, Shakespear had tried to complete the list of the clan families and branches, but the 'ignorance of the people themselves as to what clan or family they belonged to' defeated such attempts, he explained.[15] This implied the wide variety of origins from which monastic subjects could be drawn into a common politics of adherence, but colonial administrators of the early twentieth century were not to know that.

In contrast to this tradition of colonial ethnography-cum-history stood a group of Ahom-Bengali literati writings that rested on intimacy with the subjects, privileged experience of place and time, and relied on personal authority for corroboration. Men who never wrote in English, nor aspired to do so—such as the *Ahom buranji* writer or the Bengali-language poet or chronicler of this period— they nevertheless gave minute accounts of the dues and services owed to each monastic establishment and lord. Expert Sanskritists and classicists such as Achyuta Charan Choudhuri Tattvanidhi and Naobaisya Phukan produced exquisitely detailed materialist accounts of their districts and provinces. In 1911–17, Choudhuri produced a two- volume history of Kachar and Sylhet in terms of the inter-relationship between lineages of married ascetics (such as the Bara Gosain of Jayantiapur) and goddess-worshipping, water-worshipping communities identified as Dimasa.[16] Choudhuri was aware of all the material traces in the region, such as the carved pillars in the vicinity of Dimapur. A line drawing of these pillars appeared as illustration in his text. Even though he could not provide numerous photographs of the coins, Achyuta Choudhuri described the coins in use, decoded the Sylheti terms of evidence, gathered the tattered version of the law codes based on the *dharmasastra* that had been promulgated by the sannyasi-lords, and brought various kinds of resources into the discussion of the past. Notably, none of the terms of his Bengali-language discussion used the Bengali or Sanskritic equivalent for 'aboriginals', 'indigene', or 'tribe'. The word *adivasi* was simply absent from this history.

This was even more characteristic of the small group of literati who came together in Gauhati in April 1912 to found the Assam Research Society. The vernacular title of the group was Kamarupa Anusandhan Samiti. Initially made up of only twelve members, this group included Sanskritists such as Padmanath Bhattacharyya Vidyavinod, Muslim Persianate and Bengali-speaking literati such as Amanatullah Ahmed from Kuch Bihar, colonial office and title-holders such as Kanaklal Barua, Vaisnava educationists such as Sarat Chandra Goswami, and even engineers such as Raj Mohan Nath. None was formally trained in any particular method of history writing, but each had a deep immersion in the materials that would have to be interpreted for writing such histories.

They differed from Gait and the military ethnographers in the way they viewed the region that they were writing about. Achyuta Choudhuri's history of Kachar and Sylhet portrayed these places in terms of the location of various gurus, teachers, texts, and temples—the typical landscape of monastic geographicity and subjecthood. Colonial military officers wrote of the same sites and peoples in terms of extractive resources, as we have seen in Chapter 4. There is thus a great deal of continuity in the descriptions of sites, tanks, and monumental structures in the midst of the Nambhor Forest along the banks of the Dayang River (modern lower Assam) in Colonel L.W. Shakespear's *History of Upper Assam, Upper Burmah and North-Eastern Frontier* (first published in 1914) and their discussion in the colonial administrator J.H. Hutton's 'Carved Monoliths at Jamuguri in Assam' in 1923.[17] Neither of these officers referred to Achyuta Choudhuri's Bengali-language text. Instead, Hutton proposed that these monumental structures had been erected by Kacharis, a 'tribe' who were the 'principal representatives of a Bodo race.' The official non-recognition of the monastic subject, begun in the 1790s, culminated in an organized colonial ethnology of 'tribe' and 'race', the categories of the colonial census taker, military superintendent, and plantation owner. All these texts also had one other common characteristic. All their authors cited Gait as their original model.

The Ahom-Bengali literati, on the other hand, took the matter of proof and evidence very seriously. To begin with, the twelve-member body called the Assam Research Society raised money, acquired a building in Gauhati to house its collections of terracotta objects, manuscripts, plaques, old guns, swords, garments, and so on. From 1929, they were goaded into publishing a quarterly journal after the colonial government funded a rival institution—the Department of Historical and Antiquarian Studies (the current DHAS) in 1928. The latter institution had two colonial administrators and one unofficial Indian as an honorary assistant director. The two colonial directors were A.H.W. Bentinck and James P. Mills (ICS). The latter graduated from Oxford and began his colonial service as an administrator of the 'scheduled district' of 'Naga Hills' from 1916.[18] Like others before him, Mills too had participated in the suppression of the anti-colonial resistance of cotton-growing communities to the corvee demands made on them for service in distant battlefields of World War I during 1917–19 ('Kuki rebellion'). Not only were these resistance movements invisible in the ethnographies he authored—*The Lhota Nagas* (1922), *The Ao Nagas* (1926), and *The Rengma Nagas* (1937)— during his stint in office, all of them were composed in the face of an ongoing revitalization of a Vaisnava Puritanism across the highlands of Bengal and Assam at that very moment. The Tipura rajas had already warned the British government that all matters pertaining to 'social order' (*samajik visayadi*) was the domain of government of the clan administration (*kulaguru*) of the rajas.[19] In 1929, this monastic administration issued prohibitions on alcohol consumption, and attempted to curb the volatility of the Vaisnava ordination systems among the hill-based cohorts (*parbatiya jamatiya*) by establishing three separate ranks of ritualized initiation (*bhek*) of the purest, middling, and householder varieties. These closely resembled three kinds of vows among Buddhists. A similar movement had occurred in North Kachar, led by cousins who were also its priests (Jadonang and Gaidinliu), who emerged in 1925–32 and rapidly became the mainspring of a 'Naga' anticolonial movement.[20] In 1933, Mills, the deputy commissioner in Kohima, had suppressed this Vaisnava movement. His third book was written after the destruction of the Jadonang temples, the execution of Jadonang, and the imprisonment of Gaidinliu for eighteen years from 1932.

In his refusal to grant political dignity to the monastic subject in the hills, Mills echoed the eighteenth-century surgeon Buchanan. Indeed, the twentieth-century 'Tour Diary of Chittagong Hills Tract of December 1926' written by Mills lifted Buchanan's words almost entirely. Like Buchanan, Mills spoke of *Banjugi kukis*. Like Buchanan and Lewin, Mills knew no Tibetan languages. Like them, Mills too sought to 'purify' the populations of the same hills by expelling all traces of the Bengali Hindu and Muslim plainsman in the region. Thus, on the instruction of his friend, Henry Balfour, the director of the Pitt Rivers Museum, Mills collected only the most 'simple things' from these hill men: the metal objects of Bengali workmanship were left out, to establish that the Bengali plainsmen had had no influence here. Curiously, this effort on the officers' part was intended to stall the very determined effort at fostering Bengali culture that his contemporary 'native chief'—the Bohmong—had fostered at the time. Even more obvious was the fact that Mills' reports were prepared as advice for the Simon Commission of 1927. The political purposes to which such reports were put were clear. But there was something both ironic and sinister afoot in 1933, when, after being appointed as director of the DHAS, Mills lectured the Assam–Bengal literati about the proper 'scientific' historical method. Their histories, he said, suffered from the absence of a 'strictly objective standpoint—the standpoint of all true scientists'.[21] Their Bengali and Ahom-language historical chronicles and manuscripts failed as history because they were too redolent of a 'Hindu' monastic subjectivity. Like Gait earlier, Mills never specified which version of Hinduism was being referring to: was it Vaisnava, was it Sakta-tantric, Saiva? Nevertheless, he prescribed that the correct method of interpreting such records was to abstract the contents from their 'later Hindu frames', compare the narratives, and arrive at the earlier past of an Ahom court and country (before it was 'contaminated' by Hinduism and Buddhism). Yet if 'Hindu' frames of manuscripts were not suitable for the scientist's history, Mills nevertheless suggested that the Kamarupa Anusandhan Samiti undertake precisely the kind of work that would ensure its further marginalization in the eyes of Objectivists such as himself. Mills asked the members of the Samiti to leave the work of studying ethnology and 'research among the wilder tribes' for the officers of government; the members of the Kamarupa Samiti should study the Kamakhya temple premises and ceremonies, as well as the great Gosains of Majuli Island.

Their disciples number thousands, but nowhere have we a picture of their mode of life, the beliefs they hold, the buildings they inhabit, or the ceremonial connected with them. Offerings have poured in for countless years and one's mouth waters at the thought of the relics of past ages they must have brought. 'Could not some keen skilled researchers portray and describe the precious things in their possession?', he asked in the same talk.

Given the looting of the monasteries that had occurred since 1904, these exhortations were alarming. Nevertheless, the services of a man of letters, a professor of literature in Cotton College, Suryya Kumar Bhuyan, were secured for the DHAS.[22] Bhuyan collected and collated several fragments of manuscript chronicles, revised, edited, and published them as Assam's preeminent histories (*buranji*s) from

1933.[23] In response, the journal of the Assam Research Society began publication the same year. The contest over the history narrated by an officially sponsored DHAS was joined.

Mills's rhetoric of 'scientific' method only drove Assamese and Bengali-speaking and writing figures into even more determined opposition to the model of history represented by Gait's revised second edition of *History of Assam* (1926). They rejected Gait's translation strategies and historical methods entirely. They pointed out errors of fact in Gait's *History*, such as the name of the captain of the force sent against the Jaintia fort holder in 1774, or the tenure of the fort holder.[24] They pointed to errors of interpretation and raised methodological issues. One of them pointed out Gait's argument from silence in the buranjis in imputing 'illiteracy' to an Assamese ruler who had been an erudite scholar and a connoisseur poet-patron well versed in the sastra: verses to that effect were reproduced from copperplate inscriptions stacked in the office of the political agent at Sadiya.[25]

Whereas Gait's interpretative methods paired together antiquity and 'primitivism', the Ahom-Bengali literati rejected this coupling. Barua in particular objected to arguments regarding 'homelands' and 'tribes'. Pointing to the many villages in the Brahmaputra Valley which had the suffix -*kuchi*, Barua pointed out that the term stood for a village. It had the same derivation as *gucchha* or bundle. A collection of dwellings of weavers was called *Tantikuchi*, a bundle of households of astrologers was called *Ganaka kuchi*; other objects, such as fishing spikes, were called kuchi. 'Will anybody think of connecting these words with the Koch tribe?' he asked in a pointed refusal of the colonial reading of such village settlements.[26]

Another local man attempted to counter Playfair's narration about groups from 'Tibotgiri'. Playfair had apparently drawn from 'oral' sources. This local writer published a similar story about 'Tibotgiri' in the pages of the journal based on textual sources—'some worn out manuscripts in the possession of some obscure villagers' (of Goalpara district).[27] Though the Achiks had come from 'Tibotgiri' (mountains of Tibet) to the hills and plains north of Mymensingh (then Bengal, now modern Bangladesh) with many different stops along the way, the narrative named particular sites and way-stations on the migrants' path between modern Kuch Bihar, 'Ohom Bangal'

(Assamese Bengal) on the outskirts of the Himalaya mountains, ending at Sibsagar in the east and the hills and plains of Tripura on the south.

In Playfair's version of the migration account, on reaching the Manas River, the emigrants had encountered a nameless 'chief' who, attracted by the beauty of Juge-Silche, the daughter of Kangre-Jingre, tried to abduct her. In the Assamese iteration of the same account, the namelessness of the 'chief' was replaced by 'the Behari Raja', 'jealous observant of caste restrictions'. Friendship-alliance was materialized in marriage and worship. So the immigrants were said to have given a sister in marriage to the Ahom king, from which resulted 'jointness' of temple building, worship (*puja*), and commensality. In the context of the Behari Raja's 'caste' prohibitions, the Ahom raja's distinctiveness was claimed in terms of a Vaisnava equalization of dignity and the sharing of labour and subsistence: 'They took their meals of the same leaves. Their servants pounded rice in the same mortar and they together used to go in search of firewood, leaves for keeping food and of forest produce'.[28]

Like Playfair's account, the Assamese literati's account spoke of war, flight, resettlement around the vicinity of the temple of Kamakhya, of troublesome men marauding as tigers and preying on the arrivals from 'Tibotgiri'. But it presented such events as prefaces to systems of friendship and kinship. This interconnected series of relationships—a true network by any definition—was, according to this account, fragmented by the arrival of the English. In the Sangma account (1993), the English appeared in the vicinity of Habraghat when one of the significant sons-in-law had no daughters, and therefore could not acquire a son-in-law. It was at this time and place that the end of the storyteller's history arrived: 'when the English came, his kingdom was seized and partitioned among several Laskers, one Nokgil Lasker having succeeded to the portion of his capital.' The failure to have daughters meant occupation by the Company's troops.

Such orally given accounts of the past also persisted in the poetry studied in this monograph as *Sri Rajamala*, *Krishnamala*, and *Srenimala*. All these accounts—whether it was the prose account of a Sangma (1993) or the verse lyrics of a *Sri Rajamala* (1927–30)—accepted that the protagonists of their narratives had distant territorial origins. But the narrators also placed the protagonists in trajectories of kinship with other groups in the terrain and in subjecthood to common monastic lords and lineages, governed ultimately by deities. Thus, their emphasis on the marriages and friendships between groups was far more emphatic than any account provided by the colonial ethnologists.

HISTORIOGRAPHY AS 'RUPTURE'

All these engagements were in turn part of larger political and constitutional changes set afoot by the Government of India Acts of 1919 and 1935. These acts reified provisions of post-Lushai legislation such as the Scheduled Districts Act of 1874. In 1933, the Chittagong Hills and the highlands called Tippera state were categorized as 'Wholly Excluded Area'. By 1935, all these regions were put beyond the administrative remit of democratically elected nationalist Indian governments and ministries, and called the 'Excluded Areas of Assam'. First cotton, then tea, then rubber and teak, then cheap labour had continued to be sucked from these hillsides into the global economy managed by colonial governments between the eighteenth and the mid-twentieth century. The 1935 legislation therefore only formalized a process that had begun a while before. People resident in areas identified as 'excluded' after 1935 were categorically barred from experiencing themselves as connected to any of the groups in other parts of India. Voters in Assam and Bengal would also be told that they were not responsible for those 'excluded areas'.

From 1936–7, when elections to provincial legislatures occurred in presidencies such as Bengal and Assam, 'excluded' and 'partially excluded' areas remained out of the democratic process. Only a handful of scholars were permitted to enter such areas for scholarly or other purposes. Anthropologists such as C. von Fürer-Haimendorf received permission to study 'primitive societies uncorrupted by contact with the West', untouched by 'Hindu civilization of the plains of Assam and the Buddhism of Burma'.[29] Once as official policy, and a second time in scholarship, the marriages of a Ropuiliani and her Burmese husbands or the Vaisnava Manipuri Kanai Singh's marriage with local women in the hills, the other relationships of support, solidarity, and succour that have been traced in Chapters 4–6 were wiped off the board. In effect, colonial officials of the mid-twentieth century erased the substance of their own archival records of the past.

Robert Reid summed up the official policy towards the residents of these new 'reservations' when he asserted that 'neither racially, historically, culturally nor linguistically have they any affinity with the people of the plains or with the people of India proper.'[30] He insisted that these populations' common 'non-Indian origin and their backward state of development' justified their exclusion from democratic governance demanded by nationalist Indians on the plains.[31] Facing the impending partition of the subcontinent, in 1944 administrators such as Reid argued that these 'hill tribes' should be kept outside of the Indian constitution; there was 'no softening influences as ties of blood or affection' between the ministerial candidate of the plains and the hill man. Assuming the white man's burden, Reid urged, 'We are responsible for the future welfare of a set of very loyal primitive peoples who are habituated to look to us for protection and who will get it from no other source.' In having wiped out the long histories of anti-colonial resistance by these so-called primitive peoples, Reid had translated the growing official ignorance of the historical past of interconnected populations into full-blown amnesiac statist 'modernity'. He had both forgotten his own institutional past and insisted that his truncated present dictate the terms on which the future of decolonization—neocolonialism— would proceed.

Such statist amnesia might have been successfully resisted by members of the Bengal–Ahom literati if death had not thinned their ranks precipitately. Just as the Second World War loomed, many of the founding members of the feisty Kamarupa Anusandhan Samiti slipped away. The obituary notices of the 1938–9 issues of the journal came thick and fast. Padmanath Bhattacharya Vidyavinod; Nagendranath Vasu, the author of a historical study of Kamarupa; Jogendra Chandra Ghosh; and Kishori Mohan Gupta, the finder of the Sylhet copperplates, were all dead by 1939.[32] K.L. Barua died in 1940.[33] As the Asian theatre of war moved closer to Gangetic Bengal, large parts of Burma and Manipur, lower Assam and the Chittagong hills were quickly turned into scorched earth. The famine of 1943 and the migrations from Burmese and Manipuri fronts into all parts of Assam and Bengal took a heavy toll of all scholarship.

S.C. Goswami died in 1944 in the course of the war.[34] A fire in the adjacent building gutted the Samiti's buildings and collections. K.N. Dikshit, the superintendent of archaeology who had uncovered the remains of Buddhist sites in northern Bengal, died in 1946.

Then partition of homes occurred again and boundaries were redrawn through 1947–51. The knowledge of the past, even of the material traces of that past, disappeared from the academic networks of partitioned lands. Older methods of observation and verification became impossible to practice. Visits to sites, measurements, interrogation of local witnesses that classical Sanskritists such as a Padmanath Bhattacharya Vidyavinod had relied on in his debates with fellow epigraphists regarding the Nidhanpur grant (Sylhet) became impossible after 1947–8. Post-Partition scholars were immobilized by post-nationalist governments and their travel requirements. The physical conflict on the ground was directly replicated in historiography from these years as the physical traces of the ancestors—the various carved memorial pillars that colonial and missionary observers had described among populations that they had called 'Garo', 'Lakher', or 'Naga' from northern and southern segments of the same hills, left uninvestigated by the debilitated Bengal–Ahom literati, vanished from view and from scholarship of South Asia as a whole.[35] Wood decays but even the colossal carved faces in rock, high in the hills of modern Tripura and southern Assam, were forgotten by the historians of art and archaeology.

The work of the nonprofessional historians-cum-literati, such as those gathered together in the Kamarupa Anusandhan Samiti, was driven from the academic study of history. One has but to compare the social geography imagined by a lay participant member of that society in the 1930s and his exploration of the meanings of 'Assam' with the ways that professional historians defined the same region in the 1960s to see the difference a territorial Partition could make to a monastic literati's collective self-representation. In the 1930s, it had been possible for one to translate 'Shan' (mountaineers), and 'A Shan' as a Siamese derivation of Acaryya (preceptor) to suggest that in the thirteenth century, the land of 'Assam' had been settled by an influx of monks. Assam was the 'land of monks'.[36] Another had granted that, as with monastic subjects, there could be multiple connections between different sites, such as those spread across

Nepal, Assam, Bhutan, and Tibet. Referring to the finding of the *Yogasataka* (a collection of 100 verses of a Siddha Nagarjuna), the editor of the *Journal of the Assam Research Society* referred his readers to information that he had received from the Nepali Rana Suvarna Shamsher Jang, about two ascetics from Kamarupa called Machindranath (Matsyendranath) and Minanath whose arrival in Nepal cured the land of famine. 'Macchindranatha is still looked upon in Nepal as a saint by both Sakta and Buddhist, and Minanath only as Buddhist siddha'.[37] His votaries continued to insist on the place of multiple Buddhist and Sakta communities in creating a history of Assam.[38] In the course of two decades, this sense of 'Assam' as part of a wider network of monastic sites and subjects disappeared as completely as did that in 'Bengal'.

So long as there were scholars left to debate pronouncements such as Reid's, monastic subjects would not have been identified as Scheduled Tribes. But with their death, and especially with the devastation of partition and resettlement, pronouncements such as Reid's—'neither racially, historically, culturally nor linguistically have they any affinity with the people of the plains or with the people of India proper'—became self-fulfilling prophecies. The new Constitution of India preserved old colonial methods of government by exclusion. A Sixth Schedule ensured that once-monastic subjects, Buddhist-Bon-Vaisnava-Tantric, remained locked in a no-man's land of an Excluded Other, whose histories had been forgotten and whose historians were now dead. There were only Scheduled Tribes left to study.[39]

From this point on, the corrosive and colonially authorized project of ethnology drove all scholarship on Assam and lands related to it. Colonial instruction and embodiment of 'objective' history-writing, by men (and then women) who had never been part of any monastic lineage in the locality had an ominous effect on decolonizations' scholars. The expansive social geography of the past shrank. Post-Partition western Bengali and Indian historians, even of the medieval or early modern past, found it impossible to retain the cosmopolitics of the Ahom–Bengali literati of the 1930s. Even when confronted with epigraphic evidence to the contrary, post-Partition epigraphists in the Indian landmass preferred to see 'locality' and 'nation' where their predecessors had seen a 'cosmos'. Dines Chandra

Sircar's work was revealing in this regard. His treatment of a late fifth-century record was a classic example of how the cosmos shrank to fit the nation-state's boundaries. The record stated that a merchant (Rbhupala) had requested that the authorities on the plains allow him to gift permanently a plot of land for the worship of the gods Kokāmukhasvamin and the Svetavarahasvamin located at 'Himavac-chikhara', or a peak of the Himalayas. Sircar argued that this was a reference to an ancient Kokamukha Saiva pilgrimage site (*tirtha*) on a river in Nepal (Svarna Kosi) and the second reference was to a Boar incarnation of Visnu worshipped at a Himalayan peak of Dhaulagiri, part of eastern Nepal and western Bhutan. Both were Himalayan pilgrimages which the medieval merchant had visited; he had returned to the plains below and dedicated a large area in the vicinity to the worship of these two gods. But the merchant had done more: he had constructed two temples dedicated to two images of the same Himalayan gods and attached store-houses to each deity's temple. Instead of reading these gestures as attempts to materially shape the plains in the image of the Himalayas, or to establish a permanent relationship between mountains and plains, Sircar argued the opposite. While he considered it 'natural' for the people of the Dinajpur region (modern northwest Bengal) to visit the Kokamukha tirtha in the fifth century, and conceded a certain latitudinal communication between people of north Bengal and north Bihar, he simply would not admit the Nepal-Bhutan Himalayas into the medieval jurisdiction (*bhukti*) called Pundravardhana or Kotivarsa visaya (later 'Bengal').[40]

Seldom in their discussions of medieval Bengal-Assam would the scholars of the 1950s foreground the ways in which human populations shaped the terrain—by cutting paths through mountains, building bridges, constructing embankments. Relationships that preceded and made meaningful such interventions in physical and material landscapes inevitably eluded scholarly scrutiny. Thus, while Sircar found merchants from the plains going up to Himalayan peaks, he never wondered whether Himalayan residents visited pilgrimage sites on the plains below. If reciprocal visits could not be imagined on the basis of medieval records, neither could marriage relations be taken as constitutive of medieval geography. An entire generation of scholars remained silent on the significant marital connections of eminent donors and thus missed the ways in which different kinds of households may have been connected to each other. In the same vein, Sircar scoffed at a stone slab inscription in the temple of Pasupati (Nepal), dateable to 737 CE, in which the genealogy of Licchhavi kings (originating prototypically from Brahma) ended with a Jayadeva, married to a 'descendant of Bhagadatta's royal family and daughter of Sri Harshadeva', characterized as 'lord of Gauda, Odra and other lands as well as of Kalinga and Kosala'.[41] Gauda was the medieval name for western and northern Bengal. A Nepali son-in-law of a lord of medieval Bengal and Bihar suggested relationships between different geographical and social clusters that nationalist Indian scholars appeared unwilling to concede. The political effects of such histories were the segregation of Assamese and Nepali historians from the 'heartland' of Buddhist, Vaisnava, Islamicate, Bengal. The former had claimed Bhagadatta as an ancestor of the early rulers of Kamarupa (medieval Assam). Basing themselves in the continued traditions of memorizations, these scholars—among whom were the members of the Kamarupa Anusandhan Samiti—based their claims on an undatable epic (*Mahabharata*) which referred to a Bhagadatta as the leader of 'Cinas, Kiratas, Mlecchas and Sagaranupavasins' (literally, residents of lands adjacent to the oceans, or water-logged areas of an estuary).

Even when confronted with inscriptions from a variety of sites with genealogies referring to an ancestor called Bhagadatta,[42] the learned Sircar remained unconvinced that Kamrupa (Assam) and Nepali domains were connected, that a lord of one was the father-in-law of another. The Nepali inscription, he said, did not mention either Pragjyotish or Kamrupa in the list of countries that the father-in-law ruled. Such objections had already been answered in the 1930s by the members of the Kamarupa Anusandhan Samiti. Unaware of them or as unwilling as the colonial official ethnographer-historians to refer to them, historians of Bengal of Sircar's stature recommended that historians of Assam take Nepali inscriptions such as this with a grain of salt.

Such prescriptions fed the nationalist and regionalist historio-graphies but starved the 'modern' and professional historian's understanding of space, territory, family, government and the nation-state. Another kind of 'modern'—also Bengali historian and Sircar's contemporary—was condemned to spend life at the margins of the academia. Such was the Tibetologist, Nirmal Sinha, who spent six wintry months of 1955 in various monasteries in Lhasa: older Tibetans told him that the earthquake and tremors that rocked Tibet on 15 August 1947 represented earth's protest at the disruption of the ancient unity of the land of Enlightenment![43] Though the Partition had destroyed the shared cosmological map of Jambudvipa, he nevertheless found ordinary Tibetans keen to talk about places on the Indian plains—Pataliputra, Magadha, Mathura, Banaras, Kanchi, and Tirumalai. Though he had read many tomes in ancient history, he felt ignorant of the past that he then learned from the ordained monks.

His sense of regret about the history he had not learned did not infect the professional historians on the plains below. In the refashioned independent Indian metropolitan universities, a new 'ethnohistory' of state making gripped the scholarly imagination including experts such as Sircar.[44] The object of this ethnohistory was the Absolutist state of post-Reformation Europe; scholars of both medieval and ancient subcontinental pasts would use those states as standards for whether or not particular relationships and practices in precolonial India deserved to be studied as political institutions.[45] The burden of the European absolutist state was that it associated sophistication of administrative forms—a command economy—with an implicit monotheism of medieval public ritual performance. Such models allowed only *one* sacred order per temporal power instead of the concurrent practices that local literati in the 1901 survey had taken to be basic to their ideas of political subjectivity. Once devalued by colonial male military officers in the nineteenth century, practices of adherence that men and women performed as political acts faded rapidly from studies of political societies. Just as marriage across different geographies fell out of Sircar's understanding of historical geography, the political weight of adding loyal and industrious labourers through kin-making actions such as adoptions, affiliations, oaths, and blood-sacrifices all fell out of the study of the 'state' and the 'empire'.

An efflorescence of writing on 'tribes' appeared in this context from the 1950s.[46] Symptomatic of another round of state-making under the auspices of nationalist governments that had taken over from colonial administrators, this round of scholarship by regional 'experts' finally fulfilled the mandates of colonial ethnologists and politicians such as Reid. In that sense, decolonization finally led to the triumph of colonial categories of analysis. Local Indian scholars renewed their vows to alienation, convinced that people living in hill-based societies were never their friends or familiars. Illustrative instances of these were found in books that studied 'Ahom–Bhutia' relations without once mentioning Bhutanese, Tibetan, or Sikkimese Bon or Buddhist ordination lineages, lands, and estates taken over by colonial tea companies in the 1840s–70s. The relevant chapter of such a book begins: 'The Bhutanese are a Tibeto-Burman race inhabiting the sub-Himalayan range ranges from east of Darjeeling in Bengal up to the river Bhoroli in the Darrang district of Assam.'[47] Even groups that had remained Buddhist and Bengali-speaking— such as those identified as 'Chakma' in places such as Chittagong and Tripura—were described by Indian social scientists of the 1970s as though they shared neither language nor ritual nor politics with the Hindu, Muslim, and Christian others around them.[48] Ontologies of 'tribal' being, 'backward' livelihoods and cultures, once created by imperial fiat, now became foundational to a postcolonial scholarly consensus, especially in the historiography of Assam.[49] Even when critical postcolonial scholars scrutinized the literati monastic male ('elite') production of the 'tribal Santhal', they could not re-imagine the latter as a member of a monastic community.[50] Erudite students of folklore, too, forgot the orally transmitted histories of possession and dispossession that had produced Bon, Buddhist, and Vaisnava disciples, describing them as 'tribal' in the twentieth century.[51]

The devaluations of particular relationships initiated by colonial economics were sustained only in postcolonial historiography. Family formations and friendships, once forcibly exiled from politics as the East India Company officials wished to restructure it, were resolutely driven to the margins of South Asian historiography from the early twentieth century. The careers of colonially-trained anthropologists from these decades reveals that their studies followed those of the late colonial European disciplinary trends and circumscriptions: matrilineality, polyandry, levirate, and sororate were all reserved for study as largely apolitical forms for groups living in Himalayan terrain.[52] A similar pattern emerged in the study of matrilateral and bilateral inheritance systems (studied as matriliny) in those decades.[53]

While the structuralism of such studies disguised the politically contingent practices and institutions involved in such arrangments, the territorial marginality attributed to the groups studied by the anthropologists allowed Assamese and Bengali–reading historians on the plains to turn blind to the traces of identical political behaviours in their own literary and poetic records. The historiography that resulted was not created by an *absence* of records but a determined exclusion of them—by scholars who knew the languages! In the process, politics was wiped out from the study of South Asian pasts twice over—the first time by male historians who refused to study the globalizing imperialist context of a colonial ideology of monogamous marriage and reproductive sexuality, and the second time by postcolonial feminist historians who failed to study the role of intermarried lineages across hills and plains in the shaping of pro- and anti-imperialist politics of the twentieth century. This was uncanny not only because the household and family formation had remained central to all Inner Asian politics between the fourteenth and the post-Socialist late twentieth centuries. It was also uncanny because so many scholars of South and Southeast Asia who allied themselves with, or studied, riverine and deltaic cultures failed to notice that it was women-centred households that had buoyed up the 'macrohistories' of militant men, mercantile groups, and rebellious prophets in the first place. The central work done by women and children cultivators and herders, cotton-carders and wool-weavers, transporters of wood and harvests across long distances, were exiled from the 'new global histories' that were to be spun from the end of the twentieth century.

Decolonization perhaps continued the internationalization of colonial-style ignorance even as the second wave of feminist movements took off from the 1970s–90s in western Europe and the United States. As liberal Euroamerican feminists asserted 'independence' from male fathers, brothers, and husbands in their societies, demands for individual autonomous agency and subjectivity began to drive research agendas in the postcolonial Indian academe as well. In a final irony, postcolonial Indian feminists found themselves agreeing with colonial men of the nineteenth century that the family was the entire source of 'women's oppression' in India. Instead of studying the histories by which political societies became mere households, and lay disciples 'hill tribes', the attrition itself was increasingly represented as 'freedom' of the individual from the trammels of all relationships. Eminent scholars of plantation labour too treated the work of women and children in terms of classic liberal theory's option— 'force' or 'choice'. It merely extended the liberal Eurofeminist theory and history of South Asia which lauded individual women who 'gave up the veil' or went to school. Both groups of scholars completely ignored those who had never been veiled to begin with, and had fought the colonial armies tooth and nail in the nineteenth and early twentieth century. It was as though their struggles, having been defeated, had been erased forever from the books. Both liberal and socialist feminist historians thus participated alike in prolonging the shelf-life of colonial ignorance.

In the nineteenth century, colonial officers destroying monastic estates and exemptions had represented monks as 'savages', their male disciples as 'slaves', and the women who lubricated the diplomatic and economic relations between the two as 'prostitutes'. Monastic codes of gender had been undone when monastic men and their wives, daughters, sisters, and mothers were denied the 'merit' of their actions. After the 1980s, driven by liberal Euroamerican feminist imperialisms, postcolonial Indian feminists also largely ignored the ways in which colonial land-tax policies had divorced women from the merit economy, undone the political significance of levirate, and replaced women-as-wives with 'coolies' and 'labourers' on tea plantations and roads. Now, postcolonial historians would continue the work of colonial armies by denying all recognition of such women as historic actors in a monastic cosmography, refusing to even accept as a historic value the cultivation of dependence. In the mid-twentieth century, as postcolonial male scholars focused on the 'state', and forgot to talk about the central role of the households and lineages in labour-pooling and resource-sharing arrangements, postcolonial feminist scholars forgot to talk about the networks of dependence that had been built and maintained by various generations of women. Unsurprisingly, both remained equally oblivious of the extent to which they had continued old colonial military exclusions and embargoes—against those very Bon-Buddhist and Vaisnava men and women who had been 'tribalized' in the nineteenth century, and would now once more find themselves outside the professional 'critical' and literary histories that were produced.

REMEMBERING AND FORGETTING BY ERSTWHILE MONASTIC SUBJECTS: A RETURN TO FRIENDSHIP?

After the formation of India and Pakistan in 1947, populations in Tripura, the Chittagong hills, 'Naga' hills, western Burma, and southern Kachar appeared to all those reading newspapers only as 'trouble-makers' for the central government historians. On the ground, postcolonial armies took over where the colonial militaries left off. In the famine of 1952–6, it is said, the central government of India and the democratically elected government of Assam both failed to succour the populations sheltering in the hills between Chittagong and Burma. A young men's movement led by the Mizo National Front (MNF) sprang up, demanding separation from the larger province of Assam. Eventually, a state emerged there in 1987. This was called Mizoram (see Figure 7.1). Barely two decades after the formation of this new state, I arrived at Aijal/Aizawl with an updated version of the nineteenth-century military officer's quest for 'historical documents'.

Fig. 7.1 Modern Political Boundaries of Eastern India.

I had encountered the colonial archival records of expropriations of labour, time, resources, and relationships laid out in this monograph (Chapters 2–6). I was familiar with the long archival trail left by Fraser and his failed abolitionism. All that I sought was a set of 'personal' narratives from descendants of those 'liberated slaves' whom Fraser had benefitted, or descendants of those who had suffered under colonial and postcolonial regimes of deprivations. It was a desire fed by the fully developed First World traditions of memoirs, autobiographies, oral histories of the past, post-Enlightenment discursive subjectivities I had gorged on all my life.[54] I found descendants of labour servants willing to talk about their fathers as well as descendants of those who had 'liberated' their under-tenants and debtors. Both groups had continued to live in the same society, and both had photographs and memorials of their families. Both groups shared memories and memorials of their ancestors readily: descendants of the male *boi* (subjects who carried goods on the back as labour-rent) spoke of the young male's service in the 'Lushai Labour Force' during the Second World War, and the male descendant of the ex-holder also served in the same force during the same war.[55]

Yet nobody was willing to offer personal narratives of his or her own suffering, not even the suffering endured during war and famine. Trained to expect laments on suffering selves, I was stunned by this non-articulation of bereavement. What memories *did* such people have who had been through so much? Didn't even the memories of labour services performed for the colonial army during the Second World War deserve lament? Only conversations with the grandfather of one of my guides provided insight. This eighty-five-year-old man had also served as an ambulance driver in the Allied army in the Second World War. On top of the refrigerator in his home was the photograph of a British family—the man in that photograph had served alongside him in wartime as the chaplain of his military unit. The two struck up a great friendship as they spoke to each other about the Bible. After the war ended, the British chaplain emigrated to Australia, and eventually died there. His eldest son had written a long letter, in English, to his father's friend in India. It was a cherished document.

These acts of friendship, public acknowledgements of the dignity or worthiness of the human beings at their centre, were on display both within and outside the elderly man's home. A close analogue of the photo on top of the refrigerator was the round-topped staele erected by the side of the road outside his house. On the painted surface of that staele was a note in English that had been written by the state's chief minister condoling with him on the loss of his son. In the whole day that I spent with the elderly man, he never mourned the passing of a publicly honoured son. Though he lived as a widower, invisible members of the community around him provided tea and biscuits for me, the visitor. The elder also brought out various dairies he had kept through the years, and cheerfully discussed the ways in which his work during the Second World War had helped him to buy land and extend material refuge to many other destitute families. And yes, he referred to those destitute members of his own household and plantation establishments as *boi*, and even sent me off to meet one of them.

This was a young man who had the sole charge of supervising the orchards and plantations owned by the elder. The young man lived with his wife, a former domestic servant in the master's household, and their two young children. Through an interpreter, this young man told me of a flight from the food shortage of another village, of labouring in quarries owned by his current employer, from where he had graduated into becoming a house servant, and then 'resettled' as a married man, had become the supervisor of a garden. He had gone from an 'outsider' to becoming a 'trusted' steward. In his view, this was a successful transition. His only thought now focused on securing the best care and education for his children.

Refugee males finally taught me that my updated version of the colonial quest—for documented origins, memorials of selfhood and suffering—may have been misplaced from the start. Memory does not follow universal models, because neither the value of the 'self' nor the ideals of the 'good life' or of masculinity and femininity were universal. Thus a general refusal of narratives of suffering could also indicate a profusion of an ethics of enormous discipline, the commitment to and cultivation of compassionate albeit hierarchized friendships. These histories of friendships, of expansive personhood and futurity, had been erased from the historiography of a South Asia conceived only in terms of freedoms and rights, products and markets, here and now. Yet, the politics of friendship had persisted, even among those who had been the victims of colonial disavowals thereof. Even in 1922, fifty years after the expedition of 1871–2, a letter dictated to a scribe by a son of one of the men of the village addressed Lewin's widow as 'kapi' (meaning both 'aunt' and 'grandmother') and vowed that since Lewin and the man's father 'had sworn friendship', he the descendant would inherit the oath. Referring to a future, the letter went 'I will be a friend of his children if he has any, although I may never see them.'[56] This was not merely a model of exemplary forgiveness; it was also a token of the disciplining of memory, in order to fashion a future as yet unseen. It was such commitment to that future that explained the simultaneity of the past and present here: both 'masters' and 'tenants' continued to cohabit. What was more, I learnt of songs that had once been sung only by elder women but which nobody sang any more: yet the elderly women did not appear to blame anyone for the death of song.

From the perspective of those who have suffered privations of various sorts, sanctuary, friendship, the restoration of dignity were the key goals of political aspiration. It was such a politics of friendship that was enacted also within the main Baptist church in Aizawl, where three significant portraits hung in 2004–5. They were all pointed out to me as 'founders' of the nation. Two of these were the missionaries Lorrain and Savidge. The third was the doctor, Fraser. Unlike Lorrain and Savidge however, Fraser's status as a 'national ancestor' was concretized even outside the church. The Fraser Clinic is as material as the snatches of song about abolition that local informants sing to me as records of the past. Are these songs 'creative memory' at work? Cubelli tells us that there are two kinds of memory.[57] One is reconstructive memory: it is based on gist information, is concerned with everyday activities and is highly dependent on environmental and emotional contexts. Created in the context of affective states, this memory is vulnerable to incorporating information from a wide variety of different sources, either events that never happened or true episodes in the wrong contexts. Reconstructive memory creatively interprets information on the basis of previous knowledge before encoding it. In Western European clinical practice, this is considered potentially dangerous or 'faulty' memory. But in the wastelands of the postcolony, the Fraser Clinic makes reconstructive memory a pillar on which to hang the tiny gestures of friendships of a past.

If there is a 'faulty' reconstructive memory, it is that which has been encoded in writing after the 1950s–70s as the nationalist and postcolonial history of 'tribes', 'kings', and 'states'. These have been the fallible histories, fashioned in the vagaries not of affective states but of cold-blooded economics, first under British colonialism and then under the imperatives of 'Hindu Indian' and 'Muslim Bangladeshi' nationalist 'development' projects. They are dangerous because they make it possible for 'developers' to obscure their own profit-making while painting their opponents as the new barbarians. They are dangerous above all because they prevent the postcolonial feminist historian of both hills and plains from taking the full measure of her kinship with elderly men who have served as ambulance drivers as well as taking the words of the under-tenants and servants as the basis for looking at the records and traces left behind. Clinging to the 'faulty' reconstructive histories of 'tribes' and 'states' prevented historians like me from recognizing the continuity between the elderly ambulance-driver's silence about service during the Second World War, his under-tenants' silence about suffering, and their own experience of adults in post-Partition households, such as the one I grew up in, on the plains of Bengal during the sixties. All around me during my childhood and youth were men and women who had actively focused on forgetting the horrors they had witnessed and lived through, rather than on articulating it. Since Halbwachs's work *On Collective Memory*, it has been argued that survivors' memories of an event may not be shared with audiences with whom survivors do not share a language.[58] That was *not* the case of my refugee Bengali 'Hindu' parents and grandparents. They came from one literate Bengali-speaking world to another literate Bengali-speaking world. Despite sharing a common language with their host societies, neither my grandmother nor my mother nor my various aunts and uncles spoke of the horrors that drove them away. All that I was told as a child in the sixties and seventies was that suffering was the one constant fact of all forms of life, and that it was necessary to work to alleviate others' pain and suffering rather than to dwell on one's own. That common determination by members in both paternal and maternal households ensured that the particular circumstances of their own painful pasts—and part of my 'history'—remained largely shut away from me. When stories were told of the remembered village, they invoked a world of friendships, a happy past. When stories of the departures from homelands were recounted, the persons mentioned were not the persecutors but those who helped them survive, those who gave them sanctuary. The elderly ambulance driver cum plantation owner, too, remembered the friendship of a chaplain, not the horror of British colonial conscription, nor that of the Second World War. Such focused remembering rested on some other theory of mindfulness that the elderly man may well have shared with my paternal and maternal kinswomen, testaments both to the limits of a universal model of remembering and a universal model of personhood.

While my mother and grandmothers had focused on teaching me (and my younger brother and fostered siblings) not to tear paper out of a book for fear that the book 'hurts', of not stoning a cow or bird because they 'feel' pain, the ambulance driver had gone to work caring for the hurt and wounded, even if those persons came from groups that had oppressed him and his kinsmen and women. Did this ethic of care not share something vital with the plainsperson who saw life in all things? The elderly man had continued to practice this ethic of care towards other refugees. My own grandmothers and parents were refugees who refused to teach future generations to either kill or 'return' to a homeland. When asked for the 'sources' of such ideas, neither my informants in the hills nor my mother could refer me to textual or scriptural traditions. Such behaviours were probably grounded in reproductive memory, associated with high levels of fidelity to information or behaviour learned by practice, by repetition.

It was this reproductive memory that was at work in 2005 when, completely unaided by any memorials or documents at hand, descendants of men and women living in the hills in the 1915–30s remembered Mary Catherine Fraser as well as their own mothers and grandmothers. Like Mary Winchester, who remembered elderly women protectors, Reverend Zairema sang and played the songs that Mary Fraser taught him. Many of my informants rested their own claims to rectitude on a genealogy traceable to such women, female elders of some past that was rarely written down. It was apparent that the work that these women had done had neither been eclipsed nor forgotten by those who had been sustained by them. But by the early millennium, these men too were growing old and fading. Some of these stories began to be written down. That was how stories of elderly women and their attempts to restore the politics of friendships emerged in published bilingual histories, such as those of Tipura-Manipur in 2007. In the preface to a compilation of histories, a dignitary of a Manipuri lineage recorded a brief memory of a maternal grandmother, born to one of the exiled Manipuri Vaisnava men at Dhaka.[59] Colonial archival records (see Chapter 4) reveal that he had wished for his sons to be married to women from the Tipura lineage but had been fobbed off by the colonial officials in 1857; eventually, however, his daughter was successfully married there. She, in turn, tried to maintain the marital relationship between her affinal and her natal kinsmen by proposing a marital compact between her grandson (in the Tipura lineage) and a female member of the Manipur lineage. But the political superintendence of the region in the early twentieth century lay solely in British hands; the grandmother was thwarted. Yet, even in 2007, the memory of marriages that had occurred in the eighteenth and nineteenth century were kept alive. In the interstices of such memories, one could find the smudged outline of a once-disallowed widow marriage that nobody could quite name but which clearly troubled the present: thus even in the twentieth century, one of the most austere of monastic Vaisnava living between Vrindavan and Manipur reminded his audience that the practices of widow marriage was a custom enjoined by the Mahabharata.[60]

Professional postcolonial historians and scholars had learned not to read the Mahabharata to make sense of Himalayan-plains histories. Yet, the storyline of that epic—with its focus on friendships dishonoured, marriages betrayed, battles fought— is suggested by no less than the colonial archives itself. Ultimately, it was the power of stories, songs, and pictures, shared with me by various kinds of interpretative communities that told me that my learned 'history' was seriously one-dimensional, and that it was based on many different kinds of forgetting. Indeed, the stories alone remained to testify that colonized men and women had not yet written the 'scientific' or the 'complete' history of India that they had claimed as their objective. This book is a reminder that it is worth trying to recover from such teaching, if only for the sake of others who have been injured and killed by such histories. Perhaps only by recognizing the unethical nature of the histories we have consumed can postcolonial students of the Indian past finally recover from their prolonged immersion in colonial ignorance and forgetting. One can always live in hope that from among one's own students, there will emerge a better history some day.

NOTES

1. Circular No. 16, OIOC, Mss Eur E 295/10.

2. Ugyen Gyatso, Note on Buddhism in Kalimpong, 9 October 1901, encl, *ibid.*

3. Sarat Chandra Das, Rai Bahadur, in Dy Commr Darjeeling to Supt Census Operations, 25 January 1902, *ibid.*

4. Umakanta Das to Mgte Tippera, 10 November 1901, *ibid.*

5. Mgte and Collr Murshidabad to Supt of Census, 9 December 1901, *ibid.*

6. Note by Satish Chandra Acharyya Vidyabhushan, Professor in Sanskrit College, 5 October 1901, *ibid.*

7. Barua (1938). The identical verses from the *Darrang Rajvamsavali*, referring to the gifts of Naranarayan to the Kamakhya temple, have been used in Mishra (2004: 81–3). The author, unaware of Barua's critique of Gait's translation, places the shrine complex in Gauhati as the fulcrum of the process that he calls 'universalisation' of various co-resident 'ethnic' groups of the valley.

8. For human sacrifices by 'tribal priests' among many Assam 'tribes', see Gait (2004 [1926]: 39–40); for the repetition of the mis-translation of the deeds of gift as 'sacrifices' of 140 men's heads to Kamakhya and at Hajo, respectively, *ibid.*, 54, 59.

9. See Beane (1977: 59, 100–103).

10. Hodson (1908), 'Published under the Orders of the Government of East Bengal and Assam'. Subsequently, as the William Wyse Professor of Social Anthropology at Cambridge University and Fellow of St. Catharine's College, Hodson published in 1937 a census-based *Ethnography of India: 1901–1931*.

11. Hodson (1908: 96–7).

12. See proceedings under Section 110, Criminal Penal Code, 1903–1905 in Sangma (1993: 201–25).

13. Playfair (1909). This was published under the orders of the Government of Eastern Bengal and Assam; the author was Deputy Commissioner of the newly created colonial province.

14. *Ibid.*, 165–6, Appendix E.

15. Shakespear (1912: 42).

16. Choudhuri (1910, vol. 1: 12–65) for Jayantiapuri lineage of Saiva and Vaisnava initiates; for lineage of Sakta ascetics, see 87–138.

17. Hutton (1923: 150–9).
18. D. Hobson, Foreword, in Mey (2009). I thank Jacques Leider for securing this document for me.
19. Orders in Datta and Bandyopadhyaya (1976: 36).
20. Longkumer (2010).
21. Mills (1933).
22. See Neog (1966) and Chaudhury (1966). Saikia (2008a, 2008b); Purakayastha (2008). S. K. Bhuyan was born in 1894 and died in 1964.
23. The earliest to be printed was the *Tungkhungia Buranji*, a chronicle written in 1804–6 by a clerical member of the old Ahom administration, which Bhuyan translated into English and supplemented with entire sentences and passages from other chronicles as he saw fit; see Bhuyan (1990a [1933]: Introduction).
24. Ali (1933). Gait had said it was Henniker, Ali said it was Elliker. Ali had a dated coin of Bara Gosain in his possession and used it to counter Gait's chronology of rulers in the region.
25. Misra (1935).
26. *Editorial Review* (1934: 85–7).
27. Rongmuti (1933:54–60).
28. *Ibid.*, 56.
29. Von Fürer-Haimendorf (1976: 1). The anthropologist received permission from J.P. Mills, then Deputy Commissioner of the region that was closed to others.
30. Reid (1944).
31. *Ibid.*, 25.
32. Obituary Notices, *JARS*, 6, 3 and 4, 1938–9.
33. Medhi (1941); Das (1959).
34. Obituary by Umakanta Goswami, *JARS*, 1945.
35. Compare post-funeral monuments of carved wooden posts, called *Kima*, in Playfair (1909: 113–14), with the 'roughly hewn wooden figure' made for a dead man in von Fürer-Haimendorf (1976: Preface and Introduction).
36. Barua (1935).
37. Barua (1938–9).
38. Barua (1951: 156–66).
39. For narrative histories of similar populations of 1947–97 and an argument that anthropological work by E.R. Leach and Frederik Barth replaced 'tribe' with 'ethnic group' at the outset of 1960s, see Bleie (2005).
40. See 'Kokamukha' in Sircar (1971: 275–81).
41. Sircar (1971: 159–66). For the list, see A. Bhattacharyya (1994: 65–6).
42. D. Sarma (ed.) *Kamarupasanavali*, 20. The translators kept the title of the original work in deference to the original work, in Bengali, of Padmanath Bhattacharyya Vidyavinoda (1868–1938) who had compiled

twelve land grant records; this edition expanded upon those twelve, and added explanations and published the plates.

43. Sinha (2008: 62–4).

44. Sircar (1969).

45. Kulke (2001 [1993], 1995).

46. For a selection of a vast and growing literature, see Bassaignet (1958); Devi (1968, 1992); S.K. Chatterji (1974); Bose (1980); Sinha (1982); Karotemprel and Danda (1998); Medhi *et al.* (2009); Pati (2011).

47. Devi (1992 [1968]: 249).

48. Saha (1990). The volume was a publication of a conference held in Shillong in 1977.

49. Baruah (1993); A. Guha (1977, 1991); Saikia (2004).

50. Banerjee (2006).

51. See among others, Blackburn (2008); Blackburn with Tarr (2005); also Blackburn (2010); for migration stories from all parts of the vast Tibetan world to all parts of eastern Bengal, see Sangma (1993: 3–13) and maps; compare with the ethnographic accounts of 'Garo' polities with no reference to Himalayan or Tibetan pasts in D.N. Majumdar (1962); Kar (1990).

52. For the critical anthropological scholarship of Himalayan polyandry, see Prince Peter of Denmark (1955); Berreman (1962); Burling (1963); Berreman (1975); Goldstein (1976); Levine (1988); Childs (2003); Grant (2002).

53. For a survey of scholarship that excludes Himalayan matrilineal systems as available in Pain and Pema (2004), see Nakane (1961); Deb Roy (1983); review of Deb Roy by Charles Lindholm (1985); Raha (1989); Chacko (1998); Nongbri (2008).

54. Blackburn (2003).

55. I thank Reverend Zairema, Reverend Lalsawma, Dr J.V. Hhuna, the Hua sisters, Ramdini, Dr Sailo, Dinkema, Zodini, Dr Laltluangliana Khiangte and Lalsanga Sailo, the son of Khawvelthanga, Nonai, MaPuia and Pu T.K., and above all Dingi Sailo for many different conversations in the course of October–November 2005 and thereafter.

56. Lalhula Sailo, encl in J.H. Lorrain to Mrs Lewin, Ms 811/IV/66/4 (vi), Senate House, London.

57. Cubelli (2010).

58. Halbwachs (1992 [1925]).

59. M.K. Binodini's 'Preface', in Singh and Ray (2007).

60. Minesvar Sarvabhoum, *ibid.*, 97–8.

Bibliography

MANUSCRIPT MAPS

X/1280–81: Map of British Sikkim comprising hills territory and Morung pargana surveyed in 1852.

X/2172: Map of route from Gauhati to Kollakoosy surveyed by Ensign Wood and Capt. Welsh, 1792–93.

X/10150: Trade routes from Lower Provinces of Bengal to Tibet and Assam, 1874.

Mss Eur F 143/150: Map of tea gardens in northeast Assam, 1916.

Mss Eur F 174/2314: Taylor's maps of tea districts in 1910.

Private Papers: British Library, London

Letters of Major James Rennell, Mss Eur F 218.

Manipur State Diary: Royal Annals Made by Nithor Nath Banerjee, Mss Eur D 485.

Papers of T.H. Lewin, Mss Eur C 79, C 80.

Papers of H.H. Risley, Mss Eur E 295/10.

Papers of Major A.G. McCall, Mss Eur E 278/6, Eur E 361/1, 361/2–98, 361/7.

Official Diaries of Lt. Col. John Shakespear, Mss Eur Photo Eur 89.

Papers of Robert Reid, Mss Eur E 278/20.

Private Journal of Capt. Francis Jenkins, Mss Eur F 257/2.

Private Journal of Capt. R. Boileau Pemberton of a trip from Manipur to Ava and then to Arakan, OIOC, L/PS/19/36, 1830.

Tea Cultivation in Assam, Cachar and Sylhet 1868, Mss Eur F 174/2095–6.

Tea Soils of Cachar and Sylhet 1903, Mss Eur F 174/1512, 1513.

Tour Diaries of J.H. Hutton and J.P. Mills 1917–1930 and advice to Simon Commission, Eur/IOR NEG Reels 11711–12.

Manuscript Collections: Senate House, London

Papers of T.H. Lewin, Mss 811/ II/ 11–66 and Mss 811/IV/43–75.

Manuscript Collections: National Library of Wales, Aberstywyth

Church Missionary Archives 5, 27187, 27314–18.
Wills and Probates

Manuscript Collections: Bodleian Library, Rhodes House, Oxford

Mss Brit Empire S. 18 (C74–91) and 19 (D1–2).
Mss Brit Empire S. 22 G352.

American Baptist History Society, Valley Forge, Pennsylvania

Assam: Correspondence of Miles Bronson

Rutgers, State University of New Jersey, New Brunswick

Letters of Miles Bronson (1849–1857), Special Collections, Alexander Library.

Unpublished Official Correspondence: British Library, OIOC; National Archives of India, Delhi; State Archives of Assam at Gauhati; State Archives of Mizoram at Aizawl; and State Archives of West Bengal at Calcutta

Bengal Foreign Proceedings
Bengal Judicial Consultation
Bengal Judicial and Political Proceedings
Bengal Political and Secret Department Consultations
Bengal Revenue Consultations
Board's Collection 1776–1836
Home Miscellaneous 108 (Kuch Bihar)
Home Miscellaneous 219 (Bogle to Bhutan)
Home Miscellaneous 381 (Bauze Zamin Daftar/ Wastelands)
Home Miscellaneous 614 (Notes on David Scott)
Home Miscellaneous 644 (Notes on Nepal, 1814)
Home Miscellaneous 646, 648, 650, 654 (Notes on Nepal, Bhutan, Sikkim, Bengal 1814–1816)
Home Miscellaneous 687 (Buchanan Hamilton in Ava, 1798)
Home Miscellaneous 765 (James Rennell's Letters 1758–85)

OFFICIAL DOCUMENTS

Adamson, H. 1887. *Report on the Settlement Operations in the Akyab District.* Rangoon: Government Press.

Adamson, H. 1888. *Report on the Settlement Operations in the Akyab District.* Rangoon: Government Press.

Administration Reports of the Political Agency, Hill Tipperah for 1872–1878 ed. Dipak Kumar Chaudhuri. 1996. Agartala: Government of Tripura.

Administration Reports of the Political Agency, Hill Tipperah for 1878–1890 ed. Dipak Kumar Chaudhuri. 1996. Agartala: Government of Tripura.

Administrative Report on Presidency of Bengal for 1860. 1861. Calcutta: Government Printing.

Administrative Report of North Lushai Hills for 1895–96. 1896. Shillong: Assam Secretariat.

Administrative Report of North Lushai Hills for 1897–98. 1898. Shillong: Assam Secretariat.

Administrative Report of the Lushai Hills for 1898–99. 1899. Shillong: Assam Secretariat.

Allen, W.J. 1859. *Report on the Administration of the District of Kachar.* Calcutta: John Gray 'Bengal Hurkaru' Press.

Annual Report on the Administration of Land Revenue in Assam for 1874–75. Shillong: Assam Secretariat.

Banerji, Sarat Chandra. 1901. *Final Report on Resettlement of Cachar District 1894–99.* Shillong: Government Press.

Brownlow, Charles H. 1872. *Despatches of Brigadier General C.H.Brownlow Commanding Chittagong Column Looshai Expeditionary Force 1871–72.* Calcutta: Government Press.

Cachar District Records (comp. Debabrata Datta, ed. Sunanda Datta). 2007. Kolkata: Asiatic Society.

Cummings, J.G. 1899. *Survey and Settlement of the Chakla Roshanabad Estate in District Tippera, Noakhali, 1872–99.* Calcutta: Bengal Secretariat.

Davis, A.W. 1894. *Gazetteer of the North Lushai Hills Compiled under Orders of Chief Commissioner of Assam.* Shillong: Assam Secretariat Printing Office.

English Reports of the Privy Council. 1902. vol. 20. Edinburgh: William Green and Sons.

Further Correspondence on the subject of the Looshai Raids and the Consequent Hostilities. 1872.

Great Britain. House of Commons. 1859. Accounts and Papers. *Correspondence Relating to East India (Education).* Part I, Vol. 24.

———. 1863. Accounts and Papers. *Correspondence Relating to Cotton Cultivation in India.* Vol. 44.

Correspondence between the Landholders' and Commercial Association of British India, the Government of India and Government of Bengal with Reference to the Raids Made by the Looshai Tribes into the Province of Kachar, in the years 1869 and 1871. 1871. Calcutta: Stanhope Press.

————. 1872. Accounts and Papers. *Futher Correspondence on the Subject of the Looshai Raids and the Consequent Hostilities* (in Continuation of Paper no. 398 of 1871). Vol. 45.

Government of Burma. 1875. *The British Burma Code: Regulations and Local Acts in Force in British Burma.* Calcutta: Office of the Superintendent of Government Printing.

Government of India Legislative Department, 1897. *The Assam Code, Containing the Bengal Regulations, Local Acts of the Governor-General in Council, Regulations Made Under the Government of India Act of 1870 (33 Vict., C3) and Acts of the Lieutenant-Governor of Bengal in Council in Force in Assam and List of Enactments Notified for Scheduled Districts in Assam under Act XIV of 1874.* Calcutta: Superintendent of Government Printing.

Government of India. 1906. *Report of the Assam Labour Enquiry Committee.* Calcutta: Superintendent of Government Printing.

Hughes, W. Gwynne. 1881. *The Hill Tracts of Arakan.* Rangoon: Government Press.

Hutchinson, Robert Henry Sneyd. 1906. *An Account of Chittagong Hill Tracts.* Calcutta: Government Press.

McSweeney, J. 1910. *Final Report on the Settlement of Darrang District for 1905–09.* Shillong: Government Press.

Mills, A.J. Moffat. 1854. *Report on the Province of Assam.* Calcutta: Gazette Office.

Political Missions to Bhutan, comprising the reports of Hon'ble Ashley Eden (1864) Captain R. B. Pemberton 1837, 1838 with Dr. Griffith's Journal and the Account by Baboo Kishen Kanta Bose (1815). Calcutta: Government Printing Office.

Prance, B.C. 1916. *Final Report on Survey and Settlement Operations in the Riparian Area of District Tippera conducted with the Faridpur District Settlement 1909–1915.* Calcutta: Bengal Secretariat.

Relations between Looshais and Munnipoorees. 1979. Calcutta: Firma KLM.

Annual Report on the Administration of Bengal 1860–61. 1863. Calcutta: Superintendent of Government Printing.

Report of the Assam Labour Enquiry Committee. 1906. Calcutta: Superintendent of Government Printing.

Report of the Commissioners Appointed to Enquire into the State and Prospects of Tea Cultivation in Assam, Kachar and Sylhet. 1868. Calcutta: Central Press.

Report on the Revision Settlement Operations in the Akyab District 1901–92. Rangoon: British Burma Press.

Roberts, Frederick S. 1878. *Narrative of the Cachar Column Looshai Expeditionary Force.* Simla: Government Printing.

Scott, W.L. 1919. *Final Report on Resettlment of Cachar for 1917–18.* Shillong: Government Press.

Select Records on Agriculture and Economy of Comilla District 1782–1867 (comp. Ratanlal Chakraborty and Haruo Noma). 1989. Dhaka: Japan International Cooperation Agency.

Selections from Records of the Government of Bengal:

No.11, 1853: Reports on the Revenue Administration of the Province of Assam, 1851 and On the Wild Tribes of Southern Frontier of Chittagong, 1847.

No. 23, 1855: Papers Relating to Some Frontier Tribes on the Northeast Border of Assam, including Capt. John B. Neufville, 'On the Geography and Population of Assam'; Lt. R. Wilcox, 'Memoir of a Survey of Assam of Assam and Neighbouring Countries executed in 1825–28'; Correspondence and Journal of Captain Dalton on his Progress in a Late Visit to a Clan of Abors on the Dihing River; Major S.F. Hannay's 'Sketch of Singphos.

No. 25, 1857: Lt. Col. S.F. Hannay, Notes on Productive Capacities of Shan Countries North and East of Ava with Short Account of the Town of Bhamo as seen in January 1836 and its trade with China and the lower Irrawaddy.

No. 25E, 1857: Correspondence regarding the discovery of the tea-plant in Sylhet.

No. 37, 1861: Papers relative to the cultivation of tea in Assam.

Smart, Robert B. 1866. *Geographical Statistical Report on the District of Tipperah*. Calcutta: Bengal Secretariat.

Sylhet. 1898. *Final Report on Jaintia Pargana for 1892–97*. Shillong: Government Press.

Sylhet. 1903. *Final Report on Ilam Settlement*. Shillong: Government Press.

Tripura Historical Documents (comp. Maharajkumar Sahadev Bikram-Kisor and Jagadis Gan-Chaudhuri). 1994. Calcutta: Firma KLM.

Waste Land Rules for 1839 and 1841 for Arakan and for British Burma for 1863–65. 1906. Rangoon: Superintendent of Government Printing.

BOOKS AND ARTICLES

Acharjee, Jahar (ed.). 2006. *History, Culture and Coinage of Samatata and Harikela*. Agartala: Rajendra Kirtishala and Rajkusum Prakashan.

———. 2008. *Puratani Tripura*. Agartala: Jnan Bichitra Prakashani.

———. 2012. 'Tripurar Itihaser Upadane Bibhinno Puthi'. Paper at conference, Tripura University, Agartala.

Adas, Michael. 1982. *The Burma Delta: Economic Development and Social Change on an Asian Rice Frontier, 1852–1941*. Madison: University of Wisconsin Press.

Adhikary, Gajendra. 2001. *A History of the Temples of Kamrup and Their Management*. Gauhati: Kamarupa Anusandhan Samiti.

Adhikary, Surya Mani. 1997 [1988]. *The Khasa Kingdom: A Trans-Himalayan Empire of the Middle Age*. New Delhi: Nirala Publications.

Agarwal, Bina. 2009. 'Gender and Forest Conservation: The Impact of Women's Participation in Community Forest Governance', *Ecological Economics*, 68: 2785–99.

Ahmad, Khan Chowdhuri Amanat Ulla. 1946. 'Slavery in North-east India'. *IHRC*, 23(2): 73.

Ali, Daud. 2006. 'War, Servitude and the Imperial Household: A Study of Palace Women in the Chola Empire', in Indrani Chatterjee and Richard M. Eaton (eds.), *Slavery and South Asian History*, 44–61. Bloomington: Indiana University Press.

Ali, Syed Murtaza. 1933. 'An Account of the First British Expedition in Jaintia', *JARS*, 1(4): 115–17.

———. 1954. *The History of Jaintia*. Dacca: Ramna Press.

———. 1965. *Hazrata Shah Jelala O Sileter Itihas*. Dhaka: Bamla Ekademi.

Amstutz, Galen. 1998. 'The Politics of Pure Land Buddhism in India', *Numen*, 45(1): 69–96.

Andaya, Barbara. 2006. *The Flaming Womb: Repositioning Women in Early Modern Southeast Asia*. Honolulu: University of Hawai'i Press.

Aris, Michael (ed). 1979. *Bhutan: The Early History of a Himalayan Kingdom*. Warminister: Aris and Phillips.

———. 1988. *Hidden Treasures and Secret Lives: A Sudy of Pemalingpa 1450–1521 and the Sixth Dalai Lama 1683–1706*. Delhi: Motilal Banarsidass.

——— (ed.). 1992. *Lamas, Princes, and Brigands: Joseph Rock's Photographs of the Tibetan Borderlands of China*. New York: China House Gallery and China Institute in America.

———. 2005. *The Raven Crown: The Origins of Buddhist Monarchy in Bhutan*. New York: Serindia.

Arondekar, Anjali. 2009. *For the Record: On Sexuality and the Colonial Archive in India*. Durham: Duke University Press.

Arunima, G. 2003. *There Comes Papa: Colonialism and the Transformation of Matriliny in Kerala, Malabar c. 1850–1940*. New Delhi: Orient Longman.

Aruz, Joan, Ann Farkas, and Elisabetta Fino (eds.). 2006. *The Golden Deer of Eurasia: Perspectives on the Steppe Nomads of the Ancient World*. New York and New Haven: Metropolitan Museum of Art and Yale University Press.

Asani, Ali S. 1987. 'The Khojki Script: Legacy of Ismaili Islam in the Indo-Pakistan Subcontinent', *JAOS*, 107(3): 439–49.

Ashmore, Robert. 2004. 'Word and Gesture: On Xuan School of Hermeneutics of the Analects', *Philosophy East and West*, 54(4): 458–88.

Ashraf, Kazi Khaleed. 2012. *The Hermit's Hut: Architecture and Asceticism in India*. Honolulu: University of Hawai'i Press.

Aung-Thwin, Michael A. 1983. With Assistance of Jennifer Brewster. 'Athi, Kyun Taw, Hpaya-kyun: Varieties of Commendation and Dependence in Precolonial Burma', in Anthony Reid (ed.), *Slavery, Bondage and Dependency in Southeast Asia*. New York: St. Martin's Press.

———. 2005. *The Mists of Rāmañña: The Legend that Was Lower Burma*. Honolulu: University of Hawai'i Press.

Azarpay, G. 1976. 'Nana, the Sumero-Akkadian Goddess of Transoxiana', *JAOS*, 4: 536–42.

Bajracharya, Naresh Man. 1998. *Buddhism in Nepal 465 BC to 1199 AD*. Delhi: Eastern Book Linkers.

Bandhyopadhyaya, Debanath. 1986. *Rajasabhar Kobi o Kabya*. Kolkata: Pustak Bipani.

Banerjee, Prathama. 2006. *Politics of Time: 'Primitives' and History Writing in a Colonial Society*. Delhi: Oxford University Press.

Banik, Bijoykrishna. 2009. *Mainamati: Sanskrit Inscriptional and Archaeological Study*. Delhi: Bharatiya Kala Prakashan.

Barman, Ramendra (ed.). 1998. *Shaykh Manuhar Birochito Gajinama*. Agartala: Akshar Publications.

Barpujari, H.K. 1986. *The American Missionaries and North-East India, 1860–1900: A Documentary Study*. Gauhati: Spectrum Publications.

———. (ed.). 1994. *The Comprehensive History of Assam from Thirteenth Century A.D. to the Treaty of Yandabo (1826)*. 5 vols. Gauhati: Publication Board.

Bartholomeusz, Tessa. 1992. 'The Female Mendicant in Buddhist Sri Lanka', in Jose Ignacio Cabezon (ed.), *Buddhism, Sexuality and Gender*, 37–64. Albany: State University of New York Press.

Barua, Birinchi Kumar. 1935. 'A Note on the Word "Assam"', *JARS*, 3(4): 102–4.

———. 1951. *A Cultural History of Assam (Early Period)*. Vol. 1. Nowgong, Assam: K. K. Borooah.

Barua, Golap Chandra (trans. and ed.). 1985 [1930]. *Ahom Buranji trom the Earliest Time to the End of Ahom Rule*. Gauhati: Spectrum Publications.

Barua, Kanak Lal. 1933. 'Kamarupa in the Sixth Century AD', *JARS*, 1(3): 65–7.

———. 1935. 'Kausika and Kausiki', *JARS*, 3 (1): 19–21.

———. 1936. 'Rejoinder to N. Bhattasali', *JARS*, 4(3): 58–66.

———. 1938. 'Human Sacrifices in Assam', *JARS*, 6(1): 4–11.

———. 1938–9. 'Some Noted Medieval Kamarupi Authors and Their Works', *JARS*, 6 (3 & 4): 75–86.

Barua Sadaramin, Harakanta (ed. S.K. Bhuyan). 1990 [1930]. *Assam Buranji or a History of Assam*. Gauhati: DHAS.

Baruah, S.L. 1993. *Last Days of Ahom Monarchy: A History of Assam from 1769 to 1826*. Delhi: Munshiram Manoharlal.

Baruah, Sanjib. 2004. *Between South and Southeast Asia: Northeast Indian and the Look East Policy.* Gauhati: CNEISS.

Bassaignet, P. 1958. *Tribesmen of Chittagong Hill Tracts.* Dacca: Asiatic Society of Pakistan.

Basu, Kanchan (comp. and ed.). 1992. *Dusprapya Sahitya Samgraha.* Kolkata: Reflect Publications.

Bautze-Picron, Claudine. 2003. *The Buddhist Murals of Pagan: Timeless Vistas of the Cosmos.* Trumbull, Conn.: Weatherhill.

Beane, Wendell Charles. 1977. *Myth, Cult and Symbols in Sakta Hinduism: A Study of the Indian Mother Goddess.* Leiden: E.J. Brill.

Beckwith, Christopher I. 1987. *The Tibetan Empire in Central Asia: A History of the Struggle for Great Power among Tibetans, Turks, Arabs and Chinese during the Early Middle Ages.* Princeton: Princeton University Press.

——— (ed.). 2002. *Medieval Tibeto-Burman Languages.* Leiden: E. J. Brill.

Behal, Rana P. 2006. 'Power Structure, Discipline and Labour in Assam Tea Plantations under Colonial Rule', *International Review of Social History,* 51, S14, 143–72.

Bellezza, John Vincent. 2008. *Zhang Zhung, Foundations of Civilization in Tibet.* Vienna: Osterreichische Akademie der Wissenschaften.

Bennett, Judith M. 2008. 'Forgetting the Past', *Gender and History,* 20(3): 669–77.

Bernier, François (trans. A. Constable, 2nd ed. Revd. V.A. Smith). 1999 [1934]. *Travels in the Mogul Empire 1656–1668.* Delhi: Asian Educational Services.

Berreman, Gerald. 1962. 'Pahari Polyandry', *American Anthropologist,* 64(1): 60–75.

———. 1975. 'Himalayan Polyandry and the Domestic Cycle', *American Ethnologist,* 2(1): 127–38.

Bhattacharjee, Jayanta Bhushan. 1977. *Cachar under British Rule.* New Delhi: Radiant Publishers.

Bhattacharya, Gouriswar. 2000a. 'Inscribed Image of a Saivacarya from Bengal', in Enamul Haque (ed.), *Essays on Buddhist Hindu, Jain, Iconography and Epigraphy,* 309–13. Dhaka: International Centre for the Study of Bengal Art.

———. 2000b. 'Two Interesting Items of Pala Period', in Enamul Haque (ed.), *Essays on Buddhist, Hindu, Jain Iconography and Epigraphy,* 373–83. Dhaka: International Centre for the Study of Bengal Art.

———. 2003. 'Mainamati: City on the Red Hills', in Pratapaditya Pal and Enamul Haque (eds.), *Bengal Sites and Sights,* Kolkata: Marg Publication.

———. 2007. 'The British Museum Stone Inscription of Mahendrapala', *South Asian Studies,* 23: 69–74.

Bhattacharya, Malayshankar. 2008. *Glimpses of Buddhist Bengal.* Kolkata: Indian Institute of Oriental Studies.

Bhattacharya, Padmanath. 1936. 'Location of the Nidhanpur Grant of Bhaskaravarman of Kamarupa', *JARS*, 4(3): 58–66.

———. 1938. 'Dates of the Bhatera Copper-Plates', *JARS*, 6(1): 18–21.

Bhattacharyya, P.K. 1991. 'Problems of Coinage of Kamata-Kuch Behar: A Northeastern State of India', in S. Husne Jahan (ed.), *Akshaynivi: Essays Presented to Dr. Debala Mitra*, 335–43. Delhi: Sri Satguru Publications.

Bhattacharya, Shiva Chandra Vidyavinod. 1916. *Principles of Tantra*. 2 vols. London: Luzac.

Bhattacharya, Srichandrodaya Vidyavinod. 1968. *Silalipi Samgraha*. Tripura: Shikkha Adhikar.

Bhattacharyya, Alakananda. 1994. *Nepalese Inscriptions in Pre-Newari Eras: Annotated Bibliography*. Calcutta: Atisha Memorial Publishing.

Bhattacharyya, N.N. 1995. *Religious Culture of North-Eastern India* (H. K. Barpujari Lectures). Delhi: Manohar.

Bhattacharyya, S.N. 1929. *A History of Mughal North-East Frontier Policy*. Calcutta: Chukervertty, Chatterjee.

Bhattasali, N.K. 1929. *Iconography of Buddhist and Brahmanical Sculptures in the Dacca Museum*. Dacca: Dacca Museum.

Bhowmik, Dwijendralal. 2003. *Tribal Religion of Tripura: A Socio-Religious Analysis*. Agartala: Tribal Research Institute.

Bhuyan, Suryya Kumar. 1947. *Annals of the Delhi Badshahate, Being a Translation of the Old Assamese Chronicle Padshah Buranji, with Introduction and Notes*. Gauhati: DHAS.

——— (ed.). 1951 [1936]. *Kochari Buranji*. Gauhati: DHAS.

——— (ed.). 1960. *Satsari Asam Buranji: A Collection of Seven Old Assamese Buranjis or Chronicles with Synopses in Assamese*. Gauhati: Gauhati University Publication Department.

——— (ed.). 1987 [1930]. *Kamrupar Buranji or An Account of Ancient Kamrupa and a History of the Mughal Conflicts with Assam and Cooch Behar upto 1682, Compiled from Old Assamese Manuscript Chronicles*. Gauhati: DHAS.

——— (ed.). 1990a [1933]. *Tungkhungia Buranji or a History of Assam 1681–1826*. Gauhati: DHAS.

——— (ed.). 1990b [1938]. *Tripura Buranji by Ratnakandali and Arjundas Kataki*. Gauhati: DHAS and Narayani Handiqui Historical Institute.

——— (ed.). 2001 [1932]. *Deodhai Asam Buranji with Several Shorter Chroncles of Assam, Compiled from Old Assamese Buranjis*. Gauhati: DHAS and Narayani Handiqui Historical Institute.

Bidyaratna, Ramkumar. 1999. *Kulikāhinī*, in Kanchan Basu (comp), *Duṣprāpya Sāhitya Samgraha*, 2: 277–435. Kolkata: Reflect Publications.

Birge, Bettine. 2002. *Women, Property and Confucian Reaction in Sung and Yuan China (960–1368)*. Cambridge: Cambridge University Press.

Biswas, Dilip Kumar (ed.). 1997. *The Correspondence of Raja Rammohun Roy*. Calcutta: Saraswat Library.

Blackburn, Stuart H. 2003. 'Colonial Contact in the "Hidden Land": Oral History among the Apatanis of Arunachal Pradesh', *IESHR*, 40: 335–65.

———. 2008. *Himalayan Tribal Tales: Oral Tradition and Culture in the Apatani Valley*. Leiden: E.J. Brill.

———. 2010. *The Sun Rises: A Shaman's Chant, Ritual Exchange and Fertility in the Apatani Valley*. Leiden: E.J. Brill.

Blackburn, Stuart H., with Michael Aram Tarr. 2005. *Tribal Cultures in the Eastern Himalayas: Through the Eyes of Time, Photographs of Arunachal Pradesh, 1859–2006, volume 1*. Leiden: E.J. Brill.

Blackwood, Evelyn. 2005. 'Gender Transgressions in Colonial and Postcolonial Indonesia', *JAS*, 64(4): 849–79.

Bleie, Tone. 2005. *Tribal Peoples, Nationalism and the Human Rights Challenge: The Adivasis of Bangladesh*. Dhaka: University Press Limited.

The Blue Annals (trans. George Roerich). Part 1 1996a [1949] and Part 2 1996b [1951]. Delhi: Motilal Banarsidass.

Bogin, Benjamin. 2008. 'The Dreadlocks Treatise: On Tantric Hairstyles in Tibetan Buddhism', *History of Religions*, 48(2): 85–109.

Borah, M.I. (trans and ed.). 1936. *Baharistan-i-Ghaybi: A History of the Mughal Wars in Assam, Cooch Behar, Bengal, Bihar and Orissa during the Reigns of Jahangir and Shah Jahan, by Mirza Nathan*. 2 volumes, Gauhati.

Bose, Jyotsna K. 1980. *Glimpses of Tribal Life in North-East India*. Calcutta: Institute of Social Research and Applied Anthropology.

Bose, Sugata. 2003. 'Post-Colonial Histories of South Asia: Some Reflections', *Journal of Contemporary History*, 38(1): 133–46.

Botham, A.W. 1912. 'Some Kachari Coins', *Journal of the Asiatic Society of Bengal*, 8: 556–7.

Boucher, D. 1990. 'Review', *Pacific Affairs*, 63(3): 382–3.

Boulnois, Luce. 2002. 'Gold, Wool and Musk: Trade in Lhasa in the Seventeenth Century', in François Pommaret (ed.), *Lhasa in the Seventeenth Century*, 133–56. Leiden: E.J. Brill.

Bowles, Samuel, Eric Alden Smith, and Monique Borgerhoff Mulder. 2010. 'The Emergence and Persistence of Inequality in Premodern Societies', *Current Anthropology*, 51(1): 7–17.

Boyce, Mary. 1979. *Zoroastrians: Their Religious Beliefs and Practices*. London: Routledge and Kegan Paul.

Brara, N. Vijayalakshmi. 1998. *Politics, Society and Cosmology in India's North East*. Delhi: Oxford University Press.

Broadbridge, Anne F. 2010. *Kinship and Ideology in the Islamic and Mongol Worlds.* Cambridge: Cambridge University Press.

Bronkhorst, Johannes. 2011. *Buddhism in the Shadow of Brahmanism.* Leiden: Brill.

Brook, Timothy. 1996. 'Review' of Donald S. Lopez, *Journal of Asian Studies*, 55(2): 425–8.

Bruce, C.A. 1838. *An Account of the Manufacture of the Black Tea as Now Practised at Suddeya in Upper Assam by the Chinamen sent Thither for That Purpose.* Calcutta: By Author.

Buchanan, Francis. 1799. 'On the Religion and Literature of the Burmas', *Asiatick Researches*, 6: 166–308.

Burling, Robbins. 1963. *Rengsanggri: Family and Kinship in a Garo Village.* Philadelphia: University of Pennsylvania Press.

Burnham, Michelle. 1997. *Captivity and Sentiment: Cultural Exchange in American Literature 1682–1861.* Hanover: University Press of New England.

Busch, Allison. 2011. *Poetry of Kings: The Classical Hindi Literature of Mughal India.* New York: Oxford University Press.

Cabezón, José Ignacio. 1992. 'Mother Wisdom, Father Love', in Cabezón (ed.), *Buddhism, Sexuality and Gender*, 181–202. Albany: State University of New York Press.

Callahan, Mary. 2003. *Making Enemies: War and State Building in Burma.* Ithaca: Cornell University Press.

Carey, William. 1919. *A Garo Jungle Book or the Mission to the Garos of Assam.* Philadelphia: Judson Press.

Carrington, Michael. 2003. 'Officers, Gentlemen and Thieves: The Looting of Monasteries during the 1903/4 Younghusband Mission to Tibet,' *Modern Asian Studies*, 37(1): 81–109.

Carson, Elton S. 1901. 'Encouragements in Our Medical Work', *Baptist Missionary Magazine*, 81(4): 105–6.

Carson, Laura Hardin. 1997 [1927]. *Pioneer Trails, Trials and Triumphs: Personal Memoirs of Life and Work as a Pioneer Missionary among the Chin Tribes of Burma.* Calcutta: Firma KLM.

Cassinelli, C.W. and R.B. Ekvall. 1969. *A Tibetan Principality: The Political System of Sa sKya.* Ithaca: Cornell University Press.

Cederlof, Gunner. 2009. 'Fixed Boundaries, Fluid Landscapes: British Expansion into Northern East Bengal in the 1820s', Paper presented at Conference on Writing Northeast India, Center for Historical Studies, JNU, New Delhi.

Chacko, Pariyaram M. (ed.). 1998. *Matriliny in Meghalaya: Tradition and Change.* New Delhi: Regency Publication.

Chakrabarty, Dipesh. 2002. *Habitations of Modernity: Essays in the Wake of Subaltern Studies.* Chicago: University of Chicago Press.

Chakravarti, Ranabir. 2001. *Trade and Traders in Early India*. New Delhi: Oxford University Press

———. 2010. *Exploring Early India up to c. AD 1300*. Delhi: Macmillan India.

Chaliha, Deveswar. 2000 [1949]. *Origin and Growth of the Assamese Language and Its Literature*. Gauhati: Lawyer's Book Stall.

Chappell, David W. 1996. 'Searching for a Mahayana Social Ethic', *Journal of Religious Ethics*, 24(2): 351–75.

Charney, Michael W. 2006. *Powerful Learning: Buddhist Literati and the Throne in Burma's Last Dynasty 1752–1885*. Ann Arbor, Mich.: CSSEAS.

———. 2011. 'Literary Culture in the Burma Manipur Frontier in the Eighteenth-Nineteenth Centuries', *Medieval Studies*, 14(2): 159–81.

Chatterjee, Indrani. 2002. 'Genealogy, History and the Law: The Case of the Rajamala', in Partha Chatterjee and Anjan Ghosh (eds.), *History and the Present*, 108–43. Delhi: Permanent Black.

——— (ed.). 2004. *Unfamiliar Relations: Family and History in South Asia*. New Brunswick and Delhi: Rutgers University Press and Permanent Black.

———. 2006. 'Slavery, Semantics and the Sound of Silence', in Indrani Chatterjee and Richard M. Eaton (eds.), *Slavery and South Asian History*, 287–315. Bloomington: Indiana University Press.

Chatterjee, Indrani and Richard M. Eaton (eds.). 2006. *Slavery and South Asian History*. Bloomington: Indiana University Press.

Chatterjee, Kumkum. 2008. 'The King of Controversy: History and Nation-Making in Late Colonial India', in Raziuddin Aquil and Partha Chatterjee (eds.) *History in the Vernacular*, 107–41. Ranikhet: Permanent Black.

———. 2009. *Cultures of History in Early Modern India: Persian and Mughal Culture in Bengal*. New Delhi: Oxford University Press.

———. 2010. 'Scribal Elites in Sultanate and, Mughal Bengal', *IESHR*, 47(4): 445–72.

Chatterjee, Partha. 1993. *The Nation and its Fragments: Colonial and Postcolonial Histories*. Princeton: Princeton University Press.

———. 2010. 'A Brief History of Subaltern Studies', in Partha Chatterjee, *Empire and Nation: Selected Essays*, 289–301. New York: Columbia University Press.

Chatterjee, Piya. 2001. *A Time for Tea: Women, Labor, and Post/Colonial Politics on an Indian Plantation*. Durham: Duke University Press.

Chatterji, S.K. 1974. *Kirata-Jana-Kriti: The Indo-Mongoloids, Their Contribution to the History and Culture of India*. Calcutta: Asiatic Society of Bengal.

———. 1993 [1926]. *The Origin and Development of the Bengali Language*. Calcutta: Calcutta University.

Chaturawong, Chotima. 2003. 'The Architecture of Burmese Buddhist Monasteries in Upper Burma and Northern Thailand: The Biography of Trees'. Ph.D. dissertation, Cornell.

Chaturvedi, Vinayak. 2007. *Peasant Pasts: History and Memory in Western India*. Berkeley: University of California Press.

Chaudhury, P.D., and D.C. Sircar. 1951. 'Parbattiya Plates of Vanamala-varmadeva', *EI*, 29: 145–59.

Chaudhuri, K.C. 1960. *Anglo-Nepalese Relations: From the Earliest Times of the British Rule in India till the Gurkha War*. Calcutta: Modern Book Agency.

Chaudhuri, Mukundalal. n.d. [c. 1901–1911]. *Manipurer Itihasa*. Kolkata.

Chaudhury, P.D. 1966. 'Dr. Bhuyan's Association with Kamarupa Anusandhan Samiti and the State Museum', in Maheshwar Neog and H.K. Barpujari (eds.), *Professor Suryya Kumar Bhuyan Commemoration Volume*, 70–2. Gauhati: All-India Oriental Conference.

Chauley, G.C. 2007. *Art Treasures of Unakoti*, Tripura. Delhi: Agam Kala Prakashan.

Chelliah, Shobhana and Shohini Ray. 2002. 'Early Meithei Manuscripts', in Chris I. Beckwith (ed.), *Medieval Tibeto-Burman Languages*, 59–71. Leiden: E.J. Brill.

Chevalier, Jean-Baptiste (ed. Jean Deloche.). 2008. *The Adventures of Jean-Baptiste Chevalier in Eastern India 1752–1765: A Historical Memoir and Journal of Travels in Assam, Bengal and Tibet*. Gauhati: LBS Publishers.

Childs, Geoff. 2003. 'Polyandry and Population Growth in a Historical Tibetan Society', *History of the Family*, 8: 423–44.

Chirgwin, A.M. 1935. *Arthington's Million: The Romance of the Arthington Trust*. London: Livingstone Press.

Cho, Sungtaek. 2002. 'The Rationalist Tendency in Modern Buddhist Scholarship', *Philosophy East and West*, 52(4): 420–40.

Choudhuri, Achyuta Charan. 1910 [1317 BS]. *Srihatter Itibritta*, vol. 1. Kolkata.

———. 1917 [1324 BS]. *Srihatter Itibritta*, vol. 2. Silchar.

Choudhury, Sujit (ed.). 1981. *The Mutiny Period in Kachar*. Silchar: Tagore Society for Cultural Integration.

Choudhury, Sukomal. 1973 [1380 BS]. *Bangladeshe Bouddhadharma*. Kolkata: ebook digitized by Central Research Library.

———. 1982. *Contemporary Buddhism in Bangladesh*. Calcutta: Atisa Memorial Publication Society.

Chowdhury, Abdul Momin. 1999. 'Tenth Century Sylhet: Reflections on the Paschimbhag Copperplate of Srichandra', in Sharifuddin Ahmed (ed.), *Sylhet: History and Heritage*, 632–43. Dhaka: Bangladesh Itihas Samiti.

Chowdhury, Mohammed Ali. 2004. *Bengal-Arakan Relations 1430–1666 A.D.* Calcutta: Firma KLM.

Chowdhury, Prem. 1987. 'Socio Economic Dimensions of Certain Customs and Attitudes: Women of Haryana in the Colonial Period', *EPW*, 22 (48): 2060–6.

———. 1994. *The Veiled Women: Shifting Gender Equations in Rural Haryana, 1880–1990*. Oxford: Oxford University Press.

———. 1996. 'Contesting Claims and Counter-claims: Questions of the Inheritance and Sexuality of Widows in a Colonial State', in Patricia Uberoi (ed.), *Social Reform, Sexuality and the State*, 65–82. New Delhi: Sage.

Christopher, A.J. 1985. 'Patterns of Overseas Investment in Land 1885–1913', *Transactions of the Institute of British Geographers*, NS, 10(4): 452–66.

Colley, Linda. 2002. *Captives: The Story of Britain's Pursuit of Empire*. New York: Pantheon Books.

Collins, Kathleen. 2004. 'The Logic of Clan Politics: Evidence from the Central Asian Trajectories', *World Politics*, 56(2): 224–61.

Collins, Steven. 1990. *Selfless Persons: Imagery and Thought in Theravada Buddhism*. Cambridge: Cambridge University Press.

Comstock, Rev. G.S. 1847. 'Notes on Arakan', *JAOS*, 1(3): 219–58.

Cook, Joanna. 2009. 'Hagiographic Narrative and Monastic Practice: Buddhist Morality and Mastery amongst Thai Buddhist Nuns', *Journal of Royal Anthropological Institute*, NS, 15: 349–64.

Cox, Hiram. 1971 [1821]. *Journal of a Residence in the Burmhan Empire*. With introduction by D.G.E. Hall. London: J. Warren.

Cox, Jeffrey. 2002. *Imperial Fault Lines: Christianity and Colonial Power in India, 1818–1940*. Stanford: Stanford University Press.

Crosthwaite, Charles. 1968 [1912]. *The Pacification of Burma*. 2nd ed. London: Frank Cass.

Cubelli, Roberto. 2010. 'A New Taxonomy of Memory and Forgetting', in Sergio Della Sala (ed.), *Forgetting*, 35–48. Hove, Sussex: Psychology Press.

Curley, David. 2008a. *Poetry and History: Bengal Mangal Kabya and Social Change in Precolonial Bengal*. New Delhi: Chronicle Books.

———. 2008b. 'Battle and Self-Sacrifice in a Bengali Warrior's Epic: Lausen's Quest to be a Raja in *Dharma Mangal*', in Ralph W. Nicholas (ed.), *Rites of Spring: Gajan in Village Bengal*, 142–210. New Delhi: Chronicle Books.

Dai, Yingcong. 2004. 'A Disguised Defeat: The Myanmar Campaign of the Qing Dynasty', *MAS*, 38 (February): 145–89.

———. 2009. *The Sichuan Frontier and Tibet: Imperial Strategy in the Early Qing*. Seattle: University of Washington Press.

Dalton, Jacob P. 2011. *The Taming of the Demons: Violence and Liberation in Tibetan Buddhism*. New Haven: Yale University Press.

Dar, Saifur Rahman. 2007. 'Pathways between Gandhara and North India during Second Century BC–Second Century AD', in Doris Meth Srinivasan (ed.), *On the Cusp of an Era: Art in the Pre-Kusana World*, 29–54. Leiden: E.J. Brill.

Dargye, Yonten. 2001. *History of the Drukpa Kagyud School in Bhutan (12th to 17th Century A.D.)*. Thimpu: The Author.

Das, A.K. 2004. 'Buddhism and Tribal Art in Northeastern India', in Anupa Pande and Parul Pandya Dhar (eds.), *Cultural Interface of India with Asia: Religion, Art and Architecture*, 146–52. New Delhi: National Museum and D.K. Printworld.

Das, Murari Charan. 1959. 'Rai Bahadur K.L. Barua', in K.L. Barua Comemoration Volume, *JARS*, 23: 1–5.

Das, Ratna. 1997. *Art and Architecture of Tripura*. Agartala: Tribal Research Institute.

Das, Sarat Chandra. 1903. 'How I Crossed the Jon-Tsang La Pass', in Douglas W. Freshfield, *Round Kanchenjunga: A Narrative of Mountain Travel and Exploration (with Illustration and Maps)*. London: Edward Arnold.

———. 1969 [1908–9]. *Autobiography: Narratives of the Incidents of My Early Life*. Calcutta: Indian Studies Past and Present.

———. 1970 [1881–2]. *Contributions on the Religion and History of Tibet*. New Delhi: Manjusri Publishing House.

———. 1978 [1893]. *Indian Pandits in the Land of Snow*. Ed. Nobin Chandra Das. Delhi: Delhi Printers' Prakashan.

———. 1990 [1902] *Tibetan-English Buddhist Historical Glossary*. Revised S.K. Gupta. Delhi: Sri Satguru Publications.

Das, Sudhir R. 1971. *Archaeologocial Discoveries from Murshidabad District*. Calcutta: Asiatic Society.

Das, Umakanta. 2004. *Report on the Administration of the State of Tipperah for the Year 1300 Tripurabda (13 April 1890–12 April 1891)*. Agartala: Government of Tripura.

Dasgupta, K.K. 1967. 'Iconography of Tara', in D.C. Sircar (ed.), *The Sakti Cult and Tara*, 115–27. Calcutta: University of Calcutta Press.

Dasgupta, Shashibhushan. 1997 [1372 BS]. 'Foreword', in Tripur Chandra Sen (ed.), *Tripur Deser Katha 1626–1715*. Agartala: Upajati Gavesna Kendra, Government of Tripura.

Datta, Amaresh (ed.). 1987–94. *Encyclopedia of Indian Literature*. New Delhi: Sahitya Akademi.

Datta, Dvijendrachandra and Suprasanna Bandyopadhyaya (eds.). 1976. *Rājagī Tripurār sarkārī Bamlā*. Agartala, Tripura: Education Department.

Datta, Sarat Kumar (ed.). 1937. *Jayantia Buranji*. Gauhati: Narayani Handiqui Historical Institute.

Datta-Ray, Basudeb. 1977. *Assam Secretariat 1874–1947: An Administrative History of North-East India.* Calcutta: K.P. Bagchi.

Davidson, Ronald M. 2002. *Indian Esoteric Buddhism: A Social History of the Tantric Movement.* New York: Columbia University Press.

De, Sushil Kumar. 1961. *Early History of the Vaisnava Faith and Movement in Bengal.* Calcutta: Firma KLM.

Debbarma, Sukhendu. 1996. *Origin and Growth of Christianity in Tripura with Reference to the New Zealand Baptist Missionary Society 1938–1988.* Delhi: Indus Publishing.

Deb Roy, H.L. 1983. *A Tribe in Transition: The Jaintias in Meghalaya.* Atlantic Highlands, N.J.: Humanities Press.

Deb Roy, Mrinalkanti. 2008. *Rajamala.* Agartala: Gyan Bichitra.

De Filippi, Filippo (ed.). 1932. *An Account of Tibet: The Travels of Ippolito Desideri of Pistoia S.J. 1712–1727.* London: George Routledge.

Della Sala, Sergio (ed.). 2010. *Forgetting.* Hove, Sussex: Psychology Press.

Dena, Lal. 1988. *Christian Missions and Colonialism: A Study of Missionary Movement in Northeast India with Particular Reference to Manipur and Lushai Hills 1894–1947.* Shillong: Vendrame Institute.

Derounian-Stodea, Kathryn Zabelle, and James Arthur Levernier. 1993. *The Indian Captivity Narrative 1550–1900.* New York: Twayne.

Deva, Krishna. 1983. 'Sattra in Indian Epigraphy and Art', in Braja Nath Mukherjee (ed.), *SriDinesachandrika: Studies in Indology*, 317–22. Delhi: Sundeep Publishers.

Devi, Laishram Kunjeswori. 2003. *Archaeology in Manipur.* New Delhi: Rajesh Publications.

Devi, Lakshmi. 1992 [1968]. *Ahom-Tribal Relations: A Political Study.* Gauhati: Lawyer's Book Stall.

Dey, Shumbhoo Chunder. 'The Bara Bhuyas of Bengal', *Calcutta Review*, 109: 116–23.

Dhand, Arti. 2004. 'The Subversive Nature of Virtue in the *Mahabharata*: A Tale about Women, Smelly Ascetics and God', *Journal of the American Academy of Religion*, 72(1): 33–58.

D'Hubert, Thibaut and Jacques Leider. 2011. 'Traders and Poets at the Mrauk U Court: Commerce and Cultural Links in Seventeenth-Century Arakan', in Rila Mukherjee (ed.), *Pelagic Passageways*, 77–111. Delhi: Primus Books.

Dhungel, Ramesh K. 2002. *The Kingdom of Lo (Mustang): A Historical Study.* Kathmandu: Jigme S.P. Bista and the Tashi Gephel Foundation.

Diemberger, Hildegard. 2005. 'Female Oracles in Modern Tibet', in Janet Gyatso and Hanna Havnevik (eds.), *Women in Tibet*, 113–68. New York: Columbia University Press.

Digby, Simon. 2001. *Sufis and Soldiers in Awrangzeb's Deccan: Malfuzat-i-Naqshbandiyya* (trans. from Persian). Oxford: Oxford University Press.

Dikshit, K.N. 1938. 'Excavations at Paharpur, Bengal', *Memoirs of the Archeological Survey of India*, no. 55. Delhi: Archaeological Survey.

Doctor, Andreas. 2005. *Tibetan Treasure Literature: Revelation, Tradition and Accomplishment in Visionary Buddhism*. Ithaca and Boulder: Snow Lion Publications.

Dorje, Rig'dzin. 2001. *Dangerous Friend: The Teacher-Student Relationship in Vajrayana Buddhism*. Boston: Shambhala.

Dotson, Brandon. 2007. 'Divination and Law in the Tibetan Empire: The Role of Dice in the Legislation of Loans, Interest, Marital Law and Troop Conscription', in Matthew T. Kapstein and Brandon Dotson (eds.), *Contributions to the Cultural History of Early Tibet*, 3-78. Leiden: Brill.

Downs, Frederick S. 1994. *Essays on Christianity in North-east India*. Delhi: Indus Publishing.

Dreyfus, Georges B.J. 2003. *The Sound of Two Hands Clapping: The Education of a Tibetan Buddhist Monk*. Berkeley: University of California Press, Berkeley.

Dube, Saurabh. 2004. *Stitches on Time: Colonial Textures and Postcolonial Tangles*. Durham: Duke University Press.

Dutt, Sukumar. 1962. *Buddhist Monks and Monasteries of India*. London: G. Allen and Unwin.

Dutta, S.K. (ed.). 1937. *Jayantia Buranji*. Gauhati: Historical and Antiquarian Studies.

Dutta, Sristidhar and Byomakesh Tripathy (eds.). 2006. *Buddhism in North-East India*. New Delhi: Indus Publishing Company.

———. 2008. *Buddhism in Arunachal Pradesh*. New Delhi: Indus Publishing Company.

Eaton, Richard M. 1978. *Sufis of Bijapur 1300–1700: Social Roles of Sufis in Medieval India*. Princeton: Princeton University Press.

———. 1993. *The Rise of Islam and the Bengal Frontier 1204–1760*. Berkeley and Los Angeles: University of California Press.

Eden, A. 1865. *Political Missions to Bootan*. Calcutta.

Edgar, John Ware. 1969 [1874]. *Report on Visit to Sikhim and Thibetan Frontier October, November, and December 1873*. New Delhi: Manjusri Publishing House.

'Editorial Review of *Indian History Quarterly*, 10, no. 3'. 1934. *JARS*, 2(3): 85–7.

Eimer, Helmut and David Germano (eds.). 2002. *The Many Canons of Tibetan Buddhism*. Leiden: E.J. Brill.

Elliott, John. 1792. 'Observations on the Inhabitants of the Garrow Hills Made During a Public Deputation in the Years 1788 and 1789', *Asiatick Researches*, 3: 17–37.

Ellingson, Ter. 1990. 'Tibetan Monastic Constitutions: The bca'-yig', in Lawrence Epstein and Richard F. Sherburne (eds.), *Reflections on Tibetan Culture: Essays in Memory of Turrell V. Wylie*, 205–29. Lewiston, N.Y.: E. Mellen Press.

Elverskog, Johan. 2010. *Buddhism and Islam on the Silk Road*. Philadelphia: University of Pennsylvania Press.

Emmer, Gerhard. 2007. 'Dga'lDan Tshe Dbang Dpal Bzang Po and the Tibet-Ladakh-Mughal War of 1679–84', in Uradyn E. Bulag and Hildegard G.M. Diemberger (eds.), *The Mongolia-Tibet Interface*, 81–108. Leiden: E.J. Brill.

Emmerick, R.E. 2001. 'Epilepsy According to the Rgyub-bzi', in G. Jan Meulenbeld and Dominik Wujastyk, *Studies on Indian Medical History*, 57–84. Delhi: Motilal Banarsidass.

Fielder, Charles Henry. 1869. 'On the Rise, Progress, and Future Prospects of Tea Cultivation in British India', *Journal of the Statistical Society of London*, 32 (1 March): 29–37.

Firminger, Walter K. (ed.). 1914. *Rangpur District Records*. Calcutta: Bengal Secretariat.

———— 1917. *Sylhet District Records*. Shillong: Assam Secretariat.

Fleming, Benjamin J. 2010. 'New Copperplate Grant of Sricandra (number 8) from Bangladesh', *BSOAS*, 73(2): 223–44.

Flood, Finbarr B. 2009. *Objects of Translation: Material Culture and Medieval 'Hindu-Muslim' Encounter*. Princeton: Princeton University Press.

Flood, Gavin. 2004. *The Ascetic Self: Subjectivity, Memory and Tradition*. Cambridge: Cambridge University Press.

Foster, William (ed.). 1999 [1921]. *Early Travels in India 1583–1619*. Delhi: DK Fine Press.

Fraser-Lu, Sylvia. 2001. *Splendour in Wood: The Buddhist Monasteries of Burma*. Trumbull, Conn.: Weatherhill.

Froerer, Peggy. 2006. 'Emphasizing "Others": The Emergence of Hindu Nationalism in a Central Indian Tribal Community', *Journal of Royal Anthropological Institute*, March 1, 39–59.

Furui, Ryosuke. 2008. 'A New Copper Plate Inscription of Gopala II', *South Asian Studies*, 24: 67–75.

Gaenszle, Martin. 2002. 'Nepal Kings and Kashi: On the Changing Significance of a Sacred Centre', *Studies in Nepali History and Society*, 6(1): 1–33.

Gait, Edward A. 2004 [1926]. *A History of Assam*. 2nd ed. Gauhati: LBS Publications.

Gangopadhyay, Mrinal Kanti. 2007. 'Tibetan Tradition as Complementary to Indian Tradition', in Ratna Basu (ed.), *Buddhist Literary Heritage in India: Text and Context*, 37–46. New Delhi: Munshiram Manoharlal.

Gardner, Alexander Patten. 2006. 'The Twenty-Five Great Sites of Khams: Religious Geography, Revelation, Nonsectarianism in Nineteenth-Century Eastern Tibet'. Ph.D. dissertation, University of Michigan.

Garrett, Frances. 2008. *Religion, Medicine and the Human Embryo in Tibet*. London: Routledge.

Gawler, J.C. 1987 [1873] Sikkim: *With Hints on Mountain and Jungle Warfare Exhibiting also the Facilities for Opening Commercial Relations through the State Of Sikhim with Central Asia, Thibet, and Western China*. Calcutta: Bibhash Gupta, Microform Publication Division.

Gellner, David N. 1987. 'The Newar Buddhist Monastery: An Anthropological and Historical Typology', in N. Gutschow and A. Michaels (eds.) *Heritage of the Kathmandu Valley: Proceedings of an International Conference in Lubeck, June 1985*, 365–414. Sankt Augustin: VGH-Wissenschaftsverlag.

———. 1991. 'Hinduism, Tribalism and the Position of Women: The Problem of Newar Identity', *Man*, NS, 26(1): 105–25.

Gerard, Lt. Alexander. 1824 [1818]. 'Journal of an Excursion through the Himalayah Mountains from Shipke to the Frontiers of Chinese Tartary'. *Edinburgh Journal of Science*, 1(1): 41–51.

Ghermain, Dawn. 1975. '"Review" of Richard Slotkin, *Regeneration through Violence: The Mythology of the American Frontier 1600–1860*', *Journal of American Folklore*, 88(348): 209–13.

Ghosh, Jogendra Chandra. 1936. 'A Kamarupa Brahman in Kalinga in 700 AD', *JARS*, 3(4): 113–15.

———. 1937a. 'Koch-Behar Era', *JARS*, 4(4): 96–8.

———. 1937b. 'Lolarkunda Inscription of Prannarayan of Koch Behar, *JARS*, 5(3): 63–4.

Ghosh, Parimal. 2000. *Brave Men of the Hills: Resistance and Rebellion in Burma, 1825–1932*. London: Hurst.

Giersch, C.P. 2010. 'Across Zomia with Merchants, Monks and Musk: Process Geographies, Trade Networks and the Inner-East-Southeast Asian Borderlands', *Journal of Global History*, 5: 215–39.

Gill, Sandrine. 2002. 'Notes on Chronology and Style: Evidence from Mahasthan', in Gautam Sengupta and Sheena Panja (eds.), *Archaeology of Eastern India: New Perspectives*, 40–65. Kolkata: Center of Archaeological Studies.

Goepper, Roger and Jaroslav Poncar. 1996. *Alchi: Ladakh's Hidden Buddhist Sanctuary*. Boston: Shambhala.

Gogoi, Lila. 1986. *The Buranjis: Historical Literature of Assam (A Critical Survey)*. New Delhi: Omsons Publications.

Goldstein, Melvyn. 1976. 'Fraternal Polyandry and Fertility in a High Himalayan Valley in Northwestern Nepal', *Human Ecology*, 4(3): 223–33.

Goldstein, Melvyn C. and Cynthia M. Beall. 1990. *Nomads of Western Tibet: The Survival of a Way of Life*. Berkeley: University of California Press.

Goldstein, Melvyn, T.N. Shelling, and J.T. Surkhang (eds.). 2001. *The New Tibetan-English Dictionary of Modern Tibetan*. Berkeley: University of California Press.

Gommans, Jos and Jacques P. Leider (eds.). 2002. *The Maritime Frontier of Burma: Exploring Political, Cultural and Commercial Interaction in the Indian Ocean World, 1200–1800*. Leiden: KITLV Press.

Gosvami, D.N. 1994. 'The Land System of Govinda Manikya as Reflected in the Land Grants', in J.B. Bhattacharjee (ed.), *Studies in the Economic History of North-East India*, 53–72. New Delhi: Har-Anand Publications.

———. 2002. *Rajarshi Bhagyachandra: A Life History*. Agartala: Akkhar Publications.

Goswami, Sarat Chandra. 1933. 'Vaisnavism in Kamarupa', *JARS*, 1(2): 46–54.

Goswami, Surendra Kumar. 1986. *A History of Revenue Administration in Assam 1228–1826*. Gauhati: Spectrum Publications.

Graham, Kelly. 2008. *Gone to the Shops: Shopping in Victorian England*. Westport, Conn.: Praeger.

Grant, Nellie. 2002. 'Polyandry in Dharamsala: Plural Husband Marriage in a Tibetan Refugee Community in Northwest India', in P. Christian Klieger (ed.), *Tibet, Self, and Tibetan Diaspora*, 105–38. Boston: E.J. Brill.

Gravers, Mikael. 1999. *Nationalism as Political Paranoia in Burma: An Essay on the Historical Practice of Power*. Richmond: Curzon.

Gray, David B. 2007. 'Compassionate Violence? On the Ethical Implications of Tantric Buddhist Ritual', *Journal of Buddhist Ethics*, 14: 240–71.

Green, Nile. 2006. *Indian Sufism since the Seventeenth Century*. London: Routledge.

———. 2008. 'Tribe, Diaspora and Sainthood in Afghan History', *JAS*, 67(1): 171–211.

Griffiths, Paul J. 1990. 'Review', *Philosophy East and West*, 40(2): 258–62.

Griffiths, William. 1865. 'Journal of the Mission to Bootan in 1837–38', in A. Eden, *Political Missions to Bootan*. Calcutta.

Gruschke, Andreas. 2004. *The Cultural Monuments of Tibet's Outer Provinces: Kham*. Bangkok: White Lotus Press.

Guha, Amalendu. 1977. *Planter Raj to Swaraj*. New Delhi: Indian Council of Historical Research.

Guha, Amalendu. 1977. 1991. *Medieval and Early Colonial Assam: Society, Polity, Economy.* Calcutta: Centre for Studies in Social Sciences.

Guha, Devaprasad. 2007. 'Pali Literature of Pagan', in Ratna Basu (ed.), *Buddhist Literary Heritage in India: Text and Context*, 67–72. New Delhi: Munshiram Manoharlal.

Guha, Ranajit. 1963. *A Rule of Property for Bengal: An Essay on the Idea of Permanent Settlement.* Paris: Mouton.

———. 1983. *Elementary Aspects of Peasant Insurgency in Colonial India.* Delhi: Oxford University Press.

———. 1997. 'Chandra's Death', *Subaltern Studies*, V, 135–65.

Guha, Sumit. 1999. *Environment and Ethnicity 1200–1990.* Cambridge: Cambridge University Press.

———. 2004a. 'Transitions and Translations: Regional Power and Vernacular Identity in the Dakhan, c.1500–1800', *Comparative Studies of South Asia, Africa and the Middle East*, 24(2): 23–31.

———. 2004b. 'Speaking Historically: The Changing Voices of Historical Narration in Western India, 1400–1900', *American Historical Review*, 109(4): 1084–1103.

———. 2009. 'The Frontiers of Memory: What the Marathas Remembered of Vijayanagara', *Modern Asian Studies*, 43(1): 269–88.

———. 2010. 'Serving the Barbarian to Preserve the *Dharma*: Scribal Ideology and Training in Peninsular India c.1300–1800', *Indian Economic and Social History Review*, 47(4): 497–525.

Guneratne, Arjun. 2002. *Many Tongues, One People: The Making of Tharu Identity in Nepal.* Ithaca: Cornell University Press.

Gupta, K.M. 1933. 'Jaintiapur Copperplate Inscriptions of Mahadevi Kasasati, dated Sakabda 1710 (1788), 1723 (1801) and 1725 (1803)', *JARS*, 1(1): 6–9.

Gupta, Kamalakanta. 1967. *Copperplates of Sylhet, vol.1: 7th to 11th Centuries.* Rasheedistan, Sylhet: Lipika Enterprises.

Gutschow, Niels and Ganesh Man Basukala. 1987. 'The Navadurga of Bhaktapur: Spatial Implications of an Urban Ritual', in N. Gutschow and A. Michaels (eds.), *Heritage of the Kathmandu Valley: Proceedings of an International Conference in Lubeck, June 1985*, 135–66. Sankt Augustin: VGH-Wissenschaftsverlag.

Gyatso, Janet (ed.). 1992. *In the Mirror of Memory: Reflections on Mindfulness and Remembrance in India and Tibetan Buddhism.* Albany: State University of New York Press.

———. 1998. 'Review', *History of Religions*, 37(3): 286–9.

———. 1998. *Apparitions of the Self: The Secret Autobiographies of a Tibetan Visionary.* Princeton: Princeton University Press.

———. 2003. 'One Plus One Makes Three: Buddhist Gender, Monasticism and the Law of the Excluded Middle', *History of Religion*, 89–115.

Gyatso, Janet and Hanna Havnevik (eds.). 2005. *Women in Tibet*. New York: Columbia University Press.

Halbwachs, Maurice (trans. Lewis A. Coser). 1992 [1925]. *On Collective Memory*. Chicago: University of Chicago Press.

Hall, D.G. (ed.). 1955. *Michael Symes: Journal of His Second Embassy to the Court of Ava in 1802*. London: Allen and Unwin.

Hamilton, Clarence H. 1950. 'The Idea of Compassion in Mahayana Buddhism', *JAOS*, 70(3): 145–51.

Hamilton (Buchanan), Francis. 1824–5. 'An Account of a Genus Including the Herba Toxicaria of the Himalaya Mountains or the Plant with which the Natives Poison their Arrows'. *Edinburgh Journal of Science*, 1(2): 249–51.

————. 1825a. 'An Account of the Frontier between part of Bengal and Kingdoms of Ava'. *Edinburgh Journal of Science*, 2(3): 48–59.

————. 1825b. 'An Account of the Frontier between Ava and Part of Bengal Adjacent to the Karnaphuli River', *Edinburgh Journal of Science*, 3(5): 32–44.

————. 1825c. 'An Account of the Tract between the Southern Part of Bengal and the Kingdom of Ava', *Edinburgh Journal of Science*, 3(6): 201–12 and 4(7): 22–37.

———— (ed. Suryya Kumar Bhuyan). 1963 [1940]. *An Account of Assam*. 2nd ed. Gauhati: DHAS.

Hannay, Major S.F. 1847. *Sketch of the Singphos or Kakhyens of Burmah: The Position of this Tribe as Regards Baumo and the Inland Trade of the Valley of the Irrawaddy with Yunnan and Their Connection with the Northeast Frontier of Assam*. Calcutta: Military Orphan Press.

Hardiman, David. 1987. *The Coming of the Devi: Adivasi Assertion in Western India*. New Delhi: Oxford University Press.

————. 1994. 'Power in the Forest: The Dangs 1820–1940', in *Subaltern Studies*, 8: 89–147.

————. 2008. *Missionaries and Their Medicine: A Christian Modernity for Tribal India*. Manchester: Manchester University Press.

Harding, Frederic. 1974. *Christ and the Hill-Men*. Lakemont, N.Y.: North Country Books.

Harris, Elizabeth J. 2006. *Theravada Buddhism and the British Encounter: Religious, Missionary and Colonial Experience in Nineteenth-Century Sri Lanka*. London: Routledge.

Harvey, Peter. 1993. 'The Dynamics of Paritta Chanting in Southern Buddhism', in Karel Werner (ed.), *Love Divine: Studies in Bhakti and Devotional Mysticism*, 53–84. London: Curzon.

Hazarika, Sanjoy. 1994. *Strangers of the Mist: Tales of War and Peace from India's Northeast*. New Delhi: Penguin Books.

Hefner, Robert W. 1993a. 'Christian Conversion in Muslim Java', in Robert W. Hefner (ed.), *Conversion to Christianity: Historical and*

Anthropological Perspectives on a Great Transformation, 99–128. Berkeley: University of California Press.

Hefner, Robert W. 1993b. 'Introduction: World Building and the Rationality of Conversion', in Robert W. Hefner (ed.), *Conversion to Christianity: Historical and Anthropological Perspectives on a Great Transformation*, 3–46. Berkeley: University of California Press.

Hershock, Peter D. 2003. 'Renegade Emotion: Buddhist Precedents for Returning Rationality to the Heart', *Philosophy East and West*, 53(2): 251–70.

Hillman, Ben. 2005. 'Monastic Politics and the Local State in China: Authority and Autonomy in an Ethnically Tibetan Prefecture', *China Journal*, 54(July): 29–51.

Hodge, Stephen. 2009. *An Introduction to Classical Tibetan*. Bangkok, Thailand: Orchid Press.

Hodgson, Dorothy. 2005. *The Church of Women: Gendered Encounters between Maasai and Missionaries*. Bloomington: Indiana University Press.

Hodson, T.C. 1908. *The Meitheis, with an Introduction by Sir Charles J. Lyall*. London: David Nutt.

———. 1937. *Ethnography of India: 1901–1931*. New Delhi: Government of India Press.

Holler, David. 2002. 'The Ritual of Freeing Lives', in Hank Blezer (ed.), *Religion and Secular Culture in Tibet*, 207–26. Leiden: E.J. Brill.

Holmberg, David. 2000. 'Derision, Exorcism, and the Ritual Production of Power', *American Ethnologist*, 27(4): 927–94.

Hooker, Joseph Dalton. 1969 [1854]. *Himalayan Journals: Notes of a Naturalist in Bengal, the Sikkim and Nepal Himalayas, the Khasia Mountains etc.* New Delhi: Today and Tomorrow's Printers and Publishers.

Hopkins, Edward H. 1889. 'The Social and Military Position of the Ruling Caste in Ancient India as Represented by the Sanskrit Epic', *JAOS*, 13: 57–376.

Hosena, Muhammad Asrapha. 1990. *Silhater Itihasa* (History of Sylhet). Silhet: Mahbub Ahsan Choudhuri.

Hossain, Muhammad Mosharraf, Tofail Ahmed, and Mohammad Ali 1995. *Archaeological Survey Report of Greater Dinajpur District*. Dhaka, Bangladesh: Department of Archaeology and Ministry of Cultural Affairs.

Howarth, Whitney. 2010. 'Advocates and Arbiters: Travancore and Mysore Missionaries as Public Petitioners and Champions of Social Justice, 1806–1886', *Journal of Postcolonial Theory and Theology*, 1(2): 1–19.

Huber, Toni. 1998. 'Contributions on the Bon Religion in A-mdo (1): The Monastic Tradition of Bya-dur dGa'-mal in Shar-khog', *Acta Orientalia*, 59: 179–227.

———. 2008. *The Holy Land Reborn: Pilgrimage and the Tibetan Reinvention of Buddhist India*. Chicago: University of Chicago Press.

Huntington, Susan L. 1984. *The "Pala-Sena" Schools of Sculpture*. Leiden: E.J. Brill.

Hussain, A.B.M. and M. Harunur Rashid (eds.). 1997. *Mainamati-Devaparvata: A Survey of Historical Monuments and Sites in Bangladesh*. Dhaka: Asiatic Society of Bangladesh.

Hutton, J.H. 1923. 'Carved Monoliths at Jamuguri in Assam', *Journal of Royal Anthropological Institute of Great Britain and Ireland*, 53 (January–June): 150–9.

Huxley, Andrew (ed.). 1996. *Thai Law, Buddhist Law: Essays on the Legal History of Thailand, Laos and Burma*. Bangkok: White Orchid Press.

———. 1997. '"The Traditions of *Mahosadha*": Legal Reasoning from Northern Thailand', *BSOAS*, 60(2): 315–26.

———. 2001. 'Positivists and Buddhists: The Rise and Fall of Anglo-Burmese Ecclesiastical Law', *Law and Social Enquiry*, 26(1): 113–42.

———. 2002. *Religion, Law and Tradition: Comparative Studies in Religious Law*. London: Routledge.

Huxley, Andrew, with Ryuji Okudaira. 2001. 'A Burmese Tract on Kingship: Political Theory in the 1782 Manuscript of Manugye', *BSOAS*, 64(2): 248–59.

Imam, Abu. 1999. 'Ancient Sylhet: History and Tradition', in Sharifuddin Ahmed (ed.), *Sylhet: History and Heritage*, 173–201. Dhaka: Bangladesh Itihas Samiti.

———. 2000a. *Excavations at Mainamati: An Exploratory Study*. Dhaka: International Centre for Study of Bengal Art.

———. 2000b. 'Samatata Mainamati: Some Observations', in Abu Imam, *Excavations at Mainamati: An Exploratory Study*, 613–23. Dhaka: International Centre for Study of Bengal Art.

Inden, Ronald B. 1976. *Marriage and Rank in Bengali Culture: A History of Caste and Rank in Middle Period Bengal*. Delhi: Vikas.

Ingalls, Daniel H.H. 1957. 'Dharma and Moksa', *Philosophy East and West*, 7(1–2): 41–8.

Islam, Sirajul (ed.). 1978 *Bangladesh District Records: Chittagong vol. 1, 1760–1787*. Dhaka: Dhaka University.

Izzet Ullah, Mir. 1843 [1812]. 'Travels Beyond the Himalaya', *Journal of the Royal Asiatic Society of Great Britain and Ireland*, 7(2): 283–342.

Jacob, Smita. 2009. 'Tribes of Neverland', *Tehelka*, 6(36), September 12.

Jahangirnama (trans. Wheeler M. Thackston). 1999. Washington, D.C. and New York: Smithsonian Institution Press and Oxford University Press.

Jalal, Ayesha. 2008. *Partisans of Allah: Jihad in South Asia*. Delhi: Permanent Black.

Jayantia Buranji. See S.K. Dutta 1937.

Jerryson, Michael and Mark Juergensmeyer (eds.). 2010. *Buddhist Warfare*. Oxford: Oxford University Press.

Johnston, Anna. 2003. *Missionary Writing and Empire, 1800–1860*. Cambridge: Cambridge University Press.

Jonsson, Hjorleifur. 'Above and Beyond: Zomia and the Ethnographic Challenge of/for Regional History', *History and Anthropology*, 21(2): 191–212.

Kachari Buranji, or a Chronicle of the Kachari Rajas from the Earliest Times to the Eighteenth Century, with Special Reference to Assam-Cachar Political Relations (comp. and ed. S.K. Bhuyan). 1951 [1936]. Gauhati: DHAS.

Kakati, Banikanta. 1962 [1941]. *Assamese, Its Formation and Development* (rev. 2nd ed. G. C. Goswami). Gauhati: Lawyer's Book Stall.

Kamarupar Buranji, or An Account of Ancient Kamarupa and a History of the Moghul Conflict with Assam and Cooch Bihar up to AD 1682 compiled from Old Assamese mss Chronicles (ed Suryya Kumar Bhuyan). 1958 [1930]. Gauhati: DHAS.

Kamarupasasanavali. See D. Sharma et al. 1981.

Kane, P.V. 1930-1962. *History of Dharmasastra*, 5 vols. Pune: Bhandarkar Oriental Institute.

Kapstein, Matthew (ed.). 2009. *Buddhism between Tibet and China*. Boston: Wisdom Publication.

Kar, Bodhisattva. 2004. *What Is in a Name? Politics of Spatial Imagination in Colonial Assam*. Gauhati: CNISSAS.

———. 2008. '"Tongue Has No Bone": Fixing the Assamese Language, c 1800–c 1930', *Studies in History*, 24(1): 27–76.

———. 2008. 'Incredible Stories in the Time of Credible Histories: Colonial Assam and Translations of Vernacular Geographics', in Raziuddin Aquil and Partha Chatterjee (eds.), *History in the Vernacular*, 287–321. Ranikhet: Permanent Black.

Kar, Parimal Chandra. 1990. 'Outline of Akhing Polity among the Garo of Meghalaya', in Jayanta Sarkar and B. Datta Ray (eds.), *Social and Political Institutions of the Hill People of North-East India*, 42–57. Calcutta: Anthropological Survey of India, Government of India.

Kar, Subir. 2000. *Mahabidroher Drohagatha: Jongiyar Gan*. Silchar: Assam University Press.

Karim, Abdul. 1992. *Corpus of the Arabic and Persian Inscriptions of Bengal*. Dhaka, Bangladesh: Asiatic Society of Bangladesh.

Karlekar, Malavika. 1996. 'Reflections on Kulin Polygamy—Nistarini Debi's *Sekeley Katha*', in Patricia Uberoi (ed.), *Social Reform, Sexuality and the State*, 135–55. New Delhi: Sage.

Karmay, Samten G. and Y. Nagano. 2003. *Survey of Bonpo Monasteries and Temples in Tibet and the Himalaya*. Osaka: National Museum of Ethnology.

Karmay, Samten G. and Jeff Watt (eds.). 2007. *Bon: The Magic Word. The Indigenous Religions of Tibet*. New York: Rubin Museum and London: Philip Wilson.

Karmi, Madhabchandra Chakma (comp.). 1997 [1940]. *Rajnama: Chakma Rajanyabarger Itibritta.* Agartala: Upajati Gavesana Kendra, Government of Tripura.

Karotemprel, S. 1994. *Impact of Christianity on the Tribes of Northeast India.* Shillong: Sacred Heart Theological College.

Karotemprel, Sebastian and Dipali Danda. 1984. *The Tribes of Northeast India.* Calcutta: Firma KLM.

Karotemprel, S. (ed.). 1998. *The Tribes of Northeast India.* Shillong: Vendrame Institute.

Kasturi, Malavika. 2009. '"Asceticising" Monastic Families: Ascetic Genealogies, Property Feuds and Anglo-Hindu Law in Late Colonial India', *Modern Asian Studies*, 43(5): 1039–83.

Katz, Nathan and Ellen S. Goldberg. 2004 [1995]. 'The Ritual Enactments of Indian-Jewish Identity of the Cochin Jews', in Katz (ed.), *Studies of Indian Jewish Identity*, 15–51. Delhi: Manohar.

Keyes, Charles F. 1984. 'Mother or Mistress but Never a Monk: Buddhist Notions of Female Gender in Rural Thailand', *American Ethnologist*, 11(2): 223–41.

Khan, Abdul Mabud. 1999. *The Maghs: A Buddhist Community in Bangladesh.* Dhaka: University Press.

Khiangte, Laltluangliana (ed.). 2002. *Mizo Songs and Folk Tales.* Delhi: Sahitya Akademi.

Kim, Jinah. 2010a. 'A Book of Buddhist Goddesses', *Artibus Asiae*, 70(2): 259–329.

———. 2010b. 'Unfinished Business: Buddhist Reuse of Angkor Vat and Its Historical and Political Significance', *Artibus Asiae*, 70(1): 77–122.

Kirkpatrick, William. 1969 [1811]. *An Account of the Kingdom of Nepaul, Being the Substance of Observations Made during a Mission to That Country in the Year 1793.* New Delhi: Manjusri Publishing House.

Kirsch, Thomas A. 1996. 'Buddhism, Sex Roles, and the Thai Economy' in Penny Van Esterik (ed.) *Women of Southeast Asia*, 13–32. De Kalb: Northern Illinois University Center for Southeast Asian Studies.

Klein, Anne Carolyn. 1995. *Meeting the Great Bliss Queen: Buddhists, Feminists and the Art of the Self.* Boston: Beacon.

Kolsky, Elizabeth. 2010. *Colonial Justice in British India: White Violence and the Rule of Law.* Cambridge: Cambridge University Press.

Krishnamala of Dvija Ramaganga (ed. Sahadev Bikramkishor Deb Barman and Jagadish Gana-Choudhuri). 1995. Agartala: Uttam Chakrabarti.

Kulke, Hermann (ed.). 1995. *The State in India 1000–1700.* Delhi: Oxford University Press.

———. 2001 [1993]. *Kings and Cults: State Formation and Legitimation in India and Southeast Asia.* Delhi: Manohar.

Kumar, Dharma, Tapan Raychaudhuri, Irfan Habib, and Meghnad Desai (eds.) 1982–3. *The Cambridge Economic History of India, vol. 2.* Cambridge: Cambridge University Press.

Kvaerne, Per. 1975 [1958]. *Oracles and Demons of Tibet: The Cult and Iconography of the Tibetan Protective Deities.* Graz, Austria: Akademische Druck-u Verlagsanstalt.

———. 1985. *Tibet Bon Religion: A Death Ritual of Tibetan Bonpo.* Leiden: E.J. Brill.

———. 2010 [1977]. *An Anthology of Buddhist Tantric Songs: A Study of the Caryāgīti.* Bangkok: Orchid Press.

Kyles, David. 1944. *Lorrain of the Lushais: Romance and Realism on the North-east of India.* London.

Lahiri, Nayanjot. 1991. *Pre-Ahom Assam: Studies in the Inscriptions of Assam between the Fifth and the Thirteenth Centuries AD.* New Delhi: Munshiram Manoharlal.

———. 2011. 'Settlements and Economy', in Nandini Sinha Kapur (ed.), *Environmental History of Early India: A Reader,* 216–421. New Delhi: Oxford University Press.

Laidlaw, James. 2010. 'Ethical Traditions in Question: Diaspora Jainism and the Environmental and Animal Liberation Movements', in Anand Pandian and Daud Ali (eds.), *Ethical Life in South Asia,* 61–82. Bloomington: Indiana University Press.

Lalrimawia. 1995. *Mizoram: History and Cultural Identity, 1890–1947.* Gauhati: Spectrum Publications.

Lalthlengliana, C. 2004. *The Lushai Hills: Annexation, Resistance and Pacification (1886–1898).* Gauhati: Spectrum Publications.

La Touche, T.H.D. (ed.). 1910. 'The Journals of Major James Rennell, First Surveyor–General, Written for the Information of the Governors of Bengal during His Surveys of the Ganges and Brahmaputra Rivers 1764–1767', *Memoirs of the Asiatic Society of Bengal,* 3. Calcutta.

Laufer, Berthold. 1930. 'A Chinese–Hebrew Manuscript: A New Source for the History of the Chinese Jews', *American Journal of Semitic Languages and Literature,* 46(3): 189–97.

Lees, W. Nassau. 1867. *Another Word on Tea Cultivation in Eastern Bengal.* Calcutta.

Lefebvre, Henri (trans. from French by Donald Nicholson Smith). 1991. *The Production of Space.* Cambridge, Mass.: Blackwell.

Leider, Jacques P. 2002. 'Arakan's Ascent during the Mrauk U Period', in Sunait Chutintaranond and Chris Baker (eds.), *Recalling Local Pasts: Autonomous History in Southeast Asia,* 53–87. Chiang Mai, Thailand: Silkworm Books.

Leider, Jacques P. 2005/6. 'Specialists for Ritual, Magic and Devotion: The Court Brahmins (Punna) of the Konbaung Kings (1772–1885),' *Journal of Burma Studies*, 10: 159–202.

———. 2008. 'Forging Buddhist Credentials as a Tool of Legitimacy and Ethnic Identity: A Study of Arakan's Subjection in Nineteenth-Century Burma', *JESHO*, 51: 409–59.

———. 2009. 'Relics, Statues and Predictions: Interpreting an Apocryphal Sermon of the Lord Buddha in Arakan', *Asian Ethnology*, 68(2): 333–64.

Leoshko, Janice. 2003. *Sacred Traces: British Explorations of Buddhism in South Asia*. Aldershot: Ashgate.

Levine, Nancy E. 1987. 'Fathers and Sons: Kinship Values and Validation in Tibetan Polyandry', *Man*, NS, 22(2): 267–86.

———. 1988. *The Dynamics of Polyandry*. Chicago: University of Chicago Press.

Levy, Robert I. 1987. 'How the Navadurga Protect Bhaktapur: The Effective Meanings of a Symbolic Enactment', in N. Gutschow and A. Michaels (eds.), *Heritage of the Kathmandu Valley: Proceedings of an International Conference in Lubeck June 1985*, 105–34. Sankt Augustin: VGH-Wissenschaftsverlag.

Lewin, Thomas H. 2005 [1884, 2nd ed. 1912]. *A Fly on the Wheel or How I Helped to Govern India*. Aizawl, Mizoram: Synod Publication Board.

———. 1996 [1869]. *The Hill Tracts of Chittagong and the Dwellers Therein*. Rangamati: Sthaniya Sarakara Parishada.

Lhuna, John V. 1992. *Education and Missionaries in Mizoram*. Gauhati: Spectrum Publications.

Lieberman, Victor. 2003-2009. *Strange Parallels: Southeast Asia in Global Context, c 800–1830*, 2 vols. Cambridge: Cambridge University Press.

———. 2010. 'Review of James C. Scott, *The Art of Not Being Governed*: A Zone of Refuge in Southeast Asia? Reconceptualising Interior Spaces', *Journal of Global History*, 5: 333–46.

———. 2011. 'Response to Comments on *Strange Parallels*', *JAS*, 70(4): 999–1006.

Lindholm, Charles. 1985. 'Review of H.L. Deb Roy, *A Tribe in Transition*', *JAS*, 44(3): 634–5.

Lindsay, Robert. 1849. 'An Indian Life', in Lord Lindsay, *Lives of the Lindsays or a Memoir of houses of Crawfurd and Balcarres*, vol. 3. London: J. Murray.

Linrothe, Rob. 1999. *Ruthless Compassion: Wrathful Deities in Early Indo-Tibetan Esoteric Buddhist Art*. London: Serindia Publications.

Lloyd, J. Meirion. 1991. *History of the Church in Mizoram (Harvest in the Hills)*. Aizawl, Mizoram: Synod Publication Board.

Locke, John Kerr. 1985. *Buddhist Monasteries of Nepal: A Survey of the Bahas and Bahis of the Kathmandu Valley*. Kathmandu: Sahayogi Press.

Logan, Lisa. 1998. *American Literature*, 70(2): 398–9.

Longkumer, Arkotong. 2010. *Reform, Identity and Narratives of Belonging: The Heraka Movement of Northeast India*. New York: Continuum International.

Loos, Tamara. 2009. 'Transnational Histories of Sexualities in Asia', *AHR*, 114(5): 1309–24.

Lopez, Donald S., Jr. (ed). 1993 [1990]. *Buddhist Hermeneutics*. Delhi: Motilal Banarsidass.

———. 1995a. 'Authority and Orality in the Mahayan', *Numen* 42(1): 21–47.

———. 1995b. 'Foreigner at the Lama's Feet', in Lopez (ed.), *Curators of the Buddha*, 251–95. Chicago: University of Chicago Press.

Lorrain, James Herbert. 1908. *Aro Ishor-ke Doying-e (The Story of the True God in the Abor-Miri Language)*. Calcutta: American Baptist Missionary Union and Calcutta Christian Tract and Book Society.

Lorrain, James Herbert and Fred W. Savidge. 1898. *A Grammar and Dictionary of the Lushai Language*. Shillong: Assam Secretariat.

Lorrain, Reginald A. 1951. *Grammar and Dictionary of the Lakher or Mara Language*. Gauhati: DHAS.

———. 1988 [1912]. *Five Years in Unknown Jungles for God and Empire*. Gauhati: Spectrum Publications.

Luard, C.E. (trans. and ed.). 1926. *Travels of Fray Sebastien Manrique 1629–1643*. Oxford: Oxford University Press.

Luczanits, Christian. 2004. *Buddhist Sculpture in Clay: Early Western Himalayan Art Late 10th to Early 13th Centuries*. Chicago: Serindia Publications.

———. 2011a. 'Gandhara and Its Art', in *The Buddhist Heritage of Pakistan: Art of Gandhara*, 13–24. Asia Society Museum Catalogue. New York: Asia Society.

———. 2011b. 'Art and Architecture', in *The Buddhist Heritage of Pakistan: Art of Gandhara*, 73–83. Asia Society Museum Catalogue. New York: Asia Society.

Ludden, David (ed.). 2001. *Reading Subaltern Studies: Critical History, Contested Meaning and the Globalisation of South Asia*. Delhi: Permanent Black.

———. 2003. *Where Is Assam? Using Geographical History to Locate Current Social Realities*. Gauhati: CNEISSEAS.

Mabie, H.C. 1901. 'Beginning of the Work in Assam and the Early Missionaries', *Baptist Missionary Magazine*, 81(6): 207–8.

Macdonald, Alexander and Anne Vergati Stahl. 1979. *Newar Art: Nepalese Art during the Malla Period*. Warminster: Aris and Phillips.

Macneil, Denise, 2005. 'Mary Rowlandson and the Foundational Mythology of the American Frontier Hero', *Women's Studies*, 34(8): 625–53.

MacWilliams, Mark W. 2000. 'The Holy Man's Hut as a Symbol of Stability in Japanese Buddhist Pilgrimage', *Numen*, 47(4): 387–416.

Mahanta, Mohan Chandra. 1936. 'Vaisnavism in Kamrup', *JARS*, 4 (1936): 123–8.

Majumdar, Dhirendra Nath. 1962. *Himalayan Polyandry: Strucure, Functioning and Cultural Change: A Field Study of Jaunsar-Bawar*. Bombay: Asia Publishing House.

———— and Madhab C. Goswami. 1972. *Social Institutions of the Garo of Meghalaya: An Analytical Study*. Calcutta: Nababharat.

———— and Tarun C. Sharma. 1980. *Eastern Himalayas: A Study of Anthropology and Tribalism (Essays Presented in Honor of M.C. Goswami)*. New Delhi: Cosmo.

Majumdar, Rochona. 2009. *Marriage and Modernity: Family Values in Colonial Bengal*. Durham: Duke University Press.

Makley, Charlene E. 2007. *The Violence of Liberation: Gender and Tibetan Buddhist Revival in Post-Mao China*. Berkeley: University of California Press.

Malcolm, Rev. Howard. 1839. *Travels in South-Eastern Asia Embracing Hindustan, Malaya, Siam and China, with Notices of Numerous Missionary Stations and a Full Account of the Burman Empire*. London.

Marez, Curtis. 2001. 'Signifying Spain, Becoming Comanche, Making Mexicans: Indian Captivity and the History of Chicana/o Popular Performance', *American Quarterly*, 53(2): 267–307.

Martin, Dan. 1994. *Mandala Cosmogony: Human Body, Good Thought and Revelation of Secret Mother Tantras of Bon*. Weisbaden: Harrassowitz.

————. 1999. 'Ol Mo-lung-ring, the Original Holy Place', in Toni Huber (ed.), *Sacred Spaces and Powerful Places in Tibetan Culture: A Collection of Essays*, 158–301. Dharamsala: Library of Tibetan Works.

————. 2007. 'Olmo Lungring: A Holy Place Here and Beyond', in Samten G. Karmay and Jeff Watt (eds.), *Bon: The Magic Word. The Indigenous Religions of Tibet*, 99–123. New York: Rubin Museum, and London: Philip Wilson.

Marx, Karl. 1955 [1847] (trans. from the German). *The Poverty of Philosophy: Answer to the "Philosophy of Poverty" by M. Proudhon*. Moscow: Progress Publishers.

Maung Maung, U. 1990. *Burmese Nationalist Movements*. Honolulu: University of Hawai'i Press.

M'Cosh, John. 1837. *Topography of Assam.* Calcutta: Bengal Military Orphan Press.

McCutcheon, R.T. 2007. 'Words, Words, Words', *JAAR*, 75(4): 958–87.

McKay, Alex. 2007a. 'Fit for the Frontier: European Understandings of the Tibetan Environment in the Colonial Era', *New Zealand Journal of Asian Studies*, 9(1): 118–32.

———. 2007b. *Their Footprints Remain: Biomedical Beginnings across the Indo-Tibetan Frontier.* Amsterdam: Amsterdam University Press.

Mckeown, Arthur Philip. 2010. 'From Bodhgaya to Lhasa to Beijing: The Life and Times of Sariputra (c 1335–1426), Last Abbot of Bodhgaya'. Ph.D. dissertation, Harvard University.

McLane, John R. 1993. *Land and Local Kingship in Eighteenth-Century Bengal.* Cambridge: Cambridge University Press.

Medhi, Birinchi K., R.P. Athparia, and S.V.D. K. Jose (eds.). 2009. *Tribes of North-East India: Issues and Challenges.* New Delhi: Omsons Publications.

Medhi, K.R. 1941. 'Late Rai Bahadur K. L. Barua, C.I.E.', *JARS*, NS, 8(1): 7–8.

Mevissen, Gerd J.R. and Arundhati Banerji (eds.). 2009. *Prajnadhara: Asian Art, History, Epigraphy and Culture in Honour of Gouriswar Bhattacharya.* 2 vols. New Delhi: Kaveri Books.

Mey, Wolfgang (ed.). 2009 *J. P. Mills and the Chittagong Hill Tracts 1926/27: Tour Diary, Reports, Photographs.* http://archive.ub.uni-heidelberg.de/savifadok/volltexte/2009/548/, accessed 20/10/2011.

Meyer, Johann Jakob. 1989 [1971]. *Sexual Life in Ancient India: A Study in the Comparative History of Indian Culture.* Delhi: Motilal Banarsidass.

Michaud, Jean. 2009. 'Handling the Mountain Minorities in China, Vietnam and Laos: From History to Current Concerns', *Asian Ethnicity*, 10(1): 25–49.

Miller, Beatrice D. 1961. 'The Web of Tibetan Monasticism', *JAS*, 20(2): 197–203.

———. 1993. 'Is There Tibetan Culture(s) Without Buddhism?', in Charles Ramble, Gerard Toffin, Beatrice Miller, and M. Brauen (eds.), *Anthropology of Tibet and the Himalaya*, 222–8. Zurich: Ethnological Museum of the University of Zurich.

Miller, Robert James. 1959. *Monasteries and Cultural Change in Inner Mongolia.* Wiesbaden: Otto Harrassowitz.

———. 1961. 'Buddhist Monastic Economy: The Jisa Mechanism', *CSSH*, 3(4): 427–38.

Mills, J.P. 1933. 'Assam as a Field of Research', *JARS*, 1(1): 3–6.

Mills, Martin. 2000. 'Vajra Brother, Vajra Sister: Renunciation, Individuation and the Household in Tibetan Buddhist Monasticism', *Journal of Royal Anthropological Institute*, 6(1): 17–34.

Mishra, Nihar Ranjan. 2004. *Kamakhya: A Socio-Cultural Study.* New Delhi: D.K. Printworld.

Misra, Nalini Kumar. 1935. 'Was Rudra Singha Illiterate?', *JARS*, 2(4): 97–100.

Misra, Sanghamitra. 2010. *Becoming Borderland: The Politics of Space and Identity in Colonial North-Eastern India.* Delhi: RoutledgeIndia.

Mitchiner, Michael. 2000. *Land of Water: Coinage and History of Bangladesh and Later Arakan c 300 BC to the Present Day.* London: Hawkins.

Mitra, Debala. 1976. 'Antiquities of Pilak and Jolaibari, Tripura', *JASB*, 18 (1–4): 56–77.

———— (ed.). 1996. *Explorations in Art and Archaeology of South Asia: Essays Dedicated to Nanigopal Majumdar.* Kolkata: Directorate of Archaeology and Museums and Government of West Bengal.

Mohammed, Jigar. 2002. *Revenue-Free Land Grants in Mughal India, Awadh Region in the Seventeenth and Eighteenth Centuries (1658–1765).* Delhi: Manohar.

————. 2005. 'Mughal Sources on Medieval Ladakh', in John Bray (ed.), *Ladakhi Histories: Local and Regional Perspectives*, 147–60. Leiden: E.J. Brill.

Montgomery, Benilde. 1994. 'White Captives, African Slaves: A Drama of Abolition', *Eighteenth-Century Studies*, 27(4): 615–30.

Moonshee, Munphool Meer. 1868–9. 'On Gilgit and Chitral', *Proceedings of Royal Geographical Society of London*, 13(2): 130–3.

————. 1870. 'Relations between Gilgit, Chitral and Kashmir', *Journal of Ethnological Society of London*, 2(1): 35–9.

Mornang, Ngawang L. 1990. 'Monastic Organization, and Economy at Dwags-po Bshad-Grb-Gling', in Lawrence Epstein and Richard F. Sherburne (eds.), *Reflections on Tibetan Culture: Essays in Memory of Turrell V. Wylie*, 249–68. Lewiston, N.Y.: E. Mellen Press.

Morris, J.H. 1939. *Thomas Jerman Jones, a Missionary Hero.* Liverpool: English and Foreign Missions of the Presbyterian Church of Wales.

Morrison, Barrie M. 1970. *Political Centers and Cultural Regions in Early Bengal.* Tucson: University of Arizona Press.

————. 1974. *Lalmai: A Cultural Center of Early Bengal. An Archaeological Report and Historical Analysis.* Seattle: University of Washington Press.

Mukherjee, B.N. 1985. 'Epigraphic Sources of Indian Iconography: Some Illustrations from Deopani', in Frederick M. Asher and G.S. Gai (eds.), *Indian Epigraphy: Its Bearing on the History of Art*, 169–74. Oxford: Oxford University Press.

Mukherji, Ramaranjan and Sachindra Kumar Maity. 1967. *Corpus of Bengal Inscriptions.* Calcutta: Firma KLM.

Mukhopadhyaya, Sitaram. 1975. *Rajarshi Bhagyachandra*. Birbhum: Mukharji Book Supply.

Mullard, Saul. 2011. *Opening the Hidden Land: State Formation and the Construction of Sikkimese History*. Leiden: E.J. Brill.

Munshi, Jayanatha (ed. by Viswanath Das). 1985. *Rajopakhyana*. Calcutta: Firma KLM.

Murphy, Lt. 1832. 'Account of the Cossyah and of a Convalescent Depot Established in Their Country 280 Miles Northeast from Calcutta', *Journal of Royal Geographical Society of London*, 2: 93–8.

Myint, Ni Ni. 1983. *Burma's Struggle against Imperialism 1885–1895*. Rangoon: Universities Press.

Myint-U, Than. 2002. *The Making of Modern Burma*. Cambridge: Cambridge University Press.

Nakane, Chie. 1961. *Garo and Khasi: A Comparative Study in Matrilineal Systems*. The Hague: Mouton.

Nandy, Ashis. 1995. 'History's Forgotten Doubles', *History and Theory*, 34(2): 44–66.

Narayan, Rochisha. 2011. 'Caste, Family and Politics in Northern India during the Eighteenth and Nineteenth Centuries', Ph.D. dissertation, Rutgers University.

Nath, R.M. 1937. 'Notes on Certain Words of the Nidhanpur Copper-plate', *JARS*, 4(4): 99–100.

Nath, R.M. and R.D. Vidyavinode. 1938. 'Dates of the Bhatera Copper-plates', *JARS*, 5(4): 94–101.

Nebesky-Wojkowitz, Rene de (trans. from French by Michael Bullock). 1956. *Where the Gods Are Mountains: Three Years among the People of the Himalayas*. New York: Reynal.

Neelis, Jason. 2011. *Early Buddhist Transmission and Trade Networks: Mobility and Exchange Within and Beyond the Northwestern Borderlands of South Asia*. Leiden: Brill.

Neog, Maheswar. 1966. 'Professor Dr. Suryya Kumar Bhuyan: A Life Sketch', in Neog and H.K. Barpujari (eds.), *Professor Suryya Kumar Bhuyan Commemoration Volume*, 1–9. Gauhati: All-India Oriental Conference.

———. 1998 [1965]. *Sankaradeva and His Times: Early History of the Vaisnava Faith and Movement in Assam*. Gauhati: Lawyer's Book Stall.

Neog, Maheswar and H.K. Barpujari (eds.). 1966. *Professor Suryya Kumar Bhuyan Comemoration Volume*. Gauhati: All-India Oriental Conference.

Nietupski, Paul Kocot. 2011. *Labrang Monastery: A Tibetan Buddhist Community on the Inner Asian Borderlands, 1709–1958*. Lanham, Md.: Lexington Books.

Niyogi, Puspa. 1980. *Buddhism in Ancient Bengal*. With Foreword by Giuseppe Tucci. Calcutta: Jijnasa.

Nongbri, Tiplut. 2008. *Gender, Matriliny and Enterpreneurship: The Khasis of North-east India*. Delhi: Zubaan.

Novetzke, Christian Lee. 2008. *Religion and Public Memory: A Cultural History of Saint Namdev in India*. New York: Columbia University Press.

O'Hanlon, Rosalind. 2010. 'The Social Worth of Scribes: Brahmins, Kayasthas and the Social Order in Early Modern India', *IESHR*, 47(4): 563–96.

Olschak, Blanche C. 1979. *Ancient Bhutan: A Study on Early Buddhism in the Himalayas*. Zurich: Swiss Foundation for Alpine Research.

Orr, Leslie C. 2000. *Donors, Devotees and Daughters of God: Temple Women in Medieval Tamil Nadu*. New York: Oxford University Press.

———. 2005. 'Identity and Divinity: Boundary-Crossing Goddesses in Medieval South India', *JAAR*, 73(1): 9–43.

Ostrowski, Donald. 1998. 'The "tamma" and the Dual-Administrative Structure of the Mongol Empire', *BSOAS*, 61(2): 262–77, http://www.jstor.org/stable/3107652, accessed 10 June 2009.

Overmyer, Daniel L. 1982. 'The White Cloud Sect in Sung and Yuan China', *Harvard Journal of Asiatic Studies*, 42(2): 615–42.

Pain, Adam and Deki Pema. 2004. 'The Matrilineal Inheritance of Land in Bhutan', *Contemporary South Asia*, 13(4): 421–35.

Palit, Projit. 2004. *History of Religion in Tripura*. New Delhi: Kaveri Books.

Palsetia, Jesse. 2006. 'Parsi and Hindu Traditional and Non-Traditional Responses to Christian Conversion in Bombay, 1839–1845', *JAAR*, 74(3): 615–45.

Pande, Anupa (ed.). 2009. *The Art of Central Asia and the Indian Subcontinent in Cross-Cultural Perspective*. New Delhi: National Museum and Aryan Books International.

Pantha, R. (ed.). 2004. *Buddhism and Culture of Northeast India*. Nalanda: Nava Nalanda Mahavihara.

Papa-Kalantari, Christiane. 2007. 'The Art of the Court: Some Remarks on the Historical Stratigraphy of Eastern Iranian Elelments in Early Buddhist Painting of Alchi, Ladakh', in D. Klimburg-Slater, K. Tropper, and C. Jahoda (eds.), *Text, Image and Song in Transdisciplinary Dialogue*, 167–228. Leiden: E.J. Brill.

Parratt, Saroj Nalini Arambam. 2005. *The Court Chronicle of the Kings of Manipur: The Cheitharon Kumpapa*, vol. 1. London: Routledge.

Parratt, Saroj N. Arambam and John Parratt. 1997. 'Female Spirit Possession Rituals among the Meiteis of Manipur', paper at annual conference of the British Association for the Study of Religions, Oxford.

Patel, Alka. 2004. 'Architectural Histories Entwined: The Rudra-Mahalaya Congregational Mosque of Siddhpur, Gujarat', *Journal of the Society of Architectural Historians*, 63(2): 144–63.

Pati, Biswamoy (ed.). 2011. *Adivasis in Colonial History*. Delhi: Orient BlackSwan.

Patil, Parimal G. 2009. *Against a Hindu God: Buddhist Philosophy of Religion in India*. New York: Columbia University Press.

Patterson, Orlando. 1982. *Slavery and Social Death: A Comparative Study*. Cambridge: Harvard University Press.

Peletz, Michael. 2006. 'Transgenderism and Gender Pluralism in Southeast Asia since Early Modern Times', *Current Anthropology*, 97(2): 309–40.

Pemberton, R. Boileau. 1865. 'Report on Bootan 1837–38', in A. Eden, *Political Missions to Bootan*. Calcutta: Bengal Secretariat Office.

Petech, Luciano. 1984. *Medieval History of Nepal 750–1482*. 2nd ed. Rome: Istituto Italiano per il Medio ed Estreme Oriente

Peter, Prince of Denmark. 1955. 'Polyandry and the Kinship Group,' *Man*, 55 (December): 179–81.

Pinch, William. 1996. *Peasants and Monks in British India*. Oxford: Oxford University Press.

―――. 2006. *Warrior Ascetics and Indian Empires*. Cambridge: Cambridge University Press.

―――. (forthcoming). 'Guru, Master, Commander: Discipleship and Slavery in South Asia, ca. 1500–1850', in Jacob Copeman and Aya Ikegama (eds.), *The Guru*. London: Routledge.

Pines, Shlomo and Tuvia Gelblum. 1989. 'Al-Biruni's Arabic Version of Patanjali's Yogasutra: A Translation of the 4th Chapter and a Comparison with Related Texts', *BSOAS*, 52(2): 265–305.

Pirie, Fernanda. 2006. 'Secular Morality, Village Law and Buddhism in Tibetan Societies', *Journal of the Royal Anthropological Institute*, NS 12: 173–90.

Planta, Joseph. 1776. 'An Account of the Romanish Language, in a Letter to Sir John Pringle', *Philosophical Transactions of the Royal Society of London*, 66: 129–59.

Playfair, Alan. 1909. *The Garos, with an Introduction by Sir J. Bampfylde Fuller*. London: David Nutt.

Pollock, Sheldon. 1985. 'The Theory of Practice and the Practice of Theory in Indian Intellectual History', *JAOS*, 105(3): 499–519.

―――. 2003. *Literary Cultures in History: Reconstructions from South Asia*. Berkeley: University of California Press.

―――. 2006. *The Language of the Gods in the World of Men: Sanskrit, Culture and Power in Premodern India*. Berkeley: University of California Press.

―――. (ed.) 2011. *Forms of Knowledge in Early Modern Asia: Explorations in the Intellectual History of India and Tibet 1500–1800*. Durham: Duke University Press.

Pommaret, Françoise. 1999. 'The Mon-pa Revisited: In Search of Mon', in Toni Huber (ed.), *Sacred Spaces and Powerful Places in Tibetan Culture: A Collection of Essays*, 52–73. Dharamsala: Library of Tibetan Works.

———— (trans. from French by E.B. Booz and Howard Solverson). 2007. *Bhutan: A Himalayan Mountain Kingdom*. New York: Odyssey Books.

Pomplun, Trent. 2010. *Jesuit on the Roof of the World: Ippolito Desideri's Mission to Eighteenth-Century Tibet*. New York: Oxford University Press.

————. 2011. 'Natural Reason and Buddhist Philosophy: The Tibetan Studies of Ippolito Desideri, SJ (1684–1733)', *History of Religions*, 50(4): 384–419.

Poonacha, Veena. 1996. 'Redefining Gender Relationships: The Imprint of the Colonial State on the Coorg/Kodava Norms of Marriage and Sexuality', in Patricia Uberoi (ed.), *Social Reform, Sexuality and the State*, 39–64. New Delhi: Sage.

Powell, Avrill. 1993. *Muslims and Missionaries in Pre-Mutiny India*. Richmond, Surrey: Curzon Press.

Pradhan, Queeny. 2007. 'Empire in the Hills: The Making of Hill Stations in Colonial India', *Studies in History*, 23(1): 33–91.

Pranke, Patrick Arthur. 2004. 'The Treatise on the Lineage of the Elder (Vamsadīpanī): Monastic Reform and the Writing of Buddhist History in Eighteenth Century Burma', Ph.D. dissertation, University of Michigan.

Proctor, Robert and Londa Schiebinger (eds.). 2008. *Agnotology: The Making and Unmaking of Ignorance*. Stanford: Stanford University Press.

Purakayastha, Sudeshna. 2008. 'Restructuring the Past in Early—Twentieth-Century Assam: Historiography and Surya Kumar Bhuyan', in R. Aquil and P. Chatterjee (eds.) *History in the Vermacular*, 172–208. Ranikhet: Permanent Black.

Raha, Manis Kumar. 1989. *Matriliny to Patriliny: A Study of the Rabha Society*. New Delhi: Gian Publishing.

Rahman, Shah Sufi Mostafizur. 2000. *Archeological Investigation in Bogra District (from Early Historic to Early Medieval Period)*. Dhaka: International Centre for Study of Bengal Art.

Rai, Meenakshi. 2006. *Kadampa School in Tibetan Buddhism*. Delhi: Saujanya Publications.

Rajput, A.B. 1963. *The Tribes of Chittagong Hill Tracts*. Karachi: Pakistan Publishers.

Ramble, Charles. 1999. 'Politics of Sacred Space in Bon and Tibetan Popular Tradition', in Toni Huber (ed.), *Sacred Spaces and Powerful Places in Tibetan Culture: A Collection of Essays*, 3–33. Dharamsala: Library of Tibetan Works.

Ramkhe, Reverend M. 1887. *Bamla-Garo Abhidhana [Bangla-Garo Dictionary]*. Tura: American Baptist Missionary Union Garo Mission.

Rangachari, Devika. 2009. *Invisible Women, Visible Histories: Gender, Society and Polity in North India, Seventh to Twelfth Century*. Delhi: Manohar.

Rao, V. Narayan, David Shulman, and Sanjay Subrahmanyam. 2003. *Textures of Time: Writing History in South India*. New York: Other Press.

———. 2007. 'A Pragmatic Response'. *History and Theory*, 46(3): 409–27.

Rao, V. Narayan and Sanjay Subrahmanyam. 2009. 'Notes on Political Thought in Medieval and Early Modern South India', *Modern Asian Studies*, 43(1): 175–210.

Rawlins, John. 1790. '"Of the Manners, Religion and Laws of the Cucis, or Mountaineers of Tippera" Communicated in Persian by John Rawlins', *Asiatick Researches*, 2: 187–93.

Ray, Haraprasad. 2003. *Trade and Trade Routes between India and China, c 140 B.C.–A.D.1500*. Kolkata: Progressive Publishers.

Ray, Himanshu Prabha. 2003. *The Archaeology of Seafaring in Ancient South Asia*. Cambridge: Cambridge University Press.

———. 2007. 'The Stupa: Symbolizing Religious Architecture in Asia, in Ray (ed.), *Sacred Landscapes in Asia: Shared Traditions, Multiple Histories*, 63–80. New Delhi: Manohar.

Reid, Robert. 1944. 'The Excluded Areas of Assam', *Geographical Journal*, 103(1–2): 18–29.

Rennie, David Field. 1970 [1866]. *Bhotan and the Story of the Dooar War*. New Delhi: Manjusri Publishing House.

Reynolds, John Myrdhin. 2005. *The Oral Tradition from Zhang-Zhung*. Kathmandu: Vajra Publications.

Rhodes, Nicholas G. and S.K. Bose. 1999. *The Coinage of Cooch Bihar*. Dhubri: Library of Numismatic Studies.

———. 2002. *The Coinage of Tripura: With Notes on Seals, Orders, Decorations and Medals of the State*. Kolkata: Mira Bose.

———. 2003. *The Coinage of Assam*. Dhubri: Library of Numismatic Studies.

———. 2006. *A History of the Dimasa Kacharis as Seen through Coinage*. Kolkata: Mira Bose.

———. 2010. *The Coinage of Jaintiapur; Within an Account of the Last Days of the Jaintia Raj*. Kolkata: Gauhati.

Rhodes, Nicholas G., K. Gabrisch, Carlo Pontecorvo della Rocchetta Valdettaro. 1989. *The Coinage of Nepal from the Earliest Times until 1911*. London: Royal Numismatic Society.

Richman, Paula. 1992. 'Gender and Persuasion', in José Ignacio Cabezón (ed.), *Buddhism, Sexuality and Gender*, 111–36. Albany: State University of New York Press.

Riebeck, Emil (trans. by A. H. Keane). 1885. *The Chittagong Hill-Tribes: Results of a Journey Made in the Year 1882*. London: Asher.

Rockhill, W.W. 1891. 'Tibet: A Geographical, Ethnographical and Historical Sketch Derived from Chinese Sources', *Journal of the Royal Asiatic Society of Great Britain and Ireland*, vol. 23, n.s. January, 1–133.

Rongmuti, Dewan Singh. 1933. 'A Traditional Account of the Garos', *JARS*, 1(1): 54–60.

Roy, Amal. 2002. 'Nanddirghi-Vihara: A Newly Discovered Buddhist Monastery at Jagajibbanpur, West Bengal', in Gautam Sengupta and Sheena Panja (eds.), *Archaeology of Eastern India: New Perspectives*, 557–95. Kolkata: Center of Archaeological Studies.

Roy, Atul Chandra. 1986. *History of Bengal: Turko-Afghan Period*. Calcutta: Kalyani Publishers.

Roy, Jyotirmoy. 1958. *Manipurer Itihasa*. Imphal: Firma KLM.

Roy, Rammohun. 1822. *Brief Remarks Regarding Modern Encroachments on the Ancient Rights of Females According to the Hindoo Law of Inheritance*. Calcutta: Unitarian Press.

Roy, Suparna. 2007. *Land System and Management in the Colonial Period: A Study of the Barak Valley*. New Delhi: Mittal Publications.

Ruegg, David Seyfort. 1995. 'Review', *Bulletin of School of Oriental and African Studies*, 58(3): 573–7.

———. 2004. 'The Indian and the Indic in Tibetan Cultural History and Tson Kha Pa's Achievements as a Scholar and Thinker', *Journal of Indian Philosophy*, 32: 321–43.

———. 2008. *The Symbiosis of Buddhism with Brahmanism/Hinduism in South Asia and of Buddhism with 'Local Cults' in Tibet and the Himalayan Region*. Vienna: Osterreichische Akademie der Wissenschaften.

Ruppert, Brian D. 2001. 'Sin or Crime? Buddhism, Indebtedness, and the Construction of Social Relations in Early Medieval Japan', *Japan Journal of Religious Studies*, 28(1–2): 31–55.

Russell, James R. 1987. *Zoroastrianism in Armenia*. Cambridge: Harvard University Press.

Saha, S.B. 1990. 'The Chakmas of Tripura', in Jayanta Sarkar and B. Datta Ray (eds.), *Social and Political Institutions of the Hill People of North-East India*, 172–82. Calcutta: Anthropological Survey of India, Government of India.

Sahai, Nandita Prasad. 2007. 'The "Other" Culture: Craft Societies and Widow Remarriage in Early Modern India', *Journal of Women's History*, 19(2): 36–56.

Saikia, Arupjyoti. 2005. *Jungles, Reserves, Wildlife: A History of Forests in Assam*. Gauhati: Wildlife Areas Development and Welfare Trust, Assam.

Saikia, Arupjyoti. 2008a. 'History, Buranjis and Nation: Suryya Kumar Bhuyan's Histories in Twentieth-Century Assam', *IESHR*, 45(4): 473–507.

———. 2008b. 'Gait's Way: Writing History in Early Twentieth-Century Assam', in R. Aquil and P. Chatterjee (eds.) *History in the Vernacular*, 142–171. Ranikhet: Permanent Black.

———. 2010. *Forests and Ecological History of Assam 1826–2000*. New Delhi: Oxford University Press.

Saikia, Yasmin. 2004. *Fragmented Memories: Struggling to be Tai Ahom in India*. Durham: Duke University Press.

Salimallah, Munshi. 1788. *A Narrative of the Transactions in Bengal during the Soobahdaries of Azeem us Shan, translated from the Original Persian by Francis Gladwin*. Calcutta.

Samuel, Geoffrey. 1993. *Civilized Shamans: Buddhism in Tibetan Societies*. Washington, D.C.: Smithsonian Institution Press.

———. 2002. 'Buddhism and the State in Eighth Century Tibet', in Henk Blezer (ed.), *Religion and Secular Culture in Tibet*, 1–20. Leiden: E.J. Brill.

———. 2008. *The Origins of Yoga and Tantra: Indic Religions till the Thirteenth Century*. Cambridge: Cambridge University Press.

Sanderson, Alexis. 2009. 'The Saiva Age: The Rise and Dominance of Saivism during the Early Medieval Period', in Shingo Einoo (ed.), *Genesis and Development of Tantrism*. Tokyo: Institute of Oriental Culture.

———. 2010. 'Influence of Saivism on Pala Buddhism', lecture at University of Toronto, February. http://alexisanderson.com/aboutus. aspx, accessed 2/15/2012.

Sangari, Kumkum and Sudesh Vaid (eds.). 1989. *Recasting Women: Essays in Colonial History*. Delhi: Kali for Women.

Sangkima. 2004. *Essays on the History of the Mizos*. Gauhati: Spectrum Publications.

Sangma, Mihir N. 1993. *Unpublished Documents on Garo Affairs: Sonaram Rongrokgre Sangma vs. King Emperor, In the Matter of Encroachment of Bijni Zamindars on Nazarana Mehals and Lakharaj Lands of the Garos in the Habraghat Pargana etc*. New Delhi: Scholar Publications.

Sardar, Hamid. 2007. 'Danzan Ravjaa: The Fierce Drunken Lord of the Gobi', in Uradyn E. Bulag and Hildegard G.M. Diemberger (eds.), *The Mongolia-Tibet Interface*, 256–92. Leiden: E.J. Brill.

Sarkar, Jadunath. 1973. *The History of Bengal: Muslim Period 1200–1757*. Patna: Academica Asiatica.

Sarkar, Jayanta and B. Datta Ray (eds.). 1990. *Social and Political Institutions of the Hill People of North-East India*. Calcutta: Anthropological Survey of India, Government of India.

Sarkar, Sumit. 1997. 'The Decline of the Subaltern in Subaltern Studies', in Sumit Sarkar, *Writing Social History*, 82–108. Delhi: Oxford University Press.

———. 2003. 'Postmodernism and the Writing of History', in Sumit Sarkar, *Beyond Nationalist Frames*, 154–94. Delhi and Bloomington: Permanent Black and Indiana University Press.

Sarkar, Tanika. 2002. *Hindu Wife, Hindu Nation: Community, Religion and Cultural Nationalism*. Bloomington and Delhi: Indiana University Press and Permanent Black.

Sastri, Bhikshu Silachar. 1981 [1388BS]. *Chattagrame Bauddhadharma*. Chittagong: Nandankanan Bouddhavihara.

Sastri, Hirananda. 1923. 'Nalanda Copperplate of Devapaladeva', *EI*, 17: 310–27.

Schaeffer, Kurtis R. 2003. 'Textual Scholarship, Medical Tradition and Mahayana Buddhist Ideals in Tibet', *Journal of Indian Philosophy*, 31: 621–41.

Schopen, Gregory. 1997. *Bones, Stones, and Buddhist Monks: Collected Papers on the Archaeology, Epigraphy, and Texts of Monastic Buddhism in India*. Honolulu: University of Hawai'i Press.

———. 2005. *Figments and Fragments of Mahayana Buddhism in India: More Collected Papers*. Honolulu: University of Hawai'i Press.

Schram, Louis M.J. 1957. 'The Monguors of Kansu-Tibetan Border: II', in *Transactions of American Philosophical Society*, NS, 47(1): 1–164.

Scott, James C. 2010. *The Art of Not Being Governed*. New Haven: Yale University Press.

Scott, Joan W. 2008. '"Unanswered Questions": Forum on Revisiting "Gender: A Historical Category of Useful Analysis"', *American Historical Review*, 113(5): 1422–9.

Sen, Benoychandra. 1942. *Some Historical Aspects of the Inscriptions of Bengal [Pre-Muhammadan Epochs]*. Calcutta: University of Calcutta.

Sen, Kaliprasanna (ed.). 1927–1930. *SriRajamala*, 4 vols. Agartala: Rajbari.

Sen, Samita. 2004. 'Without His Consent? Marriage and Women's Migration in Colonial India', *International Labor and Working-Class History*, 65: 77–104.

———. 2009. 'Commercial Recruiting and Informal Intermediation: Debate over the Sardari System in Assam Tea Plantations, 1860–1900', *Modern Asian Studies*, 44: 3–28.

Sen, Tansen. 2003. *Buddhism, Diplomacy, and Trade: The Realignment of Sino-Indian Relations 600–1400*. Honolulu: Association for Asian Studies and University of Hawai'i Press.

Sen, Tripur Chandra. 1997 [1960]. *Tripura Deser Katha*. Agartala: Upajati Gavesna Kendra, Government of Tripura.

Sengupta, Anusuya. 1993. *Buddhist Art of Bengal from 3rd c BC to 13th century AD*. New Delhi: Rahul Publishing.

Sengupta, Gautam. 1986. 'Early Sculptures of Tripura', in Jyotibhushan Bhattacharjee (ed.), *Studies in the History of North-East India: Essays in Honour of Professor H. K. Barpujari*, 1–9. Shillong, North-East Hill University Publications.

Shakeb, M.Z.A. (ed.). 1982. *A Descriptive Catalogue of Miscellaneous Persian Mughal Documents from Akbar to Bahadur Shah II*. London: British Library.

Shakespear, J. 1909. 'The Kuki-Lushai Clans', *Journal of the Royal Anthropological Institute of Great Britain and Ireland*, 39 (July–December): 371–85.

———. 1912. *The Lushei Kuki Clans*. London: Macmillan.

Shakespear, L.W. 1914. *History of Upper Assam, Upper Burmah and North-Eastern Frontier*. London: Macmillan.

Shakspo, Nawang Tsering. 1988. *A History of Buddhism in Ladakh* ed. John Bray. Delhi: Ladakhi Buddhist Vihara.

Sharma, D. (ed.) (trans. by P.D. Chowdhury and Padmanath Bhattacharyya.). 1981 [1931]. *Kāmarūpaśāsanāvalī*. Gauhati: Assam Publication Board.

Sharma, Jayeeta. 2009. '"Lazy" Natives, Coolie Labour and the Assam Tea Industry', *Modern Asian Studies*, 43(6): 1287–1324.

———. 2011. *Empire's Garden: Assam and the Making of India*. Durham: Duke University Press.

Shastri, Lobsang. 2002. 'Activities of Indian Panditas in Tibet from the 14th to the 17th Century', in Hank Blezer (ed.), *Tibet, Past and Present*, 129–46. Leiden: E.J. Brill.

Shneiderman, Sara. 2010. 'Are the Central Himalayas in Zomia? Some Scholarly and Political Considerations across Time and Space', *Journal of Global History*, 5: 289–312.

Siddiq, Mohammad Yusuf. 2009. *Historical and Cultural Aspects of the Islamic Inscriptions of Bengal: A Reflective Study of Some New Epigraphic Discoveries*. Dhaka: ICSBA.

Silber, Ilana F. 1993. 'Monasticism and the "Protestant Ethic": Asceticism, Rationality and Wealth in the Medieval West', *British Journal of Sociology*, 44(1): 103–23.

Silk, Jonathan A. 2002. 'What, If Anything, Is Mahayana Buddhism?: Problems of Definition and Classifications', *Numen*, 49(4): 355–405.

———. 2008. *Managing Monks: Administrators and Administrative Roles in Indian Buddhist Monasticism*. New York: Oxford University Press.

Simha, Vrajagopal. 1916 [1326 Tripurabda]. *Monipuri O Kukibhashar Shikkhar Sahaja Upaya*. Koilashahar, Tripura: Published by Author.

Sims-Williams, Nicholas. 2000. *Bactrian Documents from Northern Afghanistan I: Legal and Economic Documents.* Oxford: Nour Foundation and Oxford University Press.

Singh, Daman. 2007. 'The New Land Use Policy: People and Forests in Mizoram', in Mahesh Rangarajan (ed.), *Environmental Issues in India: A Reader*, 298–315. Delhi: Pearson Longman.

Singh, Jyotsna G. 1999. *William and Mary Quarterly*, 3rd series, 56(2): 442–4.

Singh, L. Birmangal and Pannalal Ray. 2007. *Itihasera Aloke Tripura-Manipur.* Agartala and Kolkata: Akshar Publications.

Singh, L.P. 2002. 'Polyandry in Himachal Pradesh: A Socio-Cultural Analysis and Reflection', in Laxman S. Thakur (ed.), *Where Mortals and Mountain Gods Meet: Society and Culture in Himachal Pradesh*, 165–74. Shimla: IAAS.

Singh, M. Kirti. 1980. *Religious Developments in Manipur in the Eighteenth and Nineteenth Centuries.* Imphal: Manipur State Kala Akademi.

———. 1998. *Recent Researches in Oriental and Indological Studies (Including Meitology).* Delhi: Parimal Publications.

Singh, Sarva Daman. 1978. *Polyandry in Ancient India.* Delhi: Vikas.

Singha, Kailasachandra. 1984 [1896]. *Rajamala Ba Tripurar Itibritta.* 2nd ed. Agartala, Tripura.

Sinha, M. 1995. *Colonial Masculinity: the 'Manly Englishman' and the 'Effeminate Bengali' in the Late Nineteenth Century.* Manchester NY: Manchester University Press.

———. 2006. *Specters of Mother India: the Global Restructuring of an Empire.* Durham: Duke University Press.

Sinha, Nirmalchandra. 2008. *A Tibetologist in Sikkim: Remembering Professor Nirmal C. Sinha.* Gangtok: Namgyal Institute of Tibet.

Sinha, Surajit. 1982. *Tribes and Indian Civilization.* Varanasi: N.K. Bose Memorial Foundation.

——— (ed.). 1987. *Tribal Polities and State Systems in Pre-colonial Eastern and North-Eastern India.* Kolkata: K.P. Bagchi and Center for Studies in Social Sciences.

Sircar, Dinesh Chandra. 1967. 'The Tara of Candradvipa', in Sircar (ed.), *The Sakti Cult*, 128–33. Calcutta: University of Calcutta Press.

———. 1969. *Landlordism and Tenancy in Ancient and Medieval India as Revealed by Epigraphical Records.* Lucknow: University of Lucknow.

———. 1971. *Studies in the Geography of Ancient and Medieval India.* Delhi: Motilal Banarsidass.

———. 1973. *Epigraphic Discoveries in East Pakistan.* Calcutta: Asiatic Society.

———. 1979. *Some Epigraphical Records of the Medieval Period.* New Delhi: Abhinav.

———. 1983. *Select Inscriptions Bearing on Indian History and Civilization from the Sixth to the Eighteenth Century A.D. Vol. II.* Delhi: Motilal Banarsidass.

Sivaramakrishnan, K. 1999. *Modern Forests: Statemaking and Environmental Change in Colonial Eastern India*. California: Stanford University Press.

Skaria, Ajay. 1999. *Hybrid Histories: Forests, Frontiers and Wildness in Western India*. Oxford: Oxford University Press.

Smith, E. Gene (ed. Kurtis R. Schaeffer). 2001. *Among Tibetan Texts: History and Literature of the Himalayan Plateau*. Boston: Wisdom Publishers.

Smith, Frederick M. 2006. *The Self Possessed: Deity and Spirit Possession in South Asian Literature and Civilization*. New York: Columbia University Press.

Sneath, David. 2007. 'Ritual Idioms and Spatial Orders: Comparing the Rites for Mongolian and Tibetan Local Deities', in Uradyn E. Bulag and Hildegard G.M. Diemberger (eds.), *The Mongolia-Tibet Interface: Opening New Research Terrains in Inner Asia*, 136–58. Leiden: E.J. Brill.

Snellgrove, David. 1967. *The Nine Ways of Bon*. London: Oxford University Press.

Socolow, Susan Migden. 1992. 'Spanish Captives in Indian Societies: Cultural Contact along the Argentine Frontier, 1600–1835', *Hispanic American Historical Review*, 72(1): 73–99.

Sperling, Elliot. 2011. 'The Tangut/Mi Nyag Element in the Lineage of the Sikkim Chos rGyal', in Anna Balikci-Denjongpa and Alex McKay (eds.) *Buddhist Himalaya: Studies in Religion, History and Culture. Volume II: The Sikkim Papers*, 43–51. Gangtok: Nangyal Institute of Tibetology.

Spivak, Gayatri Chakravorty. 1999. *A Critique of Postcolonial Reason: Toward a History of the Vanishing Present*. Cambridge: Harvard University Press.

Srenimala of Ujir Durgamani (ed. Bikramkishor Debbarman and Jagadish Gana Choudhuri). 1996. Agartala: Tripura Rajya Upojati Sanskritik Gobeshona Kendra.

Sreenivasan, Ramya. 2007. *The Many Lives of a Rajput Queen: Heroic Pasts in India c. 1500–1900*. Ranikhet: Permanent Black.

Srinivas, Mytheli. 2008. *Wives, Widows and Concubines: The Conjugal Family Ideal in Colonial India*. Bloomington: Indiana University Press.

Srivastava, K.P. (ed.). 1974. *Mughal Farmans 1540–1706*. Lucknow: Uttar Pradesh State Archives.

Stein, Rolf. 2010. *Rolf Stein's Tibetica Antiqua* (trans. and ed. Arthur P. Mckeown). Leiden: E.J. Brill.

Stewart, Gordon T. 2009. *Journeys to Empire: Enlightenment, Imperialism and the British Encounter with Tibet 1774–1904*. Cambridge: Cambridge University Press.

Stewart, John and Tayshoo Lama. 1777. 'An Account of the Kingdom of Thibet, in a Letter from John Stewart Esq, FRS, to Sir John Fryer, Bart., P.R.S.' *Philosophical Transactions of the Royal Philosophical Transactions of the Royal Society of London*, 67: 465–92.

Stewart, Tony K. 2004. *Fabulous Females and Peerless Pirs: Tales of Mad Adventures in Old Bengal*. New York: Oxford University Press.

Stewart, Tony K. 2010. *The Final Word: The Caitanya Caritamrta and the Grammar of Religious Tradition*. New York: Oxford Univesity Press.

————. 2011. 'Replicating Vaisnava Worlds: Organising Devotional Space through the Architectonics of the Mandala', *South Asian History and Culture*, 2(2): 300–36.

Studdert-Kennedy, Gerald. 2005. 'Evangelical Mission and the Railway Workshop Apprentices: Institutionalising Christian Presence in Imperial Bengal, 1885–1914', *Journal of Imperial and Commonwealth History*, 33 (September): 325–48.

Suan, H. Khan Kham. 2011. 'Rethinking "Tribe" Identities: The Politics of Recognition among the Zo in the North-East', *Contributions to Indian Sociology*, 45(2): 157–87.

Swearer, Donald K., Sommai Premchit, and Phaithoon Dokbuakaew. 2004. *Sacred Mountains of Northern Thailand and Their Legends*. Chiang Mai: Silkworm Books.

Symes, Michael. 1800. *An Account of an Embassy to the Kingdom of Ava: Sent by the Governor-General of India in the year 1795*, vols. 1–2. London: J. Debrett.

Takeuchi, Tsuguhito. 2003. 'Military Administration and Military Duties in Tibetan-Ruled Central Asia (8th–9th century)', in Alex McKay (ed.), *Tibet and Her Neighbours: A History*, 43–55. London: Hansjorg Mayer.

————. 2004. 'The Tibetan Military System and Its Activities from Khotan to Lop-Nor', in Susan Whitfield and Ursula Sims-Williams (eds.), *The Silk Road: Trade, Travel, War and Faith*, 50–6. Chicago and London: Serindia Publications and British Library.

Tambe, Ashwini. 2000. 'Colluding Patriarchies: The Colonial Reform of Sexual Relations in India', *Feminist Studies*, 26(3): 586–600.

Tamuli, Laxminath (ed.). 2005 [c.1904]. *Naobaisha Phukanar Asom Buranji*. Gauhati: Publication Board.

Tamuli Phukan, Kasinath (comp; ed. Pratapchandra Chaudhuri). 1991 [1844]. *Asom Buranji Sara*. Gauhati: DHAS.

Taranatha's History of Buddhism in India (trans. from Tibetan by Lama Champa and Alaka Chattopadhyaya and ed. Debiprasad Chattopadhyaya). 1970. Simla: IAAS.

Tautscher, Gabrielle. 2007. *Himalayan Mountain Cults*. Kathmandu: Vajra Publications.

Taylor's Maps of Tea Districts of Darjeeling, Terai, Jalpaiguri, Dooars, Darrang, Golaghat, and Complete Index to All Tea Gardens. 1910. Calcutta: Thacker Spink.

Teltscher, Kate. 2006. *The High Road to China: George Bogle, the Panchen Lama and the First British Expedition to Tibet*. New York: Farrar, Straus and Giroux.

Templeman, David. 1999. 'Internal and External Geography in Spiritual Biography', in Toni Huber (ed.), *Sacred Spaces and Powerful Places in Tibetan Culture: A Collection of Essays*, 187–97. Dharamsala, Library of Tibetan Works.

———. 2002. 'Iranian Themes in Tibetan Tantric Culture: The Dakini', in Henk Blezer (ed.), *Religion and Secular Culture in Tibet*, 113–28. Leiden: E.J. Brill.

Thanzauva, K. (ed.). 1997. *Statistics of the Churches in Khasia, Jaintia, Sylhet, Kachar and Lushai Compiled from Annual Reports of the Foreign Missions of the Presbyterian Church of Wales on Mizoram 1894–1957*. Aizawl: Synod Literary and Publication Board.

The Friend of India, 1835–76, British Library Newspaper Reading Rooms, Colindale, London.

Thomas, F.W. (trans). 1935. *Tibetan Literary Texts and Documents Concerning Chinese Turkestan*, Part I, Literary Texts. London: Royal Asiatic Society.

Thong, Tenzenlo. 2011. '"To Raise the Savage to a Higher Level": The Westernization of Nagas and Their Culture', *Modern Asian Studies*, 45(1): 1–26.

Thurman, Robert A.F. 1978. 'Buddhist Hermeneutics', *JAAR*, 46(1): 19–39.

———. 1991. *The Central Philosophy of Tibet: A Study and Translation of Jey Tsong Khapa's Essense of True Eloquence*. Princeton: Princeton University Press.

Tickell, S.R. 1854. 'Extracts from Journal up the Koladyne River, Aracan in 1851', *Journal of Royal Geographical Society of London*, 24: 86–114.

Tirmizi, S.A.I. 1979. *Edicts from the Mughal Harem*. Delhi: Idarah-i-Adabiyat-i Delli.

Tournadre, Nicolas and Sangda Dorje. 2009. *Manual of Standard Tibetan: Language and Civilization*. Bangkok, Thailand: Orchid Press.

Tran, Nhung Tuyet. 2008. 'Gender, Property and the Autonomy Thesis in Southeast Asia: The Endowment of Local Succession in Early Modern Vietnam', *JAS*, 67(1): 43–72.

Tripura Buranji of Ratnakandali and Arjundas Kataki (ed. Suryya Kumar Bhuyan). 1990 [1938]. Gauhati: DHAS.

Troughton, Geoffrey M. 2006. 'Jesus and the Ideal of the Manly Man in New Zealand after World War One', *Journal of Religious History*, 30(1): 45–60.

Trouillot, Michel-Rolph. 1996. *Silencing the Past: Power and the Production of History*. Boston: Beacon.

Tsering, Tashi. 2005. 'Outstanding Women in Tibetan Medicine', in Janet Gyatso and Hanna Havnevik (eds.), *Women in Tibet*, 169–94. New York: Columbia University Press.

Tucci, Guiseppe. 1931. 'The Sea and Land Travels of a Buddhist Sadhu in the Sixteenth Century', *Indian Historical Quarterly*, 7(4): 683–702.

Tucci, Guiseppe. 1956. *Preliminary Report on Two Scientific Expeditions in Nepal.* Rome: Instituto Italiano Per il Medio ed Estremo Oriente.

———. 1988 [1935]. *The Temples of Western Tibet and their Artistic Symbolism* ed. Lokesh Chandra, 3 vols. New Delhi: Aditya Prakashan.

Tun, Than (ed.). 1986. *Royal Orders of Burma*, vols 1–7. Kyoto: Center for Southeast Asian Studies, Kyoto University.

Tunga, Sudhangsushekhar (comp). 1985. *Banglar Baire Bangla Gadyer Charcha.* Kolkata: Kolkata University.

Turner, Samuel. 2005 [1800]. *An Account of an Embassy to the Court of the Teshoo Lama in Tibet Containing a Narrative of a Journey through Bootan and Part of Tibet.* Delhi: Asian Educational Services.

Uberoi, Patricia (ed.). 1996. *Social Reform, Sexuality and the State.* New Delhi: Sage.

Uebach, Helga. 2003. 'On the Tibetan Expansion from Seventh to Mid-eighth Centuries and the Administration (kho) of the Countries Subdued', in Alex McKay (ed.), *Tibet and Her Neighbours: A History*, 21–9. London: Hansjorg Mayer.

Urban, Hugh. 2001. *The Economy of Ecstasy: Tantra, Secrecy and Power in Colonial Bengal.* New York: Oxford University Press.

———. 2010. *The Power of Tantra: Religion, Sexuality and the Politics of South Asian Studies.* London: I.B.Tauris.

Valantasi, Richard. 1995. 'Constructions of Power in Asceticism', *JAAR*, 63(4): 775–821.

Vanlalchhunga, Rev. (comp). 2003. *Reports of the Foreign Mission of the Presbyterian Church of Wales on Sylhet-Bangladesh and Kachar-India, 1886–1955.* Silchar: Shalom Publications.

Van der Kuijp, Leonard W.J. 1983. *Contributions to the Development of Tibetan Buddhist Epistemology, From the Eleventh to the Thirteenth Century.* Weisbaden: Franz Steiner.

Van der Veer, Peter. 1998. *Religious Nationalism: Hindus and Muslims in India.* Oxford: Oxford University Press.

———. 2001. *Imperial Encounters: Religion and Modernity in India and Britain.* Princeton: Princeton University Press.

Van Esterik, Penny. 1996. 'Lay Women in Theravada Buddhism', in Van Esterik (ed.), *Women of Southeast Asia*, 42–61. DeKalb: Northern Illinois University Center for Southeast Asian Studies.

Van Schendel, Wilhelm (ed.). 1992a. *Francis Buchanan in Southeast Bengal (1798): His Journey to Chittagong, the Chittagong Hill Tracts, Noakhali and Comilla.* Dhaka: University Press.

———. 1992b. 'The Invention of the "Jummas": State Formation and Ethnicity in Southeast Bangladesh', *MAS*, 26(1): 95–128.

———. 2005. *Bengal Borderland: Beyond Nation and State in South Asia.* London: Anthem Press.

Van Spengen, Wim. 2000. *Tibetan Border Worlds: A Geohistorical Analysis of Trade and Traders*. London: Kegan Paul International.

————. 2006. 'Chone and Thewu: Territoriality, Local Power, and Political Control on the Southern Gansu-Tibetan Frontier, 1880–1940', in P. Christian Klieger (ed.), *Tibetan Borderlands*, 209–30. Leiden: E.J. Brill.

Varma, Nitin. 2011. 'Coolie Strikes Back: Collective Protest and Action in the Colonial Tea Plantations of Assam, 1880–1920', in Biswamoy Pati (ed.), *Adivasis in Colonial India: Survival, Resistance and Negotiation*, 186–215. Delhi: Orient Blackswan.

Venis, Arthur. 1899–1900. 'Copperplate Grant of Vaidyadeva, King of Kamarupa', *EI*, 2: 347–58.

Verardi, Giovanni. 2011. *Hardships and Downfall of Buddhism in India*. Delhi: Manohar.

Vergati, Anne. 1987. 'The King as Rain-Maker: A New Version of the Legend of the *Red Avalokitesvar* in Nepal', in N. Gutschow and A. Michaels (eds.), *Heritage of the Kathmandu Valley: Proceedings of an International Conference in Lubeck, June 1985*, 43–47. Sankt Augustin: VGH-Wissenschaftsverlag.

————. 2002 [1995]. *Gods, Men and Territory: Society and Culture in Kathmandu Valley*. Delhi: Manohar.

Viswanathan, Gauri. 1998. *Outside the Fold: Conversion, Modernity, and Belief*. New York: Oxford University Press.

Vitali, R. 2001. 'Saskya and the mNga'ris skor gsum Legacy: Case of Rinchen bzangpo's Flying Mask', *Lungta 14: Aspects of Tibetan History* (Spring): 5–44.

————. 2005. 'Some Conjectures on Change and Instability during the One Hundred Years of Darkness in the History of La dwags (1280s–1380s)', in John Bray (ed.), *Ladakhi Histories: Local and Regional Perspectives*, 97–124. Leiden: Brill.

Von Fürer-Haimendorf, Christoph. 1976. *Return to the Naked Nagas: An Anthropologist's View of Nagaland 1936–1970*. New Delhi: Vikas.

Vostrikov, Andrei I. 1970 [1958]. Tibetan Historical Literature. Calcutta: Indian Studies Past and Present.

Walsh, Michael J. 2007. 'The Economics of Salvation: Towards a Theory of Exchange in Chinese Buddhism', *JAAR*, 75(2): 353–82.

————. 2010. *Sacred Economics: Buddhist Monasticism and Territoriality in Medieval China*. New York: Columbia University Press.

Wayman, Alex. 2005 [1973]. *The Buddhist Tantras: Light on Indo-Tibetan Esotericism*. Delhi: Motilal Banarsidass.

Weiss, Gillian. 2005. 'Barbary Captivity and the French Idea of Freedom', *French Historical Studies*, 28(2): 231–64.

White, David Gordon. 2003. *Kiss of the Yogini: Tantric Sex in Its South Asian Context.* Chicago: University of Chicago.

―――. 2009. *Sinister Yogis.* Chicago: University of Chicago Press.

White, Major Adam. 1988 [1831]. *A Memoir of the Late David Scott.* Gauhati: DHAS.

Whitlock, Tammy. 2005. *Crime, Gender and Consumer Culture in Nineteenth Century England.* Aldershot: Ashgate.

Wigley, F.G. (ed.). 1905. *The Bengal Code Containing the Regulations and Local Acts in Force in Bengal.* Calcutta: Superintendent of Government Printing.

Williams, Nerys W. 1990. 'The Welsh Calvinist Methodist Mission in Assam 1930–50 with Special Reference to Missionary Attitudes to Local Socity, Customs and Religion'. Ph.D. dissertation, University of London.

Willis, Michael. 2009. *The Archaeology of Hindu Ritual: Temples and the Establishment of the Gods.* Cambridge: Cambridge University Press.

Wilson, Jon E. 2005. '"A Thousand Countries to Go to": Peasants and Rulers in Late Eighteenth-Century Bengal', *Past and Present,* 189 (November): 81–109.

Wise, Thomas Alexander. 1845. *A Commentary on the Hindu System of Medicine.* Calcutta: Thackeray and Spink.

―――. 1867. *Review of the History of Medicine,* 2 vols. London: J. Churchill.

Woodthorpe, G. 1978 [1873]. *The Lushai Expedition 1871–72.* Aizawl, Mizoram: Synod Publication Board.

Woodward, Hiram. 2004. 'Esoteric Buddhism in Southeast Asia in the Light of Recent Scholarship', *Journal of Southeast Asian Studies,* 35(2): 329–54.

Yamamoto, Carl Shigeo. 2008. 'Vision and Violence: Lama Zhang and the Dialectics of Political Authority and Religious Charisma in Twelfth-Century Central Tibet'. Ph.D. dissertation, University of Virginia.

Younghusband, Francis. 1905. 'The Geographical Results of the Tibet Mission', *Geographical Journal,* 25(5): 481–93.

Zhao, George Qinghzi. 2008. *Marriage as Political Strategy and Cultural Expression: Mongolian Royal Marriages from World Empire to Yuan Dynasty.* New York: Peter Lang.

Ziarek, Ewa Ptonowska. 2008. 'Bare Life on Strike: Notes on the Biopolitics of Race and Gender', *South Atlantic Quarterly,* 107(1): 89–105.

Zou, David. 2011. 'Spiritualised Homes: Imaginative Geographies in Colonial Mizoram, India 1897–1947', Seminar at Nehru Memorial Museum and Library, November 15.

Zou, David V. and M. Satish Kumar. 2011. 'Mapping a Colonial Borderland: Objectifying the Geo-Body of India's Northeast', *Journal of Asian Studies,* 70(1): 141–70.

Zysk, Kenneth G. 1991. *Asceticism and Healing in Ancient India: Medicine in the Buddhist Monastery.* Delhi: Motilal Banarsidass.

Glossary

acarya	Teacher
akhara	'Wrestling arena'; monastery of Vaisnava warrior-monks
alim	Islamic legal scholar
amban	Chinese governor, appointed to govern regions claimed by Qing court in eighteenth and nineteenth centuries
bairagi	Vaisnava renunciant
bari	Residence, also used for land market office for tea plantation
bhakat, bhakta, bhagat	Vaisnava initiate, devotee
bhikshu	Ordained Buddhist monk, renunciant
bonjoogi	Tibetan for military force on the move
Bootea	Bhutanese
Bouddha	Buddhist
brahmottar	Tax-exempt lands whose income was dedicated to the subsistence of Brahmans, priests, ritualists
buranji	Assamese chronicle
chakaran	Rent-free lands supporting a monastery
Chakma	Member of a community following Sa-skya Buddhist teachers, currently residents of modern Bangladesh
chamua paik	Subordinate attached to a monastic or temple estate, exempted from military service
chaudhri	Headman
Cosseah/ khase/ khasi	Portuguese Jesuit term of reference for 'Cathay' or western Tibet and eastern Kashmir; also encountered as 'kashar' and 'kacchar' in English sources in eighteenth century. Also, collective of priests and followers.

dana	Gift
dana-prasad	Objects gifted by disciples, consecrated by deities and recipient power-figures, and returned to donor
desi	Officer appointed by monks to administer temporal affairs, especially for Bhutanese regime
dharmottar	Land or income from shops and tolls dedicated to the upholding of Buddhist law, or dharma.
dzongpen	Commander of fort
fakir, faqir	Sufi mendicant monk
farman	Mughal order, decree
faujdar	Mughal administrator of a subdivision of a subah (province) called a sarkar
gayal	Cross between a bison and an ox
gelong	Tibetan for ordained Buddhist monk
gosain, goswami, gohain	'Lord of cattle-wealth'; Vaisnava renunciant, devotee of Krishna
got	Group of 3 or 4 paiks
hkyaung	Burmese monastic residence; see kiaung
jhum	Swidden
jhuming	Slash-and-burn cultivation
Kachar, also Kashar and Cachhar	Term used for speakers of heteroglot Nepali and Tibetan languages, geographically associated with Himalayan foothills across Kashmir, Tibet, Sikkim, Bhutan.
Kargyupa	Colloquial for Tshalpa Bka'brgyud pa, a lineage of ordained Buddhist tantrics tracing their spiritual genealogy from Marpa in the eleventh century
kari paik	Subordinate attached to monastery who was liable to military service
Karmapa	A lineage of ordained Buddhist tantrics tracing their spiritual genealogy from Milarepa in the twelfth century
kavya	Epic poetry in Sanskrit
khanqah	Sufi dormitory
kheda	Catching elephants for use in paying taxes

khel	Corporate group, Afghan clan-formation
khangjai	Dormitory
Khasi	Tibetan term for a group made up of the ordained and the lay
khutba	Address in a mosque, usually at Friday service
kiaung, kiaung-sa	Burmese monastic dormitory; residents of or attendants upon them
Kuki, Kookie	Literally, incarnate Buddha; also, respect-payer, broadly used for subjects of Buddhist laws, even when commanded by non-Buddhist warriors and traders
kulina	Spiritually distinguished
la-khiraj	Tax-exempt
lugs gnyis	Tibetan for subjects
lu shih	Chinese for the ordained monk who taught monastic rules or Vinaya to novice monks
Lushai	colloquial rendering of above; also of co-sharers in a patrilineage or *bRu bzhi*; and of participants in 'mind-only' contemplative exercises, the root of which was *lodze* or keen perception.
masjid	Mosque
matha	Monastery, monastic dormitory
Morang	land lying between the rivers Kosi (flowing from eastern Nepal through plains of Bihar, India to join the Ganga) and the Tista in northern Bengal: included Sikkimese sites and populations
Mugg, alternately 'mog'	Tibeto-Burman for refugee from Arakan
paik	Subordinate worker, attached to lands of a temple, monastery, or lay lord
parganah	Province
Permanent Settlement	A system which authorised contracted collectors of Mughal taxes to become permanent owners of landed estates and pay fixed sums of cash as land tax to the East India Company from 1793.

pir	Sufi teacher-guide
posa	Tributary payment, payment for military protection
praja, proja	Subject of a (monastic or lay) lord
punya	Merit
raiyat, ryot	Cultivator, farmer
Rakhain	Arakanese
Ryotwari	A system of paying taxes directly by the individual farmer, both lease-holder and tiller, to a Company official
samgha	Assembly of Buddhist monks
sanad	Deed of land or confirmation of proprietorship
sannyasi	Hindu renunciant
sardar	Leader
sastra	Sanskrit for organized text
sattra	Assembly of Vaisnava initiates
seva	Service, used in both ritual and temporal contexts
silsilah	In Sufism, the 'chain of initiation'
sipahi, sepoy	Indian infantrymen in British service; esp. mutineers in 1857–8
sishya	Initiated disciple of either Vaisnava or Saiva teacher
svargadeva	Heavenly lord; commanding authority over the Brahmaputra Valley
Swadeshi	Movement to manufacture and use local goods in preference to those of European manufacture, associated particularly with the protest against the partition of Bengal in 1905
thakurbari	Temple, lit. 'house of god'
tirtha	Pilgrimage site, a 'crossing'
vihara	Buddhist establishment of monks
zamindar	A Mughal official who collected the land taxes of his district; in colonial times, a landowner paying the government a fixed revenue
zawlbuk	assembly hall for contemplative training, often associated only with young men.

Index

Abor 189, 310
abbot or adept (master, *adhikar*)
7, 24, 38, 39, 45, 71, 129, 132,
197, 199, 209. *See also sattra*
Achiks 350
Acts and Regulations: I of 1790,
98; II of 1793, 162; XI of
1793, 105; X of 1822, 191; II
of 1828, 147; III of 1828–9,
149–50; XIII of 1859, 251; VI
of 1865, 251; V of 1873, 270;
VIII & XII of 1874, 271; Assam
Wastelands Regulations (1842)
236; Inner Line Regulations
(1871) 27–8, 270
adherence, adherents and devotees
(*bhakta*s, *bhakat*s, *bhagat*s) 1, 2,
4, 24–6, 38, 358; as feudalism
176–88; fraternity of tea and
politics of monastic freindship
240, 250, 253, 255–7, 269,
271, 272, 345–6; Hodson's
negative judgement on
authenticity and purity 344–5;
military labourer, male 'savages',
216–19;& monastic governance,
geographicity and gender
41, 52, 54, 70, 72; monastic
goverments, shifts 86, 91, 95,
97–100, 115, 117; political
ecology and Hindu marriage
129, 132, 135, 148, 158; and
subjects 129; translations,

from feudalism and slavery to
savagery 173–223; —inversion
of sacral manumission in Assam,
193–202; undoing gender 287,
303, 310, 318, 320–1, 328. *See
also* East India Company; *sattra*
administrative: policies 270–1;
reforms 358; reorganization
255, 291, 352
affinal relationships and politics 57,
134, 139
Afghan(s) 46, 99, 161, 236, 339;
and Assamese lords, affinal
relationship 57; sultans of
Bengal 4, 23, 47; localization
of *ulema* 25; Luhanis 48;&
Mughal emperors 65; Muslims
161; Rajput soldiers and
Mughal-Rajput commanders,
contests 48–9, 57
Afghan-Mughal-Ahom warfare
216
Afghanistan 13, 45, 48, 237
Agent of the Governor General
(AGG) 149, 160
Agent of the Governor General in
the North-East Frontier (AGG
NEF) 209, 218
agrarian, agriculture 192, 306;
calendar 184; capitalism 213;
colonially sponsored 340
agro-pastoralist(s) 273; economy
100; women 14, 272

Ahmed, Amanatullah 346
Ahom, *Ahom* 146, 164, 194; Bhutia
   relations 359; *buranjis* 60, 131,
   346, 349–50; monarchs 203–4,
   212; monastic bureaucracy 240;
   Rajas 72; Vaisnava 116, 261. *See
   also* Assam
Ahom-Bengali literati 343–4,
   346–9, 353–6
Ahul-lup lakpa 218
Akas 204, 207
Akbar 65
akhāras 37, 67, 84, 101, 129, 154,
   329
Aksobhya Buddha 125n
Akyab 196, 242, 291, 294
Alchi Monastery 54
Alexanderpur tea plantations 259,
   262
Ali Jan Lashkar (Alichan Lascar)
   115
Aloo Raja 155
Amarapura 106, 137, 250;
   Burmese-Buddhists 127; wars
   with Siam (1785) 106
amban 112, 114
Ambari Falakata 205
Ambika, goddess 23, 132
Amitabha Buddha 125n
Amoghasiddhi Buddha 125n
Amritachand 102
Anahita-Nahid 45
Anandadeva, Saiva lord (1147–67)
   3
Anantanāga 184
ancestral cult 48, 70
Angami Naga 186
Anglo-Bhutan wars (1772–3) 90;
   (1865–6) 253, 255, 262–3
Anglo-Burmese War (1824–6) 26,
   150, 158, 162, 177, 179–80,
   188, 192, 195

Anglo-Burmese Yandabo treaty
   (1826) 147
Anglo-Nepal war 85
Anglophone 26, 340
animal(s), animal wealth 36,
   62–5, 292; as bride-wealth 62,
   137–38; exchange for humans
   57; sacrifice 133, 314, 343;
   transport 62, 89
Aniseed 62
Arakan, Arakanese 2, 17, 28,
   340; Chittagong, Burmese
   occupation 117; colonial
   governance and women 28, 289,
   292, 294; Hindus, 137, 244,
   252, 275; monasteries, monastic
   governance 39, 105, 106, 108,
   110, 112, 114; political ecology
   and Hindu marriage 150, 152,
   159, 173, 178, 181, 183, 195,
   201; tea plantation and politics
   of monastic friendship 243, 260
Areng 241
artisans 42, 194
Asad al-daulah, Nawab of Awadh
   67
Assam 2, 3, 9, 17–18, 23, 26, 27,
   340, 342, 345, 347, 354–5,
   359; buranjis 24, 53, 63, 135;
   colonial mimicry of monastic
   politics 27, 232–3, 235, 236,
   238–40, 245–6, 249–50,
   255, 268, 270–1; Labour and
   Emigration Act (1882) 315;
   monasteries 25; monastic
   geographicity, governance and
   gender 25, 43, 44, 62, 68, 72;
   monastic governments, shifts
   88, 104, 111; political ecology
   and Hindu marriage 157, 160,
   176, 213; temples 55; women
   workers/traders 14, 15

Assam Research Society (Kamarupa
    Anusandhan Samiti) 346, 347,
    349–50, 353–5, 357
Assam Tea Company, Kachar 238
Assamese 36, 39, 54, 205, 288,
    340, 350, 357, 360
Assamese-Burmese marriage of
    1793–6, 136
Ata, Mir 175
attavada (a doctrine of self) 298–9
Aung-ghio-se Tam-mang, 112
Aurangzeb 55, 65
Ava 141, 235; Burmese-Buddhists
    127; monastic geographicity,
    governance and gender 47, 62;
    monastic governments, shifts
    26, 106, 107, 109, 110; political
    ecology and Hindu marriage
    127, 128, 135, 146, 157, 164,
    181; tea fraternity and politics
    of monastic friendship 235
Ayodhya (Mi-thub-pa) 24, 44, 69,
    98–9
Ayurveda 38
Azim, Mohamed 264–5

Babri mosque demolition 16
Baharistan-i-Ghaybi 63
Baidyanath, Raja of Dinajpur 67
Bairagi, Ramgopal 129
Bairagi, Ramshah 90
bairagis (renunciants) and fakirs.
    See sannyasi (ascetics), bairagis
    and fakirs
Balaram Deb 179
Balfour, Henry 348
Balarampur 86
BaraGosain, BarGosain, Bura
    Gohain 100, 116, 140
Bara Senapati 190, 198–201, 235
Barak valley. *See* Surma-Barak
    valley

Baruah, Balramchand 205
Barua, Kanaklal 346, 350, 353
Barua, Khunchang Lama 54
Baruah, Maniram Datta 234
Baxanagar, Buddhist stupa site 23
Becher, William 212
Behari Raja 351
Bell, Charles 345
Bengal 23, 359; Buddhist
    and Vaisnava, relations
    127; monastic governance,
    geographicity and gender 44,
    47, 55, 66–8, 73; monastic
    governments, shifts 104, 107,
    111; Nawabs 82; political
    ecology and Hindu marriage
    130, 152, 164, 176
Bengal Tea Company 247
Bengal-Assam-Burma 89
Bengali 36, 57, 68, 159, 205, 240,
    253, 274, 288, 290, 340, 346,
    350, 359, 360; Sanskritic 19;
    speaking Muslims and Hindus
    252; Tibetan-inflected 19–20
Bentinck, A.H.W. 347
Bentinck, William 161–2
Bhagadatta 357
Bhagyachandra. *See* Jaisimha
*bhakat*s, *See* adherents and
    devotees; *See also* sattra
Bhatgaon. *See* Tripura
Bhattacharjee, Madhuram 105
Bhattacharya, Gouriswar 10
Bhonta 3
Bhosles 17
Bhunga, Sardar Hrang 320
Bhutan 52, 54, 88, 117, 208, 355;
    monastic government 87–8
Bhutanese-Sikkimese-Tibetan
    Buddhist 116
Bhutia, Indu, 105
Bhutiya, Jayaram 24

Bhutias. *See* Bod
Bhuyan, Suryya Kumar 18, 20, 22, 349
Bijni Raj 117, 194, 203, 205
Bir Chandra 256
birth and rebirth, cycles 5, 8
Biru Karji 59
Bod (Bodos, Bhot, Bhotiya, Bhutias, Bhuteas, Bhutiahs) domains and militia 56, 88, 152, 203, 204, 207, 212, 242, 293, 347, 359; and Ahoms 116
Bodhawhpaya, the sovereign Lord of White Elephants 128, 135, 260
Bodhgaya (Bihar) 8
*bodhisattva*s (Bodhisattva) 110, 209, 242, 341
body-mind discipline 41
Bogle, Captain 88–9
Bohmong 349
boi 330, 364
Bon-Buddhists, Bon lineage, Tantra 1, 2, 4, 5, 20, 28, 45–6, 54, 105, 129, 193, 205, 207, 240, 244, 260, 269, 272, 287–8, 315, 345, 359, 361; authority over Saiva and Vaisnava disciples 52; agro-pastoralists 273; colonial agnosia 268; practices of compassion 321
Bon-zu (Bonjoogies) 111–12
Bonpo 10, 314, 316, 317
Borahi Kochari 46
Bormon, Nandaram 154
Bormon, Rajaram 154
Bose, Krishna Kanta 152–53
Brahman(s) 7, 19, 41–2, 47, 90, 161, 176; exemption from military or other labour services 194; recipients of grants 67

Brahmaputra river and valley system 4, 7, 16, 26, 36, 38–9, 44–6, 48, 52, 54–6, 72, 81, 85, 117, 132, 134, 151, 163, 185, 187, 189, 194–5, 197, 202, 204–5, 207, 233–4, 253, 287, 350
Brahmaputra–Meghna Valley 173, 188, 196
brahmottar lands 104, 158
brides and bride wealth in the eighteenth century 136–41, 291; arrangements and gifts 62–4, 119; payments in cattle wealth 293–4
British India Tea Company 258
British: law of coverture (married women's separate estate) 26; special system of government 191–2
Bronson, Miles 193
brotherhood 293
Brown, Nathaniel 193, 196
Bruce, Charles 235
bSam.yas (Samye) 7
Buchanan, Francis 56, 106–16, 137, 141, 161, 176–8, 244, 252, 339, 348
Buddha 17, 39, 105, 313, 341
Buddhas 2
Buddhasena 8
Buddhavacana 17
Buddhism, Buddhists, Buddhist tradition 1, 5, 10, 17, 24, 38, 39, 43, 64 65, 81, 91, 115, 116, 118, 129, 145, 176, 272, 287, 342–4, 355, 357; in Bengal 340–2; in Burma 352; cosmological world 128; *dakini*s 49, 50; doctrine of debt and obligation 322, 329; estates in eastern Assam and

lower Bengal 238; and Islam
55; and Jaina subjects 236;
lineages in Sikkim 146; of
Magadha 2; male (Devakhadga)
11; Mazdaist-Bon-Nyingmapa
(Tantric) lineages 46; monastic
economies and militias 218;
monks and Vaisnava gurus
7, 39, 193; Muslim Rakhain
and Bengali subjects 179, 184,
255; and non-Buddhist others,
relations 1, 46; Raulins 260,
325; and Saivas 18, 115, 184;
samgha 288; Tantric tradition,
Tantrics 2, 4, 7, 12, 18, 21,
28, 38, 45, 46, 48–9, 51, 132,
155–7, 164, 213, 233, 236,
239, 250, 258, 342; —Saiva
and Muslim power-sharing
arrangements 107; —Saiva–
Vaisnava–Islamic populations
183; —Sufi society 105;
—Vaisnava rebels 133; teaching
traditions 2, 12; Trongsa or
Paro Penlops 205–6; and
Vaisnava, lineages, relations
127, 166, 184, 192; Buddhist-
Vaisnava-Sufi subjects 315
Buglun 134
bullion trade of the Himalayan
world 85
Burma 22, 44, 71, 108, 127, 362;
after its incorporation into the
British Empire (1852) 241;
annexation by British 106, 276;
Land Revenue Act (1876) 289
Burmese 57, 240; aid against each
other's affines and factions
141–4; authority in Assam
143; Buddhists 120, 127, 221;
hkyaung 37, 39, 118; Khiongs
252; Marjit alliance 143; royal

and Assamese marital political
relationship 135–36
Burmese-Pali-speaking groups 47

Calcutta Council 95
Canning, Lord 245
captivity and the problem of ethical
action, 259–69
care, cure, and possessions: 1905 as
revival 317–24
Carey, Felix 118, 146
Catholicism, Catholic(s) 105, 176,
252; Portuguese 191
cattle-wealth, women's control 133
caves and thatched huts 41
celibate lineages 38
cemetery-based ritual cultivation
(smasān sādhanā) 51
Central Asian (Afghan): forces
49; Sufis 138; and West Asian
(Arab) lineages, localization 25
Chaibem 175
chakaran or rent-free support lands
84
Chakmas 11, 108, 112, 325, 341,
359
Chakrabarti, Ganganarayana
129–30
chakravartin 128
Champigny 97
Chandrakala, daughter of
Nandaram Bormon 154
Chandraprabha 154
Chandrapur 120
Changidam 59
Charai 175
Charaka 38
charity (khairat) grants 82, 91, 99,
102, 138
Chatheng River 151–2
Chatterjee, Partha 15
Chattesvari, deity 50

Chaucasam (Chakrasamvara) 110
Chaudhuri, Sadruddin 117
Chaudhuri, Sona Mian 256
Chaudhuris 161
Cheitharon Kumpapa 62
Chevalier, French 89, 190, 194
Chevalier, Jean-Baptiste 68
Chhaimaar 175
Chhakaccheb 175
Chhatoi 175
childless 'Hindu'co-wives and
    widows 13, 103
*chiliarchie*s 44
Chin Byan 117
Chittagong Hill Tracts (Golangiya)
    and plains 2, 19, 28, 39, 47,
    294, 348, 353; Buddhist
    Chakmas 341; colonial mimicry
    of monastic politics 259, 271,
    275; monastic governments,
    shifts 82, 94, 104–5, 107,
    109–12; monastic subjects,
    refusal of political dignity
    348; political ecology and
    reconstructed Hindu marriage
    137, 143, 152, 173; post-
    partition 362
Cholas 260
Choudhuri, Mahindra Narain 191
Choudhuri, Tattvanidhi Achyuta
    Charan 346–7
Choudhuris 191
Chourjit, son of Jaisimha 142–4
Chowdhury, Ghulam Ali 69
Christian missionaries, Christians
    82, 164, 223, 314–16, 329
Christian Second Coming 319
Christianity 331
Christianization of newly isolated
    societies 28, 287, 288, 311
Chumna, Musammat Nur 104
Church Missionary Society 192

Chutia Kochari 46
Cinas 357
clans and households 48–9, 71, 96;
    administration 348
Cole, Major G.H. 319–21
collective: brotherhood 294;
    residential organization 36–7;
    will 15; worship community
    176
collocated monastic dormitories,
    colonial ignorance 340
colonial: agnosia about Bon,
    Tantric, Islamic and other
    collocated communities 160,
    268–9; bureaucracy 200, 221,
    297, 301, 341; development
    295; economics 302, 359;
    governance 28; information
    gathering and the constitution
    of ignorance from the late
    eighteenth century 105–16;
    knowledge formation 340;
    liberalism 234; metal currency
    288; military strategy 305;
    public discourse 247; regime
    214, 291; revenue authorities
    289; scientific knowledge
    schemes 339
colonialism 162, 173, 366
conflicts and wars: about succession
    101–2; intra and inter-monastic
    ordination lineage 134–6,
    187–8; resolution mechanisms
    290
conjugal affinity (*kutumbitā*) 58
Constitution of India 355
containment to reversal: resistant
    men, authoritative women, and
    the Company 98–101
convergence: of Christian
    missionary 193; of Muslims 115
conversion 288, 316

coolies 14, 28, 159, 188, 214, 215;
in colonial regime 291, 295–6,
299, 301–3, 307–8, 315; tea
fraternity and 258, 261–2, 266,
307; women 295–6, 301–2
co-residential monastic and
disciples' dormitories 38–9
corporate: delivery systems 197;
liabilities 197; responsibility for
repayments of loans 243
cosmological and symbolic systems
115
cosmopolitanism 105, 115, 272–6
cotton supplying hill-plains
networks, redirected subjects
94–8
cotton-growing elevations 82
Council at Calcutta 88, 90
criminal justice in British legal
system 261
criminal monks, dispersed
adherents, and dispossessed
widows 219–23
cross-lineage affinities 12
Cubelli, 365
cultivation, cultivators 8, 39, 42,
45, 47, 51, 67, 94, 95, 108,
113, 138, 158–9, 162, 178,
186, 189, 191–4, 197–8, 205,
209; of *dharmottar* lands 202;
female 14–16, 217; under
Govindachandra 147–8;
practices of monks 210; taxation
204; of tea 193, 201

Dadan Sahib 117
Dafflas (Dufflas) 24, 204, 207
Daga Penlop 206
Daikoma Raja 320
Dakkhinshik 175
dakshina 6
Dalai Lama 88; Fifth 53

Dalekmay 242, 269
Damayanti Devi 102
dana (donations) 8–9, 12, 291. *See
also* gifts
Dara, Chief of Pukpui 296–301,
305, 312–13, 327
Darpong 266–7, 270
Darrang 207
Darrang Raj Vamsavali 342
Das, Sarat Chandra 2, 252, 297,
341, 343
Dass, Gour Charan 312
daughters and widows, legal
dispossession 26. *See also* women
dauhitra lineage marriages and
births 136–7
Davidson, James 248
Davis, Samuel 88
Dayabhaga school of Hindu law
149
Dayang River 347
De Borros, Aura 105
Deb Raja (Deva Raja) 87–90, 116,
203, 205, 208, 211, 212
debt, notions of 243
Decennial and Permanent
Settlements (1790 and 1793)
101–2, 104, 107
decolonization 359, 360
Deka, Phutak 134
Delhi Sultanate 49
Delo-jio 155
denationalization 287
Desideri, Ippolito 61
Devapaladeva 12
Devasena 8
Devi Singh, Raja 92–3
devotional singing (*gayans*) 41
devotional subjecthood 176
devottar 158, 195, 212
Dhaleswari River 160
Dhansiri River 239

Dharma, a *sannyasi* 47
Dharmanarayana 54
Dharmapala, King of Magadha 12, 43, 45
Dharmapala, pandit 43
Dharmapur 185
Dharmaraja 54, 116, 190, 205, 206–7, 209, 211, 218, 342
Dharmarakshita 8
dharmasastra 346
Dharmasvamin 8
Digungpa (bKa-rGyud-pa) 4
Dihingia Sattra 70
diksha-centred lineage 130
Dikshit, K.N. 354
disciples and adherents as 'tribes', 'races', and 'slaves' 188–202
disciples' dormitories 37
discipleship and donations 51
disciple-subjects of monastics 174
Docompo 257
Dokhama 311
doljatra (procession on the occasion of the spring equinox) 100
doloi 96, 155
dominance and subordination, conceptions 210
donor(s) 10, 26, 42, 43; and recipients, political and economic relationships 9, 42
dost 4
dowry 134, 136, 137, 291
Drukpa Buddhist 88
Drukpa Kagyupa (Kagyu) 51–3, 114, 205
Drukpa Kuenley 51
Durga (goddess) 176, 182
Durgacharan 185
Durgamani/Durgamanikya 136–7, 180
dzongkha 155
Dzungari (Mongol) commanders 53

Eagleton, Mr. 251
East India Company 13, 14, 26, 27, 63, 81, 88, 90, 91–93, 106, 117, 173–4, 201–3, 219, 237, 240, 359; administrators in Goalpara 195; court's judicial process 180; encroachment on 'charity' lands 91; political ecology and reconstituted Hindu marriage 127, 135–6, 141, 143–4, 146–8, 154, 156; realignments of monastic networks against rival Europeans 81–3; revenue in restructured Hindu law 157–62 ; shifting grounds under 69–73; structuring of the monastic political economy 90; tax regime 182, 203, 207, 212; traders 99; war with Burma 146, 158
economic: activity 7; development, 16, 236; interdependence, 86; legislation 287
Eden, Ashley 261, 262–3
Edgar, John Ware 208, 289
elephant-catching operation (*kheda*) 180
elephants as bride-wealth 62, 64
Elijah 197
Elliott 133–4, 152, 156
endogamous relationships/sexual unions 12, 137
Enlightenment science and empiricism 108
epistemological traditions 18
Equitable Tea Company 245
ethical commerce and monastic subjects 242–4
ethnic consciousness 235
Ethnological Committee of the Asiatic Society 255
Euro-American colonization 259

Eurofeminist theory and history of South Asia 361
European tea plantations 219; male plantation owners 276
Excluded Other 355
exclusion strategies 270–2
exogamy 71

family-clan and ordination lineages of a guru, conflicts 152; and gender 66
famine and impoverishment and 95, 303, 306, 308, 321; (1882) 289–90; (1911) 322, 326, 328, 330; (1943) 353, 355; (1952–6) 362, 363
faujdars 67
female: adherent and kin 100; centred societies in the Himalayan foothills, 152; and child labourers 261–3; labour force, 249; male relationships 5, 103, 166; oracles, sonic regimes, and lineage of female ordination 324–31; transportation workers 89; ultimogeniture 156
feudalism, feudal system 27, 220, 263; and 'slavery' to 'savagery' 173–223
fever-demons 341
Fisher, Thomas 150, 153–6, 157, 161
Fitzgerald, Serjeant 238
followership, descent, and marriage, inter-relationships 254
forest conservation 289
Fraser Clinic 365
Fraser, Mary Catherine 320, 324–7, 367
Fraser, Peter 320–1, 323–4, 330
fraternity, friendship, and kinship 272–6

frontier making 204
Furer-Haimendorf, C. 352

Gaidinliu, priest 348
Gait, Edward A. 340, 342–4, 347, 349, 360
Galoo Dev 154
Ganaka kuchi 350
Ganga Das 217
Gangasagar 4
Ganges 2, 4, 16
Garhgaon 57
Garo (Garoo) 19, 50, 190–1, 193, 270, 271, 310, 345, 354
Gauda 357
Gaudama 244
Gaudiya 70
Gelugpa ordination lineage 52, 53, 54, 70, 88
gender, gender relations 98, 165; class and ethnicity 264; gender-generation codes 329; monastic codes 71; and rank in Northeast 18
genealogies, genealogical descent 10, 26, 65
Gharibnawaz 119, 144, 145
Ghazi, Mirza 104
Ghergong, capital of Assam 68, 135, 234
Ghose, Anoda 312
Ghosh, Jogendra Chandra 353
gift (dana) 8–9, 12, 13, 38, 55, 58, 65, 103, 136, 178, 196, 221, 234–5, 343; of daughters in marriages 136; of animals 63; gift-giving social respectability 291; of land (bhumidana) 39, 47; to temples and monasteries 42; of solidity 144–9
Godama (Gautama) 108, 110

goddess-worshipping 346
gojen-lama books 20
Gokarna 12
Gonagom (Kanakamuni) 110
gosain (gohain) lineages, (*goswamis*)
47, 85, 116, 132, 138, 182,
183, 188, 209; Chetiya Gohain
53; control over land routes
89; and East India Company,
confrontation 99, 101–2, 148,
158, 173; grants of *paik*s 42,
194–5, 198; of Majuli Island
349; recipients of gifts 65, 158;
Sadiyakhowas 200; spiritual
succession 101–2; struggle for
control of market and trade 87;
taxation 203
Gosain, Bhattacharya Parbatiya 39
Gosain, Nitaichand 101
Gosain, Purnagiri 89
Gosain, Shanti Das 70
Gosain, Shib 205
Goswami, Sarat Chandra 346, 354
*got*s and *khel*s, part of charitable
gifts 120
Government of India Acts (1919
and 1935) 352
Govinda Garo 24
Govindachandra Narayan 143–50,
153–5, 161, 163, 185, 217; khel
system 148, 214
Govindaji temple, Manipur 130
Govindram Barmanya 163, 185
Graham, Major 238
Greek Orthodox 191
Griffiths, W. 182
Gunapāla 43
Gupta, Gourishankar 179
Gupta, Kishori Mohan 353
Gurkhali regime in Nepal 112, 146
guru-shishya lineages 5, 164
Guthrie, Lieutenant, 214

Gyatso, Ugyen 297, 341, 343

Hachengsa lineage (*Hachengsa
vamsaja*) 49
Hajo 117
Halbwachs 366
Hamid, Abdul 312
Hamilton, Alexander 56, 88, 106
Hamilton, Buchanan. *See*
Buchanan, Francis
Hamilton, C.H. 277n
Haragauri 49; *Haragaurisamvad* 21;
Haragaurivivaha 21
Harshadeva 357
Hayagriva Madhava temple, Hajo
51, 52
Hayat, Mir 102
Hazareebagh Tea Company 247
Head-hunting savages 217
headship of monasteries 38
heir–apparent (*deka adhikar*) 38,
39
Herombo (Helambu, Herambo)
Raja 22, 138–40
hill-based cohorts (parbatiya
jamatiya) 348
hill states and excluded territories
344
Hill tribes 146, 190, 241, 246,
269, 353, 361; in Arakan 269;
of Chittagong Hill Tracts,
251–52
hills, commercial cultivation 344
Himalayan, Himalayas 2, 4, 49, 52,
55, 63, 71, 113, 293, 351, 356,
359; Bon-Buddhist lineages
242; Buddhist clans 57, 210,
260, 293; bureaucracy 60; lords,
133; —and their plain disciples,
diplomatic correspondence
58; monastic universities 210;
Tantrics of Tippera 21

Hindus 1, 16, 86, 156, 359; of Assam 352; law, 103; — restructured and revenue 157–62; males and British colonialism 15; marriage, reconstituted and political ecology 127–66; widows, defeat of, 149–57
Hinduism 26, 72, 155, 190, 342–5, 349
Historical and Antiquarian Studies, Department (DHAS) 347–50
Hodson, Thomas C. 344–5
Holmberg, David 113
horse, import 62
house tax 202
household formations 138, 287
household-based social reproduction 219
Howlongs (Haulong, Hualongs, Wallong), 253, 267, 275, 289, 290
Hrangvunga 320–2. See Bhunga, Sardar Hrang
human and animal, continuum 243–4
Hurnea 217
Hussain Shah, Sultan of Bengal 51; Turko-Afghan Muslim (1494–1519) 23
Huntington, Susan 9
Hutchinson, F.F. 295
Hutton, J.H. 347

ijaradars 63
Indo-Gangetic plains 22, 44, 47, 89, 99, 161
Indo-Sino-Tibetan trade 87
Indramani 139–40; Indramanikya 139
Indraprabha 144, 149–50, 153–7, 160, 163–5, 187, 217, 220, 222–3

infant king of Kuch Bihar and East India Company 88
inheritance (dāyabhāga, dāyatattva) 103, 149, 156, 359
initiants (bhakats) 39, 42; initiation and ordination rituals 5, 6, 288; relationship with teachers and disciples 43
Inner Asian system 43–5, 48, 52, 54, 287; Buddhist-Vaisnava alliance 50
Inner Line Regulations of (1871) 27–8, 270, 289
institutionalization 175
intermarried lineages of the Tipra-Manipuri Vaisnava lords 255, 294
Ishanchandra 179
Islam 55, 66, 114, 342, 357
Islamic communities 115, 244
Ismaili 48

Jacopa. See Zakapa
Jadonang, priest 348
Jafar, Mir 82
Jagannath temple, Orissa 179
Jahangir 183
Jains 86, 105, 260
Jaintia 95, 157, 343, 270
Jaisimha (Bhagyachandra, Chin-thang-khomba) 119–20, 129–33, 138, 141, 220
Jambudvipa 44, 358
Jardine, Skinner and Company, 258
Jatakas 209, 261
Jayadeva 357
Jayahari Yavana 24
Jayanti, daughter of Mohyn Dev 154
Jayantia (fort) 140
Jayantia Buranji 61

Jayantia, goddess 46, 48, 57, 139,
    186
Jayantipur 346
Jayantipura Purandhara 100
Jayasena 8
Je-khenpo 52
Jellal, Hazrat Shah 67
Jenkins, Francis 160–1, 188, 193,
    205, 208–9, 211, 234, 236,
    252, 291, 319
Jewish-Zoroastrian 71
jhuming (slash-and-burn
    cultivation) 245
Jiri 214
jiva (life-consciousness) 243
Jogendrojit 164
Jones, David Evan 311
Joobandi, daughter of Rajuram
    Bormon 154
Judaism 48
Juge-Silche 351
Jumla, Mir 58
jungle grants 237

Kachar (Khaspur) 27, 49, 94, 146,
    148, 157, 160, 164, 165, 186,
    222–3, 289, 294, 340, 347;
    based Manipuri rivals, 216;
    post-partition 362; Raja of,
    144–5; trade in elephants, ivory,
    wax etc 118
Kachar Tea Company 246,
    248–9
Kacharis (Kadzari, Koch, Kochari,
    Katsari, Kotsari) 57, 146, 161,
    205, 207–8, 236, 347, 350;
    Raja, 131; subjects of Bhutia
    lords, or Mechis 205
Kadam Rasul 115
Kadampa lineage 4
Kagyupa (Kargyupa) 4, 7, 39, 54,
    267, 313

Kaifeng 22
Kailasa-Manasarovar region 4
Kairuma 305
Kaladan River 243–4, 264, 287
Kali 341
Kalika 133
Kalikadevi 100
Kalikamatha 100
Kalinga 357
Kalla Naga 251
kalyanamitra 4
Kamakhya temple 51, 52, 55, 349,
    351
Kamrup 2, 3, 44, 45, 116, 202–3,
    205, 353, 357
Kamatapura 21
Kamboja 2, 3
Kamta Raja 52
Kanchi 358
Kangtis 190
Kanta Ram Roaja 181
Kanu Thakur 179–80
Kanungo, Krishnadas 179
Kapilavastu (Ser-skyahi-gnas) 44
karma 9, 86
Karnaphuli River 108, 112, 248
Karrani, Bayazid 48
karuna (compassion) and *dana* 261
Kasasati, Mahadevi 100
Kashi Thakur 179–80, 182;
    Kashichandra Manikya 142
Kashmir 22, 43, 49, 54, 55, 128,
    142
Kashyapa (Gaspa) 110
Kausambi 44
Kayasthas 161
Kedara 12
Khaamachheb 175
Khambo 341
Khams 17, 160, 202
Khangchai Kukis, khongjai,
    Khangjai, khonjai (dormitories

of Buddhist, Bon and Vaisnava
followers) 107, 118, 187,
214, 215, 216; Khunshai 54;
Khyongthas 242; Kiaung-sa
107–8
Khan, Burhanuddin 92
Khan, Ismail Ali (of Lungla, Sylhet)
250, 256
Khan, Jabbar 115
Khan, Muhammad Ali, Shia 65
Khan, Navazish 92
Khan, Sarmad 105
Khan, Tabbar/ Tabbo-ka/
Tauboka, Raja in Rauganea
111, 115
Khan, Zabardast 105
Khanglai Chetiya-ra 54
Khanum, Roshanara 104
khānqāh 37, 40
Khasa (Ya-tshe) 3
Khasi, Khasis 50, 95, 312, 316;
Khasi Hills 270
Khawvelthanga 320–2
khels (corporate bodies) 41, 120,
147–8, 154, 156, 161, 186,
194, 197, 198, 202, 214, 237,
246, 256; Khelwari system 240,
241
khŏ 43
Khoboom 251
Khora raja 57
Khri sron Ide'u btsan 43
khu-chung society of the hills
151–2
Khyen 241
Khyunglung 54
Kiaung-lha-pru 113
kindness, ethos 260, 273
Kinlakh (Kinloch), Captain 85
Kiranti 341
Kiratas 357
Kirtichandra 144, 154

Klein, Anne 209–10
knowledge and knower 21
Kokāmukhasvamin 356
Konbaung dynastic and monastic
lineage 105, 128, 143
Kosala 357
Koungmhoodan 118
Koutuk, a Kanaujia brahman 47
Krishna 70
Krishnachandranarayan, Raja of
Kachar 138, 141, 144, 145,
150, 154, 155, 161, 163
Krishnadas Kanungo 179
Krishnamala 21, 63, 84–5, 140,
150–3, 174–6, 180, 220, 351
Krishnamani 139–40
Krishnamanikya, Raja 84–5,
138–41, 179
Kubo valley 118–19, 184
Kuch Bihar lineages 87; and Tibetan
Buddhist order, relation 117
Kuki-gana 175
Kukis, Kookis, Kookies (Buddhists)
mosaic subjects of the Vaisnava
initiates 2, 151–52, 159–60, 163,
166, 176, 180, 186–8, 217–18,
237, 240, 242, 245, 248, 256,
288; rebellion 256, 348
Kulikahini 249
kulina 12–13
Kumilla/Tripura 2, 23, 94, 100,
106–7, 137, 141–3, 221
Kung 175
Kuranganayani 132–33
Kusiara 38
Kutilaakhi, daughter of raja of
Manipur 182

labour services, labourers 28, 36,
149, 179, 183, 213–14; as
bride-wealth 140; in colonial/
Company's regime 98–9, 161–

2, 173–4, 179, 185, 188, 195,
199–200; in form of *dana* (gift)
9, 51–2, 55, 177; by disciples 6,
12; from devoted subjects 200;
of devotion singing (*gayans*)
41; exemptions 194, 197–8;
global market 94; military 106,
111; in monastic economy/
monastic order 9, 15, 42, 55,
61, 70, 89, 94, 115, 117, 120,
187; to pay dues 147–8; power
amidst intra-monastic conflicts
136; providers 6, 188; as rent
or taxes, 16; scarcity 248; sexual
division/undoing gender 14, 89,
159, 291; tea fraternity and 27,
232, 249, 261; of women 14,
159
Ladakh 54, 65; Bhutan relationship
52–3
Lakher 354
Lakkhidi 154
Lakkhiprabha 144, 145
Lakshmi 133
Lakshminarayana, Saiva tantric 59
Lal Maham 92
Lallbuta 295
Lalpitang, Lal-poitang 253, 274
Lalruma 306
Lalsavunga 275
Lalthangvunga 298, 304
Lalthauma Vansanga 275, 305
Lamaguru, Lanmakhru 54
land, landholdings: descent-based
claims and inheritance 119;
masculinization 104; revenue
and military service, shifting
economies 27; shifting nature of
use 289
land grants (gifts) 119–20; to
deities 45; recipients 38;
Mughal imperial and sub-

imperial 101; redistributed by
Company 127
Lāndā Sultān 48, 57, 59, 63,
90
Langai Rufani Telpoi 175
Langthabal (Manipur) 186
law-enforcement personnel (*chat-
bhat*) 7
lay adherents, communities, 16,
54; householder lineages 12,
42; legal and political status of
intermarried clan-dormitories
339; male (layman) 9, 12, 42;
female (laywomen) (*upāsikā*)
9, 71, 101, 159, 287–8, 339;
—claims to merit-making 330;
—and monastic codes of gender
11–16, 287, 331
legal-moral and disciplinary
practice 5
Lenin, Vladimir 238
Lepchas 341
levirate (*karewa*) 14, 293; and
colonial conscription 291
Lewin, Thomas Herbert 246–8,
251–55, 258, 264–5, 273–4,
345, 365
Lewin, William 247
liberalism 173, 263, 272
Limbu 341
lineages: conflicts 164; the
localization of cosmopolitanism
255–9; politics of Assam,
Kachar and Manipur 145
Ling-ta and Lang-ta 111
Lister, Lieutenant Colonel 215,
238–40, 247, 252
Lohitya 38
Lorrain, James 308, 311, 331
Luchi dafa/*dapha* 175
Lungleh 294
Lungree 134

Lushai(s) (Luchayes, Loo-sai,
    Looshai, Looshais) 112, 166,
    239–40 247, 250, 255, 248,
    262, 263, 273, 290, 297, 316,
    318; armies as slave-catchers or
    slave-raiders, 259; Expedition
    (1871) 27, 340; Labour Force
    363; Sylu clan 253, 255
Lushai Hills 291, 292, 307, 309,
    310, 318, 322, 328
Lushei-Kuki 165, 345

M'Cosh, John 189–90
Macchindranatha 355
madad-i-ma'ash (subsistence) 11, 66
Madhuchandra 144, 153
Magadha 4, 8, 43, 358
Maglau king 133
Mahabharata 70, 357, 368
Mahadebi Rani 153
Mahamoony (Mahamuni) 110
Mahamuri river 114
Mahayana lineage 1, 4, 5, 6, 10,
    25, 210, 242, 253, 260–1,
    287, 313, 325–6, 329; codes of
    maternal masculinity, 209–10;
    ideas of dharmakaya and
    rupakaya 314; idealization of
    compassionate care 287
Mahendrapala 8
Mahesvar 133
Mahmudabad 92
Mairang 131, 317
Maitreya 110
Makley, Charlene 218
male: authority, 165; and female,
    hierarchical division/relationship
    5, 103, 166; householder 13;
    oral-ritual skills 10
Malla, Jayasthiti 3
Malla forces 3, 4
Malla-Narayana lineages 87

malla-vidya (wrestling, also hand-
    to-hand combat) 22
Mamluk 49
Manadeva, Himalayan Buddhist-
    Vaisnava king 23
Manas river 182, 351
Manikchand, Diwan 93
Manikya 152
Manikya, Krishnakishore 142
Manipur, Manipuri lineages,
    Manipuris 26, 27, 47, 70,
    71, 128–31, 134, 142, 144,
    146, 165–6, 255, 269, 340;
    Burmese Buddhist alliance
    143, 145, 164; and Kachari
    (Muslim) 143; negative
    judgements on authenticity
    and purity 344–5; refugees
    on the plains of Bengal 182;
    Vaisnava lineage 120, 133,
    143, 174, 220–3, 260, 368
Manipuri-Kachari-Tipra 'princely'
    (guru) lineages 249
Maniram Dewan 232
Manrique, Jesuit monk 325
Manuhar, Shaykh 55
marital. See marriage
maritime trade 46
Marjit, son of Jaisimha 141–4,
    222, 256
markets, labour markets, and social
    structures (1871–91) 288–91
marriages, marital alliances 14, 25,
    71, 293; and affinal relationships
    between lineages 141, 255;
    as anchors of monastic
    geographicity 56–65; diplomatic
    36; diversity, polygamy, and
    multiple partnerships 141–4;
    heterosexual 294; in-marrying
    grooms, practice 133–4;
    patrilateral cross-cousin 128;

politics 71, 127; preferences
between close kin 127–8;
settlement or *moranna* 104;
succession, marriage, and
inheritance laws 105
married ascetics, lineages, inter-
relationship 346
Marx, Karl 177
masjids and *thakurbaris*, 91
materials, exchange for militant
manpower 58–9
mathas, *akharas*, *masjids*, and
khanqahs 37, 67
matrilateral and bilateral
inheritance systems 359
matriliny 359
Mattak Raja 190
Matthews, John 84–5
Mazda-ists 45–6, 345
McCulloch, Major (later Colonel)
237, 344, 345
Meghan 72
Meiteis, Metei clan 47, 62, 63, 64,
138. *See also* Manipur
memorization process 316
men and their paternal uncles,
relationship 139
men, women, deities and spirits,
relations 23
mercantile and monastic
communities, polyglossia 297
merit (*punya*, moral capital)
8–10, 13, 42, 47, 86, 178, 196;
economy 9, 14, 28, 136, 160,
291, 301, 306, 329, 339; and
generosity as forms of moral
capital 9, 10; gifts of donors in
exchange for 9, 14–15, 25, 28,
160; merit-making 9, 160, 306,
329, 330; undoing of gender,
restoring of motherhood and
merit 287–331

metropolitan ethnicity 235
military, militaries: in the Bengali-
Assamese literary record 46–56;
conflicts 36, 264; diplomatic
alliances 90, 95; labour (as
chamua paiks) 198; and
liberation of women plantation
labourers 260, 263, 272; and
monastic geographicity 56;
organization 43; and planter-
missionary brotherhood 270,
273, 276, 297; politics 236,
287; science and technology
151; service corps and clan-
heads, relations 199; service-
providers (kari paiks) 197;
technology 55–6
Milky (*malki* or owned) and
Lackerage (*la-khiraj*, tax exempt)
92
Mills, James P. 347–50
Mimamsa (philosophy) 38
Minanath 355
Miris 199, 202
mission schools monastic
dormitories, restoration 315–17
Mizo National Front (MNF) 362
Mlecchas 152, 357
Moamaria Mahanta 132–4, 160,
193, 329
Momee 133
Monaikhal (Monierkhall) 258
monastic, monasteries:
administration and economies
6, 9, 11, 12, 26, 28, 44,
46, 159, 183, 206–7, 211,
295, 348; assemblages 119;
codes of gender 11–16, 71;
commitments 20; communities
12, 16, 36, 111, 120, 182;
cosmography 361; discipleship
28; dormitories, sanctuaries,

and shelters 40–1, 43, 101,
108; exemptions from taxes
26, 339; female subjects
14; gifts, devaluation 211;
geographic order. *See* monastic
geographic order; governance.
See monastic governance;
households 14; knowledge
tradition 344; males 272, 359;
Manipuris 269; mercantilism
67, 112; militias 7, 11, 23,
25, 55, 57, 71; in the mission
schools restoration 315–17;
movements and resettlements
47–50; ordination lineages. *See*
monastic ordination lineages;
structures 39–40; subjects. *See*
monastic subjects; tantric and
magic-wielding 50
monastic governance,
governmentality 6, 12, 13,
52, 66, 81, 88, 90, 116, 173,
193, 288; and Burmese forces,
conflict 117; involvement
in marriages of disciples,
12; restored 16–24; and
subjecthood, 107, 112; teachers
27, 288, 339; —as forgotten
friends and governors 4–11;
tenancy, lure of freeholding and
the erosion of 202–4; warriors,
immigration and resettlement in
dormitories 47
monastic geographic order,
monastic geographicity 22,
23, 24, 25, 26, 36, 70, 92,
110, 136, 145, 174, 179,
223, 232, 270, 347; brunt
of East India Company 117;
extra-textual fragmentation
344; intra-monastic conflicts
57; linked landscapes and shred

cosmographies 42–6; marriages
as anchors 56–65; and militaries
in the Bengali-Assamese literary
record 46–56; relational aspects
119; residence as unit 36–42;
segregation 116–20
monastic ordination lineages
(lords and lineages) 2, 4, 7, 8,
14, 24, 38–9, 40, 57, 60, 71,
72, 90, 102, 105, 107, 129,
132, 155, 174, 178, 195, 202,
212–13, 218, 221, 239, 250,
255, 300–1, 352; in Assam 70;
mercantile 67, 112; political
system, politics 36, 127, 162,
182–3, 209, 276, 288, 305;
rules (*vinaya*) 174
monastic subjects 138, 187, 195,
218, 235–6, 259, 267, 269, 270,
339–42, 343, 348; political-social
relationships 118; remembering
and forgetting by erstwhile, a
return to friendship 362–9
monasticism 1
Mongolia, Mongols 4, 6
monogamous marriages 301, 360
moral-social capital as *punya*
(merit) 86
Moran Motok 46
Moran, Ramakant 133
Mo-roong (Morung, Morang,
Moroong, Mrungs) 89, 113–15,
241, 341
motherhood and merit, undoing
gender 287–331
mountain (*parbatiya*) king of
Tripura 22; pilgrimages 46
mouzawary system 240–1
Mug (mugs) (Rakhain Muslims)
91, 111, 117, 177–9, 183, 244
Mughal, Mughals 46, 49–51, 53,
339; and Central Asian warfare

217; donors 11; governors 63; hybrid patterns of cultivation 162; inheritance 65–9; Ladakh-Tibet peace treaties 55; pattern of female holding and inheritance of monastic estates 99; provincial administration 91; sub-imperial administration 94

Muhammad Jang (Alivardi Khan, *c.* 1740s) 139

Muhammad Shahi sultans 47

Muhammad, Jigar 98–9, 100

Muhammadans 65. *See* Muslim

Mukhopadhyaya, Chandrasekhar 313

Mukundamanikya 140

Murray, C.S. 294–6, 299, 301

Murshchoi Lall 257

musicians (*bayan*s) 41

Muslim 24, 65, 86, 91, 107, 111, 113, 115, 359; Buddhist societies 106; diviner (*qalandar*) 10; lineage 81; monastic governance 86; networks 272; Rakhain 117, 184, 243–4; Shia lineage of Mughal governors (Nawabs) 342; zamindars 258

Mymuna Bibi 104

Nadia (Navadvip, Nabadvip) 47, 102, 129, 164, 174, 223

Naga(s) 165, 184–5, 193, 214–5, 238, 239, 248, 251, 270, 354; anti-colonial movement 348; chiefs of Namsang and Kungan 240

Naga Hills, 240, 347; post-partition 362

Nagarjuna, Siddha 355

Nahor Habi (Sylhet) Tea Company 247

Nako, Buddhist-Sufi monastic complex, Himachal Pradesh 17, 22

nam kirtan 41

Nambhor Forest 347

Nara Raja 57

Naranarayana, king of Assam 343

Narayana (title) 117

Narayanpala 209

Narayans 205

Narayan, Rochisha 99–100

Narottama 24

Narottamdasa 129

Narsimha, Regent at Manipur 164, 215

Naskar, Dolai Dev 163

Nath, Raj Mohan 346

Nature-worship 345

Nazim, Naib 84

necromancy and magic spells 10

Nepal 22, 43, 111–12, 236, 355, 357; Nepali-Sikkimi-Sino-Tibetan confrontations 112

Nepuitangi 305

Newars 341

Nidhanpur grant 354

Nilambar, Raja of Kamata 51, 153

Nilkrishna 256

Ningrew-la 234–5

Nokte Lama 148

non-dualist metaphysics 21

non-dualistic notion of corporeality 115

non-Gelukpa lamas 218

non-recognition: aftermath of authority within families, lineages, and landscape 162–6

non-sectarianism 8

'non-self' doctrine (*anatta*) 298–9

Northeast India: lamentable historiographical practice and

monastic governmentality restored 16–24
Nyaya (justice-legality) 38
Nyingmapa (rNyingma, Tibetan Tantric lineage) 4, 22, 51, 52, 208, 267, 297
Nyingma-Bonpo 50–1
Nyingma-Kagyu 70

Om Śakābda 23
open-border policy 255
oral communication, oral transmission of knowledge 19, 20, 71, 129
ordination lineages 6, 12, 22, 43, 45, 52–3, 186, 260, 329, 359; monastic and temple lords, disputes 70, 201–2; ordained-lay relationships 202
orthodoxy 70
orthography 107
other groups 104, 105

paiks 41–2, 50, 84, 154, 173, 186, 194–5, 343; chamua 41; kari/kanri 41, 42; khalasara 41; likcau/lixoo 41
paitou 44
Pakhoa Lushai tribes 290
Pala 43
Pala lineage, Tantric teachers and disciples 7, 8, 12
Pāngons/Bongāls (Muslim artillery and infantrymen) 47–8
Panjiham Tipperah 301
Panna 99
Paramananda, Vaisnava Goswami 24, 129
pardanashin 99
parliamentary governance 344
Partition (1947) 22, 358, 362
Pasupatinath 3, 209, 357

Pataliputra 358
patron-donors of the monastic-ascetic lords 339
peacekeeping and information-gathering services 183
Pegu 62
Pemberton, Robert B., 182, 210
Permanent Settlement 191
Phadung 180–1
phalö 43
phenomenological (vyavahar, laukika) 21
Phukan, Naobaisya 346
Phulesvari 132
Pibuk 274
Pilak, Buddhist stupa site 23
pilgrimages 46–7, 120, 130, 356
Pir Ali, Sayyid 67
plantations. See tea plantation
Playfair, Alan 345, 350–1
pluralism 243–4
political: alliances of Tantric Buddhist and Vaisnava households 132; associations 61; community 41; crisis and military conflict 140; ecology and reconstituted Hindu marriage 127–66; economy 16, 27, 90, 108, 186, 252, 287, 339; exemptions and privileges 81; fraternities 26; groups 13; identity 68; marriages 145; and military antagonism 182 moral economy 14; social and economic institutions 13, 16; society 1; subjectivity 358; warfare of the Manipuri nephews' factions in Kachar 216
politics 4, 5, 6, 71, 359, 360, 364–5; of adherence 345–6; of followership 174; of memory 331; of monastic friendship

232–76; of periodization 176; of representation and monastic community 296; of value that linked marriage to wealth and security 136
polyandry (*niyoga*) 13, 14, 26, 65, 71, 150, 153, 156, 293–4, 340. *See also* marriage
polygyny and hypergamous relationships 12, 153–4
Po-mang-gri, Pow-mang-gre 113, 115
Pooran Singh Soobadar 222
Powell, Avril 192
praja. See subjects
Prajñāpāla 43
Prananarayana 54
primitivism 350
prisoners of war 60
property management and inheritance 129
proprietary rights 91, 202
Protestant and post-Reformation 1
Puia, Rutton Singh 253–54, 264–6
Pundravardhana (Li-kho-ri-sin-hphel-ba) 44, 356
Puritanism 86

Qing regime 112
Qosot Mongol armies 70
Qutbuddin 91

racism 274
Radha–Krishna 100, 145
Radharam of Pratapgarh 68–9, 94–6, 106, 133, 147; Vaisnava–Sufi resistance 152
Ragha 132
Rahul, son of Siddharth Gautama 177
Rahuli monks 178

Rajamala (also *SriRajamala*) 21–4, 47, 50, 139–40, 351
rajavamsi or ancestors 178
rajbungshee 177
Rajdhar Manikya (*r.* 1785–1804) 141–2
Rajeh, Beeby 92
Rajesvara Simh (Pramatta Simh) 133
Rajkoowuri, Bhabanipuri 153
Rajputs 99
Rakhain 47, 48, 108–11, 114–5, 117, 177–9, 183–4, 188, 260; Muslim 117, 184, 243–4
Ram Jai Roaja 181
Rama 70
Ramadhvaja Simh 60
Rambelli, Fabio 115
Ramchandra Dhvaja Narayan, lord of Hirimbo 140
Ramdev 72
Ramganga, Dvija 150
Ramganga Manik, Raja of Tippera 180–1
Ramsingh 140
Rana-chandi (goddess of war) 138
Rang 175
Rangamati (Rangamatty) 47, 190
Ranghkhol 175
Rangpur 92–3
Rannadevi 12
rasa 130
Rāslilāmrita 145
Rastrakuta 12
Ratnasambhava Buddha 125n
Razak, Abdul 84
Rbhupala 356
Rebellion of 1857 222, 234, 242, 247, 249–50, 256; aftermath 173
rebels and refugees 178
reconstructive memory 365–7

regional dormitories 186
Reid, Robert 353, 355
relational identities 113
religious communitarian
    boundaries and marriages 132;
    cultures 176; laws of the Hindus
    and Muslims 91
remade renunciants, marriages, and
    the Company courts 101–5
Rennell, James 85–7, 90
rent-free grants 270; of lands,
    rent-exempt lands (devottar and
    brahmottar) 18, 173, 195, 249
renunciation 5, 9, 28
reproductive sexuality 360
residence as unit monastic
    geography 36–42
resource-sharing arrangements 61,
    174, 361
reuse culture 44
revenue in restructured Hindu law
    157–62
risk-sharing 141
ritual: complexities of militias
    49; and disciplinary practices,
    conflicts around 129; homage
    and economic implications 51;
    invocations 10
road-building projects 213, 241,
    250, 270; road-construction
    project 213
Roberts, J. Watkin 320
Ropuiliani 254, 275, 311, 352
Rowlands, Edwin 311
Roy, Rammohan 102–3, 149
royal clan (rajavamsi/rajbongshi)
    220
Rung 175
ryots, ryotwari pattern 162, 198,
    246

Sabbath 315–16

sacrality 268–9
Sadiyakhowa 200–1
Sagaranupavasins 357
Sahija Badshah 69
Saikia, Madhu 210
Saiva(s) 1, 5, 7, 10, 20, 21, 24, 28,
    42, 50, 52, 71, 91, 107, 115,
    117, 133, 156, 341; Buddhist
    symbols 115, 267; Sakta 7,
    156, 210, 267; Kashmiri 44;
    monastic governance 12; Natha
    ascetics (yogis, bairagis) 8;
    Pasupatas 209; Tantrics 8, 12,
    18, 38, 51, 52, 59, 153, 349
Saiva-Sakta Banesvara temple 39
Sakta tantric lineages (female
    shamanic traditions) 7, 12, 20,
    38, 50, 51, 100, 107, 114, 140,
    156, 199, 205, 218, 343, 349,
    355
Sakya (Sa-skya) Buddhist 3–4, 17
Sakyamuni, Buddha 44, 142, 341
Sakyapa 45, 266
Samarqand 49
samgha 37, 38
samhati 37
Sangermano 107
Sangma 351
Sankar river 112
sannyasi (ascetics), bairagis
    (renunciants) and fakirs 8, 68–9,
    83, 86, 91, 100; Sufi forces 106
Santhals 359
Santhi Giri, Raja of Kachar 119,
    144, 147
Santong 267
Sanandram 185–6, 236
Sanyashigotta 86
Sarasvati, Hema 21
Sardars 178
Sarkar, Tanika 98
Sarma, Baidyanath 179

Sarma, Rajkumar 312
*sattra*s (monasteries) 37, 38, 41, 71, 194, 202, 209, 329
savagery 27, 191, 239, 319; savages, barbarians, and coolies 214
Savidge, J.H. 308, 309, 311, 331
Sawbwa, Angun 142
sayrmahal (customs collections) 94
Sayyids 65
Scheduled districts 315
Scheduled Districts Act (1874) 352; (1882) 271
Scheduled Tribes 355
Scott, David 149, 192, 195, 203, 252, 319
Scott, James 184
sectarian traditions and ecological niches, sectarianism 12, 18
Sen, Binoychandra 3
sena 8, 12
sexual services 28
Shabsdrung 117; *Zhabs-drung* 52
Shaikhzadas 65
Shakespear, Colonel L.W. 347
Shakespear, Lieutenant-Colonel John 295–9, 301, 304, 305–7, 325, 345
Shambhu Chandra 221
Shan (mountaineers) 354; Shans 118
shari'a 66
Shekapas 216
Shendu 247
Shia Begams of Awadh 99
Shib Gosain 205
Shunyeupha (Lakshmi Simha) 132–3
Shutenpha (Pramatta Simha) 132–3
Shwedagon 196
Siddhapāla 43
Siddhartha 128

Sidli 117, 205
Sikkimese monastic estates of Darjeeling and Kalimpong 235
Simon Commission 349
Simha, Chait Raja of Banaras 99
Simha, Chakradhvaja 58
Simha, Chandrakanta 143
Simha, Chandrakirti Raja of Manipur 164–5, 219
Simha, Debendro 221, 255
Simha, Gadadhar 234
Simha, Gambhir 119–20, 144, 149, 157–8, 164, 184–7, 195, 212, 213–14
Simha, Gaurinath (Gaurinatha) 116, 134–5
Simha, Gokul 255
Simha, Jayadhvaja 57
Simha, Kamalesvar (Kinaram) 71, 116
Simha, Kanai (Kanhai Singh) 166, 222, 250, 251, 255–8, 270, 352
Simha, Lakshmi Ahom king (Laksmisingh) 60, 72, 134
Simha, Rajkumar Nal 221
Simha, Nawal 165–6
Simha, Pabitra 144, 153–4, 163, 187, 217, 222
Simha, Ram Raja of Jayantia 186
Simha, Tribhuvanjit 212, 215
Singphos/Chinpha/Shing-pha 207
Singh, Ganga 97–8
Singh, Kabo 221
Singh, Purandhar (Purandar Simha), raja of Assam 146, 198, 233–4
Singh, Subha 97, 140
Singh, Tilak 137
Sinha, Mrinalini 15, 147
Sinha, Nirmal 358
Sino-Tibetan 44, 207, 296
Sipuia (Seipooeya) 253–54

Sircar, Dines Chandra 355–8
Sirkar, Hemronjan 312
Siva 71, 341
Sivadeva, Himalayan Buddhist-
    Vaisnava king 23
slavery, slaves 27, 173–223, 239,
    263–4, 316, 321–2, 324, 330,
    361
Smarta Hindus 133
smarta teacher 39
Sna (golden) Langmeirempi 64
social: adherence and community
    255; formations 113; networks
    145
soil ownership 45
Somdeva (Chomdeu) 53
Song Chinese empire 22
spatial–cultural continuities 293
spiritual: accomplishments
    (siddhapurush) 220; political
    leader (adhikari gosain) 132; and
    social lineages 10
Srenimala 21, 137, 140, 142, 150,
    153, 156, 220, 351
Sri Govinda Kirtan 145
state-making 358
Stewart, Lt 275
Sthaviravada Buddhist 329
stock exchanges 340
sTon-pa-gShen-rab 45
subject(s) (praja) 6, 38, 166, 174;
    and the lord, relationship 191;
    and object 21; reconstituted,
    and landscapes of Kachar
    and Manipur 213–19; and
    sovereigns, political complex 25.
    See also monastic subjects
subjecthood 212
subsistence (madad-i-ma'ash) 11,
    66
succession order 134
Sudras 195

Sufi silsilahs/tradition, Sufis 1, 2,
    5, 8, 10, 18, 24, 38, 69, 81, 93,
    96, 176, 217, 242, 287, 344;
    pirs, 25, 65; warriors 48
Sukpilall 256–7, 274, 290
Sungboonga 253
Sunthee Karee 144
sunyata (emptiness) 48
Surma-Barak valleys 26, 36, 48, 50,
    54, 57, 58, 59, 61, 62, 71, 81,
    114, 118, 119, 156, 163, 174,
    176, 187, 214, 233, 236, 240,
    264, 315
Suvarna Shamsher Jang, Nepali
    Rana 355
svargadeva 39, 46, 53, 55, 57–63,
    71, 89–90, 131–5, 146, 206;
    power of inherited consorts of
    previous 133
Svetavarahasvamin 356
Sylhet 14, 27, 45, 38, 48, 54, 57,
    62, 64, 67–70, 81–3, 89, 92–8,
    100, 105, 118–20, 133, 137–8,
    141, 143, 146, 148, 155, 159,
    161–2, 164–6, 180, 190–1,
    213–17, 219, 221, 347
Sylhet Light Infantry 146, 217
Symes, Michael 106

Tagore, Dwarkanath 232
Tai-biak (Tai-koup) 112
Ta-kang 112
Tamang 112–13
Tamradhvaj, Raja 154
Tangloa 290
Tantikuchi 350
Tantra (ritual means) 38
Tantric 1, 10, 13, 28, 201, 312,
    315, 343; Bon. See Bon-Tantric;
    Buddhist. See Buddhist, Tantric;
    meditational practices 175;
    Saiva. See Saiva Tantric; Sakta.

See Sakta Tantric; Vaisnava. *See* Vaisnava

Tara, the female deity 10, 12,132

Tashilunpo 13

Tashischu Dzongpen 206

Tattvanidhi, Achyuta Charan Choudhuri 346–7

Tavares, Tita 105

tax collections (*jamma*), taxation 7, 84, 162, 197, 199, 208, 233, 241 in Company-administered Bengal 164; in kind 120; exemptions 41, 65–6; exempted lands and gifts (*brahmottar*) 91, 102, 103, 150, 202, 203, 213; and labour-levies 6; punitive 84; tax-free grants to Vaisnava 164; tax-paying estates (*khiraji*) 198

Taylor, Mr 299, 301

Tayshoo Lama 88

tea plantations, tea fraternity 174, 212, 232; conflicts over 27; ecology 340; effects on the social networks as well as the lands 257; establishments (*boi*) 330, 364; European management of labour 27, 219, 361; and politics of monastic friendship 232–76; —of compassion 245–55; and the transformation of Kachar, Northern Arakan, and hills of Chittagong 236–42

teacher-monks 19

teaching-disciple, teaching-learning lineage 5, 6, 8, 10, 12, 42, 72

Tekhao 62

temple building 93

temple-monastic economy 26

tenants (*bahatiya*) 24

tenurial system 106

territorial: boundaries 7; deities 45; frontiers: foregrounding making monastic subjects British 204–13; marginality 360; relationships between distinct groups of monastics, 108; supremacy 177

territorialism 118

Tetua Punji 293

Thadoi Khyong (Thado hkyaung) 187

Thakur, Ramchandra 180

Thakur, Shambhu 179–82

Thakur's *raiyat*s (subjects of the Lord) 101

Thathanabaing 276

Theravada Buddhist 86, 107, 109, 128, 260; architecture, 109; in the Burmese capital 235

Tibet (Khams) 3, 17, 22, 43, 49, 62, 85, 111–13, 253, 267, 355

Tibetan 2, 4, 19, 107, 160, 201, 236, 252; Buddhism 17, 65, 150, 212, 242, 313–4; Bootea monasteries 152; calendars 20; empire, military and civil administration 43–4; *got* 44; inflected languages 107, 178; language historiography 55; Mahayana 253; *pai* 44; Rakhain Buddhist Tantric kings 48; sects 267; speaking societies 50, 65; Tai Mahayana 329; Tantra, tantric lineages. *See* Nyingma; *tshug*s 44

Tibetan–Bengali-speaking populations 152

Tibetan-Burman prisoners of war 192

Tibetan-Burman-Bengali 67

Tibetan-Nepali 57, 138, 236

migration of Tibetanized clans 17

Tibeto-Bengali 296
Tibeto-Burmese 36, 113, 185, 207, 240, 296–7, 310, 359
Tibeto-Mongol 49
Tibeto-Nepali gosains 138
Tibeto-Sikkimese lineage 190
Tibotogiri 351
Tibukche Tol 3
Tickell, S.R. 244
Tilakchandra 84
Time 17
Timur, Amir 49
Tippera. See Tripura
Tipra. See Tripura
Tirhutiya 3
Tirumalai 358
Tlandrukpa 253
trade: routes 112; in woolens, silks, black pepper, and bullion 88
trading pilgrims of India 89
translations, debating, deflecting colonial transmission 27, 342–52
transportation: animals 62–3; labour for colonial armies and engineers 250
tribes and races 190, 232, 358; colonial ethnology 347
tribute-gathering systems 179
Tripur bhasha 21
Tripura (Bhatgaon, Tipra, Tippera, Tipura) 2, 3, 17, 24, 26, 27, 288, 294, 343, 351–2, 354, 359, 368; forces, invaded Manipur 186; lineage at war with other segments 216; Mallas 21; Manipuri alliance 250; monastic governance, geographicity and gender 39, 46, 48, 51, 62–3, 72; monastic governance, shifts 94–5, 100, 104–5, 112–15;

political ecology and politics reconstruction of Hindu marriage 131, 136, 139–41, 146, 150, 220–1; post-partition 362; raided by Sultan of Bengal 3; rajas 84–5, 180, 186–7, 216, 320, 348; Rakhain 270
Tripurasundari 3, 23
Trivedi, Ramendra Singh 342
Trongsa Penlop 209, 218
Tshalpa monasteries 7
Tughlaq 49
Tuin-kiaung 113
Tula Ram (Tularam) Senapati 157, 160, 163, 185, 187, 236
Tunghum 186–7, 214
Turko-Afghan dominion in Bengal 47
Turko-Mongols 19
Turner, Samuel 55, 88, 152
Turuskas 2

Udayaditya 61
Udbhranto Prem (Chandrasekhar Mukhopadhyaya) 313
Uighur, 339
Umaid Reza 97
Umananda temple 55
united absolute (*paramartha*) 21
United Assam Association (Assam Company) 232–3, 236, 238
universal compassion (*maitri*) 236
Upadhya, Prem Ronjon 312
Urmila, granddaughter of Durgamanikya 137

Vairocana Buddha 125n
Vaisnava tradition(dedicated to Visnu), Vaisnavas 1, 5, 10, 12, 24, 44, 48, 72, 86, 87, 91, 110, 152, 161, 164; adherence as feudalism 176, 179–80, 184,

186–90, 192–3; administration 173; Ahom order, 240; akharas 84, 129, 329; bairagis in Sylhet and Kachar 256; brides and bride wealth 136–41; British and the monastic subjects 205, 207, 208, 210, 212; Brahmans 67, 71; —and Muslim households, synchronicity 103; —and Meiteis, assimilation 47, 62; and Buddhists, alliances/relations 50, 52, 127, 132, 145, 157, 158, 164, 165, 250; cosmologies 184; donors 67; and East India Company, confrontations 81, 84, 92, 94, 96; gurus and gosains 70, 102, 129–30, 138, 173; —classified as slaves by British 193–202; iconography 243; kingdoms 260; landholders 119–20; Manipuris 120, 133, 137–38, 140–43, 145, 147, 150, 152–4, 157–8, 165–6, 174, 182, 185, 214, 217, 219–22, 238, 250, 255–6, 293; monastic economics and militias 218; monastic governmentality 116, 233; monastic lineage 129–30, 134, 142, 236, 256, 315, 329; monks 180, 216; novices and initiates, ordination system 38, 39, 51, 119, 348; poets 138, 145, 150, 153, 175; political community 160; Puritanism 348; Sahajiya 329; tantrics 21, 38, 42, 54, 50, 118, 193; temples 69, 118; traders 68–9; women 100, 102
Vaisnava–Buddhist–Muslim dvars 207
Vajravarahi, female deity 243

Vajrayana 2, 4, 5, 7, 20, 107, 108, 109, 117, 132, 178, 210, 244, 317; based *tantra, kaula, siddha* disciplines 7. *See also* Buddhism; Tantra Vanchhunga 324
Vandula 253–4, 275
Vanhnuailiana (Vanhoilien) 305
Varathregna 243
Vasanta Vihār 145
Vasu, Nagendranath 353
Vedantic order 314
Verelst, Henry 131
Verethragna 49
Vetch, Captain 235
Vidyavinod, Padmanath Bhattacharya 346, 353, 354
vihāra 37, 71
Vikramasila monastery 45
Vincent, Lieutenant 238, 247
Volonel 268, 272, 275, 290
Vonpilall (Vonpolall) 268, 274, 290
Vrindavan and Mathura 129, 158, 329, 358, 368
Vyas 116

Walsh, Michael 9
Wangma clan 52
Wangyal, Lama Tashi 52
warrior monks 218
warrior-traders 89
waste lands in Assam and Kachar 146, 242, 245, 272
water-worshipping 346
Wa-the Mroo 113
Wazir, Durgamani 21
Welsh Presbyterian Mission 270, 319, 328
widows 13, 98, 99, 102–4, 136, 163, 200, 274, 293, 323, 326, 331, 368; criminal monks, dispersed adherents and

dispossessed widows 219–23; and daughters' claims in lands 158, 161; gift-giving 100; Hindu 103, 149–57; inheritance rights, deligetimation 40, 66, 103, 127; disqualification of titles to lands 158; matrilateral kin 154. *See also* women

Winchester, Mary 259, 262–5, 273–6, 326, 367

Winchester, Mr. 259, 262

Wise, Josiah Patrick 238

Wise, William 238

witchcraft and superstition 119

women, women's lineages 294, 306; adherence, as well as catholicity 100; authority and power 134, 339–40; centrality to social and disciplinary lineages 102; headed households 11, 250, 276; inheritance and property rights 101–4, 127, 149; membership in Methodist Church 329; merit-making activities 306; kin relationships 66; oppression 360; plantation labourers/owners 275, 293, 301, 306–7; in monastic communities 120; sexual and social work for a lineage 295; as wives, public authority 133, 156, 361

Wood, Browne 240

World War I 348

World War II 22, 353, 363, 364, 367

Xi Xia state 17

yoga (and *prayoga*) 5

Yogini tantra 21

Younghusband 317

Zaduna 305

Zairema 325, 367

Zakapa (Jacopa) 295, 299–303, 305

zakat (mandatory charity) 8, 11, 86

zamindars 68, 91, 104, 180, 234, 270, 320; colonial government as 237–8; and East India Company 82, 83, 92, 99, 178, 191, 205, 212; gifts to sacred figures 67, 93; Mughal/Muslim 82, 97, 101, 139, 258; of Tipra 139, 256; Vaisnava 180

Zhabs-drung 52

Zhang Zhung (variation Zhangzhung) 45, 54

Zoroastrianism 48–9

Zunghari invasion of Central Tibet 70

About the Author

INDRANI CHATTERJEE is the author of *Gender, Slavery and the Law in Colonial India* (Oxford University Press, 1999). Apart from having contributed essays in scholarly journals, she has edited *Unfamiliar Relations: Family and History in South Asia* (Permanent Black and Rutgers University Press, 2004) and co-edited *Slavery and History in South Asia* (Indiana University Press, 2007). She has taught at Miranda House, University of Delhi, Rutgers University, the State University of New Jersey, and is going to teach at University of Texas at Austin from September 2013.